Digital Economic Policy

Digital Economic Policy

The Economics of Digital Markets from a European Union Perspective

Mario Mariniello

OXFORD
UNIVERSITY PRESS

OXFORD
UNIVERSITY PRESS

Great Clarendon Street, Oxford, OX2 6DP,
United Kingdom

Oxford University Press is a department of the University of Oxford.
It furthers the University's objective of excellence in research, scholarship,
and education by publishing worldwide. Oxford is a registered trade mark of
Oxford University Press in the UK and in certain other countries

Published in the United States of America by Oxford University Press
198 Madison Avenue, New York, NY 10016, United States of America

British Library Cataloguing in Publication Data
Data available

Library of Congress Control Number: 2021952604

ISBN 978–0–19–883147–1(hpk)
ISBN 978–0–19–883148–8(pbk)

DOI: 10.1093/oso/9780198831471.001.0001

Printed and bound by
CPI Group (UK) Ltd, Croydon, CR0 4YY

General, your tank is a powerful thing.
It can break down a forest and crush a hundred men.
But it has one defect:
It needs a driver.

General, your bomber is powerful.
It flies faster than the wind and carries more than an elephant.
But it has one defect:
It needs a mechanic.

General, a man can be turned to many uses.
He can fly and he can kill.
But he has one defect:
He can think.

Bertolt Brecht (tr. Tom Kuhn, The Collected Poems of Bertolt Brecht, 2019)

To Birutė, at the origin of the beauty that surrounds me.

Contents

List of Figures

List of Tables

List of Boxes

List of Abbreviations

3D	Three-dimensional
3G	3rd Generation
4G	4th Generation
5G	5th Generation
AI	Artificial Intelligence
API	Application Programming Interface
AR	Augmented Reality
ATM	Automated Teller Machine
AVMSD	Audio-visual Media Services Directive
AWS	Amazon Web Services
B2B	Business to Business
B2C	Business to Consumer
B2G	Business to Government
BEREC	Body of European Regulators for Electronic Communications
CAAS	Country As A Service
CDC	Centers for Disease Control and Prevention
CEO	Chief Executive Officer
COVID-19	Coronavirus Disease 19
CPF	Compte Personnel de Formation
CSIRT	Computer Security Incident Response Team
CV	Curriculum Vitae
DESI	Digital Economy and Society Index
DGA	Data Governance Act
DG-COMP	Directorate-General for Competition
DIY	Do It Yourself
DLT	Digital Ledger Technology
DMA	Digital Markets Act
DSA	Digital Services Act
DSL	Digital Subscriber Line
DSM	Digital Single Market
EC	European Commission
ECJ	European Court of Justice
ENISA	European Union Agency for Cybersecurity
EUIPO	European Union Intellectual Property Officer
EQF	European Qualification Framework
EU	European Union
FRAND	Fair Reasonable and Non-Discriminatory
FTTx	Fibre To The x
G7	Group of Seven
G2B	Government to Business
G2G	Government to Government
GDP	Gross Domestic Product

GDPR	General Data Protection Regulation
GFT	Google Flu Trends
GPS	Global Position System
GPT	General Purpose Technology
HLG	High-Level Group
HM	Her Majesty
HPC	High-Performance Computing
ICT	Information and Communication Technology
I-DESI	International Digital Economy and Society Index
IP	Internet Protocol
IPR	Intellectual Property Right
ISA	Interoperability Solutions for Administrations
ISP	Internet Service Provider
IT	Information Technology
JRC	Joint Research Centre
LLU	Local Loop Unbundling
M2M	Machine to Machine
MFF	Multiannual Financial Framework
MFN	Most Favoured Nation (clause)
MNO	Mobile Network Operator
MVNO	Mobile Virtual Network Operator
MOOC	Massive Online Open Course
MS	Member State
NATO	North Atlantic Treaty Organization
NGA	Next Generation Access network
NGN	Next Generation Network (see, NGA)
NGO	Non-Governmental Organization
NIS	Network and Information Systems
NYC	New York City
OECD	Organisation for Economic Cooperation and Development
OFCOM	Office of Communication
OJ	Official Journal
OSCE	Organization for Security and Co-operation in Europe
OTT	Over-The-Top
PEBCAK	Problem Exists Between Chair And Keyboard
PIMS	Personal Information Management System
PPP	Public-Private Partnership
PSI	Public Sector Information
QR	Quick Response (code)
R&D	Research and Development
RPM	Resale Price Maintenance
RTB	Real-Time Bidding
SARS-CoV-2	Severe acute respiratory syndrome coronavirus
SIM	Subscriber Identification Module
SM	Single Market
SME	Small and Medium Enterprise
SOC	Security Operation Center
SQL	Structured Query Language
STEM	Science, Technology, Engineering, and Mathematics
TFEU	Treaty on the Functioning of the European Union

TTC	Trade and Technology Council
TV	Television
UBI	Universal Basic Income
UCPD	Unfair Commercial Practice Directive
UGC	User Generated Content
UK	United Kingdom
UNCTAD	United Nations Conference on Trade and Development
UNESCO	United Nations Educational, Scientific and Cultural Organization
URL	Uniform Resource Locator
US	United States
USD	United States Dollars
VAT	Value Added Tax
VBER	Vertical Block Exemption Regulation
VP	Vice President
VR	Virtual Reality
WHO	World Health Organization

Introduction: Why You Should Read This Book

In April 2016, I received an invitation to teach a Master course on the "Digital Economy" at the College of Europe in Natolin, Poland.

I was at the time Digital Adviser for the European Political Strategy Centre, a European Commission in-house think-tank reporting to President Jean-Claude Juncker. My job was to provide policy advice on anything that related to the EU digital agenda. One day I could be asked to double-check the arguments of a telecom company demanding higher investment subsidies. The day after, I could be giving a presentation on artificial intelligence—on how to address its destabilizing effects on society. Or I could liaise with the European Commission's antitrust department and discuss their strategy to tackle market power in online markets.

I was deeply enjoying my job. The digital economy generates novel questions, for which a straightforward answer often simply does not exist. Its study can thus be challenging, stimulating, and enriching at the same time: it requires mastering traditional analytical tools, conceived to understand an "analogic" society, to tackle new problems. Or to come up with new instruments that could replace the old ones, sparking lively discussions amongst academics and practitioners. A good example is with the role of antitrust enforcement in the digital domain: a growing number of academics, particularly in the US, has recently started asking whether traditional enforcement tools, geared to protect consumers, are too narrowly focused on being able to address the emerging challenges posed by concentration in specific areas of the digital economy.

But until I had received the College of Europe's invitation, I had not realized that the value-added of my contribution was not so much in the analysis of the single issue I was dealing with. Nor in the creative solution I could have proposed to tackle it. Most of my value-added was in the broad perspective I could bring to the debate in the attempt to connect the dots between areas that seemingly had little in common. A lot has been written or said about digital policy puzzles such as telecom regulation, copyright or the impact of technology on labour markets. However, the literature offers little or no guidance on how all the different dimensions of the digital economy interact with each other. On the *fil rouge* (the broad perspective) that a policymaker should follow to have a consistent approach across the board, to avoid the intervention in one area that hampers what is done in the other.

When I received the invitation to teach, I was suddenly confronted with the job of calling what I was doing at work by its name; I just did not know what that name was yet. Moving from applied economics and policy making to classroom work was not at all automatic. It not only required acknowledging that the *fil rouge* was the real value-added that I could teach to students. It most prominently required moving from that implicit recognition to a clear plan. A course needs a sensible structure. A framework where all the puzzle pieces can naturally come together and make sense of each other.

This book is the result of that exercise. In many ways, it transposes and extends the lectures that I have been giving to students in Natolin (and, lately, at the University of Namur, Belgium) following the same structured approach.

Similarly to the aim of my lectures, this book aims to provide students with the background knowledge and analytical tools necessary to understand, analyse, and assess the impact of EU digital policies on the European economy and society. The approach is both theoretical and applied. The primary goal of the course is to prepare students to give informed and economically sound advice to a hypothetical EU policymaker for digital affairs. Incidentally, the course aims to stimulate students' curiosity, laying down the basis for further research, for a deeper look at one of the many questions that this book necessarily leaves open.

If I had to describe the job of a policy advisor in a "tweet", I would say that this primarily consists of disentangling legitimate concerns from artificial concerns, designing optimal solutions to address the former and gaining evidence to rebut the latter. Legitimate concerns may merit public action if the market, by itself, cannot deliver what is considered desirable from a societal point of view. It is legitimate, for example, to be concerned about workers made redundant by automation, about the spread of disinformation online, or about small companies' inability to scale up within the EU Single Market because of cross-border limitations to e-commerce. Conversely, stakeholders may put forward artificial concerns to steer policy action towards protecting specific vested interests. Market players often present those interests disguised as legitimate concerns. For example, they may attempt to pull policymakers to intervene to protect privacy rights, while the fundamental objective is to prevent competitors from accessing valuable data. Regulation may be necessary to ensure that companies can compete on an equal footing and that unfair business practices do not harm users. Yet often, stakeholders would attempt to steer its design to get an advantage, such as being shielded from stronger competitors. The ultimate ironic effect is to penalize those users the regulation meant to protect at its inception.

Factors contingent on the digital environment make that advising job particularly tricky in digital policies, especially in this historical moment. We are in the midst of a societal and economic revolution (someone would refer to it as a *fourth industrial revolution*, as we shall see in the book). Traditional business models are being challenged and disrupted by entirely different models; very different actors are replacing old incumbent market players. Those actors play by a rulebook that is hardly intelligible to companies that prospered in the traditional, pre-digital economy. It is sufficient to look at, for example, the publishing industry and how the emergence of the Internet and the use of smartphones have, in a very short interval of time, radically affected the viability of publishing businesses, dramatically changing the expectations around the long-term evolution of the publishing industry.

The implication of this extensive and radical disruption is a significant reshuffling of power in markets. New incumbent players are replacing old ones, economic gains are shifting from one company to another, between industries, and across societal segments. The technological revolution is bringing enormous benefits, as we shall see, and a primary objective of policymakers should be to foster the digitization of the economy. However, societies are converging to new power and value allocation settings that are not necessarily more symmetric than the old ones. As we shall see in Chapter 13 on inequality, despite the promise of significantly improving the human condition, technological progress and the adoption of digital technologies have surprisingly not been associated with a generalized reduction of inequality within society. If anything, we observed the opposite—for reasons that I will explain later.

The generalized reallocation of economic gains and power has been met by strong resistance. And that explains why digital policymakers are heavily lobbied. Stakeholders are very well aware of the peculiarity of the historical moment: after the initial shock brought about by the emergence of new technologies and business models, such as the Internet, data analytics, online platforms, artificial intelligence, and fast, portable communication technologies in recent years, it became apparent that public authorities must take a proactive role to define the rules of the newly emerged markets before potential issues and concerns cement. How rules are currently written determines who will exert a stronger influence on the economy and society in the coming years; this is yet another reason why digital policymakers are currently exposed to tremendous pressure by stakeholders.

Because technological markets are in continuous and rapid evolution, it is not easy to anticipate concerns that may emerge in the future, with societies becoming increasingly digitized. With that in mind, the book's goal is not to provide students with universally applicable ready-made solutions to the future problems they will encounter on their way. Instead, students are offered the opportunity to learn an approach, an applied methodology from the analysis of current issues and the corresponding EU policy implemented in response. Hopefully, that methodology will allow them to address tomorrow the problems we cannot yet foresee today.

The book is structured in four parts. Each part contains four chapters. Except for the chapters contained in Part 1, every chapter in this book has the same section structure: it starts with a general illustration of the context (*background* section); it then discusses the relevant economic dimensions, the dynamics within a particular area of study that are conducive to benefits or costs for society (*opportunities and challenges* section); it analyses the possible solutions from a public policy perspective (*dilemmas for policymakers* section); and, finally, it describes the policies that have so far been implemented at European Union level (*the European Union's perspective* section). Each chapter also includes a brief case study and review questions that students can use to test their understanding of the chapter.

This chapter structure serves two purposes: first, it ensures a systematic approach, allowing the reader to identify similarities and connect policy responses across different topics easily; second, it separates definitions, economic analysis, and general policy challenges (sections one to three) from actual policy responses (section four). A clear separation between analysis and measures implemented can mitigate a risk to which this book is inevitably exposed: to be, in some ways, *short-lived*, if not updated frequently, given that digital markets tend to change so rapidly. But core economic questions and policy puzzles are likely to change at a slower pace than the actual policy solutions that are attempted in response. So the bulk of the updates that the book will inevitably require in the future are most likely to concentrate in section four (*the European Union's perspective*) of each chapter.[1]

Part 1, *Towards a Digital Economy*, contains a general overview of the transformation propelled by technological development. It is about the context the reader is about to venture into. It describes the general features of a **digital economy**, discusses the challenges of digital policy, and introduces the overall EU strategy in the digital domain (Chapter 1). It also reports **facts about the European digital economy** illustrating the current status of the digital transformation in Europe, including a discussion on measurement challenges for the digital economy (Chapter 2). Finally, it contains an overview of digital technologies' role during the **Covid-19 pandemic crisis** that started in 2020 (Chapter 3).

Part 2, *Digital Infrastructure*, Part 3, *Digital Markets*, and Part 4, *Digital Society*, are the core analytical parts of the book. An inverse-pyramid relationship may help represent the relationship between each part (Figure 0.1): digital infrastructures are key inputs from which digital markets stem, ultimately affecting the whole society.

Part 2 focuses on infrastructure and the key inputs necessary for the economy to digitize. Chapters 4 to 7 focus on: **telecom markets**, how to stimulate investment in infrastructure and ensure wide access to high-quality connectivity (Chapter 4); the **data economy**, policies to unlock the potential of data analytics and tackle market

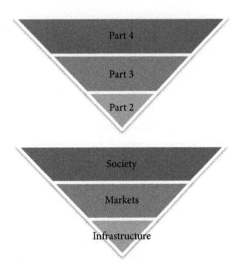

Figure 0.1 Structure of the book

---

[1] Regular updates can be retrieved on the author's website: http://mariomariniello.com

failures in the data ecosystem (Chapter 5); the **public sector**, what prevents public administrations from digitizing and what steps can be made to speed up their transformation (Chapter 6); **cybersecurity**, the safety risks the digital economy is exposed to and how can public policy mitigate that risk increasing the resilience of the digital environment to security failure (Chapter 7). Notably, the digitization of the public sector could also be considered an "output" of the digital economy. But it is placed in Part 2 to emphasize its role as an enabler of digitization: the ability of individuals and businesses to interact with a digitized public administration can be of a great impulse to the technological progress of society.

Part 3 is dedicated to digital markets: the most apparent aspect of the digital economy; those services people tend to interact with in their daily life—checking their e-mail, surfing the Internet, or ordering a pizza through an online delivery platform. Central to Part 3 are **online platforms**, their functioning, the general issues they generate and the interplay of regulation and competition policy in the online platform environment (Chapter 8). The following chapters provide for a deeper look at essential dimensions of the platform economy: online **platforms' liability** for the (illegal) content they may host and how to deal with the dilemma of protecting online users while avoiding censoring legal content (Chapter 9); **e-commerce** and digital taxation, how to pull down barriers to cross-border supply and demand of digital goods and services, and how to ensure that digital services pay taxes where they create value (Chapter 10); the **sharing economy**, the dynamics underpinning online business models that allow private individuals to share their physical assets or spare time for a profit, the economic and societal issues they give rise to, and how can we address them (Chapter 11).

Finally, Part 4 focuses on the broader societal implications that a digitized economy entails. It discusses the effect of technological adoption on **labour markets** and suggests how policymakers should protect workers that are negatively affected by digitization (Chapter 12). It contains an analysis of the effect of technology on **inequality** and the relationship between the "digital divide" and the distribution of the value generated by technological progress within society (Chapter 13). It explains why online **disinformation** is so widespread and discusses potential short-term and long-term solutions to alleviate that problem (Chapter 14). Finally, Chapter 15 is a deep dive into the world of **artificial intelligence**, the transformational effects on the economy and society due to its wide adoption, and the need for a European Union strategy to foster its development and uptake, while preserving the EU fundamental values and principles.

The last part of the book contains tools that students may use to complement their reading: the **Appendix** is a toolkit designed for students who do not have background studies in economics; it briefly explains concepts that I often use throughout the book, such as "network externalities", "market failures", "asymmetric information", and so forth. Similarly, the **Glossary** should help readers quickly navigate the book's terminology (not a straightforward task, as there is significant complexity and variation in terms across the different areas of study covered by the different chapters).

A final caveat for the reader: I wrote this book with the idea of making it as accessible as possible to a broad audience, regardless of the reader's background. This book is thus not specifically designed for students with an economic background. However, an economist wrote the book. The description of the digital environment's dynamics, the interpretation of the issues, and the analysis of possible solutions are all coming from an economist's perspective. That simple fact should be kept well in mind by readers: the digital economy can be looked at from many different angles, through the lens of many different scientific disciplines (such as anthropology, sociology, informatics, psychology, philosophy, or law), none of which can claim to have the best answer to the challenges the digital economy confront us with. Instead, each of them can contribute to form our understanding and help to shape policy intervention in the best possible way. This book hopes to be one crucial contribution of the many that are necessary to pursue that goal.

Acknowledgements

I wrote the greatest part of this book during the Covid-19 pandemic. I was among the privileged ones who could safely work at home without fearing losing their job or being exposed to a health hazard. The loss of human contact was nevertheless a hardship that I struggled to endure. Being aware that millions of others were simultaneously sharing similar feelings was of no help—I still felt a profound solitude. Ironically, I found myself writing a book on digital technology, the epitome of humans' endeavour to go beyond the limits of their biology while nurturing an ever-deeper belief about the importance of those limits to define us. The pandemic reminded me how much we need to be physically close with no technological mediation, breathe the same air, touch each other, accept each other's fallacies, be real and present, together, at the same moment in the same place, to feel human. I am convinced that no technology will ever be able to change that.

However, this book also generated many occasions to feel loved. I may have been writing this book all alone in the basement of a *maison de maître* in Brussels. But if this book saw the light in this shape, it is also thanks to the contribution of all those who did not hesitate to help me when needed. While the responsibility for any inaccuracy in the content of this book is solely mine, I would like to take the occasion here to express my gratitude to all of them.

I should first mention my former and current students at the College of Europe and the University of Namur. Teaching the material I used in this book was the best way to test its didactic power; this book benefited significantly from my students' feedback and the exchanges I had with them during our classroom work.

Marianna Wysocki supported this project from the beginning. Marianna has not only been carefully reading everything I was writing (providing detailed feedback and suggestions on how to improve the clarity of my message), she also often raised intellectually challenging questions on content, pushing me to back up my statements with solid evidence from the literature.

Hèctor Badenes helped me extensively by enhancing and streamlining all the graphics reported in the first draft of the manuscript. Monika Grzegorczyk and Tom Schraepen helped make order in the long references I used in the book.

I owe an outstanding debt to Bertin Martens and Alexandre de Streel. They read the final manuscript and took the time to give me extensive comments, which significantly improved the book's structure, content, and shape.

Finally, I would like to thank everyone who helped throughout the editing and publishing process from the Oxford University Press and Integra teams: Sivanesan Ashok Kumar, Prabhu Chinnasamy, Duncan Baylis, Henry Clarke, Jade Dixon, Jenny King.

But the list of the "indirect contributors" could be much longer: the book is only the endpoint of a journey that started a long time ago. Thus, it was also shaped by all that I learned talking to friends and colleagues throughout my academic and professional career. The book owes a lot to my long-standing mentors Massimo Motta and Alessandro Petretto, and my former colleagues at the European Commission Daniela Bremer, Anne Bucher, Filomena Chirico, Marigael Duriez, Carles Esteva Mosso, Natacha Faullimmel, Kamil Kiljanski, Kim-Hoang Le, Klaudia Majcher, Ann Mettler, Mihnea Motoc, Damien Neven, Penelope Papandropoulos, Enrico Pesaresi, Leonardo Quattrucci, Agnieszka Skuratowicz, Lucilla Sioli, Oliver Stehmann, Pavel Swieboda, Luís Viegas Cardoso, Roberto Viola, and Hans Zenger. The book also greatly benefited from the debates and the exchanges I had with the whole Bruegel community, starting from Guntram Wolff and Maria Demertzis (Guntram and Maria did not hesitate to offer me a space to work on the book, even though the pandemic then prevented me from using it!), Grégory Claeys, Zsolt Darvas, Alicia García-Herrero, Mia Hoffmann, Scott Marcus, Benedicta Marzinotto, Diane Mulcahy, Laura Nurski, Francesco Papadia, Georgios Petropoulos, Jean Pisani-Ferry, Niclas Poitiers, André Sapir, Nicolas Véron, Reinhilde Veugelers, Simone Tagliapietra, Georg Zachmann, Makfire Alija, Stéphane Asse'e, Alma Kurtovic, Paola Maniga, Delphine Michel, Scarlett Varga, Emanuela Dimonte, Giuseppe Porcaro, and Stephen Gardner (Stephen's editorial tips have been invaluable to me since the moment I attempted to write my first opinion piece). The book also immensely benefited from the support I felt from my close friends and family. I would never have been able to walk this journey without the support of my friends in Florence, my friends in Brussels (the friends from Viola Club Bruxelles were always there when needed!) and my family: Tommaso Mariniello, Luana Pistozzi, Susy Mariniello, Irene Traversi, Jacopo Traversi, Alice, Bobute, Antanas Stančius, Ivona Stančiūtė, Lina Stančiūtė, Martynas Gecevičius, Ema, and Aja.

Yet, by all means, my biggest debt is towards the two loves of my life, Jurga and Lulu. Jurga not only first came up with the idea of the book, she actually believed that I could be the one writing it! Throughout the whole drafting time, from the beginning until the end, she was next to me, trusting, supporting, encouraging me unconditionally. Even when, admittedly, having me around all the time at home during lock-downs must have been a much tougher challenge than writing a book . . .

And finally, Lulu, who is still not fully aware of how important she is for everything her dad does, just filling his heart with joy every day, making sense of it all.

Brussels, April 2022

****

PART 1
TOWARDS A DIGITAL ECONOMY

1
A Digital Economy

Abstract

Throughout history, economies and societies have always been deeply affected by technology. Radical technological innovations, such as steam-power, electricity, or electronics,
prompted the first, second, and third industrial revolutions. Now, countries worldwide
are experiencing a fourth, equally disruptive, industrial revolution, thanks to the Internet and powerful emerging technologies such as artificial intelligence. As society becomes
more and more reliant on digital applications, action by public policy is required to correct
markets where they fail to deliver optimal outcomes, namely: creating significant value
and ensure that everyone can enjoy it. The job is not easy, and digital policy needs to
address complex challenges: it needs to balance dynamism and stability, to address regulatory fragmentation in a highly fluid, fast-changing, environment; to solve novel economic
puzzles and to answer profound philosophical dilemmas. Nations around the world are deploying digital policy strategies in an attempt to secure an overarching consistent public
approach to emerging issues.

1.1 A new digital era

Defining the *digital economy* is an elusive and risky exercise. It is elusive because
the societal transformation induced by recent technological developments is profound, and the boundaries between what is digital and what is not are increasingly
blurred. I could argue that it is misleading, for example, to attempt to separate policies for *economic* development from policies for *digital* development: to the extent
that digitalization is mediating an overwhelming share of interactions between society's members, that digital has become the primary vehicle of public and private
communication, and that advanced technologies are radically reshaping the way we
work, think, or experience life, economic and digital development are more and
more the same thing.

Defining the digital economy is also a risky exercise because it entails a false
sense of security: practitioners, policymakers, researchers, and students alike may
be compelled to believe that the *digital economy* can be reduced to some categories,
where specific issues can be studied in isolation and viable self-standing solutions
identified. To a certain extent attaching a label to observed dynamics and propose
categories of action is, of course, part of any analytical and strategic policy process.

Digital Economic Policy. Mario Mariniello, Oxford University Press.
© Mario Mariniello (2022). DOI: 10.1093/oso/9780198831471.003.0001

This book itself is an example of that: Chapters 3 to 15 are each dealing with specific dimensions of the digital economy, be that infrastructure development, the platform economy, the future of work, or artificial intelligence. However, as I hope it will become apparent in the course of this book, this classification is mainly artificial. All dimensions of analysis are deeply intertwined, and no issue within the digital world can be looked at in isolation from each other. That applies to measurement as well, as we shall see in the next chapter.

This chapter aims not to provide a proverbial "textbook" definition of the digital economy and explain it. Not only because there does not exist a univocal one;[1] the main reason is to avoid being captured in unhelpful narrow categories. Instead, the purpose of this chapter is to describe the features that characterize the economy and society as transformed by current technological development. The chapter aims to frame the general policy challenge and describe the main motor that has so far guided the European Commission's policy action in the digital space.

1.1.1 The big picture

Commentators have started to refer to the existence of a digital economy as of the late 1990s. The emergence of the Internet radically changed the way people communicate; computing performance dramatically increased, and powerful computing machines, such as personal computers or, more recently, smartphones, became affordable and widely available. What came to be known as *Moore's Law*[2] (that is, the empirical observation that transistors on a chip tend to double every eighteen months, halving computers' size while doubling their power) led to an explosion of technological development and the massive computerization of society. Fast wired and wireless connectivity infrastructure challenged the relevance of physical constraints in limiting the ability of individuals to work, study, and communicate across the territory. Online platforms (operative systems, social networks, search engines, e-commerce platforms) have reshaped the way individuals relate to each other and enabled the creation of business models that only a few years ago could not exist. Consider, for example, ride-sharing applications, such as Uber or Lyft. They crucially rely on individuals owning smartphones, on Global Position Systems (GPS), on mapping services, on Internet connection, and mobile Internet payments (we will see the functioning of these businesses, in detail, in the following chapters).

This profound transformation has also concerned the industry. The **Internet of Things** (namely the universe of objects that automatically communicate with each other with a constant flow of data through *machine to machine* or **M2M** communication) is changing how goods and services are produced and supplied. For

---

[1] The expression "digital economy" has been used in numerous contexts and many definitions put forward. The term went mainstream after having been proposed by Information Technology expert Don Tapscott in Tapscott, D. (1996).

[2] See Moore, G. E. (1975, pp. 11–13); the article corrects a first prediction based on Moore, G. E. (1965).

many, the economy is undergoing a true new *technological revolution*. A first revolution is deemed to have occurred towards the end of the eighteenth century, with the discovery and diffusion of steam power and mechanization; a second revolution occurred about a hundred years later, with the emergence of electricity and mass production. Automation, electronics, informatics, and computing facilities reshaped the industry a third time in the 1960s. A final fourth revolution is now ongoing, thanks to connectivity, artificial intelligence, data analytics, the Internet of things, and, more generally, the digitalization of the production value chain (Schwab, K., 2017).

The digital economy manifests itself in countless ways. The most critical aspects from a policy perspective will be analysed in-depth in the following chapters; hence readers should expect to have a good understanding of what a digital economy means only after having gone through the whole book.

Yet, we can use some compelling facts to provide an order of magnitude of the transformation that technology is inducing in societies around the world:

- **Online platforms** allow Internet users to communicate, interact, and benefit from each other. The most popular of them could be described as clubs where membership is offered for free in monetary terms (that is, you do not need to pay any monetary fee to get in). As we shall see in Chapter 8, online platforms tend to become bigger and bigger. The bigger they are, the more beneficial to their users, who can enjoy a bigger pool of users to interact with. This natural tendency to expand has led some platforms to become more "crowded" than the most populous countries in the world. In 2019, Facebook had more than 2.4 billion active users; YouTube, 2.2 billion; WhatsApp, 1.6 billion; WeChat, 1.1 billion; Twitter, 330 million. By comparison, in 2021, China and India each had a population of 1.4 billion individuals; the European Union, 447 million; the United States, 331 million. Online platforms have also made the world look smaller, enabling individuals to meet and stay in contact even if geographically distant. As an illustration, consider this figure: between 2012 and 2015, the proportion of monthly active Facebook users with at least one international friend tripled, from 15% to 50% (45% in advanced economies, 55% for emerging economies).
- A key input for the digital economy is **data.** Data is considered the *new oil* of the economy (the expression is suggestive even if somehow inaccurate, as we shall see in Chapter 5). The ability to process large amounts of information makes artificial intelligence-powered machines outperform humans when carrying out specific tasks. To have an idea of the amount of data produced and collected in the digital economy, consider Figure 1.1 (Jenik C., 2020): every minute of 2020, on average, has seen Netflix users streaming more than 400,000 hours of videos; 42 million messages shared on WhatsApp; nearly 6,700 parcels shipped by Amazon; and over 208,000 participants in Zoom meetings.

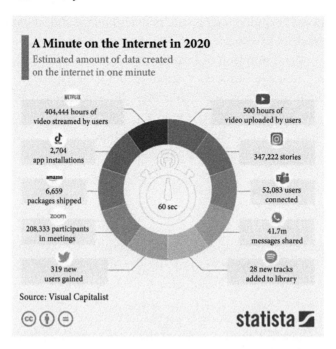

Figure 1.1 A minute on the internet in 2020. Jenik, C. (2020).
Statista Inc. Accessed: April 12, 2021. https://www.statista.com/chart/
17518/data-created-in-an-internet-minute/. Made available under the
Creative Commons License CC BY-ND 3.0

- The **pace of development and uptake** in digital economies is unprecedented. As an illustration, consider that it took 160 years for Indonesia to adopt steam power since its invention widely; 60 years were necessary for Kenya to provide widespread access to electricity; conversely, it took only 15 years for Vietnam to introduce computers (World Bank, 2016). The speed of adoption of online services seems to grow at an exponential rate. It took eight years for Facebook to reach 1 billion users, seven years for WhatsApp, three years for TikTok.
- Digital economies are fertile ground for invention. In particular, the contemporaneous availability of fast connectivity infrastructure, computing power, and massive amounts of data contribute significantly to creating the conditions for the development of technologies that can radically transform people's lives. In this book, I analyse some of the emerging technologies that are looking more promising at the time of writing. Artificial intelligence, for example, has a dedicated chapter (Chapter 15) because of its extensive general implications. I discuss other technologies in the context of the relevant relating chapter. 5G wireless communication technology is discussed in Chapter 4 dedicated to connectivity, for example. *Blockchain* and *digital ledger technologies* are discussed in Chapter 6 on digital government. But the list of promising technologies that

are capturing the imagination of policymakers and the collectivity alike is long. Here are just a few examples:[3]

- **High-performance computing (HPC) and Quantum technologies.**[4] HPC is used to solve highly complex computational or data-intensive problems (hence HPC technologies are also referred to as *supercomputers*). On the other hand, quantum technologies use the physical properties of small particles (i.e. *quantum objects*) to achieve significant breakthroughs in computing, cryptography, communication, and measurement.
- **Connected or automated mobility** refers to the development of driving systems that can replace or assist human drivers with different levels of autonomy. Such systems have the potential to reduce vehicles' environmental impact, and car crashes, significantly. However, they do pose new challenges. For example, how to ensure smooth wireless connectivity while on the move, how to address potential new cybersecurity threats, and how to deal with tricky ethical questions, such as whether a driver-less car should prioritize the safety of its occupants or that of pedestrians.[5]
- **3D printing** refers to automated manufacturing processes where robot-arm printheads deposit or fuse material on multiple layers. Materials can be of different nature, such as metal, glass, or wood. 3D printing can also be used to print biological material, for example, to print skin or organs, such as bone or cartilage scaffolds. The impact of 3D printing on the economy can potentially be powerful: it can radically change the manufacturing value-chain, dramatically reducing production costs, prompting reshoring of work processes and changing the pattern of trade.[6]
- **Wearable technologies** refer to personal equipment that individuals can wear with the intent to monitor or enhance their experience. Smart watches, smart-jewellery or smart-clothing, for example, can provide accurate information on the possessor's health status. Sensors can also be implanted or tattooed on people's skin. Wearable technologies can be very useful at the individual and public level. For example, they could be used to accurately monitor the level of pollution to which individuals are exposed. Their use, however, may increase privacy and security risks, or may even constitute a violation of human rights (for example, if imposed by an employer to an employee).[7]
- **Virtual reality (VR) and augmented reality (AR).** Virtual reality is used to simulate real-world experiences using scenarios that are generated by

---

[3] For an overview of how digital technologies reshape the entrepreneurial process, see: Elia, et al. (2020).

[4] On the relevance of HPC for different economic actors, see Gupta, et al. (2013).

[5] Students may test their ethical views in this context by visiting the MIT "moral machine" website: https://www.moralmachine.net/

[6] For an introduction to the international trade implications of 3D printing, see Pierrakakis, et al. (2015).

[7] Kalantari (2017) has a good review of the literature on consumers' adoption and acceptance of wearable technologies.

specific software. Augmented reality is used to enhance individuals' performance while carrying on a task by combining their real-life experience with computer-generated content (Eurofound, 2019). For example, a carpenter could use some AR-powered goggles to improve the precision of her woodcut.

- Digital technologies have radically **reshaped the allocation of economic power**. Figure 1.2 compares the most valuable publicly quoted companies in the world in 2009 and 2019. In 2009, the wealthiest companies were almost all active in the energy or financial sector. In 2019, seven out of ten are large digital companies with an online platform business model[8] (note, moreover, that none of those companies is European; they are either US companies or Chinese companies).

2009

Ranking of companies:	Market Capital [$B] :	Sector:
1. Petrochina	367	Energy
2. Exxon	341	Energy
3. ICBC	257	Financial
4. Microsoft	212	Technology
5. China Mobile	201	
6. Walmart	189	
7. China Construction Bank	182	Financial
8. Petrobras	165	Energy
9. Johnson and Johnson	157	
10. Shell	156	Energy

2019

Ranking of companies:	Market Capital [$B] :	Sector:
1. Microsoft	1,050	Technology
2. Amazon	943	Technology
3. Apple	920	Technology
4. Alphabet	778	Technology
5. Facebook	546	Technology
6. Berkshire Hathaway	507	
7. Alibaba	435	Technology
8. Tencent	431	Technology
9. VISA	379	Financial
10. Johnson and Johnson	376	Technology

Figure 1.2 Largest global companies 2009 vs 2019
https://www.visualcapitalist.com/a-visual-history-of-the-largest-companies-by-market-cap-1999-today/

---

[8] A general discussion on the economic changes induced by the platform economy is in Kenney and Zysman (2016).

- Digital economies have also most recently been shaken by **techlash** (a technological backlash). Major online platforms, in particular, have attracted mounting criticism: for their powerful position in increasingly concentrated markets; for the explosions of cases in which personal data of individuals were compromised, showing that privacy and security risks are the effective cost borne by users to access allegedly "free" online services; and for the massive spread of disinformation on the Internet, which is believed to play a crucial role in the raise of populism and polarization of societies.
- Finally: the **Covid-19 pandemic has accelerated the digitalization process of the economy,** forcing the workforce to work remotely when possible. But it has also exacerbated an already strong tendency towards an asymmetric distribution of the benefits of technological development, which has become worryingly typical of digital economies. Because of the *digital divide,* during the pandemic the gap between those who had the means to profit from the Internet and those who did not (such as students from low-income households with no access to connectivity infrastructure) increased, leading to more unequal societies.

1.2 Digital policy

Digital economies escape universally accepted definitions and are challenging to measure (as we shall see in the next chapter). Their inherent elusiveness makes pinning down potential societal and economic issues tricky. Digital economies trigger complex novel policy challenges for public decision-makers for other reasons too. **Four dichotomies** are most relevant to explain why digital policy is challenging (Figure 1.3):

First, as we have seen, digital markets tend to evolve very rapidly. New technologies can quickly emerge and be widely adopted. They can induce major changes in production and consumption processes; new business models can quickly reshape markets, shifting the allocation of profits between different players in the value chain. Thus, a significant feature of digital markets is their **dynamism**. Yet, digital services and goods crucially depend on connectivity and computing infrastructure. Infrastructure can only be set up through significant long-term investment, as we shall see in the dedicated chapters. But investment requires stability, some visibility on the future evolution of the economy, and some **certainty** that the initial investment will pay off in the long term. This tension between dynamism and the need for stability is a first source of troubles for policymakers. One of the most commonly used selling points for regulatory intervention, for example, is that regulation can help dispel uncertainty for investors. However, in a very dynamic environment, that may quickly turn into a disadvantage: by the time regulation comes into force, regulated markets may have already significantly changed and regulation is born obsolete.

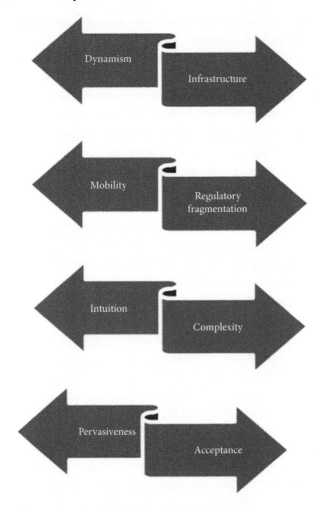

Figure 1.3 The four dichotomies of digital policy

The second dichotomy relates to the **geographical fluidity** of digital markets. Digital technologies allow services and goods to travel the world in the blink of an eye; thanks to the Internet, physical distance is no longer a relevant issue affecting work, production, consumption, or communication. Small start-ups can quickly scale up and reach the whole globe at an insignificant fraction of the cost they would have had to bear a few years ago. This geographical fluidity, however, implies that digital markets are very vulnerable to **regulatory fragmentation**. Scaling up for digital businesses is not a nice add-on—it is an essential part of the business itself (in the following chapters, I will often stress the importance of network externalities, i.e. the advantage of becoming bigger and bigger). That means that the chances of success of a digital business can be hampered by multiple regulatory frameworks, with different geographical regions or countries imposing different requirements to players. It is straightforward to see how this dichotomy, *mobility vs regulatory fragmentation*, is relevant for the European Union, where Member States have much to gain from creating a uniform regulatory approach across the whole continent (the EU *Digital Single Market*, see Section 1.3 below).

The third dichotomy concerns the economics of digital markets. On the one hand, digital businesses owe their success to their immediacy, their simplicity. Social networks, Internet search engines, rental sharing platforms, lift peer-to-peer services, and dating apps are widely used because their operating principle is **intuitive**. Tinder is a dating app where users browsing potential dating mates' photos can either swipe right to flag interest or left to move on to the following user—as simple as that. Yet the underlying economic dynamics of most digital services are very **complex**: multi-sided platforms connect groups of players that are very different from each other, such as consumers, business users, content producers, infrastructure owners, and virtual operators. Moreover, service and goods production and consumption often involve costs and benefits that do not have a monetary appreciation, such as effects on privacy risks or the benefits of customization and the prosumer role of consumers that, with consumption, contribute to the production of the product themselves. These features tend to create novel problems for economists, who are still looking for the correct answers.

Finally, the fourth dichotomy concerns the role that technology is playing within society. Digital applications are everywhere: many are glued to their smartphones in their daily life; Internet search engines have become indispensable tools to study, work, plan leisure activities, and retrieve health information; social networks and *over the top* platform communication services (such as WhatsApp or Telegram) are the main channels people use to stay in touch with friends, family, and acquaintances. Technology is, in other words, **pervasive**. And yet, technological adoption comes together with profound ethical dilemmas for which a "right" answer often simply does not exist. Often, digital technologies push humans beyond the limit of their *bounded rationality*. In the following chapters, we will discuss the privacy paradox, i.e. an inconsistency between individuals' behaviour online and offline in terms of how cautious they are regarding the risk of endangering their privacy when publicly disclosing personal information. Despite wide adoption, digital technologies are looked at with suspicion: one may feel she cannot live without them, while at the same time not being entirely convinced or aware of the consequences that their use entail. Wide **social acceptance**, despite the apparent success suggested by adoption, is still far away. The challenge for public policy is evident, as the answers put forward cannot merely address technical economic puzzles; they also entail deep consequences for the societies' underlying value structure.

1.2.1 The goals of digital policy

Policymakers should aim to extract the maximum value from digital technologies for society despite this novel and complex context. Naturally, policymakers have their political agenda to pursue, and goals differ across different public administrations worldwide.

Economists can provide some technical guidance on how to actionize the overarching principle that public policy should foster society's long-term welfare (this principle tends to be universally accepted, at least in its nominal shape, by policymakers everywhere in the world).

In the digital environment, this boils down to fostering and steering technological development towards creating the maximum possible value for the economy and ensuring that this value is fairly shared among the members of society. *Value* is a purposely vague term: it does not coincide with *richness in monetary terms,* and its specifications depend on individuals' preferences. A value-generating technology may well not make a country more prosperous but can ensure that its economic activities are more environmentally sustainable, for example.

More specifically, it is possible to identify **five areas** where policy can intervene to pursue that overarching objective:

- **Development** – the aim of policymakers should be to incentivize investment in the development of valuable new technologies. To create a fertile environment that stimulates value-enhancing invention from a societal perspective. To ensure that the economy can access the physical resources (such as natural raw materials), infrastructures (such as telecommunication), and intangible capital (such as skills and knowledge) that are necessary to be at the frontier of technological development. That also means to increase an economy's *strategic autonomy*, or, in other words, its ability to stand on its feet, should trade with other economies suddenly stop. The no-trade scenario may seem a theoretical exercise: value chains are so intertwined internationally that it may seem absurd to consider the possibility that countries would stop trading with each other. However, the extreme of the no-trade *thought experiment* may help assess a country's strength when entering into trade agreement negotiations. A simple example that I will later discuss in Chapter 10 is taxation on digital services and its repercussion on trade talks between the EU and the US.
- **Adoption** – the aim of digital policy should be to facilitate and incentivize the uptake of new value-enhancing technologies by any potential user: inhabitants, public administrations, small and medium companies, or large enterprises. *Adoption* is a general term that should not be considered to apply only to access and use of digital infrastructure, technological equipment, or digital applications. Adoption also refers to the endorsement of a new mindset, a new way to create and enjoy value within the economy thanks to the new opportunities generated by digital means, particularly in the online space. In Chapter 6, we shall see, for example, how this aspect of adoption matters in the context of the *e-government* discussion.
- **Seamlessness** – policymakers should be particularly concerned with removing any obstacle hampering the flow of digital goods and services. These may be

physical obstacles, like adverse geographical conditions that, for example, may impede connectivity in remote rural areas. They may be artificial barriers, such as unnecessary regulatory restrictions preventing small companies from selling across borders (this is a critical issue within the EU Digital Single Market, as we shall see). But they also may be intangible barriers at an individual level, preventing potential users from enjoying the full potential of technology, for example because they lack the knowledge or the skills that are necessary to use it. Elderly people, for example, are the population group that is likely to benefit the most from digitized health services, as they rely less on personal mobility. However, they are also the least likely to be able to access them, given their average low digital skills levels.

- **Inclusivity** – technological development and adoption may generate significant value but, if that value is concentrated and only a tiny share of society can enjoy it, the ultimate dominant effect is to exacerbate inequality, widening the gap between the haves and the have-nots. Making the distribution of the value generated by technology and digital goods and services more symmetric, by allowing all members of society to enjoy it, is a fundamental task of digital policy. This does not only concern the removal of the obstacles to access technology, feeling the *digital divide*. It also concerns the set-up of a regulatory framework that would prevent abuse of technology by the powerful against the vulnerable. For example, it should be ensured that employers do not exploit artificial intelligence to worsen their employees' working conditions.

- **Protection** – finally, policymakers must ensure that the environment where technology is developed, endorsed, and used is safe. This goal is not only about the apparent need to adopt and implement a framework that protects the digital environment from cyber-threats, i.e. a *cybersecurity* framework. Policymakers should ensure that digital markets are not liable to abuse and exploitation. Online disinformation content may, for example, not qualify as illegal but cause significant harm at an individual and societal level, as we shall see in Chapter 14. The high level of granularity of the data that can be collected and processed in the digital economy significantly expands the scope for discriminatory behaviour. Policymakers should feel compelled to prevent discrimination that is harmful to individuals and a threat to social cohesion.

These five areas of action overlap as policy action can affect multiple areas at the same time. The most obvious example is competition policy (this will be discussed in Chapter 8 in the context of online platform markets). Competition policy enforcement dissuades powerful companies from abusing their dominant position. Hence it ensures *protection*. It prevents acquisitions that would lead to a harmful concentration of market power. Hence it ensures that value is *shared*. And it stimulates the development and adoption of technology by preserving the incentives of companies to invest in innovation. Similar considerations can be made, for example, about data protection policies, consumer protection, telecom regulation, and cybersecurity.

How digital policies can pursue those objectives in practice will be discussed in each dedicated chapter. Crucially, any policy intervention should be informed by the identification of a well-defined **market failure**. That is the specification of why the market economy cannot reach the optimal outcome from a social perspective, absent public intervention. It is not sufficient, for example, to point out that the spread of disinformation on online platforms is causing harm to users to justify public action to tackle it. It is necessary first to understand why online platforms are not tackling the problem themselves in the first place, or why users are not able to react, for example abandoning that communication platform. This two-step logical approach (namely: first, identify the market failure, *and only then* intervene to correct it) is needed because public policy intervention is always costly. An obvious cost is linked to the public resources needed to mobilize public action, from inception, design, adoption of laws to their enforcement, for example. But the main cost is the risk of distorting market players' incentives and determining a misallocation of economic resources. Public decision-makers are less apt to "select the winners" than (functioning) markets: the value of a technology is best tested by its adoption rate, not by its political support. Provided that, of course, the market is *frictionless*, and no market failures are hampering the valuable technologies' chances to emerge (we will discuss the relationship between market failures and state aid intervention in Chapter 10, in the context of digital taxation).

Identifying market failures is a process as delicate as the one necessary to design the best way to address them. The challenge for policymakers is to focus on legitimate concerns proposing efficient solutions for them while rebutting artificial or protectionist concerns that players may have put forward to steer policy action in their favour. For example, policymakers may decide to impose a tax on adopting new technologies to limit the growth in their use (it would not be a good idea, as we shall see, but let us consider this just for illustration). They may be moved to do so by a *legitimate* concern that artificial intelligence is destroying certain jobs, increasing the unemployment risk for specific categories of workers. Or they may be driven by a *protectionist* concern since artificial intelligence may be increasing the competitiveness of foreign companies, thereby eroding domestic companies' profits.

This challenge is familiar to any economic policy. Digital policy is, however, a bit special, at least in the historical moment in which I am writing this book. Digital policy is heavily lobbied, and disentangling legitimate concerns from protectionist concerns is often particularly hard. It is not by chance that when the European Commission launches a public consultation seeking feedback from stakeholders for a regulation or directive it is considering to propose for a digital area, it usually gets a high number of submissions. Digital policy is heavily lobbied for two reasons: first, because digitization is radically reshaping the economy and our society, as we have seen above. In other words, digitalization is challenging the traditional allocation of wealth, re-shuffling the cards, massively shifting power and value from one player to another. Just think about the effect that the Internet had on traditional news publishers, with most of their customers switching from paper to online to read their daily news (see Chapter 9). Or the telecom sectors and the impact that online platforms had on telecoms' revenue from messaging services (see Chapter 4). Thus, it is only natural that the **disruption** caused by digitization is triggering significant resistance by traditional industries and incumbent players. As well as catalysing the efforts of new dominant players in the digital space, such as major online platforms, interested in creating more and more room in the economy so that they can occupy it, replacing old incumbent industries.

The second reason is that this "clash" is happening at a moment of great dynamism and uncertainty—it probably has never been harder to predict how the economy will evolve in the next few years. Moreover, many technologies with a vast disruption potential are emerging (think about artificial intelligence) posing very novel issues, as we shall see. Thus, the stakes are high: holding the pen for a digital regulation today means having the potential to shape the future evolution of society, determining winners and losers of the *digital revolution*. The result is an intensely emotional and polarized public debate. At one extreme, techno-optimists may hail technology as the way to salvation. For example, they may emphasize the role of *geo-engineering* (i.e. a large-scale attempt to use technology to affect the Earth's natural system) to address climate change rather than focusing on reducing the consumption of non-renewable resources. At the other extreme, techno-pessimists may see technology as humankind's damnation. For example, they may suggest that artificial intelligence will lead to the extinction of humankind, with machines replacing humans as dominant species on Earth, see Chapter 15.

Thus, sound economic analysis seems all the more needed today to complement the political democratic lead and guide digital policy towards picking social-welfare maximizing choices.

1.3 The EU strategic approach to digital policy

By the end of 2020, 34 out of the 37 OECD countries[9] had developed an overarching national digital policy strategy defining policy priorities, goals, and implementation patterns to favour the digitization of their economy while addressing emerging issues. According to the OECD (2020a), countries tend to consider top priorities as: digitize the public sector, foster innovation in digital technologies, *develop skills for the digital transformation,* and *develop telecommunication infrastructure.* A second tier of priorities is: *fostering security, designing data governance frameworks, and fostering the adoption of digital technologies by the business. Consumer protection* and *improvement of Internet governance* tend to get lower attention than the other areas of action and come last in the OECD ranking of countries' priorities. However, as we shall see in Part 4 of the book, governments increasingly pay attention to the effect that digitization has on individual well-being. As a result, a growing effort by public

[9] The full list of OECD countries can be retrieved here: http://www.oecd.org/about/members-and-partners/

institutions to prevent online harm should be expected everywhere globally for the years to come.

Most recently, the international dimension of the digital economy has become prominent in the political discourse. Countries are more and more concerned about their chance to win an alleged *race for technological supremacy*.[10] Digital technologies are (probably rightly) indicated as a primary tool to achieve commercial, political, and military primacy in the international landscape (we will discuss this at length in Chapter 15, dedicated to artificial intelligence). The urge to *move fast* to regulate the digital space is also dictated by the urgency to prime the direction of the evolution of technology, and help international efforts converge to develop technologies that tend to be more aligned with the preferences in the domestic jurisdiction. The European Union's efforts to define an ethical framework for artificial intelligence-powered technologies or prevent personal data misuse can also be seen through this light, as we shall see in the dedicated chapters.

The rhetoric of *strategic autonomy* is increasingly apparent in public decision-makers' statements: in the US, "America First" was the slogan that informed former President Trump's line of action. "Made in China 2020" is the overarching principle guiding China's approach to digital technologies. The European Commission has similarly increasingly emphasized preserving (or, more appropriately, achieving) *technological sovereignty*. In her first "State of the Union" address (European Commission, 2020a) to the European Parliament Plenary in September 2020, European Commission President Ursula von der Leyen mentioned, explicitly, **digital sovereignty** as the ultimate goal of her Commission's action in the digital domain. In that spirit, she announced an investment of €8 billion on *supercomputers* (see above on HPC and Quantum computing technologies). This *arms race* rhetoric is easy to understand: by 2020, China had almost half of the world's 500 supercomputers (226) while EU countries altogether had only 79 (European Commission, 2020b). The following year, during her second State of the Union address in September 2021, she unveiled her plan to propose a **European Chips Act**.[11] Chips are considered an indispensable resource for the geopolitical technological competition engaged by the biggest world economies such as China, the US, and the EU. Chips are indispensable for smartphones, for artificial intelligence applications, for automated cars, and for the Internet of Things. With the Chips Act, the European Commission is flagging its intention to raise the stakes, prioritizing research, development, and chip design to attempt reverting a worrisome trend of a declining share in the global production of semiconductors in favour of its Asian counterparts. Whether it will succeed will very much depend on the concrete efforts that the European Union will exert in the coming years (particularly, but not only, in terms of the amount of monetary resources it will be able to commit to this area).

---

[10] Cave and ÓhÉigeartaigh (2018) discuss the risk of the "technology race" rhetoric and the need for a more pro-active involvement of the academic community.

[11] See: https://ec.europa.eu/info/sites/default/files/soteu_2021_address_en.pdf

Notably, the EU efforts to boost Europe's computing performance are rooted in a broader, far-reaching plan to **digitize the European industry**. In its 2016 Communication (European Commission, 2016a), the European Commission proposed a multi-dimensional set of actions to complement EU countries' national initiatives supporting the digitalization of their domestic industries. The plan entailed using policy and regulatory tools, financial aid and non-binding guidance to favour supra-national coordination of the different national strategies. The most significant regulatory measures envisaged by the Commission will be discussed in the dedicated chapters (for example, the regulation on the "free flow on non-personal data"-see Chapter 5-is meant to help companies improve their access to data and foster their technological development). The 2016 Communication also aimed to mobilize investment through public-private partnerships, namely: supporting the co-financing of projects targeted to the modernization of the economy by EU and national public institutions and private investors. The 2016 Communication promoted the creation of **digital innovation hubs**, i.e. excellence centres based in universities or research institutions that aggregate technologies, expertise, data, resources, technical know-how, digital skills, and funding tools that companies (in particular start-ups and small-medium enterprises) can access, to reduce scale-up costs and exploit cross-sectoral synergies. For example, the European Commission reports the story of two small companies, Spanish Podoactiva and Italian Base Protection that teamed up and designed a scanner needed to process data that feed in on-demand high-performance computing cloud services. Podoactiva and Base Protection could rely on the help of Spanish Digital Innovation Hub "Lnycom".[12] The 2016 Communication also prompted the set-up of large-scale pilot projects to foster the development of the Internet of Things and advanced manufacturing technologies. It supported investment in cloud computing: a parallel initiative launched at the same time of the 2016 Communication supported the creation of a **European Cloud** (European Commission, 2016b) to boost the share and re-use of data across the borders, through high-performance computing, storage, and connectivity infrastructure for European researchers and business (see further in Chapter 5).

Finally, the 2016 Communication aimed to smoothen and speed up **standard-setting processes,** particularly for cybersecurity, 5G, cloud computing, Internet of things, and data technologies. Standardization is a crucial step for the development and wide adoption of technologies; it refers to the definition of technical properties that ensure that technologies are safe and interoperable (i.e. they can communicate with each other). However, the process is very complex, as it requires concerted action by industry stakeholders with different, potentially conflicting, interests (standard-setting bodies help mitigate that by attempting to coordinate stakeholders). That means that, despite being an important step to make to promote the adoption of a specific technology in the market, standardization can take

---

[12] More information about digital innovation hubs supported by the European Commission, together with more successful examples, can be found here: https://digital-strategy.ec.europa.eu/en

a long time, and it may even result in sub-optimal outcomes, for example, increasing the likelihood of antitrust abuse.[13] Thus, the Commission proposed new rules to attribute political priority in the validation and monitoring of standardization priorities, to be sure that the technological standards with a more substantial strategic relevance for the digitization of the EU industry (e.g. 5G or cloud computing) are prioritized. Where necessary to speed up the process, the Commission also envisaged financial help with EU funding to support testing and experimentation of essential standards.

Note that the "digitize the European industry" strategy should be also seen in the broader European Union economic context. In its Communications on a **"New Industrial Strategy"** (see: (European Commission, 2020) and (European Commission, 2021)), the European Commission emphasizes the need for mapping EU's strategic dependency from foreign economies and addressing them expanding its industrial capacity. This is particularly relevant for the digital economy, since strategic dependencies are identified in areas such as semiconductors, cloud and edge technologies (see Chapters 5 and 15 for a discussion).

1.3.1 The European Digital Single Market Strategy and A Europe Fit for the Digital Age

At a broader level, the European Union's policy action in the digital area since 2015 has been shaped by the **Digital Single Market Strategy** (usually referred to as *DSM Strategy*) (European Commission, 2015a). The strategy laid down in the 2015 European Commission's Communication fits the approach launched by the Commission in its 2010's *Digital Agenda*; namely: to single out the digital space as a critical area for the European economy and to indicate the need for a coherent set of policy actions geared to reach well-defined long-term objectives (European Commission, 2010a). The DSM Strategy, however, is a crucial milestone because it was drafted at a historical moment where the political *hype* around digital technologies, both in terms of their potential beneficial effect for the economy and of the societal concerns they give rise to, was at its peak. In many ways, the DSM Strategy has set a path for the years to come.

The DSM Strategy contained a set of 16 concrete actions (most of them are covered in details in the chapters of Part 2, Part 3, and Part 4 of this book). The actions are structured in three "pillars" (Figure 1.4):

Pillar I is titled **Better access for consumers and businesses to digital goods and services across Europe.** It presents actions that the European Commission intended to undertake to pull down barriers to the flow of digital goods and services. In particular, it indicates the need to:

---

[13] For an overview of antitrust concerns with standardization, see Contreras (2015).

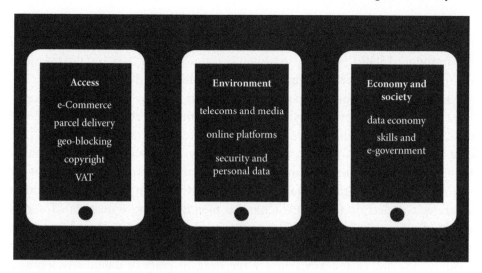

Figure 1.4 The Digital Single Market strategy
European Commission: https://ec.europa.eu/commission/presscorner/detail/en/IP_15_4919

- Make **cross-border e-commerce** more straightforward, for example harmonizing consumer protection when buying online
- Decrease the cost of cross-border **parcel delivery**
- End unjustified **geo-blocking**, a practice that allows sellers to discriminate against online buyers based on the place they connect from
- Modernize European **copyright law** taking into account the revolution caused by digital in the audio-visual sector.

Pillar II is titled **Creating the right conditions and a level playing field for digital networks and innovative services to flourish**. This pillar is concerned with establishing rules favouring fair competition between market players and preventing potential harm for end users. Actions include, for example:

- A massive review of the **EU Telecom regulatory framework** with the intent to stimulate investment in connectivity infrastructure and make that infrastructure universally accessible
- An in-depth analysis of the concerns generated by the **online platform** economy and the definition of potential legislative or non-legislative intervention to tackle them
- Initiatives in the realm of **personal data protection** such as a review of the e-Privacy Directive
- Actions to foster **cybersecurity** throughout the whole EU Single Market.

Finally, Pillar III is named **Maximizing the growth potential of the digital economy**; this pillar contains actions that are believed to have tremendous boosting potential for growth within the digital economy. These are:

- The creation of a European data space where **data can flow freely** from one entity to another (this action also includes the European Cloud initiative that I introduced above)
- The definition of prioritizing to speed-up **standardization**
- Initiatives to support the acquisition of **digital skills** by citizens and workers
- Initiatives to favour the **digitalization of the public sector.**

Most recently, in 2020, the European Commission launched a new digital policy strategy framework which, on many counts, appears a natural continuation of the path undertaken with the Digital Single Market strategy in 2015, with a stronger geostrategic projection (as the EU Chip Act mentioned above suggests). The new strategic framework is called **A Europe Fit for the Digital Age,**[14] and it rests on an overarching programme called **Shaping Europe's Digital Future** (European Commission, 2021a) and a 'vision' for the next 10 years of digital development (called **Europe's Digital Decade**). The Shaping Europe's Digital Future programme is structured in four categories of action:

- Technology that works for people
- A fair and competitive digital economy
- An open, democratic, and sustainable society
- Europe as a global digital player.

Similarly to the DSM Strategy, the first category, *technology that works for people*, envisages initiatives geared to empower and protect citizens, workers, and business alike: actions to favour digital skills, artificial intelligence, and other emerging new technologies, connectivity, cybersecurity, and inclusion, for example. The second category, *a fair and competitive digital economy*, entails actions directed to preserving market competition and favouring business' competitiveness, such as online platforms regulation, data governance, and copyright. The third category, *an open, democratic, and sustainable society*, is concerned with actions tailored to enhance trust in the digital environment. These are initiatives that tackle disinformation issues, that foster the use of e-health services, that aim to create a thriving media and digital culture. Finally, category four projects the EU action in the digital domain to the broader international landscape. In particular, the European Commission envisages steps to support the digitization of developing economies and promote EU technology standards internationally. That applies also to initiatives designed to respond to China's Belt and Road Initiative, or China's strategic plan to develop a global infrastructure connecting with a significant number of countries in Asia and Africa, such as the EU-Asia, EU-Africa or EU-South America connectivity strategies. Most recently, in September 2021, the European Commission and the US Government launched the **Trade and Tech Council** (or TTC): a periodic high-level meeting between senior US and EU officials to increase cooperation between

---

[14] See https://ec.europa.eu/info/strategy/priorities-2019-2024/europe-fit-digital-age_en

the two economies, particularly on technological matters, with the scantly disguised intent to contrast China's increasing power in the global digital arena.

Regarding **Europe's Digital Decade**, in March 2021, the European Commission published its latest Communication with the Commission's vision on Europe's digital transformation by 2030 (European Commission, 2021): **"2030 Digital Compass: the European way for the Digital Decade"**. The document hinges on what the Commission calls "four cardinal points": *Skills, Infrastructure, Government,* and *Business*. Each of the four dimensions links to a well specified target, to *be reached by 2030*:

- **Skills**: 80% of the population should have at least basic digital skills; 20 million Europeans to be employed as ICT specialists (the Commission also aims to address gender balance in the sector)
- **Infrastructure**: universal 5G coverage and a "gigabyte speed" access for everyone in Europe; doubling the EU share of cutting edge semiconductor world market; 10,000 environmentally friendly, highly secured "edge nodes"; deploying the first computer with quantum acceleration
- **Government**: 80% of EU citizens using digital identification; 100% of citizens being able to access medical records online; 100% of citizens able to access key public sector services online
- **Business:** 75% of EU companies using cloud, data analytics, or artificial intelligence-powered technologies; double the number of EU "unicorns"; at least 90% of EU small and medium enterprises to achieve a basic level of digitization (see Chapter 2 for a definition).

The meaning of those targets will become clear in the following chapters. After having gone through the whole book, readers should also become able to appreciate how ambitious those targets sound. At the time of writing the book, it seems unlikely that the European Commission will be able to reach all of them within the envisaged time line.

****

2

Facts about the European Digital Economy

Abstract

Measuring the digital economy is a critical first step to identify where digital policy intervention is needed. Reliable and comparable metrics for digital phenomena are, however, hard to come by, given the novelty and often immaterial nature of digital markets; or they may get quickly outdated, given the rapid evolution pace of the digital economy. Even with these limitations, data on the digital economy can give an order of magnitude of the economy's performance in terms of adoption, development, and access to digital technologies, guiding policymakers into where policy action is more needed. This chapter focuses in particular on the European digital landscape. It describes the European Commission 2020 Digital Economy and Society Index. This chapter is our base of departure for the analysis of the different dimensions of the digital economy that I present in the following chapters.

2.1 Measuring the digital economy

It could be argued that the purpose of the Digital Single Market strategy or, more generally, of any strategy guiding the European Commission's actions in the digital area is, ultimately, to digitize the economy and to make sure that everyone in Europe can profit from it. However, we cannot discuss how to pursue that objective without first having an idea of our starting situation, where we are now, and how far we are from that end goal.

This chapter illustrates the *status quo*, the level of digitization of the European economy based on the available data at the time of writing. Looking at the European digital landscape is a natural first step in the journey that we are embarking on with this book. Policy intervention should always come after accurately identifying where the economy is not performing as hoped for. For example, identifying where the level of access, acceptance, or adoption of digital technologies is below the level that is desirable from a social standpoint.

Before looking at the figures, students should be aware of the inherent limitations that characterize the exercise that I am about to describe. For several reasons, measuring the *digital economy* is a tricky task unlikely to yield precise results.

From the outset, the digital economy poses critical measurement puzzles to macroeconomists and policymakers alike. The Gross Domestic Product (GDP), defined as the total value-added generated by the production of goods and services in a particular economy, is a standard variable used in most, if not all, macro-economic

Digital Economic Policy. Mario Mariniello, Oxford University Press.
© Mario Mariniello (2022). DOI: 10.1093/oso/9780198831471.003.0002

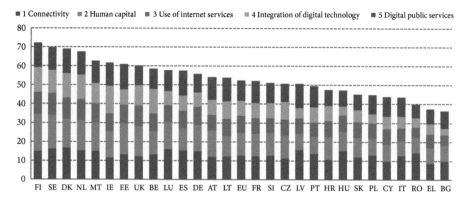

■ 1 Connectivity   ■ 2 Human capital   ■ 3 Use of internet services   ■ 4 Integration of digital technology   ■ 5 Digital public services

Figure 2.1 The Digital Economy and Society Index (DESI), 2020
Source: European Commission's Digital Scoreboard https://ec.europa.eu/digital-single-market/en/digital-economy-and-society-index-desi

analyses. Policymakers check countries' GDP performances and their over-time evolution to decide whether they should worry about their country's growth level or about public finances being unable to cope with increasing public debt burdens. While many[1] have questioned GDP's accuracy in providing information about a country's well-being (that is, what actually should be the ultimate goal of elected public decision-makers), GDP is still widely used because it is easy to calculate and compare across different jurisdictions.

Yet, the emergence of the digital economy has come to question that advantage too. Ahmad & Schreyer (2016) and Watanabe, et al. (2018), for example, point out that the digital economy makes measuring goods' and services' added-value challenging, because, inter-alia:

- The digital environment is subject to strong disruptive dynamics; new economic and social phenomena appear quickly and are difficult to anticipate
- Traditional statistical indicators fail to keep track and capture value generated by new business models powered by online platforms
- An increasing number of goods and services are available free of charge
- There are increasingly blurred boundaries between producers and consumers (with the latter often being part of the production process, without necessarily knowing it)
- The value generated by the use of massive amounts of data is becoming a primary component of the economy, but good metrics for it are still not available.

The above list is non-exhaustive, but it suffices to hint at how challenging it can be to measure value in the digital economy (the meaning of the mentioned challenges will

---

[1] See, for example: Stiglitz, et al. (2010).

become more apparent in the following chapters, when we will, for example, discuss them in detail).

According to the International Monetary Fund (IMF, 2018), in 2018, still, less than 10% of the employment, income, or value-added produced by a majority of economies worldwide could be officially accounted to the "digital sector". Yet, as we know from the previous chapter, digital technologies permeate the whole economy, enabling new opportunities for individuals and companies, transforming and disrupting traditional businesses, generating intangible benefits that are hard to pin down.

Speaking about a digital economy just with reference to the Information and Communication Technology (ICT) sector is thus very reductive: the proportion of value-added the creation of which is enabled or otherwise affected by digital technologies is arguably much higher than that 10%. For example, according to the OECD, approximately 25% of jobs in G20 economies are in digital-intensive sectors, accounting for 43% of the new jobs created between 2006 and 2017 (OECD, 2020b). That is why the OECD proposes a much broader definition for the **digital economy** as *"all economic activity reliant on, or significantly enhanced by the use of digital inputs, including digital technologies, digital infrastructure, digital services and data. [the digital economy] refers to all producers and consumers, including government, that utilise these digital inputs in their economic activities"* (OECD, 2020b).

Figure 2.2 illustrates the approach suggested by the OECD; it consists of the identification of four levels, or tiers, for measuring the digital economy:

- A **core tier**, encompassing only economic activities that are strictly recognizable as technological (e.g. ICT goods and services). For example, a personal computer would belong to this category

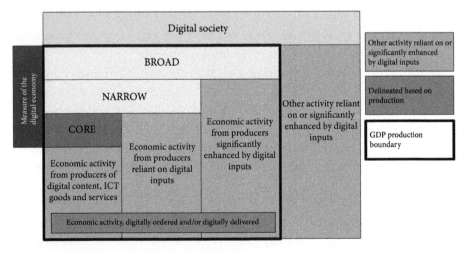

Figure 2.2 A tiered definition of the digital economy

Source: OECD (2020) A Roadmap toward a common framework for measuring the Digital Economy, Report for the G20 Digital Economy Task Force, 2020, OECD

- A **narrow tier**, which includes products and services that crucially depend on digital inputs to be produced or to exist. For example, online platforms, such as Uber or Netflix, would not exist without an Internet connection (and AI, as we shall see in the following chapters)
- A **broad tier**, including all products and services that are significantly enhanced by digital technologies, though not necessarily depending on them. For example, financial services relying on electronic payments belong to this category
- Finally, a **digital society tier**, that refers to any economic activities with a meaningful relationship with digital technologies. The OECD suggests using this category to capture those immaterial activities relevant to calculate benefits and costs of the digital economy but that are not tangible and cannot be included in the first three tiers, such as privacy, personal data and digital well-being.

What motivates the OECD (2020) classification's proposal is creating a **coherent international measuring framework** to which all OECD economies could converge, overcoming one of the critical obstacles to measurement in the digital economy: lack of uniformity in statistical approaches.

An intrinsic difficulty with the digital economy (and particularly with artificial intelligence-enabled applications) is with **elusive definitions:**[2] it is often challenging to develop a unique way to describe what we mean with *digital technology* and when can that technology be considered *adopted*. We shall see in Chapter 15, for example, that today there still no agreed definition for artificial intelligence. That makes measurement a challenge because any quantitative exercise always requires cross-unit comparison and some form of data aggregation. It should be possible to add up the figures of digital usage by each active company in the economy to measure how many companies use digital technologies in a specific jurisdiction. However, while measuring manufacturing output or the number of machines used in a manufacturing production process may be relatively easy, it is hard to measure companies' levels of integration of digital technologies simply because companies have different ways of classifying technology. Some companies (or even individuals) may adopt AI-powered applications without being aware that they do so (a simple email interface may, largely, depend on AI) or have an otherwise different understanding of what AI means in practice. Adopting AI-powered technologies requires computational infrastructure, human skills/capital, software, data, and organizational changes – all of these dimensions are difficult to measure and compare in practice.

As we have seen in Chapter 1, moreover, **the digital environment is incredibly fluid**, with new technologies and business models emerging and rapidly gaining ground in the economy, so that keeping up with measurement is tricky. Metrics

---

[2] For a very nice review see: Mishra, et al. (2020).

just adopted may become quickly obsolete, making overtime comparison very difficult. The European Commission, for example, has only recently adopted indicators capturing the extent to which EU companies perform data analytics, use cloud computing, or rely on AI technologies. Those technologies did not exist (or did not exist in the current shape) just a few years ago. Setting up new indicators to measure new phenomena needs time. To start with, national statistical offices must know what to ask or look for when performing their periodic data collection exercises.

Another problem with measurement in the digital economy is that, as we shall see particularly in Chapter 5 (on the *data economy*) and Chapter 8 (on *online platforms*), often **transactions are non-monetary**. Internet users often access online services by implicitly bartering information on their habits or preferences instead of paying them with actual money. That poses a direct challenge for measuring the benefits and the costs of the digital economy since non-monetary parameters (such as the generation of new opportunities in the social network space, privacy risks, security risks, or psychological costs) are intrinsically harder to associate with numbers objectively. Digital technologies tend to progress towards an ever-increasing ability to capture very granular information about individuals or processes to refine the supply of products and services, making them closer and closer to what customers want. This customization or personalization of the economy has a cost in terms of our ability to measure and capture its real effects: the more personalized our goods and services, the more difficult it is to measure and aggregate them in a statistically meaningful way.

Other measurement challenges concern the sale and **purchase of goods or services through the Internet** (*e-commerce*), which often escape administrative-accounting because trade registries do not capture small parcel trade (see Chapter 10 for a discussion). Or, more simply, because immaterial goods and services that are easily transferred through digital means are difficult to measure. Think about an intra-company exchange of data across multiple jurisdictions: how should the value of data be calculated and allocated to the different economies involved in the transaction?

Likewise, the impact of digitization on **job markets** is hardly quantifiable. For example, there is no uniform definition of the skills that are necessary to perform in the digital economy. Companies have their subjective definition of the skills they look for in digitally-savvy employees. Statistics on online platform workers with hybrid jobs that cannot be neither classified as employed nor self-employed (i.e. jobs in the "sharing economy" sector, see Chapter 11) tend to be inaccurate and hardly comparable, given the complexity and diversity of arrangements and the different regulatory and monitoring approach adopted by countries around the world.

These observations lead to one important conclusion: statistics related to the digital economy can be helpful and should be used to improve practitioners' understanding of digital dynamics and their impact on the broader economy and society. However, students, researchers, and policymakers should take them with a *pinch of salt*: figures may provide an idea, an order of magnitude for effects that we would like to understand better. But they are unlikely to be conclusive on their own and should always be complemented by information from other sources of qualitative nature too. The need to be careful with statistics is arguably true with any economic phenomenon (econometrics *is not* an exact science). Still, for the reason discussed above, the need for complementary sources of information is particularly acute when we are studying phenomena related to the digital economy (for this book, that complementary exercise is carried out in the following chapters that are dedicated to the relevant area of analysis of the digital economy).

2.2 Data sources

Data on the digital economy can be collected by researchers and practitioners using a multitude of data sources. Sources may be of public nature, such as national statistical offices; semi-public, such as databases compiled by research institutes and made available to the wide public with open access; or private, such as data indexes compiled by consultancies or large companies, with the caveat that these datasets are more likely to suffer from bias, as the compilation process may be affected by the company's agenda (a telecom company may have an interest in showing that infrastructure investment is lower than desirable absent governmental support, for example).

Notable examples of international public data sources are the European Commission, the OECD, and other intergovernmental organizations. The OECD regularly updates its **Going Digital Toolkit** (OECD, 2021), which currently contains 33 core indicators and several complementary indicators allocated to these seven policy categories:

- Access to communications infrastructures, services, and data
- Effective use of digital technologies and data
- Data-driven and digital innovation
- Good jobs for all
- Social prosperity and inclusion
- Trust in the digital age
- Market openness in digital business environments.

It is possible to compare indicators across OECD countries and look at indicators' performance over time. Similarly, UNCTAD (2021), The World Bank (2019), and UNESCO (2021) publish useful indicators to monitor ICT sector production, infrastructure development and access, and digital trade across a variety of countries. For Europe, the most comprehensive source is the European Commission's Digital Scoreboard (European Commission, 2021b), which relies primarily on data from Eurostat (2021), the statistical branch of the European Commission. I will discuss the European Commission's indicators in the next section. Any national statistical office would typically survey the ICT sector, both from the supply side (i.e. the development of technology) and from a demand-side (i.e. the use made by business customers or consumers of digital technologies).

A notable example of a semi-public data source is **Stanford's AI Index project**.[3] The index collects data mostly about artificial intelligence from several sources, including surveys. It is an independent initiative by Stanford University but is supported by many companies or partners from the private sector. According to their authors: *"the AI Index Report tracks, collates, distils, and visualizes data relating to artificial intelligence. Its mission is to provide unbiased, rigorously-vetted data for policymakers, researchers, executives, journalists, and the general public to develop intuitions about the complex field of AI".* All data used to compile the index are accessible for free by the wide public. As of 2019, the initiative also includes the publication of a Global AI Vibrancy Tool (Stanford HAI, 2020) that allows cross-country comparison on metrics such as: number of AI conference papers, AI skills and hiring, AI investment, number of start-ups created, and companies' adoption of industrial robots.

More generally, the *datafication* of the economy also offers excellent opportunities to researchers to efficiently collect data at the origin, from every single unit of observation, and aggregate them, using dedicated software to survey the Internet. A good illustration is with labour markets.[4] Researchers can collect information about the evolution of skills' demand and supply by collecting information from job and employment platforms, such as LinkedIn, Monster or CareerBuilder. Typically, the information that can be retrieved online has a high level of granularity: it may include workers' employment history and great detail of the characteristics looked for by employers opening vacancies. Similarly, data can be retrieved from social networks, compatibly with personal data protection laws. Researchers can use *application programming interfaces* (API, see Chapter 5 for a definition) to access data directly or even extract them through *web-crawling*, i.e. through the use of special "spider" software automatically searching for information on the web *scraping* the content they find online.

2.3 The European Digital landscape

The Digital Economy and Society Index, or **DESI**, is an annual statistical exercise performed by the European Commission to measure the progress of digitalization throughout the European Union. The primary source of data is Eurostat (in turn, Eurostat draws most of its data from national statistical offices). DESI also uses as sources ad-hoc data collection methods, and specific studies to capture certain

---

[3] See Perrault, et al. (2019). The 2019 AI index report can be retrieved here: https://hai.stanford.edu/research/ai-index-2019

[4] A great review on methodologies for empirical investigation of labour markets using online sources is in Horton and Tambe (2015).

phenomena of the digital economy that are not accurately described by traditional statistics compiled by national statistical offices.

The description that follows is strictly based on the European Commission's **DESI 2020 report**.[5] Before describing the data, let me flag an important caveat. The data described in this section refers to the pre-pandemic period—the 2020 DESI was published in June 2020 and it is based on data up to the year before, *2019* (for obvious reasons, as sources such as accounting data is submitted by companies to national statistical offices on a yearly-cyclical basis).[6] However, we know that the Covid-19 pandemic had a massive impact on the economy, among other things inducing the lay-off or furlough of many workers and the market exit of many small companies everywhere in the world. The pandemic also gave significant impulse to the digitization of the economy, forcing companies to offer their workers the opportunity to telework whenever feasible during lock-down or dramatically expanding the demand (and thus the supply) of e-commerce services. This impact is not reflected in the figures we are about to discuss.

Some figures available at the time of writing are discussed in Chapter 3, which is specifically dedicated to analysing the effect of the Covid-19 pandemic on the digital economy. The figures described in this chapter should nevertheless be considered as a baseline reference for the European digital economy by students. They illustrate where Europe was in terms of digitization at the beginning of the third decade of the twenty-first century; whether the pandemic (or, for what it matters, other unforeseen events) will permanently switch the transformation gear and render some of those figures obsolete is still to be seen. For example, it is reasonable to expect that after the end of the Covid-19 pandemic, there will be a drop in demand for e-commerce services compared to the lock-down period, when physical retail shops were closed to the general public and buyers could not stick their nose out of their house, simply because a significant number of customers prefer physical interaction to online shopping. Likewise, companies (small ones and big alike) will necessarily reduce the proportion of work performed by employees in teleworking, converging to new equilibria, where the balance between on-premise and telework will be somewhere between the pre-pandemic balance and the lock-down balance.

The pandemic's effect most likely to have long-term consequences is the exacerbation of the *digital divide,* or the gap between individuals who can and those who cannot access and profit from the digital economy (see Chapter 3 and 13). In fact, the pandemic hit the hardest those who could not access or use proficiently digital technologies, to work, study, or use public services. Kids from less privileged backgrounds, for example, were more likely to be cut off from distance learning during lock-downs. Thus, they are more likely to become disengaged with learning and educational systems and are more likely to experience long-term losses in terms of their

---

[5] Retrievable here: https://ec.europa.eu/newsroom/dae/document.cfm?doc_id=67086
[6] See here for data source and methodology used for the Digital Economy and Society Index: https://ec.europa.eu/newsroom/dae/document.cfm?doc_id=67082

overall life satisfaction (OECD, 2020d). That is a clear-cut call to duty for policymakers who are now, more than ever, pressed to take action against digital inequality, as we shall see in the coming chapters.

2.3.1 The 2020 Digital Economy and Society Index Report

DESI may alternatively indicate the whole set of figures collected by the European Commission, which I am about to describe, or a composite index which attempts to summarize in one single figure the level of digitization of each Member State. The composite index has 5 different components, as illustrated in Table 2.1. Figure 2.1 represents the DESI 2020 composite index by Member State. It suggests that three Scandinavian countries are lead-digital performers: Finland, Sweden, and Denmark; Malta, Ireland, and Estonia follow them. On the other hand of the spectrum, the least digitized economies of the European Union appear to be Bulgaria, Greece, Romania, and Italy. An essential complement to DESI is the **I-DESI** index, namely: the *international* version of DESI, compiled by the European Commission normalizing data of other economies to make them comparable with the European figures. Thanks to I-DESI 2020 (European Commission, 2020c), it is possible to see how Europe is faring in the international landscape (Figure 2.3). The most compelling observation we can derive from these figures is about the variety of development within the European Union: the EU *Top four* countries are, on average, the most digitized in the world; the EU *average country* is, however, performing worse than US, Australia, Japan, or Korea; the EU *Bottom four* countries are less digitized than Chile, Russia, China, and Serbia.

Let us now discuss each of the five dimensions of analysis, but in a slightly different order than the one adopted by the authors of the DESI 2020 report.

We will first look at the indicators providing a sense of the level of digitization of the private sector: *the use of digital technologies by business* and *citizen's use of the Internet*. We will then move to discuss *connectivity, human capital and digital skills* in Europe and the *digitization of the public service* (with the addition of *cybersecurity*).

Table 2.1 The 5 different components of DESI

1 Connectivity	The deployment of broadband infrastructure and its quality (see Chapter 4 for a definition)
2 Human capital	Skills and knowledge needed to benefit from the opportunities offered by the digital economy
3 Use of Internet	The diverse activities performed by European Internet users
4 Integration of digital technology	The level of digitization of business and the development of online sales channels
5 Digital public services	The level of digitization of the public sector

Source: European Commission (European Commission, 2020d)

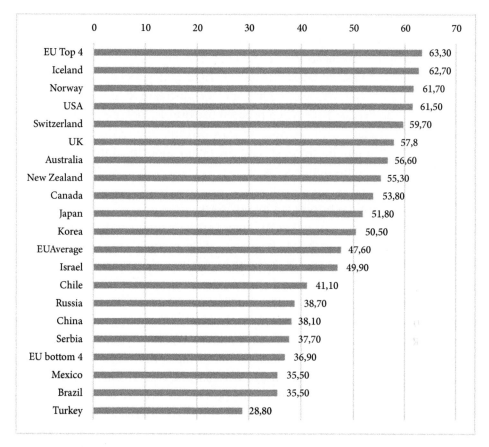

Figure 2.3 The International Digital Economy and Society Index (I-DESI) 2020
https://digital-strategy.ec.europa.eu/en/library/i-desi-2020-how-digital-europe-compared-other-major-world-economies

Bear in mind that it is challenging to identify unidirectional effects between the different variables that we observe, particularly in the digital domain. For example, a low degree of connectivity infrastructure may explain why citizens in a specific area do not access Internet services frequently. However, low demand for services can explain the lack of interest by telecom companies in infrastructure investment (I explain the underpinning economic dynamics in Chapter 4). Likewise, a cyber-safe online environment incentivizes use by business and citizens. But the higher the number of users, the higher is the likelihood of a security failure. As we will see in Chapter 7, companies' and single individuals' negligence are essential factors to consider when looking for the origin of a cybersecurity breach. And so forth.

However, it is possible to consider the private sector as the "pulse" of the digital economy. That is why it is preferable to start our discussion from there: it indicates how far we are from the goal that digital policy aims to pursue. In many respects, the private sector comes at the endpoint of the digital value chain. A digitized private sector suggests that all the necessary inputs to adopt and implement digital technologies, such as infrastructure, know-how, or the presence of a secure online environment, are available to the broad economy and society. Conversely, the lack of digitization in the private sector suggests the existence of bottlenecks in the digital value chain that may be tackled using the right policy tools. We are, in other words, adopting a backward logic: we first look downstream to see if digitization is taking place at the desired pace. Then proceed backwards, looking at the upstream inputs that may explain what we observe downstream. The relationship between downstream digitization, bottlenecks, and the policy tools to address them is the core object of study of this book.

2.3.1.1 Use of digital technologies by business

Figures on business' use of digital technologies are very different depending on the company size, the sector, and the Member State of observation. Large companies, for example, tend to be much more digitized than smaller ones. A simple explanation is that they have the means to be so. For example, they can afford to have dedicated ICT personnel, while small companies usually do not have the budget. DESI 2020 reports an index called "digital intensity", which aims to capture companies' level of technological adoption. It tracks down companies' performance along 12 different adoption dimensions (the list includes, for example, the adoption of customer relationship management software, the use of electronic orders from extra-EU countries, and whether at least 20% of workers use portable devices for work). Companies ticking "yes" to at least 10 of these dimensions are deemed to have a very high level of digitization. Companies with low (or very low) digitization levels are ticking "yes" to 4 to 6 dimensions (or less than 4). As it turns out, in 2019, 75% of EU companies had a low or very low level of digital technology adoption, according to the European Commission's figures (Figure 2.4). This result is strongly affected by the lack of digitization amongst smaller companies. For example, only 17% of Small, Medium Enterprises (SMEs) use cloud and only 12% of them use big data applications (see Chapter 5 for an explanation of these technologies), compared to almost 40% and 35% respectively for large companies. But the gap in technological adoption between large and small companies not only concerns advanced technologies. It also concerns e-commerce and other basic technologies such as "enterprise resource planning" software. 75% of large enterprises employ ICT specialists compared to 15% of small businesses (Figure 2.5).

Besides the obvious one, Information and Communication Technology (ICT), the sectors with the highest level of business digitization are publishing, films, TV and music, and travel agencies or touristic activities. Conversely, manufacturing sectors tend to be the least digitized. As we shall see throughout this book, the likely reason for such a result is the significantly disruptive competitive pressure that online platforms have come to put on the publishing and travels sectors, forcing them to digitize to stay competitive. The manufacturing sector has so far been comparatively protected from disruption, but that is likely to change in the years to come (see, for example, the emergence of AI-enabled applications, Chapter 15).

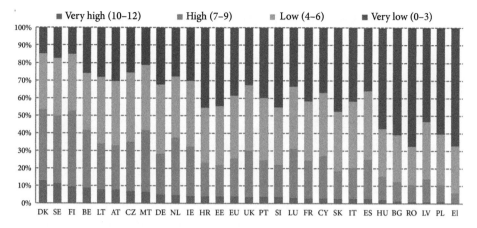

Figure 2.4 Business Digital Intensity Index (2019), DESI 2020
https://ec.europa.eu/newsroom/dae/document.cfm?doc_id=67086

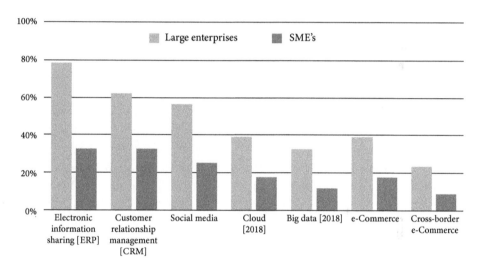

Figure 2.5 Adoption of digital technologies by company's size (2019), DESI 2020
https://ec.europa.eu/newsroom/dae/document.cfm?doc_id=67086

As for **e-commerce** (bearing in mind that these are pre-Covid-19 pandemic figures), only 17.5% of SMEs sold products through the Internet in 2019, compared to 39% of large companies. The most compelling figure for e-commerce concerns cross-border sales (Figure 2.6), as we shall see in Chapter 10. In 2019, only 7% of enterprises sold products or services to customers residing in other EU countries (while almost all of them, i.e. 16% of companies, sell to customers within their country of origin). This is a yet powerful indication that the European Union is far from being a Digital Single Market: cross-border barriers such as different language, legislation, and operational costs that cannot be tackled lacking scale, hamper companies' abilities to move goods and services freely from one EU country to the other.

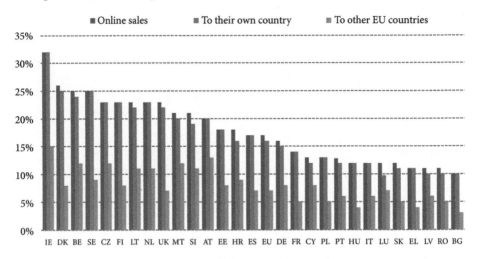

Figure 2.6 E-commerce sales by country of purchase (2019), DESI 2020
https://ec.europa.eu/newsroom/dae/document.cfm?doc_id=67086

2.3.1.2 Citizens' use of Internet services

The Covid-19 pandemic has dramatically boosted the use of online services by EU users. The level of Internet use was already high in 2019 though, with 85% of Europeans going online at least once per week, ranging from 95% for users residing in Denmark to 67% for users residing in Bulgaria. Yet, Figure 2.7 indicates that, still in 2019, there were significant chunks of the EU population that had never used the Internet before: almost 10% on average at EU level, but up to 24% of Bulgarian residents, 22% of Greek residents, and 22% of Portuguese residents. Tellingly, the number of non-users is exceptionally high among individuals with no or low educational level (24%), elderly people (23%) and the unemployed, retired, or inactive (26%).

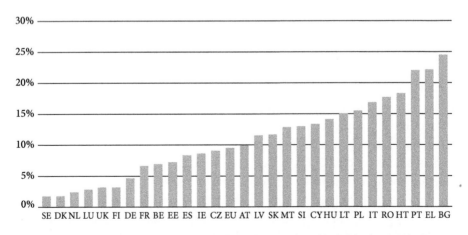

Figure 2.7 People who have never used online services (% of individuals, 2019), DESI 2020
https://ec.europa.eu/newsroom/dae/document.cfm?doc_id=67086

In 2019 there were huge gaps between countries regarding their residents' attitude to online purchase: 86% of Danish users in 2019 had shopped online, compared to 29% of Romanian users. Younger users and users with a higher level of education have a higher propensity to shop online. Once again, e-commerce attitude provides a strong indication of the lack of integration within the Digital Single Market: 87% of online shoppers made at least one purchase in their home country, but only 35% bought a good or a service from another EU country. Common actual or perceived barriers to buying online cross-border are: delivery costs, high return shipping costs, long delivery times, and security concerns (i.e. potentially challenging procedures to solve problems if something goes wrong during the purchasing process).

2.3.1.3 Connectivity

Connectivity refers to EU residents' ability to access telecommunication infrastructure and the quality and cost of communication services. As we will extensively discuss in Chapter 4, telecommunication infrastructure is the backbone of the digital economy—online services crucially depend on their ability to transfer large quantities of information at a high speed between different connected users.

In 2019, Europe fared relatively well in terms of overall connectivity, with an 86% average coverage in terms of Next Generation Access networks (NGAs, that is: connections that guarantee at least a 30Mb per second of download speed, see Chapter 4). It means that if, in 2019, you would pick randomly 100 households across Europe, 86 of them would indicate that they can access the Internet at high speed. Another compelling figure concerns fixed *very high capacity networks* which allow ultra-fast connection at rates no slower than 100Mb per second. In this case, the overall coverage in Europe is 44%. The average figures, however, do not tell the whole story. In fact, there still exists a significant gap in connectivity between urban and rural areas (Figures 2.8, 2.9, and 2.10). Coverage for NGA in rural areas was only 60% still in 2019, despite the recent years' progress, and 20% for very high capacity fixed networks.

In terms of wireless connectivity, by 2019, 4G mobile technology covered almost the entire EU population. Conversely, the latest wireless technology developed, 5G, has to still overcome some critical hurdles before starting wide deployment (this in particular concerns Member States' wireless spectrum management, as we shall see in Chapter 4). The countries that appear more ready in terms of the proportion of assigned spectrum as a proportion of the total harmonized 5G spectrum in 2020 are Germany, Finland, Hungary, and Italy (Figure 2.11). By March 2020, more than 120 European cities had started 5G trials, and several countries had deployed 5G "digital cross-border corridors" to test automated mobility solutions (such as self-driven cars): between Portugal and Spain; Belgium and the Netherlands; France, Luxembourg, and Germany; Germany and the Czech Republic; Germany, Austria, and Italy; Poland and Lithuania; Lithuania, Latvia, and Estonia; Denmark, Sweden, Finland, and Norway; and Greece and Bulgaria.

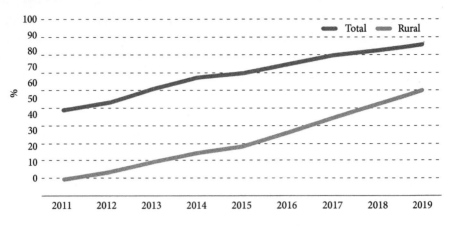

Figure 2.8 Next Generation Access networks – coverage of urban and rural areas vs rural areas (% of households, 2019), DESI 2020
https://ec.europa.eu/newsroom/dae/document.cfm?doc_id=67086

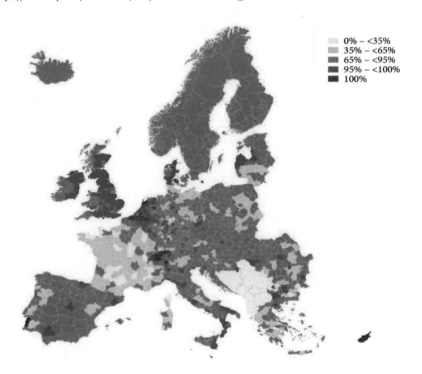

Figure 2.9 Next Generation Network Coverage (European Map, % of households, 2019), DESI 2020
https://ec.europa.eu/newsroom/dae/document.cfm?doc_id=67086

Finally, a comparison of connectivity prices across the EU can be misleading. National borders strongly define telecom markets. Users cannot pick operators that offer telecom services in a country that is different from the one where they reside. For that reason, prices depend on local supply and demand features: local competition between operators, for example, and users' average income. As it turns out,

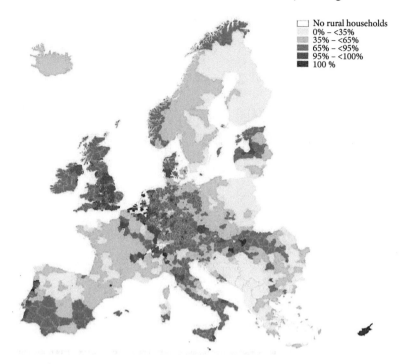

Figure 2.10 Next Generation Network Coverage in Rural Areas (European Map, % of households, 2019), DESI 2020

https://ec.europa.eu/newsroom/dae/document.cfm?doc_id=67086

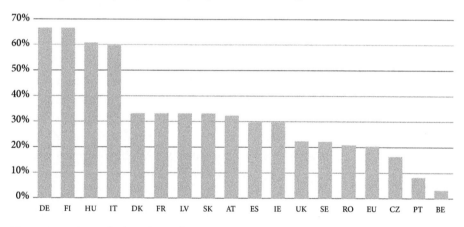

Figure 2.11 Countries' readiness for 5G spectrum assignment (assigned spectrum as a % of total harmonized 5G spectrum, 2019), DESI 2020

https://ec.europa.eu/newsroom/dae/document.cfm?doc_id=67086

Romania, Poland, and Lithuania offered the most affordable connectivity price in 2019, while Belgium, Cyprus, and Ireland are the countries where accessing telecom infrastructure is most expensive. As we will see in Chapter 4, current EU rules have fostered the use of mobile communication while "roaming" in other EU countries. At the same time, those rules prevent operators' cross-border competition: users cannot be roaming permanently. They cannot buy a mobile SIM card in a foreign country and use it where they reside. The Roam Like At Home regulation has caused retail data roaming traffic to increase from 7.3 million Gigabytes in Q4 of 2015 to 273.4 million Gigabytes in Q3 of 2019.

2.3.1.4 Use of digital technologies by the public sector

The digitalization of the public sector is generally progressing everywhere in Europe, as recorded by the annual DESI exercise as of 2014. To assess the level of digitization of public administrations across Europe, DESI 2020 uses a composite indicator based on:

- The proportion of public service users that *need* to submit online forms to access those services
- Whether public institutions propose to users pre-compiled forms when they connect online (giving an idea of how smooth is users' experience with the services)
- The proportion of public services that are accessible online
- The number of public services that are available to the business (including for cross-border purposes)
- Public institutions' open data policies.

The DESI digital public sector indicator goes from 0 to 100. The EU average score is 72% for 2019; the EU top performers are Estonia, Spain, and Denmark (a score above 87%), while the worst performers are Romania, Greece, and Croatia (scores below 60%).

Open data is a particularly relevant figure, as we shall see in Chapter 6. The level of maturity of an open data policy of a country is assessed, among other things, based on: the presence of specific norms regulating the licensing of access to public sector's data; the level of coordination between national and local administrations; the development of national open data online portals; the likely impact that open data has on the economy, society, politics, and environment of the country; and the quality of the data that are shared (for example, whether they are shared in easily accessible/standard formats). As shown in Figure 2.12, Member States that fare better are Ireland, Spain, and France. At the other end of the spectrum, Hungary and Slovakia are lagging behind, with a performance that the European Commission considers less than half as good as the ones of the top performers (less than 40% score compared to almost 90% for top performers).

Another significant figure concerns cross-border mobility, which indicates the extent to which residents from other EU countries can use digital public services in the Member State of observation. Generally, DESI records a better performance for cross-border access by business than by citizens. Smaller countries with a high level of digitization and infrastructure, such as Malta, Estonia, Austria, and Luxembourg, lead the EU ranking of cross-mobility of online public services. Romania, Hungary, Poland, and Greece figure at the end of the ladder.

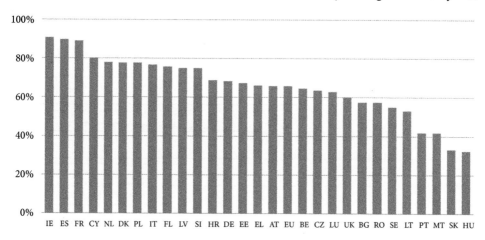

Figure 2.12 Open Data, Member States ranking, (2019), DESI 2020
https://ec.europa.eu/newsroom/dae/document.cfm?doc_id=67086

Finally, when it comes to putting users at the centre of their digital policies, EU public administrations have made the most progress in recent years by increasing their "mobile friendliness". That is, increasingly allowing citizens to use their mobile phones to connect to public administration, prove their identity online, fulfil their obligations, or benefit from the offered public services.

2.3.1.5 Human capital and digital skills

Digital skills refer to the competencies that individuals acquire to use digital technologies and profit from them. They are critical enablers of the digital economy and society – consumers need them to feel empowered and protected when accessing online services; workers more and more need them to find a job; companies, sometimes desperately, look for individuals who can master technologies they need to adapt to keep up with the competition. Digital skills (or a lack thereof) are, in other words, a key factor contributing to the digital divide, as we shall see particularly in part 4 of this book.

According to DESI 2020, the proportion of individuals with at least some basic digital skills in Europe is 58% (Figure 2.13). That is a compelling figure: while slow progress has been recorded in the last years, it suggests that still almost half of the EU population lacks even those very basic digital skills, such as copying or moving files on a computer or sending/receiving emails, that are likely to become more and more indispensable even to find a job outside the ICT sector. Quite surprisingly, though, "lack of need or interest" is mentioned by the majority of citizens that do not have Internet at home, followed by other barriers to access such as "equipment costs" or "insufficient starting skills". This figure is likely to be strongly affected by the Covid-19 pandemic: it would be hard to find anyone unaware of Internet usefulness in 2021, after the experience with pandemic lock-downs.

DESI 2020 reports that, in 2018, 3.9% of European employees (or 9.1 million people) had a job as an ICT specialist. Note, however that most of them are men:

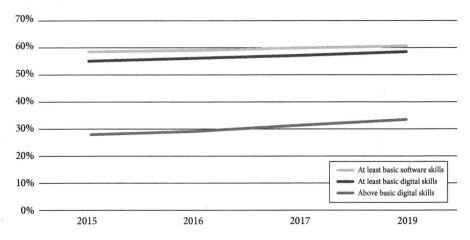

Figure 2.13 Digital skills over time evolution (% of individuals), DESI 2020
https://ec.europa.eu/newsroom/dae/document.cfm?doc_id=67086

only 1.4% of employed females are ICT specialists. As we shall see in the following chapters, finding ICT specialists is still perceived as a top challenge by companies of any size. 64% of large companies and 54% of small and medium enterprises that have hired an ICT specialist in 2018 flagged that it is hard for them to fill ICT specialist vacancies.

Companies are increasing their training efforts to foster the development of the digital skills of their employees. In 2018, 24% of EU companies provided ICT training for their personnel (ranging from 37% in Finland and 36% in Belgium to 6% in Romania). The most important predictor for internal training offer is companies' size: 70% of large companies train their employees compared to just 23% of small ones.

2.3.1.6 Cybersecurity

An increasing proportion of citizens experience security issues while being online. It is no surprise that security concerns top users' concerns when they surf the Internet. In 2019, 50% of surveyed users flagged that security concerns limited or prevented them from performing online activities. Figure 2.14 illustrates the kind of issues that online users more commonly experience. In 2019, phishing, or the receipt of messages attempting to lure users to perform a particular activity, was experienced by 30% of users. False websites crafted to steal users' personal information were experienced by 15% of users. A minority of users experienced other illegal activities. Note, however, that these figures are based on the reporting of individuals who realized that their security was compromised. As we shall see in Chapter 7, this is likely to be just the tip of the iceberg, as many security breaches simply go unnoticed.

On the business side, in 2018 (the most recent year in the data) slightly more than 12% of companies experience a problem due to a fallacious ICT security system (23% of large companies and 12% of SMEs). Large companies are more likely to experience incidents (for example, because they are more likely targets of hacking

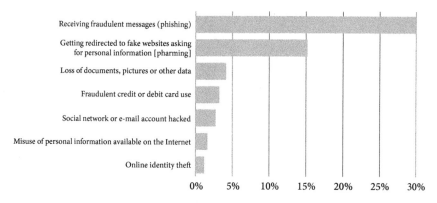

Figure 2.14 Types of issues experienced by internet users in 2019 (% of internet users), DESI 2020

https://ec.europa.eu/newsroom/dae/document.cfm?doc_id=67086

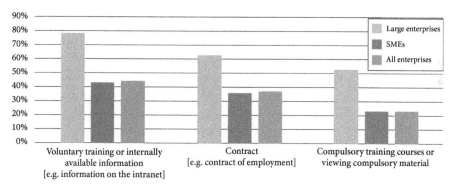

Figure 2.15 EU companies' cybersecurity policy (% of enterprises, 2019), DESI 2020

https://ec.europa.eu/newsroom/dae/document.cfm? doc_id=67086

activities). Still, they are also more likely to monitor and notice ICT failures; these two factors can explain the difference with SMEs. The most common cause of issues at the company level is the breakdown of ICT services. Two other common causes, albeit less frequent, are the destruction or corruption of the companies' data and the breach of confidential data.

Figure 2.15 finally provides a good indication of the level of companies' commitment to anticipate potential digital security issues. It suggests that a good proportion of companies offer voluntary training or provide information to their employee to improve the enterprise's cybersecurity performance (80% of large enterprises in 2019 and more than 40% of SMEs). However, a much smaller proportion of companies appear to consider cybersecurity as a top priority, imposing compulsory training to employees or compulsory material that employees must get accustomed to (about 50% of large firms and just slightly more than 20% of SMEs).

✶✶✶✶

3
Technology and the Covid-19 Pandemic

Abstract

The Covid-19 pandemic had a brutal impact on the life of human beings around the globe. As of March 2020, SARS-CoV-2, a virus provoking severe acute respiratory syndrome, had spread from China to the rest of the world. Billions of people experienced severe limitations to their fundamental rights to move, work, and engage in physical contact with other human beings. Technology supported the global effort to respond to the health emergency and provided a lifeline for economies. Digital services allowed families to be in contact through videoconference applications or social networks. E-commerce fuelled home-delivery services to locked-down households. Technology made telework possible when offices were not accessible. But technology played a double role. It exacerbated the opportunity gap between those who could use it for studying or working and those who could not, facilitating the spread of misleading information on the virus, and shifting economic value to dominant digital companies, aggravating those concentration tendencies that have been increasingly observed in online markets. While the pandemic has undoubtedly pushed the economy to become more digitized, the outstanding question is how much of that level of digitization will be retained by business and users alike after the pandemic is over.

3.1 The Covid-19 pandemic

This book was written almost entirely during the Coronavirus Disease 19 (**Covid-19**) pandemic. Covid-19 is caused by SARS-CoV-2, a virus provoking severe acute respiratory syndrome. The virus was recorded initially in China in December 2019; it spread throughout the entire world in less than three months, becoming a global pandemic. By January 2021, Covid-19 had caused more than 2.2 million deaths. Its impact on the life of billions of people has been dramatic. Respiratory viruses can be transmitted in three ways: (1) through physical direct or indirect contact (for example, touching the same surface); (2) through respiratory droplets, which can be spread through a sneeze or cough; or (3) through airborne transmission, namely through breathing lighter droplets that are spread by infected individuals in the air through their normal breathing (Lancet, 2020). Thus, in a desperate effort to stem the virus' progress, as of 2020, countries around the world have been implementing draconian measures, imposing drastic restrictions to the freedom of movement

Digital Economic Policy. Mario Mariniello, Oxford University Press.
© Mario Mariniello (2022). DOI: 10.1093/oso/9780198831471.003.0003

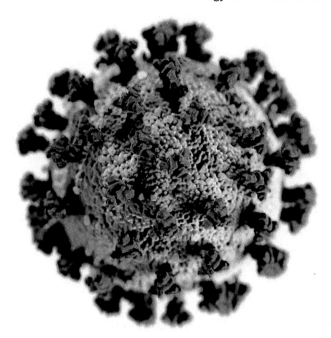

Figure 3.1 SARS-CoV-2, a graphical illustration
https://pxhere.com/en/photo/1608796

and work through physical or social distancing, home lock-downs or curfews. That quickly translated into the worst economic downturn since the Great Depression in 1919 (IMF, 2020), with a global drop in gross domestic production of 3% in 2020 compared to the preceding year. Many economic sectors will require years before they would recover to pre-pandemic levels. Global unemployment increased by 33 million in 2020 (ILO, 2021).

Digital technologies have played a primary role during the Covid-19 pandemic. Before 2020, access to the Internet had already emerged as a fundamental resource to study, work, and communicate. But during the pandemic, for many, access to the Internet instead became an indispensable resource for survival. Technology allowed working from home when legal restrictions imposing physical distancing prevented workers from performing their tasks at their employer's premises. Technology allowed e-commerce and delivery services to bring groceries, medicines, and other essential goods to the door of locked-down families. Technology helped to monitor the spread of the pandemic, to track down outbreaks, to improve medical treatments and ultimately to develop the vaccines that, at the time of writing, are seen as the "light at the end of the tunnel", the ultimate solution that may help humanity to recover its pre-pandemic "normality". Perhaps most importantly, digital technologies have filled the physical distance by connecting people, if just through video and audio devices. Small children could still play with their grandparents using video-conferencing services. Friends and family were never out of reach, thanks to social networks or over-the-top communication platforms, such as WhatsApp or Telegram. Hospitals began to use tablets to allow dying patients to say goodbye to their dear ones on their deathbeds (Bergeron R., 2020). Nothing of this would have been possible without digital technologies.

But the pandemic also placed the spotlight on technology's dark side. Or, more accurately: it emphasized technology's potential to decrease social welfare, without public policy guidance or regulatory control. The digital divide has exacerbated inequality, for example favouring students who could rely on good connectivity infrastructure to attend their classes or workers who could more easily perform their task remotely. Digital platforms have contributed to spreading harmful content online, with dramatic consequence for some, for example when people felt compelled to use false harmful remedies to cure or prevent the disease. Employers could use artificial intelligence to surveil employees. And digital technologies have exhausted the energies of remote workers, hampering their ability to set well-defined boundaries between their professional and personal lives.

This chapter contains a short overview of the role played by technology during the Covid-19 pandemic and its short and long-term economic and societal implications.

3.2 Technological solutions to address the health crisis

Technology played a critical role in the direct global response to the Covid-19 pandemic. It had a significant impact on three areas:

(1) Diagnosis
(2) Drug development (treatment and prevention)
(3) Tracing and monitoring

(1) Diagnosis

Digital technologies have been widely used to improve the identification of Covid-19 in cases of suspected infection. Digital applications made diagnosis faster and more accurate. That helped to unburden hospitals that, during the pandemic, struggled to treat an overwhelming number of incoming patients. Dananjayan & Raj (2020) report a few examples: AI diagnostic tools based on a machine learning model called *XGBoost* can analyse blood samples and predict infected individuals' chance of survival with a 90% accuracy rate. AI has been used to rapidly screen CT scan images and attribute the origin of identified lungs' lesions to either Covid-19 or common pneumonia. Similarly, Covid-Net is a deep learning application that uses deep convolutional neural networks to identify Covid-19 cases, scanning X-ray images.

Digital applications have been implemented to facilitate self-detection by individuals. For example, researchers have been using machine learning to develop smartphone applications that could recognize Covid-19 symptoms based on the sound of recorded cough (Laguarta, et al., 2021). More generally, connectivity infrastructure and technologies enabling remote communication have made it possible to use telemedicine as a means for practitioners to diagnose suspected Covid-19 cases and suggest follow up without the need for a physical visit.

(2) Drug development (treatment and prevention)

Technology helped speed up drugs and vaccine development. Researchers used machine learning to study the features of SARS-CoV-2 and sequence its protein structure, for example (Dananjayan & Raj, 2020). AI and big data analytics accelerated the process of "drug repurposing", i.e. using existing drugs to treat Covid-19. Cloud technology has favoured collaboration between researchers, facilitating data sharing, fostering the creation of synergies between labs around the world, increasing transparency, and promoting a continuous process of cross-verification between peer-researchers and with the general scientific community. Websites such as Our World in Data (2021) helped to provide researchers from any background (from medical sciences to economics, from sociology to psychology) with the resources needed to monitor the pandemic's evolution in real-time and its impact on society.

Digital applications also play a role in the roll-out and distribution of vaccines. For example, it increases the efficiency in the allocation of slots to individuals who need to get their shot. In addition, it may make the whole process more transparent and accountable. Notably, however, relying on online booking systems can have the perverse effect of disadvantaging those who find it difficult to access the Internet because they do not have access to the necessary connectivity infrastructure or lack familiarity with the digital environment. In other words, the digital divide exacerbates the unequal effects of Covid-19 on society because those who cannot use technology to study or work are more exposed to the virus (see Section 3.3). But also because, ironically, those very same individuals may find it more difficult to access treatment and prevention tools, such as vaccines.[1]

Finally, digital technologies such as the *blockchain* have been considered to create "immunity passports". Namely, digital certificates that would attest that a particular individual has been vaccinated and could thus enjoy privileged access to workplace or travel. As of July 2021, after a proposal by the European Commission, Member States have agreed to adopt a EU Digital COVID Certificate system.[2] The digital certificate allows a person to certify that she satisfies at least one of these three conditions: (a) has been vaccinated against Covid-19; (b) has received a negative test result; or (c) has recovered from Covid-19. The certificate allows lifting restrictions to the freedom of movement within the EU Single Market. It relies on a QR code with a digital signature to protect against falsification attempts.

---

[1] For a deeper analysis see Guetta-Jeanrenau and Mariniello (2021).
[2] See https://ec.europa.eu/info/live-work-travel-eu/coronavirus-response/safe-covid-19-vaccines-europeans/eu-digital-covid-certificate_en

(3) Tracing and monitoring

Artificial intelligence has been used to check travellers at airports or to scan walking crowds to identify individuals with symptoms that could raise the suspicion of SARS-CoV-2 infection (e.g. a body temperature higher or equal to 38 degrees Celsius). A notable example is *FluSense*: researchers have developed a contactless "surveillance" platform that captures bio-clinical signals in crowds through thermal scanners and microphones, and compares them with influenza-like physical symptoms captured in hospital waiting areas (Al Hossain, et al., 2020). The platform had been developed initially to monitor the spread of seasonal flu, but its relevance for Covid-19 became quickly apparent with the outbreak of the pandemic.

More generally, Internet of Things systems, whereby a network of sensors from "intelligent" machines or applications constantly interacts with individuals in their daily life, are incredibly effective tools to monitor and control the spread of diseases and to verify the observance of behavioural rules (such as mask wearing) or quarantine measures. But, conversely, sensors networks pose critical questions for the protection of privacy and personal data of individuals (a topic that we will discuss at length in Chapter 5 on the data economy).

The (actual or so-perceived) trade-off between the advantage of monitoring and enforcement of rules that would limit the spread of the Covid-19 pandemic on the one hand and, on the other, the protection of individuals' right to privacy became most apparent with **contact tracing smartphone apps**. Contact tracing apps have been widely adopted by countries worldwide and the vast majority of EU countries (Figure 3.2). Users can install them on their smartphone and permit them to communicate with the smartphones of nearby strangers through Bluetooth connectivity. If a user is tested positive, she can share that information with any person she has

Figure 3.2 Contact tracing smartphone apps in the EU

https://ec.europa.eu/info/live-work-travel-eu/coronavirus-response/travel-during-coronavirus-pandemic/how-tracing-and-warning-apps-can-help-during-pandemic_en

been in contact with within the previous two weeks (typically a contact for more than 15 minutes at less than 2 metres distance is considered to at "high risk of infection"). The European Commission has been proposing a framework to facilitate cross-border interoperability of national applications, with the purpose to facilitate international mobility.

While the idea of contact tracing apps is valuable on paper, it did not achieve much when translated into practice. Apps must be downloaded and activated by a large share of the population (at least 60% to 80%, according to the general indication of epidemiologists) to be helpful and offer a potential alternative to manual contact tracing. However, contact tracing apps faced significant resistance by potential users, particularly in those countries where the trust towards the government was the lowest or where privacy concerns tend to be widespread. The information-sharing prompted by the apps does not require the transfer of any personal information and is thus generally considered safe by data protection authorities. Yet, this has not been convincing enough for users, most of whom decided not to opt-in. At the time of writing, Iceland and Singapore, with a 40% adoption rate by their population, were the most successful countries globally; Germany had a 21% adoption rate; France 15%; Italy 14%.

The failure of contact tracing apps suggests that policymakers must still do much substantive and communication work to reassure citizens that their data can be used to pursue general interest goals without endangering their privacy (see Chapter 6 for a discussion).

3.3 The role of technology for the economy and society during the Covid-19 pandemic

During lock-downs, digital technologies were instrumental in preserving people's access to the world outside their homes. First and foremost, digital technologies mediated most (in some cases, all) of contacts with other human beings. The number of users of video-conferencing platforms boomed from one day to another (Figure 3.3). Smartphone applications that were not widely known before the pandemic, such as Zoom or Houseparty, became popular in segments of the population lacking familiarity with digital technologies, such as amongst elderly people, who needed to rely on video-conferencing to stay in touch with families and friends. The Internet became by far the primary source of information and entertainment: 70% of global consumers increased their usage of smartphones; video-streaming services spiked: popular subscription-based streaming platform service Netflix saw sudden massive increases in demand; Netflix's share price has jumped up by more than 60% since the beginning of 2020. In some cases, industries responded to the pandemics by transforming their supply, starting to offer online content. That is the case of the fitness industry, for example, with training classes moving from gyms to live stream or pre-recorded videos that could be used for exercising at home.

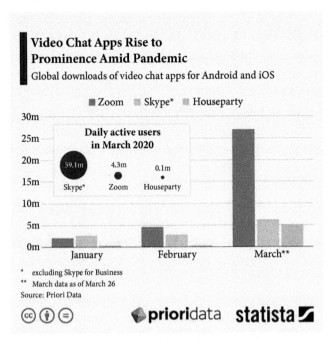

Figure 3.3 The boom in videoconferencing apps. Richter, F. (2020). *Video Chat Apps Rise to Prominence Amid Pandemic.* Statista.

Statista Inc. Accessed: April 12, 2021. https://www.statista.com/chart/21268/global-downloads-of-video-chat-apps-amid-covid-19-pandemic/. Made available under the Creative Commons License CC BY-ND 3.0

The pandemic triggered a significant increase in e-commerce. For non-essential brick-and-mortar retailers, e-commerce has been the only option to do business. Likewise, customers, particularly those most vulnerable to the effects of Covid-19, saw in e-commerce a safe alternative to going out from their homes for shopping. As a result, in April 2020, e-commerce sales in the European Union increased by 30% compared to April 2019. At the same time, total retail sales had decreased by almost 18% (OECD, 2020c). Notably, the largest online platforms thrived during the pandemic – that is rather obvious for Amazon since home delivery is its core business model. But the same held for Microsoft, Facebook, Alphabet, or Apple: after an initial setback, driven mainly by the drop in sales in hardware and revenue losses from reduced advertising turnover, they all significantly prospered, arguably because, after the initial shock at the beginning of the pandemic, consumers' purchasing habits adjusted to greater consumption of technological goods and services. Thus, the pandemic may have aggravated a fundamental problem with online platform markets: concentration of market power (this issue will be extensively discussed in Chapter 8).

Overall, the pandemic has indisputably pushed the economy to digitize more. However, it remains to be seen how much of this shift is structural, how many buyers and sellers will retain their digital habits or business strategies after the end of the pandemic. Some industries, such as those active in the travel sector, will certainly bounce back. Restaurants will likely go back to on-premises service rather than entirely relying on home delivery for their sales. But the economy will most likely not go back to the pre-pandemic equilibrium. As we shall see in the following chapters, digitizing an economy depends on factors such as lack of skills or experience with the technological environment. In a certain sense, the pandemic has forced individuals and companies to "learn by doing", and the acquired knowledge capital can undoubtedly contribute to speed up digitization in the future.

The resulting increase in Internet traffic put countries' connectivity infrastructure under extreme stress regarding their speed, capacity, reliability, and security (Figure 3.4). Generally it appears that, where connectivity is widespread (that is, in urban areas), European communication networks responded well to the pandemic. Those who could access the Internet before the pandemic did not experience a significant disruption in the quality of the service they could access. The pandemic may even have triggered structural changes in the economy, implying higher Internet traffic levels in the post-pandemic future. It could thus be argued that more opportunities for investment in infrastructure are being created, with the prospect of higher profits for telecom companies (see Chapter 4 for a discussion). For example, it is likely that bringing high-speed Internet to peripheral or rural areas will become

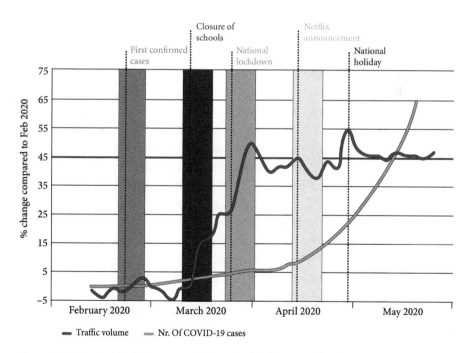

Figure 3.4 Internet traffic increase during the Covid-19 pandemic
ENISA/Fastly. https://www.enisa.europa.eu/news/enisa-news/telecom-security-and-resilience-during-covid19

significantly more profitable in the future, if the telework trend will continue after the pandemic, with a proportion of workers leaving their habitual residences to move outside cities.

3.3.1 Effects on society and labour markets

The pandemic has exacerbated the effects of the digital divide: those lacking access to connectivity or lacking digital skills experienced significant opportunity losses compared to their digitally equipped and digitally savvy peers. According to UNICEF (2020), two-thirds of the world's school-age children have no Internet access at home; in the US, 4.4 million households with children did not have consistent access to computers for online learning during the pandemic (USA Facts, 2020). As we shall see in Chapter 13, those who could not attend school because of lack of Internet access are likely to experience significant long-term effects on perspective life opportunities. The effect materializes mainly through disengagement: students left behind are less likely to get back on the same schooling path they were walking before the pandemic.

Inequality also increased because of how technology shaped labour markets' response to the pandemic. Before the Covid-19 pandemic, teleworking (namely, the possibility of employees to perform their assigned tasks physically separated from a traditional workplace and her supervisor (Fenner & Renn, 2010)) was not widely adopted. According to Sostero et al. (2020) in 2019, around 11% of dependent employees were teleworking at least sometimes during their working week; only about 3% of employees did that regularly. Not all workers can perform their task remotely, of course. Economic sectors such as information and communication technologies (ITC), the publishing, creative, or educational sectors tend to provide a higher number of telework opportunities than manufacturing. Particularly striking is the socio-economic profile of pre-pandemic teleworkers: telework tends to be much more prevalent among highly educated employees, with higher income and more stable jobs (Figure 3.5). Tasks that require physical presence are more likely to be performed by *blue-collar* employees. Office work that can be carried on also remotely is usually performed by *white-collar* employees, and white-collar employees have, on average, a higher level of education than blue-collar workers.

This segregation between workers who can and who cannot telework has exacerbated the unequal effect of the pandemic. While highly educated, high-income employees could work from home with a high chance to retain their job and with minimal exposure to the risk of infection by SARS-CoV-2, low-income, uneducated workers bore the heaviest burden: a much higher proportion of them lost their job or were furloughed; when they did retain their job, they were exposed to higher Covid-19 risks, working in crowded warehouses where physical distancing was hardly implementable, or operating public transportation and having no control on potentially infectious passengers, for example. Darvas (2020) finds that 8% of

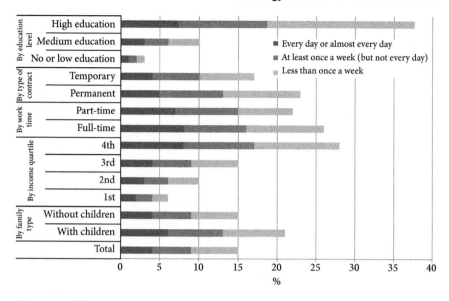

Figure 3.5 The socio-economic profile of teleworkers before the Covid-19 pandemic

Source: Sostero M., Milasi S., Hurley J., Fernández-Macías E., Bisello M., *Teleworkability and the COVID-19 crisis: a new digital divide?*, Seville: European Commission, 2020, JRC121193

workers with a lower secondary level qualification or below lost their job during the first six months of 2020; during the same period, jobs for middle-level qualification employees declined by 5%, while jobs for workers with a university degree *increased* by 3%.

Generally speaking, thanks to remote connectivity, those who could do so worked from home during the pandemic. Eurofound (2020) reports estimates of 37% of European employees starting to work from home by April 2020. Notably, new technological solutions emerged to substitute human workers in dangerous jobs and preserve their safety. For example, hospitals have sometimes used robots to disinfect Covid-19 patients' rooms. The long-term effects of the pandemic on labour markets are difficult to predict; it seems reasonable to expect that a significant proportion of those workers who teleworked during the pandemic will not go back to pre-pandemic teleworking levels.

Technology is an enabler of telework; however, its increased use carried its risks. For example, cybersecurity threats have increased dramatically during the pandemic: email scams increased by more than 6 times during the pandemic and video-conferencing apps, such as Zoom, have been subject to criticism because of an allegedly higher vulnerability to cyber-attacks. Artificial intelligence has also enabled employers to exert stricter control over their teleworking employees, possibly stepping over their workers' rights.[3] The demand for monitoring software increased during the pandemic: employers used remote desktop control, algorithms tracking the use of keywords of files by employees, live video feed or location tracking

---

[3] See for example: The New York Times (2020a) and The New York Times (2020b).

services, for example. Wearable devices may have been used to collect data of work-ers' performance, checking the time dedicated to breaks or away from their desk (Kritikos, 2020).

3.3.2 Harmful Covid-19-related content online

Social networks are increasingly considered natural repositories of people's senti-ments. The pandemic only accelerated that process, as communication and relation-ship turned from physical to digital due to home lock-downs. During the pandemic, Internet users relied on social networks such as Facebook or Twitter to gather in-formation about how to prevent Covid-19, how the virus spread, and what are the likely consequences of infection. They looked for emotional support, sought chan-nels that could alleviate pandemic-induced stress, such as groups of individuals sharing common concerns. They used social networks to vent their frustrations vis-à-vis harsh political decisions, such as those implying restrictions on the free-dom of movement or their bewilderment towards inconsistent communication from public institutions. All this created a fertile "emotional" environment where misin-formation about the Covid-19 pandemic could prosper, notably as users with a low degree of experience and digital skills (and thus more vulnerable to manipulation) increased their use of online platforms.

The harmful content that circulated online during the pandemic took the form of *misinformation*, whereby self-styled health "experts" provided inaccurate, poten-tially harmful information about the disease, or *disinformation*, that is: deliberate attempts to manipulate users into behaviours that could lead to their harm. Harm-ful content spread at any level. Users proposed false remedies; made-up evidence in support of the alleged inefficacy of the use of masks, or the role played by po-litical adversaries or foreign countries in fostering the spread of the coronavirus (Figure 3.6). Heads of State such as Brazil's Jair Bolsonaro or the US' Donald Trump supported and amplified on social networks false claims about the alleged efficacy of hydroxychloroquine as a method to treat Covid-19 while being potentially harmful.

Online platforms have exerted significant efforts to promote accurate information while limiting the spread of harmful content. According to EU Disinfo Lab (2020), an NGO focusing on disinformation research, online platforms have in particular implemented the following measures that turned out to be helpful:

- Surfacing and prioritizing content from authoritative sources, such as the World Health Organization
- Enacting closer cooperation with fact-checkers and public authorities to speed up the removal of content and increasing automated content moderation
- Offering free advertising to public authorities to promote evidence-based health advice.

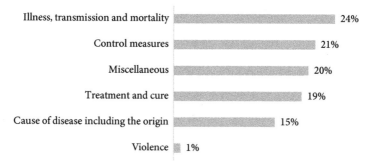

Figure 3.6 of 500

Figure 3.6 Disinformation during the Covid-19 pandemic (Composition of Covid-19 rumours, stigma and conspiracy theories circulating on social media/online news platforms)

Source: Statista, 2021. Accessed: April 12, 2021. https://www.statista.com/chart/22527/composition-of-covid-19-misinformation/. Made available under the Creative Commons License CC BY-ND 3.0

Yet, those efforts were not sufficient to halt the "misinformation pandemic", as that would have required structural changes in platforms' business models. For example: in May, a video titled "Plandemic" went viral on Facebook. The video claimed that pharmaceutical companies had created the coronavirus to profit from vaccine development. Facebook took the video down after just a few days but, by then, almost 2 million users had seen it (The New Yorker, 2021). Technical and economic reasons (such as the emphasis placed by online platforms' business models on content virality and its direct link with advertisement profitability) can explain this dynamic. We will discuss them at length in Chapter 14, dedicated to harmful content online.

✶✶✶✶

PART 2
DIGITAL INFRASTRUCTURE

4
Connectivity

Abstract

Fast and reliable connectivity is the first indispensable input for a digitized economy and society. However, telecom markets are highly complex. Their structural features, such as the need for high sunk investment to deploy infrastructure and the relationship between networks' size and services' quality, make it unlikely that they would work efficiently without public intervention. Thus, public policy is needed, particularly to pursue two overarching goals: (1) to incentivize investment to achieve high speed, reliability, responsiveness, and security of data traffic; and (2) to incentivize access under reasonable terms for everybody everywhere. Concretely, the success of the EU long-term telecom strategic plan should be measured against two indicators: the deployment of wired optical fibre networks and wireless 5G networks, especially where services are less profitable (in rural areas, for example); and the degree of cross-border connectivity. A variety of public policy tools are available to pursue those plans: "push" policies to directly support the deployment of new networks; "pull" policies to attract investment stimulating demand of digital services; spectrum management policies; and regulation and competition policy to stimulate and preserve a dynamic, pro-competitive telecom environment.

4.1 Background

Digitization needs telecommunication infrastructure. Most users, consumers, and public or business customers are familiar with downstream services, such as Internet search engines, social networks, or messaging apps. They may be using them every day. They may be less familiar with what lies behind them, though—how data can travel from one place to another through intricate telecommunication networks that cover the whole globe. Those networks provide the first, indispensable input that allows those services to exist and flourish: *connectivity*.

The global pandemic of Covid-19 has provided the bluntest example of the importance of reliable telecommunication networks. With billions of people locked down at home during quarantine, telecom networks went through a heavy stress test, accommodating a sudden boost in data traffic. As a result, video-conferencing applications, such as Zoom, experienced a massive boom in their market value (see Chapter 3).

Digital Economic Policy. Mario Mariniello, Oxford University Press.
© Mario Mariniello (2022). DOI: 10.1093/oso/9780198831471.003.0004

As societies and economies become ever-more digital, they are increasingly reliant on connectivity infrastructure (Figure 4.1 shows constant global progress, particularly in terms of download speed). Telecoms or, more generally, Information Communication Technologies (ICT) are thus the **backbone of any digital economy**.

The need for high speed and reliable connectivity is pressing. In 2020, the European Commission projected a 530% global increase in data volume by 2025, soaring from 33 zettabytes in 2018 to 175 zettabytes (1 *zettabyte* is equal to a *trillion gigabytes*, where a gigabyte is roughly equivalent to almost 600 copies of *War and Peace*, 20 music albums, or one hour of average quality film footage—it is *a lot!*). In 2025, the *Internet of Things* market is set to boost, with worldwide spending at US $1,100 billion compared to US $646 billion in 2018 (Statista, 2020a). So are cloud services, connected cars, e-health applications, and virtual reality—to mention only a few examples—, as we have seen in Chapter 1. Developing new networks or upgrading legacy ones is essential to keep up with the highly dynamic, fast-evolving digital environment. It comes as no surprise, therefore, that connectivity is globally increasing, with the number of fixed-broadband subscriptions projected to reach 15.7 for every 100 individuals and the average broadband connection speed to reach almost 35Mb per second in 2024 (from, respectively, a number of subscriptions of 14.6 for every 100 individuals and an average speed of 17Mb per second in 2019 (Statista, 2021)).

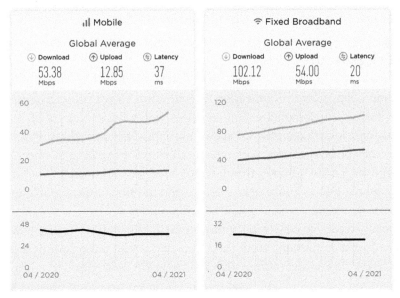

Figure 4.1 Global connectivity speed (April 2021)
https://www.speedtest.net/global-index

Responding to a survey carried out by the European Commission in 2015, an overwhelming majority of users indicated that good connectivity is an essential condition to achieve the Digital Single Market for citizens, industry, business, schools, and research and innovation centres (European Commission, 2016o). Almost 90% of respondents flagged their pessimism that the required speed and quality of connectivity can spontaneously emerge in the market and wished for proactive action by public authorities to support investment and take-up of connectivity services and network deployment.

In this chapter, I describe the functioning of telecom markets and discuss where those markets may fail to provide what is needed by a rapidly digitizing society. I also analyse the potential policy options, such as regulation, competition policy, and proactive stimulus policies, that can facilitate access and incentivize investment, expanding telecom networks and increasing the quality of services. However, telecom regulatory policy is a highly complex subject, backed by dense economic literature, cumulated through decades of telecom history. An in-depth review of that literature escapes the purpose of this chapter, which aims to provide students with just the essential tools needed to understand telecom policy in the context of the wider digital policy strategy, and not to train them to perform a telecom regulators' job.[1]

In this section, I thus present a simple illustration of the functioning of the different technologies. The purpose is to shed some clarity on the terminology commonly used, which can be somewhat cryptic. Students may feel overwhelmed by the number of acronyms they encounter, and I will try to keep it to a minimum (the glossary at the end of the book can also be of help).

4.1.1 Telecom markets: Infrastructure and technology[2]

Nowadays, data is mainly transmitted through **broadband**. Following the European Commission's definition, broadband is a term that applies to "*high-speed telecommunication systems capable of simultaneously supporting multiple information formats such as voice, high-speed data services, and video services on demand*".[3] **Basic broadband** is intended for a connection speed of up to 30Mb (megabytes) per second, **fast broadband** from 30Mb to 100Mb per second, and **ultra-fast broadband** are networks that can allow a speed greater than 100Mb per second.

"Next Generation Access" networks, or **NGA networks,** is yet another subjective term to indicate new or upgraded networks that allow significant improvements to speed and quality compared to traditional networks.[4] Improvements can be

---

[1] For those interested in a thorough description of telecom markets, the advice is to start from a good basic textbook. See for example: Penttinen (2015).

[2] This part draws extensively from the EC 'guide to broadband investment'. See: European Commission (2014a).

[3] Broadband is a *subjective* term as 'broad' is a relative concept—so any entity may have its own view of what can be considered broad and what cannot. Definition from European Commission (2021c).

[4] Sometimes the term NGN (next generation networks) is used in a similar fashion to NGA, though the two terms do not have exactly the same meaning.

obtained through several different technologies, as explained below, but often NGA networks indicate networks that primarily rely on fibre technology. To give an idea of adoption in the EU (more in Section 4.4): the possibility to access basic broadband is already guaranteed to all EU citizens; and the European Commission's targets for NGA coverage by 2020 were for 100% of EU households to have access to at least 30Mb per second connectivity, and 50% of EU households to have access to at least 100Mb per second connectivity (European Commission, 2021d).

Connectivity is provided through **passive physical infrastructure** and **active equipment**.[5] Examples of the former are masts, ducts, and cables. Routers, switches, and transponders are examples of active equipment. The deployment of new or upgraded passive infrastructure is one of the most important policy puzzles to be figured out.

Infrastructure's deployment tends to be very expensive: it requires significant capital investment, it has an exact geographical location, and it is thus *sunk*, meaning that it cannot be reused somewhere else. It can provide a stable stream of profits to the investor in the long term, but it is naturally subject to regulatory pressure, as it is likely to generate monopolistic power in the hands of the infrastructure owner (see Section 4.2 below).

It is important to note that the high investment needed to place fibre cables is not due to the cost of the cable itself. The costly part is represented by the civil engineering works that need to take place to place the cables: this entails digging trenches and laying ducts and cables (to the final users' premises, if this is necessary). This fact has important implications: when the fibre is deployed, it is typically deployed in hundreds of cables (once you have started digging, you take the opportunity to stick in as much fibre as you can!). That means that fibre capacity is usually very high, and that cables can be easily leased to telecom operators, or even cable TVs, banks, or large companies, that might have the resources and interest to operate the fibre themselves (or, using a slightly more technical terminology: to *light up* the *dark fibre*—i.e. make use of the passive infrastructure they lease).

When it comes to the physical make-up of a broadband network, three sections can be identified (Figure 4.2):

- A **backbone network**, usually made of a ring of fibre optic cable. The backbone aggregates all the data traffic at the regional level. It then connects it to the *Internet*, namely to the national or international network
- The **backhaul**, which aggregates traffic at local (village or town) level, receiving the traffic from the local *access nodes* (namely: the switching points where end-users are connected to the network)
- The **last mile** (sometimes referred to also as the *first mile*; it all depends on which position you are looking from!). This is the last connection segment,

---

[5] As explained in European Commission (2014a).

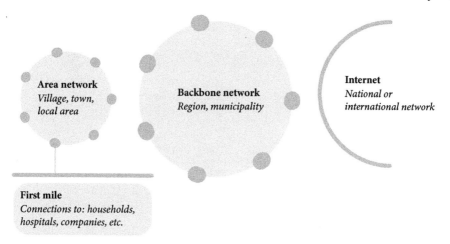

Figure 4.2 Scheme of the physical components of a broadband network
European Commission, 'Broadband Investment Guide' (23 September 2014), p. 16. https://ec.
europa.eu/digital-single-market/en/news/broadband-investment-guide

from the *access node* to every single user, be that a single household, a school, a bank, or a hospital.

The *last mile* has critical importance in defining the characteristics of the connection that the final user can experience. Broadband's most important quality parameters are:

- **Maximum (Advertised) Speed**. This is what operators claim they can pro- vide to users, when transmission conditions are optimal. It is measured in the amount of data (usually megabytes) that can be transmitted over a specific in- terval of time (usually seconds). Hence the most common expression of speed is in *Mbs*: megabytes per second
- **Actual Speed**. This is the speed users *actually* get to experience when they con- nect. It is often different from the advertised speed, as actual speed depends on the available bandwidth, for example, or, depending on the infrastructure used, the distance between the user and the access node
- **Bandwidth**. Bandwidth is a feature of broadband that is related to actual speed. It is an indication of the capacity of a network to transfer data. It is usually measured in GHz (gigahertz)
- **Latency**. Latency is the amount of delay which is to be expected from the mo- ment in which the command to start the data transfer is given, to the moment in which the actual traffic begins. Latency is a significant factor for time-critical applications—it may not be so important if downloading a movie takes a few seconds to start, not quite so if a surgeon is operating remotely (Figure 4.3)
- **Symmetry**. With a symmetric connection, speed is equal whether the user is uploading or downloading. But, again, it is the use made of the network that determines whether this feature is relevant. If the user needs the connection

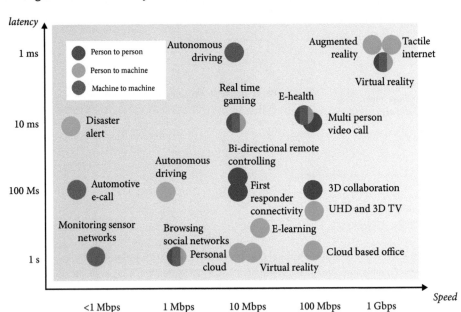

Figure 4.3 Need for speed and latency for use of application and services by a single user

European Commission, 'Connectivity for a Competitive Digital Single Market – Towards a European Gigabit Society' (14 September 2016), p. 4. https://ec.europa.eu/newsroom/dae/document.cfm?doc_id=17182

primarily for inflow traffic (for example, to watch a Netflix movie), symmetry is not that important. Conversely, applications that require lots of outflow traffic from the user (for example, video-conferencing) critically rely on similar performances for data download and upload.

Connection in the *last mile* can be made possible through five different types of passive infrastructure (see Table 4.1). **Wired infrastructure** tends to be the most reliable, as it does not depend on external factors such as the weather. It can, however, be expensive to set up. The least expensive solution is *copper*, where a broadband connection is obtained through a twisted pair of the legacy copper cables that were traditionally used for phone calls. Copper tends to be very asymmetric and slow, but it is also the infrastructure that requires the least investment and disruption for users since it relies on legacy cables. Copper is usually indicated through the terms *x*DSL (where *x* can be an **A** indicating "asymmetric" connection (ADSL), or **S** indicating "symmetric" connection (SDSL), for example). **Vectoring** (or *VDSL*) is a technology that can significantly increase copper's speed (up to 60Mbs). Vectoring, however, prevents *local loop unbundling* or LLU (I will explain what LLU is in the next section) therefore preventing competition in the last mile. Another option for wired infrastructure is *coaxial cable* (often referred to with just the term "cable"). As in the case of copper, cable primarily relies on the legacy network, this time TV distribution networks. Cable can reach very fast download speed rates (up to 300

Table 4.1 Types of Infrastructure

Wired Infrastructure	Pro	Cons
Copper	Low investment cost	Performance depends on number of users, length of last mile segment, total traffic and technology
Cable	Low investment cost	Actual speed may be much lower than advertised as bandwidth shared with multiple users. Does not allow competition as last mile cannot be unbundled
Fibre	Best performance in terms of speed and latency. Symmetric	High investment cost
Wireless Infrastructure	**Pro**	**Cons**
Terrestrial Wireless (Mobile)	Last mile not needed	Requires backloading; signal depends on traffic, distance, weather
Satellite	No need for investment in backbone network	High cost for end-user equipment, limited user capacity by region, high latency; signal depends on weather

(modified version of European Commission, (European Commission, 2014a, p. 21))

Mbs) but is also very asymmetric (maximum upload speed about 50 Mbs), its performance is heavily affected by the number of connected users and the length of the last mile segment, and it does not allow for competition in the last mile since unbundling is not feasible.

The best, future-proof, wired infrastructure is **fibre** (often referred to with the acronym **FTTx**, which means *Fibre To The x* where *x* can be, for example, P – premises, H – home, S – subscriber, B – business, C – cabinet, N – node, hence **FTTH** indicates fibre connection that connects directly with the household, while **FTTC** indicates fibre connection that connects only to the access node, leaving for other infrastructure to connect the last mile from home to the access node). Fibre can reach ultra-fast speeds—more than 1Gbs or 1,000 Megabytes per second for download and upload—and it is very reliable, secure, stable, and symmetric. However, it also requires a heavy investment, as mentioned previously.

When it comes to **wireless infrastructure**, the options are essentially twofold: terrestrial wireless and satellite. The first case is commonly referred to as **mobile connection**, which is currently provided through 3G ("Third Generation") or 4G/LTE ("Fourth Generation"/"Long-Term Evolution") technologies. 5G is the new terrestrial wireless standard; its commercial deployment had just started in 2020, but it is expected to be widely available only as of 2025. 5G has the potential to enable significant improvements compared to 4G, in terms of speed, symmetry and latency: theoretically, 5G could reach a download speed of up to 20Gbs, although users should initially experience an average speed of about 100Mbs before the technology is fully developed. 5G is considered the indispensable step to unlocking the development of new applications of the *digital economy*, such as e-health or autonomous vehicles. Because of its crucial strategic importance, 5G is also at the centre of a high-profile geopolitical controversy revolving around the activities of Huawei, a Chinese 5G infrastructure provider. In Sections 4.2 and 4.4, I will briefly touch upon this dispute. However, it should be noted that 5G and wireless infrastructure will never be able to fully replace wired infrastructure. 5G, even at its best, requires backloading, which relies on wired (fibre) infrastructure. Offloading data from cellular to fixed lines is, in fact, necessary to maintain a mobile connection's performance levels. In other words: one cannot expect to set up a single mast to cover a vast geographical area using only radio spectrum. Instead, masts are only able to cover geographical areas of limited size, and they always need to be connected to a network of fibre dug into the ground. So rather than substitutes, wired and wireless technology should primarily be conceived as complementary (Peña-López, 2017).

Moreover, the key—indeed, indispensable—input necessary for mobile communication is **radio spectrum**. Radio spectrum is a scarce resource managed by national public authorities which typically allocate its frequencies through spectrum auctions. It is sought after by various actors that would like to use it for different purposes, for example for radio or TV broadcasting. I discuss **spectrum management** in Section 4.2, in the context of the policies necessary to stimulate broadband uptake.

As regards **satellite**, this can be used to reach users that are very dispersed in remote areas. The investment needed is not so much on the passive infrastructure side; instead, it is the active equipment for users that can be pretty expensive. Moreover, satellite speed rates are never really high (maximum 20Mbs in download), and latency is intrinsically high, given that the signal must always travel back and forth between the users and satellites orbiting in space.

Finally, again along the lines of the definitions proposed by the European Commission, it is possible to identify the following **actors** in the broadband value chain (European Commission, 2014a):

- The owner/operator of the **backbone physical infrastructure**. It could be an incumbent telecom company or even the local municipality
- The owner/operator of the **access area** (i.e. the last mile segment). Again, a telecom operator or a public entity
- The **network provider**: the company that "lights up" the passive equipment, providing connectivity. Typically a telecom operator
- The **service provider**: the company which provides a digital service relying on the connecting infrastructure (Google, for example, is a service provider, in this terminology)
- The **end customer**: households, enterprises, schools, hospitals, etc.
- The **wholesale customer**: an actor who has the interest and resources to lease dark fibre for its own use. It could be a large business entity, for example.

Often the backbone infrastructure operator, the access area operator, and the network provider roles are played by the same incumbent vertically integrated telecom company.

Infrastructure markets generate important economic dynamics that often justify public policy intervention. Let us look at them in the next section.

4.2 Opportunities and challenges

Expanding connectivity within a particular geographic area can have potent effects on its economy. There are plenty of quantitative estimates supporting this statement in the literature. For example, Czernich, et al. (2011) show that increasing broadband penetration by 10% stimulates GDP per capita by 0.9 to 1.5%. Vu, et al. (2020) review 208 academic papers exploring the causal link between growth and ICT (Information Communication Technologies, a general term that includes any telecommunication application or infrastructure).[6] They reach the following conclusions, among other things:

- ICT contributes significantly to growth and productivity, and the effect tends to increase over time
- Countries and regions differ significantly in terms of their ability to reap the benefits of ICT for growth
- Long-term effects are much greater than short-term effects
- There are three main channels through which ICT affects growth: (1) learning and diffusion of technology and innovation; (2) improved quality in decision-making; (3) significant decreases in costs and expansion of choice, implying a boost in demand and supply.

Note that the empirical exercise mentioned above requires a certain level of statistical sophistication. It is not sufficient to observe, for example, that high broadband infrastructure coverage is often present in more prosperous economies to conclude that broadband increases economic performance. It may indeed be the reverse. Richer geographical areas are more likely to afford higher investment levels or have a stronger demand to tap in to support the expansion of telecom infrastructure (higher demand means higher potential profit, hence higher incentive to invest). In other words, correlation does not mean causation. A good policy adviser should ascertain whether a particular claim is backed by solid empirical analysis where causal effects are disentangled or if that claim crucially rests on correlation results. In the latter case, the claim may be unfounded (in the appendix, I briefly describe some common pitfalls in empirical quantifications that a policy advisor may fall into while analysing complex markets like telecom ones).

---

[6] Other examples of relevant contributions in the economic literature: Roller and Waverman (2001); Datta and Agarwal (2004), Sridhar and Sridhar (2008), Pradhan, et al. (2014), and Pradhan, et al. (2018).

The most important effect of the deployment of fast connectivity infrastructure is, in any case, hardly quantifiable. **Infrastructure is the key, indispensable enabler** to allow the leap to the digital economy and society. Most of the recent digital applications I described in Chapter 1 (such as automated cars, the Internet of Things, smart wearables, augmented and virtual reality, cryptocurrencies, e-health applications, anything enabled by the advance of artificial intelligence and data analytics) would not see the light of day without fast connectivity infrastructure. More than that, predicting the potential use of ultra-fast connectivity in the future is tough as, presumably, many new applications will be invented in the years to come. We currently have no idea what those applications will look like (a similar consideration can be made about new, today unimaginable, jobs that will be created in the future—see Chapter 12). Besides the quantitative indications from empirical research, we should thus be inclined to rely on an *intuition*, albeit a solid one: that a society without fast connectivity is likely to develop at a much slower pace in the years to come.

The crucial role of telecom infrastructure in the development of the digital economy also helps explain the nature of the puzzle that policymakers need to solve. Connectivity has powerful positive beneficial effects for society (**positive externalities**, as economists say). No matter how high the long-term profit is of a private stakeholder investing in infrastructure deployment, that profit is unlikely to match the magnitude of the positive spill-over that building the infrastructure has for the whole affected community. Perhaps a telecom operator would not see the point of investing a significant amount of resources in digging a 50km trench connecting a small rural village on a Greek mountain. And yet, that cable may enable a whole economic community to flourish.[7] Or allow isolated children to access the highest level of education through online courses (see Chapter 12), perhaps nurturing the emergence of new geniuses who could make a breakthrough scientific discovery that would benefit the whole world.

Laying down the groundwork for achieving those goals, as far-fetched as they may appear, is the central task of public policy, though it is certainly not the main motor driving private profit-seeking market players' investment decisions. As explained in the appendix, **strong positive externalities** are a source of market failure. If market operators would not receive additional incentives (such as public financial support), they would tend not to invest in what a society considers desirable, because they base their investment decision on the profits they make and not on the benefits they generate for society.

Oulton (2012) reports a very telling finding: the most significant contribution of ICT to the economy is a consequence of *using* communication equipment (including hardware and software) in *other industries*, rather than from the growth of the ICT sector itself.

---

[7] See, for example: Dartford (2019).

The critical take-away for students is that, when it comes to telecom policy, poli-cymakers should always keep in mind that their **primary goal is to develop the *use* of communication technologies** and not to foster prosperity in the telecom sector as such. The health of the European telecom industry should certainly be of primary interest for European policymakers; but only to the extent that it is instrumental to the achievement of a **connected society**. Thus, for example, comparing US telecom companies' profitability with that of EU telecom companies can be misleading: big-ger profits do not necessarily translate into more connectivity for society, as we are about to see. Infrastructure investment, as such, should therefore not be considered a goal in itself. Instead, it is a *means* to achieving the overarching goal of a digitized economy.

Let us consider in greater detail the **challenges** that public policy is called to address.

Two leverages need to be activated to achieve connectivity: **investment** and **access**.

Investment is required to ensure high-quality connectivity across the territory. As we have seen in the previous section, investment is needed to expand geographi-cal coverage and improve the actual speed at which data is transmitted, eliminating latency, the stability and security of the connection, and its "symmetry". Fibre is the burdensome investment *par excellence*. Stimulating investment in rural areas, where profitability is arguably low and bridging the "digital divide" (see Chapter 13), is one of the biggest challenges for policymakers.

Access implies that not only should high-quality connectivity (infrastructure and technology) be potentially available to everybody everywhere; it should also be possible to access it at a reasonable price. Qualitative superior connectivity infras-tructure is pointless if only a few can afford it. It would run the risk of ending up with the opposite result and making society less inclusive by exacerbating income inequalities. Those who can afford it would have a head start compared to those who cannot, as we have seen happened during the Covid-19 pandemic (see also Chapter 3).

In the digital space, investment decisions are very tricky. On the one hand, the ex-pansion of the digital economy, the hype around digitization and the general push to migrate from copper to fibre, points to a gold mine investors should be eager to tap into. And it is undoubtedly true that demand for fast connectivity is only set to further increase in the years to come (at the time of writing this book, the Covid-19 pandemic has increased Internet traffic by 25%–30% worldwide). But, on the other hand, investment requires long term stability—and **digital is a great source of uncertainty**, given how dynamic and fast-changing the digital environ-ment is. For example, telecom operators themselves are subject to heavy disruption by **Over-the-Top players** (namely: platforms that use the Internet to offer commu-nication services, such as WhatsApp, Zoom, Telegram, or Facebook Messenger) and may be wary that potentially high long-term rents brought about by infrastructure investment may be quickly eroded by sudden reshuffles of market dynamics.

Strong positive externalities and high **future uncertainty** explain why markets cannot deliver what society would hope for in terms of connectivity infrastructure and access to it; that is why public policy comes into play.

Another crucial economic feature of ICT markets that prevents markets from functioning efficiently, relates to the *size* and the *type* of investment needed. In ICT, investment is **large** compared to operational costs, and it is often **sunk**, meaning that it cannot be recovered, for example, by selling infrastructure or reconverting it for other uses. Remember: the costly part of infrastructure investment is often the civil engineering works needed to install it.

Moreover, telecommunication markets rely on networks. That implies that their value increases at a higher rate than the speed of expansion of the network: the more users are connected, the more valuable is the network for everybody who connects to it (see the appendix for a description of the meaning of **network externalities**).

High fixed sunk costs, low variable costs, and *strong network externalities* are a recipe for **natural monopolies**. Natural monopolies occur when a single market player is better suited to supply a good or provide a service than multiple players. Increasing the number of players would increase total costs while possibly decreasing the value that is generated.

To see this, compare a market A where every user is connected to the same network belonging to a single player, and a market B where half of the users are connected to the network of one player and the other half to the network of a second player. Assuming that regulators do not force the networks to be interoperable, users would prefer to be in market A, where they can be connected to all other users in the market, instead of just half of them. Market A also implies lower aggregate deployment and maintenance costs since only one network is needed, not two.

Telecom services and other utilities such as water or energy provision tend to qualify as natural monopolies. They are therefore subject to heavy regulatory pressure. If having only one operator is the best option to minimize costs, public authorities (the regulators) may allow the single operator to sell access to the network or supply the connectivity service. Still, they may constrain its pricing policy or force it to open up some of its infrastructures to access by other players.

In some ways, regulators are called to substitute for the role that is normally played by market competition: instead of competitors pushing players to lower their prices, for example, it is the regulator that constrains the natural monopolist's pricing and quality decision.[8]

---

[8] As mentioned in the introduction of this Chapter, detailing the functioning of telecom regulation is outside the scope of this book. In Chapter 8 on online platforms, I will shed some further light on the relationship between regulation and competition.

4.2.1 Investment vs Access?

The traditional "legacy networks" puzzle has seen *investment* and *access* juxtaposed, often in a contrasting fashion. Historically, telecommunication infrastructure, technology, and services have been provided by vertically integrated telecom operators. A whole ecosystem was owned and operated by one single company. Telecom markets naturally evolved from state-owned enterprises holding the service monopoly; to vertically integrated monopolists of a private nature; to oligopolies, where a few other players could challenge at least some segments of the market; to liberalization, where competition is fostered wherever possible. The shift of the core business from *calls* to *data* has triggered significant changes in business models, allowing the emergence of players of different natures active at different levels of the value chain (see Section 4.1). The result being, from the perspective of the final user, that receiving or sending data from a device entails dealing with several companies and not just one (even if that user may not realize it).

A milestone in the public policy approach to telecom markets in Europe since the beginning of the twenty-first century is the mandating of incumbent operators to provide access to their network infrastructure to potential competitors that could challenge them in the **last mile**, from the cabin to the user (Figure 4.2). The obligation applies to operators that hold *significant market power* (SMP) or that have received public support in the form of state aid to build the network. That approach goes under the name of **Local Loop Unbundling** (LLU). If access is mandated at the active equipment level, that is called **bitstream**. LLU and bitstream have had a significant impact on the development of connectivity in Europe: those policies pushed companies to increase the quality of their networks and technologies, and dramatically reduced prices for end-users.

Note the importance of the history that led to LLU and bitstream: vertical separation (that is: separating wholesale and retail businesses) and competition has yielded a significant hit to incumbent players' profitability. From an investment and innovation perspective, this could be a problem. For example, suppose an incumbent player is penalized for holding significant market power. In that case, this could affect the incentives of new players to follow the same path and aggressively pursue a strategy to become the next incumbent player. Knowing that they would ultimately be penalized if very successful, challengers may refrain from pursuing their (pro-competitive) plans. This dynamic would ultimately undermine societal welfare because it would hamper investment and innovation from smaller, *wannabe-big* market players. However, incumbent telecom operators most often did not *earn* their market power thanks to a successful pro-competitive strategy. They instead *inherited* it from past public monopolies.

This historical insight is essential. It marks a crucial difference with other successful players who may enjoy comparable power levels in digital markets and have some features (namely, *network externalities*) in common with telecoms services. That is **online platforms**, such as Google, Amazon, or Facebook. Incumbent online platforms did not inherit their market power. They earned it through breakthrough inventions (see, for example, the spectacular success of Google's proprietary algorithm in the search engine market). Students should keep that in mind when asking whether platforms should be treated as utilities and be broken up to tame their market power. I will discuss this issue extensively in the dedicated Chapter 8 on online platforms.

Not surprisingly, since liberalization started, the telecom industry has been increasingly vocal about the alleged adverse impact that *competition* (which puts downward pressure on *access prices*) would have on *investment*.[9] As a result, calling for a rethinking of the EU approach to competition in telecom markets to stimulate fast and ultra-fast connectivity infrastructure deployment throughout Europe has become a mantra of the telecom industry. Relaxing merger control, for example, and allowing markets to consolidate, would reduce competition and increase prices and revenues for operators, providing them with the necessary resources to deploy new infrastructure.

That logic is flawed. There is no guarantee that increased profits would be reinvested in infrastructure rather than kept in companies' shareholders' pockets. Private investment is always driven by potential profit. And if the prospect of profit is concrete, financial markets can provide the necessary resources for investment, particularly when the demand for it comes from well-established incumbent market players.

A more subtle objection to policies favouring competition in telecom markets is based on a famous 2005 paper (Aghion, et al., 2005). The authors report empirical results supporting the existence of an inverse-U relationship between competition

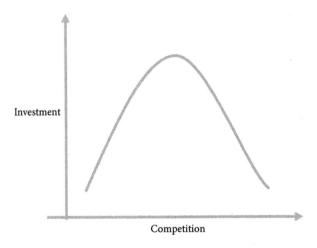

Figure 4.4 Competition and Investment – An Inverse-U Relationship?

[9] See, for example: Telecoms chiefs back overhaul of EU competition policy, Financial Times, 1 December 2019 https://www.ft.com/content/89a0c4a8-12b0-11ea-a7e6-62bf4f9e548a

and innovation/investment (Figure 4.4). The underlying intuition is straightforward: when competition is too high, profits are too low to incentivize investment. Taken at the extreme, if competition is perfect, prices are just enough to offset costs and market players would make no profit investing in them. So why would they do it in the first place?

The paper has been criticied by a number of researchers, and indeed its empirical findings appear to be based on shaky grounds.[10] Its theoretical intuition is nevertheless compelling—shouldn't the prospect of lower profits act as a brake for investment? That certainly is the case. However, such an effect should not be considered in isolation as other forces act in the opposite direction. Competition lowers profits, but it also provides for dynamic incentives to invest: it stimulates investment by companies that are afraid that their competitor may challenge their market share with a higher quality product or service. Or it pushes companies to open new markets. For example, suppose competitors in the last mile see their profits reduce too much in a dense urban area. In that case, an operator may have an incentive to escape that competition by deploying infrastructure somewhere else where competition is less daunting (an extended description of the static and dynamic effects of competition is reported in the appendix).

Thus, ultimately, which of the effects mentioned above prevails is an empirical question: are we on the left or right side of the peak in Figure 4.5? If we are on the left side, increasing competition increases investment. Conversely, being on the right side, increasing competition achieves the opposite result.

Generally, observing how telecom markets have evolved in recent years indicates that increasing competition in telecom markets has largely benefited investment. Take, for example, Figure 4.5. When LLU started in Europe, US policymakers took the opposite route and endorsed the logic backed by the telecom industry: companies were allowed to enjoy significant degrees of market power under the assumption that this would have incentivized them to invest more. Figure 4.5 compares the 2003 OECD country ranking for fixed broadband penetration with the OECD ranking of 2014. After 11 years of US pro-market power policies, the US dropped from the 10th to the 16th position. Countries that implemented a pro-competition policy had a better investment performance.

4.2.2 Europe and the United States

As it turns out, up until recently, Europe has been better placed than the US in terms of basic connectivity. It has almost universal coverage for standard broadband speed (fewer than 30Mbs); the average actual download speed in most EU Member States

---

[10] Correa (2012) points out that a structural break due to the establishment of the Court of Appeals for the Federal Circuit is behind the results in the Aghion, et al. (2005) paper. Once that is taken into account the relationship between competition and innovation is positive. Correa (2012) and Correa (2014) find a similar positive relationship in a dataset of US firms. This may suggest that the shape of the inverted-U is such that the empirically relevant part is the increasing one, with the decreasing part covering unrealistic competition levels that exists only in stylized theoretical models. Shapiro (2011) provides a critique of the use of this theory to argue in favour of less pro-competitive policies (Mariniello & Salemi, 2015).

is higher than in the US. And access is much cheaper: final users' prices tend to be significantly lower than in the US (even if comparisons are hard to make, as connectivity services are often purchased in bundles or with complex tariff schemes that are dependent on the amount of data consumed). The US' more unsatisfactory performance in access price should not come as a surprise since many US citizens cannot choose their operator, particularly for fast or ultra-fast *NGA* networks.

However, Europe is not currently equally well-placed to face future demands for fast connectivity. The US is doing better than the EU regarding the deployment of high-speed connectivity wired and wireless infrastructures.

There are two main reasons behind that outcome, and they are not related to the different levels of competition observed in the two geographical areas. First, in terms of wired connectivity, the US could rely on a much more widely spread deployment of *cable*, traditionally used for TV purposes by a large proportion of US households. Demand for high-speed download has also been historically higher in the US, given the popularity of video streaming and video gaming (and hence it has always been more profitable to invest in fast connectivity infrastructure in the US, *ceteris paribus*).

Second, more centralized control in the allocation and assignment of radio spectrum has helped to speed up the deployment of 4G mobile technologies and is likely to help with 5G as well. Europe, on the contrary, did not fare as well with its wireless spectrum management. And that resulted in a delay in deployment of 4G and 5G.

To understand the importance of this second reason, first note that the vital limit of Europe's single market (compared to the US) is its inherent fragmentation. Telecom markets are essentially national in their scope and cross-border competition between operators is limited. That is problematic: the absence of a uniform, borderless market hampers the creation of pan-European operators, i.e. operators that are

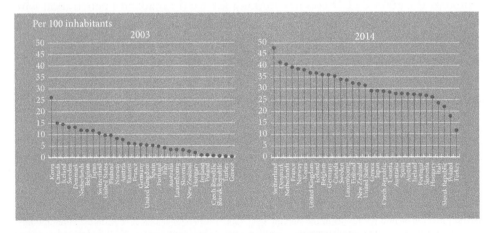

Figure 4.5 OECD rankings fixed broadband penetration, 2003 vs 2014

https://wayback.archiveit.org/12090/20170202151808/http://ec.europa.eu/epsc/sites/epsc/files/strategic_note_issue_19.pdf

active in every single EU country offering similar conditions across the continent. Those operators could increase their profits leveraging on their scale to reduce their investment and operational costs. Arguably that would make markets more efficient, and thus increase the supply of connectivity services.

Fragmentation in mobile telecom markets is particularly disturbing. There is an increasingly pressing need to ease cross-border wireless connectivity services to support the creation of a single, unified digital market. Imagine automated cars travelling across Europe and the importance of smooth transition across the territory of different Member States.

The lack of a uniform pan-European approach is especially apparent in the case of **radio spectrum management**. Spectrum management consists of two categories of action: **allocation**—which refers to the decision regarding the use of a given band of spectrum, e.g. TV, radio, or communication, and **assignment**—the decision to award a specific player the rights to employ a proportion of the spectrum band already allocated for a particular use. So a specific band of spectrum could be *allocated* to mobile communication, for example. Then part of that band could be *assigned* to a specific mobile network operator, which could use it to supply mobile communication services.

Radio spectrum management is traditionally mostly a Member State's national competence. The fundamental reason for this is that spectrum management represents an important source of revenue for national governments. In particular, spectrum is typically allocated through **spectrum auctions**; depending on the design of the auction, the final outcome can be very lucrative. For example, Germany's 5G mobile spectrum auction raised €6.5 billion for the German government. Therefore, it comes as little surprise that Member States are reluctant to yield their control over spectrum to favour a more centralized approach, as can be observed in other jurisdictions, such as the US.

However, lack of coordination and fragmentation in spectrum management can explain why Europe struggles to nurture the emergence of pan-European mobile operators and, therefore, fall behind in terms of next-generation mobile networks deployment. For example, as national auctions do not take place simultaneously, operators cannot precisely anticipate the costs of providing services in every Member States. This uncertainty prevents them from factoring in the economies of scale that they would achieve by packaging a single offer to cover the whole EU territory at the same time. It is one thing to participate in a single auction for a whole continent, but quite another to participate in one auction after another, in each Member State, facing a much higher degree of uncertainty regarding the final outcome.

Fragmentation in the EU mobile telecom market also implies **high international roaming costs**, without intervention by regulators. International roaming refers to users that temporarily use their mobile devices outside their home country. Lack of international competition in the roaming market can explain high roaming costs. But they are also due to an economic effect called **double marginalization** (I explain the effect in detail in the appendix). Double marginalization translates into higher tariffs for final users. It occurs when multiple companies selling complementary services are necessary for the final product. In the case of international roaming, more than one company is involved in the provision of the service, namely the home country operator and the host country operator. For example, a Belgian user travelling to Italy and using her mobile to call home needs to access the Italian operator's infrastructure *and* the Belgian operator's infrastructure.

The EU has gradually curbed *retail* roaming costs within the Single Market, achieving their complete elimination in June 2017, with the *Roam Like At Home* initiative (European Commission, 2015b). European consumers welcomed this measure as an example of the most concrete benefits that the EU's action can have. And yet, the new regulation did not escape criticism. Wholesale charges were not eliminated, and some operators found themselves squeezed between guaranteeing low home tariffs to their roaming customers and paying high access prices to network operators in host countries. For example, in the case described above, the Belgian operator must offer "roam like at home" tariffs to her customer who is travelling to Italy. However, if the Italian infrastructure owner asks a high wholesale price to the Belgian operator to access its Italian network, the Belgian operator may risk incurring a loss. That occurs if the "roam like at home" tariff charge to the user is lower than the wholesale access price. For that reason, regulators had also to set wholesale **caps** (that is: maximum limits to how much a wholesale network service provider can charge a retailer).

Moreover, there was a concern that users could game the roaming regulation, purchasing SIM cards in countries where charges are lower and using them in their home country. This dynamic could put upward pressure on prices in countries where tariffs were lower, for example, because of a lower average income. For example, imagine if all of a sudden French customers bought SIM cards from Bulgarian operators: the increase in demand would push prices up in Bulgaria, making mobile less affordable for Bulgarian citizens. Regulators thus established a *fair use* clause that allows operators to identify and block users attempting to use foreign SIM cards at home permanently. Note that while the economic concern is genuine, the *fair use* clause contrasts with the fundamental principle of the EU Single Market (whereby anybody should be able to buy goods or services from anywhere in Europe and use them wherever she wants). This tension between the ideal of the Single Market and a conflicting approach adopted by EU regulators for pragmatic reasons is a recurrent issue with EU digital policy. We will note it again, for example, in the context of the discussion around geo-blocking (see Chapter 10).

A final source of concern relates to **5G and its potential cybersecurity risks** (see Chapter 7). According to an analysis published by EU Member States in October 2019, the novelty of 5G technologies will increase the likelihood of security incidents. For example, certain parts of the network equipment, such as base stations, become more sensitive (Dartford, 2019). The sensitivity of networks would depend on the type of impact (e.g. whether a threat could compromise confidential information) and the scale of the impact (e.g. the number of users affected). Given that 5G is likely to be used widely, where possible also substituting for wired connectivity, both the type of impact and its scale point to an increased general vulnerability compared to 4G.

Moreover, 5G may have more entry points for cyber attackers. Since 5G is comparatively more reliant on software than previous technologies, it is more exposed to potential software vulnerabilities. *Backdoors* generated by attackers could expose a whole network to several cyber threats, including data breaches from foreign state actors (see Chapter 7). The report stresses how these 5G risks can be exacerbated if the deployment of networks is primarily dependent on one single supplier. Without naming it, the report alludes to the Chinese company Huawei: in 2020, the company owned the lion's share of the 5G infrastructure deployment world market. Therefore, the European concern has an apparent geostrategic root: Huawei is considered close to the Chinese government, so some consider a firm reliance on Huawei for Europe's future mobile infrastructure to be a threat to national security.[11]

4.3 Dilemmas for policymakers

Incentivizing investment in higher-speed connectivity and favouring access are the two conundrums of telecom public policy. One key puzzle to solve is how to expand connectivity where the market is most likely unable to provide it by itself. This market failure could be expected, for example, in rural areas, where isolated communities could greatly benefit from connectivity, but services would not yield much profit to operators. Likewise, stimulating access to fast connectivity for vulnerable categories – the older, less educated, and poorer segments of the population – is a fundamental step to addressing the digital divide (more on that in Chapter 13 on inequality).

Countries have implemented a variety of measures to achieve those goals. One common trend has been updating policies and regulations to account for supply-side and demand-side **convergence** in communication markets. Convergence occurs because industries that were once separated are now significantly intertwined: computing industries, telecommunication, and broadcasting rely on data transmission over the Internet (or, more precisely, over IP—*Internet Protocol*). On the demand side, advancement in wireless technologies allows for a certain degree of substitution between fixed and mobile networks. Even though, as we have seen in Section 4.1, mobile can never get away without fixed backloading, so fixed and mobile are also largely complementary: one cannot do without the other.

Likewise, final users can obtain access to multiple services through even a single online platform: services such as communication, video, audio broadcasting, and

---

[11] Public policies needed to address cybersecurity risks are discussed in Chapter 7 and are therefore not treated in Section 4.3 of this Chapter.

other data-based services. Therefore, policymakers and regulators are required to consider convergence, for example, when they need to assess the level of competition in a market because multiple sources can now generate competition.

Similarly, policymakers need to take convergence into account when they make their plans to ensure connectivity for a specific geographical area since connectivity can now be provided in many different ways. Again, bearing in mind the role that different actors and technologies can play along the value chain.

A closely related term is **technology neutrality**. Maxwell & Bourreau (2015) describe three different implications associated with this concept. Technology neutrality means that:

- *regulations should define the objectives to be achieved, such as guaranteeing a certain security level, but the means of achieving them should be left to companies to define*. Companies should be allowed to select the technology they consider most suitable to achieve those goals
- *the same regulatory principles must be applied*, no matter the nature of the technology which is being regulated
- *regulators should be neutral* as regards which technology should prevail in a particular market. They should not "pick the winner". They should instead allow markets to select the technology that better serves to pursue the public policy goals.

For example, a *technology-neutral* regulator should not care whether users can access fast speed connectivity through fixed networks, mobile networks, or a combination of both; what matters is that access is possible and the price is affordable.[12]

In the next section, we will focus on the latest developments in telecom policy at the EU level. This section takes a more general approach, analysing **four potential action areas** to address the concerns identified in Section 4.2.

The four areas of actions are:

- *Push* public policies
- *Pull* public policies
- Spectrum management
- Regulation and competition policy.

4.3.1 Push public policies

Push policies aim to stimulate investment by leveraging the supply side of connectivity. They may consist of direct financial support for private operators investing

---

[12] The definition of what can be considered 'affordable' is an inherently subjective exercise. A good attempt is made by Alliance for Affordable Internet. See for example their 2019 report: The 2019 Affordability Report. *Alliance for Affordable Internet Washington DC: Web Foundation.*

in infrastructure where expected profits are low. Alternatively, the public sector could play a more active role, getting involved in deploying the networks and their wholesale supply.

Governments can reduce barriers to entry, particularly at the backbone network level, by easing legislation, cutting administrative costs, or more directly through **state subsidies** or tax breaks.[13] Direct subsidies should generally be associated with a specific project and follow strict criteria for selecting the beneficiaries. The best way to allocate subsidies is through public tenders. With an efficient design, the public authority allocating the subsidy minimizes the risk that the money given is too much or too little compared to what the private operator needs to deploy the network. Resources can also be transferred through soft loans or guarantees, essentially giving access to a private borrower to a cheaper loan at the state's expense, which acts as a lender or guarantor and hence bears part of the risk that financial markets would bear. Finally, the state can provide physical assets in its ownership, such as ducts, for free or at a below-market price. All of these measures would qualify as *state aid*.

State aid is subject to EU competition control. Governments can subsidize entry into telecom markets, but they are obliged to limit distortion of competition within the Single Market.[14] This limit to state subsidies is specific to the EU context. However, the rule is based on a sound economic principle that is universally valid. Subsidies should be used **only when strictly needed,** not to *crowd out* private investment that would have taken place otherwise. Students should keep in mind this general principle. If private players can efficiently pursue the goal, there is no need to spend taxpayers' money on subsidizing entry.

The need for state aid in the telecom market can be defined in different ways. The European Commission, for example, adopts a classification based on *shades of grey*: **white areas** are geographic locations where there are no Next Generation Access (NGA) networks, nor plans to have one in the near future; in **grey areas,** only one NGA network is present or planned to become operational soon; and in **black areas,** two or more NGA networks are present or set to be operating soon. State aid is usually easily authorized in white areas, and it may be acceptable in grey areas, subject to a specific analysis of the market conditions. In black areas, state aid is, by default, not permitted, although it may still be possible if there is strong evidence of a market failure which can only be corrected through subsidies.

Another way to implement supply push policies is through the direct involvement of the public sector. Policies can hinge on the involvement of local and regional authorities or rely on *public-private partnerships* (**PPP**). Local municipalities can, for example, directly deploy broadband networks. They can then keep the network

---

[13] See The Broadband State aid rules explained: A Guide for Decision Makers, https://ec.europa.eu/regional_policy/sources/conferences/state-aid/broadband_rulesexplained.pdf

[14] Art 107 of the Treaty on the Functioning of the European Union (TFEU) states that: '*any aid granted by a Member State or through State resources in any form whatsoever which distorts or threatens to distort competition by favoring certain undertakings or the production of certain goods shall, in so far as it affects trade between Member States, be incompatible with the internal market*'. A level of distortion is, however, accepted where it would provide overwhelming benefits. This may be the case in telecom markets.

ownership and responsibility for its maintenance but lease access to it at a fair price (typically based on the FRAND—fair, reasonable, and non-discriminatory principle).[15]

Another possibility is **community-based broadband investment** models, which are essentially private initiatives by groups of residents in local communities that generally receive support from local public authorities. These models proved to be very successful and hugely popular in the Nordic countries, particularly in Sweden, one of the best-performing EU countries in terms of broadband connectivity. As proponents of these models like to say: at the end of the day, deploying infrastructure boils down to taking up your shovel and digging it yourself.

4.3.2 Pull public policies

Pull policies leverage the *demand side*. The logic is simple: an increase in demand makes markets that depend on connectivity more profitable, which incentivizes private investment in infrastructure. Policies supporting the development of a digitized society, such as those discussed in this book, all have a potentially strong indirect positive effect on the development of connectivity infrastructure. Data-hungry applications, such as those enabled by artificial intelligence (see Chapters 5 and 15), boost data traffic and increase operators' potential profits. Strong pan-European demand for cross-border digital content (Chapter 10), or applications that are by nature cross-border, such as automated driving, can make the supply of pan-European connectivity more appealing.

Investment in digital skills and education, retraining of the workforce, and awareness schemes for the general population are equally effective. As we have seen in Chapter 2, and I will further analyse in Chapter 13, demographics play an important role in explaining access to digital: Internet usage is lowest among the unemployed, poorest, oldest, and most isolated segments of the population. Therefore, policies that encourage Internet use by those segments also have the indirect effect of stimulating investment in connectivity.

Policies aimed to push business customers and, in particular, small and medium-sized enterprises to increase their digital activity, are extremely important. Tax credits to invest in ICT equipment, for example, or policies to support the hiring of a digitally skilled workforce, can become essential pull factors for broadband investment. Likewise, the public sector has a significant role to play in its capacity of "digital customer": the more connected are hospitals, schools, and public institutions, the more national and regional public entities "go digital" (for example, through e-Government strategies) and the greater the profitability of broadband (see Chapter 6 for an analysis of public policies for the digitization of the public sector).

---

[15] The FRAND principle has important implications for market competition, although its implementation is very complex.

As suggested in the European Commission's guide to high-speed broadband investment directed to public authorities: "[your] *broadband plan should define how the
public sector can include its own demand for services and thus act as an **anchor tenant**
to reduce demand risks in the short/medium term (while waiting that demands pick
up over the medium/long term)*" (European Commission, 2014a).

4.3.3 Radio spectrum management

As we have seen in the previous two sections, **radio spectrum** is a scarce resource
that is indispensable for mobile operators to supply terrestrial wireless connectivity. Policies that favour an efficient use of spectrum can entail, for example,
spectrum trading and secondary markets. Generally speaking, from the European Union's perspective, a considerable advantage would be achieved with better
coordination throughout the Single Market in the allocation and assignment of
band use.

Supra-national authorities, such as the European Commission, can set the timing of national auctions (similarly to the US Federal Communication Commission)
and coordinate national regulatory authorities in the design of the auction. This
could ensure a certain uniformity in the approach by Member States and minimise
participation costs for bidders (i.e. telecom operators), while safeguarding the speci-
ficities of single national markets Participating in spectrum auctions is costly: it
entails complex planning by operators. Sequential auctions are usually considered
even more burdensome as they increase uncertainty, particularly for operators
seeking to supply mobile services in multiple countries.

Notably, Member States should always retain revenue won through spectrum auctions. Coordination in spectrum management is a tool to lower bidding costs by
pan-European operators. It is not a way to shift revenue from Member States to
the EU.

4.3.4 Regulation and competition policy

Finally, **regulatory policies and enforcement** are indispensable tools to address failures in telecom markets, stimulating competition and fostering investment while
favouring access at competitive prices. As mentioned previously, telecom market
regulation is a complex subject, and its complete analysis lies outside the scope of this
book. However, policymakers must have some familiarity with telecom regulation
basics, so let us have a general look at it.

Regulation and competition policy in telecom markets are a means to stimulate competition, innovation, and investment. But, as we have seen in the previous
section, there is always a careful balance to strike, considering the static, short-
term and dynamic long-term effects. We can grasp the complexity of the exercise

by considering extreme scenarios. For example, if regulation forced network access price to zero, it would lead to a collapse in retail prices, stimulating access but eliminating long-term incentives to invest. Conversely, if telecom operators were free to use their market power, they would ask too high retail prices to guarantee a wide access to connectivity (but long-term investment would not necessarily be high).

Aside from (theoretical) extreme scenarios, policies that promote healthy and fair competition in telecom markets positively affect their development in the short and long-term (see Section 4.2.1).

One of the most critical jobs of regulation is to define the conditions at which potential competing operators can access the network at different levels of the value chain (see Section 4.1). The general idea is to identify where bottlenecks exist—where significant market power allows incumbents to limit access to key inputs for the provision of connectivity services—and impose remedies (European Commission, 2020e). Remedies often take the form of mandating access. In the EU, national regulators define the conditions for access, enforcing the national laws that transpose the European Electronic Communication Code (more on that to follow in Section 4.4) and cooperating with the European Commission (European Commission, 2018a). They define and analyse the relevant markets and impose conditions. For example, they could fix the wholesale price to access a fixed broadband network in specific geographical locations. Likewise, conditions may be imposed upon Mobile Network Operators (MNO) to provide access for their mobile network to Virtual Mobile Network Operators (MVNO) at a specific rate. The European Commission monitors the analysis and conclusions of the national regulators. It can veto them in case the proposed remedies are considered to be incompatible with the rules of the Single Market. Traditionally, the European framework has endorsed a "**ladder of investment**" principle, according to which entrants are allowed to access the network of the incumbent but at decreasingly favourable terms: the entrant is given the opportunity to grow and to build its competitive stance over time while "climbing" the regulatory ladder (Cave, 2006).

Telecom regulation defines the *ex-ante* rules by which market players must abide. **Competition policy enforcement** instead takes place *ex-post*, sanctioning behaviours that harm the competitive process and ultimately harming final users (in Chapter 8, I will discuss the interplay between regulation and competition policy extensively). Depending on the size of the companies involved, either the national competition authority or the European Commission's competition department (DG-Competition) would intervene in the case (1) of an **attempted merger** or (2) of an alleged **antitrust infringement**. State aid is an exclusive competence of the European Commission (see also the appendix for a description of what competition policy enforcers do and why; merger control, for example, is used to avoid that too few companies remain active in the market).

(1) **Mergers** in the telecom sector in Europe often concern mobile operators (MNOs). There are many elements that are considered in the analysis performed

by enforcers. However, typically two critical elements in the analysis of a proposed merger between MNOs stand out:

a. *The definition of the market.* The European Commission's baseline assessment considers the geographical scope of mobile telecom markets to be national, meaning that there is no significant cross-border competition from other EU countries that can compensate harm to competition when two national operators merge (MNOs strenuously contest that approach, but until now no evidence has proven the Commission wrong)

b. *The definition of the "counterfactual" scenario.* Merger analysis must always consider what would happen if the merger would not go through. Perhaps there are scenarios in which synergies between companies could be obtained without a reduction in competition. In the case of mergers in mobile networks, such alternative scenarios are often plausible and entail "**network sharing agreements**". These agreements allow companies to share their network, reducing costs and incentivizing investment. However, since the operators are still separate entities, they retain the incentive to compete against each other (which would not be the case if they would merge). Therefore, network sharing agreements tend to be preferable to mergers from a competition authority's perspective.

(2) **Antitrust cases** in telecoms instead often concern fixed networks operators and can entail a variety of abuses. For example, using non-compete clauses operators may agree to split their markets without competing with each other. In *margin squeeze* cases, an incumbent operator significantly lowers its retail prices while simultaneously increasing its wholesale access prices. In this way, its competitors at retail/service levels are "squeezed" by the high wholesale prices they have to pay to access the network and the low price they need to charge for the sale of their service if they want to be competitive in the retail market. The final consequence is that competitors may be forced to exit the market, allowing the incumbent to preserve its market power.

Let me make a final remark about the **net neutrality** debate. *Net neutrality* generally refers to the principle that Internet Service Providers (ISPs, or network operators) should treat all Internet traffic in the same way, regardless of its origin or destination. This principle has been endorsed in the EU telecom framework as of October 2015 (European Commission, 2015b). The term was first introduced by Tim Wu in 2003 and has been subject to a lively debate in the telecommunication arena ever since (Wu, 2003). Advocates of net neutrality point out that ISPs have the ability and, often, the incentive to *throttle* (i.e. impair or degrade) certain types of web traffic, particularly if that traffic threatens the ISP's retail profits. For example, ISPs may reduce the speed of video streaming platforms such as Netflix, YouTube, or Amazon Prime if those services threaten to erode their profits from their own video broadcasting services. Likewise, operators may apply throttling to hamper over-the-top

(OTT) platforms. On the other hand, opponents of net neutrality point out that preventing operators from offering different bandwidths to different services renders traffic management less efficient. Some *data-hungry* applications may need more bandwidth than others, and it makes sense to offer different tiers of services to optimize the use of the network.

In a sense, the *net neutrality debate* mirrors the more general debate about price discrimination in competition policy (in Chapter 8 I briefly explain this point). The basic idea is that *discrimination* is not necessarily bad for end-users. For example: contrary to the principle of net neutrality, end-users could be offered to pay less in exchange for receiving lower-quality/downgraded data traffic; depending on the user's preference and income, this may suit them well. However, discrimination tends to be more harmful and likely to give rise to antitrust concerns when market concentration is high. That happens because the more market power ISPs have, the higher their incentive and ability to penalize competitors at the retail level. Therefore, the general conclusion is that net neutrality laws are more useful where market competition is low. This may also explain why the debate is particularly lively in the US, where network competition tends to be limited (see Section 4.2 above).[16]

4.4 The European Union's perspective

From the previous three sections, we can conclude that:

- Fast connectivity is crucial for the development of the digital economy
- If left alone, telecom markets cannot provide for the required quality and accessibility of connectivity
- Public policy tools can tackle telecom market failures to foster investment and access.

In this section, I focus on the most recent policy solutions deployed by the EU. Based on what we have seen in the previous sections, the ideal overarching goal could be summarized in a nutshell as below:

To provide the maximum level of connectivity to **end-users** – consumers and business customers – in terms of **low prices, coverage, speed, quality, security,** and **reliability of Internet connection** – for **everybody, everywhere** in Europe.

To achieve what it dubbed "*A European Gigabit Society*", the European Commission established in September 2016 the following strategic objectives to be achieved by 2025 (European Commission, 2016e):

---

[16] In 2015 the Federal Communication Commission adopted a net-neutrality order which was overturned by a then Republican-controlled FCC in 2017.

- Gigabit connectivity for all European main socio-economic drivers. That means guaranteeing a download speed of at least 1Gbs and a latency lower than 10 milliseconds to every European school, airport, train station, hospital, local municipality, as well as to digitally intensive enterprises
- All European urban areas, highways, national roads, and railways to be covered by 5G technology
- At least 100Mbs broadband download speed everywhere, including rural areas, for all European households.

These are ambitious targets on paper, given that, in 2018, Europe was still lagging behind its potential in terms of fast connectivity: in rural areas, for example, only 52% of households had access to a broadband connection of at least 30Mbs of download speed, and ultrafast technologies could reach only 16% of them (see the figures discussed in Chapter 2).

To reach its targets, the European Commission envisaged the use of three leverages:

- Direct Funding
- A new regulatory framework
- A plan for 5G deployment.

Direct EU financial support for broadband deployment comes from several European Funds: the European Fund for Strategic Investment (EFSI), the European Regional Development Fund (ERDF), the European Agricultural Fund for Rural Development (EAFRD), and the Connecting Europe Facility Programme 2 within the Multiannual Financial Framework (MFF—the overarching instrument setting the limits to EU budget). Financial support can take the shape of direct monetary transfers or loans to support infrastructure projects by Member States or private investors. The Connective Europe Facility 2 initiative is geared explicitly towards fostering cross-border connectivity; hence it would support, for example, the creation of "5G corridors" along transport paths, having in mind automated driving in particular.

4.4.1 The European Electronic Communications Code

Directive 2018/1972 establishes the European Electronic Communications Code (the *Code*) (Directive (EU) 2018/1972). This Directive is the cornerstone of the European Commission's *Gigabit Society* strategy. Since its entry into force in December 2018 (Member States are supposed to have transposed it by December 2020), it has defined the enforceable EU telecom regulatory framework, replacing previous legislation.

While attempting to preserve the pro-competition spirit of the legacy regulation (the one that embraced the local loop unbundling principle, see above Section 4.2), the code shows some openness by the legislator towards the idea of relaxing competition in well-defined circumstances to stimulate infrastructure investment. Notably, the code explicitly indicates that EU regulation should be used as leverage to incentivize the deployment of "very high-capacity networks" and slightly softens the regulatory approach to network access. For example, it introduces some limitations to national regulators' power to mandate network access obligations (though only when specific market failures are identified). The code defines "very high capacity networks" as "*either an electronic communications network which consists wholly of* **optical fibre** *elements at least up to the distribution point at the serving location, or an electronic communications network which is capable of delivering, under usual peak-time conditions, similar network performance in terms of available downlink and uplink bandwidth, resilience, error-related parameters, and latency and its variation*" (Art. 2.2 of the code).

To further incentivize investment, the code promotes **co-investment** and **wholesale-only** investment models. In the co-investment model, the network is deployed jointly by multiple operators. In short, it encourages potential competitors to join their resources to reduce the costs they have to bear to roll out new high capacity networks, particularly in rural areas. The code mandates specific pro-competitive conditions, such as FRAND access conditions for all co-investors. But these business models can favour collusive behaviours and may thus result in lower incentives to compete after the deployment of the network. In wholesale-only models, on the other hand, players may obtain the financial resources needed for the roll-out of a network and then sell or rent access, abstaining from competing at the retail/service level. In this case, the code provides for lighter regulatory conditions for the network owner (this is quite intuitive: being absent from the downstream or retail market, wholesale-only players have fewer incentives to "squeeze" their customers).

The code also sets the grounds for greater coordination in the timing and management of radio spectrum. It obliges Member States to free certain spectrum bands from other uses—such as TV or radio—3.6GHz, and a significant part of the 26Ghz band by January 2021) to foster the deployment of 5G technology (the 700MHz band was already supposed to be freed by July 2020). It also introduces parameters to coordinate some features of national spectrum auctions. For example, auctions must assign spectrum to the winning operators for at least 20 years, a measure that intends to improve long-term stability and favour investment. Moreover, the code incentivizes spectrum sharing to facilitate the roll-out of 5G; national authorities are urged to define conditions that maximize efficiency in the use of spectrum (and therefore also the conditions that facilitates its sharing between market operators).

The code also partially addresses telecom operators' concerns regarding the "unfair competition" exerted by OTT players, such as WhatsApp or Zoom. Operators have been pointing out that OTT players should be subject to similar regulatory requirements to retail telecom operators to preserve a *level playing field*. The code introduces three categories of obligations for OTTs:

- they must ensure the security of their servers
- they must provide access on equal conditions for users with disabilities
- they must give their users the possibility to call 112 free of charge – the EU emergency number.

It remains to be seen whether these conditions are enough to ensure a level playing field. One controversial area where the European Commission could attempt bolder steps is *interoperability* between OTT players. After all, telecom operators must ensure interoperability between themselves. And this may be appropriate also for OTT players, even if OTT applications users can relatively easily **multi-home**. Namely: if you are on WhatsApp and your friend is on Telegram, either of you can easily download the necessary application to communicate with each other. The multi-homing objection to the need for interoperability between OTT players is, however, not fully convincing. Indeed users are compelled never to leave their original platform unless they are prepared to lose the ability to connect with their contacts that are only on that platform. So a user can easily install Telegram to communicate to a friend that is only on that platform. But that user would likely never abandon WhatsApp because she would still want to stay in touch with her friends who are only on WhatsApp.

This observation helps explain why it is essential to foster competition in the online platform space. Platforms do not have much incentive to provide a high service quality if customers cannot *punish* platforms that offer a low-quality service by abandoning them. "Quality" in the case of messaging apps could mean, for example, better safeguards for users' privacy. This reasoning was probably in the back of the European Commission's mind when it proposed the Digital Markets Act in December 2020 (see Chapter 8).

Finally, together with the approval of the code, a regulation strengthening the role of BEREC—the Body of European Regulators for Electronic Communications, which represents national telecom regulators—was introduced (Regulation (EU) 2018/1971). With the new regulation, BEREC becomes a fully-fledged EU agency and acts as a one-stop-shop for operators who submit a notification for network access to the agency. In particular, BEREC's role in fostering cross-border connectivity markets is emphasized: for example, one of BEREC's tasks is to provide guidance to national regulators to align them with common remedies in the case of cross-border connectivity markets (BEREC, 2021).

4.4.2 The 5G Action Plan and the 5G Toolbox

Another critical element of the European Commission's strategy for a Gigabit Society is the 5G Action Plan, released by the Commission at the same time as the strategy in September 2016. The idea was to have a well-defined roadmap to favour private and public investment in the roll-out of 5G networks across Europe in the years to come. The plan entailed coordination mechanisms for Member States to promote convergence in targets, such as:

- the introduction of large-scale commercial 5G by 2020 (we know by now that this target has been missed; see Section 4.2)
- support for cross-border and multi-stakeholder trials
- the promotion of roll-out of 5G networks, in particular in major urban areas and along the most important European transport paths. For example, Member States were encouraged to develop 5G national deployment roadmaps and to identify at least one major city to be covered by 5G before 2020; to work together towards the freeing of spectrum bands above 6GHz; and to set up 5G-PPP (*Public-Private-Partnerships*) to stimulate experimentation and support industry-led pre-commercial 5G trials.

We know from Section 4.2 that a critical aspect of 5G is cybersecurity. The 5G "toolbox", adopted by Member States in January 2020 and subsequently endorsed by the European Commission, attempts to address the main security concerns (European Commission, 2020f) (European Commission, 2020g). Its key recommendations are:

- Member States should set up a framework that empowers them (or their national regulatory authority) to act swiftly in restricting 5G or imposing conditions on the provision of 5G services should significant threats emerge. In particular, Member States are encouraged to:
  - define strict security requirements for mobile operators
  - make risk profile assessments of market players and exclude them if necessary from the most vulnerable and sensitive assets—such as 5G core networks
  - favour *multi-homing* by operators. Member States are, in other words, encouraged to limit dependence on a single supplier to diversify (and hence, mitigate) risk.
- The European Commission should in particular help to promote competition along the 5G value chain, again having in mind the goal of limiting long-term dependence on single operators and facilitate coordination between Member States on security standards and EU-wide certification schemes (see also Chapter 7 on cybersecurity)

- The NIS cooperation group (a working group established in 2016 to favour cooperation and information exchange between Member States on cybersecurity, see Chapter 7) should review periodically the risk assessments made by Member States, monitor and evaluate the implementation of the toolbox, and support EU-wide cooperation to tackle 5G security risks.

The toolbox, therefore, does not prevent Member States from taking strong measures against specific vendors, like the US or Australia have been doing vis-à-vis Huawei, for example. However, the cybersecurity risk is always to be balanced against the cost of addressing it: as we shall see in Chapter 7, pursuing a *zero-cyber-security-risk* strategy may not only be unrealistic; it may also slow down Europe's pace towards a *gigabit society*.

****

4.5 Case Study: The Ludgate Hub

Skibbereen is a small town in a rural area on the Irish south-west coast. In 2015 a group of 11 people launched an initiative called "Ludgate Hub". The project aimed to transform a disused bakery into a digital hub. It crucially rested on Skibbereen's inclusion as a pilot town by SIRO, a joint venture between Vodafone and the Irish Electricity Supply Board to provide access to FTTB (fibre to the building) with up to 1Gb download speed connectivity guaranteed in Irish rural areas. The Ludgate Hub is a success story: primarily thanks to high-speed connectivity, it achieved its ultimate goal of setting up a local ecosystem with a vibrant tech community, stimulating innovation, attracting start-ups and multinational companies. By April 2021, the Ludgate Hub had created 146 entirely new jobs, supplied 3,100 "hot desks" for remote workers and contributed to the local economy with more than €4 million. Vodafone had estimated that setting up similar digital hubs in every Irish county could create more than one thousand new businesses and create more than eight thousand new jobs.

More information on the Ludgate Hub can be retrieved here:
https://www.ludgate.ie/

4.6 Review questions

- Explain the relationship between competition in telecom markets in the short term and the long-term effects on investment, network accessibility, and quality of service.
- Who benefits from increased connectivity in peripheral and rural areas? Identify the affected actors and describe the economic dynamics at the origin of direct and indirect (spill-over) effects.
- Why does international roaming tend to be expensive?
- Can you think about possible push policies and pull policies to favour investment in connectivity infrastructure that are not described in the book?
- Do you expect that the new EU Telecom Code can level the playing field between traditional telecom operators and Over-the-Top players? Why so or why not?

5

The Data Economy

Abstract

Data is an essential input to the digital economy. As we have seen in the case of connectivity, a digital economy and society cannot prosper without a flourishing data economy behind it. However, the data value chain poses difficult challenges to policymakers, giving rise to complex and novel issues. Several important economic structural features associated with data and lack of transparency or competition often lead data markets to malfunction. Public policy can intervene, fostering competition and realigning the incentives of market players with those of society to achieve higher welfare levels. The European Union's institutions have been very active in the area, setting global standards for privacy protection with the 2018 General Data Protection Regulation (GDPR) and designing actions to support the development and uptake of data analytics in Europe.

5.1 Background

In the previous chapter, we looked at telecom infrastructure and *connectivity* as one of the essential ingredients of the digital economy. The other indispensable input to the digital economy is **data**. Data has some commonalities with telecoms. According to the OECD (2015), data should also be considered an infrastructure because of its fundamental role in the production of a vast range of products and services.[1] Moreover, like connectivity, data is not consumed for the sake of it. The demand for data is primarily driven by its use as a resource in producing something else. For example, data may be of help for forecasting weather, improving farming efficiency.

However, differently from telecom infrastructure, data infrastructure and data analytics as a core business model are, to a large extent, a **new economic phenomenon**. Of course, data and statistical analysis have been used in business for a long time. But the level of granularity, accuracy, and size of datasets has become so high today that it has given rise to an entirely new game with new business dynamics, creating opportunities and puzzles for policymakers that are unprecedented, as we shall see in this chapter.

Data should not be described as the "**new oil**" though. This often used simile is appealing: it underlines the role of data as an indispensable input in many digital activities. For example, in 2017, The Economist had titles such as "The world's

---

[1] Oussous, et al. (2018) report a comprehensive survey of significant 'big data' technologies used worldwide.

Digital Economic Policy. Mario Mariniello, Oxford University Press.
© Mario Mariniello (2022). DOI: 10.1093/oso/9780198831471.003.0005

most valuable resource is no longer oil, but data" (The Economist, 2017b). However, the association with oil is somehow misleading as, unlike fossil fuels, data is *non-rivalrous*: multiple users can use it without depleting its value. The fact that data is non-rivalrous has important implications for economic policy, as further discussed in Section 5.2.

The amount of data created worldwide has been increasing exponentially in recent years, and it shows no signs of slowing: it is projected to break record after record in the years to come. No wonder, then, that the European Commission has resorted to the moon to illustrate the phenomenon's scale. According to the European Commission (2021e), the amount of data produced in 2018 could be stored in as many as 512 gigabyte tablets as needed to build a tower that would reach the beloved natural satellite. With the amount of data created in 2025, *five* of those towers could be built, for a total of 175 zettabytes. I suppose the European Commission imagines placing one of about 1.2cm-width tablet over each other to build the tower (see Chapter 4 for a definition of zettabytes). For 2035, the projection is 2,142 zettabytes (Figure 5.1). Similarly, the European Commission predicts an increase in the value of the data economy for the EU27 area from €301 billion in 2018 (or 2.4% of EU27 Gross Domestic Product) to €829 billion in 2025 (or 5.8% of GDP).[2] In 2025, there will be as many as 10.9 million data professionals in Europe, compared to 5.7 million in 2018 (data professionals can refer to data engineers—those who work on infrastructure, and data analysts or data scientists—those who read and interpret the outcomes of data analytics).

As will become apparent in this chapter, the increase in data production is not only owed to an increase in the activities reliant on data. Above all, it is **our capacity to capture, store, and process information that is growing significantly**, thereby enabling the supply of more data analytics services. The exponential nature of such

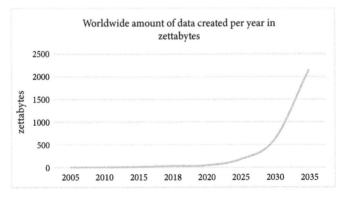

Figure 5.1 Worldwide amount of data created per year in zettabytes

'Digital Compass', Statista (2019), p. 6. https://www.statista.com/study/52194/digital-economy-compass/

---

[2] For a theoretical framing to how big data contributes to value creation, see Urbinati, et al. (2019).

growth is due to the fact that digital economies and societies enact a virtuous cycle: the more digitized the economy, the easier the monitoring and data capturing. It is not hard to see why—billions of Internet users share information about what they like on social networks or reveal what drives them while browsing the net and typing keywords in search engines; demand continues to rise for wearables devices, such as smart watches, which collect information on people's habits 24/7; and the number of connected cars, machines, utility meters, and consumer electronics interconnected between themselves is expected to reach 16 billion worldwide in 2021 (the *Internet of Things*, as described in Chapter 1).

5.1.1 The features of data

A terminology students may have encountered is **Big Data**. The hype with the term has gradually faded away in the digital-savvy circles, possibly because of its vagueness (how big is "big"?). Nevertheless, *data analytics,* as I refer to in this chapter, can be defined with reference to the same dimensions usually used to describe "big data".[3] Namely the **Four Vs**:

- **Volume** – *the scale of data.* The scale of datasets is often so large that it requires treatment with special software and hardware equipment with high processing and storage capacity
- **Velocity** – *the speed of data processing.* Often speed is exceptionally high as data feed into a process that requires immediate feedback for taking a decision based on the outcome of the data analysis. Think about self-driven cars and the response rate of their sensors to what happens on the road
- **Variety** – *how differentiated the dataset is* within itself. Variety can be a source of statistical power, providing information on a particular phenomenon from different angles. However, it can also be counterproductive if data cannot easily be aggregated, for example, because it is structured in different formats that are not compatible with each other
- **Veracity** – *the quality of the data.* High veracity means that the source of data is trustworthy and thus meaningful insights can be extracted from the dataset. Conversely, low data accuracy may generate noise in the analysis and lead to erroneous conclusions.

Data volume is possibly the most compelling of all "big data" characteristics. Volume, however, cannot compensate for other failing features. For example, if a dataset has poor veracity, a bigger volume does not help. A huge dataset could never lead to meaningful conclusions if the inference is based on inaccurate information. Likewise, leveraging data size to identify strong correlations does not imply getting any

---

[3] See also: Ammu and Irfanuddin (2013) and Lee (2017).

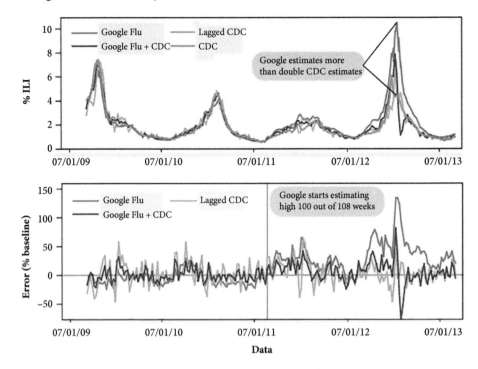

Figure 5.2 The Parable of Google Flu: Traps in Big Data Analysis
https://science.sciencemag.org/content/343/6176/1203/F2

closer to inferring causality between two different events (see the appendix for a discussion).

A good example of big data's pitfalls is what Wired called *"The Epic Failure of Google Flu Trends"* in 2015,[4] illustrated in Figure 5.2 (Lazer, et al., 2014). In February 2013, Google developed a data analytics tool named Google Flu Trends (GFT). GFT was tasked with inferring where the next flu outbreak would occur by leveraging a large dataset of searches made by Google users. Users searching for a flu-related symptom, for example, would suggest that the virus may have spread in that user's location. Initially, GFT appeared to work successfully. The GFT orange line and the "CDC" (the US national health protection agency) light blue line in Figure 5.2 largely overlap. That suggests that Google could anticipate outbreaks identified with the official metrics from the CDC by about two weeks. But when the flu epidemic numbers rose significantly, GFT completely missed the target, reporting double as many cases as the CDC. That happened because GFT failed to account for false correlations—a problem that becomes more acute when datasets become bigger. In addition, GFT used a relatively static algorithm that did not adapt as fast as users to the changing environment, including the Google Search algorithm. Users would change their

---

[4] See https://www.wired.com/2015/10/can-learn-epic-failure-google-flu-trends/

interest search habits the more information they received, while GFT suggested inference based on users behaviour observed at the beginning of the epidemic.[5]

The general lesson to learn is that data can be a powerful resource, but only if analysts know how to use it, understand what they can do with it, accept its limitations, and correct potential biases.

Data collection has improved dramatically in recent years, as has data storage and data processing. A determinant factor in this advancement is **cloud computing**. Cloud computing refers to a service offered by providers to business customers and private users to store or process data on demand. It essentially boils down to renting software applications, storage, and computing infrastructure from cloud computing providers who have the resources (equipment and skills) to operate large data centres and servers, leveraging their scale to minimize costs. **Data centres** are physical locations where computing and storage infrastructure is concentrated. In 2020, there were approximately 8 million data centres in the world. Thanks to cloud computing, even small enterprises can process large amounts of data without investing in IT infrastructure or hiring a specialized workforce. They can also benefit from the "knowledge spill-over" of cloud computing companies, and data processing can be made more cyber-secure at a lower cost (see Chapter 7). That is why cloud processing is likely to become a dominant model in the handling of data (current projections estimate that around 70% of worldwide data will be stored on cloud servers by 2025, as opposed to 30% in 2010). The most prominent players in the cloud market are currently Amazon Web Services—AWS, Microsoft's Azure, IBM Cloud, and Google Cloud (together representing approximately 60% of the global cloud market in 2018). It should be mentioned that cloud and data centres tend to generate environmental concerns. Data centres are expected to represent 3.2% of the total EU electricity demand in 2030. As a result, we should expect increasing political pressure on tech companies to deploy greener technologies and uses in the years to come.

At the other extreme of the spectrum of data-handling models, there lies another solution that is also becoming very popular: **edge computing**. Edge computing implies that data processing is done where the data is collected, namely at the *network's edge*. This can be pretty handy with the increase in the adoption of "Internet of Things" devices (Gyarmathy, 2019). First, because local processing dramatically reduces latency, as data do not need to travel from the sensors to data centres. Second, for the same reason, data that stays where it is collected avoids overloading the network's bandwidth, making connectivity more efficient (see Chapter 4). The European Commission estimates that, in 2025, 80% of data analysis will be processed at the level of smart connected objects rather than in centralized computing facilities. By definition, however, edge computing limits data aggregation. It, therefore, may limit data analytics based on the volume of big datasets. In that sense, cloud and edge

---

[5] Einav and Levin (2014) nicely describes the challenges that the 'data revolution' implies for economics as a science discipline.

computing should not be seen as substitutes for one another but as complementary tools. They can also be combined with **fog computing**, which is a *"distributed"* system extending the power of storage and processing of cloud computing to the local level across a whole network.[6]

5.1.2 The data value chain[7]

What we call "data" is ultimately just a by-product of reality: information is generated spontaneously by humans, animals, machines, or any other entity for the mere fact of existing. The actual value creation occurs when that information is collected, aggregated, processed, stored, and analysed; hence, the primary actors in value creation are those who own the means to make the leap from the *single observed information* to the *final outcome* of the data analysis. Part of the generated value is captured in the form of profits for the market players who work directly with the data. And part of it spills over the economy, for example in the form of better or cheaper products or services, as we shall see shortly.

For the purpose of this chapter, let us identify four categories of actors along the data value chain:[8]

   a) **Data Generators**
   b) **Data Services**
   c) **Data Business Users**
   d) **End-Customers**

To a certain extent, this classification is artificial: its purpose is to simplify the description of the different elements of the data analytics process. Bear in mind, however, that one actor can play different roles simultaneously, and this is often the case: single individuals can generate data while being the end-customers of a company using that data to produce its products. Vertically integrated companies can collect, process, and directly feed data into their business model.

Figure 5.3 illustrates the different categories with the help of a fictitious example. A user plays a smartphone application, a game named Mushroom-GO.[9] Mushroom-GO uses augmented reality to let players see, on their phones, virtual mushrooms they need to "virtually collect" in the physical space around them. A player of Mushroom-GO produces information while playing, for example locational data identifying where the user tends to be around lunchtime. The player is, therefore, a *data generator*. DATA-REAP is a company offering a *data service*. It could, for

---

[6] See Varghese and Buyya (2018) for a good description of cloud computing technologies, development trends, and relative societal impact.
[7] This part follows closely European Political Strategy Centre (2017).
[8] Another description of big data value chain is in Faroukhi, et al. (2020).
[9] This example has been purely invented for illustrative purposes; I made up the names of the applications and the commercial activities that are mentioned.

THE DATA VALUE CHAIN

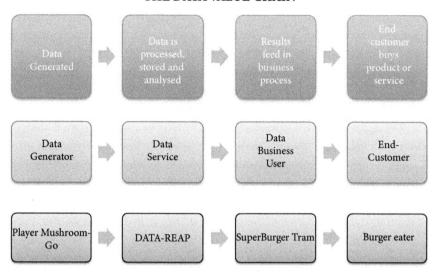

Figure 5.3 The Data Value Chain

example, analyse locational data from Mushroom-GO users, provided that these were purchased by a *data business user*, such as the fast-food restaurant chain SuperBurgerTram's (possibly in an anonymized fashion, to avoid privacy pitfalls). DATA-REAP's analysis feeds into SuperBurgerTram's business process and leads the company to take a decision: open a new restaurant. The chosen location is an area that appears to be very popular amongst potential end-customers around lunchtime.

5.1.2.1 Data Generators

Data generators are the origin of the information. They can be machines: a smartfridge or a manufacturing robot in a factory. They can be humans: a smartphone app user; somebody buying a train ticket online; a friend placing a "like" on a Facebook post. Anything can be a data generator, even *nature* in its broad sense: snowfall on a spring day can generate any number of data points.

Data generators can **actively** supply data, for example, if an Internet user is required to fill in a form with her email and preferences to access a newspaper's website. Data can otherwise be generated **passively** if the data generator does not need to be aware that she conveys information while performing a particular action. This would be the case, for example, for navigation apps, whereby drivers get route directions but, at the same time, they provide data that is used to estimate the average journey time.[10]

Web cookies are files that are stored in a user's device and are updated with passive information about users' characteristics, preferences, or online habits. Cookies can help smooth a user's experience; for example, they allow a website to remember

---

[10] Choe, et al. (2014) analyse the compelling case of "quantified-selfers", or individuals keen to diligently collect data about themselves.

a user's login details or shopping cart. But they can also be perceived as invasive and raise privacy and discrimination concerns (see Sections 5.2 and 5.4). The distinction between "actively" and "passively" generated data is relevant, particularly when assessing whether the data generator has provided its consent to the use of their data for a specific purpose, as will be further discussed in Section 5.4.

Data may be *personal* or *non-personal*. According to the EU's General Data Protection Regulation (or GDPR),[11] **personal data** means "*any information relating to an identified or identifiable natural person [. . .]*". An identifiable natural person "*is one who can be identified, directly or indirectly in particular by reference to an identifier such as a name, an identification number, location data, an online identifier or to one or more factors specific to the physical, physiological, genetic, mental, economic, cultural or social identity of that natural person.*" In the terminology applied in the GDPR, human data generators of personal data are called **data subjects**. Personal data may be **pseudonymized** if they are processed in such a way that they cannot be re-associated with their original source, unless a "key code" or additional information is used to "crack" the pseudonym. Or they can be **anonymized**, if such key code does not in principle exist. That means that it is theoretically impossible to attribute anonymized data to single individuals.[12] **Non-personal data** are most easily defined as the *residual set*: any data that cannot be considered personal is non-personal. Non-personal data can originate from non-human data generators (for example, weather information), or a human data generator may initially generate them before the data is subsequently anonymized.[13]

The distinction between the two categories of data—"personal" and "non-personal"—is of crucial importance: it has substantial implications in terms of understanding privacy risks. It thus defines the scope of the law, as we will see in the following sections. However, in practice, it is challenging to distinguish between these two categories when data is actually processed.

A view with significant traction amongst practitioners is that there is always a risk that anonymized data can be re-identified and linked to individuals (see Finck & Pallas (2020), for example). If anything, it is possible to imagine that technological advancement may eventually allow the reversal of anonymization processes that today may appear secure and definitive. Indeed, studies suggest that it is already possible to ascertain from an anonymized dataset an individual's identity: Rocher, et al. (2019) show that knowing fifteen attributes such as gender, age, or marital status would allow researchers to identify an individual from an anonymized dataset of Americans with 99.98% probability. Also, note that, because individuals and machines are increasingly interconnected, "mixed datasets," where personal and non-personal data are mixed, are the norm; this only adds to the complexity of disentangling one type of data from another.

---

[11] see https://gdpr-info.eu/ GDPR Art. 4—we will discuss the GDPR extensively in Section 5.4.
[12] Hintze and El Emam (2018) compare the benefits of pseudonymization and anonymization under the GDPR.
[13] For a good description, see European Commission (2019).

Finally, note that companies or governments do not strictly need personal data about a single individual to *draw inference* about that individual's features or preferences. For example, if you live in a low-income neighborhood, it is more likely that you are *also* low-income. Information about some individuals in a relatively homogeneous group can be enough to build accurate expectations about individuals that already belong or could belong to that group. The ultimate purpose of statistical analysis is to infer individual insights from representative samples. The conclusion is that personal data protection alone cannot shield users from discrimination, as I will explain in the next section.

5.1.2.2 Data Services

Companies that extract value from data are called *data services*. The following steps can describe the process of value creation through data analytics:[14]

- **Data are collected**. Collection can happen through the use of sensors from machines, for example, "crawled" from the web, actively submitted by users, provided by public agencies, and so forth. It can also be acquired through intermediaries or *data brokers*, companies that aggregate information from different sources, often packaging it in a structured and clean way for the purpose of selling it or licensing it to other companies
- **Data are transferred.** Transfer can rely on wired or wireless telecommunication networks, if not processed locally (in which case data does not need to be transferred)
- **Data are prepared and integrated**. Analytic service providers run several operations to ensure the accuracy of the information collected and integrate it into a single, intelligible dataset
- **Data are stored**. Storage can occur in localized data centres or through cloud services
- **Data are analysed**. Analytic service providers process the information, and the output of the analysis is displayed, for example, through visualization techniques. Sophisticated, artificial intelligence-enabled applications may be used to extract the most value from data. These include **Data Mining** and **Machine Learning** (we will look at those technologies in Chapter 15 on artificial intelligence).

5.1.2.3 Data Business Users

These are public or private entities that use the outcome of data analytics (the OECD defines them as "data-driven entrepreneurs"). Data can be used to improve the quality of products or services, cut administrative costs, facilitate monitoring, and improve customer-targeting strategies. It can allow *dynamic pricing*, adapting the price to fit customers' willingness to pay, or responding to competitors' market moves. It can be used to predict potential failures in production processes,

---

[14] Based on: GilPress (2016), TNO report: Esmeijer, et al. (2013), and OECD (2015). See also Curry (2016).

to allow deeper investigation of customers' or citizens' satisfaction. It helps optimize the allocation of capacity over infrastructure networks and make water or energy distribution more efficient. Data can also unlock innovation, allowing the supply of entirely new products or services, such as a personalized e-health service or a sophisticated robot to optimize a manufacturing production process (OECD, 2015).

A particular type of data business user is vertically integrated companies that collect, process, and analyse data themselves. Google, for example, is a vertically integrated online platform with a vast range of activities. It collects data from users of its services, such as Gmail, YouTube, or Google Search, and uses those data to improve the supply of its services (for example, to refine Internet search). But it also sells data to advertisers who can use it to improve their targeting of customers.[15]

5.1.2.4 End Customer

Finally, the *end customers* of data business users are simply the buyers or takers of the services or products that have been "enhanced" through data analytics. They can be readers of an online newspaper or citizens who enjoy a cleaner air quality thanks to more efficient traffic management enabled by data analytics in their town. Or they could be farmers who purchase automated trucks that can provide real-time feedback on the status of their crops and anticipate future challenges; the examples are manifold.

The most direct effect of data analytics for end customers is a reduction in prices or improvement in the quality of what they buy. Some goods or services would not exist without data: many smartphone applications, such as navigations apps, would not work without the data feedback from other drivers on the road.[16]

5.2 Opportunities and challenges

5.2.1 Benefits of a data economy

The previous section gave us a hint: that the data economy can significantly contribute to societal welfare, generating **benefits for everybody across the value chain spectrum**.

Perhaps its primary (and hardly quantifiable) contribution is in its role of "innovation enabler", particularly within the digital environment. Take artificial intelligence (AI), for example, which will be discussed extensively in Chapter 15. AI is considered by many a powerful tool that can allow a level of progress humans have never

---

[15] Marr (2016) describe a number of case studies focusing on companies that have successfully used big data analytics to enhance their business' performance.

[16] Roberts, et al. (2014) survey consumers to explore their motivations to engage in co-creation activities, such as the ones enabled by data analytics.

experienced before. For example, AI gives rise to hopes for dramatic improvements in cancer care or in the global fight against climate change. These priceless achievements may even escape the human imagination. But AI needs *data*: data (as well as connectivity and computing infrastructure) is an indispensable input factor for AI. Hence, a society that invests in data infrastructure opens up to the possibility of unquantifiable benefits for its future generations.

On a more concrete level, in 2020, the European Commission provided some illustrative estimates of the value generated by data. For example, real-time traffic avoidance navigation can save up to 730 million hours, or €20 billion in labour costs, and a better allocation of resources to fight malaria achieved through more intense use of data analytics could save up to €5 billion in healthcare costs globally (European Commission, 2021e). Researchers have estimated that firms that adopt data-driven decision making have a 5–6% output and productivity increase compared to what they could expect from investing in other traditional Information Technologies (Brynjolfsson, et al., 2011). These figures can only give a glimpse of what can be achieved by improving the production process, cutting costs and enhancing quality, customer targeting, and precision in making business predictions.[17]

Single individuals or organizations—consumers, citizens, private or public entities—also enjoy significant benefits from the data economy in their capacity as *end-customers* of entities that use data analytics (as we have seen in the previous section), and as *data generators*. The most striking example of this is that data can be used as a **kind of currency**. Since information generated by users is valuable to data services, it may be exchanged for a reduction in the price of goods or a services, even if most of the time this transaction is implicit. For example, **advertisement business models** allow consumers to access a service (e.g. using Instagram, Twitter, Facebook, Gmail) without paying a monetary price.[18] Users may be induced to believe that they get the service *for free*, but they are *de facto* paying with the information they provide while consuming the product, such as a smartphone application, a website or a game (such as Mushroom-GO). Figure 5.4 gives an idea of the average price at which data brokers sell data points. Intimate and private information appears particularly valuable: data points regarding health conditions are the most expensive.

Companies such as online platforms usually aggregate data of single users from multiple sources to profile them. Profiling consists of associating physical attributes, behaviours, and preferences to a specific user each time they manifest them, possibly over different activities that may well be online and offline. Google, for example, could use its profiling tools to verify whether the advertisements that its users see online on its webpages translate in higher visit rates to brick and mortar stores. It can do so by matching a user's web track record with their GPS location when using

---

[17] Saggi and Jain (2018) report a good survey of ways through which companies can extract value from data. See also Akter, et al. (2016).

[18] For a review of the main findings of the literature on online advertising, see Liu-Thompkins (2019).

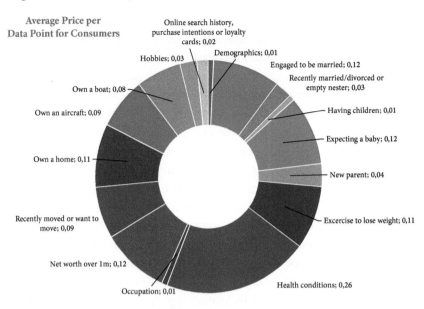

Figure 5.4   Average Price per Data Point for Consumers in US$ in 2017
https://www.statista.com/study/52194/digital-economy-compass/

Google Maps (Reilly, 2017). Platforms monetize their users' data profiles primarily through online advertisement.[19] Ads are often displayed online using a tool called **real-time bidding (RTB)**, which essentially boils down to advertisers participating in an auction for the web page's slot that displays the ad on the screen of the user (which is called *impression,* in reference to the fact that a user can potentially have seen the ad and been "impressed" by it). The auction happens in real-time, that is: as soon as the user accesses the page. The more accurate the profile, the better targeted the ad, and the higher the bids.[20]

To go back to my Mushroom-GO fictitious example, imagine a player using her phone to chase a tasty porcini. In the game, some ads may be displayed on the phone screen.[21] With RTB, it could happen that, as soon as the user turns a corner and reaches a specific location, several advertisers bid in real-time. The winner gets to display their advert on the phone of the Mushroom-GO player. Similarly, a Facebook, Twitter, or Google user sees ads from the winning advertiser who made the highest bid for that specific user in a specific moment on that specific platform. The advertisement market is the motor of online business models. In 2018, more than €250 billion was spent on online ads worldwide, although scepticism is rising as to whether the ad market is generating a significant "value bubble" (Jesse & Maurits, 2019). It is unclear what proportion of web traffic is genuinely generated by ads: users that click on advertised links may often have ended up on the advertiser's website

---

[19] See also Lambrecht, et al. (2014) and Kannan (2017).
[20] See Bourreau, et al. (2017).
[21] See Maffei L. (2016) for a real-life case example with Pokemon-GO.

through other channels (for example, through an organic or general web search engine). In those cases, ads are just a useless expense for advertisers. And this could suggest that the value of users' data may be over-estimated.

In addition to using their data as currency to access services without paying in monetary terms, users can also directly benefit from targeted advertising. For example, users may be happy to see the ad of a brand new pillow that can help with their headache after *googling* remedies for neck stiffness. In that case, Google could have added to the user's profile information about her physical problems, and a medical pillow-maker could have won the RTB to display the ad to that user.

Targeted advertising can have positive effects on welfare because it dramatically reduces search costs. By handing out their data, users allow sellers to know them better and come forward offering what they like, meaning that buyers need to exert a smaller effort to satisfy their needs. Likewise, *price discrimination*, receiving a customized price for what is purchased, can be welfare-enhancing, as we shall see below.

5.2.2 Sources of concern

Having said that, despite the considerable benefits they can bring to the economy, data markets give rise to concerns that require policymakers' attention.

Let us identify two broad categories of concerns:

1) concerns due to **potential data abuses;**
2) concerns due to **suboptimal supply of and access to data.**

Potential data abuses

Data markets are **complex** and **murky**. Data generators often lack the resources (time, for example) or the ability to grasp the complexity of the commercial relationship they enter into when using their data as a currency. As a matter of fact, they may not even realize that there is no free lunch and that they are paying for the service they are using, just not in the traditional monetary way. Similarly, users are unlikely to be able to read through the "terms and conditions" of the contracts they often casually accept when accessing a service or installing an application on their smartphone. The Norwegian Consumer Council read out word-by-word the terms and conditions of thirty-three apps typically found on a user's smartphone: 900 pages took thirty-two hours to read.[22] They would have taken more if one wanted to fully understand them (Kaldestad Ø., 2016).

Moreover, individuals often do not act rationally (for a discussion on the limits to human rational behaviour, see Chapter 14 on disinformation). It is a well-known fact that individuals tend to reveal online preferences that are inconsistent with their

---

[22] On users' "privacy fatigue" see Keith, et al. (2014).

offline habits. For example, customers in a restaurant would start whispering when talking about a particular subject if the waiter gets closer but would not show the same wariness when posting precisely the same content publicly on a social network. That is commonly referred to as the **privacy paradox** (see Acquisti (2004), for example). Complexity and bounded rationality hamper the functioning of markets, particularly when it comes to enhancing the "hidden quality" aspects of the goods or services supplied by market players. For example, typing a search term on a web search entails entering an implicit *data contract*. Since users are not aware or sensitive to the privacy risks of data contracts, they do not exert significant pressure on market players to improve their services to be more privacy-friendly. Why would platforms offer more privacy if users cannot grasp the privacy implications of joining a platform in the first place? As we will often see in this book, this situation falls into the general category of **asymmetric information**, whereby the buyer cannot fully assess the quality of what they are buying (see the appendix for a description). Information asymmetries contribute to explaining why markets fail to provide what is best for society (in this case: higher privacy protection for users).

Kshetri (2014) describes an anecdote of harmful effects of data predictive analytics. A US retailer tracked a high school-aged girl. The company's pregnancy prediction score based on the information on the girl that it collected suggested that the girl was pregnant. The company thus sent to her home address promotional material for pregnant women. The material was delivered to the girl's home before her parents actually knew that she was pregnant.

Concerns with privacy and security issues can only be expected to significantly increase in the future with the advent of the Internet of Things. According to PwC (2016) the wearable industry is expected to boom in the coming years. Wearables have the potential to capture/store more personal data than any other device ever owned by users, including health information, habits, details about employees, and political and sexual preferences.

Privacy risks are exacerbated by the fact that data markets are often not competitive enough. Featuring **strong network externalities** and **economies of scale**, markets hinging on data tend to concentrate;[23] and concentration partly explains the success of the supplied services. Simply put, the more data is fed into the analysis, the better and more efficient the service becomes (it is easy to see here a resemblance with the "natural monopoly" discussion of Chapter 4 on telecom markets; we will discuss this further in Chapter 8 on online platforms).

Privacy risks are higher if markets are concentrated because market players cannot lose privacy-wary customers to competitors and are therefore less inclined to address those risks.[24] There are not many alternatives customers can turn to if they feel that an application's service is not privacy-friendly in concentrated markets.

---

[23] On market power in data markets see Graef (2015).
[24] See also Day and Stemler (2019).

The exploitation of fine-grained insights about individuals and multifaceted intrusions into their private spheres—with or without their knowledge or consent—can therefore be trust-corrosive and disempowering. As Apple Chief Executive, Tim Cook, said in 2018 (BBC, 2018): "personal information is being 'weaponized with military efficiency' by tech companies." Some even claim that we have entered the age of privacy nihilism (Boogost I., 2018), where citizens are gradually losing control over their most intimate and detailed information, such as political preferences, sexual preferences, or personality characteristics. As revealed in the Ranking Digital Rights 2018 Index (The Ranking Digital Rights, 2018), insufficient transparency about what types of data are collected and how they are handled is pervasive across the tech industry. The avalanche of privacy scandals, such as the 2018 Cambridge Analytica scandal that affected the privacy of 87 million users, reveals that troves of insights are increasingly used for purposes that are far from legitimate or desirable.

Privacy is recognized as a fundamental human right in the Universal Declaration of Human rights,[25] and it has a foundational value for democracy.[26] Privacy, therefore, has value per se. As food-makers are obliged to provide food that does not poison their clients, laws can oblige those who hold data not to risk the privacy of data generators for the simple purpose of protecting privacy. A clear example of such laws is the GDPR, as we will see in Section 5.4.

However, lack of privacy also has important indirect economic implications. Algorithms coupled with sophisticated tracking technologies can enable companies to set dynamic, tailored prices. Amazon, for example, is reportedly able to update prices for consumers every 10 minutes (Retail Touch Points, 2016).

Dynamic pricing can in principle give rise to **price discrimination**, or a company's practice to set different prices for different groups of customers, despite bearing the same unit production costs.[27] The overall welfare effects of price discrimination or personalized pricing are context-dependent: it may lead to lower prices for certain customers (an intuitive illustration is "discriminatory" discounts for students and elderly people in museums) but higher prices for others. Yet price discrimination is more likely to have adverse welfare effects when market concentration is high, since suppliers, facing fewer constraints, have an increased power to extract value from their customers. Unconstrained incumbents also have fewer incentives to be transparent, aggravating the consequences of the "black box" nature of algorithmic functioning and rendering it very difficult to detect instances of discriminatory treatment, assign responsibility, and hold a company accountable. Unfair trading practices can also translate into platforms charging an excessive price for data both for consumers and business customers or lead them to engage in tactics to exclude competitors by leveraging their market power. Echoing the Google Shopping case (European Commission, 2017a), dominant platforms may favour their own services or embark on differentiated treatment between third-party

---

[25] United Nations (1948), Art.12.
[26] See, for example, Rouvroy and Poullet (2009)
[27] On dynamic pricing online, see Weiss and Mehrotra (2001).

suppliers (in the case of Google, the European Commission concluded that Google had favoured its own services by ranking them higher in the results list of its general web search engine).

The conclusion is that, if left unconstrained, market forces are unlikely to address on their own the risks for data generators by reducing them to a minimum (that being the minimum risk level necessary to enjoy the benefits of the data economy from a social standpoint). This is a first reason explaining calls for public policy intervention, as we discuss in Section 5.3.

Suboptimal supply of and access to data

Data, as we have seen in Section 5.1, are *non-rivalrous*. That means that the information collected and used by different data services could be shared and used by other market players without necessarily making it less valuable.

A similar feature is traditionally observed in Research & Development (R&D). Investment in research benefits the whole economy. That may seem nice at first sight: R&D can benefit everyone, kicking off progress and more innovation by other players who can capitalize on discoveries made by others to innovate as well. However, R&D positive spillover has a significant economic implication: market players do not *internalize* this positive general effect that innovation can have on society. And that means that when they decide how much to invest in R&D, they do it suboptimally from a social perspective. Market players invest *less* than what would be desirable, given the value of the potential innovation for the whole economy. That is why there are public incentives to invest in R&D (for example: R&D tax cuts). Tax exemptions are meant to realign the incentives of the single market player with those of society by increasing the private value that R&D may have for the single-player.

An equivalent logic can be applied to data markets. For instance, mobile data may be collected for analysing wireless connectivity by telecom companies. However, the same data could be used to track users' movements during an epidemic, such as in the case of Covid-19, because, **as R&D, data is non-rivalrous**. Likewise, data collected for advertising purposes could also be used by researchers to refine our understanding of human behaviour, and so forth.

Because the value of collecting and processing data from the perspective of the collectivity is not taken into account, there is a concrete risk of an **under-supply of data analytics** compared to what could be considered optimal from a social point of view. Students may note the similarity with the problem faced in the context of the connectivity puzzle (Chapter 4). Telecom operators' investment decision in a rural area, for example, does not take into account the beneficial spillover that infrastructure can have on society at large, as we have seen, often requiring subsidization by the government.

Another angle to consider along similar lines concerns the fact that data has a strong complementary nature. Data is a key input that enhances the value of production processes of products; therefore, **restrictions that limit access to data tend**

to reduce social welfare (unless they are strictly necessary to incentivize market players to invest in data collection and data analytics).

In the digital economy, access to data lies at the heart of innovation. It allows companies to boost productivity and provide improved services or entirely new and innovative market offerings, as we have seen above. Yet many companies lag behind the data-powered innovation frontier set by the incumbent tech companies that can enjoy considerable market power thanks to network economies (see above). And even though data as such do not necessarily have a competitive nature (they are non-rivalrous), **access to data continues to be a barrier to entry to online markets.** Datasets owned by incumbents are often truly unique and unlikely to be replicated by nascent businesses.

Market power along the data value chain can be an important source of ineffi-ciency, leading to **suboptimal access to data**. For example, a data supplier could set a price that is too high compared to what would be desirable from a social point of view (this often happens when competition is lacking along the value chain—see Chapter 4 and the appendix for a description of the *double marginalization* issue). Or it could limit access to its data by potential competitors, de facto excluding it from the market where it is active or from other potential markets. Imagine a developer wishing to use data to develop a messaging app that could rival a large online plat-form, for example. Or a car company, preventing a third-party spare parts reseller getting access to a driver's car's data.

Market power can also lead to hold-up problems. Consider[28] a start-up with an innovative idea for a new service. Before investing in its development, it would need to be reassured that it will get access to data from a particular online platform; other-wise, the new service may not work. But once the start-up has made its investment, it may be held up and forced to pay a high price for accessing the data.

Moreover, data tend to exhibit **economies of scope**: it is proportionally less costly to collect, store, process, or otherwise analyse data altogether, instead of analysing them separately. So there is a clear benefit from fostering data ac-cess and sharing from a collective point of view, as this increases efficiency by eliminating costly cost duplications and reducing the overall costs of working with data.

Finally, national governments can impose restrictions on data flow across juris-dictions (the most typical type of data facing restrictions in Europe is accounting information and financial statements). Security or data protection reasons can sometimes justify restrictions. However, often **data localization measures** are pro-tectionist, meaning that countries implement them to limit cross-border trade. In recent years, there has been a progressive increase in the number of measures im-posed by countries worldwide, including EU Member States. These restrictions can entail significant losses for companies that are prevented from processing data

---

[28] I borrowed this example from Martin Peitz (Peitz, 2018).

where is less costly. The burden is proportionally higher for Small and Medium Enterprises.[29]

5.3. Dilemmas for policymakers[30]

The two families of concerns, *potential data abuses* and a *sub-optimal supply of or access to data*, can be addressed through a set of policy instruments, ranging from tools of a regulatory nature to proactive public measures in support of data markets. The attentive reader may have noted that **lack of competition** lies at the roots of many of the concerns we analysed in the previous section. One way to deal with that is through **ex-post competition policy enforcement.** Ex-post enforcement can help address many of the problems related to market power in the data value chain. For example, it may prevent incumbents from leveraging their access to large datasets to exclude potential competitors from the market. A comprehensive analysis of the competition policy tools available to tackle issues in data markets is outside the scope of this book, although in Chapter 8 I discuss key insights on competition policy in the digital environment, most of which apply to data markets (in fact, to a large extent, any digital market is also a data market, since data is the motor of the digital environment).[31] As we shall see, the overarching question is whether policymakers should intervene *ex ante* (defining, for example, rules for accessing data) or let competition authorities intervene *ex post* (for example, sanctioning a company that limits data access to its competitors).

For this chapter, let us focus on regulatory instruments that are specific to data markets and that can directly address the issues identified in Section 5.2 (while often also affecting, one way or the other, on competition, as we will see shortly).

5.3.1 Legislative action to protect from data abuse

A first direct approach is regulation to protect human data generators from data abuse. **Personal data protection laws** serve that purpose. It is a largely shared opinion that with the General Data Protection Regulation (GDPR), the European Union set a worldwide standard for privacy protection followed by numerous other jurisdictions (Scott M.; Cerulus L., 2018). Hence, the GDPR is a good template to use to discuss the properties of data protection laws: we will look at the GDPR in the next section. However, it is important to note that, generally speaking, laws that impose significant obligations on all market players may have unintended consequences on market structure. For example, the GDPR had asymmetric effects penalizing smaller

---

[29] See Alharthi, et al. (2017) for a number of case studies on barriers to adoption of data analytics from a company perspective. See also Cohen, et al. (2017) and Selby (2017).

[30] This part follows closely the EPSC note (European Political Strategy Centre, 2017) and Majcher and Mariniello (2020).

[31] For a deeper analysis, begin from Crémer, et al. (2019).

companies (and, in particular, smaller platforms) while benefiting big companies, the latter being better equipped to deal with its burdensome requirements. (Johnson & Shriver, 2020) found that one week after the entry into force of the GDPR, web technology vendors for EU users reduced their website presence by 15%. Websites were reported to be more likely to drop smaller vendors, increasing the relative concentration of the vendor market by 17%. Asymmetric effects may be mitigated in the longer term, as smaller companies have the time and resources to catch up with the new rules. Moreover, new rules can stimulate the creation of innovative businesses, such as business designed specifically to cater for some of the dispositions of the new law. In the case of the GDPR, this could be a business focusing on smoothing the portability of data from one platform to another, as we will see further below. So the long-term economic effects of data protection laws are unclear.[32] Yet this is something policymakers must keep an eye on: the enforcement of data protection laws must go hand-in-hand with monitoring the evolution of the structure of data markets.

Protecting the right to privacy in itself is not a "silver bullet" addressing all potential risks of data abuse. Another way to protect users from potential data abuse is to empower them to reduce information asymmetry. Empowerment can be achieved through legislative actions to render explicit the actual value of products and services in the digital marketplace, which may ultimately encourage competition on quality (e.g. level of privacy protection). **Transparency requirements** belong to this category: companies may be obliged to reveal what they may do with the users' data or explain how their algorithms work. However, often requirements of transparency and provision of information are not enough. They can create a well-known fallacy: "terms and conditions" and explanations may end up mirroring the technological complexity of the algorithms that they aim to explain, thereby leaving individuals perplexed rather than empowered and more knowledgeable. As it turns out, laws that impose transparency require a great amount of effort by public authorities to ensure that the implementation of the rules effectively achieves the objective of increasing users' knowledge of data contracts. Templates that allow for a simplified and intuitive way of providing information to users can be made mandatory and necessary to verify meaningful consent. Individuals must be fully aware of the services for which they are exchanging their data and have the information to assess to the best of their ability the trade-off with which they are confronted (i.e. what do they really *pay* and what do they really *get*).

Data market dynamics are still not fully understood due to their complexity and novelty. For that reason, laws that clarify what may happen should things go wrong are particularly effective. Imagine a surgeon carrying out a remote surgery through a data-powered AI application and a surgical robot. If the outcome of the surgery is

---

[32] See Degeling, et al. (2018) for an analysis of the GDPR on privacy online.

worse than expected, who should be blamed for it? The surgeon, the robot manu-facturer, the service that collected the data, the service that processed the data, the software developer, or the connectivity provider?

Liability laws establish which market player bears responsibility along the data value chain under any circumstance that may arise. This increased certainty fosters the incentives to provide safer, more secure products and services, and promote the creation of data-driven business, particularly in the case of the Internet of Things. If the allocation of responsibility is clear *ex ante* (i.e. it is defined before the product or the service is supplied on the market), it is easier for all players to calculate the expected profits and costs that their business entails. In other words, liability laws can dispel uncertainty and thus favour investment in data-powered applications.

Liability can be allocated according to straightforward economic principles. Bertolini (2016), for example, suggests allocating **liability to the party that is best placed to minimize costs** and litigation, provide compensation, and ensure product safety. Generally, that party would correspond to the market player that is best-placed to assess what can go wrong in the data value creation process, and act accordingly. Consider the case of self-driven cars. It could be argued that liability should be allocated to car manufacturers, which are the actor with the greatest con-trol and vision of the car production and marketing process. So it would be up to the manufacturer to make sure that, for example, the data that are collected by the car's sensors and the software that processes them are accurate and meet the highest standards of safety. In turn, manufacturers can enter insurance schemes to mitigate risks while guaranteeing that harm caused to users or their property would be duly compensated.

An important ongoing debate in the public policy sphere concerns the desirabil-ity of the introduction of *data property rights*. The debate is often referred to using the term "**data ownership**".[33] The idea is that data generators should have formal recognition that they are the primary source of the collected data. They should be identified as the legitimate owners of the data, and they should be entitled to dis-pose of their data property right formally. A car manufacturer, for example, could not simply use a driver's data to get a secondary stream of revenues on top of the revenues strictly related to the sale and maintenance of the car. With data property rights, it would need to formally "buy" the right from the driver, who would be free to trade her data at her convenience.[34]

While the concept may intuitively seem appealing (users would appear enriched and empowered), the creation of data property rights is fraught with significant limitations. Three limitations stand out:

- First and foremost, enforcing property rights on data would be costly and com-plex to implement in practice. It would necessarily increase transaction costs

---

[33] For a discussion of the relevant issues see Thouvenin, et al. (2017).

[34] The car example is not coincidental, as the data ownership debate is particularly lively in Germany where the impact of digitization on the car manufacturing sector is of significant concern.

and reduce data sharing, introducing inefficiencies in the system. Keep in mind that we are concerned with potential data abuses and stimulating the collection, sharing, and supply of data. Data ownership rights would necessarily push in the opposite direction

- Moreover, it would be very difficult to attach a price tag to the single data point sold on a stand-alone basis (the values reported in Figure 5.4 are averages over a large dataset; data brokers do not sell single data points). The marginal value of a single piece of information from a single customer is often negligible. That is because the value of data comes from their aggregation: you cannot draw statistical inference from a single piece of data – a large enough dataset is required. This underlines an indisputable fact: in the data value chain, data services generate most of the value, even though data generators are the ones who provide the required information at the beginning of the process. Croll (2011) rightly points out that the most critical question to ask is not who owns the data, but who owns the means of analysis
- Finally, data ownership rights, together with their cumbersome implementation, would make data-powered business more uncertain and tricky, particularly for smaller companies, reducing their profitability and contributing to making the market stiffer and possibly more concentrated. Larger data companies would enjoy a comparative advantage vis-à-vis their smaller competitors, given that they would enjoy a higher bargaining power at the "data right" trade table. In Chapter 10 we will discuss a similar argument in the context of copyright and the creation of "neighbouring rights" for publishers vis-à-vis online platforms; the creation of property rights often runs the risk of increasing market concentration, favouring incumbents.

Leaving aside these limitations, possibly the strongest objection towards the introduction of data property rights is that there are better tools to empower users without incurring the same potential issues. As the UK's HM Treasury puts it in a 2018 discussion paper (HM Treasury, 2018): "[it is not] *clear what advantages data ownership would confer to the individual over and above a strong rights framework around consent, portability, and removal of data.*"

5.3.2 Legislation to favour flourishing data ecosystems: flow, share, and access

From a public policy perspective, measures that favour data flow from one entity to another, across players and the territory, are superior tools compared to data ownership. Ultimately, the goal should be to prevent the lock-in of users' data in a single place or a single company. If achieved, that goal would naturally entail empowerment for data generators. To go back to our self-driven car example: if the driver can easily access her data and freely transfer them to a spare car part reseller in the secondary market, she would stimulate market competition between the original manufacturer and the reseller, and still get the most out of her data. Thus, the driver does not need data property rights. Likewise, users and data services should enjoy the maximum freedom of movement within a geographical area that shares the same level of data protection, such as is the case in the EU since the entry into force of the GDPR in May 2018. Thus, maximizing data accessibility is a much more promising avenue to empower data generators while boosting the data economy, compared to establishing data ownership rights.

Measures that allow more **data sharing** between market players can significantly contribute to society's welfare. Note that a set of four acronyms is often used when referring to data sharing:

- **B2B**: *"Business-to-Business"* data sharing refers to companies sharing data between themselves
- **B2G**: *"Business-to-Government"* data sharing refers to companies sharing data with the public sector. You may also hear the expressions **Data4Policy** or **Data4Good**, meaning that data of a private nature that is shared with public authorities with the stated goal of pursuing the common good. The "tracing apps" for the Covid-19 pandemic belong to this category of data sharing
- **G2B**: *"Government-to-Business"* data sharing refers to the public sector sharing data with the outside world. Here, the key reference term is **Open Data**, or data that the public sector makes accessible to anyone wishing to use it for personal or business purposes. For example, Propeller Health (Propeller, 2021) is an application that helps those with chronic conditions like asthma to foresee environmental conditions, thanks to its access to a continuous stream of data from environmental public agencies
- **G2G**: *"Government-to-Government"* data sharing refers to data shared across different entities within the public sectors. G2G may well include entities from different jurisdictions, such as the health authorities of different EU Member States.

I analyse the cases of B2G, G2B and G2G in Chapter 6 on the digitalization of the public sector. As regards B2B, this can take the form of **data pools**, for example, whereby companies are allowed to "pool" together the data they hold and leverage economies of scale and economies of scope to minimize costs and maximize the value that can be extracted from their data. Data pools are very appealing; as we will see in the next section, the European Commission thinks highly of them, particularly in the context of the sharing of industrial data. However, they hide risks that need addressing and that could be tackled upfront through *ex ante* regulation such as monitoring and transparency requirements. Following the Crémer, et al. (2019) report on Competition Policy for the Digital Era, we can emphasize four of these risks:

- Data pools may tantamount exclusive clubs. The club members can thus deny "membership" to foreclose market entry by other companies potentially competing with them
- Data pools increase the likelihood of collusive behaviour amongst their participants since information exchange can facilitate coordination between competitors. That is why EU competition law generally prohibits information sharing between competitors (European Commission, 2011)
- Data sharing can discourage investment and innovation, feeding a **free-rider** problem: *why bother collecting and processing data if other members of the data pool's club does it for me?* If all players think alike, the result is a lower aggregate amount of data collected and processed than scenarios where data pools are not formed
- Data pools may enjoy considerable market power, controlling all data necessary as input for other vertically related markets. That implies that data pools may have the ability and the incentive to pursue abuses such as excessive data prices—asking an unfair (or non-FRAND, see Chapter 4) price to access the pool's data.

Regulation can likewise foster the growth of data ecosystems while increasing competition along the value chain, by pulling down all the artificial barriers that lock data within a particular company. For example, **format standards** and the opening up of **Application Programme Interfaces (API)** can be made mandatory to guarantee platforms' **interoperability**. API are interfaces that allow services to smoothly communicate with each other with no need to share business-sensitive information (such as software coding). For example, the smartphone application *Itsme* (Itsme, 2021) allows its Belgian users to identify themselves vis-à-vis public sector services, such as unemployment offices or tax authorities. One way it does so is through the API of banks' web applications. With its user's consent, Itsme uses an API to communicate with the user's bank, obtain their personal credentials, and confirm the user's identity with third parties. A closely related concept to interoperability is **data portability**. As we shall see in Section 5.4, the GDPR introduces data portability as the right of individuals to reuse their data by transmitting them from one platform to another. Data portability is thus expected to prevent online lock-in and facilitate switching to another provider. The right does not only help rebalance the relationship between users and companies by providing the former with more control but also encourages interoperability and innovation, going to the heart of market competition. Consider the case of social networks: data portability can help users win the "fatigue" that filling in all personal information for building a new profile entails and, in this way, stimulate the emergence of competing social network models.

Various innovative solutions can be set up to facilitate portability. A promising one is based on **Personal Information Management Systems**, or **PIMS**. Through PIMS, users can access a personal digital deck where all their data is stored. Services then run based on this deck, giving users the ability to keep track and control the information they share and, above all, easily use that information for multiple platforms. This solution echoes the principle of *edge computing* (see Section 5.1 above), whereby data are kept locally, close to their primary source. Once again, PIMS show that ownership rights are not necessary to empower users with more control on the information they generate.[35]

Ultimately, interoperability and portability aim to create user-centric platforms of competitive interoperable services without depriving companies of the added value brought by their innovation. For example, in line with what scholars call "**the empowering approach**," or "**the fusing scenario**" (De Hert, et al., 2018), users should be able to export or import the data they explicitly provide (e.g. photos or social media posts) and the information collected by companies (e.g. location data, cookies, preferences), while not necessarily removing them from the first platform.

At the same time, access solutions and portability rights should be crafted carefully **not to undermine companies' business models**. For example, sharing economy platforms tend to rely on feedback systems through which users and service providers build their online reputation or "ranking" (for example, a host on Airbnb gets a score of up to five stars after the visit of guest; more on ranking in Chapter 11). It is questionable whether users' rankings should be made portable, since that information is generated through interactions enacted by the platform itself, and the accuracy of the ranking is one of the parameters of the quality of the platform's service. Making ranking information portable could therefore reduce incentives to create higher quality services.

Finally, public policy can **proactively foster** prosperity in data markets, along the same lines of what is traditionally observed with financial framework programs in support of R&D. We have seen in Section 5.2 that data analytics and R&D share critical structural features, such as being non-rivalrous goods. In the specific case of the EU, this may include:

- the definition of ambitious targets, for example, data analytics to represent a significant proportion of the European economy (along the lines of the "Barcelona target," agreed to by Member States in 2002, of increasing the overall investment in R&D in Europe to reach 3% of gross domestic product)
- active monitoring of data processes take-up, particularly by Small and Medium Enterprises and the public sector across the Single Market
- investment in the development of professional skills needed by employers to push forward their data-related businesses (see Chapter 12)
- direct financial support from EU funds, particularly for cross-border data pooling initiatives
- and possibly the extension of the R&D state-aid framework to include also data-related activities.

---

[35] Some authors are more sceptic about PIMS' potential to address data concerns, pointing to PIMS' lack of economic viability (PIMS may face significant operational costs to manage personal data). See: Krämer, et al. (2020). My gratitude to Bertin Martens for flagging this point.

5.4 The European Union's perspective

This section is dedicated to the EU policy framework for data markets. Data are the "bricks" upon which digital services and products are built. That basic fact implies that almost all initiatives taken by the European Commission or the EU legislator in the digital area have at least the potential of significantly affecting data markets. This may generate some confusion, which is only reinforced by the often unclear allocation of responsibilities in public governance models. In a typical public body with executive power (such as the European Commission or a Member State's national government), data markets' prerogatives could indeed fall into any portfolio, from economic issues to justice and home affairs, from security to trade or technology.

To not add to the confusion, in this section, I only focus on EU policies that strictly relate to data markets. All the other policies that can affect data markets are analysed in the chapters dedicated to the main subject they relate to. So, for example, EU policies for data technologies and standards are described in Chapter 1 in the context of the digitizing European industry initiative. EU policies on the two-way data flow between the public and the private sector are described in Chapter 6 on the digitization of the public sector. EU policies affecting data security are discussed in Chapter 7 on cybersecurity. Policies to foster the creation of skills in data analytics are described in Chapter 12 on technology and employment, and so forth.

With that in mind, let us identify two broad categories of EU data policies to be discussed in this section:

- Policies to *protect citizens'* privacy
- Policies aimed to support the *development of the data economy*, also known as **Policy4Data**.

5.4.1 Privacy protection Initiatives[36]

At the heart of the EU privacy protection system lies the General Data Protection Regulation, or GDPR (Regulation (EU)2016/679, entered into force in May 2018). The GDPR has had a significant impact within the EU and outside its borders, influencing jurisdictions in South America, to the Middle East, to California in the United States (for a complete overview, see Petrova (2019)).

Not only did the EU set a global privacy standard by being a first-mover in the space. It could also leverage its market size to induce multinationals to adopt GDPR-compliant rules across the world. Indeed, it is often more efficient for international

---

[36] In this section, I do not cover the E-Privacy Directive (Directive 2009/136/EC). The E-Privacy Directive regulates, inter-alia, the confidentiality of communications and it has become known to the wide public particularly because of its effect on cookie consent pop-ups from websites. A detailed analysis of privacy measures for the electronic communication sector is outside the scope of this book and a major overhaul of the directive is indeed under discussion at the time of writing.

companies to endorse just one *modus operandi* rather than adapting their policies locally.

The GDPR limits the transfer of personal data outside the EEA (European Economic Area, which covers the EU plus Iceland, Liechtenstein, and Norway) to jurisdictions covered by an **"adequacy decision"** or fall into a specific exception. An "adequacy decision" is an EC decision finding that the foreign jurisdiction ensures a level of adequate protection within the meaning of the GDPR. A notable adequacy decision is the **EU-US Privacy Shield.** Adopted in 2016, the Privacy Shield allowed companies to transfer data from the EU to the US under certain strict conditions (for example, it contains safeguards on the US government's access to personal data transferred from the EU (European Commission, 2016c)). The EU Court of Justice, however, invalidated the adequacy decision[37] stating that the Privacy Shield does not offer the same level of protection of European citizens' personal data as the GDPR. Since then, the European Commission and the US Government have been negotiating to design an adequate framework for cross-border data transfers. A still valid adequacy decision concerns Japan, instead. According to the European Commission, the 2019 Japan adequacy decision created the "world's largest area of safe data flows" (European Commission, 2019a).

In the mind of the EU legislator, a primary goal of the GDPR was to offer companies uniform, harmonized rules of personal data protection across the Single Market. That would favour the flow of external investment, as companies would find it easier to establish their business in Europe. And it would facilitate scaling-up by EU companies wishing to expand cross-border, as being GDPR-compliant at home would imply being compliant everywhere else in Europe.

It should be pointed out that the GDPR fails to achieve EU-wide uniformity of privacy rules, despite that being its main selling point. The GDPR is an EU Regulation, meaning that it is automatically embedded in Member States' legal systems. But Member States need to define the rules for applying it. And there are sixty possible exceptions that each Member State can adopt. For example, the GDPR defines the age at which a minor can consent to data processing. Member States have, however, a margin of discretion: they can pick between thirteen and sixteen years old (below thirteen years old consent is never possible, above sixteen years old consent is always possible). In addition, the GDPR must be enforced, and every national regulator has its own approach. Although the GDPR introduces measures to favour coordination between authorities, **it is no one-stop-shop.** In case of potential cross-border infringement, the location where the company collecting or processing the data (the "data controller," in the terminology of the GDPR) has its main establishment determines the authority that takes the lead of coordinating an investigation. But all

---

[37] Case C-311/18 Data Protection Commissioner v Facebook Ireland Ltd and Maximillian [2020], European Court of Justice. See: https://curia.europa.eu/juris/document/document.jsf;jsessionid=E8C2F17447C9C22E52872 38837C61EA5?text=&docid=228677&pageIndex=0&doclang=EN&mode=req&dir=&occ=first&part=1&cid =4426307

national data protection authorities *de facto* retain their autonomy in pursuing the investigation.

By the time of writing (two years after the entry into force of the GDPR), almost 145,000 complaints were filed across the EU. They targeted the "usual suspects" from the Big Tech club (Google, Facebook, Amazon, and the like), as well as small local companies. Regulators, however, often lack the budget and the human resources to handle all the queries and complaints. A common criticism has been that the GDPR still had to "show its teeth": despite the possibility of sanctions up to 4% of a company's global turnover for a GDPR breach, only few significant fines have so far been imposed. In 2019, the French data protection authority has imposed a fine on Google for failing to disclose to users how it collects their data properly, for example. Even if the fine was at the time the biggest ever imposed for a breach of the GDPR, it totalled "only" €50 million, which is 10% of the revenue that Google generates in one day (Satariano A., 2020). It is hard to see how that level of enforcement can effectively dissuade companies from infringing personal data protection rules. Most recently, in July 2021, the Luxembourg data protection authority set the GDPR record imposing a €746 million fine on Amazon (at the time of writing the authority's decision had not yet been published, pending the completion of the legal process).[38]

While a full review of the GDPR[39] is outside the scope of this book, let us consider some of its most significant provisions. First, let us recall that in the terminology used by the GDPR, a "data generator" that generates personal data is called a "**data subject**". In contrast, a company managing the use of personal data is called a "**data controller**".

An essential requirement for data processing imposed by the GDPR is "**consent**". According to Article 4 of the GDPR, "*'consent' of the data subject means any freely given, specific, informed and unambiguous indication of the data subject's wishes by which he or she, by a statement or by a clear affirmative action, signifies agreement to the processing of personal data relating to him or her.*" "Freely given" implies that data subjects must be in a position to say "no" and still be able to access the service (unless the data is indispensable for the service to be delivered). Data subjects must be given the possibility to revoke their consent, they must be correctly informed in an intelligible and plain language, and their consent must be straightforward. Their consent cannot be simply assumed, for example, using default settings such as pre-ticked boxes on web pages. Importantly, consent must be *specific*, meaning that the data provided can be processed only for the purposes for which the data subject has expressly given consent.

Article 4 and its interpretation are, however, not controversy-free. For one, all of the requirements mentioned above for consent appear seldom applied. Often, organizations do not adequately inform data subjects and do not offer the opportunity to access the service without consent to process their data. Most notably, Article 4

---

[38] See: https://cnpd.public.lu/fr/actualites/international/2021/08/decision-amazon-2.html
[39] For a good, accessible description of the main features of the GDPR, see: Lomas (2018).

prevents data "**repurposing**". This provision has been perceived by many in the data economy sector as an extreme measure imposing an unnecessary limitation. In fact, it is quite common for organizations to collect or hold data without yet knowing how those data could be used. That is part of the "dynamic nature" of the data economy, as we have seen in the previous section. New services and products are developed through use, and it is often impossible to anticipate what the next innovation may be. Therefore, it could be argued that a less stringent provision on repurposing could have been adopted by the GDPR, safeguarding data subject's rights while stimulating potential innovation.

The impact of the repurposing limitation may even be exacerbated by Article 25 of the GDPR, which introduces the principles of **data minimization** and **data protection by design**. That implies that when organizations collect or process personal data, they need to minimize the potential impact on data subjects. Hence, they are required to implement appropriate measures to ensure they process only the personal data that is strictly necessary to pursue their specific purposes.

Likewise, the GDPR has been criticized for "pushing" too far the rights of individuals in a highly uncertain environment that can sometimes escape the control of organizations. A notable example comes from Art. 22 GDPR and Recital 71 GDPR, whereby individuals that are subject to an automated decision (i.e. algorithmic decision, see Chapter 15)—including profiling—should, *inter alia*, be entitled to obtain an explanation of how the decision was reached.[40] While that seems theoretically sensible, it has been pointed out that machine learning, by definition, relies on algorithms to learn autonomously throughout the data processing. The learning often unfolds to the extent that a complete understanding of how the outcome was reached is impossible, even for the very same developers who created the algorithm. So it may seem an overshoot to require organizations to offer an explanation to data subjects whenever they would require it.

Moreover, that may not even be strictly necessary to protect individuals from data abuse. What is necessary is to explain the outcome of the decision and ensure that it is compatible with the protection principles established by the law. To use an analogy: when sentencing a person to jail, a judge does not need to explain all the factors that led them to take a decision. That may well include the books they read or the teachers they had during their studies. But the judge must nevertheless be accountable for their decision and must be able to explain the logical link between the evidence examined and the final outcome expressed by their judgement. In the case of the algorithm, there is arguably no need to break down and explain every single passage in that "learning process" that led it to achieve the outcome. But the *humans* using the algorithm should be accountable for it (see also Chapter 15 on artificial intelligence and deep learning technologies).

Art. 17 GDPR empowers data subjects with the right to ask organizations to delete their personal data if, in particular, the data are no longer necessary to pursue the

---

[40] Some even question whether that right really exists: see Wachter, et al. (2017).

purpose for which they were originally collected. This right has been popularized as **"the right to be forgotten"**. The GDPR transposes into hard law a judicial precedent set by the EU's Court of Justice in 2014 (Google Spain vs Gonzalez). Five years after the sentence, almost one million people had requested the removal of 3.3 million web links in Europe. The right established by the GDPR is, however, not indiscriminate. For example, it can be overridden if the data are used to exercise the right to freedom of expression and information (see more about this in Chapter 14 on Disinformation).

Moreover, an important sentence by the CJEU in 2019 (GC and Others v Commission nationale de l'informatique et des libertés (CNIL)) established that the right to be forgotten applies *only to Europe*. This means that a web search engine such as Google may be forced to remove a link pointing to personal information within the EU. But that link may still be accessible outside the EU. While it would be hard to see how Article 17 could be fully enforced beyond the EU's borders, the sentence exposes all the limitations of the right to be forgotten. It is in fact sufficient to use a "virtual private network" (or VPN) application to change the Internet protocol (or IP) of a device and "pretend" that the device is located outside the EU when connected to the Internet. Hence, personal information which is not removed globally remains readily available to anybody interested in accessing it.

Art. 20 GDPR establishes a fundamental right: the **right to portability**. Data subjects can ask data controllers to provide them with their personal data in *a structured, commonly used, and machine-readable format*. Data subjects may then transmit those data to another data controller without hindrance from the original data controller from whom they are exporting their data. Art. 20 GDPR is arguably one of the theoretically most incisive of the GDPR provisions: it can unlock a great potential of the data economy and address many of the issues we discussed in Sections 5.2 and 5.3, bringing more competition to the data value chain. At the time of writing the book, though, there were no indications that the right has been effectively implemented throughout the Single Market.

Finally Art. 33 GDPR requires companies that have been subject to a personal data breach to notify the supervisory authority within seventy-two hours of becoming aware of it. As we shall see in Chapter 7 on cybersecurity, this requirement is extremely important. Companies do not have an interest in disclosing a security issue, and that gives rise to well-known *market failures* that can undermine a whole ecosystem's security and expose it to a high risk of cyber-threats, as we shall see in Chapter 7.

5.4.2 Policy4Data Initiatives

Policy4Data Initiatives are a set of legislative and non-legislative EU policies that are geared to nurture the creation of data ecosystems. They aim to favour the adoption of data processing, facilitating data access, and sharing and ensuring that the value generated by data markets spills over to the whole economy and society, including citizens and companies.

Four European Commission strategy papers (or "Communications") offer the best overview of such initiatives: "Towards a thriving data-driven economy (2014)" (European Commission, 2014b); "Building a European Data Economy" (2017) (European Commission, 2017b); "Towards a common European data space" (2018) (European Commission, 2018b); and "A European Strategy for Data" (2020) (European Commission, 2020i).

The European Commission's Communications reflect, on the one hand, the need to reach a deeper understanding of data markets: they emphasize the importance of discussing open questions related to ownership, interoperability, security, access, and data flow with stakeholders to develop effective solutions. On the other hand, however, they express a clear intent to invest in creating synergies to develop data markets further while stimulating data flow, access, and sharing.

By the time of the drafting of this book, possibly the most concrete and impactful follow-up to the European Commission's strategy was the adoption of Regulation (EU)2018/1807 **on a framework for the free flow of non-personal data**. The regulation entered into force in May 2019, and its goal is to pull down all barriers to the free movement of non-personal data across Member States and IT systems in Europe. Former European Commission Vice-President for the Digital Single Market, Andrus Ansip, used to refer to this as "the establishment of a fifth EU right to the freedom of movement within the Single Market: *data* after *goods, capital, services,* and *labour*" (Stolton S., 2018). As it focuses on any data that cannot be qualified as "personal," the regulation has a residual and complementary function with respect to the GDPR (which, as we have seen, already establishes the right to portability for personal data). It explicitly prohibits Member States to impose data localization requirements, which are sometimes misconceived "as a proxy for assurances in terms of privacy, audit, and law enforcement". The prohibition does not apply only if Member States can justify the localization requirements on public security grounds. It remains to be seen whether Member States will abide by the regulation: it is too early to know how it will affect data flows within the Single Market. The regulation, moreover, makes an attempt, albeit a weak one, to address vendor lock-in, by encouraging stakeholders to adhere to "self-regulatory" codes of conduct that would facilitate data portability across different IT systems, with the purpose of fostering growth in **Cloud computing** solutions. As we shall see in the course of this book, however, self-regulation is seldom effective. Market players often lack the incentives to set rules that would expose them to increased competition, if not forced by the law (note in particular the discussion on self-regulation in Chapter 14 on Disinformation in the Digital Age).

Other important aspects of the European Commission's overall data strategy have not yet been expressed in a concrete form. Among these, the most intriguing concerns the plan of the von der Leyen Commission (the European Commission under President Ursula von der Leyen, 2019–2024), which primarily focuses on the creation of **fully-fledged common European data spaces**, both *across* sectors and *within* sectors (dubbed by the Commission "*High Impact Projects on European data spaces and federated Cloud structures*"). The idea is to equip these spaces with everything that is needed to generate data synergies and flow:

- a common data governance framework
- cross-sector data format standardizations to favour interoperability
- a package of incentives to stimulate B2B and B2G data sharing and data pooling (that would include the clarification of ground rules, for example, as regards usage rights of data co-generated by multiple companies)
- rules to prevent abuse such as Fair Reasonable Non-Discriminatory (FRAND) mandatory data access terms where competition policy cannot remedy it
- measures to ensure within sector data quality and interoperability, the deployment and sharing of key IT infrastructure and technologies such as cloud, edge, and fog computing technologies.

The European Commission aims to raise up to €8 billion of investment across the EU to support its common data spaces strategy. The plan looks good on paper but, again, its effectiveness will have to be judged in the years to come.

In November 2020 the European Commission proposed a Regulation on European Data Governance, (European Commission, 2020j), commonly referred to as the **Data Governance Act** (DGA).[41] The proposed regulation covers three main areas:

- **Data held by the public sector**. The DGA aims to foster the sharing of public data by reassuring that personal data must receive adequate protection through a number of safeguards (I will discuss in the next chapter, Chapter 6, the importance of *open data* initiatives)
- **Data intermediaries**. These are companies that should facilitate the sharing of data between companies. The DGA lays down several conditions that apply to them, including their "neutrality", namely: they cannot use the data they get for anything else than their intermediation service. Once again, the proposed regulation attempts to provide reassurances that should incentivize data sharing between private entities
- **Data altruism**. The DGA lays out the conditions under which the private sector can share data with the public sector to pursue objectives of public interest (see also in Chapter 6, the discussion on *data4good*).

At the time of writing this book, the text of the DGA is being discussed by the EU co-legislators (the European Parliament and the European Council). As it

---

[41] Note: formally, the one proposed is a regulation, not an *act*. The EU legislative system includes: treaties, regulations, directives, decisions, recommendations, opinions, delegated acts, and implementing acts. Hence the terminology used to promote the proposed regulation by the European Commission is somehow misleading, although, I guess, catchier, at least in the mind of the European Commission's officials.

stands now, the regulation's text is unlikely to create a major breakthrough in the EU data economy. The European Commission is, however, set to propose a set of stronger and possibly more effective provisions in a **Data Act** set for release in early 2022. The Data Act will aim to foster access and use of data, particularly leveraging on increased interoperability to smooth data flow in B2B and B2G data sharing relationships.

A final note on **liability**. There is an ongoing effort by the European Commission to assess the adequacy of the current liability framework to tackle issues generated in data-powered markets. A recent manifestation of such endeavour is the European Commission "Report on the safety and liability implications of Artificial Intelligence, the Internet of Things and robotics" (European Commission, 2020h). The report suggests that EU national liability frameworks have so far worked well, thanks also to the parallel application of the EU Product Liability Directive, which favoured cross-border harmonization of liability regimes and compensated national laws where they failed to provide coverage on new issues brought about the digital economy. The report, however, points out that new technologies (AI, the Internet of Things and other data-powered applications) give rise to novel and demanding challenges. Those challenges suggest that the Product Liability Directive should be updated soon.

****

5.5 Case Study: Dawex

Dawex is a French data company founded in 2015. It is an online platform interme-diating between companies willing to sell data or to buy them from other companies. Dawex's typical users are companies from the health, energy, automobile, and retail sectors and can be of any size: from start-ups to large enterprises. Dawex itself does not buy data or use them for commercial purposes. Instead, it allows companies to profit from data they control. For example, it offers the chance to the owner of a smart-factory plant to monetize the machine data it generates during production— selling them to other companies that may use them to predict potential breakdowns in their factories. Companies that register on Dawex's platform must ensure the le-gality of the process (e.g. they need to guarantee that they own the right to hold, share, and use the data) and part of the platform's service consists in double-checking companies' claims through an objective validation process. Dawex's "neutral" in-termediation service encapsulates one of the main channels through which the European Commission hopes to incentivize more business-to-business (B2B) data sharing between European companies; that is: trustful intermediation (see the discussion on the *Data Governance Act* in Section 5.4.2).

More information on Dawex can be found on its website: https://www.dawex.com/en/

5.6 Review questions

- What are the risks of being too confident with the results of "big data" analytics? Look for a real-case scenario in which too much confidence in the size of the sample misled researchers (do not use the example given in the chapter), or make up your own fictitious example.
- Why are edge computing and fog computing attractive, especially from a European Union's point of view? (Tip: consider the privacy angle.)
- Illustrate the value data chain with a different example than the one used in the book.
- A Member of the Parliament proposed creating a new property right for the data collected from single individuals. According to the proposal, before us-ing individuals' data, companies need to purchase a license to use from them (through the help of an intermediary). Identify and explain the benefits and drawbacks of the proposal.
- How do data pools, and data spaces where data sharing is incentivized, benefit the European economy?

6

Digital Government

Abstract

Digitizing the public sector has become imperative for every country in the world. A digitized public administration is leaner, faster, and more efficient. It can better identify and anticipate its constituency's issues; it is transparent and accountable. That is all the more necessary to enable governments to perform increasingly challenging tasks, such as dealing with shrinking public budgets, meeting citizens' raising expectations, and relating with a highly dynamic surrounding economic environment. Transformation is, however, far from easy. Technological adoption, the modernization of infrastructure, and the upskilling of the public workforce are just the first steps. A digital public sector requires a radical cultural change for public employees and citizens alike. It begs for significant investment and efforts to establish a mutually beneficial communication flow between public administrations and citizens, business, and society at large. Of particular relevance is the use of data in the public sector. Data is a powerful enabler of innovation. But to unleash its full potential, it needs the proper governance framework. As we shall see in this chapter, the European Commission and the EU legislators have recently started making their first steps in the direction of a more integrated EU public sector's data system.

6.1 Background

In Chapter 1, I introduced the digital disruption challenge that legacy industries must face. Well-established industries often fail to keep up with their new digital competitors because they struggle to innovate their business *internally*, for example, reshaping how they organize the hierarchical relationship between employees. Or *externally*, for example, changing the way companies relate with the rest of the value chain. An all-around change by incumbent corporations, including a cultural shift, is needed to adapt to the new digital normality.[1]

To a certain extent, public institutions are facing a similar challenge. Developed economies are increasingly vulnerable to an adverse demographic trend. The European Commission has estimated that by 2070, 30.3% of the European population will be aged 65 or older, compared to the 20.3% of 2019 (European Commission, 2021f). The proportion of people aged 65 and above compared to those between 15 and 64, (the *old-age dependency ratio*) will increase from 29.6% in 2018

---

[1] See Sebastian, et al. (2020) for several illustrative case studies of digital transformation in traditional companies.

Digital Economic Policy. Mario Mariniello, Oxford University Press.
© Mario Mariniello (2022). DOI: 10.1093/oso/9780198831471.003.0006

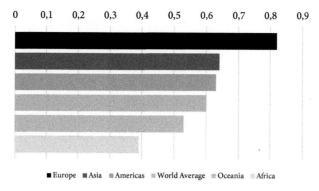

Figure 6.1 2020 E-Government Development Index
https://www.statista.com/study/25866/e-government-statista-dossier/

to 51.2% in 2070 (European Commission, 2018d). That is: the workforce, those paying taxes and social security contributions, will become smaller compared to the non-working population, which instead will require increased spending for health, long-term care, and pensions, putting enormous pressure on public budgets (European Commission, 2020k).

On the other hand, there is a parallel growing trend in citizens' expectations vis-à-vis public administration. Better informed citizens expect the public to keep up with the private sector, demanding a better understanding of their needs, effective solutions tailored to their personal preferences, efficiency, accountability, openness, and transparency (see, for example, Melchor (2008)). Governments have been struggling to transform to meet that increasingly pressing demand, often causing disappointment (Figure 6.2). This contributes to explaining the global erosion of trust in the public sector occurring, perhaps not surprisingly, exactly when policy action is more needed (OECD, 2017a). OECD (2017a) identifies three major "pressure points" eroding trust in public administration: concerns about lack of economic growth and inequality; anger against corrupted behaviour by public officials and tax evasion; and disillusionment towards the meagre outcome of governments' action against a global threat such as climate change, migrations, and other geopolitical issues (see also Chapter 14 on disinformation for a discussion on the consequences of miscommunication and lack of trust on polarization).

The 2020 Covid-19 pandemic (see Chapter 3) may have further undermined citizens' confidence in the public sector, wherever the policy answer has not been perceived to stand up to the challenge (with lack of clear communication by decision-makers playing a decisive role).

Thus, despite public administration is generally not subject to the hardship of market competition to the same extent that private corporates are, it is nevertheless under increasing pressure to transform itself and adapt to a fast-changing surrounding environment.

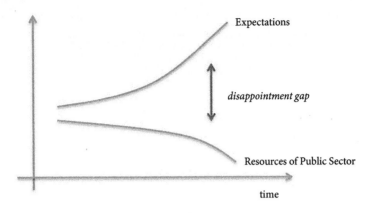

Figure 6.2 The disappointment gap

As we shall see throughout this chapter, moving towards an innovative and digitized public sector may be one of the best ways to shrink the disappointment gap, improving the quality of public service while efficiently employing public resources.

Furthermore, public institutions and their processes as we observe them today successfully emerged in traditional economies and societies. Still, they now look obsolete in the face of the significant societal transformation prompted by digitization. Legacy institutions cannot foster digital development and address its challenges without embracing the challenge themselves: it is hard to think about an efficient regulation drafted and enforced by a regulator that has no experience with the target of its rules.

6.1.1 Opportunities to grab

Recent technological developments can be linked to suitable and often desirable applications within the public sector. In particular, three technological areas are worth mentioning: data analytics and cloud computing technologies, artificial intelligence, and distributed ledger technologies (DLT). The background of the first two areas is described elsewhere in the book (respectively: Chapter 5 on the data economy and Chapter 15 on artificial intelligence). Thus let me just briefly introduce the last one. **Distributed ledger technologies** enable the sharing of databases between peers. Possibly the most famous type of DLT is the **blockchain**, the underlying technology of cryptocurrencies such as *Bitcoin*. The name blockchain derives from the fact that this particular DLT takes the shape of an ever-growing chain of "blocks". Each block contains data relative to a specific transaction and it is cryptographically sealed to the block that precedes it and to the block the follows it (European Commission, 2018e). Changing the content of a block would require changing the entire chain and of all its copies that rest with every user; this is considered impossible.[2] Blockchain hinges on three fundamental principles (OPSI, 2018):

(1) It is *distributed*. Thus every user has a copy of the database, and every copy is continuously updated and synchronized
(2) It is *shared*. All transactions are visible to every user
(3) It is *immutable*. Once information is registered in the distributed ledger, it cannot be changed.

Such features can enable powerful, breakthrough applications: they eliminate the need for a middle-man, a central authority (such as a bank, a notary, or a public authority) to ensure the validity of a particular act or transaction. In other words, they allow bypassing a (costly and potentially unreliable) central authority fostering trust between users that have no information about their counterpart. As a result, marriage licenses, property deeds, financial statements, birth and death certificates, and votes can all be registered in the blockchain with no further validation need.[3]

Naturally, blockchain has a significant potential to profoundly disrupt and enhance the work of public administrations (Figure 6.3 reports blockchain initiatives backed by governments around the world). Blockchain can, for example, allow for quick and secure validation of individuals' *digital identity*. It can thus facilitate access to public online services. Or it can be used by public administrations to increase their efficiency while managing public registries. Substantial cost and time can be saved for operations such as the cross-validation of the data collected by public administrators (European Commission, 2018e). We shall see in Section 5.3 below what kind of policies may be needed to foster the use of DLT by the public sector.

Technological adoption is, nevertheless, only the most apparent of the clues suggesting that the public sector is going through a process of digital transformation. Digitization indeed more radically entails a change of culture within the institutions.

The Joint Research Centre (2020) defines **Digital Government Transformation** as: "*the introduction into government operations of radical changes, alongside more incremental ones, within both internal and external processes and structures, to achieve greater openness and collaboration within and beyond governmental boundaries. [Such transformation] is enabled by the introduction of a combination of existing ICTs and/or new data-driven technologies and applications, and by a radical reframing of both organizational and cognitive practices. It may encompass various forms of public sector innovation across different phases of the service provision and policy cycles, to achieve key context-specific public values and related objectives including*

---

[2] It would be more correct to say that the resources needed to change the content of a block would entail a cost so high as to make it unsustainable at the current state of technological development. It cannot be excluded that, in an undefinite future, new technologies will allow to challenge the immutability of blockchains. However, it is fair to say that the blockchain is the tool currently most difficult to hack, and hence the most secure available.

[3] On the blockchain economy and its governance, see: Beck, et al. (2018).

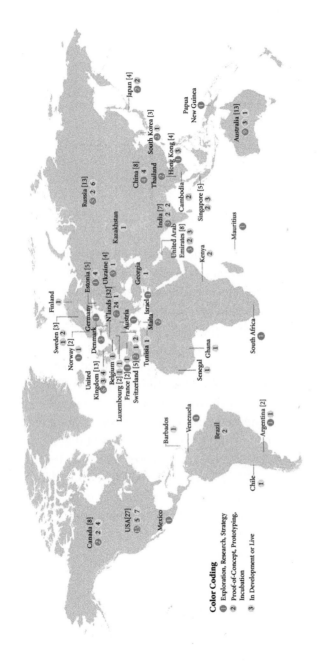

Figure 6.3 Government's blockchain initiatives around the world (by 2018)
https://oecd-opsi.org/new-opsi-guide-to-blockchain-in-the-public-sector/

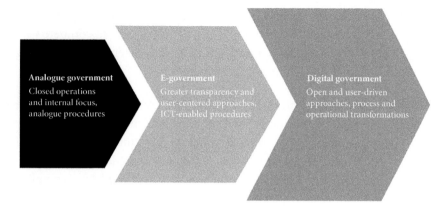

Figure 6.4 The path to a digital government

OECD (2019), *The Path to Becoming a Data-Driven Public Sector*, OECD Digital Government Studies, OECD Publishing, Paris, https://doi.org/10.1787/059814a7-en

increased efficiency, effectiveness, accountability and transparency, in order to deliver citizen-centric services and policies that increase inclusion, and enhance trust in government".

As pointed out by the OECD (2019a), the path towards a public sector capable of designing policies and enacting processes that are consistent with the digitally native and networked societies that are increasingly surrounding, has often been incremental.[4] It starts with an *analogue government*, focused on internal processes and closed to external scrutiny. It then moves to *e-government*, where technology is considered the best solution to achieve efficiency gain and ensure greater transparency towards the outside world. And it finally reaches *digital government*, where technology is only one of the necessary means to achieve the primary goal of re-engineering and re-designing services and processes to make them genuinely open, tailored to users, and capable of addressing citizens' diverse needs (Figure 6.4). Similarly, the Joint Research Centre (2019a) identifies four historical steps in the progress towards a digitally transformed public sector:

(1) *e-government 1.0*, started in the late 1990s, with public administrations progressively going online (e.g. setting up a website to publicize information) and investing in ICT

(2) *e-government 2.0*, until the early 2010s, with an ever-growing interest by public institutions to become *open* and to create spaces for cooperative collaboration with citizens

(3) *e-government 3.0*, until the mid-2010s, with an increasing reliance on "smart" or "intelligent" technological solutions, the Internet of Things, data analytics and artificial intelligence-enabled applications

---

[4] For an analysis of the digital government's evolution, see Janowski (2015).

(4) *e-government 4.0*, in the late 2010s, with governments focusing on more radical transformations that would allow the public sector to compete with the private one, crafting personalized solutions for citizens while pursuing the overarching goal of sustainable development.

Thus the digital transformation of governments is a complex phenomenon that is hard to capture through quantitative analysis. Accurate measuring of the progress made by public administrations towards their digitization is inherently tricky: data often relate to just the adoption or use of technologies without necessarily capturing the shift in the internal culture which is needed to accomplish the change.

With all these caveats, the European Commission runs a yearly exercise to monitor progress in e-government (we have briefly touched upon this in Chapter 2). That is the annual **eGovernment Benchmark.**[5] The 2020 eGovernment Benchmark constantly records over time progress by European countries towards the digitization of their public administrations, at a pace that is often faster than their global counterparts (Figure 6.1). It focuses on four key benchmarks:

(1) *user-centricity*, or the extent to which services can be easily accessed online
(2) *transparency*, or the level of administrations' openness to their users, for example, about how their personal data are collected and processed
(3) *key enablers*, namely: what kind of technological solutions have been adopted
(4) *cross-border mobility*, that is: how easy it is to access public sectors' services from abroad.

On the positive side, the 2020 benchmark report indicates good overall progress, particularly on governments' transparency. Moreover, it finds that the gap between frontrunner countries, such as the Baltics and Scandinavian countries, and the laggards, such as Eastern and Central European countries, is narrowing. Likewise, differences between *national* and *local* administrations within countries are also getting smaller. Differences in the budget for technological adoption usually drive differences between national and local administrations. Conversely, the two outstanding performance gaps recorded by the 2020 eGovernment Benchmark are: (a) the still too slow progress in making business-related services available online, and (b) lack of smooth cross-border access and mobility of Member States' public services. We will see in the following sections what may originate these issues and how can policy contribute to addressing them.

---

[5] The 2020 report can be found here: https://ec.europa.eu/digital-single-market/en/news/egovernment-benchmark-2020-egovernment-works-people

6.2 Opportunities and challenges

Measuring progress towards a digitized public administration is tricky; so is quantifying its benefits for citizens. That should not surprise since public institutions often do not operate in markets as private operators would. So monitoring and analysing supply and demand dynamics often do not provide good indications on the quality of the supplied public services. Moreover, students should be aware of a typical statistical pitfall: investing in digitalization requires the design of forward-looking strategies, careful planning, and effective implementation. These features usually are associated with efficient public institutions *as such*. Thus, observing a better performance of highly digitized public administrations may not necessarily mean that digitalization improves services' quality. Instead, there may be more digital adoption wherever governments tend to be more efficient (a case of *reverse causality*, see the appendix for an explanation).

Twizeyimana and Andersson (2019) survey the then existing literature on creating value for citizens by public service delivered by a digitized public administration. They analyse 53 papers and suggest that six channels through which value can be created are generally considered most relevant by researchers (arguably the boundaries between the different dimensions identified are blurred, as the effect overlaps— reinforcing each other):

- **Improved public service** refers to offering a responsive, effective, efficient, cost-minimizing, transparent, and collaborative service, for example, through governments' digital platforms or any other type of digital interface favouring communication within and between public institutions
- **Improved administrative efficiency** refers to gains due to the streamlining of administrative processes. It includes reduced administrative burden, fewer bottlenecks, and queues for the delivery of services to citizens. A digitized public sector can reach out to a broader public: it is easier for citizens with limited mobility to access governments' services, for example (on the other hand, access may be limited if people do not possess basic digital skills, see below)
- **Open Government (OG) capabilities**. Open government empowers citizens by favouring public engagement, enhancing transparency, favouring information and data sharing, nurturing skills, and expanding the resources on which administrations can count
- **Improved ethical behaviour and professionalism**. Public employees of a digitized administration tend to have an increased sense of responsibility towards citizens. They are more accountable and thus have a higher likelihood of behaving honestly, with integrity, impartiality, and openness
- **Improved trust and confidence in government** refers to the increase in public trust due to a better public organization, management of the economy, use of public resources, and delivery of services. Digital administrations are more

flexible and reliable; hence, they tend to be perceived as more able to respond to citizens' needs

- **Improved social value and well-being**. Digitalized governments have a higher capacity to stimulate growth and well-being within communities, can create better economic conditions, favour public engagement, ensure better health services, provide better security, address discrimination, and protect human rights

Generally speaking, digitization in the public sector can have effects comparable to those already studied for the private sector. Automation can significantly reduce the need for human resources by minimizing human involvement, for example. The Estonian X-Road strategy—a digital one-stop-shop for public services—led to saving up to 1,400 years of working time annually (Joint Research Centre, 2019a). It is unclear how much of this saving can be translated into labour costs saving, however, since public sector employees universally enjoy stronger protection from lay-off than their private sector's counterparts. But savings can also arise through better, more integrated technology. It was estimated that in Singapore, machine-to-machine communication enabled savings by public agencies of up to 60% of their ordinary storage costs (Joint Research Centre, 2019a). Likewise, the UK HM Revenue and Customs Department saves processing costs by 80% and cuts calls by 40% using dashboards to automate customers' queries.

6.2.1 The use of data in the public sector

Digitized administrations are more efficient, accountable, trustworthy, transparent, and effective to address citizens' challenges; it may be difficult to pin down all the factors that contribute to such achievement. Yet, consistently with what we have seen in Chapter 5, one key enabler stands out to explain digital governments' superior performance: **data**. Data-driven innovation is at the core of a digitized government, within the meaning of the definition discussed above in Section 6.1.

Following the OECD (2019a), it is possible to list three broad areas of impact for data analysis within the public sector (Figure 6.5):

1) *Anticipation and planning*
2) *Implementation and delivery*
3) *Monitoring and ex-post evaluation.*

(1) Planning

Data analysis can improve policy action with better insights, allowing evidence-based agenda setting and policy design. It helps to forecast the state of the world if no public action is taken and anticipate one policy choice's effect compared to others.

Evaluation   Planning

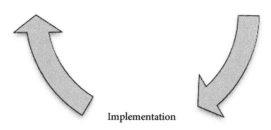

Implementation

Figure 6.5 Use of data in the public sector
(author's own elaboration of OECD (2019))
The Path to Becoming a Data-Driven Public Sector, OECD
Digital Government Studies, OECD Publishing, Paris,
https://doi.org/10.1787/059814a7-en

The Hungarian Health Ministry has implemented "big data" mapping techniques to monitor patients' movements between hospitals according to their pathologies. The government could thus grasp the underlying reasons that prompted patients to migrate. For example, the closest hospital to the place where they usually reside lacked the equipment or the skills to treat their pathology. Hence, data analysis helped the Hungarian government identify hospitals' issues and reallocate resources, leading to significant savings and healthcare improvements. For another illustration, consider AI-powered applications using data from different governmental departments to anticipate people's future needs. A country's educational department could, for example, provide mapping information on average school dropouts to the health department to identify geographical areas where future poor health risk is higher and take adequate measures in time (there is a strong relationship between good education and good health, see for example: Freudenberg and Ruglis (2007)). Data can back *foresight analyses*, namely: horizon-scanning exercises aimed to identify possible, not necessarily likely, future scenarios with the ultimate goal to inform present policy with forward-looking insights.[6]

(2) Implementation

Data allows a more efficient policy implementation and service delivery. Thanks to data, public administrations can have a more accurate grasp of the heterogeneity of the needs of citizens that interact with it and tailor service delivery accordingly. For

---

[6] For example, see the European Commission Competence Centre on Foresight: https://ec.europa.eu/knowledge4policy/foresight/about_en

example, imagine a social subsidy programme targeted at low-income households that ends up with unsatisfactory enrollment levels. Data analytics could help to understand the reasons for such poor outcome and act accordingly. Suppose enrolment is low due to lack of awareness amongst target families. In that case, data analytics can suggest the best ways to foster communication, increase knowledge, or provide beneficiaries with the necessary resources, where needed.

Furthermore, data analytics can help to engage directly with citizens and the private sector. Open data initiatives (see below, Section 6.3) can create value by allowing private entities to address social issues. Governments can share granular data on the environment collected by sensors owned by public entities and provide anybody with the opportunity to match climate data with business opportunities, for example. Data-driven applications can be particularly effective when governments are required to respond to emergencies or manage unexpected crises (see Chapter 15 on AI for an illustration of the use of AI-powered applications to address pandemic emergencies).

(3) Evaluation

Data analytics can, finally, be used to provide policymakers with an accurate picture of the effectiveness of ongoing policies through regular and real-time automated monitoring. That goes hand-in-hand with digitization's goal of increasing governments' accountability and transparency. Data analytics can help back up policy choices with quantitative evidence showing whether those choices had any significant return on investment and prompt voters' support. Note that, as illustrated by Figure 6.5, monitoring and *ex-post* valuation come at the end of a policy process but also at the beginning of new policy processes, to the extent that the lessons learned from the implementation of past policies can inform policy agenda setting and implementation.

Data analytics can also help with enforcement. As an illustration, consider a government agency mapping doctors' prescriptions data to spot whether doctors have a systematic upward bias towards prescribing more expensive drugs. Such a programme led the government to identify the issue and tackle it in Hungary, reaching savings of up to 50% of drugs' prices. The Estonian government asked companies to provide data on B2B transactions, processed them and made real-time predictions on potential tax frauds (for example, estimating employment changes based on the volume of ongoing B2B business).

6.2.2 Challenges with government digitization

Making progress towards a more digitized public sector is universally considered a good thing. Yet, the transformation of the public sector requires policymakers to proactively commit to it, winning resistance to change, accelerating the shift of mentality, and addressing all potential issues that a digitized public administration may give rise to.

The first, most apparent obstacle to digitizing the public sector is **lack of resources**: digitization requires investing in technological equipment and developing relevant skills by public employees. Gartner (2020) predicts an overall global spending in IT by governments worldwide of $438 billion for 2020. The most significant expenditure is for IT services, followed by software, telecom services, devices, and data centres. Financial barriers are particularly relevant for local administrations and agencies with a peripheric structure (imagine digitizing schools or hospitals in rural areas). Note, moreover, that public sector digitization does not only require high investment in technology adoption. It also requires a commitment to potentially high ongoing implementation programmes, employee skill training, maintenance, and updates. Costs are exacerbated by the fact that public offices often "do not speak the same language" in the sense that they do not adopt the same communication standards, and digital information sharing becomes cumbersome, if not unfeasible.

A more subtle obstacle resides with **resistance to change within the public sector** itself (the **internal challenge**).[7] As we have seen, digitization implies a radical change in the public sector's mainstream culture. It implies, for example, accepting that public service has to adapt to the needs of its customers (namely: the citizens) and not the other way round. It is a shift from a traditionally vertical system, where information control had a strong hierarchical shape, to a horizontal system, where the public system engages with citizens and incorporates and processes their input in a cooperative fashion. That also implies the need for a reshuffle of power within institutions – that does not go well with public administrators who need to let control go. This issue is not necessarily limited to top managers. From the family doctor to a local post office, from a policeman to a school director, any public official who exerts a certain degree of discretion vis-à-vis other individuals enjoy a form of power. By increasing transparency and accountability, digitalization erodes that power and thus may prompt resistance.[8]

Furthermore, public institutions are run by professionals (e.g. administrators, lawyers, economists) who have been bred by traditional textbook. They are thus often constrained by what they know, finding it difficult to depart from it to look at the world with different lenses. Public institutions do not only need people with new skills, e.g. those who understand technology. They actually need experts in traditional disciplines who are open to adapt their knowledge and can think about reshaping the tools they use to grasp new dynamics and deploy non-orthodox responses.

---

[7] See also: Fernandez and Rainey (2017).

[8] There is an extensive economic literature aimed to analyse public officials' motivations taking into account their self-interest. It goes under the headling of *Public Choice*. Interested students could start their journey here: Tullock (2004).

Digitization of the public sector requires addressing several **external challenges** too. A digitized public sector needs to address issues with cybersecurity. Essential public services such as those provided by a country's key public infrastructure, for example, for transport or healthcare, may be more efficient if digitized but also vulnerable to cyber-attacks. An increased dependency on ICT infrastructure also implies an intrinsic fragility: if technology fails, vital services cannot be supplied anymore. Hence the need for a reliable cybersecurity framework that would minimize that risk (cybersecurity is discussed in next Chapter 7).

Digital governments may also encounter public resistance due to the risk of privacy violation or, more generally, the risk that the information collected by the state would be used without the data subject's consent against her interest. The fear of a surveillance state is a primary driver behind the lack of adoption of coronavirus-tracking apps, for example (as of September 2020, only 4% of French smartphone users had downloaded the government-backed tracking app, as we have seen in Chapter 3). Public administrators can misuse citizens' data to monitor citizens' behaviour, screen and profile individuals to be considered a threat from the perspective of who controls public institutions (for example, in authoritarian regimes). Or citizens' data can be used to perpetrate discriminatory acts, such as imposing more burdensome sanctions in court to black offenders, based on a biased assessment and a biased predictive analysis (see Chapter 15 on artificial intelligence for an extensive discussion).

A third dimension of difficulty with the external world concerns accessibility. A digitized public sector can certainly facilitate access by users. The most straightforward illustration is that digital services often offer the possibility to citizens to avoid going to public offices in person and be physically present when interacting with the public administration. However, not everybody can experience the same level of easiness of access to digital public services. Citizens may lack the skills (consider the case of elderly people) or have disabilities that prevent them from being fully functional with online interfaces. Or, more simply, they may not be able to access the necessary technology; even a reliable Internet connection can be an outstanding barrier for low-income households, for example.[9]

A good illustration of the potentially magnifying effect of digitization of public service on social inequality is again from the Covid-19 pandemic. A survey by Stelitano et al. (2020) of American teachers found that those of them who operate in high-poverty schools were much more likely to indicate that their students had difficulties following classes during the pandemic lock-down because they lacked Internet access at home (83% of teachers in low-poverty schools indicated that almost all of their students had Internet access at home, compared to 30% of teachers in high-poverty schools). Digitizing public administration without addressing the digital divide thus would run the risk of achieving precisely the opposite goal of a

---

[9] Helsper (2011) noted the emergence of a digital underclass of citizens unable to have full access to public services in the UK already in 2011.

digital government: it would be *less* inclusive and less participatory, and it would increase the gap between the haves and the have-nots.

Finally, it should be noted that digitized public institutions may also run the opposite risk: to become **too transparent** or participative. Public administrators should be fully accountable for the outcome of administrative processes; they should not, however, be under the constant pressure of external monitoring by the public audience they work for. Any corporation, be that of private or public nature, requires a certain level of opacity vis-à-vis the external world to function correctly. That is because decisions are taken by professionals who are supposed to possess the technical know-how to process information that is not necessarily available to the public. Suppose public administrations were required to fully disclose and justify every single step that led to their decision. That could undermine the health of the debate within the institutions since administrators would be conditioned by external pressure rather than their knowledge to stick to less risky options to avoid public criticism. Paradoxically, this would result *in less responsibility* and *less accountability* by public administrators.[10]

In this sense, the public sector is not exempted from the risk that digitization would inject too much transparency and democratize too much processes, taking away control from those who have the knowledge to take the best decision in that context. Democratic control should be implemented in a way that does not impede democratic institutions' functioning. This is a common principle of democracies: the Italian Constitution, for example, forbids the use of referendum for tax laws.[11] Citizens are not considered able to collectively express a vote on this matter that would pursue their best interest (it is hard to believe that a referendum to abolish income taxes would not succeed to achieve a widespread consensus). I discuss these dynamics and the limits of human rationality extensively in Chapter 14 on disinformation in the digital age.

6.3 Dilemmas for policymakers

Policymakers can accelerate the transition to a digitized public sector. However, that requires a solid long-term commitment to invest monetary and human resources, address internal resistance to the necessary cultural shift, and favour external acceptance, ensuring safe and secure access. Bear in mind that all these dimensions of actions are equally relevant: increasing spending for technological adoption is essential, in particular to support financially constrained public agencies on peripheral territories. Yet, monetary investment cannot make up for lack of cultural change or acceptance, for the same reason that counting the number of personal

---

[10] On excess of transparency in public process, see Roberts (2015).

[11] Italian Constitution, art. 75: "*Non è ammesso il referendum per le leggi tributarie e di bilancio [cfr. art. 81], di amnistia e di indulto [cfr. art. 79], di autorizzazione a ratificare trattati internazionali [cfr. art. 80]*".

computers in public offices is, as such, not a good indicator of the level of digitization of a public administration. This observation is well encapsulated by the expression "**eGovernment paradox**" as suggested by Savoldelli, et al. (2014). The researchers collected evidence on public investment for the deployment of online public services over approximately twenty years, starting in the mid-1990s. They find that e-government adoption was lower than expected based on the exerted efforts (hence the paradox). Resources had been mostly invested in technological and operational matters without addressing the institutional and political barriers that hinder e-government adoption, and that may explain the paradox.

Furthermore, investment in technological adoption and maintenance needs to be accompanied by a parallel effort to equip administrations with the necessary skills to operate the newly adopted technologies. That not only means training (which, in itself, bears its own challenges, see Chapter 12). It also implies introducing more flexibility in the hiring process of public employees, possibly modernizing ranking criteria that are traditionally skewed to reward applicants with a public institutions' knowledge, gearing them also to attract technological talent.

Welby (2019) proposes six dimensions for action by governments to step up their efforts and move from mere technological adoption to a whole approach to public sector digitization:

- **Digital by design.** This implies endorsing the digital approach from the outset of any transformational phase. Digital solutions should be prioritized when public administrators are confronted with new challenges, such as rethinking or reengineering old administrative processes. The digital paradigm is the basis from which any public action should start
- **Data-driven public sector**. Gear public administration to exploit the full potential of the data economy. That should affect how data are collected, store, processed, analysed, and shared
- **Open by default.** Digitization of governments goes hand-in-hand with the adoption of a new mentality that emphasizes public agencies' need to open up to citizens and share data and information that can create collective and individual value. To be transparent and accountable
- **User-driven.** Administrative processes must be designed around users, similarly to what successful digital businesses do in the private sector. Digital governments must thus place citizens at the centre of their strategy (the ultimate goal should be to satisfy their needs) and of their implementing processes (a smooth and bi-directional information flow between administrations and citizens must be ensured)
- **Government as a platform.** A digitized public sector requires an efficient interface mechanism that allows horizontal cooperation between citizens, business, civil society, and public administrators
- **Proactiveness.** The idea is that public administrations must be in constant listening mode, be open to external input, and accountable for the way they

operate. They should also leverage their privileged position as a catalyst of information and act proactively, anticipating issues that citizens may not yet see coming.

These six dimensions of action may appear somewhat abstract. They, however, have concrete implications. So let us focus on the most significant of them.

6.3.1 Addressing the internal challenge

Securing senior management support is necessary to facilitate acceptance of a digital culture within the public sector. That applies especially when it comes to reengineering processes or establishing new relationships and working methodologies (OECD, 2003). However, doing that requires adopting a consistent overarching vision, which should guide the transformation of an institution as a whole, and not with uncoordinated initiatives by their different departments or units.

A practical way to do that is to create ad-hoc offices or roles as *digital architects, data stewards,* or *chief data officers.* That is, offices that directly coordinate with the management to shape a long-term digital transformation strategy and take responsibility for its implementation everywhere in their organization.

In that respect, an important area of action concerns **data governance** (OECD, 2019a). Data governance refers to the design of a general framework that would promote data as a key resource or asset for the institution and indicate specific and concrete ways for extracting value from it. For instance, data governance implies the definition of standards for data communication between departments of the same institution and between institutions across the territory, at any level of government: local, regional, national, and international (for the EU, the cross-border dimension is extremely relevant as we have often seen in this book; see also Section 6.4 below for a discussion of the cross-border measures taken by the EU legislators). Estonia, for example, has developed an innovative concept that goes under the expression of *country as a service* or CAAS. CAAS is a framework that allows the cross-border sharing of information, for example for tax collection for freelancers that are registered in Estonia but operate in other EU countries. CAAS may furthermore help address the issue of allocation of tax revenues for online activities and foster cross-border e-commerce (see Chapter 10 for a dedicated discussion).

Data governance frameworks would define which types of information can be shared, through which channels, and in what format. This can allow the creation of *data hubs* or *data lakes* within institutions, that is: data repositories, infrastructures containing large databases that aggregate and centralize information from several sources and are accessible from all departments in the institutions. These **data one-stop-shops** can lead to significant efficiency gains: saving in data maintenance, storing, and processing; saving in time; and avoidance of duplications, for example in data collection.

6.3.2 Addressing the external challenge

In parallel, to address the *external challenge*, a first step is to favour **access**. This means supporting the deployment of telecom and ICT infrastructure in the first place (see Chapters 4 and 5). In particular, ensuring fast and reliable connectivity where there exists a market failure, for example in rural areas. At the same time, it is possible to implement dedicated subsidy schemes to reduce the digital divide. For instance, low-income households can be granted benefits to incentivize the purchase of technology and its use (see also Chapter 13). Inclusiveness should be constantly monitored: if engagement indicators suggest that participation by specific population groups drops (such as visually impaired individuals), services should adapt accordingly. Being inclusive also entails envisaging ways to involve individuals who would drop out of public services for cultural or psychological reasons. For example, older citizens may not be used to interacting through digital interfaces and may prefer dealing with public officials in person. These kind of challenges cannot be addressed with knee jerk reactions. They require careful planning and tapping in a diverse set of expertise (for example: professionals from a sociological background) to understand the impact of the use of digital interfaces within a particular local community and have a strategy for unanimous acceptance.

Naturally, external acceptance increases with the degree of perceived benefits from using digital services compared to their traditional counterpart. Simplifying online procedures and ensuring ways to easily prove citizens' identity, allowing portability and interoperability of users' data between different public services, can significantly impact adoption rates. Imagine a national system where all the relevant information linked to a single resident is submitted only once (the **once-only principle**). In that system, residents could transport their personal information and easily use it with any public administration. They could use it to get access to schooling or healthcare services, for example. At the same time, the success of the system very much relies on its security: users should not be concerned with potential monitoring abuse, government surveillance, discriminatory acts, privacy violations, and cybersecurity threats (I deal with the policies necessary to deal with each of these issues in the dedicated Chapters: 4, 5, 7, and 15). Public administration should thus be incentivized to use digital-ledger technologies to ensure the maximum level of data protection.

Within the limits defined by data protection laws, governments can also maximize accessibility to data by any entity capable of generating value from them (European Political Strategy Centre, 2017). **Open Data** refers to this type of approach. Open data means that public institutions may share their data with the outside world anonymously.[12] The aim is to provide an opportunity to create new businesses, support economic growth, help address societal challenges, and increase citizens' participation in policymaking (we have seen some concrete examples in the previous section). The reverse of open data is **B2G data sharing** policies (sometimes referred to also as **data4good** policies). Data4good policies refer to the creation of a secure

---

[12] On open data, see Janssen, et al. (2012), Zuiderwijk and Janssen (2014), and Ayre and Craner, (2017).

framework for the sharing of data by private entities (e.g. companies) with the public sector to pursue a goal of public interest. The 2020 European Commission's report of the *High-Level Expert Group on Business-to-Government Data Sharing for the Public Interest* (European Commission, 2020m), suggests a number of illustrations for data4good. For example, data from retailers such as supermarkets can help build accurate indicators to monitor prices or households' well-being. Cities' sensor data can help address environmental issues such as sound or air pollution. Governments can use transport data to craft effective policies that favour cross-border mobility. Harvard (2014) describes how telecom data was used to monitor and anticipate the spread of the Ebola pandemic in West Africa.

To favour B2G data sharing it is necessary to design regulatory frameworks that clearly define the scope of the liability by data collectors. For example, data collectors should not be held liable for the violation of the privacy of the data subjects if they adhere to the guidance provided by the public administration they share data with, for example. Furthermore, to not reduce the incentives to collect data in the first place, solid guarantees should be given to the data collectors that competitors cannot use those data to pursue goals that contrast with the data collector's ones.

6.4 The European Union's perspective

The eGovernment policy landscape in Europe features a multitude of strategies at a national, regional, and local level. Strategies may also vary across institutions over the same territory. They are in continuous evolution: public services are subjects to the same dynamism observed in markets, technology is continuously innovating, citizens' needs and expectations evolve quickly, the environment that surrounds public institution is changing fast.

A comprehensive overview of what is being done in Europe would require a chapter on its own, and it would necessarily run the risk of being quickly superseded. So, for this section, let me focus on the supranational EU level of action, particularly on the latest, most significant initiatives taken by the European Commission. Which, as we know, aims to promote a more harmonic approach within the single market. In this case, by national and local public administrations.

The basis of the European Commission's most recent eGovernment strategy is the 2016 **EU eGovernment Action Plan 2016–2020** (European Commission, 2016f). The overarching goal of the plan is stated in the Communication as follows:

> By 2020, public administrations and public institutions in the European Union should be open, efficient and inclusive, providing borderless, personalised, user-friendly, end-to-end digital public services to all citizens and businesses in the EU. Innovative approaches are used to design and deliver better services in line with the needs and demands of citizens and businesses. Public administrations use the opportunities offered by the new digital environment to facilitate their interactions with stakeholders and with each other.

Based on what we have seen in Section 6.1, it seems evident that this (ambitious) goal has not been achieved yet, particularly regarding cross-border interoperability. But it is fair to say that considerable progress has been recorded in recent years, and EU public administrations seem to be set on the right track to reach it—if just a bit later than what was hoped for.

The Action Plan lists several principles that, if implemented, would push administrations forward towards that ultimate goal. The principles resound the analysis that we have seen in the previous sections: administrations should be *digital by default*, they should ask for information only once (the *once-only principle*), they should be *inclusive* and *accessible*, *transparent* and *open*, *secure* and *trustworthy*, *cross-border*, and *interoperable by default*. The actionable version of those principles has been organized into three pillars:

1. Modernizing public administration with ICT, using key digital enablers
2. Enabling cross-border mobility with digital public services
3. Facilitating digital interaction between administrations and citizens/businesses.

The actions in Pillar 1 aim to support technological developments that can, in particular, facilitate the information flow between citizens and public administrations, and between administrations themselves (for example, electronic identity or electronic signature, more below). It includes actions to foster connectivity and promote the use of cloud computing in EU public services. Pillar 2 is mainly geared at making going cross-border more simple for citizens or business alike. It contains initiatives such as a *single digital gateway*, namely a web portal where all the necessary information, administrative procedures, and assistance are provided for anybody willing to perform any activity in any EU country. The web portal, named "Your Europe", should contain administrative procedures such as corporate tax declarations, car registrations, and business registrations. Actions in Pillar 2 are primarily aimed to implement the *once-only* principle in a cross-border fashion. For example, facilitating the flow of information on companies' solvency, or simplifying VAT collection. Pillar 3 is centred around individual citizens and contains actions within data-enabled applications and *open data*. That is, actions to favour the flow of data between citizens and administrations to improve public services (see below).

Parallel to the actions linked with the strategy laid down by the plan, the European Commission has funnelled significant monetary support to innovative projects by EU public administrations. For example, Horizon 2020 (European Commission, 2020l), an €80 billion budget EU fund financing research and innovation in Europe, has supported ICT-enabled public sector modernization: for example, projects to enable open data, to favour co-creation between different public administrations, and to favour a smooth migration from older technologies. By 2018, the total Horizon 2020 funding of innovation projects within the EU public sector amounted to €110 million (European Commission, 2019b). Equally important are actions that are taken at the sectorial level. Possibly the most significant of those is **eHealth**; eHealth refers to the digitization of the EU public health and care system. The European Commission has launched its strategy with the 2018 Communication (European Commission, 2018f) on **Digital Transformation of Health and Care in the Digital Single Market**. The strategy lists three priorities:

(1) allow citizens to access their health data cross-border
(2) ensure that the infrastructure is deployed to enable personalized medicine throughout the EU
(3) and empower citizens to use digital to get access to care and communicate with healthcare providers.

A set of concrete initiatives to be undertaken in the coming years is associated with each of the three priority areas. They include, among other things: funding for technological development; a recommendation for the specification of technical standards that would allow easier sharing of health record across the EU; the set-up of a mechanism for voluntary coordination for the sharing of data or infrastructure between health authorities and other stakeholders for prevention and personalized medicine; and support for cooperation and sharing of best practices.

Let us now have a closer look at two broad policy areas on which the European Commission has been recently active and where it is most likely to achieve significant results: (1) the **European Interoperability Framework** and eIDAS; and (2) open data (the revision of the Public Sector Information Directive).

6.4.1 The European Interoperability Framework and eIDAS

Interoperability between public services is a pre-condition to smooth free movement within the EU and creating functioning cross-border markets. Public services of different Member States must interact with each other, rapidly and securely, using the same communication standards. The European Commission has been working for the establishment of such a framework as of the late 1990s. The most recent attempt was launched in 2017 with the **European Interoperability Framework—Implementation Strategy** (European Commission, 2017c). The framework provides guidelines, principles, or recommendations to favour interoperability of EU public services. It addresses *legal barriers* (e.g. it prompts the removal of unjustified conditions imposed by a Member State when a public service from another EU country attempts to interact with it). It addresses *organizational barriers*, favouring coordination between institutions of different nature. It ensures that the *same communication standards* are used across the single market. It prompts *technological innovation and convergence*, in particular to facilitate data flow.

ISA (*Interoperability Solutions for Administrations* in Europe, from 2010 to 2015) and **ISA^2** (from 2015 and 2020) are the two main implementing programmes of the framework. ISA^2 envisages a set of 54 actions that are considered instrumental to the development of digital solutions in the area of interoperability. For example, an ISA^2 action aimed to simplify e-procurement and e-invoicing adoption. This should increase participation in public procurement tenders and improve their outcomes, with greater cost savings and higher quality of the job delivered by the tender winner. The ISA^2 action supported the adoption of standardized electronic certification forms or funded the publication of procurement code lists on the metadata registry to enable smoother reuse of data that originated from different sources (European Commission, 2016d). In 2018 the European Commission ran an interim evaluation exercise consulting experts and stakeholders. It concluded that ISA^2 has overall been a success, but it has three areas of potential improvement. ISA^2 should increase its efforts to raise awareness amongst national, regional, and local public administrators. It should upgrade its strategy, from placing the user at the centre of the supported solutions, to place the user in the driving seat (solutions should thus become user-driven, in a more bottom-up fashion). Finally, ISA^2 should pave the way for ensuring that the successes achieved do not vanish in the long term. The interoperability achieved must be truly embedded in the modus operandi of Member States' public administration, so that ISA^2 successor programmes will be able to efficiently build on ISA^2 achievements.

Within the European Interoperability framework, one of the most important and tangible initiatives taken by the EU legislators concerns *identification*. The 2014 **eIDAS** (electronic IDentification, Authentication and trust Services) **Regulation** (Regulation (EU) No 910/2014) defines an EU-wide framework for facilitating a smooth interaction between citizens, business, and public administrations based on a secure system that verifies the identity of the actors that operate online. Thanks to eIDAS, for example, a Lithuanian citizen should be able to sign a document with a Portuguese public administration online without the need to provide that administration with any further document than her electronic identification (eID) obtained in Lithuania. Notably, the system can allow for the sharing of selective information, and thus guarantee a high level of privacy—a public administration may need to only access information regarding a citizen criminal record, for instance; thanks to an efficient eID system, that information can be provided without necessarily disclose information on gender, age, or marital status. The eIDAS regulation also aims to stimulate a market for trust services within the EU. Namely, services that ensure the authentication of signatures, seals, eCommerce delivery, or any other sort of online action requiring authentication. Within the eIDAS regulation, the interoperability of the identification infrastructure is warranted by a Cooperation Network between Member States. The Network reviews and potentially approves national eID schemes when notified by a Member State. However, this procedure is somewhat complex and cumbersome, and until 2020 only 14 Member States had submitted any eID schemes for approval. Similarly, the private sector had not picked up and leveraged eID for business as it was hoped for, leading to a general sense of disappointment amongst observers (Echikson, 2020).

Thus, it was no surprise that the European Commission proposed an updated eIDAS Regulation a few years later, in June 2021 ((European Commission, 2021); at the time of writing, the proposal had still to be adopted by the EU legislators). The proposal aims to simplify the framework to incentivize adoption. It proposes the provision of "**digital identity wallets**" by public authorities or private entities recognized by a Member State. EU citizens should be able to use their digital wallet linking it to certificates such as driving license, bank account, birth certificate, and diplomas. Wallets should be valid across the whole Single Market and should help their possessor certify their identity and attributions in any EU national jurisdictions. While the 2014 eIDAS regulation did not oblige Member States to offer the digital identification system to their citizens, the new proposal is binding: Member States will have to offer the option to citizens willing to have one. Likewise, any public or private entities will be obliged to accept the digital identity as ID proof. If the proposal is adopted, the European Commission plans to begin testing the digital identity wallet app as of October 2022. The framework for Digital Covid-19 certificates launched in July 2021 to ease restrictions to the freedom of movement in the aftermath of the Covid-19 pandemic is likely to spark momentum that may facilitate the endorsement of the new digital ID framework.

6.4.2 Open data (the revision of the Public Sector Information Directive)

The EU framework that regulates and incentivizes public administration to open and allow re-use of their data by the public dates back to 2003 with the **Public Service Information (PSI) Directive** (Directive 2003/98/EC). The PSI Directive was revised (Directive 2013/37/EU) in 2013 and, more recently, in 2019 with the new PSI Directive (Directive (EU) 2019/1024), sometimes referred to as the **Open Data Directive**, to be implemented by Member States by July 2021.

The definition of "public sector" has been widened by the Open Data directive: it currently also includes utilities, the transport sector, and research institutions when research has been funded through public budget. The previous framework defined by the 2003 PSI directive was limited to public sector bodies governed by public law. Hence it excluded undertakings supported by public funding. Furthermore, the Open Data Directive supports the use of APIs (application programming interfaces, see Chapter 5) to favour the re-use of real-time data and introduces several safeguards to avoid agreements between public and private entities that would exclude other potential users from accessing public data. The intent of the EU legislators to maximize open data value creation leveraging on higher transparency, competition, and technological innovation is evident. Assuming a complete and correct transposition of the Open Data directive by Member States, public sector content should become accessible for free or at minimal cost by anybody who wants to use it, *by default* anywhere in the EU. Public entities cannot make a profit when they supply data to external users. Thus, they are not allowed to charge more than their operational costs for collection or processing when supplying data to a company using that information to innovate their business, for example. The Open Data directive also emphasizes the relevance of certain types of data that have a greater potential to enable significant value generation: the **high-value datasets**. High-value datasets are so important for the economy, the environment, and society that access to them must be as smooth as possible. The directive mandates that those datasets must be made available for free, in machine-readable format, via APIs and, if necessary, allowing bulk download. The European Commission is tasked to list high-value datasets motivating its choice by 2021. The Open Data directive, however, already offers a track. High-value datasets should correspond to six thematic categories: *geospatial*; *earth observation and environment*; *meteorological*; *statistics*; *companies and company ownership*; and *mobility*. Examples of datasets that could enter the list are postcodes and national or local maps, demographic indicators, energy consumption, satellite images, and road signs.

It is fair to say that open data is a critical area of action, with a great potential to generate value. But it is also an area that requires an ongoing effort by institutions at all government levels. It would be unreasonable to expect an EU directive to suddenly pull down all the barriers and win public administrations' resistance to open up. That is why the European Commission is accompanying the implementation of the Open Data directive with several non-legislative actions to support the re-use of public data across the EU (European Commission, 2021g).

Parallel to the Open Data initiative, the European Commission has attempted to promote **B2G data sharing**, albeit with a more cautious, non-legislative approach. In its 2018 Communication "Towards a Common European Data Space" (European Commission, 2018b), the Commission provided guidance on business data sharing, emphasizing the need to create the right environment to avoid reducing the incentives to collect and process data in the first place. It laid down six principles:

- *Proportionality*: any request of data from the public sector must be motivated by a well-identified public interest and should not exceed what strictly needed
- *Purpose limitation*: business data should be used only for the specific purpose they are requested for (see here the echo of the GDPR logic limiting the scope of use for personal data, see Chapter 5)
- *"Do no harm"*: the data request should not result in a loss for the business entity that shared the data with the public sector. Therefore, public administrators should not deplete data relative value, for example, failing to protect

commercially sensitive information that could be used by competing market players

- *Conditions for data re-use*: public services should provide adequate compensation for the data they get in relation to the significance of the public interest pursued
- *Mitigate limitations of private sector data*: public administrations should exert quality control on the data they get from a private entity and take the necessary measures to address potential sources of bias
- *Transparency and societal participation*: the agreement between public and private entities underlying data sharing should be transparent and publicly available (under the condition of not compromising the confidentiality of the data).

After the Communication, initiatives were put in place to foster the dialogue between stakeholders and move forward to more concrete action, from the mere definition of the underlying principles of the data-sharing framework. Those included convening the expert group on B2G data sharing that I mentioned in the previous section. However, by the end of 2020, not much progress had been achieved, except for the proposed Data Governance Act regulation discussed in Chapter 5. As a result, there is currently no regulatory basis for B2G data sharing at the EU level. That is all the more disappointing, given the vital role that private data may play in pursuing public interest goals (the most straightforward example is how mobility of data could have been used to contain the spread of the Covid-19 pandemic). Addressing legal uncertainty in this area should be a priority for EU legislators.

****

6.5 Case Study: Barcelona Digital City

Since 2011, the City Council of Barcelona has been pursuing a broad digital transformation strategy to improve the general functioning of the city and its management, foster its economic growth, and enhance Barcelona's citizens' quality of life. In 2016, the City's Council announced that any public service would be provided from the outset through digital channels, strictly abiding by the "open data" principle and applying solid ethical guidelines to foster transparency, protect privacy and individuals' digital rights. Central to the Barcelona Digital Plan is a digital participatory platform called *Decidim* which is used to get citizens involved in the city's policy design and better address their needs. As of 2017, 13,000 proposals were voted on *Decidim*, involving 40,000 participants; more than 70% of the Barcelona government's agenda come from *Decidim*. The approach endorsed by the City Council emphasizes the will to establish a "technological sovereignty" by the local community, regaining control over the data generated by digital technologies, investing in the deployment of public digital infrastructure, and promoting the use of open-source standards and software. Several projects stemming from the Barcelona Digital Plan have so far proved very successful. For example, *open budget* is a project to increase public funding transparency and accountability; *ethical mailbox* allows citizens to denounce corruption episodes safely; *digital market* is a project that aims to speed up, increase transparency and improve outcomes of public procurement.

More information about Barcelona Digital City can be found here: https://ajuntament.barcelona.cat/digital/en/digital-transformation

6.6 Review questions

- Rank the most important aspects of a digitized public administration. Which ones, in your view, are the most likely to improve residents' well-being?
- Look up for a real-case scenario in which data analytics have successfully been used to improve a public administration's functioning. Which of the impact areas (anticipation and planning; implementation and delivery; monitoring and *ex-post* evaluation) was most affected and why?
- Describe all the reasons why a local public administration may resisting digitization.
- What are the economic or regulatory obstacles that can limit the scope and use of open data?
- What are the main advantages of more health data sharing cross-border within the European Union?

7

Cybersecurity

Abstract

Cybersecurity policies aim to ensure that digital technologies are safe and resilient. It is impossible to guarantee that technology is fully cyber-incident proof. However, it is possible and desirable to increase technologies' resilience to incidents and malicious attacks to minimize the risk of using technology. For this reason, cybersecurity is an essential ingredient of any public strategies geared to fostering the digital economy: lowering risk implies lowering the economy's expected costs and increasing the likelihood of adoption through greater trust. Cyber-risk can entail enormous costs for the economy, businesses, and ordinary users alike. However, markets do not autonomously converge to the optimal level of investment in cybersecurity from a social point of view, and public policy is needed to create the right incentives and steer all actors to contribute to the safety of the cyberspace.

7.1 Background

Cybersecurity is a wide-encompassing term capturing a set of public and private policies, rules, and actions to protect the digital space from harmful intentional activities, such as malicious cyber-attacks, technological breakdowns, accidents, and human error.[1] The ultimate goal of cybersecurity is to build a resilient digital space. Cybersecurity is thus a vital element of the technological layer on which the digital society and economy is grounded. According to the European Commission, the frequency of cyber-attacks is increasing, averaging one every minute worldwide; at least one million users fall victim to a cybercrime every day, possibly without even being aware of it. 47% of European SMEs and 74% of large enterprises (companies with more than 1000 employees) were targets of a cyber-attack in 2019. This number likely underestimates the total number of attacks, as a significant part of them is not reported. In response, the size of the worldwide information security market increased by 27% between 2016 and 2018 and is projected to double, reaching a total of US $151 billion by 2022 (Figure 7.1). The size of the global market for protection from "advanced persistent threat" (namely: an unauthorized access to a system or network by a user who then remains undetected for an undetermined amount of time) is projected to reach US $9.4 billion in 2023, up from US $1.95 billion in 2015.

---

[1] Definition and meaning of cybersecurity are discussed in Craigen, et al. (2014). An accessible popular introduction to cybersecurity issues is Singer and Friedman (2014).

Digital Economic Policy. Mario Mariniello, Oxford University Press.
© Mario Mariniello (2022). DOI: 10.1093/oso/9780198831471.003.0007

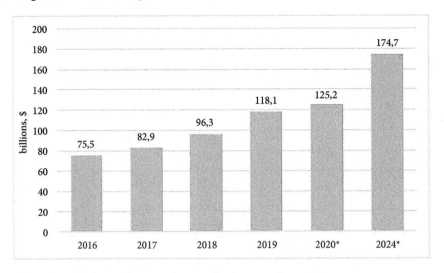

Figure 7.1 The increasing prominence of cybersecurity markets

Statista, 'Information Technology security' (2019), p. 2. https://www.statista.com/study/15503/information-security-statista-dossier/

Cyber-resilience is, however, not spontaneously generated by private operators in digital markets. Cyber-attacks are costly to the victims, but without reinforced incentives, the economy does not converge to the optimal level of cybersecurity investment by itself. In the next section, we will look at the reasons why these market failures occur, justifying the need for public intervention.

Lack of security in the cyberspace is an increasingly relevant issue for any economy, and governments must keep up with the challenge. However, digitization implies a dispersed distribution of power to state and non-state actors, making enforcement challenging. Public authorities are increasingly confronting harmful activities that are fluid and geographically hard to pin down.

The public interest in cybersecurity can be easily grasped.[2] First, and most intuitively, cyber incidents are a drag for the economy. An average company's loss due to cybercrime in 2018 amounted to more than US $27 million in the US, US $13 million in Germany, US $11.5 million in the UK, and almost US $10 million in France. Second, in an increasingly interlinked world where every infrastructure, private appliance, industrial machine, or public service is somehow connected to the Internet, the spill-over from cyber accidents can have dramatic consequences. Imagine if the victim of a cyber-attack is a company with links to critical infrastructure such as power grids or the transport network: such an attack could have repercussions for the entire economy of a country. The Internet of Things can only exacerbate economies' vulnerability. This is particularly worrisome for Europe: it is estimated that more than half of the world's total of Distributed Denial-of-Service attacks (see further below) in 2017 targeted a European country (Bell L., 2018). Finally, without cyber-resilience, technological adoption cannot take off. A 2017

---

[2] For a cost-benefit analysis of cybersecurity see Gordon and Loeb (2006).

Eurobarometer survey (European Commission, 2017d) found that 87% of surveyed citizens consider cybercrime an important challenge to the internal security of the EU; 86% believe that there is an increasing risk of being a victim of cybercrime, and 65% are concerned that public authorities do not keep their personal information security. When the level of trust is low, it is hard to imagine a speedy adoption of services. That is caused by demand and supply effects: citizens are less likely to buy digital products or use private or public digital services. Consequently, the private and public sector reduces their supply. For example, in Chapter 10 we will see how security concerns are limiting cross-border e-commerce in Europe.

A primary source of concern is merely technical: cyber attackers can exploit software limitations to hack it. The European Agency for cybersecurity (ENISA) defines a **vulnerability** as *the existence of a weakness, design, or implementation error that can lead to an unexpected, undesirable event [G.11] compromising the security of the computer system, network, application, or protocol involved* (ENISA, 2021). It should be well accepted that **software can never be fully attack-proof**. As extensively explained in (Sen, 2018), there are many reasons for this. First, software coding is exceptionally complex (Facebook's software, for example, has more than 60 million strings of code (Sen, 2018)). Second, software always requires interplay with other software (for example, compiler software that translates source code to executable software or the operating system in which the software is grafted), which may itself have vulnerabilities. Third, software coding is necessarily built upon previously coded software, which may have vulnerabilities that have never been patched. Most importantly, making software fully "cyber-attack-proof" would entail assessing all possible interactions that that software could have with the surrounding data environment, implying the employment of vast amounts of resources to the point that the costs would well outweigh the benefits. That is why software developers typically do not aim to create a perfectly cyber-proof product. Their preferred strategy is instead to develop a software and then provide patches to fix vulnerabilities *when they are discovered*. At the same time, users rely on other complementary software such as antivirus, firewall, and traffic monitoring software (which can also be vulnerable to attacks) to monitor and counter potential attack attempts.

7.1.1 Categories of cyber-attacks

Cyber-attacks can generally be grouped into three broad families:[3]

- Access Attacks
- Control Attacks
- Denial Attacks

---

[3] This classification has been proposed by Joss Wright, Oxford Internet Institute. A survey of emerging threats in cybersecurity is in Jang-Jaccard and Nepal (2014); bear in mind, though, that the paper is from 2014 and the cybersecurity landscape changes quickly over time.

Access attacks aim to infiltrate a digital appliance or a network to extract data or monitor the outside environment. This would typically occur by cracking a user's password, for example. With **control attacks**, malicious agents can use the system they infiltrated using it as if it were their own. Finally, **denial attacks** aim to prevent users from using the infiltrated appliance or accessing their data.

Threats may have elements of all types of attacks: access, control, or denial. The following section presents a non-exhaustive list of some of the most common cyber-threats in Europe in 2018.[4]

- **Malware: Trojan horses, Worms, Viruses, Ransomware**

Malware is the most common cyber-threat, making up 30% of all data breach incidents according to ENISA (ENISA, 2019). It refers to malicious software that is installed on a digital appliance without its user's consent. ENISA also reports an increasing trend of malware threats targeting mobile devices. Typical malware software are:

- *Trojan horses.* A Trojan hides in a programme with a specific harmful function, such as establishing a backdoor that hackers can use to break into a system
- *Worms.* Worms are stand-alone programmes that infect an appliance and propagate themselves to other connected appliances (for example: through emails), possibly overburdening the system and preventing its normal functioning
- *Viruses.* Viruses change the coding of software applications and replicate themselves, exploiting the system they have infected
- *Ransomware.* Ransomware prevents users from accessing their data on their digital appliances or threatens to use it against them (for example, sending compromising photos of the users to friends and family), demanding a ransom in exchange for setting the user "free" by restoring control over their data. Encryption techniques can be rather sophisticated, making it unlikely that the user would independently circumvent the ransomware. See Figure 7.2 for a real-life example: the *WannaCry* ransom attack of 2017 (see also the case study at the end of this chapter). Ransomware has been popularised by mainstream TV series such as "Black Mirror".

- **Web based attacks and Web application attacks**

Web-based attacks and web application attacks use web services to reach their victims. They are increasingly frequent for two reasons: (a) the gatekeeper role of websites for any commercial activity, including for small companies; and (b) the growing complexity of web services, giving rise to potential opportunities for sophisticated malicious activities.

---

[4] Source: ENISA (2019). Other sources: Cisco (2021), Melnick, J. (2018), IT Governance (2021).

Figure 7.2 The 'WannaCry' ransom attack – screenshot of message to the victims
Publicly shared on the Internet

Web-based attacks may take different shapes, from malicious advertisement to search engine results redirection. A popular one is called SQL Injection Attack: attackers identify a vulnerability in the database running behind a website, where the information of users interacting with the website is stored. The attackers can then inject malware (for example, a trojan software) into the database of the website and infect users that visit it.

- **Phishing**

Phishing refers to a technique used by cyber-criminals to lure users into opening a compromised file or clicking on a deceptive URL through messages crafted to get users' attention. It is an increasingly popular hacking method, with 90% of malware infections and 72% of data breaches in organizations originating from phishing attacks (ENISA, 2019). Phishing is a key by-product of personal data hacking: personal data can indeed be used to tailor the message to the target, making its content look more realistic. The more information the attacker has of their victim, the more likely it is that the victim mistakenly believes that the source of the message is credible.

- **Denial of Service and Botnets**

Denial of service attacks aim to over-burden a particular network or system with a large amount of traffic, ultimately exhausting its bandwidth and preventing it from functioning correctly. Distributed denial of service (DDoS) attacks rely on taking control of a high number of host machines (Botnets) that, possibly unknowingly, are used by the attackers to connect with the target of DDoS simultaneously. The more the Internet of Machines expands, the more opportunities there are for DDoS: imagine attackers taking control of a vast number of smart-fridges to launch an attack on a nuclear power plant.

- **Spam**

Spam is defined as unsolicited emails targeting a large number of recipients grouped in specific lists. Most spam has a commercial purpose. It is probably the oldest form of cyber-threat—*as old as the Internet.* Despite its decreasing relevance, thanks in particular to the technological advance in AI-enabled email filtering, spam remains one of the major types of attack observed by cybersecurity experts, representing almost 40% of total inbound emails in 2017 (down from 85% in 2008).

- **Data breaches, data leakage, and identity theft**

Although listed as cyber-threats by (ENISA, 2019), "data breaches" are often the *outcome* of a successful cyber-attack. They consist of the appropriation, leakage, or exposure of valuable or sensitive information related to single individuals or organizations. Almost half of data breaches are caused by outsiders, while a significant proportion is caused by human factors or negligence (27%). Data is continuously exposed or compromised everywhere globally: a daily average of 25 million records were compromised or exposed during the first half of 2018 (ENISA, 2019). Most data breaches occur in the health sector (approximately a quarter of the total). Data leakage is a form of data breach occurring when data is transferred digitally or physically from an internal system to an outsider recipient. Finally, a cyber-criminal may access detailed information about a single individual and consequently be able to create a plausible profile to commit a variety of frauds, a cyber-threat dubbed "identity theft" by ENISA. That includes the use of counterfeit credit or debit cards, phishing, networks' or systems' access, for example.

- **Insider threat**

Current or former employees may pose an "insider threat" to the organization they belong to (or belonged to). They may intentionally perpetrate a cyber-attack. They may unintentionally become a tool for attackers to infiltrate the organization's system. Or, they may negligently expose their organization to potential sources of cyber-attacks by omitting to observe the organization cybersecurity internal code.

Almost 77% of companies' data breaches are caused intentionally or unintentionally by insiders (ENISA, 2019).

- **Physical manipulation, damage, theft, loss**

Physical threats are considered a cybersecurity threat by ENISA to the extent that they may involve the criminal appropriation of users' data (for example, through the theft of a digital device such as a smartphone, laptop, or tablet). A significant proportion of data breaches are due to physical attacks (between 11% and 16%). At the time of writing, ATM physical attacks are on the rise in Europe and the US.

- **Cryptojacking**

Cryptojacking is a relatively new phenomenon whereby hackers take control of the target's device or system and use its processing power to mine cryptocurrencies, often without the target being aware of it (see Chapter 6 for a description of the functioning of blockchain, the technology underlying cryptocurrencies). ENISA 2019 report that during the first quarter of 2018, cryptojacking malware grew by 629%. This type of cybercrime is on the rise, particularly as an alternative to ransomware. It indeed confers several advantages to the attackers, for example, because it relies on the exploitation of informatics systems' unused computing power (from powerful computers to smartphones). Victims are not prompted to pay any "ransom" for their data, meaning that it is less likely to attract attention from law enforcers. It is also a relatively simple threat to implement, making entry into this illicit activity particularly easy (ENISA, 2019).

- **Cyber espionage**

Cyber espionage is typically a threat from state actors. It can target a strategic economic sector of a specific country, for example key infrastructures such as transport, telecommunication, energy, health, and banking systems. According to (ENISA, 2019), China, Russia, and Iran stand out as the actors most capable of exerting a cyber-espionage threat on other countries.

7.2 Opportunities and challenges[5]

Despite the costs of malicious activities in the cyberspace, markets do not autonomously converge to society's optimal levels of cybersecurity.[6] Several economic dynamics contribute to the emergence of this *market failure*. Most importantly:

---

[5] This section draws extensively from Sen (2018). For an economic analysis of cybersecurity issues, see also Anderson (2001), Anderson and Moore (2006), and Moore (2010).

[6] It would be hard to quantify an "optimal level of cybersecurity" for society. As explained above, that level cannot be "the level where no cyber incident occurs", since that level is not attainable: any digital system will always entail some cyber vulnerability. We know, however, that the optimal level of cybersecurity in the EU is above what

- **Asymmetric information and moral hazard.** Some actors know more about the vulnerability of the system to cyber-attacks and may exploit their greater knowledge to their advantage, or may simply be unable to signal the quality of their security options
- **Negative externalities.** Actors that fail to implement security procedures do not bear all the costs of a cyber-attack; they hence have less interest in investing in protection than if they took into account the cost they impose on the economy and society when a cyber-incident occurs
- **Positive externalities**. Implementing security procedures has a beneficial spillover effect on every other actor in the system. But that positive spillover effect is not taken into account by single agents, who thus invest in security less than the optimal level from a system's point of view. Students may note the similarities with the market failure generated by telecom or data investment, as discussed in Chapter 4 and 5.

To see this in detail, let us identify the following categories of actors:[7]

(1) Organizations
(2) Single users
(3) Software developers
(4) Public enforcers

(1) Organizations

Security in the cyberspace depends on the contribution of everybody in the system. Despite the potentially high cost of cyber-attacks, however, companies may be reluctant to dedicate a significant part of their budget to cybersecurity expenses. Costs may be high and not easy to justify in the short term, especially for smaller enterprises. It is likewise expensive to invest in monitoring activities to keep track of potential new vulnerabilities that emerge in the software used by companies.[8]

Companies offering Internet-related goods or services, Internet service providers, and platforms interact in the same ecosystem. However, because the security of that space depends on the efforts of all involved actors, any of them has **incentive to free-ride** on the efforts of the others. Therefore, instead of investing in security, they may expect others in the value chain to do it (Kunreuther & Heal, 2003). An Internet service provider can, for example, provide some security for the other actors in the ecosystem by monitoring traffic. Likewise, if others in the value chain do not implement security measures, they are likely to affect the vulnerability of the whole

---

is currently observed in EU markets, because the trade-off between (a) the cost of increasing security and (b) the expected cost of cyber incidents for the economy is still in favour of the latter.

[7] Note however that this is a simplification, as market players may well be in multiple categories at the same time.

[8] For a review of the literature on cybersecurity for company in "industry 4.0", see Lezzi, et al. (2018).

system. Hence, companies have little incentive to invest in security, knowing that their organization's overall level of security is largely dependent on what the other actors do. No matter what they do, they are potentially exposed because of others' negligence.

The problem of this disincentive to invest in security is exacerbated by the **difficulty of attributing liability in a highly complex environment**. If a security breach occurs, companies may be able to quickly shift the blame away from themselves, instead of calling into question the behaviour of other actors in the value chain. Or they may hide it to avoid paying its reputational cost. By doing so, they prevent their clients, users, or companies affected by the breach to take the necessary precautionary measures. For example, the ride-hailing company Uber was subject to a data breach exposing data of 600,000 US drivers in November 2016. Still, it publicly acknowledged the breach only a year after in November 2017: a neat example of failure to report a cybersecurity incident.

It is also unclear how much companies really pay in terms of reputational loss after being the victim of a cybersecurity incident. It may be possible to observe a disconnect between the perception of threats in the digital space and those of a more "traditional" nature in the physical world.[9] If the bank where an individual keeps their savings could be easily robbed and their loss not refunded, customers would surely run to that bank, take back their money, and bring it to another bank. Not so if the company is not a bank but a software company exposing users' data to potential data breaches. After the Cambridge Analytica scandal (see Chapter 5), 26% of Facebook users claimed that they used Facebook more, while 49% reported unchanged habits.[10] Ablon et al. (2016) find that only 11% of respondents to their survey stopped dealing with the affected company following a data breach. Other studies[11] have shown that cyber-attacks can affect companies' stock value, but only in the short term. In the long term, the effect of the cyber-incident fades away, leaving little incentive for companies to increase their cyber-resilience to reassure their investors.

(2) Single users

Similarly to the case of organizations, the security of the system depends on every single user. It is sufficient for one user not to abide by the security guidelines to generate a vulnerability in the entire system that cyber-attackers can exploit. The **weakest link** of a system determines the overall level of security of that system. And yet, often, users have very little understanding of the importance of cybersecurity in the context in which they operate. Experts use the acronym **PEBCAK** to indicate that, often, when there is a security breach, the *problem exists between chair and keyboard*. It is not the software, but the human who uses it that is ultimately causing

---

[9] Bounded rationality and users' inconsistent behaviour is analysed in Chapter 14 on disinformation.
[10] Source: Ipsos, Thomson Reuters.
[11] See, for example, Cavusoglu, et al. (2004), Acquisti, et al. (2006).

the trouble. In 2017, an analysis by Verizon (Verizon, 2017) suggested that 65% of security breaches involved the exploitation of a vulnerability caused by a human. According to the 2019 update (Verizon, 2020) of the Verizon report, 35% of security breaches could be attributed to human error. There were more than 4.5 billion Internet users worldwide in 2020. The vast majority of them do not encrypt sensitive data; do not run the necessary updates to patch discovered vulnerabilities in the software they use; do not regularly change their passwords; they share passwords with friends or family, or use passwords that can be easily hacked. It is not surprising that malware, web-based attacks, and phishing still top the ENISA ranking of cybersecurity threats in Europe (see Figure 7.3). Users may not update their software for a variety of reasons: because they are not fully aware of the importance of the update; because it takes time to do so, and they, therefore, prefer to postpone

Top Threats 2017	Assessed Trends 2017	Top Threats 2018	Assessed Trends 2018	Change in ranking
1. Malware	➲	1. Malware	➲	→
2. Web Based Attacks	⬆	2. Web Based Attacks	⬆	→
3. Web Application Attacks	⬆	3. Web Application Attacks	➲	→
4. Phishing	⬆	4. Phishing	⬆	→
5. Spam	⬆	5. Denial of Service	⬆	↑
6. Denial of Service	⬆	6. Spam	➲	↓
7. Ransomware	⬆	7. Botnets	⬆	↑
8. Botnets	⬆	8. Data Breaches	⬆	↑
9. Insider threat	➲	9. Insider Threat	⬇	→
10. Physical manipulation/ damage/ theft/loss	➲	10. Physical manipulation/ damage/theft/loss	➲	→
11. Data Breaches	⬆	11. Information Leakage	⬆	↑
12. Identity Theft	⬆	12. Identity Theft	⬆	→
13. Information Leakage	⬆	13. Cryptojacking	⬆	NEW
14. Exploit Kits	⬇	14. Ransomware	⬇	↓
15. Cyber Espionage	⬆	15. Cyber Espionage	⬇	→

Legend: Trends: ⬇ Declining ➲ Stable, ⬆ Increasing
Ranking: ↑ Going up, → Same, ↓ Going down

Figure 7.3 Top cybersecurity threats according to the European Network Information Security Agency (ENISA), 2019

https://www.enisa.europa.eu/publications/enisa-threat-landscape-report-2018 page 19

it for an indefinite amount of time; or because they are afraid that the system may not work smoothly after the update. Training programmes have been found to have minimal effect on changing users' habits. Conversely, software developers refrain from imposing hard constraints on their users (such as, imposing the use of strong passwords or following mandatory programme updates), as this would impact the appeal of their software. Customers are less likely to buy software that is known to impose a "burden" on users.

(3) Software developers

Software developers may lack incentives to develop secure software for a "miscoordination dynamic", typically observed in markets with strong asymmetries of information (Akerlof, G. A., 1978). Given its complexity, companies and users cannot verify the strength of the software they are buying from a security standpoint. Unfortunately, this happens also with repeated purchases, as a security incident does not necessarily provide evidence to the buyer that the software they bought was unsafe. As we have seen above, it is often difficult to pin down where the system's security failed and who is to blame for it. As a result, software developers have little incentive to invest in increasing the security of their product: if they did so, they would not be able to monetize the higher quality with a price premium because buyers, failing to appreciate it, would not be ready to pay that premium. As pointed out in Sen (2018), this problem may be exacerbated by lack of competition. If customers have little choice when deciding which software to buy, developers have little incentive to develop secure software or to patch vulnerabilities when discovered.[12]

Conversely, software developers may reward programmers for spotting and fixing vulnerabilities in their software or rely on *zero-days markets* to identify "exploits". Zero-days exploits are vulnerabilities that have not yet been discovered or patched by the software developer. When discovered, the information about the bug may be sold to the vendor in exchange for a "bounty". The reward can be very high: in the past, bounties as high as US $250,000 for an iOS bug, US $200,000 for a bug in Internet Explorer or Chrome, and US $120,000 for a vulnerability of Windows have been paid. The legitimacy of these markets and strategies by software vendors is debated amongst experts. While it is generally accepted that those markets may help identify vulnerabilities, they may also generate a perverse dynamic by creating the incentives to open vulnerabilities in the first place.

It is believed that **open source software** is paradoxically *less exposed* to cybersecurity risks. This is because when many programmers are involved in the continuous development of software, there is a higher chance that vulnerabilities are spotted by someone throughout the development or update process.

---

[12] The effect of competition on digital markets is explored in detail in Chapter 8. See also: Jo, A.M. (2017).

(4) Public enforcers

Cybercrime is putting growing pressure on public enforcement systems: an increasingly digitized economy and society is accompanied by a parallel trend in crime, which is progressively migrating from the physical to the cyber space. Criminal activities thus become more elusive and harder to pin down geographically. A whole global underground economy is flourishing using the Dark Web as a safe space for illegal activities. The Dark Web is a subset of the Deep Web, the Internet layer where websites are not indexed and are therefore not reachable through search engines. Criminals can now find new targets and vulnerabilities to exploit: *crime 4.0* can target the "Internet of Things" space, from surveillance cameras, TVs, smart kitchen appliances to pacemakers and self-driving vehicles. The more connected the world is, the easier it is to spot a weak link to exploit. Yet, public law enforcers, such as *cyber-police* units, struggle to match the same level of technological progress achieved by cyber-criminals. Attackers can exploit a first-mover advantage, accessing information at a level of granularity that is often out of reach for enforcers, implying that defenders tend to always lag behind hackers (Chia, et al., 2016). The entry barriers for hackers are falling, together with the cost of accessing the technological tools that allow committing crimes in the cyberspace. Any teenager with a computer and access to the Internet can potentially become a hacker from their own bedroom. Likewise, the psychological cost of committing a cyber-crime is mitigated by the distance between the attacker and the victim. Robbing a bank may entail psychological distress for perpetrators. Criminals may fear for their own safety. They may be disturbed by the perception of the harm inflicted on the actual victims and by the breaking of institutional, cultural, or moral constraints. Pursuing a cybercrime instead may often feel less real and tangible, despite having similar consequences to robbing a bank, precisely because it is played out in a physically distant context. This may contribute to explain the emergence of crypto-jacking as an increasingly frequent form of cybercriminal activity (see above, Section 7.1). Cybercrime is perceived as a relatively safe and cheap crime activity, and it has thus exploded in a variety of forms that are extremely difficult to capture by the enforcers.

7.3 Dilemmas for policymakers

Three key insights can be drawn from the previous two sections:

- digital systems always display vulnerabilities exploitable by cyber-attackers
- cybersecurity is nevertheless essential to minimize risk and therefore to ensure that the digital economy can flourish
- markets alone do converge to the optimal level of cybersecurity.

The conclusion is that public policy is needed to render the risk of cyber-threats manageable. It can do so by aligning the different public and private actors' incentives to minimize exposure to security failure while still promoting the production, supply, and adoption of digital technologies. Once again, it is helpful to emphasize that public policy should not aim to eliminate cyber risks entirely. This is arguably impossible, given the complexity of digitized systems, nor desirable, as costs would likely outweigh benefits. As the OECD (2015c, p. 35) points out:

> It is impossible to protect an activity against every potential threat, vulnerability and incident. Therefore, choices have to be made with respect to the selection and implementation of digital security risk management measures ("security measures"). Further, security measures are unlikely to be neutral with respect to the activity they protect. They can create different kinds of barriers and constraints for this activity. For example, they can increase financial cost, system complexity and time to market, as well as reduce performance, usability, capacity to evolve, innovation, and user convenience. They can also generate privacy threats (. . .) and other adverse social consequences. These constraints and adverse effects can be addressed and mitigated, but at a cost.
>
> Digital security risk management roots security-related decisions in the economic and social reality of the activity at stake. It prevents decisions from being made in isolation, from a separate technical or security point of view. It drives the selection of "security measures" which are appropriate to, and commensurate with, the risk and activity at stake. In so doing, it ensures that the security measures will support the economic and social activities at stake, and will not undermine them, for example, by inappropriately closing the environment or reducing functionality in a manner that would limit the possibility of taking advantage of ICTs to innovate and increase productivity.

To create a **cyber-secure environment**, policymakers should look at solutions that address the issues identified in the previous sections from multiple angles. Similarly to other areas of policy interventions analysed in this book, cybersecurity strategies should rely on a careful mix of non-binding guidance, regulatory action, and enforcement action (see Chapter 8 for an extensive discussion on the relationship between *ex-ante* regulation and *ex-post* enforcement). These may entail new laws, co-regulatory and self-regulatory measures, sectoral guidelines, and the definition of industry standards, for example.

A general observation should be made here. As much as digitalization concerns every aspect of the economy, any cybersecurity policy strategy should not be narrowly focused on the ICT sector. Instead, it should encompass the whole economy. This could imply, for example, broadening the definition of *critical infrastructure*, or infrastructure which is of crucial importance for the functioning of the economy, such as transport or health. A new definition could include a whole ecosystem of interconnected infrastructures, public entities and organizations of a private nature that do not necessarily belong to that sector but are intimately related to it in such a way that their vulnerabilities are vulnerabilities for the ecosystem as a whole.

Likewise, fostering competition at any level of the cybersecurity value chain (software developers, adopters, business customers) has significant beneficial effects. It increases actors' incentives to adopt more cyber resilient strategies: the more competitive the environment where they operate, the higher the likelihood of being "punished" by their customers if they do not offer safe products.

From a micro perspective, strategies may target market failures that affect organizations, business, and public entities in particular. A key measure is to introduce **mandatory disclosure obligations** in case of security failure.[13] Fostering transparency helps attribute responsibility to the organization that may not have invested enough in cyber protection, thereby heightening the likelihood of an incident. These obligations incentivize companies to adopt solid cybersecurity measures through their potential impact on the reputation of organizations ("naming and shaming" mechanisms). They also allow other affected actors to adopt the necessary measures to avoid further attacks: for example, prompting individual users to change their passwords if the account they have with the attacked company has been compromised. Finally, transparency can help improve the overall resilience of the cyberspace by providing the public with information about the nature of the attacks. It rings a useful bell to remind everybody of the potential costs of being excessively exposed to cyber risks. As we have seen in Chapter 5, Art. 33 of the General Data Protection Regulation envisages a 72-hour maximum delay to notify the supervisory authority that a personal data breach occurred; failure to notify can incur a fine of up to €10 million or 2% of global turnover (whichever is higher). Additional measures could aim to correct the asymmetry of incentives between different actors in the value chain. If, for example, Internet Service Providers (ISP) would be best placed to identify and block certain types of cyber-attacks (e.g. *malware attacks*), they could be compelled to take a more active role in the prevention of attacks and in the reporting and clean-up of affected machines after the attacks have taken place (Moore, 2010).

From a user perspective (both as a single private consumer and as a single actor within an organization), the most straightforward public policy measures aim to increase users' awareness of cybersecurity risks through effective communication strategies. Their goal is to educate users about how to implement basic or advanced security measures. For example, employees can be trained to enhance their alertness to potential external threats such as phishing (see above) and adopt more secure behaviours, such as frequently changing the password they use to login into their company's system. However, training is not necessarily an effective solution to insider threats: training can be too general or infrequent to shift habits. Anecdotal evidence from several case studies shows, for example, that there is no significant difference in the likelihood of clicking on phishing links between employees receiving training and those not receiving training (Sen, 2018). Likewise, awareness campaigns can do little to enhance private users' ability to stay safe online: users tend to underestimate the risk they run online. For example, they often ignore warnings

---

[13] On cybersecurity disclosure and its impact on companies' market valuation, see: Berkman, et al. (2018).

prompted by the system they are connected to (Sen, 2018). A solution to overcome this "security fatigue" could be to compel software developers to oblige users to update their software, therefore addressing discovered vulnerabilities with the released patches. Or to nudge them towards secure behaviours, e.g. with increasingly frequent reminders to run security checks of their system.

Technology suppliers and software developers bear the responsibility to provide products that are *as cybersecure as possible*. Public authorities can deploy guidelines and regulatory frameworks ensuring that technology is **secure by design**, namely that its development follows strict security principles throughout its whole life-cycle: during the definition of concepts and requirements; the design of the software, its development, and implementation; testing, deployment, and integration with different technologies and informatic systems; maintenance; and disposal (see ENISA (2019), for an extensive description).

Certification systems can be used to address the information asymmetry between developers, sellers, and adopters/buyers, described in the previous section.[14] Independent bodies can verify the reliability of a particular technology, vis-à-vis a set of potential cyber-threats, and issue a conformity stamp to be used by the seller to signal the quality of its product. Certification has its own limitations, though: it is intrinsically complex to ascertain the level of security of a software, the vulnerabilities of which may hide within millions of coding strings. Moreover, the certification process can be slow, and by the time it is completed, new, sophisticated cyber-threats may have emerged, rendering vulnerable a certified cyber-secure software. Certification can, in other words, give a false sense of security to users. Alternatively, cybersecurity certifications can target software's design and deployment process rather than the final outcome, i.e. the software or the technology itself. This approach can enable more flexible certification, better able to adapt to the fast-evolving cyber-threats context.

Finally, **developers may be held liable** if an intrinsic vulnerability of their software ultimately harms its users. However, ascertaining liability in this context is a highly complex and lengthy exercise. It is challenging to determine whether the origin of the cybersecurity failure is in the negligence of the software developer. The origin may lie somewhere else, and the developer may have taken all measures expected to guarantee what authorities deem a reasonable level of security for the software they developed.

Cybersecurity enforcers' challenge is to create the conditions for effectively responding to attacks in an environment where identifying sources and assigning responsibility is complex, and the boundaries of relevant jurisdictions are blurred.

This may entail providing enforcing agencies with tools to access informatics systems for monitoring purposes while guaranteeing safeguards to protect privacy. Enforcers need to keep up with the fast-evolving criminal environment around

---

[14] See also: Matheu-García, et al. (2019).

them. That means they must be equipped with the necessary skills (experts in cybersecurity, AI, data analytics) and access to the same sophisticated technology available to cyber-attackers. Most importantly, the effectiveness of enforcement in the context of cybersecurity crucially depends on enforcing authorities' ability to **cooperate**: to share the information they acquire during their investigations, to coordinate action on the ground at different levels of government, from local to central, and to actively participate in the creation of efficient cooperation networks at international level.

It is equally important to foster cooperation between public and private entities, facilitating the flow of information regarding past experiences, creating an environment of mutual trust and increasing the economy's overall ability to anticipate and react to emerging threats.

7.4 The European Union's perspective

In the previous sections, we have seen that one of the crucial challenges for cybersecurity is keeping up with a fast-changing criminal environment. Cyber-criminals may have easy access to sophisticated technologies while being highly fluid and geographically dispersed. Unsurprisingly, we have concluded that policy initiatives to target this issue must entail a high degree of consistency across the Digital Single Market.

To reinforce the point made in Section 7.2: the level of security of technology value chains is defined by the *weakest link*: a vulnerability in a single, seemingly minor part of the system implies a vulnerability for the whole system. Similarly, jurisdictions that are strongly interrelated exert potentially negative externalities on each other. A negligent approach to cybersecurity by one Member State in the European Union can imply a higher vulnerability for the whole Single Market. Therefore, the European Commission plays an essential role in deploying a supra-national approach to creating a secure European cyberspace.

The first important step in the cybersecurity space taken by the European Commission was the release of the European Union Cybersecurity Strategy in 2013 (European Commission, 2013). The strategy relies on five pillars:

1. *Increasing cyber-resilience*. Increase Member States' capacity to anticipate and react to cyber-attacks and incidents and create the conditions for closer cooperation and information exchange between public and private bodies across the whole European Union. This includes expanding the role of the **European Network and Information Security Agency (ENISA)**, established in 2004 and based in Greece (see Box 7.1 below), as a point of reference for Member States in the process of developing stronger national cyber-resilience strategies

---

Box 7.1   The European Union Agency for Network and Information Security (ENISA) (ENISA, 2021)

Set up in 2004, ENISA is the EU Agency for cybersecurity policy and enforcement. The Agency works closely with Member States and the private sector to deliver advice and solutions to cyber-threats and improve their capabilities. This support includes, inter alia:

- the pan-European Cybersecurity Exercises;
- the development and evaluation of National Cybersecurity Strategies;
- CSIRTs cooperation and capacity building;
- studies on IoT and smart infrastructures, addressing data protection issues, privacy-enhancing technologies and privacy on emerging technologies, eIDs and trust services, identifying the cyber-threat landscape, and others.

ENISA also supports the development and implementation of the European Union's policy and law on matters relating to network and information security (NIS) and assists Member States and EU institutions, bodies and agencies in establishing and implementing vulnerability disclosure policies on a voluntary basis.

Since 2019, following the coming into force of the Cybersecurity Act (Regulation 2019/881), ENISA has been tasked to prepare "European cybersecurity certification schemes", which serve as the basis for certification of products, processes, and services that support the delivery of the Digital Single Market.

The European Cybersecurity Act introduces processes to support the cybersecurity certification of ICT products, processes, and services. In particular, it establishes EU comprehensive rules and European schemes for cybersecurity certification.

---

2. *Drastically reducing cybercrime*. Empower enforcers with stronger investigative and prosecution powers and coordinate the work of the enforcing agencies of different Member States. For example, the European Commission committed to supporting the European Cybercrime Centre (EC3) that Europol launched in the same year, 2013, as the European focal point in the fight against cybercrime

3. *Developing EU cyber defence policy and capabilities related to the Common Security and Defence Policy (CSDP)*. Create an institutional environment where civilian and military entities cooperate, complementing each other to protect cyber assets

4. *Developing the industrial and technological resources for cybersecurity*. Favour the flourishing of a cybersecurity single market, stimulating the growth of the production, supply, and demand of cybersecurity technological tools and increasing public and private investment in Research and Development in the cybersecurity field

5. *Establishing a coherent international cyberspace policy for the EU and promote core EU values.* Foster cooperation with different international organizations such as the Council of Europe, OECD, UN, OSCE, NATO, the African Union, the Association of Southeast Asian Nations (ASEAN), and the Organization of American States (OAS), as well as strengthening bilateral cooperation, particularly with the United States in the context of the EU-US Working Group on Cybersecurity and Cybercrime.

In other words, since its inception, the EU approach to cybersecurity envisages five areas where action is broadly necessary: building resilience, fighting cybercrime, developing cyber-defence, fostering cybersecurity in the Single Market, and steering a coherent international approach.

A couple of years later, cybersecurity featured prominently in two broader European Commission strategies. Fighting cybercrime was one of the three key priorities of the **European Agenda on Security,** adopted by the European Commission in 2015 (European Commission, 2015). And building a trusted and secure digital economy through enhanced cybersecurity capabilities was listed as a crucial element of the **Digital Single Market Strategy** in 2015 (see Chapter 1 for a description).

The strategies laid down the basis upon which the EU cybersecurity puzzle has been gradually built. That includes several complementary initiatives relevant to the cyberspace but naturally "belonging" to other broad policy areas. Such as defence or education. In 2020, the European Commission launched its Digital Education Action Plan, see Chapter 12, which could potentially be very beneficial to cybersecurity given the relevance of insider cyber-threats and the issue with skills in combatting threats, as discussed in Section 7.2. In 2017, the EU Council endorsed the creation of a framework to address cyber-attacks by foreign powers from a defence policy perspective: the *Cyber Diplomacy Toolbox.* The Toolbox provides Member States with the ability to coordinate and impose international sanctions for cybercrimes. While the coordination of a consistent EU approach is essential, it is, however, unclear how effective a tool sanctions can be in the cyberspace: researchers have noted, for example, that US sanctions imposed on Iran, North Korea, and Russia did not significantly affect their cyber-offence policy (Soesanto, 2018).

7.4.1 The Network and Information Security (NIS) Directive

The first notable EU legislative act specific to cyberspace is the **Directive on Network and Information Security** (NIS Directive) (Directive (EU) 2016/1148). It was adopted by the Council and the European Parliament in July 2016 and entered into force in August 2016, while Member States had until May 2018 to transpose the Directive into their national laws. The Directive targets[15]

[15] art. 4(1).

network and information systems. These are defined as electronic communication *networks*, *devices* performing automatic processing of digital data, or *the digital data* stored or processed by those networks or devices. According to the Directive, "security of network and information systems" refers to the ability of network and information systems to resist, at a given level of confidence, "any action that compromises the availability, authenticity, integrity or confidentiality of stored, transmitted, or processed data or the related". The NIS Directive rests on three key action areas:

- leverage on Member States, pushing them to prepare to respond to cyber incidents, for example, through a national "Computer Security Incident Response Team" and establishing a national authority responsible for the enforcement of the NIS Directive
- facilitate cooperation and exchange of information between Member States
- requiring operators of "essential services" to:
  o "take appropriate and proportionate technical and organizational measures to manage the risks posed to the security of network and information systems which they use in their operations",
  o to prevent and minimize the impact of potential incidents and swiftly notify the competent national authority or the CSIRT when an incident occurs.[16]

The NIS Directive considers "essential sectors" to be the following: energy (electricity, oil, gas), transport (air, rail, water, and road transport), banking, financial market infrastructures, health sector, drinking water supply and distribution, and digital infrastructure.

The idea of the NIS Directive is to create an environment of cyber-responsibility around key services: it does not list specific measures or rules that organizations must follow. Instead, it provides an overall framework whereby operators are incentivized to adopt efficient security policies, adapting them to address evolving threats, if necessary. If operators fail to comply, they run the risk of being heavily fined: Member States can impose their maximum penalty level; the UK, for example, can levy a fine of up to £17 million for a breach of the NIS Directive transposition law.

A 2019 European Commission report (European Commission, 2019c) assessed the consistency of the approaches taken by Member States in the identification of the operators of essential services. In fact, a uniform approach by Member States is deemed crucial to reduce the risks of internal market distortions. The report stresses that the process of identifying Member States' essential services has triggered an overall assessment of the risks associated with operators in almost all countries, which has to be considered an important achievement of the NIS Directive. The report, however, stresses that Member States adopted diverging approaches in their methodology, resulting in significant fragmentation, including in terms of the scope

---

[16] art. 14 NIS directive.

of application of the NIS Directive. The very same operators may be identified as a provider of an essential service in one Member State but not in another. Some Member States have also expanded the scope of the NIS Directive, adding other sectors to the list of essential services, such as: *information infrastructures* (e.g. data centres, server farms), *government services* (e.g. electronic services for citizens), *environment* (e.g. disposal of hazardous waste), and *education* (e.g. authorities in charge of national exams). This suggests that other key sectors are potentially vulnerable to cyber-attacks and the NIS Directive failed to take that into account. Moreover, the 2019 report underlined the lack of proactive coordination between Member States and called for stronger cross-border cooperation to achieve convergence in applying the NIS Directive. As we have seen above, cross-border coordination is an essential element of any effective cybersecurity strategy.

In December 2020, the European Commission proposed a revision of the NIS Directive. The proposal was dubbed **NIS 2 Directive** ((European Commission, 2020); at the time of writing, the proposal had still to be adopted by the EU legislators). The proposed NIS 2 Directive aims to address the shortcoming of the NIS Directive, also taking into account the evolution of the cyber-threat landscape from 2016. As we have seen, threats have become increasingly widespread in the economy. Therefore, the NIS 2 Directive attempts to expand the scope of the NIS directive. For example, it targets additional economic sectors (such as food production, manufacturing of medical devices, postal and courier services) and indicates clearly that all medium or large companies in the relevant sectors are within the directive's scope. The proposal also suggests to supersede the definition of essential service provider of NIS by classifying entities based on their importance and apply to them different supervisory regimes. Admittedly, the European Commission recognized that the NIS Directive failed to trigger a satisfactory level of cyber-resilience of EU business and an homogeneous approach by public authorities across the Single Market. For that reason the proposed NIS 2 directive envisages stronger supervision and enforcement by the competent national authorities. For example, authorities can impose fines of up to 2% of a company's worldwide turnover if "essential and important" entities (as defined by the directive) are found in breach of the cybersecurity risk management framework or their reporting obligations. For the first time companies are deemed responsible for the security of the entire supply chain: companies are required to address cyber vulnerabilities in their relationship with suppliers, for example. Similarly, the proposal attempts to foster more coordination and harmonization by strengthening cooperation between Member States, ENISA, and the European Commission, particularly in their assessment of cyber vulnerabilities in critical supply chains. Along with the NIS 2 Directive, the European Commission also proposed a new directive specifically targeted to increase cybersecurity of "critical entities" in ten sectors (such as health, energy, or transport), proposing a specific framework to "*prevent, resist, absorb and recover*" from critical incidents such as natural hazard or terrorism (see (European Commission, 2020)).

7.4.2 The Cybersecurity Act and the 2020 New Cybersecurity Strategy

In 2017, with its Communication on an "EU Cybersecurity Act," (Regulation (EU) 2019/881), the European Commission released its second package to tackle risks in the cyberspace. The Communication stems from the Digital Single Market Strategy. It is yet another attempt by the European Commission to sharpen its security tools while fostering a homogeneous and organic approach by Member States at the EU level. It defines cybersecurity as *"any activity necessary to protect network and information systems, their users and persons affected by cyber-threats"*.

In contains measures to (a) increase EU-wide cybersecurity capacity (such as the creation of competence centres to help deploy tools to be used in cyber-attacks) and (b) strengthen Member States' criminal law responses in case of non-cash fraud (i.e. to tackle cybersecurity issues in the context of electronic payments such as credit card frauds).

In addition to those measures, the two most significant actions prompted by the Cybersecurity Act are:

(a) the introduction of a series of measures to **strengthen the European Union Agency for Cybersecurity** (ENISA, see box above). The Act expands ENISA's human and budgetary resources from a staff of 84 employees and €11 million budget, to 125 employees and €23 million budget. It tasks ENISA with:
   a. *policy development and implementation*: to provide support to Member States and the European Commission in the design and deployment of cybersecurity policies
   b. *operational cooperation*: to act as focal point for coordination of Member States in response to incidents
   c. *knowledge and information*: to be a "research centre" for cybersecurity—perform analysis, launch information campaigns, foster awareness, become a "hub" for institutional bodies in need of information on cybersecurity
   d. *capacity building*: provide training programmes; support Member States in their efforts to increase their expertise in the cyber space
   e. *market-related tasks*: be in charge of the set-up and roll-out of the Cybersecurity Certification Framework (see below)
(b) the establishment of a **EU Cybersecurity Certification Framework**. Certification schemes are to be based on sets of rules, technical requirements, standards, and procedures proposed by ENISA and endorsed by Member States. Multiple schemes are to be created for several categories of ICT products, processes, and services. The aim is to allow businesses (particularly smaller ones, facing a proportionally higher burden for investment in security) to signal that the technology they use meets strict cybersecurity safety

criteria valid for cross-border, intra-European trade. Notably, the adoption of a scheme is voluntary. Hence companies are not obliged to certify their products or services. However, in the mind of the EU legislator the market should be driving the widespread adoption of EU certification schemes across the whole Single Market.

In December 2020, the European Commission presented an updated Cybersecurity Strategy: **Towards a New Cybersecurity Strategy** (European Commission, 2020). The new strategy is in continuity with the plans set out by the previous strategic communications (particularly the Cybersecurity Act). It hinges on three tools (*regulation, investment,* and *policy*) to intervene in three areas (with a timeline of seven years):

1. resilience, technological sovereignty, and leadership
2. operational capacity to prevent, deter, and respond
3. cooperation to advance a global and open cyberspace.

Specifically concerning investment, the European Commission envisage financing of cybersecurity spending lines of about €2 billion at the EU level by 2027 (the figure does not include investment at a country level and from private corporates).

At the core of the 2020 Cybersecurity Strategy, there lies a legitimate concern: the European Union lacks the ability to leverage its collective strength to protect its economy and react to cyber-threats. Quite the contrary: fragmentation in response has played against cyber-resilience in Europe until today.

Actions for the first area ("**resilience, technological sovereignty and leadership**") include updating the NIS Directive that we discussed above. Indeed, as we have seen, the proposed NIS 2 Directive tries to foster greater cooperation across authorities within the Single Market. The European Commission also proposes the creation of a **European Cyber-Shield**. Private and public entities of significant size rely on Security Operations Centers (SOC) to monitor, analyse, and react to cyber-threats. The proposed cyber-shield would consist of a network of SOCs across the European Union, enhance existing SOCs and help deploy new ones. For example, the European Commission plans to support investment in the training of SOCs' staff. The strategy also envisages the completion and effective implementation of the 5G Toolbox (see Chapter 5) and it flags the possibility of adopting new horizontal regulatory measures to improve cybersecurity in the Internet of Things. For example, manufacturers of connected devices could be required to abide by stringent duty of care standards.

Actions in the second area ("**operational capacity to prevent, deter, and respond**") include the establishment of a **Joint Cyber Unit** at the EU level, with the goal of improving response to cross-border cyber-threats. The Joint Cyber Unit would not establish a new EU body similar to ENISA. Still, it would work as a backstop aggregating the expertise from different EU communities (such as civilian, diplomatic, law enforcement, and defence communities) engaged in cybersecurity matters. It would promote information sharing and prompt awareness across communities, and it would foster the communities' ability to respond and recover in the aftermath of a cyber incident. The European Commission considers the Joint Cyber Unit an essential piece of the puzzle of its cybersecurity crisis management framework. Furthermore, the European Commission considers strengthening its *Cyber Diplomacy Toolbox* (for example, through the release of implementation guidelines) and boosting cyber defence capabilities by leveraging on synergies with the military sector, both at the research and operational level.

Finally, actions in the third area ("**cooperation to advance a global and open cyberspace**") focus on proactively engaging with non-EU partners to enhance cybersecurity globally. Here the goal is to increase the cyber-resilience of the European economy by leveraging on its external dimension. For that purpose, the European Commission places significant emphasis on the importance of international standard-setting processes. The Commission aims to empower the European Union to steer international **standard-setting** processes towards more cyber-secure, "human-centric" standards – for example, strengthening the EU's role to coordinate Member States to "speak with one voice" in international fora. The Commission also plans to establish an informal EU Cyber Diplomacy Network to favour exchanges with non-EU countries and "*promote the EU vision of cyberspace*". At last, the Commission proposes the setup of an **EU External Cyber Capacity Building** Framework (which would include an *agenda*, a *network*, and a *board* encompassing relevant EU institutional stakeholders) to support investment in cyber-resilience and capacity of EU partners (such as the western Balkans).

****

7.5 Case Study: WannaCry Ransomware Attack

The WannaCry ransomware attack took place in May 2017. It had a broad geographic scope, potentially targeting any computer in the world using a Microsoft Windows operating system. It was the first massive-scale global attack in years, infecting more than 200,000 systems worldwide. The UK National Health Service was heavily hit: doctors had to send their patients home, and hospitals' emergency departments had to close. The attack exploited a vulnerability of an old version of the operative system called "EternalBlue", and it affected all systems that had not been updated. In fact, Microsoft had released a patch to the exploit before the attack, but many organizations, from the private and the public sector, had simply not used it or were still running older versions of the Windows operative system that could not be updated.

WannaCry encrypted users' files, holding them hostage and demanding a ransom in bitcoins to "free" them. It employed an incentive scheme crafted to progressively increase pressure on victims to transfer the money (Figure 7.2): the requested payment was $300 initially, then $600, followed by the threat to delete the files permanently if the transfer would not have been made within three days. Cybersecurity experts often suggest not to give in and pay the ransom during a ransomware attack. There is indeed no guarantee that the attackers would abide by their promise and unencrypt the files after the payment is made. In the case of WannaCry, the attackers could not even link each paying user with her computer.

The global cyber-attack was halted by two security researchers, Marcus Hutchins and Jamie Hankins, who discovered the existence of a "kill switch" in WannaCry. Before infecting any system, WannaCry needed to connect to an unregistered web domain. Hutchins and Hankins discovered that registering that web domain and publishing a web page on it would halt further infections. Hutchins and Hankins became known as the "heros" who "saved" the Internet.

The story, as it is told on TechCrunch can be found here: https://techcrunch.com/2019/07/08/the-wannacry-sinkhole/

7.6 Review questions

- Search for three real-life cyber-attacks cases, one for each of the three categories of attack: access, control, and denial. Which one was more harmful from a society perspective and why?
- Explain how a stricter cybersecurity policy can penalize or favour investment in innovation.
- What are the differences between small and big companies regarding their ability and will to become more cyber-secure?
- Can privacy laws affect the level of cybersecurity in a country? How?
- Explain why more coordination at EU level is necessary in order to achieve a higher level of cybersecurity at national level in each Member State.

PART 3

DIGITAL MARKETS

8
An Introduction to Online Platforms

Abstract

The emergence of online platforms has radically changed how goods and services are produced, supplied, and consumed. Online platforms became the primary vehicle of information flow between market players and now play a pivotal role in the economy and society. The magnitude of benefits brought by platforms cannot be overstated. Day-to-day benefits and gains range from easier communication thanks to social media and new types of online services, to the convenience and reduced transaction costs related to online purchases and home delivery, to the ubiquitous access to information offered by Internet search engines. But at the same time, as a small number of tech companies grow in dominance in the globally integrated business environment, non-negligible downsides have emerged: platforms have a great potential to cause harm. Given the complexity and the novelty of their business dynamics, market failures are particularly tricky to identify and address. It is the job of policymakers to verify whether the current regulatory framework is still adequate to ensure the correct functioning of markets and, if not, to propose efficient solutions. Updating competition policy and regulatory tools may be amongst those.

8.1 Background

The rise of the "**platform economy**" is one of the most prominent digital-age phenomena.[1] It is expected that, by 2021, 20% of all activities any individual will have engaged in would involve at least one of the top seven digital giants (by market capitalization: Google, Apple, Facebook, Amazon, Baidu, Alibaba, and Tencent; all seven have business models revolving around online platforms) (Gartner, 2017b). Today, the biggest online platforms have user bases comparable to the most populated countries in the world (Figure 8.1). In January 2021, Facebook reached more than 2.7 billion active users; in 2021 China's and India's populations were 1.44 billion and 1.39 billion respectively.

Platforms are not a recent discovery. Before the advent of the digital economy, the "physical" world flourished with examples of successful platform business models. For example, credit cards are multi-sided platforms allowing buyers to buy

---

[1] The economic literature on online platforms is vast. To mention few relevant contributions on the general background and definitions: Tiwana, et al. (2010), Gawer (2014), Hagiu and Wright (2015), Parker, et al. (2016), Martens (2016), de Reuver, et al. (2018).

Digital Economic Policy. Mario Mariniello, Oxford University Press.
© Mario Mariniello (2022). DOI: 10.1093/oso/9780198831471.003.0008

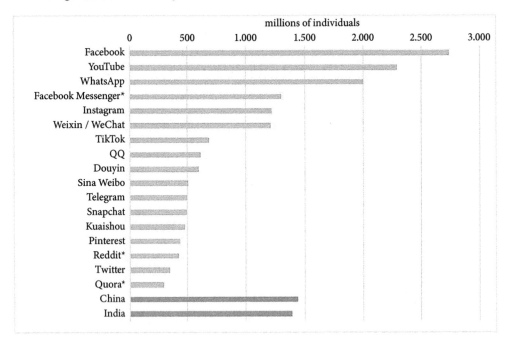

Figure 8.1 Online platforms' user base and countries' population, January 2021
https://datareportal.com/social-media-users

from merchants interconnecting their respective bank accounts. Newspapers are platforms where advertisers meet readers. Shopping malls attract shoppers and retailers: the shoppers find it convenient to access a wide range of supply in the same place; the retailers exploit their collective power of attraction and enjoy a higher demand for their products.[2]

With the Internet, however, physical barriers have become less relevant. And platforms that use the Internet to interconnect different groups of market players have become highly successful. Online platforms leverage the Internet in order to meet their users' needs everywhere and at any time, tackling economically inefficient uses of resources and inducing an explosion of market opportunities. For example, young cyclists in need of money may have some spare time to lend but may not be able to commit to a full-time job; small restaurants may wish to reach hungry clients unwilling or unable to leave home, but may not be able to afford the investment necessary to set up their own delivery network. Online platforms such as Deliveroo and UberEats provide an easy way to meet the two needs and create economic value mutually: in fact, a transaction bringing benefits to all parties involved—the platform, the cyclists, the restaurants, and the clients—was unlikely to materialize had it not been made possible by the platform itself.

---

[2] For an economic analysis of platforms which is not strictly confined to the digital environment, see: Rochet and Tirole (2003), Rochet and Tirole (2006), Boudreau and Hagiu (2009), and Evans and Schmalensee (2013).

Box 8.1   The Platform Economy

Online platforms emerged as the most profitable business model worldwide. Platforms can be very light on assets since they can generate value leveraging on the scale of their network. Despite being the world's largest accommodation company, Airbnb, for example, does not own any real estate. Thanks to minimal marginal costs, online platforms can often expand very quickly, in stark contrast with traditional companies.

Currently, the most successful online platforms can be found in the US and China. By 2020, Apple, Amazon, Alphabet (Google), and Microsoft had surpassed the $1 trillion market valuation: they are all *platform* businesses. European platforms instead struggle to scale up and to be competitive at a global level.

(Evans & Gawer, 2016) classify platforms based on their primary purpose:

- Transaction – they facilitate the exchange of value between users, e.g. eBay;
- Innovation – they provide a basis allowing other complementary technologies to develop, e.g. Intel;
- Integrated – they are both transaction and innovation oriented, e.g. Amazon;
- and Investment – they hold a platform portfolio and act as holding company or active platform investor, e.g. Naspers.

Europe is lagging far behind North America and Asia in Transaction and Integrated platforms; it can achieve reasonably good performance levels on innovation, but it fails to develop that innovation into significant commercial activities. This is a recurrent problem of the European economy, as we have often seen throughout this book.

8.1.1   What is an online platform?

A definition that would single-out online platform business models from any other type of business is hard to come by.[3] The online platforms' ecosystem is very heterogeneous. One may wonder whether Tinder has more in common with Wikipedia and Android than with Netflix or Kayak.com. And there exists no comprehensive characterization that experts unanimously recognize as most accurate.

A definition was proposed by the European Commission in its 2015 "public consultation on the regulatory environment for platforms, online intermediaries, data and cloud computing and the collaborative economy" (European Commission, 2015c).

---

[3] Hein, et al. (2019) have a good overview of platform ecosystems' definition. A general overview of definitions in the literature is in de Reuver, et al. (2018). Hagiu and Wright (2015) propose a definition which is well grounded in the traditional economic theory on multi-sided platforms. That definition is however narrower than the one adopted by the European Commission (for example: they emphasize the need for each side of the platform to make a platform specific investment, such as compiling a profile on a social network).

"online platforms are undertakings operating in two (or multi)-sided markets, which use the Internet to enable interactions between two or more distinct but interdependent groups of users so as to generate value for at least one of the groups."

Consistently with Gawer and Srnicek (2021), I believe that the European Commission's definition is a good starting point for the analysis that follows. Quite tellingly, however, one of the goals of the European Commission consultation was to test the suggested definition with stakeholders. The majority of respondents contested it, pointing out that it was **either too narrow** or **too broad**, while potentially overlapping with the definitions of online intermediaries and "information society service" providers (European Commission, 2015c).

Accordingly, as we will see in Section 8.4, the European Commission concluded that to propose a *one-size-fits-all* general regulation for online platforms would be inappropriate and dangerous. That is because the definition exercise is inherently elusive. And a general regulation hinging on a single definition of online platforms would necessarily apply asymmetrically in online markets.

Generally speaking, **rather than coming up with a synthetic definition encompassing all platforms, it is more helpful to identify a set of features** that tend to be displayed by the majority of online platforms.

Multi-sided platforms supply products or services to multiple groups of users. Each group uses the platform to make transactions because the platform can significantly reduce transaction costs between groups of users. Importantly, each group is affected indirectly by the size of the other group. It is easy to see this in the offline examples quoted above: with newspapers, the bigger the pool of readers, the higher the value for advertisers; for credit cards, the bigger the pool of merchants that accept a particular circuit, the higher the value of holding a card belonging to it to make purchases.

Box 8.2   Examples of online platforms

- Internet search engines: *Bing, Google, DuckDuckGo, Baidu*
- Vertical/specialized search tools: *Google shopping, Kelkoo, Twenga, Tripadvisor, Yelp*
- Online market places: *Amazon, eBay, Allegro, Booking.com, Facebook*
- Audio-visual and music platforms: *Deezer, Spotify, SoundCloud*
- Video sharing platforms: *YouTube, Dailymotion*
- Payment systems: *PayPal, Apple Pay*
- Social networks: *Facebook, LinkedIn, Twitter, Tuenti, Tinder, Snapchat, Clubhouse, TikTok*
- Sharing economy platforms: *Airbnb, Uber, Taskrabbit, Bla-bla Car*

Online platforms crucially rely on network effects[4] (students may recall from Chapter 4 that network effects are very important also in telecom markets). Typically, the greater the number of users, the more valuable it is for others to join the platform. Generally speaking, the group of users that generates the strongest positive network effects is also the one that pays the lower price to access the platform's related services. At the extreme, the platform may offer products or services for free on one side of the market (newspaper websites, web search engines, social networks) to maximize the value generated and charge higher joining fees on other sides of the platform (to advertisers, for example). The incentive for platforms to attract users is higher when users cannot "**multi-home**"; that is, when users are unable, or cannot afford, to join more than one platform simultaneously.[5]

Network effects can materialize on the same side of the platform (such as in the case of social networks, where a bigger pool of users tend to be more attractive for those who wish to join) or between sides (such as in the case of sharing economy platforms, where the size of the network of service suppliers and that of buyers increase the value for buyers and suppliers respectively—see Chapter 11). Network effects may also be adverse: from a user perspective, there may be an optimal size on same-side networks. If the network is bigger than the optimal level, increasing the size of the network diminishes the value of the platform for those users. For example, think of an online dating application that needs large networks for each of the involved gender or taste-related sides to be successful. A large pool of users on the women side increases the incentive for heterosexual men to join the dating app. So when the network is relatively small, any other heterosexual woman joining would exert a positive externality on the women already in the pool because she would make the platform a little bit more attractive for men. However, after a certain point, an additional woman in the pool would not increase the value for men (who may already think the pool of female users is large enough to make joining the platform worth the effort or cost). Still, she would increase competition between women and make it less likely for women to match with a partner on the other side. In other words, users may have **complementary** or **substitutional effects** on each other, and that depends on the size of the network.

Online platforms also tend to collect and analyse **large amounts of data** of personal and non-personal nature. As we have seen in Chapter 5, data analytics usually benefits from economies of scale and can help companies to tailor their services on the preferences of their client, enhancing their perceived quality and optimizing the production process. Yet, the ownership of such information confers established online platforms a significant power vis-à-vis users and emerging competitors,

---

[4] On network effects and online platforms, see: Belleflamme and Peitz (2018).
[5] On competitive effects of multi-homing, see: Armstrong and Wright (2007).

leaving scope for potentially harmful practices, explored in greater depth in the next section.

8.2 Opportunities and challenges

8.2.1 The benefits of online platforms[6]

Most of the benefits of online platforms are rather apparent to users, explaining their popularity. Figure 8.2 is based on the results of a public consultation run by the European Commission in 2015. Improved access to information, facilitated communication and interaction, and an increased range of choice were the benefits that achieved the highest consensus amongst respondents. Platforms may have strong pro-competitive effects since they facilitate the emergence of markets and boost the supply of services and goods in the economy. Pro-competitive effects translate into higher quality and lower prices for consumers and business customers. The total effects on the economy are difficult to quantify. Still, estimates may give a sense of magnitude: Brynjolfsson and Oh (2012), for example, report over $100 billion per year in terms of value for consumers in the US generated by free Internet services.

More specifically, online platforms can:

a) *Reduce information asymmetries and facilitate the flow of information between market players*

As we have seen earlier, in economics, the notion of *asymmetric information* is used to indicate a situation in which one of the parties involved in a potential

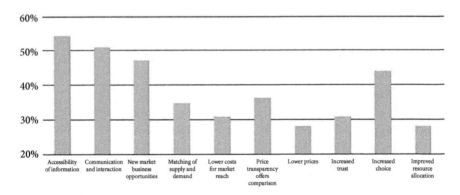

Figure 8.2 The perceived benefits of online platforms (% of respondents to EC's 2016 survey)

European Commission https://www.researchgate.net/figure/Perceived-benefits-of-online-platforms-EuropeanCommission-2016_fig2_320065590

---

[6] For an overview of how platforms create value, see, for example: Hein, et al. (2019).

transaction has a higher level of knowledge about the value of the good or service being exchanged. Information asymmetries are a widespread source of market failure, preventing markets from allocating resources efficiently and maximizing the value generated for society as a whole (see also the appendix). Online platforms can reduce asymmetric information since they intermediate between groups of users with different levels of knowledge. This can happen through a vouching system: the reputation of the platform extends to the sellers that use the platform, reassuring other users that they can trust what they buy from it. Typical examples are GooglePlay or the Apple Store, where the platforms filter bad quality apps out of the ecosystem. Asymmetric information can also be tackled through reputational systems based on users' feedback: TripAdvisor, for example, reduces travellers' risk of eating low-quality food by allowing users to share their experience of different restaurants; in fact, platforms may be able to transform goods or services traditionally considered "experience goods" (that is: goods or services that need to be experienced before a customer can get to know their quality) to "search goods" (that is: goods or services that can be evaluated before being bought or experienced).

b) Make resource allocation more efficient

Central to **sharing economy** platforms (see Chapter 11) is the idea that the full potential of physical or immaterial economic assets (such as time) is often not exploited because actual or perceived transactions costs are too high. Platforms can directly affect those costs and make it very easy to unlock assets' value. For example, Airbnb allows users with excess capacity – in this case, home owners who need to leave their flat vacant for a short period of time or who have a spare unused room at home – to gain a profit from it by making it very easy and safe to rent it out. Thanks to this mechanism, a potentially wasted resource (an empty flat or room) creates economic value (for the owner of the flat and the visitor who rents it).

c) Capture value from economies of scale

Platforms can significantly reduce their operational costs thanks to strong economies of scale: that is, their average costs decrease with the expansion of their user base. Much of the success enjoyed by Amazon, for example, is due to its very low marginal distribution costs, which are made possible by aggregating large quantities of goods in distribution hubs. Amazon's savings are partially passed on to consumers, who may be able to pay lower prices for goods purchased through Amazon's portal.

d) Increase the choice of products and services

Users can use online platforms as coordination devices. The supply of specific products or services may not be profitable if their demand is too weak. However, thanks to platforms' **digital ubiquity**, it may be possible to aggregate a geographically scattered demand and coordinate buyers to make supply economically sustainable. YouTube has significantly increased the accessibility of old movies because it was able to aggregate a large group of potential viewers worldwide, generating enough demand for movies that would otherwise not be broadcast elsewhere.

e) Increase products' value through network effects

As explained in Section 8.1, the exploitation of network effects to create value is central to all online platform business models. Sometimes, however, network effects are not clearly apparent to users, because platforms can rely on complex technologies or economic models. As an example, consider the algorithm behind Google Search: the higher the number of users that search for keywords on Google's universal search engine, the higher is the quality of the search results that are returned to them, because the algorithm "learns" from each user what they really look for when they use one word or another.

f) Shift individual risks and increase trust between peers

Platforms may indirectly work as insurance companies. They aggregate individual transaction risks sustained by single risk-averse individuals and shift that risk from user to the platform itself. For example by offering compensation (such as a full refund) if something goes wrong when the platform is used for a purchase. Like with insurance companies, platforms rely on large numbers of users to reduce the volatility of adverse events. PayPal is an online platform that enables transfers between individuals with no personal connection, offering coverage against potential fraud or misuse.

g) Negatively affect costs for business/prices for consumers

Typically, online platforms reduce **search costs** by aggregating supply in a single place and making it easily accessible and comparable. That also has an indirect negative effect on prices and a positive one on quality, as lowering search costs increases competition between different suppliers. For example, LinkedIn allows employers to easily browse potential candidates to fill a vacancy amongst the numerous users who uploaded their CV on the platform (more than 450 million worldwide as of 2017). Kelkoo, meanwhile, makes it easy to compare the offers of different shops selling online.

h) *Create new products or markets; favour innovation*

Online platforms may allow the emergence of goods and services that would not have existed otherwise because their production strongly depends on the business structure of online platforms. For example, Waze is a GPS-based map service that can suggest the best way to reach a driver's destination based on an accurate estimation of current traffic conditions. That estimation is extrapolated from the aggregated information received by all drivers using Waze at the same time.

8.2.2 Potential risk factors of online platforms

We have seen that online platforms can be very effective in tackling economic inefficiencies. They rely on very low marginal costs and economies of scale to quickly penetrate markets with no geographic boundaries, save for those dictated by the application of different regulatory regimes. Most significantly, online platforms' market power tends to increase with the size of their network because network externalities are often at the core of their business models. These features make platforms very valuable from a societal standpoint, but they also suggest that the malfunctioning of online platform markets can have highly detrimental effects on the economy.

Let us explore the most significant risks associated with online platforms:

a) *Lack of transparency vis-à-vis users (consumers or business)*

As we have seen in Chapter 5, it can be difficult for users to understand how data are collected and processed by online platforms, often because the algorithm used is too complex to be intelligible to the outside world. Users may not realize, for example, when web search results are tailored to users' location or online history. Uber has been blamed for its lack of transparency on surcharge fares, which are believed to lead to unfair prices for drivers as well as for clients (Chen & Sheldon, 2015). Concerns over lack of transparency may explain why Europeans tend not to trust online businesses (see Figure 8.3 for a comparison across different institutions/business types).

b) *Dependency on potentially unreliable reputational mechanisms (ratings, reviews, certifications, trust-marks)*

Studies show that users tend to rely on other users' reviews significantly. For example, a 2014 survey revealed that American and Canadian consumers tend to trust what they read online: 88% of them said they trust online reviews as much as personal recommendations (Anderson M., 2014). Despite that, one may wonder whether reviews are sufficiently reliable and, most importantly, whether they can in

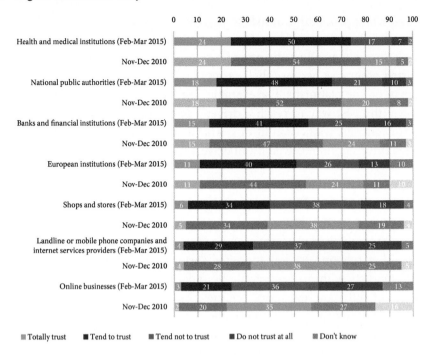

Figure 8.3 Survey on trust towards public and private institutions (% of respondents)
Eurobarometer 2016

practice be considered a substitute for regulatory measures that are meant to protect consumers.[7] For example, EatWith allows private chefs to set up pop-up restaurants in their homes, preparing dinner for guests they do not know in exchange for a payment. After the dinner, users can leave feedback with stars from 1 to 5 to rate the experience. The question is whether the feedback system can successfully replace hygiene and safety regulations applied to restaurants to avoid putting clients' health at risk.

c) Violation of privacy; misuse of personal data

Because of the lack of transparency, users are often unable to control the use of their personal data by online platforms. Lack of transparency exacerbates the risk of privacy violation[8] or misuse of users' personal information, potentially violating their fundamental rights (Articles 7 and 8 of the Charter of Fundamental Rights of the European Union) or leading to discriminatory practices (forbidden by Article 21 of the Charter). As we have seen in Chapter 5, the General Data Protection Regulation aims to protect users from that type of risk.

---

[7] Zervas, et al. (2021) for example suggests that Airbnb ratings tend to be inflated. See also Chapter 11.
[8] Papacharissi and Gibson (2011) argue that, because of social networks, *"in the future, one may be truly private* [only] *for 15 minutes"*.

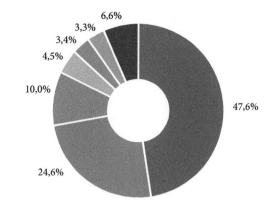

Figure 8.4 shows (in legend): ■ Google ■ Facebook ■ Alibaba.com ■ Amazon ■ Baidu ■ Tencent ■ Other

Figure 8.4 Digital advertisement global market shares, 2019 (% of total revenue) Statista

d) Lack of competition/alternatives

The platform economy is particularly susceptible to the creation of bottlenecks. When network externalities and economies of scale are strong, a natural tendency for markets to concentrate may exist: the bigger the scale, the more efficient and successful the business. For example, Figure 8.4 shows that, in 2019, almost three-quarters of the global market for digital displayed ad revenue was controlled by just two players: Facebook and Google.

The tendency to concentration is all the more evident when companies have data at the core of their business. As Shapiro and Varian (1998) put it: "*Positive feedback* [in the data domain] *makes the strong get stronger and the weak get weaker, leading to extreme outcomes*". The continuous accumulation of a large amount of data makes it very difficult for potential entrants to challenge the incumbent, as they would lack a key input to offer a competitive service. The stability of Google's market share in the search engine market in Europe over the last ten years (Figure 8.5), despite sizeable investments by Microsoft in its rival, Bing, seems to demonstrate well that dynamic (Akerlof, et al., 2018).

Companies may consolidate their market power through "**platform envelopment**" strategies (Eisenmann, et al., 2011). A platform enters into another platform's market by bundling its own functionality with that of the platform which is challenged through entry to leverage shared user relationships and common components. Google, for instance, is active in the markets of search advertising and mobile operating systems, which allows it to have a strong position in mobile search, thanks to data from Android users. In other words, platforms are incentivized to expand into various new markets and diversify their business portfolios to acquire data and create users' "**super-profiles**" (De la Mano & Padilla, 2018). Datasets owned by powerful incumbents often become genuinely unique and very unlikely to be replicated by nascent businesses. Access to unique datasets partly explains the success of services supplied by today's digital leaders: the more data is fed into the analysis, the

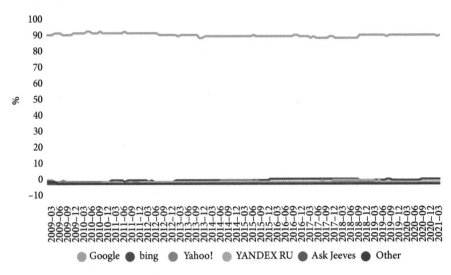

Figure 8.5 Trends in search engines market shares 2010–2021 (Europe)
https://gs.statcounter.com/search-engine-market-share#monthly-200901-202103

better, more tailored, and efficient the service becomes (see also Chapter 5). Data that allows the creation of eerily accurate personal profiles is also crucial to generate cash flow from online advertising that targets citizens at scale: Facebook and Alphabet generate a huge portion of their revenues from ads. The rise of "*digital conglomeratism*" and bundling of different services may result in higher entry barriers for smaller innovators seeking to enter a specific market niche (Bourreau & de Streel, 2019).[9]

When online platforms face little actual or potential competition, they may be able to extract excessive profits from at least one of the users' groups dealing with the platform. Market power is a traditional issue explored by industrial organization theory: a lack of market competition may imply inefficient outcomes. It is important to remember, however, that **market power per se is not necessarily a problem**. Market power may simply be the prize that rewards companies for their superior quality product. And indeed, it would be hard to question the revolutionary quality that Google brought to the web search engine market. Even platform envelopment strategies are *prima facie* pro-competitive: by expanding in different new markets, big platforms increase competitive pressure and generate benefits for the customers of those markets.

Yet the absence of concrete alternatives to powerful online platforms exacerbates all potential issues described in this section, as customers are not really able to exert

---

[9] Another economic dynamic leading to more concentration that may be favoured by online platforms is called "text economics". The dynamic occurs when, for example, search engines tend to always display the most popular links or products (*superstar* products) at the top of the rank page. Users tend to only look at those products: for a company, being on the second page of a Google search often implies very few clicks from Google search users. That dynamic thus tends to entrench superstars' products' popularity at the expense of potential competition from products in the "tail" of the search ranking distribution. See Martens (2016), for example.

a constraint on powerful platforms' behaviour, lacking a credible threat to switch to competing services.

Making the right call—distinguishing what is pro-competitive and beneficial from what is instead anti-competitive and harmful to the economy—is often the tricky job of competition authorities.

e) Lack of media plurality

Citizens increasingly consume online news (for an extended discussion, see Chapter 14 on disinformation). Even if readers and viewers tend to *multi-home*, accessing multiple sources of news (including offline), access to the news online is increasingly mediated by a handful of online platforms such as Facebook, Twitter, and Google. In principle, online platforms could abuse their power to selectively promote (or demote) specific sources of information, having a significant impact on economies and societies.[10] This issue, and its consequences for civil participation, is discussed extensively in Chapter 14.

f) Tax avoidance

Online platforms, including those based on sharing economy business models, have often been blamed for circumventing tax laws through a very blurred definition of their fiscal responsibilities. Online platforms have traditionally emphasized their role as intermediary, leaving the responsibility for fulfilling tax obligations to service providers. This approach has fostered worries that online platforms may have an unfair competitive advantage compared to traditional businesses. Quite interestingly, an increasing number of attempts are being made by local and national authorities to address that issue, also in collaboration with the platforms themselves (note, for example, Airbnb imposing a levy of €0.83 per night on bookings in Paris to collect the Parisian *taxe de séjour*). It may be particularly tricky to distinguish between public measures aimed to establish an efficient tax system and measures aimed to protect incumbent industries from the disruptive power of online platform business models. In Chapter 10 I will discuss the merits of digital taxations in the e-commerce environment.

g) Foreclosure of competitors

Online platforms that hold a significant degree of market power may leverage that power to increase their market shares in complementary markets, foreclosing actual or potential competitors. The first European Commission antitrust case against Google[11] was based on the finding that Google had leveraged its market power in online search to support its downstream affiliate Google Shopping in the market for price-comparators or vertical web search engines, at the expense of its competitors.

---

[10] See also: Parcu (2020).
[11] European Commission Case 39740—Google Search (European Commission, 2017a).

h) Anticompetitive price discrimination

Online platforms foster information flow. Thanks to platforms, advertisers can tailor targeted ads to users surfing the Internet, and sellers can significantly increase their knowledge of potential buyers' habits and preferences. This enhances their ability to *personalize* to the greatest extent possible the price of the products or services they sell, a practice described in economics as "price discrimination". Price discrimination as such does not necessarily have bad welfare effects. To see this, consider the following simple example. Two users would like to view the latest episode of Game of Thrones through online streaming. One of the users is a young professional; the other is a student. While the young professional would be willing to pay up to €7 to view the episode, the student can only afford to pay up to €3. Let us assume for simplicity that the movie can be distributed at zero marginal cost (i.e. an additional viewer does not affect the distributors' cost function). If the distributor cannot distinguish between the young professional and the student, it will fix the price at €7 to earn €7 of profit. In fact, to get both customers on board, the price would need to be set to €3, but in that case profits would only be €6, assuming both users opt to use the service. If, instead, the distributor knows who is who and can discriminate between users, it could set the price to €3 for the student and to €7 for the young professional. The result is a higher total welfare, since both users can now watch the movie, and the distributor earns €10 in profit (in the appendix I discuss price discrimination extensively and propose another numerical example). Price discrimination, however, can cause welfare losses, as it typically implies a shift of value from buyers to sellers. Moreover, it may have anticompetitive effects, increasing suppliers' market power and increasing overall market concentration.[12]

i) Intellectual property rights infringement

A key principle enshrined in the 2000 e-Commerce Directive (Directive 2000/31/EC), is that intermediary service providers are not responsible for the content they transmit, cache, or host (see Chapter 9). In that sense, online platforms would not, in principle, be liable for infringements of intellectual property rights made by their users. Since platforms greatly facilitate the exchange of content online, the concern is that expanding the platform economy would de facto reduce creators' ability to receive a fair price for their intellectual creations, reducing the incentives to innovate and create new content. There is an increasing debate as to whether platforms should be more involved in protecting intellectual property rights.[13] A similar set of concerns relates to the distribution of illegal content online. I discuss these topics extensively in Chapter 9.

---

[12] For a review of potential pro-competitive and anti-competitive effects of price discrimination, see Papandropoulos (2007).

[13] For example see the European Parliament resolution of 9 July 2015 on the implementation of Directive 2001/29/EC of the European Parliament and of the Council of 22 May 2001 on the harmonization of certain aspects of copyright and related rights in the information society.

Table 8.1 Table summarizing the benefits and risks associated with online platforms

Benefits	Risks
• Reduce information asymmetries; facilitate the flow of information • Increase efficiency of resource-allocation • Capture value from economies of scale • Increase choice of products and services • Increase products' value through network effects • Increase trust between peers • Negatively affect costs for business/prices for consumers • Create new products or markets; favour innovation	• Lack of transparency vis-à-vis users • Excessive dependency on potentially unreliable reputational mechanisms • Violation of privacy; misuse of personal data • Lack of competition/alternatives • Lack of media plurality • Tax avoidance • Foreclosure of competitors • Anticompetitive price discrimination • Intellectual property rights infringement • Excessive economic, social, security dependency

j) Excessive economic, social, and security dependency on a limited number of global market players

The power of online platforms may well go beyond dominance in several product or service markets. A restricted number of global players may significantly affect national security if, for example, information concerning the private habit of the political leadership is disclosed or if services to public institutions are discontinued. Such reasoning can be extended to anything, to the extent that platforms may become unavoidable gateways to any economic or social activity.

8.3 Dilemmas for policymakers

Box 8.3   To Regulate or Not To Regulate?

"Regulation is itself imperfect and can lead to costly and unanticipated firm responses to the incentives created by regulatory rules and procedures. The costs of regulation may exceed the costs of unregulated naturally monopoly or significantly reduce the net social benefits of regulation. These considerations lead to a very important policy-relevant question. Are imperfect unregulated markets better or worse than imperfectly regulated markets in practice?"

(Joskow, P. L., 2007)

8.3.1 The challenges of an ex-ante ad-hoc regulatory framework

To a certain extent, it could be said that the platform economy has emerged in a regulatory vacuum. Online platforms have generally been spared from assuming responsibility for any harm caused through the use of their services. Law-makers have emphasized their role as intermediary: it therefore seemed illogical to blame platforms simply for being the vehicle used by clients to cause damage. Moreover, policymakers in the US and Europe deliberately adopted a *laissez-faire* approach at the platform economy's inception. The intention was to let the platform economy grow without putting many obstacles to it. However, as we have seen, online platforms have grown rapidly to become a key infrastructure for the functioning of society and the economy. As a result, the role of platforms as pure intermediaries has been called increasingly into question, particularly given their enhanced ability to exert control on the content of the activities that take place through their services. There is now a tendency in public debate to believe that public authorities should find smart ways to put an end to what *The Economist* called "digital exceptionalism" and equip society with the regulatory tools to address the issues aggravated or generated *ex novo* by the platform economy (The Economist, 2017a).

Before addressing the core question related to that debate, let me make an important distinction. It is somehow possible to distinguish two approaches to address the issues I presented in Section 8.2.2 above. The distinction is based on whether the emphasis of regulatory intervention is placed before a particular behaviour by online platforms occurs (**ex-ante ad-hoc regulation**) or after it has been observed (**ex-post enforcement**). We have touched upon this dichotomy in Chapter 4 in the context of telecom policy. Let us now analyse it in detail.

An **ex-ante ad-hoc regulatory framework** is defined as a set of specific rules that certain market players must abide by from the outset. I use the expression *ad-hoc* here to underline that the rules are specific to platforms; they do not apply to the whole economy. For example, online platforms could be specifically prevented from attributing an advantage to services they own to favour them against competitors. Ex-ante regulation is often juxtaposed to ex-post enforcement. With **ex-post enforcement**, players know the general rules that apply to any kind of business, but they are left with some flexibility in their business strategy. If they enact a behaviour that is suspected of infringing the general rules, they can then be sanctioned, after an investigation of the enforcing authority. For example, an Internet search engine could be sanctioned by an antitrust authority for favouring its own services in a manner that is incompatible with the general competition policy framework. It is called *ex-post* because the most meaningful effect of the regulation is observable *after* the market player has implemented the behaviour. With ex-ante ad-hoc regulation, instead, behaviours are prevented *before* they are actually implemented.

The discussion around what to do about online platforms' *exceptionalism* revolves around the above dichotomy, and could be framed in this question:

> *"should we not move from a system which is predominantly based on ex-post competition policy enforcement to a system in which certain players (i.e. online platforms) are told from the outset what they can and cannot do and therefore rely more on an ex-ante ad-hoc regulation approach?"*

Identifying relevant risks associated with the online platform economy is a first indication that regulatory intervention may be needed. Yet, to warrant the design of an ad hoc ex-ante regulatory framework one has to be sure that the new rules may improve the performance of the markets compared to the status quo.

That would be the case if the following conditions hold:

a) Markets are not able to efficiently self-correct
b) The available regulatory tools cannot efficiently address the identified issues
c) The new regulatory framework would not distort the market so that the net effect of regulatory intervention is negative.

a) Markets are not able to efficiently self-correct

By its nature, the online platform's ecosystem is very dynamic and subject to a significantly high pace of technological change. Today's successful disruptive businesses may be replaced tomorrow by yet another idea based on fundamentally different business principles. Unless insurmountable and long-lasting entry barriers protect markets, high prices, for example, tend to be self-correcting. High prices signal that the market is profitable; entry should therefore be expected to occur eventually and, over time, erode platforms' market power (this is the principle around the contestable market theory, see the appendix).

Moreover, even if market power were persistent in the primary market served by the platform, new applications or tools may emerge in other neighbouring markets producing countervailing effects on the main market. For example, a group of developers created an app called SquaredFare, which keeps track of rides to help Uber drivers ensure that Uber pays drivers the amount they are entitled to. Therefore, the app helps to curb Uber's strong bargaining power vis-à-vis one side of the platform (the drivers).

The exercise of market power is often a necessary condition for the existence of the market. One of the reasons explaining why so many new online platforms models are being developed lies in the ambition of developers to dominate a new market which they aim to create. In that sense, **competition *within* the market is replaced by competition *for* the market**. Any intervention attempting to mitigate such market power would inevitably affect the incentive to create new successful markets/platforms in the future.

b) *The regulatory tools currently available cannot efficiently address the issue*

It is possible that the issues identified in Section 8.2.2 may be efficiently tackled with laws that are already in force. If that is the case, ex-post enforcement may often be preferable to ex-ante ad-hoc regulation, particularly in a dynamic environment where regulation risks being outdated from its inception (see point (c) below). For example, competition laws can address abuse of market power through vertical foreclosure: Article 102 of the Treaty on the Functioning of the European Union explicitly forbids exclusionary conduct by dominant companies, a provision that would extend to online platforms. Likewise, privacy, criminal, consumer, and data protection laws can tackle other issues (see Box 8.4 for an example; this is discussed further below).

Box 8.4   Privacy law and online platforms

The following extract from *Politico* provides an example of how privacy law in Belgium is being applied to tackle privacy issues related to online platforms.

"Belgium's privacy commission will this week finally issue the cease-and-desist order that will stop Facebook tracking non-users around the web with its "data" cookie. Facebook uses the cookie to make sure automated bots aren't scraping public content or repeatedly clicking "like" buttons for cash, but it will introduce new controls in Belgium. Non-users will be unable to access public Facebook pages, such as those of businesses and celebrities, and even users might need to go through extra security steps when logging into the service from a new browser."

(From Politico, 3/12/2015)

Sometimes, however, the specific features of online business models may be such that traditional *ex-post* enforcement tools are not effective in tackling potential problems. For example, antitrust may not be fast enough to correct the distortion caused by an abuse of market power compared to the pace of development of technological markets. We will look at this scenario in Section 8.3.2.

c) *The new regulatory framework would not distort the market in such a way that the net effect of regulatory intervention is negative*

Joskow's quote (Joskow, P. L., 2007) in Box 8.3 elegantly describes the last condition, although the quote refers to the extreme situation of "natural monopolies", i.e. markets in which it is more efficient for just one company to supply the service or good. It is debatable whether certain online platforms may be considered natural "quasi-monopolies". But it is undeniable that where network externalities are very strong, market concentration is a natural outcome. The gist of Joskow's quote could be summarized as: "*mind the alternative*" or "*be careful what you wish for*". Indeed, the introduction of regulation is never exempt from risks in itself. So the design of new rules is never a light-hearted job; a careful assessment of the counter-factual, i.e. of the consequences of new regulation on markets, should always be made by policymakers before moving in that direction.

Often ex-ante ad-hoc regulation is tantamount to dictating the best outcome that a market should yield from a societal perspective. That happens, for example, when regulation forces market players to set "fair prices" for their products; "fairness" is, however, an inherently subjective concept, and that implies a high level of uncertainty around the process of defining fair prices (and thus, a high likelihood of mistakes). Generally speaking, such an invasive intervention by regulation may sometimes be necessary if there are no alternatives. But, if possible, the best approach is always to remove all frictions in the market, address market failures, and let markets converge to their equilibrium with no further intervention. It is more likely that a market with no frictions (thus, with no market failures) returns socially optimal outcomes rather than a market in which that outcome has been pre-determined by regulators.

For example, high prices are sometimes a necessary reward that justifies the risky investments made when the market is still developing. Defining a fair price in that context is particularly challenging: what is the price that would have triggered the interest of investors, had they known it once they started the investment plan in the past? Unfortunately, public authorities may lack the ability to get price-setting right.

Moreover, direct price or quality design is often subject to intense political pressure. By directly intervening in markets processes, authorities risk undermining the natural competitive process, reducing the incentive to enter a market, innovating, or investing in the development of new products. They may alter the allocation of economic value in such a way that the most efficient firms are no longer rewarded for their efforts and, ultimately, subverting consumers' interests to the interests of power-seeking politicians.

Any new ad hoc ex-ante regulatory framework would thus need to take that risk into account. Extra care in the design of new regulation should be taken to avoid altering the incentives to compete on merits and develop successful ideas. For example, introducing data portability requirements would possibly mitigate lock-in effects, allowing users to switch between different online platforms more easily. However, this must happen without removing the platform's incentives to develop technical solutions specific to its business. Suppose the data that are made portable are a core aspect of the platform's business (for example, a seller's reputation). In that case, it is possible that the new rules would negatively affect the chance that new platforms will arise in the same markets in the future.

The new ad hoc ex-ante regulatory framework would need to be sufficiently time-proof to guarantee a certain stability to the economy, allowing companies to craft their business strategies to abide by the new rules and form reasonable expectations around future profits and costs. Finally, the new ad hoc ex-ante rules would require identifying a set of sufficiently homogeneous businesses to ensure that the effects of regulations would be broadly similar for all market players.

As we have seen, however, this is tricky ground, and conditions (a), (b), and (c) above are difficult to meet. Designing a time-proof regulation could be a daunting challenge in an environment that is exposed to constant change; rules may come into force when they are already de facto obsolete. Moreover, as we have seen, online platforms tend to display huge asymmetries in business models, size, and cost structure, for example.

It is therefore very challenging to design a regulation that would have consistent effects across the board.

All these considerations contribute to explain why the European Commission has tended to endorse a careful approach, avoiding the proposal of radically new solutions to emerging issues in the platform economy for a long time. But the European Commission finally tilted its approach with the Digital Markets Act proposal released in December 2020, as we shall see in Section 8.4.

8.3.2 Stimulating competition in the platform ecosystem

To summarize the discussion above, we could say that the policy "coin" vis-à-vis online platforms has two faces: the *ex-ante* **ad-hoc regulatory** face and the *ex-post* **competition policy enforcement** face.

I have discussed the ex-ante ad-hoc regulatory framework in the previous Section, 8.3.1. Let us now briefly look at competition policy enforcement and how it plays out in the online platform space.[14]

Competition policy is enforced by the European Commission at EU level and by national antitrust authorities at Member States level. As we have seen already in Chapter 4 and as explained in the appendix, the European Commission vets **mergers** between large enterprises (Council Regulation (EC) No 139/2004), sanctions dominant companies **abusing their market power** to penalize competitors,[15] sanction companies setting up **anti-competitive agreements**[16] (including cartels), and prevents Member States from **subsidizing** companies distorting competition within the Single Market.[17] The goal of the enforcement of competition policy is to *protect consumer welfare*.[18] In other words, competition authorities aim to ensure that mergers or anti-competitive behaviours do not hamper competition in markets in a way that consumers and business customers are harmed.

---

[14] A review of the EU competition policy framework and its application is outside the scope of this book. In addition to the aforementioned Motta, M. (2004), students interested in starting an exploration of the competition policy world should take this book in their hands: Whish and Bailey (2015).

[15] Art. 102 TFEU https://eur-lex.europa.eu/LexUriServ/LexUriServ.do?uri=CELEX:12008E102:EN:HTML

[16] Art. 101 TFEU https://eur-lex.europa.eu/LexUriServ/LexUriServ.do?uri=CELEX:12008E101:EN:HTML

[17] Art. 107 TFEU https://eur-lex.europa.eu/legal-content/EN/ALL/?uri=CELEX%3A12008E107

[18] There is a debate amongst economists whether this or *total welfare* should be the goal of competition policy. Yet, in practice, competition authorities pursue a consumer welfare standard. For a general overview of competition policies, its purposes and implementation see the excellent Motta, M. (2004).

Consumer welfare is to be intended in a *dynamic way.* That is: competition policy does not only focus on lower prices in the short term but also consider trade-offs with innovation effects in the long term, for example, which could as well affect the welfare of users (for a description of the mechanisms through which competition can positively affect the economy, see the appendix).

Developed countries' competition laws and the relative enforcement tools were conceived in a context that predates the digital economy. Those laws and tools often proved effective in the past, but it is debatable whether they are now capable of tackling new emerging issues in the digital economy. Some may argue that this is the case, that competition policy is a tool that is flexible enough to adapt to the new challenge. But an increasing number of experts suggest that competition policy tools **may now require fine-tuning**, mainly to ensure that intervention is timely and effective, particularly to tackle issues in online platform markets. Merger control may need revisiting to more effectively capture the challenges brought about by the importance of potential competition in the digital domain, for example. Or competition authorities could be equipped with additional sectorial expertise and resources to be able to fully enforce the law.

Note that dealing with disruptive technologies does not necessarily need *disruptive changes in the law.* Competition enforcement can remain faithful to its basic principles, such as prioritizing consumer welfare, also in a platform economy. The ideal of fairness in the digital market should never sabotage the well-established principle that enforcement **should protect competition, not competitors**. Even if tech giants do put companies at a competitive disadvantage, this does not automatically imply adverse effects on final customers, and that is what ultimately matters for competition policy enforcement.

Yet, it is necessary to identify those areas that clearly require concrete improvements. Let us focus on two areas: (1) **merger control** and (2) **enforcement against antitrust abuse.**

8.3.2.1 Improvements in merger control

There is a growing concern that large platforms are buying small, promising start-ups that could become their competitors in the future, cementing their market power by killing potential competition at its infancy. Over the last decade, the "GAFAM" companies—Google, Apple, Facebook, Amazon, and Microsoft—alone completed over 400 acquisitions worth more than $130 billion. Facebook, which acquired WhatsApp and Instagram, is unrivalled in the social platforms market by far in Europe and the US. Venture capitalists even talk about "kill zones" around tech giants whereby successful start-ups are either squashed through imitation or bought up when perceived as an emerging threat (The Economist, 2018).

Merger control by competition authorities worldwide must strive to fully capture the current fast-changing market dynamic. Two main challenges can be identified regarding the enforcement of merger control in the platform economy. First, **there is a procedural issue.** The thresholds used to determine whether a merger must be notified to get approval by competition authorities—*companies' turnover*[19] —may not be sufficiently effective in the digital marketplace as they may fail to capture the real perspective value of tech start-ups.

Indeed, a typical business strategy for nascent platform companies is to first expand the number of users, possibly even at a loss, and *only later* monetize their success on the market. Currently, in Europe, some relief comes from the referral system by national authorities: smaller mergers with cross-border effects can be captured and referred to the European Commission by Member States. Yet, this system relies entirely on a set of 27 different enforcement approaches. This was the case with the *Facebook/WhatsApp* merger: despite the purchase price of $19 billion and the fact that, at the time of the transaction, WhatsApp had 450 million users worldwide, WhatsApp's annual revenue was below the thresholds set in the EU Merger Regulation, and the transaction was not initially subject to notification to the European Commission. As the transaction did not have a Union dimension within the meaning of the Merger Regulation, it was assessed by the European Commission only following a referral request. Other mergers such as *Facebook/Instagram* or *Google/Waze* were never referred to the European Commission, and instead scrutinized by the national competition authority.

Second, when performing their analysis, antitrust officials must also consider the likely impact of the merger on **potential competition** (indeed, the EU Horizontal Merger Guidelines contain a provision on potential competition).[20] In other words, in theory, enforcers must consider if the merger prevents a future competitor from emerging in the market (that looks like a textbook definition for *killer acquisition*).

However, in practice, the bulk of the analysis is directed at ascertaining the impact that the merger has on **actual competition**. Namely, the analysis often focuses on whether the merger may remove from the market a company *that is already* exerting a significant competitive constraint on the acquiring entity. And not on whether that company can potentially emerge as a credible competitor in the future.

Part of the problem is practical: **antitrust authorities have insufficient tools to accurately visualize how markets will evolve in the future**. And that issue is particularly prominent in the highly dynamic digital environment. Conversely, tech giants possess a great foresight ability, often superior to the acquired start-ups themselves. In 2013, Facebook acquired the security app Onavo that helped it to get access to app usage data and monitor the evolution of Snapchat—the frequency and the duration of its use by users—before attempting to buy it (Fingas J., 2017). The confidential documents released by the UK's digital, culture, media, and sport parliamentary committee show that Facebook also relied on Onavo to track WhatsApp's performance before acquiring it. The published Onavo data had suggested that WhatsApp

---

[19] In line with Article 1 of the EU Merger Regulation, a concentration has an EU dimension where the combined aggregate turnover of all the undertakings concerned is more than €5000 million, and the aggregate EU-wide turnover of each undertaking is more than €250 million, unless firms achieve more than two-thirds of its EU-wide turnover within the same Member State.

[20] Guidelines on the assessment of horizontal mergers, OJ C 3, paragraph 60.

was on its way to grow significantly in the social messaging market in the US (Warzel & Mac, 2018). Competition authorities can require companies to provide such internal documents displaying market's analytics, and the European Commission uses those powers extensively.[21] While there is no absolute guarantee that the authority scrutinizes all potentially relevant documents, the European Commission has powers to carry out inspections and to enforce its requests for documents, including by suspending the merger review timetable until all documents are provided or by imposing fines for the submission of incorrect, misleading, or incomplete information.[22]

Converting a "competition-kill-zone" into a "competition-scale-zone" for nascent companies could require a subtle shift in the European approach to concentrations. For example, changes in the existing bodies of laws could be made to make acquisitions of start-ups more difficult to approve. Suppose an acquirer with significant market power purchases a small company that has the economic capability to scale with a concrete chance of becoming a credible future competitor. In that case, the transaction could be approached as presumptively anti-competitive. As noted by Shapiro (2018), it is sound to *"tolerate some false positives—blocking mergers involving targets, only to find that they do not grow to challenge the incumbent—in order to avoid some false negatives—allowing mergers that eliminate targets that would indeed have grown to challenge the dominant incumbent"*. This suggestion seems exceptionally sensible in markets that are somehow dysfunctional, in which the issues we discussed in Section 8.2.2 above are becoming increasingly significant for a vast number of users.

We still do not have solid quantitative evidence supporting a stronger presumption of anti-competitiveness when powerful platforms acquire smaller companies. However, it is fair to note that the higher the actual market concentration, the higher the likelihood that a merger is harmful. Given the current level of our knowledge, it would arguably be better to have a cautious approach and err, if anything, on the side of more competition rather than keeping the status quo. Bearing in mind that competition authorities must still face the inherent challenge of generating evidence solid enough to prove the anticompetitive nature of a merger in Court.

Exerting a more stringent merger control on acquisitions of promising start-ups would require overcoming a very concrete implementation problem. It would not be realistic (and certainly not desirable) for antitrust authorities to scrutinize *all mergers* taking place in the market regardless of the size of the transaction. Therefore, **new notification thresholds** should be adopted where companies' turnovers cannot

---

[21] See the EC Decision M.7217 FACEBOOK/WHATSAPP: for the purposes of calculating market shares, estimating apps penetration rates, and assessing the extent to which the merging parties' app networks overlapped, the Commission relied in its decision on data provided by Facebook, as notifying party, which is based on the market intelligence source Onavo (see paragraphs 41, 96, 140 and footnotes 13 and 44 of the decision). The decision relies on Onavo data for the period between November 2013 and May 2014 at EEA and national level.

[22] The European Commission fined Facebook €110 million for providing incorrect or misleading information during the Commission's 2014 investigation of Facebook's acquisition of WhatsApp. See European Commission (2017e).

provide a good indication of the potential market effects of the merger. Key parameters triggering notification could hinge on the number of impacted customers or the purchasing price (a reasonable proxy of the value of data assets, for example). Germany (Bundeskartellamt, 2018) and Austria have already reacted to this digital challenge by introducing a new size-of-transaction test: such a test may include cash payments, the transfer of assets, securities and voting rights, or interest-based liabilities. Thus far, however, there is no evidence that the test has effectively responded to the identified shortcomings.

Inevitably though, the number of notified transactions could increase. A possible solution would be the creation of notification screening offices within competition authorities. Merging companies would be required to submit a limited amount of information to the office (a one-page pre-notification form). On that basis, the notification screening office would establish whether the merger should go through a complete notification procedure. This process would ensure that the competition enforcer is not overburdened with minor transactions that do not pose a competitive challenge and can, instead, devote the necessary resources to thoroughly assessing more problematic instances.

Such a tightening of merger control would not be controversy-free. On the one hand, the prospect of a start-up being purchased in the near future could have chilling effects on investment incentives for those expecting the business idea to sustain and evolve into an independent success story. In this case, more vigorous competition enforcement would be innovation-enhancing. On the other hand, the start-up founders' strategy is increasingly to build **companies that are for sale**, not for scale.[23] High-tech entrepreneurship is considered by many to be about bringing new ideas with a view of commercialization and exit. In this context, a presumption of anti-competitiveness would then have adverse effects on innovation. Acquisition deals may also lead to increased competition. IBM's acquisition of US software company Red Hat for 34 billion US dollars, cleared in 2019 by the European Commission (European Commission, 2019d), could possibly enable IBM to diversify its portfolio and compete with Amazon, Alphabet, and Microsoft in the cloud business, for example.

For that reason, the introduction of a more stringent merger control should be accompanied by the adoption of sophisticated analytical tools (e.g. making use of artificial intelligence) and by a careful monitoring of markets' evolution. To base their decisions on a correct presumption, competition authorities should place more emphasis on evaluating the more granular impacts that their interventions have on markets and companies' **incentives to innovate** and compete. Establishing closer cooperation with academics and independent research institutions, possibly opening up cases' data (in a proportionate way, to the extent possible and with all the necessary safeguards for confidentiality), would be one way of obtaining

---

[23] 90% of startups as reported in The Economist, "American tech giants are making life tough for startups". See The Economist (2018).

more in-depth insights concerning the effect of new merger approaches on market performance.

8.3.2.2 Improvements in enforcement against antitrust abuse

Contrary to the case of merger control, there does not seem to be a case to advocate a tougher intervention against antitrust abuse. However, enforcement **needs to speed up** since, regardless of the final outcome of antitrust investigations (infringement, settlement, or acquaintance decision), markets and companies should not be kept long on the hook in the digital sector.[24] Solutions include implementing **interim measures** to halt the alleged infringement and prevent irreversible damage before sanctioning it. This happened, for example, in the 2019 EU antitrust case against Broadcom (European Commission, 2019e).

In order to avoid changes in market structure that may be very difficult to reverse due to network effects and tipping (see Section 8.1 above), it is also important that competition authorities can intervene once it is established with sufficient probability that the conduct at issue is likely to lead to harm, for example through foreclosure of a competitor. Competition authorities should not have to wait until actual detrimental effects on the market can be shown, for example, until companies have exited the market.

It is all the more necessary that antitrust authorities are equipped with the **computing infrastructure** and the **technical expertise** necessary to keep up with the sophistication of the outside world. Such an upgrade would guarantee early detections of possible infringements and more accurate analysis of an ever-complex digital world during the investigation phase.

Generally speaking, both in antitrust and merger control, enforcers should be ready to **expand the scope of traditional theories of harm.** Traditionally, competition authorities have built their cases against potential infringers of competition laws focusing on price effects. This does not seem to be very appropriate in the case of online platform markets, where the monetary dimension is irrelevant from a user's perspective. Competition authorities should thus take into account other dimensions where harm could occur. For example, if it is very likely that the approval of a merger would result in the violation of data protection law, a thorough reflection and cooperation with data protection authorities would be warranted to ensure coherent enforcement of EU law. As the European Commission has acknowledged in the Microsoft/LinkedIn merger decision,[25] data privacy may be "an important parameter of competition". Competition authorities should in privacy-sensitive cases more closely cooperate with data protection authorities.[26] Ultimately, competition

---

[24] Whereas the merger review has to be conducted by the European Commission within a specific timeframe (25 days for phase I investigation and 90 for phase II investigation, with a possibility of extension), no corresponding deadlines apply to antitrust investigations.

[25] European Commission, Case M.8124 *Microsoft/LinkedIn*, June 2016.

[26] See for example the UK "Competition and data protection in digital markets: a joint statement between the CMA and the ICO", published in May 2021 and retrievable here: https://ico.org.uk/media/about-the-ico/documents/2619797/cma-ico-public-statement-20210518.pdf

authorities could develop a consistent new framework to identify, assess and measure the harm that mergers or antitrust infringements can cause. Parameters such as "users' attention", "users' privacy", "transparency vis-à-vis users", and "users' exposure to low quality/detrimental content" should be factored into the valuation of competition policy enforcers in a systematic and quantitatively relevant way.

8.4 The European Union's perspective

The basic EU framework for legal reference on the functioning of online platforms is currently defined by the **2000 e-Commerce Directive** (Directive 2000/31/EC). The Directive was a first attempt to move towards a homogeneous approach to online activities within the Single Market. It endorsed a **country of origin** principle according to which online services are subject to the Member State law in which they are established and not to the law of the Member State(s) from which they are accessible. This principle has arguably increased transparency and facilitated cross-border operations by avoiding a situation whereby the same service is forced to comply with 27 different regulatory frameworks to remain active throughout the whole EU territory. The Directive also set consistent standards to be applied by all EU countries, such as online contracting and commercial communication. I will discuss the e-Commerce Directive extensively in Chapter 9 on online platforms and illegal content.

Several other EU legislative initiatives have major effects on online platforms. These include, *among other things*: the General Data Protection Regulation (GDPR), the Regulation on a framework for the free flow of non-personal data (Regulation (EU)2018/1807), the Audiovisual Media Services Directive (Directive (EU) 2018/1808), the Copyright Directive (Directive (EU) 2019/790), the unfair commercial practice directive (UCPD) (Directive 2005/29/EC), and the (recently updated) guidance on its application (European Commission, 2016h). Each of these is discussed in-depth elsewhere in this book,[27] so here let me limit myself to just a few general observations. In addition, an important piece of the legislative framework was added in 2019 with the *EU Regulation on fairness and transparency in online platform-to-business relationship*,[28] which is described further below.

As we have seen in Chapter 5, the GDPR is a comprehensive set of rules regulating the use of personal data within the European Union. Adopted in 2016, it came into force in 2018. Because it is an EU regulation, it was directly applicable

---

[27] GDPR and free-flow of non-personal data: Chapter 5 on the Data Economy; Audiovisual Directive and Copyright: Chapter 9 on Online Content and Platforms' Liability; the UCPD: Chapter 10 on e-Commerce.

[28] Regulation (EU) 2019/1150 of the European Parliament and of the Council of 20 June 2019 on promoting fairness and transparency for business users of online intermediation services.

everywhere in Europe, regardless of national legislation. It had significant implications for online platforms, given that, as we have seen, their business model often heavily relies on the use of data. Most notably, as we have seen in Chapter 5, the GDPR clarifies the **"right to be forgotten"**, which refers to the right of individuals to have their data deleted if they no longer want them to be processed by "data controllers" such as a search engine. The GDPR also establishes a right to personal **data portability**, meaning that platforms are required to make it possible for users to shift personal data from one platform to the other. The regulation for the free-flow of non-personal data ensures the right of data portability also for non-personal data. The Audio-visual Media Service Directive (AVMSD) updated the common EU regulatory framework for all audio-visual media: traditional TV broadcasts and on-demand services. Therefore, it is applicable to platforms that stream videos online, such as YouTube, and online retailers/intermediaries providing video on demand, such as Netflix. Platforms organizing and tagging a large quantity of videos have to protect minors from harmful content and protect all users from incitement to hatred. The Copyright Directive aimed to address what has come to be known as the **value** gap. The value gap originates in the allegedly unfair distribution of economic value between, on the one hand, online platforms that host content online and make profits mostly through advertising and, on the other, content producers, such as music labels or news publishers. One of the consequences of the proposed Copyright Directive was that online platforms which offer news aggregator services, such as Google News, would need to pay a "neighbouring right" to publishers for the use of small exerts of news articles extracted from their websites ("snippets"). I will discuss value distribution and intellectual property rights extensively in the following chapter. Finally, the Unfair Commercial Practice Directive (UPCD), together with the Guidance document on the application of the UCPD, protects users of online platforms in their capacity as consumers of a traded good or service. For example: online market-places such as Amazon or eBay should bear the burden of proof for non-conforming goods or non-delivery; platforms using feedback systems should not mislead consumers by leading them to believe that reviews come from real users if they cannot be certain about it; app stores should not mislead the presentation of games as "free" or provide inaccurate information about payment settings or users' consent for their purchase, and so on.

8.4.1 The European Commission's 2018 Communication on online platforms

In its 2015 *Digital Single Market Strategy* (see Chapter 1), the European Commission announced the launch of a comprehensive assessment of the role of platforms, including the sharing economy and online intermediaries. The assessment covers issues such as transparency, the use of information collected by platforms, platforms' business relations, the existence of lock-in preventing players from switching platform, and the role of platforms in tackling illegal content on the Internet (European Commission, 2015a). The proposed regulations and directives described above stem from that assessment.

The Communication on Online Platforms (European Commission, 2016i), published in May 2016, was the first document drafted by the European Commission specific to the online platform economy. It contained the results of the assessment run by the Commission on the role of platforms and explains how the Commission plans to address any emerging issues.

The key insight provided by the Communication was the European Commission's decision **not to propose an ad hoc ex-ante regulatory framework specific to online platforms**: after a thorough one-year investigation into online platform markets, the Commission concluded that online platforms play a key role in the development of the Digital Single Market and that, given the heterogeneity of their business models, a principle-based, problem-driven approach is the best way to address emerging issues and associated risks for society and the economy. In other words, rather than proposing broad, across-the-board rules, the Commission identified several problematic areas and explained how it would act on them, not necessarily through regulatory actions, to improve the functioning of online platforms. It also suggested that self- and co-regulatory measures by the industry should also play a role in ensuring the application of legal requirements and monitoring mechanisms.

In its Communication on Online Platforms, the European Commission identified four areas of actions:

1. Ensuring a level playing field for comparable digital services
2. Ensuring that online platforms act responsibly
3. Fostering trust, transparency and ensuring fairness
4. Keeping markets open and non-discriminatory to foster a data-driven economy.

The first area aims to ensure that comparable digital services are subject to comparable rules. The key reference here is to over-the-top (OTT) players: online platforms that compete downstream with traditional telecom companies, for example, offering free messaging services or **peer-to-peer IP** communication (e.g. WhatsApp or Skype). The new Telecom Code proposed by the European Commission in September 2016 (see Chapter 4 on the telecom regulation) indeed proposes measures to extend to OTT some obligations which traditional telecom operators are subject to, such as the obligation to offer the possibility to call emergency numbers for free or to take measures to allow access to users with disabilities.

The second area pertains to the issue of platforms' liability. In this regard, the measures to be taken include the review of the audio-visual media services directive, the new copyright directive, and a proposal for the formalization of the notice-and-action procedure (see Chapter 9). The European Commission also proposed that online platforms should be encouraged to put in place voluntary, good-faith, measures to fight illegal content online.

The third area concerns measures to increase safety and security (and hence trust) in the online world. Besides the guidance on the application of the unfair commercial practice Directive, mentioned previously, the Commission also proposed to encourage platforms to recognize different kinds of secure electronic identifications (eID) in order to strengthen the reliability of the systems in recognizing single-users, while at the same time guaranteeing the maximum level of interoperability between platforms. The Commission also announced its intention to carry out a targeted fact-finding exercise on business-to-business practices in the online platform environment, to identify potential market failures affecting small- and medium-sized enterprises "forced" to deal with online platforms that have a considerable amount of market power. The result of that exercise is the *EU Regulation on fairness and transparency in online platform-to-business relationship* (see further below).

Finally, the fourth area highlighted in the Communication on Online Platforms aims to foster competition in online platform markets with significant actions to mobilize the use of data within the Single Market, notably through *free flow of data* initiatives. These actions are at the core of the "Building a European Data Economy" package adopted in September 2016 and discussed extensively in Chapter 5 on the data economy.

8.4.2 The Platforms-To-Business Regulation

The European Commission's commitment to avoid legislating in favour of an ad-hoc ex-ante regulatory framework targeted explicitly to online platforms began to squeak in 2019 with the approval of the *EU Regulation on fairness and transparency in online platform-to-business relationship,* commonly known as **P2B regulation**. While this initiative had been announced in the 2018 Communication (see above), the end result was a departure from the key indication put forward by the 2018 Communication itself, that is: there should be no specific regulatory regime just designed for online platforms.

Instead, in an effort to address bargaining power asymmetries in platform markets, increasing transparency and fairness in trade, "business-to-business" relationships, the P2B regulation imposes the following rules:

- Platform's services' "Terms and Conditions" must be clearly presented, in a simple and intelligible language. Platforms are prevented from making sudden and unexplained changes to them
- Platforms must explain why they are preventing a certain business user from accessing the platform's service
- Platforms must be fully transparent about their data policy: who can access their data and at what conditions.

- Platforms should inform their business users on the main reasons affecting those users' ranking (for example, with web search engines)
- Search engines must disclose in their Terms and Conditions if any differentiated treatment is applied to services (particularly to the treatment of *own* services). See the echo of the Google Shopping antitrust case (European Commission, 2017a)
- Platforms should explain why they impose contract clauses such as *Most Favoured Nation* or *MFN* clauses, namely: why they oblige their users to offer their best prices on the platform. A typical example is Booking.com preventing hotels from undercutting the price of rooms posted on its platform[29] (in the appendix, I explain why this is not necessarily bad)
- Bigger platforms (generating, inter alia, more than €10 million turnover) must establish procedures that allow smooth and prompt handling of complaints, and they must favour out-of-court dispute settlements using external mediators.

The regulation also creates a EU Observatory for the Online Platform Economy with the goal of monitoring the evolution of online platform markets and the efficacy of regulatory solutions to address potential emerging market failures.

The P2B Regulation entered into force in July 2020 and at the time of writing of this book it was too early to judge its impact on the economy. However, the regulation gives rise to a number of question marks, particularly as it endorses a rather "invasive" approach that could hamper platforms' business models, especially in the case of smaller, emerging platforms. For example, it is unclear why companies that do not hold a dominant position in the market should be forced to explain to trading counterparts how their business works. Conversely, competition policy enforcement should be capable of capturing issues arising where market power is significant. If not, it would probably make more sense to see how enforcement could be improved, rather than an increasing regulatory burden on a sector of the economy that still struggles to emerge in Europe.

8.4.3 The December 2020 Package: The Digital Markets Act

After the P2B Regulation, the European Commission marked its definite switch of mind to ex-ante ad-hoc regulation with the **Digital Markets Act** (European Commission, 2020o) (or **DMA**) and **Digital Services Act** (European Commission, 2020p) (or **DSA**) **proposals** that were released in December 2020. The DSA focuses on illegal content online and it is thus covered in Chapter 9, when I am discussing online platforms' liability. Here let me briefly discuss the DMA.

---

[29] For an overview of this issue in the online booking sector, check the European Commission's DG-Competition's "Report on the monitoring exercise carried out in the online hotel booking sector by EU competition authorities in 2016" https://ec.europa.eu/competition/ecn/hotel_monitoring_report_en.pdf

The proposed DMA is a perfect example of ex-ante ad-hoc regulation.[30] It specifically targets a subset of players, namely **online gatekeepers**. An online gatekeeper is a platform that satisfies several conditions, such as:

(1) it operates in at least one of what the European Commission considers the digital world's eight *core services*:
- online intermediation services (including, for example, marketplaces, app stores, and online intermediation services in other sectors like mobility, transport, or energy)
- online search engines
- social networking
- video sharing platform services
- number-independent interpersonal electronic communication services (such OTT players, e.g. WhatsApp or Telegram, see Chapter 4)
- operating systems
- cloud services
- advertising services, including advertising networks, advertising exchanges, and any other advertising intermediation services, where these advertising services are being related to one or more of the other core platform services mentioned above

(2) it is active in at least three EU Member States

(3) it has a significant impact on the internal market (defined quantitatively as an annual turnover of €6.5 billion or a market capitalization of €65 billion)

(4) it serves as an important gateway for business users to reach end-users (user base larger than 45 million monthly end-users and 10,000 business users yearly) and

(5) it enjoys an entrenched and durable position or is likely to continue to enjoy such a position (meets the first and second criteria over three consecutive years).

A platform that meets these quantitative thresholds is labelled a gatekeeper. However, the European Commission retains the right to confer or remove the "gatekeeper" status by qualitative assessment. According to the proposed DMA text, the European Commission would also be empowered to alter the thresholds as technologies change and conduct market investigations to look for new gatekeepers. In this way, the European Commission aims to retain some flexibility, in a fast-changing environment such as the digital one, despite resorting to a "static" ex-ante regulation approach. Sure enough, even if the European Commission does not name them, companies like Google, Facebook, Amazon, Apple, Microsoft will certainly be caught within the scope of the DMA.[31]

---

[30] For an extended analysis, see Anderson and Mariniello (2021).
[31] For an analysis of the DMA's potential catchment area, see Mariniello and Martins (2021).

Once a company qualifies as a gatekeeper, it should abide to a number of obligations: the DMA constrains gatekeepers' behaviour while forcing them to proactively open up to more competition. If in breach of the rules, gatekeepers may face penalties of up to 10% of their yearly turnover. Repeat offenders could even, in principle, be broken-up (along the lines of what has been done in the past with telecom companies, see Chapter 5).

In practice, the DMA attempts to address two problems: anticompetitive practices by gatekeepers and high barriers to entry in online platform markets. The ultimate objective seems to be thus to make digital markets both contestable and fair for existing and future rivals.

For example, the DMA prevents gatekeepers from combining end-user data from different sources without consent. Combining data from multiple sources can give gatekeepers a significant advantage over smaller rivals. Indeed, data gleaned from one source, say online searches, can be used to predict users' preferences in other markets, say music streaming. A gatekeeper that knows a user's web browsing history is much better positioned to predict her musical tastes than a data-poor rival. Restricting the combination of data from multiple sources, therefore, restricts the ability of gatekeepers to leverage their market power from one market to another to the detriment of small players.

Other prominent rules include:

- no self-preferencing: a prohibition on ranking their own products over others;
- data portability: an obligation to facilitate the portability of continuous and real-time data
- no "spying": a prohibition on gatekeepers on using the data of their business users to compete with them
- interoperability of ancillary services: an obligation to allow third-party ancillary service providers (e.g. payment providers) to run on their platforms and
- open software: an obligation to permit third-party app stores and software to operate on their OS.

The DMA also includes a requirement for gatekeepers to notify regulators of all acquisitions they intend to pursue, even when the target is too small to be subject to merger control (see the discussion we had in Section 8.3.2).

The timeline for the definite approval of the DMA text by the EU co-legislators and the subsequent entry into force is not short (the EU Parliament and the EU Council may approve a final text by spring 2022; that would be exceptionally fast by EU standards). Yet the DMA is an important milestone marking a major shift in the approach of the European Commission. Looking at the list of behaviors that the DMA bans, it is impossible not to note a strong overlap with past or ongoing antitrust cases run by the European Commission against, in particular, "GAFAM" companies. With the DMA, the European Commission is essentially flagging that ex-post competition policy enforcement may no longer be suitable to tackle the issues we observe in online platform markets.

There is no consensus among experts on whether the European Commission's change of approach will positively impact digital markets. Students should be able to make up their own judgement, based on the analysis discussed in Section 8.3 above. Is a shift from ex-post enforcement to *ex-ante ad hoc regulation* needed, considering all benefits and risks that this may entail?

****

8.5 Case Study: DuckDuckGo

DuckDuckGo is a privacy-focused web search engine that recently emerged as a credible potential alternative to Google. Web search engines collect personal information about their users, such as their browsing or purchase history. They then monetize that information helping advertisers to craft ads that specifically target certain users' profiles. DuckDuckGo instead does not track its users' history. Instead, it makes money through the placement of ads that are not based on the user's profile but on what the user is searching for at the moment in which the ad appears. If a user searches for online courses on digital policy, she may see an ad for this book. She, however, won't see an ad about hotels in London, even if the day before she flagged online interest in the British Museum by visiting its opening hours web page.

As of April 2021, DuckDuckGo averaged more than 95 million daily searches worldwide, with more than 73 billion searches performed since its inception. A primary driver of its success is raising awareness amongst Internet users about the potential misuse of personal information by online platforms. Another factor contributing to DuckDuckGo's growth is its collaboration with browsers such as Safari, Firefox, or Chrome. DuckDuckGo also recently entered into a partnership with Linux and has its own smartphone application for iOS and Android.

More information about DuckDuckGo can be found on its website: https://duckduckgo.com/

8.6 Review questions

- The European Commissioner for Digital Affairs suddenly summons you. She has heard about online platforms, but she is not sure what they are or how they work. Give her your best definition (not the one given in the book).
- List three benefits and three potential risks in online platform markets. For each of those, describe a real-life example. Do not use the examples given in the book.
- In your view, what is the main advantage of ex-post competition enforcement compared to ex-ante ad-hoc regulation? What's the foremost drawback?
- Could a law specifically crafted to target online marketplaces make sense? What are the necessary and sufficient conditions for such a regulation to be a good idea?
- You are the adviser to the CEO of a Canadian online platform. The CEO intends to enter the European market in the next five years. He needs your help to understand what to expect in terms of the regulatory framework that will be applied to the company. Write down a short summary with a few examples or hypothetical scenarios of what could happen if the CEO moves forward with his plan.

9

Online Content and Platform Liability

Abstract

In their early days, online platforms were considered neutral intermediaries with no direct editorial responsibility. That is the approach enshrined in the 2000 e-Commerce EU Directive, whereby information society services are not considered liable for the illegal content they unknowingly host. That principle may be not entirely suitable to address today's challenges. In particular, platforms have been subject to increasing public pressure to take on a proactive role to limit the ever-growing spread of harmful content online: from incitement to hatred, from violence to child pornography. A change in platforms' liability approach seems all the more sensible since platforms have, over time, outgrown their mere intermediary role and acquired the sophisticated technological means necessary to monitor their users' behaviour. Yet entrusting platforms with a proactive screening role for the content they host entails a significant risk: hampering users' freedom of expression. Ultimately, it has the potential to undermine the functioning of the Internet as we know it today. Reconciling the two sides of the dilemma is the fundamental goal of an policy action.

9.1 Background

One key insight from Chapter 8 is that the term "online platform" can indicate many businesses which share some common features, such as the intermediation between different groups of users, despite being very different from each other. The absence of a precise definition for online platforms makes the job of legislators rather tricky, as we have seen, as picking one set of general rules for "online platforms" may prove inefficient and often counterproductive. In this chapter, we shall take a deeper look at platforms' legal responsibility for the content they host—platforms' exposure to legal liability, mostly in their capacity of *intermediaries* between different groups of users.[1]

Using Sartor's definitions (Sartor, G., 2017), we can identify two types of legal exposure for platforms:

---

[1] See Taddeo and Floridi (2015) on the increasing importance of establishing clear responsibilities for online platforms for their increasingly relevant role in society.

Digital Economic Policy. Mario Mariniello, Oxford University Press.
© Mario Mariniello (2022). DOI: 10.1093/oso/9780198831471.003.0009

1. **Primary liability** – this occurs whenever the platform is directly responsible for an illegal activity
2. **Secondary liability** – whereby platforms may be indirectly liable when a third party (such as a platform user) infringes the law.

Platforms may infringe the law directly in several ways. They can violate privacy law by mismanaging the data they process and committing a breach of the GDPR (see Chapter 5). They may violate an explicit or implicit contract with their customers (see, for example, Chapter 10 regarding the protection of consumers for online contracts). Platforms may also breach specific legislation, such as the "Platforms-to-Business" Regulation or the Digital Markets Act, if approved by EU legislators in the future (see Chapter 8). Alternatively, they may infringe competition laws: competition policy is probably the most vivid example of the enforcing power of the European Commission vis-à-vis online platforms. As primary liability of platforms is dealt with in the relevant chapters of this text, this chapter predominantly focuses on **secondary liability**. Secondary liability is an exceptional area of debate regarding appropriate policy action, given the role that online platforms have come to acquire. With a large part of society's communication migrating online, platforms tend to mediate a significant part of public and private social interaction. Online platforms tend to portray themselves as *neutral middlemen* with no responsibility regarding the ends for which their users employ those means. But there is growing public pressure on platforms to take a more proactive role and limit the harm caused by the communication channels they cater for.

Examples of illegal content uploaded by users that can trigger secondary liability for platforms are sexual abuse of children, illegal hate speech, incitement of terrorism, and tobacco or alcohol advertisement.

Before moving forward, it is essential to clarify that, in this chapter, I specifically focus on content that is deemed "**illegal**". Content that may be perceived as harmful *but it is not illegal* would fall in the "disinformation" category. A claim that drinking hot water would mitigate the risk of a coronavirus infection, for example, can be deemed as false given the current scientific acquis, and it may expose people to significant harm. The claim, however, may not be illegal as such and therefore raises different questions in terms of choosing the appropriate policy response. Disinformation *that cannot be deemed illegal* is dealt with in Chapter 14, which complements the current chapter to address the whole set of issues concerning harmful content online. As depicted in Figure 9.1, this chapter covers areas A and B;[2] Chapter 14 covers area C.

In this chapter, I also cover **copyright**. Copyright laws generate a particularly intriguing case for the legal responsibility of intermediaries. *Copyright infringement* lies right at the intersection between the primary and secondary liability of

---

[2] Area B relates to fabricated information which can be deemed illegal. Consider, for example, the case of defamation.

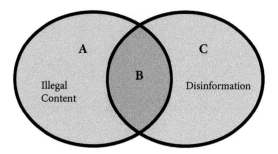

Figure 9.1 Illegal content vs disinformation

online platforms. Platforms themselves can infringe copyright. For example, if they "scrape" proprietary content from another website and use it without compensating the source. But platforms' users can also infringe copyright, for example when a user uploads copyrighted material to a video-streaming platform.

A typical illustration of content potentially infringing copyright is **User Generated Content** or **UGC**. UGC refers to content that private individuals have uploaded in an effort to be useful to others, such as a post on Wikipedia or a customer review on Yelp, or to be entertaining, for example.[3] It is easy to see how an amateur video by a private user may unwittingly infringe copyright. For example, if the user's video features a copyrighted song played in the background without authorization from the copyright holder. Daugherty et al. (2008) find that a main motivator behind UGC is its *"ego-defensive"* function. Users tend to contribute to the creation of online content to "shield" themselves from what they perceive as potential external threats (e.g. somebody in their network challenging their authority on a certain subject) and to reinforce their self-confidence, growing a sense of community. Thus a user of Quora (an online platform collecting questions on any topic) may reply to a question by another user on how to paint a wall to reinforce her confidence and authority on DIY matters.

YouTube videos are primarily categorized as UGC. As illustrated in Figure 9.2, there has been a dramatic increase in uploads in the latest years, particularly as of 2014, reaching approximately 500 hours of video uploaded on YouTube every minute globally in May 2019. The controversy around UGC is at the centre of an open fight between record labels and "YouTubers" (Alexander J., 2019). We will look into these dynamics closely in the following sections.

9.1.1 Actors in the illegal content value chain

Let us focus on the following group of actors in the illegal content online ecosystem:

- Offenders
- Victims

---

[3] For an introduction to the role of internet users as co-creators, see Van Dijck (2009).

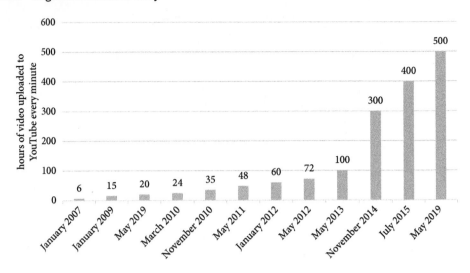

Figure 9.2 Growth in videos uploaded to YouTube over time
https://www.statista.com/statistics/259477/hours-of-video-uploaded-to-youtube-every-minute/

- Intermediaries
- Third parties with a policing role.

9.1.1.1 Offenders

Offenders upload material for various purposes: they may seek a monetary return, they may pursue ideological objectives, or they may simply be unaware of the illegal nature of the content they upload. There is no universal definition for content that may be deemed illegal: content is illegal if it breaches the laws enforced in the jurisdiction where the content is displayed.[4] Hence it may well be that an online platform operating in multiple jurisdictions could display content that would be simultaneously deemed legal and illegal in different geographical locations. Even the EU lacks harmonization as legality tends to be defined by Member States' national laws. However, the EU has recently introduced some degree of harmonization in areas that are relevant specifically to online intermediaries (see also: (De Streel, et al., 2020)). These are:

> *Terrorist content* – Directive 2017/541 (European Parliament and the Council, 2017) lists several crimes (such as an attack on a person's life) as *"potential terrorist offences"* if they are intended to *"seriously intimidate a population, to unduly compel a government or an international organisation to perform or abstain from performing any act, or to seriously destabilise or destroy the fundamental political, constitutional, economic or social structures of a country or an international organisation"*.[5]

---

[4] It is fair to say that laws from different jurisdictions share common traits. For an overview of *natural law* theories, see Finnis (2011).

[5] See point (8) of the Directive preamble.

Child pornography – Directive 2011/92 on child exploitation and abuse defines as illegal *"(i) any material that visually depicts a child engaged in real or simulated sexually explicit conduct; (ii) any depiction of the sexual organs of a child for primarily sexual purposes; (iii) any material that visually depicts any person appearing to be a child engaged in real or simulated sexually explicit conduct or any depiction of the sexual organs of any person appearing to be a child, for primarily sexual purposes; or (iv) realistic images of a child engaged in sexually explicit conduct or realistic images of the sexual organs of a child, for primarily sexual purposes".*[6]

Hate speech – Council Framework Decision 2008/913/JHA (The Council of the European Union, 2008a) defines *hate speech* as (among other things): *"public incitement to violence or hatred directed against a group of persons or a member of such a group defined on the basis of race, colour, descent, religion or belief, or national or ethnic origin"* (The Council of the European Union, 2008b).

Criminal persecution at Member State level for crimes committed in the three areas described above is encouraged. Member States must, for example, adopt measures that effectively prevent child pornography or terrorist content from circulating. However, on a global level, little success in achieving this goal has been recorded so far: 45 million videos and photos of sexually abused children were reported to have been posted online in 2018 by tech companies, with an exponential increase compared to previous years (Bursztein, et al., 2019). Likewise, the terrorist group Daesh disseminated, on average, 1,200 propaganda items every month between 2015 and 2017 (European Commission, 2018h).

A fourth area of harmonization for the definition of illegal content is **Intellectual Property Rights** and, in particular, *copyright*, which I cover in Section 9.4. Generally, *piracy*, or the consumption and distribution of copyrighted material online (music, movies, newspapers, books, magazines), is an endemic phenomenon (see Figure 9.3 for an example) that fuels a longstanding controversy between rights holders and supporters of widespread access to content. In 2020, the European Union Intellectual Property Office (EUIPO) reported that access to pirated content in the EU had fallen by more than 15% between 2017 and 2018 (The European Observatory on Infringements of Intellectual Property Rights, 2020).

9.1.1.2 Victims

Victims are stakeholders who pay for the consequences of the dissemination of illegal content online. They may be hurt directly, for example, in the case of buyers who purchase online a counterfeited good or who are otherwise subject to fraud through the provision of a faulty service or product. Intellectual property rights holders such as publishers or content creators can be directly affected, as piracy has the potential to erode the legitimate reward they gain from the creation of content (see Section 9.2). But individuals or organizations can also be harmed indirectly by

---

[6] Art. 2 of the Directive.

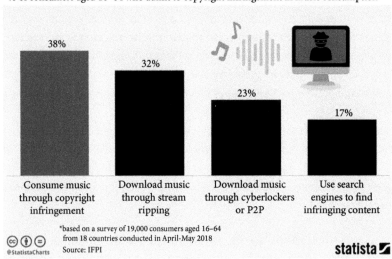

Figure 9.3 Music Piracy Online

Richter, F. (2018. *Music Piracy Still Prevalent in the Age of Streaming*. Statista. Statista Inc..
Accessed: April 16, 2021. https://www.statista.com/chart/15764/prevalence-of-music-
piracy/ Made available under the Creative Commons License CC BY-ND 3.0

illegal content shared online, even if they stay offline, for example, if they are subject
to defamation or hate speech. Finally, society at large is harmed when criminal law
is infringed, as is the case in the offline world. That is clear in the case of terrorism
offences or child pornography.

Generally speaking, it is a challenge for harmed third parties to access compensation, particularly for individuals or small organizations. The Internet makes it
extremely difficult to pin down where offenders are located and pursue any criminal law or civil law action against them (this echoes the challenges we have seen in
Chapter 7 on cybersecurity).

9.1.1.3 Intermediaries

The category of "online intermediaries," which connect the offender (those who
upload or distribute illegal content) and those who consume online content, often
overlaps with that of online platforms, though this is not always the case. According to estimates from the European Commission in 2018 (European Commission,
2018h), more than 10,500 hosting providers (that is: companies keeping web content
on their servers) are established in Europe, 90% of which are small or medium enterprises (SMEs) and 45% are micro-enterprises. Dealing with illegal content requires
investment in monitoring systems, meaning that small companies lacking resources
are more exposed to challenge. The European Commission also finds that more than
50% of hosting companies offer file storage and file-sharing services, around 20%
are online media sharing services, and just 10% are social networking and discussion forums. However, this does not tell us much about the market size since, as we

know from other chapters (see in particular Chapter 5 and 8), the market for social networks is particularly concentrated.

9.1.1.4 Third parties with a policing role

Content can be deemed illegal only by (primarily national) judicial or public administrative authorities. As we will see below, policymakers' efforts are geared towards facilitating the flow of information between online hosting services and public authorities, both in terms of the *completeness* and *accuracy* of the information provided and in terms of the *speed* at which the information is passed on. Similarly, certain public authorities may issue removal orders, compelling intermediaries to take content down within a specific timeframe. As we will see in Section 9.4, the time constraint mandated by the law is the object of a heated debate within national and EU institutions.

An important role may also be played by *"trusted flaggers,"* as defined by the European Commission in its 2017 Communication on Tackling Illegal Content Online (European Commission, 2017f). These are individuals or organizations with specific expertise endowing them with the ability to spot illegal content with greater accuracy. They may therefore be fast-tracked when reporting content that may be deemed unlawful to the hosting provider. For example, a non-governmental organization focusing on child protection may have special communication channels with online platforms to identify child pornography material. Likewise, Europol's Internet Referral Unit may have a privileged position when assessing whether certain content should be deemed of a terrorist nature. Individual users may also flag content they believe is unlawful to hosting platforms. For example, Google's users can flag to Google if they encounter content they believe qualifies as child pornography when doing a web search.

The procedure entailing the removal of content after a particular entity (such as a public authority, an IPR owner, a trusted flagger, or an individual user) has reported its alleged illegality to a platform is referred to as "**notice and take-down**."

9.2 Opportunities and challenges

An often-heard mantra within the public policy debate is *"whatever is illegal offline should also be illegal online"*.[7] This principle appears straightforward, although its application may be challenging in practice. And it does not necessarily correspond to sound economic reasoning: the offline and the online environments are in many ways very different from each other. Geographic borders have little meaning online, where online services tend to be more fluid and market dynamics more unpredictable (see Chapter 1). Laws crafted to address issues in the offline world

---

[7] See, for example, the introduction to the European Commission's Communication on Tackling Illegal Content Online https://ec.europa.eu/digital-single-market/en/news/communication-tackling-illegal-content-online-towards-enhanced-responsibility-online-platforms

may not be directly applicable to the online world. They may have been conceived to tackle market failures that simply do not materialize online or emerge in a different shape. To give an example, Martens (2016) points out that search rankings and online platforms' rating systems may create new types of market failures requiring a different balance of public policy instruments between hard law and self-regulation (see Chapter 8). New challenges have arisen in the online environment which were inconceivable in the offline world.

The online world is, as we know, far from static: markets and technologies evolve rapidly, generating new issues that may render the applicable law obsolete. The 2000 e-Commerce Directive (Directive 2000/31/EC), for example, has embraced the principle that online intermediaries should not be held liable for *mere* conduit, *caching*, or *hosting* illegal content, if they do so unknowingly (I discuss articles 12–14 of the Directive in greater detail in Section 9.4). A similar approach (though not entirely identical) is enshrined in Section 230 of the US Communication Decency Act (Cornell Law School, 2021) which was adopted by the US legislator just a few years before the EU's e-Commerce Directive in 1996. Among the reasons that motivated the adoption of that principle on both sides of the Atlantic was the acknowledgement of intermediaries' technological limitation *at that point in time*. In the eyes of policy-makers, online platforms in the late 1990s looked more like telecom companies than the sophisticated data-gathering technological services that we know today. Hence, holding online platforms liable for their intermediation service possibly looked as outlandish as it would to hold a telecom company liable for having allowed two criminals to set up a murder over a telephone conversation. However, technology today is not the same as it was two decades ago. Online intermediaries appear today much better equipped for monitoring the content they host and the behaviour of their users, even though this may remain cumbersome for smaller platforms.

Along with the "platformization" of the economy and the increasing migration of services from offline to online, the likelihood of illegal behaviour online, its scale, and potential harm have also dramatically increased. As I will explain in detail in Chapter 14 on disinformation, digitalization has dramatically decreased the costs for production, replication, and online distribution of content. Thus, some of the issues that are traditionally observed offline have been magnified by online platforms.

These elements taken together are forcing public institutions around the world to rethink their approach to online intermediaries and their responsibility vis-à-vis the content they host. For example, the European Commission has been working on a *Digital Services Act* which aims to tackle these issues, including the possible modification of some of the principles enshrined in the e-Commerce Directive (see further below).

We are, however, interested in a question that lies upstream. Why is it necessary for public policy to intervene beyond what is already envisaged with the current legal framework to capture illegal behaviour offline? Within that framework, why do online markets not spontaneously evolve to minimize the availability of illegal content online? In other words, why do online content markets *fail*?[8]

9.2.1 Market failures linked to illegal content online

Illegal content generates Internet traffic. Therefore, there is no a priori reason why online platforms should spontaneously limit the spread of illegal content online: the higher the traffic, the higher their profits. Assuming a baseline scenario where intermediaries are not held legally responsible for the content they host, the main cost they may experience is reputational drawbacks. Online platforms that are riddled with hate speech, for example, may be perceived as less appealing by potential users. Likewise, advertisers—which are frequently a major source of revenue for online platforms—may opt to withdraw their ads from a social network or search engine, should they feel their branding image is endangered by the association with content perceived harmful by their target buyers. In July 2020, Coca-Cola, Starbucks, Sony, Ford, Unilever, and other major brands committed to boycotting Facebook, asking it to revise its *hands-off* policy and take a stance against hate speech and disinformation (Lyons K., 2020). However, there is scepticism as to the effectiveness of such initiatives (and Facebook indeed has declared it has no intention of changing its content moderation policy in response to the boycott). Reputation is an effective constraint on companies only to the extent that alternatives in the market exist. As Facebook largely dominates the social network market, it has little to fear from being blamed for taking a hands-off approach to harmful content (we have seen this problem often throughout this book, such as in Chapter 5). The Facebook example can be easily generalized to any other online market where platforms hold significant market power.

The spread of illegal content online can be very harmful to the victims. But that harm is not *internalized* by platforms. The **negative externality** generated by illegal content is not, as such, accounted for by profit-maximizing companies when they plan their business strategies. Students may note a similarity with the cybersecurity context, for example, in which companies do not internalize the cost they impose on the economy if they do not invest resources to mitigate the risk of a cyber-attack.

Conversely, monitoring can be very costly. In the first instance, it is costly to set up and operate the necessary technology. Buiten et al. (2020) point out that the development of detection software and its maintenance and follow-up (namely: the actions required after illegal content has been identified) are a function of four distinct factors:

(i) **the platform's size**: as we have seen in Chapter 7 on cybersecurity, monitoring entails fixed costs that tend to be more cumbersome the smaller the company that has to invest in it

---

[8] For a general analysis see: Lefouili and Madio (2021).

(ii) **the nature of the victim**: if the harmed party is also better placed to flag the presence of illegal content, it reduces the need for active monitoring

(iii) **the platform's business model**: it may be easier for trading companies to monitor the presence of counterfeited good on their platforms than for social network companies to identify hate speech and

(iv) **the type of illegal content**: more nuanced illegal content, such as alleged hate speech that can be disguised as freedom of expression, is far more complex to identify than copyright infringement, for example, which can often be detected through automated technologies.

Monitoring is also costly because it exposes intermediaries to liability. Active monitoring signals that the platform is taking responsibility. As we have seen above, the e-Commerce Directive exempts platforms from liability *if they do not know* that they are hosting illegal content. Thus, *"awareness"* is a reason for falling outside the scope of the e-Commerce Directive's *safe harbour*, and that has a significant dissuasive effect on platforms willing to proactively find out if the content they host is illegal. Moreover, removing content that could later be deemed as lawful may motivate actions for a damages claim.

The mismatch between the optimal level of illegal online content from the perspective of online intermediaries and from the perspective of society is apparent: platforms that do not monitor illegal content benefit from higher Internet traffic and minimize costs, despite the huge harm that illegal content can cause society in a variety of shapes. Therefore, policy action is required to **realign the incentives** within online platform markets and push intermediaries to take action against what harms social welfare, even if that comes at a cost for them.

9.2.2 The case for IPR protection

Intellectual property rights (IPR), including copyright, are the means to address a structural problem related to the creation of content. **Content is a *non-rivalrous* good**. Consumption by one extra user often implies no extra cost for the content producer. For example, the production cost of a newspaper article does not change if it is read by one or one hundred thousand readers (students may recall from Chapter 5 that *data* is another example of non-rivalrous good).

From a societal perspective, this means that the optimal price to access news content should theoretically be set to zero. The intuition is simple: if there is no extra cost to allow additional consumption but there is a benefit for some (the person who accesses the content, for example, but also society more broadly, who may benefit from better-informed citizens), then setting the price to zero must necessarily increase welfare. However, that logic does not hold if we move from a static to a dynamic setting. If the prospect is that no price will be paid for the content after it is created, it would be hard to have an incentive to produce it in the first place.

The purpose of IPR and copyright is to limit access to content in order to guarantee a revenue stream to content producers to preserve their incentive to create new content.

It follows that the establishment of new rights should only be sought when strictly necessary to preserve the incentive for content producers to create content, i.e. when producers would experience a loss without the establishment of that right. Keep this consideration in mind, as it relates to a structural flaw of the EU's 2019 Copyright Directive (Directive (EU) 2019/790), as we shall see in Sections 9.3 and 9.4.

9.3 Dilemmas for policymakers

The core dilemma faced by policymakers consists of a delicate trade-off. On the one hand are the significant benefits of the platform economy, the emergence of which has been nurtured by the recognition of platforms as "neutral" intermediaries with no editorial responsibility. In his 2019 book, *The Twenty-Six Words that Created the Internet* (Kosseff, 2019), Jeff Kosseff refers to the article of Section 230 of the US Communications Decency Act granting immunity from liability. He states that it would be impossible to separate the success of US technological companies from the adoption of Section 230 (Wiener A., 2020). On the other hand, though, there is mounting evidence that the expansion of freedom of expression allowed by the platform economy is increasingly being abused, leading to significant societal harm.

Arguably platforms should bear part of the costs sustained to address illegal content online, being the primary recipients of the benefit of the higher Internet traffic that illegal content generates. But solutions are not straightforward. Particularly in this area, regulatory obligations may endanger users' freedom to express themselves and access information online, cementing market asymmetries by favouring the strongest players vis-à-vis smaller, resource-constrained competitors, ultimately leading to more harm than good (see Chapter 8).

Sartor (2017) lists the following possible approaches regarding secondary liability of intermediaries:

- **Strict liability** – implying that the intermediator is de facto liable for any illegal activity it contributes to enabling
- **Negligence liability** – the intermediary is liable if it has some kind of active or passive involvement in the illegal activity. For example, it may be liable if it is aware that the illegal activity is taking place, or if it fails to implement specific duties established by the law such as monitoring possible illegal activities it may be enabling
- **Liability under "safe harbour" conditions** – the intermediary may take specific measures to address illegal content (e.g. removal of content) that grants it exemption from liability for that content (i.e. safe harbour)

- **Immunity from sanctions** – the intermediary may be ordered to implement specific measures in response to illegal content (such as taking down some content from an online platform), but suffers no direct consequence for the illegal activity itself.
- **Immunity from sanctions and injunctions** – the intermediary is not liable, and it cannot be obliged by any public authority to take any action vis-à-vis the illegal content it contributes to enabling.

The optimal solution or combination of solutions selected by regulators depends on a balance between a number of factors. The researcher suggests the following arguments in favour of establishing a secondary liability for intermediaries:

(i) it contributes to *internalizing* the negative externality on society, meaning that it creates an incentive for platforms to remove illegal content, even though doing so implies reduced Internet traffic and hence profits

(ii) similarly, secondary liability generates an incentive for platforms to put in place policies that prevent or filter out illegal content posted by users in the first place, and finally

(iii) it allows victims to seek compensation where it would otherwise be impossible for them to do so, as offenders having primary liability are often untraceable or can easily escape law enforcement.

However, other arguments suggest that secondary liability for intermediaries may be hard to implement or, in certain circumstances, even not desirable:

(i) liable intermediaries may decide to drop some of their services or considerably limit them, ultimately preventing users from fully benefiting from engaging with the intermediary (the obvious risk is with the potential curtail of freedom of expression)

(ii) secondary liability may be not viable for certain business models that, by nature, crucially depend on outsourced contributions by their users: "classic" examples are Reddit, Quora, or Wikipedia, and

(iii) facing increased risk, intermediaries may err on the safe side and enact policies that filter out content that is not illegal. Again, this would have significant consequences on users' freedom of expression and access to information.

The latter is probably the most compelling argument against platforms' secondary liability. The relative legal term of art is **collateral censorship**. Balkin (2013) refers to it as the consequence of "*the state* [holding] *one private party, A, liable for the speech of another private party B,* [while] *A has the power to block, censor, or otherwise control access to B's speech. This will lead A to block B's speech or withdraw infrastructural support from B. In fact, because A's own speech is not involved, A has incentives to err* *on the side of caution and restrict even fully protected speech in order to avoid any chance of liability."*

An illustration of how collateral censorship dynamics could unfold comes from a now-infamous "misstep" by Facebook in 2016. Despite legal safe harbour, platforms often have internal rules determining which content should not be allowed to be posted online. In the 2016 case, Facebook found that an iconic photo by photographer Nick Út picturing a naked girl fleeing a napalm attack during the Vietnam War was in breach of Facebook's "Community Standards" against child pornography and thus ought to be removed. The case is illustrative of the challenge for platforms to play an editorial role for the content they host. It gives an idea of the potential implications of stricter secondary liability policies, which naturally would exert a much stronger constraint on companies' behaviour than their internal policy rules, for freedom of information. Note that the removal of Út's photo is just the tip of the iceberg: Facebook apologized and backed down, recognizing the mistake, but this was ultimately because the mistake was glaring and gave impulse to significant public criticism. Instead, the risk of collateral censorship is somewhat subtle: it concerns a potentially vast number of small cases that would not necessarily capture widespread public attention.

9.3.1 Possible ways forward

An efficient approach from an economic perspective would entail allocating liability to the party that is best suited to mitigate risks (we have seen this principle already in the broader context of the data economy—see Chapter 5). Arguably, in the case of illegal content, platforms are the party best placed to mitigate risks given their potential to monitor and control the process of content publication from the uploading phase to the consumption and distribution phase. This means that liability rules should be designed to **incentivize platforms to take a proactive role**, bearing in mind two further considerations: (i) that role should also entail minimization of collateral censorship risks, and (ii) other parties should also be involved when they can contribute to addressing the problem, for example if they are in a good position to spot or report the allegedly illegal content (Buiten, et al., 2020).

A key issue for policymakers concerns the distinction of the role of the intermediary between *passive* and *active*. As we have seen above, the general principle endorsed by the EU and US legislators with the e-Commerce Directive and the Communication Decency Act is that platforms should be exempted from liability if they are unaware of the illegality of the content they host. That is: if a platform remains passive and does not proactively look for illegal content, it is liable only if it becomes aware of the content incidentally, for example, if a judge explicitly flags it as such. To incentivize companies to take proactive roles, **Good Samaritan clauses** may be envisaged by the liability system. Such clauses would extend the exemption from liability also in case of proactive monitoring, provided that the platform has acted in good faith.

Automatic monitoring and detection would arguably minimize the risk that il-legal content is published online, although detection and identification is a tricky business, as we have seen. The extent to which platforms should be compelled to get proactively involved in identifying and removing illegal content they host (i.e. the platform's *duty of care*), should be determined by: (a) the magnitude of the harm that the illegal content may cause; (b) the feasibility and implementation burden of monitoring and removal measures; (c) the technology available for detection; and (4) the likelihood of side effects (such as collateral censorship).[9]

In parallel, platforms may facilitate communication from victims and third par-ties to complement their detection system with an outsourced reporting system. Establishing a notice-and-take-down system can be an effective way of tackling ille-gal content, provided that the system is smooth, transparent, and accountable. For example, users should systematically receive feedback on the content they flag with a clear explanation of the platform's follow-up action (or non-action).

To address the issue of *"over removal"*, Buiten et al. (2020) suggest a two-tier ap-proach. First, a **general system of counter-notice**, whereby the potential offender that originally uploaded the alleged illegal content is given the possibility to argue in favour of its legality before the platform takes any follow-up action. And second, an **exceptional approach** in case illegality is manifest and the magnitude of potential harm is high, whereby content is taken down immediately without waiting for the potential offender's counter-argument. Such an approach would crucially rely on the set-up of an out-of-court dispute resolution system, ensuring that counter-notices are taken seriously by the intermediary. If they failed to do so, they would risk being asked to pay compensation to the affected parties.

For the EU Single Market, De Streel et al. (2020) propose adopting harmonized rules on procedural accountability so that national authorities (or even an ad-hoc supranational authority) could supervise and, if necessary, sanction online plat-forms for their actions vis-à-vis the content they host. To mitigate the problem of asymmetric effects of the regulation (smaller companies would find it challenging to comply with a burdensome liability system), the authors suggest the identification of a threshold for the number of users above which platforms should be consid-ered "Public Space Content-Sharing Platforms" and be subject to stricter control and liability measures. That "positive" discrimination, with big platforms hit harder, is intuitive and appealing. However, it entails potential drawbacks: it may under-mine the incentives of smaller platforms to catch up and competitively challenge the big players, contrary to the explicit objective of EU policies in the digital area. And it may facilitate the migration of illegal content from bigger to smaller commu-nication channels, where illegal content may become more elusive and difficult to track. Bigger platforms could as well be required by public authorities to share their technology and know-how to facilitate monitoring and detection by smaller hosting services.

---

[9] See Sartor, G. (2017).

9.3.2 Primary liability for hosted content

As we have seen, platforms may also be held directly liable for the content they host. A peculiar case that gave rise to a harsh controversy within the EU public policy debate concerns the **use of copyrighted content by online platforms**. The controversy refers, in particular, to web search engines or social networks using *"snippets"*— short excerpts of copyrighted articles located on third-party publishers' websites. For example, news aggregators such as Google News may display links to articles with a short preview of their full content in response to a specific query by users.

European publishers (Scott M., Clark N., 2015) have voiced concerns that Google News was depleting their authors' intellectual property value. As a result, they pressured the European Union to establish a new right that would entitle copyright holders to receive a payment from news aggregators for the use of excerpts of their articles: the technical name for such rights is **neighbouring rights** (sometimes referred to with the more general term: **ancillary rights**).[10]

However, theoretical and empirical evidence[11] suggest that news aggregators tend to benefit the publishing industry, rather than harming it. Rather than being in a competition-substitution relationship, they play a complementary role: users often do not limit themselves to reading only the snippets displayed by aggregators. Instead, they get "hooked" as one might to a movie trailer, and often they follow through by clicking on the news aggregator's listed link to land on the publishers' website.

Two real-life examples have confirmed this observation. First, Germany introduced a law to establish *ancillary rights* for publishers and newspaper magazines in 2013.[12] In response, Google opted to de-index German publishers unless they would grant it permission to publish snippets for free. A 2015 decision from the Bundeskartellamt, the German antitrust authority (Bundeskartellamt, 2015), confirmed that such behaviour does not infringe antitrust laws. Axel Springer, one of the most vocal publishers supporting the introduction of the new copyright, ended up granting a free licence to Google. This comes as no surprise: since the feeding of Internet traffic from Google News is beneficial to publishers, they have an interest in favouring it.

Second, in 2014, the Spanish legislator adopted a similar levy. It was dubbed the "Google Tax" by commentators.[13] In response, Google News and other online service providers exited the Spanish market before the law entered into force in January 2015. This provided for a helpful case study: within hours of their removal from Google News, Spanish media sites saw their external traffic falling by double digit

---

[10] For a perspective on neighbouring rights, see Ricketson and Ginsburg (2006).

[11] See, for example: Chiou and Tucker (2017) or Huang, et al. (2013).

[12] Art. 87f of the German body of copyright laws 'Urheberrechtsgesetz—UrhG' see: https://www.gesetze-im-Internet.de/englisch_urhg/englisch_urhg.html

[13] Ley 21/2014, de 4 de noviembre, por la que se modifica el texto refundido de la Ley de Propiedad Intelectual, aprobado por Real Decreto Legislativo 1/1996, de 12 de abril, y la Ley 1/2000, de 7 de enero, de Enjuiciamiento Civil.

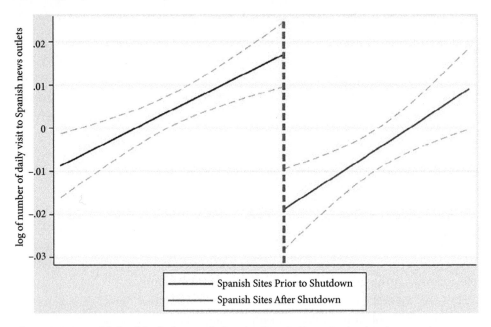

Figure 9.4 Log of daily visits before and after the Google News Spain shutdown
Joan Calzada and Ricard Gil, 'News aggregators and the reform of the copyright legislation in Europe', VoxEU
(30 April 2019). https://voxeu.org/article/news-aggregators-and-european-copyright-legislation

percentages. As shown by Calzada and Gil (2019), news outlets in Spain experienced a decrease in Internet traffic of between 8% and 14%, with the starkest impact during the first six months of the shutdown (see Figure 9.4).

At the end of the chapter, the case study summarizes another high profile neighbouring right case, this time outside the European Union, in Australia.

The introduction of neighbouring rights can often end up being counterproductive, as it has effects that run contrary to the very purpose of intellectual property rights. By reducing traffic to publishers, neighbouring rights reduce the revenue stream for creative work, lowering the incentive for authors to create content in the first place.

In addition, the introduction of neighbouring rights is likely to have adverse effects on a vast array of market players. In the market of online platforms/news aggregators, increasing the cost for news aggregators may have a shrinking effect on the market. News aggregators may exit, causing users to end up with a more restricted choice and lower quality services. Additional levies can create regulatory uncertainty and stifle innovation: new players could refrain from introducing new services (such as customer-tailored news), fearing that they may be infringing publishers' neighbouring rights. Moreover, as the German case shows (where Axel Springer granted free access only to Google News), ancillary rights tend to create a comparative advantage for established players. For example, smaller, emerging European platforms may not be able to negotiate favourable conditions with publishers while their bigger competitors (such as Google or Facebook) can. In that sense, a "Google Tax" could be more accurately dubbed a "smaller competitors' tax".

Similarly, adverse effects are expected in the news market. The reduction of traffic from news aggregators would penalize smaller publishers disproportionally. Small publishers lacking a well-known brand tend to rely more than others do on redirection from news aggregators. With the exit of news aggregators, the publishing market would therefore become more concentrated. Less competition implies lower quality, less choice, and reduced innovation for users/readers. Moreover, the market shrinking effect could also negatively affect advertisers, who could experience a loss of revenue due to the reduced Internet traffic generated.

It is worth noting that even if the net effect on publishers' revenues were positive (i.e. the revenue stream from neighbouring rights minus the loss of web traffic from news aggregators), neighbouring rights may have undesired medium- to long-term effects on the industry, because publishers would have a lower incentive to innovate, being shielded from platforms' competitive pressure. As we have seen in previous chapters, almost every industry in the world has either been disrupted, is currently going through disruption, or is likely to be disrupted in the near future. The video and the music industries, for example, are evolving in radical ways as a result of technological innovations, market dynamics, and consumer demands. Nevertheless, from a customer perspective, it is hard to complain about the variety and the quality of movies or music that can be accessed today. Likewise, readers can today access an extremely wide choice of high-quality readings. Thus, a neighbouring rights "life-line" would only serve to slow down a process the publishing industry will eventually need to go through, adapting their business model to cope with digital disruption.

9.4 The European Union's perspective

The 2000 **e-Commerce EU Directive** (Directive 2000/31/EC) is at the cornerstone of the European approach to online intermediaries' liability for hosted content. As with Section 230 of the Communication Decency Act in the US, the e-Commerce Directive played a crucial role in allowing the emergence of the platform economy in Europe. It is not by chance that, despite growing pressure to "do something" to address harm caused by abuses in platform markets, EU policymakers have so far resisted the temptation to begin the process for a revision of the law. A law that, in many respects, has worked very well since its inception. The debate around a *Digital Services Act*, ongoing at the time of writing and more than twenty years since the adoption of the e-Commerce Directive, is possibly the first time a step is being taken to challenge some of the Directive's provisions explicitly.

As we shall see in Chapter 11 on the sharing economy, the e-Commerce Directive endorses the important **Country of Origin** principle. This principle implies that platforms are by default subject to the Member State's law *where they are es-tablished*. It granted platforms greater legal certainty and the freedom to provide services across Europe, representing an essential contribution to creating a Digital Single Market.

For the purpose of secondary liability, Articles 12 to 15 of the e-Commerce Directive are specifically relevant. Art. 12 states that Member States "*shall ensure that the service provider is not liable for the information transmitted*", something that the Directive refers to as "mere conduit", provided that the platform does not have an active role in it (e.g. it does not initiate the transmission or select the information or its receivers).[14] Art. 13 forces Member States to exempt platforms from liability triggered by the automatic, intermediate, and temporary storage of information, or "caching", again provided that the platform plays no active role in it. Art. 14 refers to *hosting* and obliges Member States to ensure that platforms are not liable for the information they store, provided that the platform does not have actual knowledge of the illegal activity or information or that it acts expeditiously to remove access to that information upon becoming aware of it. Art. 15 prevents Member States from imposing general monitoring obligations on platforms where carrying out *mere conduit, caching,* or *hosting* activities.

The safe harbour principles of the e-Commerce Directive have come under indirect pressure in recent years, with the EU legislator taking action to prompt the more direct involvement of platforms for the content they host. That was the case with the revision of the Audiovisual Media Services Directive (Directive (EU) 2018/1808) (or AVMSD) adopted in 2018 (with a transposition deadline of September 2020). The AVMSD requires Member States to take appropriate measures to ensure that platforms do not display harmful content to minors or content inciting violence or hatred to the general public. It also imposes obligations for platforms to ensure that at least 30% of their catalogue contains European content and to ensure its prominence. This latter measure appears not only protectionist in nature, but also of uncertain efficacy. On-demand video services, such as Netflix, are by definition guided by users' preferences, no matter the composition of platforms' movies' catalogue. In other words, users cannot be compelled to consume a particular type of content as perhaps sometimes happens with radio or TV, where the user's control is limited to switching channel (or turning the device off). With on-demand content, users choose what they want to consume and when they want to do it, leaving little scope for attempts to boost a country's cultural sector production through induced consumption (rather than its greater appeal).

Another critical injury to the e-Commerce Directive was caused by the 2019 Copyright Directive (Directive (EU) 2019/790). Article 17 of the Copyright Directive regulates the "*use of protected content by online content-sharing service providers.*" It imposes an obligation for platforms to seek authorization to

---

[14] The e-Commerce Directive refers to the broader category of 'information society services'. I use the term platform for simplicity, as this is the category of services we are interested in.

use copyrighted work "*covering also acts carried out by users.*" If no authorization is granted, platforms are to be found liable for "*unauthorised acts of communication to the public, including making available to the public, of copyright-protected works.*" In other words, the Directive introduces a liability for platforms as regards copyrighted work posted by their users, raising concerns that this would lead to an excess of zeal. For example, platforms such as YouTube may choose to set up automatic filtering procedures, increasing the risk of collateral censorship and limiting users' creativity and freedom of expression. Most strikingly, it is unclear the extent to which Art. 17 truly "protects" content creation. To my knowledge, there is currently no sound academic evidence suggesting a significant negative impact of platform users' use of copyrighted content on content creators' streams of profits.

Moreover, Art. 15 of the Directive relates to platforms' *primary liability*, introducing neighbouring rights to "protect" press publications for online uses. As we have seen in Section 9.3, in the best-case scenario this provision will have no significant effect. In the worst-case scenario, Art. 15 may lead to higher concentration on the platforms' and news publishing markets, to the detriment of the European Digital Single Market.

Finally, yet another wound to the safe harbour principles of the e-Commerce Directive was made by the EU legislator with the **Regulation on addressing the dissemination of terrorist content online**, adopted in April 2021.[15] The Regulation mandates a one-hour removal rule for terrorist content in response to a removal order issued by the competent national authority. Terrorist content is defined as, for example, "*content that by the glorification of terrorist acts advocates the commission of terrorist offences, thereby causing a danger that one or more such offences may be committed*". It also encourages platforms to protect their services by taking specific measures against the dissemination to the public of terrorist content. Therefore, it may indirectly incentivize the use of automated filtering technologies (increasing the risk of collateral censorship).

The Regulation has been criticized for its potential effects on freedom of expression and on the platform economy, since its measures are indiscriminately imposed on platforms regardless of their size, scope, or purpose. Yet, as we have seen above in Section 9.3, an asymmetric regulation would increase the risk that harmful content would migrate from big to smaller platforms, de facto reducing the regulation' effectiveness. However, as we shall see in Chapter 14 on disinformation, it is unclear whether the removal of harmful content, even if done quickly, is an effective measure to address harm. Once posted, the content may immediately achieve its goals if it becomes viral, reaching numerous users. Addressing the problem at the root thus requires addressing platforms' business model. In particular: the dynamic through which content becomes viral.

---

[15] Regulation (EU) 2021/784 of the European Parliament and of the Council of 29 April 2021 on addressing the dissemination of terrorist content online, OJ 2021 L 173/79.

9.4.1 The Communication on Tackling Illegal Content Online

Besides prompting action on specific areas (audio-visual, copyright, terrorist content), the European Commission has also directly tackled online illegal content with non-legislative initiatives. The most relevant of those is the **2017 Communication on Tackling Illegal Content Online** (European Commission, 2017f). The Communication describes guidelines and principles aiming to help platforms step up their efforts to tackle illegal content they may host. These entail:

- measures to facilitate a **bidirectional flow of information between competent authorities** (such as judges or regulatory authorities) and platforms, such as the appointment of points of contact or the development of technical interfaces to allow smooth and continuous cooperation
- a fast-tracked system of notice-and-take-down for **trusted flaggers** (see above Section 9.1). The Commission also committed to exploring the possibility of defining EU-wide criteria to identify who can be considered a trusted flagger
- an accessible, user-friendly system of notice-and-take-down for platforms' users that should entail **easy notification and detailed feedback** explaining the reason for the notice follow-up by the platform. This also means adopting measures to **favour transparency** in general, such as a platform's commitment to publishing regular reports with information on the number and types of notices received and the follow-up action undertaken by the platform
- measures to facilitate the contest of take-downs (**counter-notice procedures**) by the affected parties and to provide them with transparent feedback as regards the motivation of the action taken. Platforms are also encouraged to use out-of-court dispute settlement bodies to address potential controversies with counter-notices
- reassurances that **proactive automatic detection measures** implemented by platforms do not necessarily imply falling outside the scope of the e-commerce safe harbour (*Good Samaritan* principle)
- encouraging platforms to implement **automated technologies that would prevent the re-appearance** of illegal content after it had been taken down.

The 2017 Communication was followed by a European Commission Recommendation (European Commission, 2018i) in 2018 that contained several concrete measures that Member States and platforms could take to operationalize the Communication's suggestions.

9.4.2 The Digital Services Act

In December 2020, the European Commission proposed a package of legislative actions to tackle issues in online platform markets. As we have seen in Chapter 8,

one of those initiatives is called the Digital Markets Act and it is aimed at imposing a number of ex-ante obligations on sizable platforms (online gatekeepers, see
chapter 8.4.3). The other notable legislative initiative is the **Digital Services Act** (or
DSA) (European Commission, 2020p). The DSA contains some provisions for online gatekeepers, but its scope is much broader than the DMA. The DSA aims to set
rules for any kind of intermediary services, including Internet service providers (see
Chapter 5), cloud and web-hosting services (see Chapter 6), and online platforms of
any size. Failing to respect those rules could result in fines up to 6% of a company's
annual turnover. Keep in mind that both the DMA and the DSA are legislative *proposals*. That means that the text needs to be adopted by the EU co-legislators before
turning into law (in this case: a EU Regulation). The process may take months, if
not years, and the final text is probably going to be different from the one that the
European Commission proposed in December 2020.

The DSA proposal does not challenge the basic principle of liability enshrined by
the e-Commerce Directive. According to the DSA, platforms are still not liable for
the content they host if they are not aware of its illegality. The DSA, however, makes
it more difficult for platforms to actually claim that they were ignorant about the
presence of illegal content on their servers once that content is actually identified.
For example, the DSA obliges online platforms to put in place smooth mechanisms for users to flag content and to cooperate with trusted flaggers (see above).
It may thus simply suffice that a user has flagged a specific content in order to make
platforms liable.

Being aware that the increased risk for online platforms could push them to
be overzealous (increasing the likelihood of collateral censorship), the European
Commission also proposes safeguards for users. They can, for example, challenge
platforms' content moderation decisions. Moreover, the DSA contains a *Good
Samaritan* clause (art. 6) stating that liability exemptions should not be disapplied
when intermediary services providers carry out voluntary own-initiative investigations or comply with the law. The DSA also imposes obligations of traceability of
business users in online market places, in order to favour the identification of sellers
selling illegal goods.

Notably, the DSA imposes more substantial obligations for very large online platforms. This category of intermediaries could loosely overlap with that proposed in
the DMA for gatekeepers (see Chapter 8). In the DSA however, the criterion applied
is much simpler: very large platforms are platforms that serve on average at least
45 million users per month. Very large platforms are supposed to show a continuous effort in tackling abuse of their communication channels. For example, they may
be forced to provide access to researchers for independent scrutiny of their data. Or
they are required to regularly assess and report the systemic risks implied by the use
of their services and attempt to implement effective measures to mitigate those risks.
Note that in this case, the risk could also be related to harmful, not necessarily illegal,
content platforms may host (e.g. *disinformation*, to be discussed in Chapter 14).

****

9.5 Case Study: Australia's Copyright Law

In February 2021, Australia's House of Representatives approved a law called "News Media Bargaining Code". The goal of the Code is to push large online platforms, such as Facebook and Google, to sit at the negotiation table with publishers and enter into a monetary agreement for the use of their content.

The Australian Code goes a step further compared to the EU Copyright Directive (see Section 9.4) in that it envisages the involvement of an independent arbitrator if negotiations fail. The arbitrator would be able to set the price platforms must pay Australian news publishers. The Code also commits Facebook and Google to invest a significant amount of money to support the creation of local digital content. According to the Code's explanatory memorandum, the Australian Government was concerned that the Australian media sector was already under significant pressure, a pressure exacerbated by a sharp decline in advertising revenue due to the Covid-19 pandemic.

Publishers around the world are increasingly demanding policymakers to provide them with stronger bargaining power vis-à-vis large online platforms, taking an example from Australia. Google and Facebook have been trying to fend off that pressure, financing expensive projects to support traditional national news outlets and local newspapers, helping them adapt to the "digital revolution".

The News Media Bargaining Code can be found here: https://www.accc.gov.au/focus-areas/digital-platforms/news-media-bargaining-code

9.6 Review questions

- What is the difference between primary and secondary liability from an online platform's perspective? Which one has the highest potential to affect platforms' profits? Why?
- What is illegal offline should also be illegal online. Do you agree? Justify your answer.
- Look for three real-life examples (or make up your own) for online "collateral censorship". Do not use the examples used in the book.
- Why are the 2000 EU e-Commerce Directive and Section 230 of the US Communication Decency Act considered milestones in the development of the platform economy? Do they contain core principles that would be desirable to preserve in future legislative action, despite new challenges emerging in the digital economy?
- You have been hired by the publisher of a small media outlet. Please lay out all possible benefits and costs entailed by any new law strengthening primary or secondary liability regimes for online platforms for your employer.

10

E-Commerce

Abstract

E-commerce is a general term encompassing any trade activity facilitated by the use of a digital interface. The vast majority of e-commerce transactions involve business customers. However, consumers are increasingly relying on e-commerce to fulfil their shopping needs. E-commerce brings significant advantages to the economy: it boosts companies' productivity, reduces costs, and increases convenience. But its growth is hampered by several obstacles, such as regulatory frictions, access to digital infrastructure and skills, logistical costs, lack of trust and compliance costs, and uncertainty due to outdated taxation frameworks. These issues can, in particular, limit the expansion of e-commerce cross-border and prevent the completion of a functioning EU Digital Single Market. Policy measures of different nature are thus needed to foster regulatory harmonization, increase trust and security, and eliminate potential distortions of competition.

10.1 Background

E-commerce is one of the most direct manifestations of the digital economy. The OECD (2019b) defines it as *"the sale or purchase of goods or services, conducted over computer networks by methods specifically designed for the purpose of receiving or placing orders"*. It can thus refer to the purchase of a book from a bookshop's website, the use of an online movies' streaming service, the delivery of an online teaching course, the online booking of a hotel, the online purchase of wholesale grocery stocks, or the acquisition of IT consulting online services by a local public administration, for example.[1]

This broad definition of e-commerce encompasses most of the topics that I have treated in the previous chapters and that I will treat in the following ones. For example, the sharing economy (see Chapter 11) relates to transactions that ultimately qualify as e-commerce because web applications enact them. Likewise, the *data economy* is inherently e-commerce, to the extent that data is exchanged using electronic means to generate value (see Chapter 5). But this chapter covers the **trading layer** of the digital economy: it specifically concerns two or more parties entering in a commercial agreement thanks to the use of the Internet or, more generally, to the exchange of electronic data through computer networks.

---

[1] Other definitions for e-commerce that can be found in the literature are in Khan (2016) and Kwilinski, et al. (2019).

Digital Economic Policy. Mario Mariniello, Oxford University Press.
© Mario Mariniello (2022). DOI: 10.1093/oso/9780198831471.003.0010

Digitization has a profound implication for trade. The OECD (2019b) suggests three dimensions where that effect unfolds:

- On the **scale of trade**: digitization makes reaching geographically far away customers much easier. It also allows companies from different countries to interconnect, facilitating the creation of global value chains, reducing transaction costs, and increasing production efficiency
- On the **scope of trade**: digitization is affecting companies' business choices, for example allowing retailers to *expand* the scope of the services that they can offer to the buyer to include logistic services, credit card and insurance coverage, e-payment, and remote assistance
  Similarly, companies may *narrow* the scope of their activity to the business segment where they can extract the most value. Digitization reduces transaction costs for complementary goods and services, reducing the need for companies' vertical integration. For example, suppose that the production of vacuum cleaners requires two core inputs, (a) manufacturing and (b) post-sale service. It may have been relatively inefficient in the pre-digital world to have one company supplying (a) and a different company supplying (b). For example, the company supplying post-sale service may have lacked the necessary information on the product hardware to do a good job. For that reason, it generally made more sense to have just one vertically integrated company to supply both (a) and (b). Conversely, digitization dramatically decreases transaction costs and, therefore, may allow companies to specialize in providing (a) or (b) without a significant efficiency loss
- on the **speed of trade**: e-commerce is associated with fast trading, up to real-time delivery and assistance (consider the simple example of downloading an application for smartphones).

These three elements help explain why e-commerce is becoming increasingly relevant. Figure 10.1, for example, indicates a global increase in the share of retail sales represented by e-commerce from 7.4% in 2015 to a forecasted proportion of 22% in 2023. The European Commission's 2020 Digital Economy and Society Index (DESI) reports a steady overtime increase in the proportion of EU companies' turnover represented by e-commerce sales, from 8.5% in 2015 to 11% in 2020.

E-commerce transactions mostly fall into three categories: **B2B**, **B2C**, and **B2G**, referring, respectively, to business' sales to other companies (for example: wholesale deals), to final consumers, or to public administration. Most e-commerce transactions are B2B, representing between 70% and 85% (Coppel, 2000) of the total; yet, direct e-commerce sales to final consumers B2C are increasing at a faster pace. As we have seen in Chapter 3, the Covid-19 pandemic generated a strong impulse especially for B2C e-commerce.

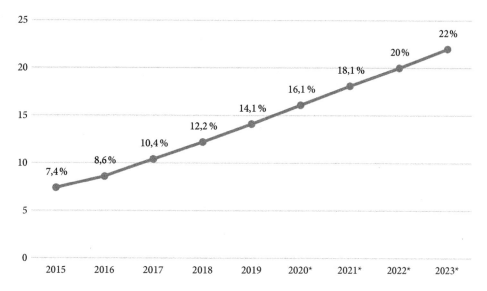

Figure 10.1 E-commerce share of total global retail sales
https://www.statista.com/statistics/534123/e-commerce-share-of-retail-sales-worldwide/

Consumers that rely on e-commerce for their purchases are typically younger and have a higher educational level. Similarly, employed individuals tend to have a higher propensity to buy online than the unemployed. Digital skills and access to the Internet through connectivity (both higher among young, educated, and employed users) are likely to be the drivers underlying those correlations. According to the DESI 2020, the most popular categories of purchases made online by EU consumers in 2019 were clothes and sports goods (65% of online shoppers indicated they purchase goods from this category), travel and holiday accommodation (54%), household goods (46%), tickets for events (41%), and books, magazines, and newspapers (33%).

The most compelling finding of the DESI 2020 is that among online shoppers, only 35% of them purchased goods or services from another EU country, compared to 87% of them buying from their home country. On the supply side, only 8.3% of EU companies in 2020 sold their products or services cross-border. That indicates very clearly that, despite the efforts to implement a Digital Single Market Strategy (see Chapter 1), we are still far from creating one single homogeneous geographical area where digital goods and services can travel smoothly from one EU country to another.

Before moving to analyse the reasons that motivate business or consumers to practice e-commerce and the obstacles they may encounter, some general consideration can be made (López González & Ferencz, 2018).

E-commerce relies on complex networks of complementary goods and services. In the first place, it relies on connectivity infrastructure and on critical services that can enable it (think about shipping and delivery services or electronic payment systems, for example). That begs for policy measures that have a broad scope: stimulating e-commerce requires considering all possible horizontal regulatory layers that affect the whole value chain underlying e-commerce transactions. Moreover, digitization makes it increasingly challenging to identify well-defined boundaries between goods and services. A case in point is 3D printing. When data are transferred from one country to the other, and data are used to print a 3D object, should we qualify that e-commerce transaction as the *sale of a good* (the printed object) or as *the sale of a service* (the transfer of the data)? This decision is crucial because it affects how e-commerce is accounted for in statistical figures and how regulation is implemented. Different geographical areas may diverge in the substance of their regulatory approach to e-commerce and the definition of its scope, undermining one of the core benefits of e-commerce. That is, its ability to *scale beyond borders*.

10.2 Opportunities and challenges

López González and Ferencz (2018) attempt to quantify the positive impact of digitization on trade in goods and services (Figure 10.2). They show that when digital connectivity is increased by 10% on both trading sides, the absolute amount of trade in goods increases by 2% and the absolute amount of trade in services by 3%.

10.2.1 The advantages of e-commerce

E-commerce yields substantial advantages over traditional non-digitized trade. Business, especially smaller companies, can benefit from:

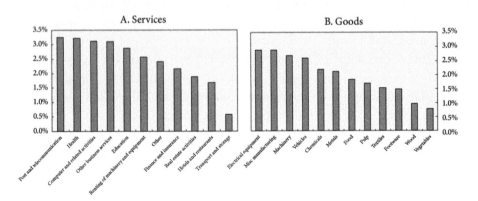

Figure 10.2 The impact of digitization on trade
https://www.oecd-ilibrary.org/trade/digital-trade-and-market-openness_1bd89c9a-en

- **higher visibility**, thanks to web page display and Internet search engine
- no **geographical constraints**, as e-commerce can theoretically reach any potential client anywhere in the world if that client has access to the Internet. There are, however, barriers to cross-border trade that are not geographical in nature, such as language differences, shipping costs, and regulatory barriers, as we discuss below
- **lower production and transaction costs**. For example, e-commerce reduces or eliminates the need for the physical display of the goods sold. Goods can be stored more efficiently at lower storage costs; likewise, inventory costs are reduced if goods are stored more efficiently. Staff costs are reduced, as the dealing process is carried out virtually online
- The opportunity to **stay open 24/7/365**: the web interface allows businesses to be continuously receptive to clients' queries
- **Increased income** from complementary revenue streams. Consider, for example, the case of customer data that can be easily collected during the product selection and transaction process and then used for data analytics or sold for a profit, within the limits defined by data-protection laws (see Chapter 5 for an extensive discussion)
- **Higher flexibility** together with an higher ability to **grasp customers' preferences** and habits. Customers' collected data can be used to aggregate customer groups, tailor offers and discounts, nudge customers to pursue certain activities, and so forth (Amazon built an empire thanks to this feature of e-commerce, as discussed in Chapter 5). This feature also leaves scope for abuse, such as anti-competitive price discrimination and geo-blocking (see further below).

Customers can likewise benefit from the convenience of accessing online stores. They may enjoy reduced prices thanks to the savings in the production process that are partially passed on to final customers *and* to increased competition between suppliers, which is enacted by the Internet. They can get around the clock availability and real-time assistance. With e-commerce, customers find it easier to locate desired products or services.

That explains the increasing popularity of e-commerce and countries' decision-makers' desire to find an effective way to stimulate its expansion within the economy. That equally applies to the European Union: students may recall from Chapter 4 that one of the three key pillars for the Digital Single Market Strategy is Access or ensuring *"better access for consumers and businesses to digital goods and services across Europe"*. For the launching of the strategy in 2015, the European Commission used powerful infographics showing that, on average, the turnover from online sales of an EU country could be split in 42% to domestic online sellers, 54% from US-based online sellers and *only 4%* from an online seller of another EU country. In other words: there is not much cross-border e-commerce in the EU Digital Single Market yet.[2]

---

[2] On barriers to cross-border e-commerce in Europe, see Coad and Duch-Brown (2017).

10.2.2 Issues with e-commerce

Many economic issues that pertain to e-commerce have been discussed in previous chapters or will be discussed in the following ones. Three areas merit a dedicated analysis, though: (a) obstacles that hamper business ability to sell online, (b) issues that reduce consumers' likelihood to purchase online, and (c) taxation and unfair competition between online and traditional business models.

10.2.2.1 Obstacles to business selling online

Companies may opt not to sell online because their product **is not suitable** for e-commerce. This obstacle is possibly the main reason behind not selling online for companies of any size, but it particularly affects small and medium enterprises. Consider, for example, a bakery, the producer of a perishable dairy product, or the seller of tailor-made suits. As noted in OECD (2019b), this observation emphasizes the existence of a potential in e-commerce that could be unlocked through technological or business model innovation. For example, a plumbing company could ship clients AR goggles and guide the client to perform maintenance work by itself; bakeries could join an online platform for the real-time distribution of out-of-the-oven pastries, and so forth.

Companies may also refrain from selling online cross-border because they are afraid to breach local regulations. They may lack the knowledge of the rules or simply consider it too expensive to adapt to them instead of just observing the domestic country's rules and selling online only domestically. Countries may even purposely adopt regulations that make it more difficult for foreign business to compete with domestic business. While this is in principle prohibited by the EU law, according to which goods should have freedom of movement within the Single Market, Member States have historically shown a tendency to *gold plate* directives that addressed regulatory fragmentation to limit cross-border competition. When EU legislation leaves flexibility to Member States on how to adapt their national laws to EU laws, Member States may abuse that flexibility and impose unnecessary regulatory requirements that dissuade companies from other countries to compete. Imagine the imposition of complex bureaucracy to have one's own website's content "cleared" by national authorities before being able to promote discounts to its users. The European Commission's (2020) communication "Identifying and addressing barriers to the Single Market" indicates burdensome and complex administrative procedures as one of the most severe obstacles to cross-border sale, particularly for small and medium companies.

Another critical obstacle to e-commerce sales is logistics: companies may find shipping and return processes too costly, especially when parcel delivery requires border crossing. A 2015 study by the University of St Louis (prompted by the European Commission) suggests that cross-border delivery costs may be as high as 4 to 5 times similar deliveries that occur domestically (Figure 10.3). That can be due

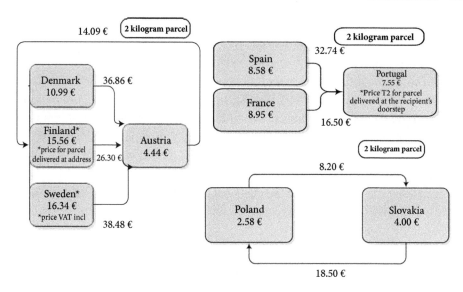

Figure 10.3 Domestic vs cross-border prices in parcel delivery (2015)
https://ec.europa.eu/transparency/regdoc/rep/10102/2016/EN/SWD-2016-166-F1-EN-MAIN-PART-1.
PDF

to the structural features of shipping markets. For example, parcel deliveries operate through networks requiring delivery also to geographical areas that are less profitable (because peripheral or scarcely populated). As in the case of telecommunications (see Chapter 4), high fixed network costs imply a tendency to **natural monopoly**. That is: it may be more efficient to have fewer companies in the market than many, with a duplication of network costs, even though this can imply higher prices than in a competitive market. Thus, those markets require regulatory intervention to keep services of general "universal" utility accessible at fair prices. Regulation, however, can be tricky to enforce, particularly for cross-border transactions, when markets are not transparent and competencies between national regulators are not clearly allocated. The result is that cross-border delivery costs hamper the creation of a Digital Single Market for e-commerce in Europe. Moreover, lack of transparency in delivery prices makes it difficult for sellers to compare different operators and enhance competition between them.

Other obstacles for sellers include: lack of the necessary digital skills for their employees; high perceived cyber-security risks, for example regarding e-payments; and lack of access to the necessary communication infrastructure. These topics are dealt with in their dedicated chapter (respectively: Chapters 12, 7, and 4).

10.2.2.2 Obstacles to online purchase

As for the case of online selling, it should be well accepted that not all products or services can be purchased online. There may be structural reasons motivating customers' choice not to buy online. And policy cannot or should not attempt to affect them. For example, customers may simply prefer to shop in person—to see, try, touch, or smell the product before buying it. Or they may feel loyal to supporting the local community. For the same reasons, we may expect a reduction in e-commerce sales after the Covid-19 pandemic is over: a significant proportion of consumers that were forced to buy online during lock-downs may get back to in-person purchase.

For that reason, it is important to keep in mind that the goal of **policymakers should not be to maximize the growth of e-commerce as such** but to remove the obstacles that prevent e-commerce from growing. Policymakers should not force buyers to increase their e-commerce purchases but should ensure that buyers have that opportunity if *they wish to.*

E-purchases may indeed also be held back by issues that *can* and *should* be addressed through policy intervention. In that respect, two areas of action stand out:

1. issues related to customers' trust
2. issues related to potential artificial restrictions imposed by the seller

Trust is an essential condition for e-commerce: buyers need to rely on the photos and description of products and services they see online.[3] They cannot touch or try them before proceeding with the payment. Thus, customers may be worried that the good or service they purchase may not correspond to its description; that the delivery may take longer than expected or that the good may be damaged during transport; that they may not be able to return or repair a faulty or damaged product, if needed; that their personal data may be used for purposes other than the transaction itself; that their credit card details may be stolen or; more generally, that they will get no reimbursement if something during the transaction does not go as expected. As we know from previous chapters, **asymmetry of information** (the seller has a much greater knowledge about the product sold compared to the buyer) and **moral hazard** (the seller has an incentive to reduce the quality of the service after the payment has gone through) are a source of market failure. These two economic dynamics thus hamper potential growth in the e-commerce market. Moreover, cross-border contexts exacerbate market failures because language and cultural differences may generate even more uncertainty in the communication between counterparts.

As we shall see in the following sections, regulatory action can correct those market failures and increase buyers' trust. However, markets may also be able to self-correct. As we have seen in Chapter 8, for example, online platforms can help reduce asymmetry of information enacting reputational mechanisms based on feedback and ranking by other buyers. That comes at a cost for sellers, though, as platforms' business models may imply acquiring a proportion of the seller's revenue (see, for example, the peer-to-peer business model, discussed in Chapter 11).

Buyers may also not be able to access certain products because of **artificial restrictions** strategically imposed by sellers. Such restrictions may sometimes have

---

[3] For a model on trust and its relation to e-commerce, see Oliveira, et al. (2017).

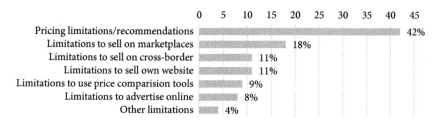

Figure 10.4 Proportion of e-commerce retailers applying restrictions to sales (% of companies)

https://ec.europa.eu/competition/antitrust/sector_inquiry_final_report_en.pdf

anti-competitive effects. However, competition policy[4] may not be applicable if e-sellers do not hold significant market shares. Thanks to e-commerce, however, even small sellers can access vast amounts of buyers' information. For example, collecting data when buyers process their online transaction. Likewise, sellers are increasingly able to control what customers can access on the website and adapt prices to their characteristics. The 2017 European Commission "Final report on the E-commerce Sector Inquiry" finds that pricing limitations/recommendations are applied by more than 40% of e-commerce retailers in Europe. For example, a wholesale supplier may require a retailer to charge a minimum price for the products it markets on-line. Many others impose limitations on selling on specific marketplaces (e.g. eBay), selling cross-border, selling on their own website, using price comparison tools, or advertising online (Figure 10.4).

Restrictions may significantly hamper the expansion of e-commerce, particularly if widespread. Of specific relevance for the Single Market are restrictions to cross-border sales, commonly referred to as "**geo-blocking**" restrictions. Geo-blocking can manifest itself through sellers' refusal to deliver outside the domestic country, through the refusal to accept a payment with a credit card registered in another country, to re-routing of customers to their domestic websites or directly preventing access to the website from outside the seller's domestic country. Imagine, for example, a customer residing in Belgium and interested in buying a pair of shoes from the Italian website of a multinational supplier with shops in Italy and Belgium. The customer may see her payment declined because her credit card is registered in Belgium. Or, she may be re-routed from the Italian website to the Belgian counterpart.

Most of the time, geo-blocking serves the purpose of preventing customers' arbitrage when the same goods are priced differently across the territory. Preventing arbitrage is not necessarily bad for consumers as price discrimination may positively affect welfare (see the appendix for a discussion). For example, price discrimination

---

[4] The current Vertical Block Exemption Regulation (VBER) (Regulation (EU) 330/2010) assumes that no infringement takes place if the restriction concerns a seller and a buyer each not possessing significant market power (quantified by the VBER as a market share above 30%). For a discussion of what the digital economy means for competition policy in general terms, see Chapter 8.

allows a multinational to sell online at lower prices in countries where the average income is lower.[5] However, by preventing the free circulation of goods and capital between European countries, geo-blocking and price discrimination clearly go against the core principles of the Single Market.

10.2.2.3 Taxation and unfair competition between online and traditional business models

Trade digitization has important implications for taxation policy. As noted by the OECD (2019c) three factors contribute to creating uncertainty in the application of taxation systems to business relying on digital applications:

- Digitalization enables **cross-jurisdictional scale without necessarily increasing the mass** or the physical presence of a business. Thanks to digital, companies can fragment their production process and locate different segments of the production chain in different geographical areas
- Digitalization implies relying more extensively on **intangible assets** such as Intellectual Property Rights. Software, websites, algorithms underpinning AI-based applications, for example, are all valuable assets, but it is much harder for a public authority to assess them from a taxation perspective
- A key component of digital business is **users' data**. As we know from previous chapters (see, for example, Chapter 5), users' data are an important source of income for digital business. They are often central to the creation of value around the product or service that the seller supplies. Users may often play the role of *prosumers*[6] in that their passive or active provision of information implies their participation in the value creation.

Tax systems have were designed in a pre-digitization era. They have evolved through time. For example, countries worldwide have been entering bilateral treaties to avoid double taxation following the emergence of multinational companies. Treaties indicate which country is entitled to tax companies that are active in different geographical areas and by how much. However, the allocation of competencies provided by international treaties is driven by the assumption that the *physical presence* of a company is a good indication of where that company is creating (taxable) value. That may have been true for traditional businesses. But that assumption is far-fledged, with economies that turn more digital and become more immaterial. Geographical boundaries lose their meaning online, and value creation increasingly occurs at the place of consumption, thanks to *prosumers'* data, and not only where companies are located (European Commission, 2018o). **Digitization, in other words, propels uncertainty in the taxation of trade** (see Figure 10.5).

---

[5] Duch-Brown, et al. (2020) discuss distributional effects due to the elimination of geo-blocking. They indicate that preventing discrimination within the Single Market implies a redistribution of profits from consumers in low-income countries to those in high-income countries.

[6] The term was first proposed in Toffler (1970).

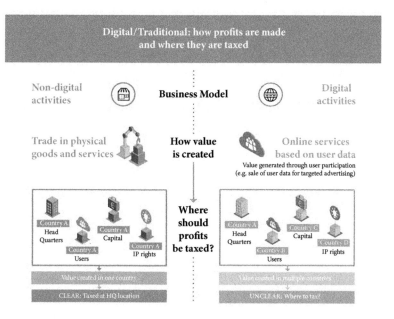

Figure 10.5 Infographics on the difference in taxation for digital and traditional business

https://ec.europa.eu/taxation_customs/sites/taxation/files/factsheet_digital_taxation_21032018_en.pdf

Uncertainty is generally bad for investment: investors may refrain from expanding their business activities if they cannot quantify the future costs they may incur in the future. That may well entail unforeseen taxes, should a specific country establish different taxation rules to mitigate the erosion of the tax base brought about by the digitization of the economy.[7]

Uncertainty in taxation may also be a source of distortion of competition, particularly in so far that traditional business may be subject to higher fiscal pressure compared to their "digitized" competitors. However, it should be noted that such a difference is difficult to quantify because digital businesses models tend to be complex and very different from each other. For example, a study requested by the European Commission and performed by ZEW (see, ZEW 2017) attributed to cross-border digital business an effective average tax rate of 9.5% compared to 23.2% of a traditional cross-border business. That study was, however, later on criticized for its flawed methodology by ZEW itself. Similarly, other authors did not identify significant differences between digital and traditional business taxation (Bauer, 2018).

Moreover, digital business may be subject to lower taxation by construct, since incentivizing digitization is a core objective of public policy. It is generally common for governments to incentivize investment in intangible assets (such as those related to Research & Development) through favourable taxation regimes or subsidies (which

---

[7] Yapar, et al. (2015) analyse the role of taxation on the development of e-commerce.

are tantamount to negative taxation). So it should not surprise if companies that *go digital* tend to pay lower taxes.

It is indisputable that multinational companies of significant size and market presence have the means to pursue aggressive tax planning, shifting profits between countries to minimize their tax burden, and often do so. Implementing such strategies is the more easy, the more intangible the companies' assets are (Dischinger & Riedel, 2011). If left unaddressed, tax avoidance by bigger technological companies may undermine the competitive dynamics within the Single Market, with smaller companies penalized because they're unable to escape taxation as their bigger competitors do. In public commentaries, this is commonly referred to as an **unlevel playing field**.[8]

Tax avoidance by technological companies also generates frustration for the lost opportunity from a public budget perspective. And the average taxpayer may rightfully feel that there is something wrong and unfair in the system if platforms generating sizable turnovers in their country end up paying little or nothing in terms of national taxes. This sentiment is one of the critical drivers of the increasing pressure on policymakers to take action against "big" multinational digital companies, as we shall see in the following sections.

10.3 Dilemmas for policymakers

As we learned from the previous sections, e-commerce is a phenomenon that should generally be considered beneficial for the economy and society. It generates efficiencies that can be passed on to customers with lower prices and higher quality products. It expands markets, increases competition, provides for innovation opportunities, and improves businesses' health and profitability. Conceivably, there could be arguments *against* e-commerce. For instance, e-commerce could be associated with a **negative net effect on environment**, for example, because it incentivizes residential deliveries instead of professional bulk purchases and thus may entail transport inefficiencies (OECD, 2019b). That is not necessarily true since e-commerce can also lower emissions, for example reducing transportation for accessing "brick and mortar" stores. But even if that would be the case, it would be more appropriate to study how e-commerce can reduce its energetical impact in the context of more general environmental policies, the analysis of which is outside the scope of this book.

Likewise, e-commerce may be perceived by some as an existential threat to physical stores, while physical stores may be a value in themselves. I undoubtedly include myself amongst those who lament the progressive disappearance of small bookshops from the streets of my hometown, Florence, for which Amazon certainly can take some blame. And yet, limiting the growth of e-commerce and releasing its competitive pressure on traditional to "save" small brick and mortar stores may not be a good

---

[8] See, for example: European Commission (2018p).

idea, as that would imply foregoing all the positive effects mentioned above. On the contrary, competition may be incentivized; but small physical stores may take the opportunity to recreate their business, innovating, providing an experience to customers that cannot be replicated online. Bookshops may thus not need to exit the market because of Amazon. They can transform themselves in aggregation points where readers and potential buyers enjoy being *physically*, such as drinking a coffee while participating in a debate over the latest novel on the shelves. Students should keep well in mind that message: even when competitive pressure seems prima facie harmful (for example, to small competitors), the best solution is rarely to reduce that pressure. Instead, the solution is to help business react to it in a manner that is generally welfare increasing.

For those reasons, it is safe to assume a straightforward policy goal in this context: policymakers should aim to **remove barriers to the growth of e-commerce** while ensuring that market competition unfolds on a level playing field.

10.3.1 Supply-side measures

Pulling down barriers in the supply-side of e-commerce requires providing access to infrastructure and other essential inputs. Policy actions geared to expand connectivity, create a cyber-secure environment, and foster digital skills (which we cover elsewhere in the book)[9] can incentivize companies to digitize their production and sale process, especially smaller ones.

Measures can be taken to reduce prices and increase quality in complementary markets such as postal delivery: the lower the cost of shipping and the higher its reliability, the stronger is the incentive for sellers to digitize their selling process.[10] Postal delivery prices can be lowered and quality can be increased by injecting more competition within the market, lowering barriers to entry and releasing regulatory constraints for potential new entrants. Or public authorities can act directly on the markets regulating price and quality levels accounting for the *positive externality* that lower prices in the postal market exert on complementary e-commerce markets.

Another important leverage to stimulate e-commerce supply is providing regulatory certainty. Companies must find it easy to understand, anticipate, and comply with the rules that govern all aspects of the production process. Consider, for example, the normative covering the handling of personal data. Or the regulatory framework underlying the application of artificial intelligence where it has potentially discriminatory implications (see Chapter 15).

Regulatory harmonization is particularly important for cross-border e-commerce. Companies need to know which regulation applies to their products or services; they need to overcome cultural or language barriers through simplified

---

[9] Namely: Chapter 4 for connectivity, Chapter 7 for cyber security, Chapter 12 for digital skills.
[10] On the impact of delivery costs on e-commerce, see Duch-Brown and Cardona (2016).

compliance procedures as similar as possible to the ones they go through within their country of origin. As a result, trade agreements are increasingly including entire chapters dedicated to cross-border data flows. Trade agreements may aim to limit or eliminate restrictions in the flow of data, for example requiring a commitment by the affected countries not to impose the use of domestic computing networks or national ICT equipment for data processing. Or requiring not to impose data localization measures (which may also imply a prohibition to store or process data in the territory of the other country party of the agreement).[11]

10.3.2 Demand-side measures

On the **demand side**, regulatory provisions can prevent artificial restrictions on sales. The most straightforward example is a regulation forbidding companies to "geo-block" users (see Section 10.4 below for a description of the EU measures adopted in 2018). Bear in mind, though, that banning price discrimination does not necessarily imply expanding the market. To see this, consider this simple example. Imagine that there are two countries, A and B. People living in B are on average poorer than people living in A. Geo-blocking may allow a multinational company to set two different prices for the same product: a high price in A and a low price in B. If geo-blocking is prohibited, customers from A arbitrage and buy from country B. The result is upward pressure on demand in country B and thus an increase in prices in B. Ultimately, prices converge to be the same in A and B. That could cause some customers from B to drop out of the market and stop buying the product. In other words, prohibiting geo-blocking, in this case, may induce a substitution of customers from country B with customers from country A. The total net effect on the demand depends on several factors. However, the important takeaway is that such **net effect may also be negative** if the drop in customers in country B is higher than the increase in customers from country A (also note that this substitution effect would have implications for equality).[12] For a discussion of the welfare effects of price discrimination, see the appendix.

Policy action can aim to **foster trust in buyers** when making their purchases online. Fostering trust is particularly important when sellers are geographically distant, thus generating worries in the buyer that she may be out of reach if something goes wrong during the transaction. Here are some examples of possible measures based on OECD (2016):

- Design consumer protection laws that are transparent and effective. Establish dedicated consumer protection authorities with the power to investigate and

---

[11] See for example: the *Horizontal provisions for cross-border data flows and for personal data protection* (in *EU trade and investment agreements*). https://trade.ec.europa.eu/doclib/docs/2018/may/tradoc_156884.pdf
[12] This analysis is formalized in Duch-Brown, et al. (2020).

sanction abuses in e-commerce. Promote international coordination between consumer protection authorities to address cross-border issues
- Design strict rules to prevent business from engaging in deceptive, misleading, fraudulent, or unfair behaviour through unfair contract terms
- Ensure customers' freedom to leave negative reviews. They should find support when reacting to unfair treatment through extra-judicial (for example, through alternative dispute resolution mechanisms) or judicial (for example, through collective redress) means
- Ensure that customers have the right to easily return damaged, defective or otherwise purchases they made online and the online description of which does not correspond to the actual object or service they received
- Guarantee standard minimum levels of protection for electronic payments. Likewise, an adequate level of assurance should be provided regarding privacy and protection of personal data
- Launch public programmes to educate users to avoid pit-falls in e-commerce, such as how to spot fraudulent advertisement, and increase their awareness about potential means to obtain compensation in case of harm
- Promote the development of technologies that empower consumers, provide them with the ability to screen e-commerce deals and protect them after making their purchase (for example, imagine a technological interface facilitating the submission of feedback from the customer to the producer concerning the performance of the purchased product).

10.3.3 Taxation

A third key area of policy action is **taxation**. Here, the driving goal of policymakers is to adapt traditional tax systems to the new business dynamics enabled by digitization, preserving a "level playing field" between competitors and tapping into an important stream of revenue for public budgets.[13] Note that taxation is just one of the many ways public authorities can attempt to establish a level playing field. The enforcement of competition policy, for example, is the most apparent tool dedicated to achieving fairness in the market that comes to mind. Yet, taxation is specifically salient to e-commerce; it thus deserves to be explicitly treated in this chapter.

Besides the core goal of raising money to support their public system, countries' taxation policy is generally guided by some well-recognized overarching principles (OECD, 2015b):

- *neutrality* – taxation should not be shaped to affect different business models differently; taxation should not discriminate based on the economic choice made by the tax-payer

---

[13] Agrawal and Fox (2017) analyse taxation frameworks and resulting effective rates in different jurisdictions in the e-commerce context.

- *efficiency* – compliance costs for companies and enforcement costs for the public sector should be minimized
- *certainty and simplicity* – tax systems must be clear and transparent so that tax-payers can easily understand the burden they are subject to; transparency and simplicity also make tax-payers less likely to attempt to game the system to avoid paying taxes
- *effectiveness and fairness* – the same income should not be subject to taxation twice (no *double taxation*), and public authorities should endeavour their best efforts to prevent tax evasion and tax avoidance
- *flexibility* – tax systems should adapt to the evolution of business, particularly in light of technological progress.

Two main categories of taxes stand out: taxation may be imposed on income (e.g. *income tax*) or consumption (e.g. *value-added tax* or VAT). Corporate income taxes are levied on the income generated by companies, encompassing the return on capital and their economic rents i.e. their *net profits*. As noted in OECD (2015), a state's sovereignty has historically come to be defined as a state power over a certain territory—the enforcement jurisdiction—and the power over a particular group of individuals—the political allegiance. A state's sovereignty is what makes it able to require subjects to pay taxes. Thus a legitimate tax claim must be based on the relationship between the tax-payer and a specific territory ("territorial attachment") or between the tax-payer and a specific person ("personal attachment").

That logic is an important starting base to understand why, as we have seen above, tax treaties tend to address the issue of cross-border corporate taxation allocating the taxing right to the country where the taxed company has a *permanent establishment*. In other words: before the emergence of digitization, the existence of a permanent establishment by a company on a particular territory was assumed to be the best indication of the company's integration of that territory's economy. It thus followed that the government of that territory could legitimately require the company to pay taxes. But, as we have seen in Section 10.2 above, that may not be the case anymore, at least for certain types of firms. That assumption is now challenged by the emergence of new digital business models that are more immaterial and difficult to pin down geographically than the legacy ones. Thus, the main[14] policy challenge is to shape new corporate income taxes that respect the general principles exposed above, but that are yet capable of capturing these new business dynamics.

---

[14] Another challenge concerns consumption/value-added VAT taxes: for example, because it is more difficult to apply it to intangible products like a movie streamed on the web, or because e-commerce allows businesses to exploit loopholes in VAT systems to minimize their tax burden. In fact, small parcels bought from abroad are usually exempted from VAT, as compliance and enforcement costs would outweigh the VAT revenue. E-commerce businesses can thus fragment their supply in such a way that their single sales are small enough to fall below the size threshold, hence avoiding taxation (for a discussion, see OECD (2015), Addressing the Tax Challenges of the Digital Economy, Action 1—2015 Final Report, OECD/G20 Base Erosion and Profit Shifting Project, OECD Publishing, Paris). The European Commission has been addressing this issue too, we will look at it in Section 10.4 of this chapter.

The work carried out by the OECD on digital taxation is a good analytical base from which to progress towards a solution to the policy challenge.[15] Bear in mind, though, that the OECD is an international organization representing the interests of its member countries. Hence, despite the arguably very high quality of its economic analysis, the OECD's broad policy proposals on controversial subjects such as cross-border taxation are necessarily conditioned by international political compromise. As we shall see in the following section, the background work of the OECD paved the way to a global agreement between 136 countries in October 2021.

The OECD background work around digital taxation hinged on finding a solution particularly along three dimensions (OECD, 2019e):

- **Scope**: new taxes should cover: (a) *automated digital services*, such as online search engines, social media platforms or online advertising services, that are provided on a standardized basis to a large population of users cross border; and (b) more generally, those business models that are mainly *focusing on consumers*. Note that this second category may also include traditional businesses to the extent that they can increasingly rely on technologies to interact and engage with their customer base. In other words, the OECD aims to create a homogeneous taxation approach for businesses that are increasingly competing in the same markets, despite still not necessarily digitized. Examples of consumer-oriented businesses are companies selling personal ICT products such as smartphones and their apps, clothes, toiletries, cosmetics, and luxury goods
- **Nexus**: the *nexus* is the link between the tax-payer and the tax authority that justifies the imposition of taxation. The new nexus should not be dependent on the physical establishment. Instead, it could be derived from the place where the actual value is created, using *sales* instead of physical presence to determine the taxing right of states. Notably, the nexus would also depend on meeting a **revenue threshold** that would suggest that the company has *a significant and sustained engagement with market jurisdictions*. The base proposal of the OECD indicated **€750 million** as the revenue amount for the threshold
- **New Profit Allocation Rule**: scope and nexus rules may indicate that a particular state has the right to tax a company that does not have a permanent establishment in its territory (this is somewhat "a revolution" compared to the legacy taxation systems). The next step is to define *by how much*. The OECD suggests a formula that allocates profits between jurisdictions, avoiding double taxation and respecting existing transfer pricing rules.[16]

---

[15] For an overview of the OECD work on digital taxation see OECD (2019d).

[16] Transfer pricing refers to trade transactions between separate internal entities within the same multi-national enterprise. Transfer pricing may be used to artificially shift profits and losses so to escape taxations. Thus, transfer pricing requires international cooperation. The approach promoted by the OECD to regulate transfer pricing is based on the *arms-length principle*. For a broad explanation, see: Neighbour (2002).

The three dimensions of analysis were at the centre of the negotiations between countries coordinated by OECD for years, after finding a compromise solution in October 2021 (see further below).

10.4 The European Union's perspective

From what we have seen in the previous sections, we can conclude that most of the issues hampering growth in e-commerce tend to relate to its cross-border vocation. As a result, supra-national institutions, such as the European Union, are usually best placed to deploy policy leverages to pull down barriers and stimulate the expansion of e-commerce markets.

Thus, not surprisingly, e-commerce figures prominently in the European Commission's Digital Single Market (DSM) strategy. The whole first pillar of the strategy concerns facilitating access for consumers and businesses to digital goods and services across Europe.

Since the inception of the DSM strategy, the European Commission has prompted action in four key areas:

- cross-border parcel delivery
- buyers' protection
- geo-blocking
- taxation.

Let us look at each of them:

10.4.1 Cross-border parcel delivery

The European Commission proposed a regulation to address parcel pricing and quality within the Single Market. The new regulation for cross-border parcel delivery services, 2018/644, was adopted by the EU legislators in April 2018 and entered into force the month after (Regulation (EU) 2018/644). The regulation attempts to leverage on three channels to improve parcel delivery in Europe: (i) it **strengthens regulatory oversight** by national authorities; (ii) it **fosters transparency** of tariffs for cross-border parcel delivery; and (iii) it obliges delivery operators to provide clear **information to customers**, for example on the specific sales contract and charges or on how to make a complaint if things go wrong.

According to the new rules, *parcel delivery service providers* are defined as (cross-border) service providers involved in the clearance, sorting, transport, and distribution of parcels. Service providers that are only active domestically are not subject to the regulation. Cross-border providers have to provide the national authority of their country of origin (i.e. where they are established) with a public list of tariffs related to their single-piece postal delivery services. The tariffs collected by the national authorities are then submitted to the European Commission which publishes them on a dedicated website.

National authorities have the prerogative to assess whether tariffs for cross-border delivery are *unreasonably high* based on, for example, a comparison of the cross-border tariffs with the domestic tariffs charged in the two Member States involved in the delivery. To help national authorities to perform that inherently complex exercise, the European Commission (2018l) issued detailed guidelines. Yet, it is not clear what would happen next once unreasonably high cross-border tariffs are identified, since the regulation does not suggest that authorities can impose any price cap accordingly.

The European Commission will, in the years to come, take stock of the progress made in cross-border delivery following the introduction of the Regulation and draw conclusions as to whether more "invasive" steps are to be deemed necessary.

10.4.2 Consumer protection

Yet another critical obstacle to the expansion of e-commerce cross-border markets is the lack of trust by buyers that they may not be harmed during the transaction. Potential sources of harm include the risk of electronic payment fraud, of receiving defective products or experiencing poor quality services, or not receiving the products at all. The EU legislators have attempted to address these general concerns in a number of ways in recent years. The European Commission prompted three actions that may help enhance consumers' trust across the EU and increase demand in e-commerce cross-border markets.

(1) First, in 2015, the EU legislators adopted Directive (EU) 2015/2366 or the **revised payment services directive (PSD2)**; Member States had to transpose it in their national laws by January 2018. The PSD2 directive aimed to **strengthen payment security**, stimulate competition and integration in the EU payments market, and enhance consumer and business protection. Most notably, the PSD2 directive prohibits surcharging (merchants cannot make consumers pay additional fees depending on the payment method they choose to use); it defines clear security boundaries for the use of consumers' financial data, in particular for online payments, to minimize the risk of fraud; and it mandates the refund of payment services' users if they are victims of data breaches, hacking attacks, credit card cloning, or similar frauds.

(2) Second, in 2019, the EU legislators adopted a Directive to improve enforcement and modernize consumer protection rules within the EU (Directive (EU) 2019/2161). Member States are supposed to transpose the directive by November 2021, in view of the entry into force as of May 2022. The directive came to be known as the **New Deal for Consumers**. It contains a number of

innovations compared to the legacy consumer protection laws,[17] that are supposed to increase e-commerce **transparency** and **empower** final consumers.[18]

In particular, the New Deal for Consumers makes it easier for consumers to assess risks when shopping online. Consumers must be told if the seller is a private individual or a trader, who is responsible for the shipping or delivering of the product, and what must be done to return the purchase exercising their withdrawal rights. Consumers are also supposed to be informed about the factors that affect the ranking of the offers appearing on their screen when purchasing online. For example, they should be allowed to easily spot if an offer on the search page is a paid advertisement. Furthermore, the New Deal for Consumers directive contains measures to enhance the reliability of consumers' reviews, for example, through the express prohibition to submit or commissioning someone to submit fake reviews or endorsements. It is, however, questionable whether this prohibition tackles a genuine market failure. E-commerce businesses that do not address fake reviews are likely to be directly penalized by consumers who could choose not to buy from them, knowing that they are unreliable. Hence the market may not need public intervention: it likely already has the means to self-correct.

The EU directive also forces traders to inform consumers if the price or offer they received has been tailored on them thanks to the analysis of their personal data and AI-driven profiling (i.e. *price discrimination*, see above). Finally, the directive extends the standard guarantees that are typically provided by traditional sellers also for digital services that are not provided on a monetary basis. Hence the supplier of a *free* application (which, as we know from Chapter 5, is only apparently "free" as it is paid for by users with their data) such as a social network smartphone app is subject to the same obligations of any other seller of more "traditional" goods. Thus, for instance, users should be able to cancel their contract within 14 days without the need to justify it.

The empowerment of consumers comes through stronger enforcement and the ability to access compensation. Consumers can claim compensations if they are victims of unfair commercial practices, for example if they were misled to believe that the product or service was different from the one they actually purchased. National consumer protection authorities can impose penalties for cross-border infringements of up to 4% of the seller's annual turnover. Notably, the New Deal for Consumers directive tackles the so-called "dual quality" of consumer goods: products that are marketed across the EU with the same brand and packaging should be of the same quality regardless of the place of sale. For example, a specific branded cheese cannot contain a different proportion of fat if sold in Spain rather than in Austria.

(3) Finally, still in 2019, another two important legislative initiative were adopted: the **Directive on Contracts for the supply of digital content and digital services**

---

[17] That is: Council Directive 93/13/EEC and Directives 98/6/EC, 2005/29/EC and 2011/83/EU.

[18] For a concise summary, see European Commission (2019i).

(Directive (EU) 2019/770) and the **Directive on Contracts for the sale of goods** (Directive (EU) 2019/771). Both directives should start to apply throughout the EU Single Market by the end of 2021, assuming that all Member States transpose them within the standard 2-year limit.[19] The two directives aim to provide for a similar protection level to consumers regardless of whether they do their purchase on-line or off-line.

According to the **digital content directive**, if a supplier sells defective content (e.g. a movie that does not stream properly), she will always be liable for it: her liability does not limited in time. Moreover, the users should not need to prove that the content is defective. It is for the supplier, who has a superior technical knowledge about the content sold, to show that the content *is not* defective (*reversal of the burden of proof*). The directive also indicates that consumers must be able to terminate long-term content contracts and that the seller should stop using users' data if the contract is ended.

Similarly, the **goods directive** extends and harmonizes throughout the whole EU Single Market the *reversal of the burden of proof* for two years. If a purchased good is considered defective by the buyer, it is up to the seller to show that *it actually is not defective*, until two years from the purchase have elapsed. Additionally, consumers do not lose their right if they do not notify about the defect in the good they purchased within a certain time limit. And if the seller is unable to repair or replace a defective product, the contract can always be terminated.

10.4.3 Geo-blocking

The EU geo-blocking initiative was one of the flagship action of the Juncker's Commission (2014–2019).[20] That resulted in the adoption of an EU regulation in February 2018 (Regulation 2018/302) or **Geo-blocking Regulation** (Regulation (EU) 2018/302). The regulation entered into force in December 2018. It aims to prevent customer (consumers but, in some instances, also business customers) discrimination based on their nationality or residence to the maximum extent. The regulation does not force sellers to *ship* a product or otherwise to provide a service to buyers at their place of purchase. That would certainly be an excessive obligation to be fulfilled by EU traders. But, as of December 2018, EU sellers cannot treat foreign buyers differently from local buyers. To the extent that a product is available to local buyers, it should also be available to those making a cross-border purchase, and under the same conditions. Sometimes that could mean that the product is available to foreign buyers only if they are ready to physically come to the shop

---

[19] For an explanation of the procedure underlying the adoption and implementation of EU directives, see European Commission (2018m).

[20] Mazziotti (2015) suggests that any (anti)geo-blocking regulation should be backed by a clarification of the conditions under which territorial restrictions are necessary to preserve cultural diversity and value allocation within a specific territorial area.

and take the product home by themselves. The EU legislators may hope that the geo-blocking regulation will stimulate the creation of an independent intermediary shipping market. Intermediary services could help complete transactions when domestic sellers are not willing to themselves ship cross-borders to foreign buyers.

Thanks to the geo-blocking regulation, customers should be treated precisely like local buyers are. They must be able to access websites that are available locally and cannot be redirected to other websites based on their IP (Internet protocol—which indicates from where they are connecting), for example. Customers must also be able to use whatever means of payment is offered by the seller on her website: if the buyer uses a foreign credit card, the purchase cannot be blocked.

However, the EU legislators left outside the scope of the regulation any services with a focus on the provision of access to copyrighted content. Moreover, sectors such as audio-visual, transport, healthcare, and social services are not subject to the geo-blocking regulation because they are already being regulated with sector-specific regulation.[21] The exclusion of audio-visuals from the geo-blocking regulation generated a significant degree of frustration amongst the public.[22] EU residents may find it hard to understand why they should be prevented from buying access to a song or a movie in another EU country since the Single Market predicates no borders to the flow of goods or services in Europe. And indeed, prohibiting geo-blocking practices also for audio-visuals may make sense in terms of economics.[23]

However, the EU legislators opted to first address the issue related to EU *copyright regulation* before moving forward prohibiting geo-blocking. The European Commission arguably worked under the assumption that a no-geo-blocking law for audio-visuals would contrast with the EU copyright framework (which, by definition, allows geo-blocking if copyright is not cleared for a particular Member State). That may not be entirely true: anti-competitive geo-blocking may be implemented by a film producer who has already cleared copyright for all Member States, for example.

10.4.4 Taxation

Taxation is the last area of EU action that is of significant relevance for e-commerce and that I examine in this chapter.

Until the end of 2020, the only relevant concrete initiative taken by the EU legislators concerned in the taxation area was related to the **Value Added Tax (VAT)**. VAT is a tax that is generally applied to any commercial activity for the consumption of a good or service. Because VAT affects intra-EU trade, there are limits to the discretion

---

[21] For audio-visual, see for example the AVMSD directive: Directive 2010/13/EU.
[22] See, for example Teffer (2017).
[23] Duch-Brown and Martens (2016) estimate that both consumers and producers would gain from removing geo-blocking restrictions. See also Marcus and Petropoulos (2017).

that EU countries can exercise when fixing VAT rates: for the vast majority of goods and services, the minimum VAT rate within the EU is 15%.[24] Moreover, VAT rates and compliance costs can significantly affect e-commerce. Hence in 2017 and 2019, EU Member States agreed to modernize the EU VAT framework which would facilitate its growth (Directive 2017/2455 and Directive 2019/1995, the **VAT e-commerce Directives**). Their entry into force was set for July 2021. The key elements of the reform are as follows (European Commission, 2020u):

- Companies that sell goods online can comply with their EU VAT obligations using a single online portal operated by the tax authority of their country of establishment. That is a "one-stop-shop" that attempts to make the life of companies that want to sell cross-border easier since they would not need to deal with different administrations speaking a different language
- Platforms that are operating marketplaces are responsible for collecting VAT for the transactions that happen on their websites
- There will be a yearly threshold of €10,000 below which cross-border sales will be considered domestic and hence paid in the country of residence, to simplify procedure and support smaller businesses. Conversely, the new framework removes the exemption from VAT of small products priced below €22 and imported from outside the EU. That is meant to address unfair competition by e-commerce businesses fragmenting their supply to escape VAT (European Commission, 2018o).[25]

VAT compliance simplification and EU harmonization can undoubtedly favour cross-border e-commerce, addressing obstacles that are perceived as high, especially by smaller companies, as we have seen in the previous sections. A **reform of corporate digital taxation systems** to capture new dynamics enabled by the digitization of the economy is however the most ambitious goal of the European Commission's strategy for taxation of e-commerce. The goal is so ambitious that by the end of 2020, no concrete result had yet been achieved. Contributing to explain the lack of progress is the inherent complexity of finding agreements on taxation within the EU Single Market since Member States tend to have very different views and approaches, especially on this matter, and the interplay with trade policy. The US, in particular, has been displaying a high degree of sensitivity to potential "digital" taxes that could hurt the profitability of US multinational companies and affect the US public budget with smaller streams of tax revenues. In June 2020, Politico (Scott, et al., 2020) reported: *"Earlier this month, President Donald Trump's administration launched a series of trade investigations that could lead to tariffs on countries in Europe, Asia and South America if they adopt digital service taxes"*.

---

[24] For an overview of the EU VAT framework, see European Commission (2021h).
[25] See footnote 14.

Lacking a common EU approach, however, can lead to worrisome scenarios: with single countries endorsing their own specific solution to an issue of global nature such as digital taxation, the risk is to reduce efficiency and transparency in taxation, increase compliance costs, hamper the growth of e-commerce worldwide, and exacerbate trade conflicts. Figure 10.6 gives a snapshot of the situation in Europe as it was standing in June 2020, with seven European countries having already implemented a digital service tax and four others having laid out a proposal to do so. Approaches differ widely in terms of rates (from 3% to 7.5%) and taxation scope (some focus only on online advertising, while others, like France, attempt to capture a much broader base, including any provision of digital interface). Arguably, these should be considered temporary solutions until countries finally converge to a common approach (see below).

In 2018 the European Commission attempted a first, ambitious proposal for a uniform approach to digital taxation within the EU. It rested on two prongs (European Commission, 2018n):

(a) a reform of corporate tax rules
(b) an interim solution for the taxation of digital services within the EU

The reform of corporate tax rules was the Commission's first-best scenario. It was a proposal for a long-term solution to the potential distortion of the taxation burden between digital and traditional businesses. According to the proposal, a business supplying digital services through a digital interface had to be considered to have

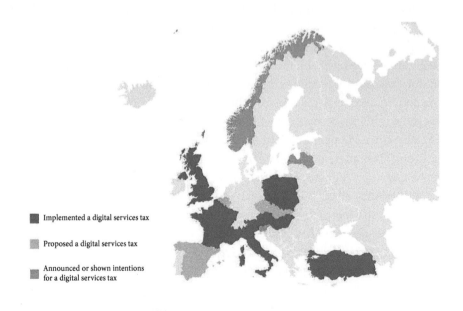

Figure 10.6 Digital Services Taxes in Europe (June 2020)
https://taxfoundation.org/digital-tax-europe-2020/

a "significant digital presence" in a country when at least one of the following conditions was met:

- Its country's annual turnover exceeded €7 million
- It had more than 100,000 users in that country for the taxable year
- It had concluded more than 3,000 business contracts for digital services within the country during the taxable year.

Profits would then have been attributed to the countries where the company had a significant digital presence based on their digital services' market value, including the profits that the company can extract from analysing users' data. The general idea was to shape the tax system to account for *where* the value was actually created.

The second prong was instead a temporary solution to be kept in place until the EU Council and Parliament would endorse a more structured approach.

The interim solution was supposed to apply a **3% corporate tax** to **revenues** rather than companies' profits. The choice was motivated by the fact that calculating the profitability of digital services can be very tricky: it entails deciding how to allocate the operational costs of immaterial activities, for example. Yet, taxing revenues is quite unusual and generally not desirable. A company would be taxed even if it is making losses, for example, and thus would have lower incentives to invest. According to the proposal, only bigger companies active in the provision of digital services (such as online advertising, platform intermediation, or the sale of users' data) should have been taxed. Namely, companies with a total worldwide turnover of €750 million and EU revenues of €50 million.

The 2018 proposal of the European Commission did not go far: neither the corporate tax nor the interim solution succeeded to gain the necessary support from EU Member States to be transposed in EU law.

However, in June 2021, the G7 countries reached a historic agreement on a global approach to taxation that was finalized in October 2021 at OECD and endorsed by 136 countries and jurisdictions representing 90% of global GDP.[26] The agreement consists of two "Pillars." Under Pillar One, taxing rights for (approximately) the 100 largest and most profitable companies in the world will be reallocated to countries where they operate, regardless of where the company is physically located (more precisely: affected countries will be able to tax international companies with a turnover above €20 billion and profitability above 10% for 25% of the profits above the 10% profit threshold). Pillar Two, instead, sets a global minimum tax rate of 15% for any multinational. The intent of Pillar Two is clearly to remove the incentive of multinationals to avoid taxes shifting profits across jurisdictions. Following the agreement, Austria, France, Spain, the UK, and the US announced that they would roll back their digital service tax and retaliatory tariffs once the agreement on Pillar 1 had

---

[26] See: https://www.oecd.org/tax/international-community-strikes-a-ground-breaking-tax-deal-for-the-digital-age.htm

been implemented.[27] In December 2021, the European Commission released a new proposal that aims to transpose the October 2021 OECD Pillar Two agreement on the 15% minimum tax rate for all EU countries (European Commission, 2021).

Before closing this chapter, let me spend a few words on a subject closely related to taxation: **state aid control**. Besides mergers, potential market abuses, and anti-competitive agreements, the EU competition policy framework also envisages scrutiny of Member States' subsidization policies (*state aid control*, exercised by the European Commission's competition policy department, DG-Competition). Accordingly, Member States cannot subsidize a specific company and distort competition within the Single Market by equipping it with an unfair advantage (there are exceptions to this general rule, for example if subsidies are necessary to correct well-identified market failures). From an economic point of view, taxes and subsidies are the same thing: a negative tax is a subsidy; a negative subsidy is a tax. A reduction in the tax rate paid by a single company compared to the one generally paid by similar companies thus qualifies, in all respect, as **state aid** and it is therefore subject to scrutiny by the European Commission.

This is particularly relevant for the digital sphere. Since digital services are very mobile (it does not really matter where their providers are physically established), they often trigger competition between countries wishing to attract them in their jurisdiction with lower tax rates. That is the background behind one of the highest-profile cases dealt by the European Commission's antitrust department in recent years: the alleged illegal tax benefit that Ireland granted to Apple, amounting to €13 billion of taxes that were unpaid by Apple throughout the period from 2004 to 2014 (European Commission, 2016j). The European Commission took the decision in 2016, and the European General Court later overturned it in 2020 (Ireland and Others v European Commission) (the European Commission has appealed the verdict to the Court of Justice of the European Union). An analysis of the details of the case is outside the scope of this book. However, students should be aware of the interplay between state aid control and taxation policies in the EU digital space. Notoriously, the enforcement of competition policy is one of the most incisive prerogatives of the European Commission. Therefore, if an agreement on coordinated solutions at the EU level to address digital taxation issues is not found, it would not be surprising to see an increasing number of similar cases being brought forward by the European Commission in the coming years.

****

---

[27] See: https://taxfoundation.org/digital-tax-europe-2020/

10.5 Case Study: geo-blocking in PC video games

In January 2021, the European Commission imposed a €7.8 million fine to Valve, the owner of an online PC gaming platform called "Stream", and five video games publishers (Focus Home, Koch Media, ZeniMax, Capcom, and Bandai Namco). The companies were deemed in breach of the EU antitrust rules because they limited cross-border sales within the Single Market through "geo-blocking" arrangements.

Stream is a PC video gaming platform. Authenticated users can play games directly on the platform or download them on their PC. They can also buy games on physical supports such as DVDs to activate them and play with them on the platform. The owner of Stream, Valve, allows the publishers of the games to restrict the geographic scope in which those games can be played: buyers of games receive "activation key-codes" which, for example, cannot be used outside certain geographic areas such as Czechia, Poland, Hungary, Romania, Slovakia, Estonia, Latvia, and Lithuania. These geo-blocking restrictions affected around 100 video games of any types, such as sports or action games.

The European Commission's antitrust investigation began in 2017, and it has no legal basis in the geo-blocking regulation. But the investigation benefited from the insights that the European Commission acquired during its e-commerce sector inquiry in 2016, which indicated that almost 60% of digital content providers have geo-blocking contractual agreements with rights holders. The PC video games antitrust case and the geo-blocking regulation thus share the same roots: the results of the sector inquiry also pushed the European Commission to propose a regulation against geo-blocking.

More information on the antitrust case can be found here: https://ec.europa.eu/commission/presscorner/detail/en/ip_21_170

10.6 Review questions

- Explain why small and medium enterprises tend to rely less on e-commerce than large enterprises.
- Does expanding e-commerce affect customers all the same? If not, which categories are set to benefit the most? Conversely, which ones are set to lose?
- Provide three real-life examples of geo-blocking (or make up your own). Do not use the examples used in the book.
- Could the Covid-19 experience have affected trust in e-commerce, both from the supplier and the buyer side? Justify your answer.
- Assume country A decides to adopt a digital tax hitting all digital services with a turnover above a certain threshold. List all significant direct and indirect effects on A's economy that could result from that decision. Does the size of A's economy matter for your discussion?

11

The Sharing Economy

Abstract

Nothing better represents the meaning of digital disruption than the "sharing economy".
Online sharing platforms allow owners of under-used assets (for example, a car, a house, or
even a specific knowledge or expertise) to compete with established businesses, offering
services of comparable, if not enhanced, quality and exploit their assets in a profitable way.
Users can access services often supplied by non-professional "peers" at advantageous conditions compared to those offered by professionals. The resulting impact on markets and
legacy businesses can be wide and significant, though not always positive: it may concern
the environment, labour markets, and society at large, with important implications for
policy-making. This chapter provides an overview of the sharing economy and analyses
its main features.

Background

The **sharing economy** refers to trading activities enabled by a specific online platform category (see Chapter 8). It deserves special treatment and a dedicated chapter
because of its broad, disruptive impact on the product, service, and labour markets
(see Figure 11.1).

First, note that the term *"sharing economy"* is only one of the many terms used
to indicate the same phenomenon. Others include: *"collaborative economy"* (a term
used by the European Commission, as we will see shortly), *"gig economy"*, *"peer-
to-peer"* economy, and *"peer economy"*. The use of one term rather than another
is tantamount to an expression of personal preference. Görög (2018), for example,
finds fourteen core definitions used in the literature which are largely overlapping
for their meaning. I have opted for the term "sharing economy" as this is the most
commonly used in the economic literature as of 2020.

As in the general case of online platforms, it is challenging to identify sharp
boundaries delineating elements belonging to the "sharing economy", and literature
still lacks a universally accepted definition of this term.[1] For this book, I rely on

---

[1] For an extensive discussion, see Codagnone and Martens (2016).

Digital Economic Policy. Mario Mariniello, Oxford University Press.
© Mario Mariniello (2022). DOI: 10.1093/oso/9780198831471.003.0011

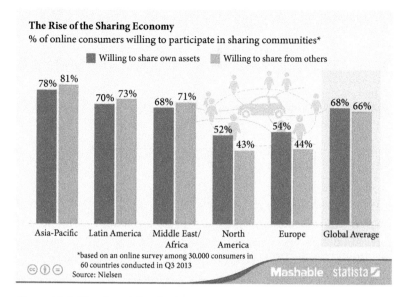

Figure 11.1 The rise of the sharing economy

Source: Richter, F. (2014). *The Rise of the Sharing Economy*. Statista. Statista Inc. Accessed: April 16, 2021. https://www.statista.com/chart/2323/the-rise-of-the-sharing-economy/. Made available under the Creative Commons License CC BY-ND 3.0

the definition laid out by the European Commission in its "Communication on A European Agenda for the Collaborative Economy" (European Commission, 2016k):

> the collaborative economy refers to *"business models where activities are facilitated by collaborative platforms that create an open marketplace for the temporary usage of goods or services often provided by private individuals."*

Popular examples include transport services such as Uber or Lyft, whereby the platform coordinates drivers to offer rides to users with their own vehicles; Airbnb, through which home-owners can rent out spare rooms or their entire place; and TaskRabbit, a platform that allows private individuals to respond to a demand to perform small tasks such as irregular home-cleaning, gardening or pet care (see Table 11.1 for more examples).[2] Because the sharing economy ecosystem is very diverse, it gives rise to a multitude of different issues. That means that a single straightforward policy answer does not exist. Instead, a well-crafted set of different initiatives is needed to maximize the benefits of the sharing economy while minimizing risk, as we shall see in the following sections.

The total value of the sharing economy worldwide is projected to increase to $335 billion in 2025, from $15 billion in 2014 (Statista, 2020c). A 2018 survey (Lloyd's London, 2018) found that 54%, 47%, and 60% of, respectively, British, American, and Chinese respondents had been a consumer of a service or product in the sharing economy. The same survey found that 13%, 8%, and 25% of respondents, British, American, and Chinese, respectively, have provided a service or an

---

[2] For a nice and accessible introduction to the world of the "gig economy", see Mulcahy (2016).

Table 11.1 Examples of platforms operating in the sharing economy (Zorn, 2019)

Sector	Example of Platforms
Transport	Uber, Lyft, Gett, Juno, Curb, Zimride, HopSkipDrive
Accommodation	Airbnb, LoveHomeSwap, HomeAway, CampinmyGarden, Short Term Stays
Vehicle sharing	ZipCar, Getaround, Tubber, Spinlister
Dining	Mealsharing, EatWith, Feastly
Child Care	BSit, Care.com, UrbanSitter, GoNannies
Task Performing	TaskRabbit, Zaaryl, TakeEasy, Handy, Your Mechanic
Cloths, Crafts	Etsy, Zibbet, SwapStyle

asset through a sharing economy site (Lloyd's London, 2018). The number of car-sharing users in Europe was projected to reach 15 million by 2020, a 21-fold increase compared to the 700,000 car-sharing users in 2011 (Frost and Sullivan, 2016). It has been calculated that over 150 million guests worldwide have used its services since its foundation in 2008 (iPropertyManagement, n.d.).

Such trends have led many commentators to refer to this as the "the rise of the sharing economy" phenomenon.[3] "Sharing", as such, is an historically typical behaviour among human beings of any culture. We share for functional reasons such as survival, strengthening social bonds, and establishing or respecting moral norms.[4] Yet, a compound of different factors has created the conditions to scale-up sharing from an activity confined to a restricted number of peers, such as family, friends, and neighbours (that is, between individuals interlinked through a trust bond supported by regular personal interaction—a behaviour defined as "*sharing in*") to sharing as a significant form of economic activity **involving predominantly strangers**. That is, between individuals who, without the "sharing activity", would not have known each other or had no direct understanding of the counterpart's reliability in a transaction potentially involving the use of personal assets (a behaviour defined as "*sharing out*").

As indicated by Hatzopoulos and Roma (2017), the emergence of large scale "sharing out" was recently catalysed by three key factors:

(1) with the consolidation of Web 2.0 and the emergence of **online platforms**, the technological evolution created the technical conditions to allow easy, reliable, and immediate communication between peers, regardless of their geographic location. Online platforms also offered the necessary guarantees to ensure the reliability of online payments (see Chapter 8)

(2) **societal trends**, such as the progressive concentration of population in urban areas, the increase in global interconnections propelled by social networks,

---

[3] See, for example: Botsman and Rogers (2010), Belk (2014) and Celikel Esser, et al. (2016).
[4] See Belk (2014).

and the pressing need to incentivize economic activities that are environmentally sustainable

(3) and, finally, the **economic crisis**, which started in 2008 with the collapse of global finances, led many people to lose their physical assets, such as their car or house, and, most importantly, to lose their jobs. This unemployment, the "hollowing out" of the middle-class, and the current instability of post-crisis labour markets (see Chapter 12) fuelled the need to resort to creative solutions to generate value, a principle which is at the core of the sharing economy's "*mindset*". Arguably, the Covid-19 pandemic has also significantly contributed to increased demand and supply in the sharing economy.

Three categories of actors are necessarily involved in the sharing economy:

- **Service providers**: actors that supply resources they own (such as time, physical assets, knowledge) on a professional or non-professional, peer-to-peer basis
- **Users**: actors who demand the use of assets or services offered by the service providers, often in return for paying a service fee (to the service provider and the platform). The platform typically prompts users to provide feedback on their user experience after the service has been completed
- **Intermediaries**: platforms that interconnect service providers with users, exerting a variable level of control on the transaction, and offering a specific guarantee that the transaction is satisfactory for both involved parties, typically receiving a commission on the value of the transaction (though also it should be noted that there are sharing platforms which do not operate for-profits).

Figure 11.2 sketches the relationship between the three different categories of actors.

11.2 Opportunities and challenges

The secret of the success of the sharing economy resides in the combination of three key ingredients – actual or potential markets must feature a great deal of:

(1) **excess capacity**, of which the platform enables the profitable exploitation
(2) **asymmetries of information**, which are addressed through trust-enhancing mechanisms such as insurance policies and, most importantly, online feedback systems
(3) **oligopolistic rents**, which the platform can dissipate by lowering barriers to entry and increasing market competition.

11.2.1 Significant excess capacity

Sharing economy platforms hinge on the untapped potential of people's resources in their daily life. As pointed out by Rachel Botsman in her 2010 TEDx speech: a "*power drill will be used around 12 to 15 minutes in its entire lifetime* [...] [that's] *kind of ridiculous* [...] *because what you need is the hole, not the drill*" (Botsman, 2010). Rough (but realistic) estimates (Barter, 2013) suggest that cars are parked (and are, therefore, unused) for 95% of the time. Owning a drill, a car, a flat with an empty room; mastering general knowledge or possessing the skills to perform specific skills such as home repair or decorating; possessing a small amount of money which is not invested in any profitable economic activity; or, most simply, having spare time to share: these are all resources which do not usually generate value but are potentially valuable to a group of customers who are able to aggregate their demand thanks to online sharing platforms.

11.2.2 Strong asymmetries of information

Most of the added value of online sharing platforms comes from their quasi-public role as guarantor in an environment which is perceived as highly uncertain, both by potential users and service providers. Airbnb has successfully created a market where homeowners often rent out the place where they live (or a place they own but do not live in) to use by strangers. Likewise, tourists rely on Airbnb to select private homes that may host them during their holidays with a minimized risk that the rented house does not correspond to what they read in the description displayed on Airbnb's website. The stronger the asymmetry of information, the fewer elements available to customers and service providers to assess the reliability of their

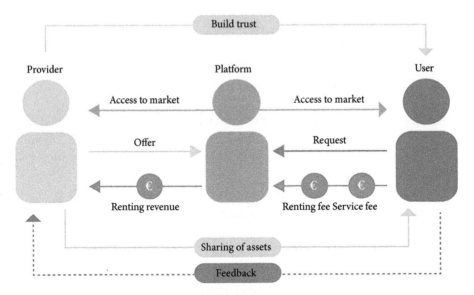

Figure 11.2 The sharing economy business model
https://app.emaze.com/@AOIZCIOLO#1

counterpart, and, subsequently, the higher the value-added of the online sharing platform.

Trust can be enhanced directly through the offering of insurance policies. For example, for each transaction, Airbnb may cover up to $1 million against damages potentially caused by guests to hosts' property. Most importantly, sharing platforms typically rely on a feedback system that feeds into the profiles of service providers and users: the counterpart's reputation is a key element of assessment at the moment in which the decision of buying or supplying a service is taken.

Mazzella et al. (2016) surveyed 18,289 users of BlaBlaCar across 11 countries in Europe, finding that 88% of respondents highly trusted members with complete digital profiles, while only 58% would highly trust a colleague and 42% a neighbour. The authors indicate that the BlaBlaCar feedback system achieves trust levels comparable to those associated with family members (highly trusted by 94% of respondents) or friends (highly trusted by 92% of respondents). While these results can hardly be generalized (the respondents are members of BlaBlaCar and therefore are more likely to trust BlaBlaCar's feedback system than the average individual) they nonetheless provide a strong indication about the **value that reputation** has for those using online sharing platforms.

A 2017 study (Teubner, et al., 2017) on 86 German cities finds that an increase by one star in the rating of an Airbnb's host is associated with an average price mark-up of $18 (for a two-person, two-night stay). The same study finds that the number of received ratings has a negative and significant effect on prices (Figure 11.3). This suggests that potential customers value not only the actual rating as a signal of the host's reliability. They also value **the retaliatory power** that leaving feedback yields

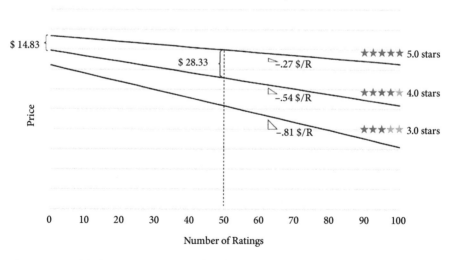

Figure 11.3 Airbnb: Impact on price of number of ratings

Timm Teubner, Florian Hawlitschek, and David Dann. 2017. 'Price Determinants on Airbnb: How Reputation Pays Off in the Sharing Economy'. *Journal of Self-Governance and Management Economics* 5 (4) (April): pp. 53–80. DOI: 10.22381/JSME5420173

to them. The impact of a negative review is, indeed, *higher* the smaller the number of reviews one host has. A host with 10 reviews can hardly afford a negative review: it would greatly impact his average rating. On the other hand, a host with 1000 reviews may afford a negative review because that review does not significantly change his average rating. Customers likely anticipate that a host with fewer reviews has a stronger incentive to offer a higher quality service, and this is reflected in the price (which tends to be higher, when the host has fewer reviews).

Feedback systems are, however, far from perfect. Feedback is often given after the transaction has taken place, and is revealed publicly only after all involved parties have left it to avoid retaliatory biases (a negative feedback could prompt an equally hostile response from the other party). However, the effectiveness of ratings can deteriorate over time. As Filippas et al. (2018) point out:

> "The problem is that ratings are prone to inflation, with raters feeling pressure to leave 'above average' ratings, which in turn pushes the average higher. This pressure stems from raters' desire to not harm the rated seller. As the potential to harm is what makes ratings effective, reputation systems, as currently designed, sow the seeds of their own irrelevance".

In other words, to the extent that the user and the service provider establish an emotional connection during the transaction, the higher the cost to the service provider of negative feedback, the lower the user's incentive to leave negative feedback. For example, Uber or Lyft drivers can be discontinued if their rating falls below a certain threshold. And ride hailers may feel that such "punishment" is exaggerated so as not to justify negative feedback even if their experience was not fully satisfactory.[5]

11.2.3 High oligopolistic profits to be dissipated

The sharing economy prospers in particular where markets are, by nature or regulatory construct, dysfunctional. For example, a suboptimal number of players enjoy oligopolistic profits, prices are above competitive levels, or barriers to entry are high enough to prevent potential competitors from contending incumbents' market shares. By giving the opportunity to non-professional service providers to compete with the established industry, online sharing platforms de facto significantly lower barriers to entry. This sudden injection of competition leads to an expansion of total supply, a reduction in prices, and positive effects on the average quality of provided services. As an illustration, Figure 11.4, showing the impact of Uber's entry on the price of taxi medallions in New York City and on the average number of monthly trips by traditional taxi, both of which are significantly reduced.

Using an Uber database of almost 50 million individual-level observations, Cohen et al. (2016) estimate that UberX has generated $2.9 billion in consumer

---

[5] For Airbnb, see also Zervas, et al. (2021).

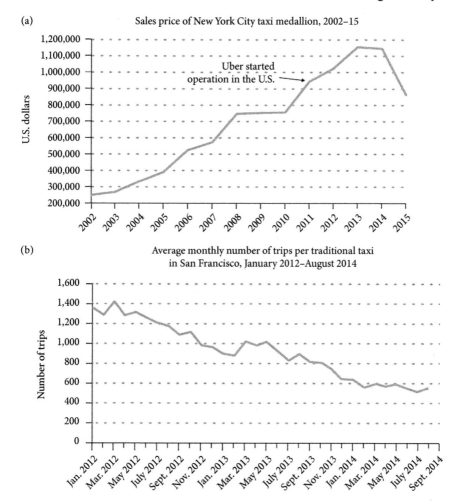

(a) Sales price of New York City taxi medallion, 2002–15

(b) Average monthly number of trips per traditional taxi
in San Francisco, January 2012–August 2014

Figure 11.4 Impact of Uber entry on NYC taxi industry

World Bank. 2016. 'World Development Report 2016: Digital Dividends', p. 68. http://www.
worldbank.org/en/publication/wdr2016. Accessed on 20 November 2018

surplus for the cities of San Francisco, New York City, Chicago, and Los Angeles,
leading the authors to conclude that for each dollar spent by consumers, about $1.60
of consumer surplus is generated.[6]

Moreover, traditional industries that are exposed to the disruptive competitive
pressure of sharing economy platforms are forced to change, find innovative ways
to generate profits, and improve their products to match the quality of the new competitors. BMW has successfully reacted to the likely contraction in vehicles sold

---

[6] It should be noted that one of the researchers involved in the study, Jonathan Hall, was, at the time of writing,
Uber's Chief Economist. This explains why the authors were able to access such a rich dataset. At the time of writing,
the paper by Cohen, et al. had not yet been published in any peer-reviewed journal, so it is not yet possible to address
doubts about the absence of bias in the results, given, in particular, the affiliation of one of the authors. The paper
also highlights one key problem with research and online platforms: unless researchers are working for the platform
itself, they are normally prohibited from accessing platforms' databases (data being at the core of their business
interests). External validation of studies on online platforms is therefore problematic.

Figure 11.5 Map indicating regions in which Uber is fully or partially banned (2017)
(Karen Hao, 2017). 'Map: All the places where Uber is partially or fully banned' Quartz (September 23)
[online]. https://qz.com/1084981/map-all-the-places-where-uber-is-partially-or-fully-banned/ Accessed
on 20 November 2018

due to expansion of shared mobility by launching its own share mobility service DriveNow, for example. Taxi companies everywhere have started offering the possibility to order a taxi and track the driver's position through mobile applications. The whole tourism industry has begun the process of digital transformation under the pressure of online sharing platforms offering complementary services to travellers (see figures reported in Chapter 2).

Traditional industries have also been responding to the appearance of the sharing economy through strenuous opposition and lobbying of policymakers. They pointed to the alleged unfairness in the treatment of sharing economy services, which are often not subject to the same rules and constraints by which incumbent industries must abide. The clash between the taxi industry and Uber, which has escalated to large-scale strikes and led a significant number of countries to fully or partially ban services by ride-sharing companies (Figure 1.5), is perhaps the most apparent manifestation of such a strategy. But any incumbent industry would have an incentive to react to the pulling-down of barriers by trying to put them back and protect their revenues, now threatened by external competitors, albeit doing it more quietly. In an article titled "Inside the Hotel Industry's Plan to Combat Airbnb" (Benner, 2017), the *New York Times* reported a document from the American Hotel and Lodging Association with their plan to take-on Airbnb with the following exert:

> "*Objective: Build on the success of 2016 efforts **to ensure comprehensive legislation in key markets** around the country and create a receptive environment to launch a wave of strong bills at the state level while advancing a national narrative that furthers the focus on reining in commercial operators and the **need for common sense regulation** of short-term rentals*"

Such "regulatory resistance" can be harmful to society as a whole. As further discussed in the appendix, competition has significant benefits on the economy: it not only lower prices and increase services' quality, it also pushes businesses to become more efficient and innovate. Policymakers should thus not be misled to take actions that cement established industries' power.

However, it should be pointed out that the significant increases in competitive pressure brought about by the sharing economy also impacts smaller businesses which do not necessarily enjoy high revenues, but may instead be at the margin of their subsistence level. That impact can have dramatic social implications. In March 2018, Wired reported the story of four taxi drivers from NYC who committed suicide feeling oppressed by the financial destabilization and demoralization afflicting taxi drivers due to the expansion of ride hailing services (Katz, 2018). Small bed and breakfast hotels can hardly compete with Airbnb, just as professionals are unable to compete with online sharing platforms that create the conditions for the supply of expertise by private individuals. Zervas et al. (2017) estimate that the entry of Airbnb in the Austin's (Texas) accommodation market caused a decline in hotel revenue in the range of 8%–10%. Still, they also find that the impact is unequal: the adverse effect is significantly stronger for lower-priced hotels and hotels that do not cater to business travellers.

The human and social implications of the sharing economy should not be underestimated, and policy action is often warranted. Besides the impact on product and service markets, the emergence of the sharing economy has fostered a debate around the potential consequences for the economy and society as a whole—and about the possible implications for policymakers. Below I analyse three areas in particular: the impact on the environment, on labour markets, and on the wider society.

11.2.4 Impact on the environment

It is generally believed that, by promoting a more intensive use of existing assets and reducing the need for new purchases, the sharing economy can contribute to reducing the economy's environmental impact (Frenken & Schor, 2019). However, such effects are not obvious: the sharing economy has a negative impact on transport and travelling costs, for example, and it could therefore be argued that the resulting expansion in the number of trips made could result in higher pollution levels compared to the counterfactual (pollution in the absence of the sharing economy). Martin and Shaheen (2011) surveyed 9,635 households which were members of a car-sharing organization in North America, and found that, indeed, the majority of households participating in car-sharing are increasing their emissions by gaining access to automobiles. However, because households also reduced their total driving or got rid of their vehicles entirely, the total net effect on pollution is expected to be negative: –0.84 tonnes greenhouse emissions per year per household. Other subsequent empirical analyses confirm similar findings,[7] but a general equilibrium

---

[7] See, for example: Chen and Kockelman (2015) and Nijland and van Meerkerk (2017).

analysis, i.e. one that would take into account the general impact on the economy by the sharing economy, is still lacking. It is not known, for example, whether the increase in disposable income of users generated by lower transport costs could result in activities that are equally or more polluting.[8] Airbnb is a case in point: it may be argued that home hospitality is less polluting than hotels that use energy-intensive facilities. But an increase in travellers' disposable income due to the reduction in accommodation costs can be associated with increased incentives to travel and buy flight tickets (hotel rooms and transport services are *complementary* goods: you often need both to visit a foreign place). The result is hence increased greenhouse gas emissions (Skjelvik, et al., 2017).

11.2.5 Impact on Labour Markets[9]

Without a doubt, the sharing economy is having a revolutionary impact on work habits: anybody with a physical or intangible asset, such as knowledge, can become a *service provider*, and do so normally under highly flexible conditions, to adapt to one's own needs. Such flexibility may explain why so many individuals are potentially engaged in sharing platform work (namely, are registered with an online sharing platform) while not necessarily actively performing any tasks. The Joint Research Council (Pesole, et al., 2018) reports estimates suggesting that an average of 10% of the adult population in Europe has used online platforms to provide any kind of labour service at least once in their life. However, less than 6% of adults spend a significant amount of time providing services through platforms and earning a significant income in this manner. Service providers who earn more than 50% of their income through online sharing platforms are classified as "*platforms workers*", and these currently represent about 2% of the adult European population, although this figure varies significantly among different European countries.

The sharing economy model entails blurred boundaries between users and service providers, self-employed workers and employees, professionals, and non-professionals. The reasons that motivate people to become service providers are thus relevant in ascertaining the nature of the work performed via sharing platforms and accordingly designing the legal framework that should be applied to it (as we shall see in Section 11.4).

Manyika et al. (2016) present a helpful classification of independent workers. They identify four categories:

- **free agents**, who rely on their independent work as their primary source of income;
- **casual earners**, who use independent work to complement the income received through other primary sources without having a strict need to do so;

---

[8] For a discussion on this issue, see Frenken and Schor (2019).
[9] For an excellent overview of the challenges faced by platform workers, see Kilhoffer, et al. (2019).

- **reluctants**, whose primary source of income is independent work but who would prefer switching to a traditional job; and
- **financially strapped**, who rely on independent work to complement their income out of strict necessity.

They also find that low-income households (in a survey of about 8,000 respondents from the US and the EU) are more likely to do independent work, often out of necessity. Other demographic studies suggest that the "service providers" crowd tend to be younger and with a higher educational level than the average worker population.[10]

Flexibility is certainly a key driver for service providers. Berg (2016) reports that individuals working with Amazon Mechanical Turk and CrowdFlower (two platforms enabling businesses to post adverts outlining small, unskillful tasks to be completed by individuals working remotely) tend to mention the ability to work from home as their second main motivation to join the platform, second to complementing their other source of income.

Yet strong competition exerts downward pressure on earnings, particularly in the case of platforms that create globalized labour markets (as is the case for virtual task-performing services, whereby the geographical location of the provider is irrelevant). Moreover, competition between platform workers had become particularly problematic during the Covid-19 pandemic, when many workers who had lost their "traditional" employment reverted to the platform economy to earn a living. That exacerbated downward pressure on platform workers' earnings.

According to a CEPS study (De Groen & Maselli, 2016) a significant difference exists between the earnings of suppliers of physical or local services and the earnings of virtual services. The study details the telling case of CoContest, a platform that allocates monetary rewards to the three best submissions by designers out of an average of ten submissions received for each posted request. If taking into account the time spent by designers to participate in the contest without necessarily being rewarded, the average remuneration has been calculated to be €3.50 per hour for Italian designers. That reward is far too low, according to several members of the Italian Parliament who questioned CoContest on the fairness of their business model (Camera, 2015).

Other studies point to low earnings also in the case of local services. Zoepf et al. (2018) surveyed over 1,100 Uber and Lyft drivers and paired the results with a dataset with information on costs associated with owning and keeping a vehicle. They found that the median profit from driving is $3.37 per hour before taxes; that 74% of drivers earn less than the minimum wage in their state; and that, for

---

[10] See, for example: Berg (2016).

a significant proportion of them (30%), driving for Uber or Lyft is actually counterproductive, in that they make negative profits once vehicle expenses are included in the total costs incurred. Often drivers do not know in advance how far they will have to go to reach the passengers' destination, being forced to accept the ride while running the risk that the payback from the platform will not cover its cost.

It is not uncommon for service providers to manifest criticism towards their working conditions. While flexibility is a key feature of their work, online sharing platforms tend to maintain a degree of control over the quality of the service, possibly to minimize running costs and maintain common standards across the board. As illustrated by Rosenblat and Stark (2016), Uber applies dynamic pricing to its fares to increase prices during demand booms. Drivers are then nudged to provide the service, for example, through guaranteed gross fares if they accept 90% of the trips offered and stay connected for at least fifty minutes of the rush hour.

All platforms exert high pressure on service providers by affecting their reputation/visibility online. Airbnb reveals hosts' speed of response to potential customers' messages, and it nudges hosts with reminders to keep up their average response timing. TaskRabbit applies a set of conditions regarding the proportion of tasks that must be accepted and the speed of response. If service providers fail to meet those requirements, they are taken off search results and hence do not get requests anymore (De Groen & Maselli, 2016).

Generally speaking, most of the earnings are concentrated on a few service providers that display the highest ratings and serve the majority of clients. Seeking to maximize the quality of service, platforms maximize competition among *their* service providers.

Competition generally has positive effects on welfare (as I often stress in this book), and, indeed, competition is the motor that allows online sharing platforms to offer services of high-quality standards at competitive prices. However, it should be kept in mind that, in this case, competition is not triggered between companies **but between individuals operating individually**. While it is not a problem, as such, if companies exit the market, the social effect of direct competition between individuals can instead be dramatic. Therefore, public intervention is warranted to guarantee that adequate safety nets of a private or public nature are put into place to protect the most vulnerable categories.

Service providers often find themselves in a vulnerable situation, particularly if earnings from the sharing economy represent a substantial part of their total income. Although the conditions of their employment may sometime resemble those of an employee with a traditional job, they are not entitled to equivalent basic rights such as minimum wage, holiday, sick leave, health insurance, unemployment insurance etc. (see Box 11.1 for risks associated with offering services through the sharing economy).

Box 11.1   A Beauty or a Beast for On-Demand Workers (Celikel Esser, et al., 2016)

On-demand workers can benefit from greater diversity and flexibility in their work patterns and commitments. They face, however, several challenges concerning career and skill development:

- They do not have a certain prospect of long-term career development
- They bear the responsibility for their skill development and training
- They face a number of risks from which they are typically not protected from through the online sharing platform: income insecurity, fluctuation in their performance or rating, accidents, sickness, or another impediment to their ability to continue working
- They need to rely on self-marketing and face typical entrepreneurial risks
- Their work on the platform may require increasingly technical competencies, for example, on how to deal with data and privacy issues
- They need to be able to entirely self-manage their time, separating work life from private life

The vulnerability of platform workers explains the increasing public criticism to which online sharing platforms are exposed.[11] Such criticism and political pressure have led some platforms to take steps to address such concerns. In 2018, Uber launched a free insurance package covering personal accidents, severe sickness, certain types of injury, and third party liability up to €1 million for all of its Uber Eats couriers in nine European markets, for example. But public regulation is also expected to play a role. It has also been proposed to define an intermediate category between the *traditional employee* status and *fully fledged self-employed* status that could be consistently applied to service providers in the sharing economy. Over the latest years, courts around the world have come to fill a gap in the law, with judges determining whether platform workers working for a certain platform had to be considered a de facto employee. A notable example is that of Uber drivers, who were deemed as *Uber's employee* in by the UK Supreme Court in February 2021.[12]

A particularly thorny issue limiting service providers' bargaining power vis-à-vis online platforms concerns their inability to export the reputation they have acquired working for a platform to another one. Service providers are de facto locked-in to the platform where they accumulated significant on-the-job experience. Arguably, a regulatory action to foster the **portability of service providers' reputations**

---

[11] See, for example: Hyman (2018).

[12] Uber BV and others (Appellants) v Aslam and others (Respondents) [2021] UKSC 5 On appeal from: [2018] EWCA Civ 2748. See press summary here: https://www.supremecourt.uk/press-summary/uksc-2019-0029.html

could enhance service providers' bargaining power and lead to improved working conditions (Celikel Esser, et al., 2016).

11.2.6 The wider impact on society

The disruptive economic effect of online sharing platforms is not limited to increasing the competitive pressure on traditional business and reducing high supra-competitive profits in oligopolistic markets. The sharing economy can also have strong externalities on other parts of the economy and society. For example, Airbnb's negative effect on accommodation prices has led to an expansion of tourism, particularly in big cities. Complementary services (such as restaurants and tourist attractions) benefit from such effects: they enjoy Airbnb's *positive* externalities. For others, Airbnb generates **negative externalities**. This is the case for residential areas which have seen a significant increase in the influx of tourists and have witnessed increasingly significant changes in the life of the neighbourhood: Airbnb short-term rentals transform the social fabric, contribute to a new form of urban gentrification, and have significant redistribution effects, displacing economic value between different social actors and different geographical areas (Wachsmuth & Weisler, 2018). Note that, traditionally, negative externalities are addressed through the use of taxation policy: this is the case if the supply of a good or service is suboptimal from a social perspective (for example, because the suppliers, not bearing the entire societal cost of production, produce too much quantity of the good or service). Yet, the taxation of online platforms – and, indeed, of digital companies more generally – is a thorny issue, especially when it comes to the geographic allocation of revenues and collection (see Chapter 10 for an extensive discussion).

Particularly worrisome is the potential impact that Airbnb short-term rentals may have on house prices. Residents of big cities such as Los Angeles, San Francisco, New York, Paris, London, Barcelona, Berlin, and Amsterdam have been complaining about the unavailability of options for long-term accommodation (Dickinson, 2018). Statista (2017) calculates that, in Los Angeles for example, renting out a flat with Airbnb can be more than five times as profitable as renting out with a standard contract. It can take as little as renting out a flat for 57 nights with Airbnb to earn the equivalent of long-term yearly rental. In response, municipalities worldwide are introducing regulatory restrictions to the house-sharing market, for example, limiting the number of nights per year during which a flat can be used for short-term rental. At the moment of writing, it is illegal in New York to rent out short-term (less than 30 days) unless the owner is present during the rental. In San Francisco, permanent residents can rent out their primary home but not their second homes. If the host is not present, the property cannot be rented out for more than 90 days per year. Hosts in Paris can rent their home for a maximum of 90 days. In Barcelona, hosts must buy a tourist licence for an annual fee. Amsterdam hosts can only rent out their home for a maximum of 30 days per year.

More generally, some authors have suggested that the sharing economy can have **significant redistributive effects**, potentially contributing to increased inequality. Frenken and Schor (2019), for example, suggest that online sharing platforms may be displacing tasks once performed by lower-educated blue- and pink-collar workers to highly-educated service providers that capitalize on their familiarity with digital technologies, contributing to increased inequality within the poorer quintile of the income distribution.

The unregulated framework in which online sharing platforms operate favours discriminatory behaviours. Edelman and Luca (2014) find that male Afro-American Airbnb hosts charge rents that are approximately 12% lower than non-black hosts. Edelman et al. (2017) find that guests with Afro-American names are 16% less likely to be accepted by potential Airbnb hosts. And Ge et al. (2016) find that Uber and Lyft drivers tend to let Afro-American customers experience longer waiting times (as much as a 35% increase) and more frequent cancellation (up to twice as much as with passengers with "white-sounding" names).

11.3 Dilemmas for policymakers

The conclusion from the discussion above is that:

- On the one hand, the sharing economy has a powerful disruptive effect; it prompts an efficient use of assets; and it injects competition into dysfunctional markets: with high barriers to entry, low competition, and high service prices
- On the other hand, several concerns about the harmful effects of the sharing economy for customers, service providers, and third parties, emerge. Customers may be harmed by services that escape consumer protection and can be exploited through nudging or discrimination. Service providers may be defenceless towards potential abuse by algorithms, and have little or no social protection. The general public may be subject to negative externalities. And public finances lose streams of revenues because platforms may pay significantly lower taxes than their traditional economy counterparts.

As we have seen often in this book, the abrupt impact of new, digital technologies-enabled services creates the premises for a polarized conflict between, on the one hand, those who unconditionally welcome innovation and, one the other hand, those who stress its negative impact and possibly call for regulatory intervention to prevent the disruption to legacy industries.

From a policy perspective, the trick is not to position public action in either of these two camps. In the case of the sharing economy, the emergence of new disruptive services should be welcomed as an opportunity to restructure dysfunctional markets and eliminate profitsoften originating in artificially low competitive pressure. At the same time, platforms should not have a *carte blanche* and, where necessary, new laws should be adopted and existing laws enforced to guarantee an adequate level of protection for citizens, users, service providers, and business customers.

For an illustration, consider local transport markets and taxis: medallions allow traditional taxi drivers to exercise their profession, but their maximum number is limited by local regulation. The number of medallions is often sub-optimal from a social welfare perspective: exercising a high degree of market power, taxi agencies can extract artificially high profits, leading customers to pay artificially high prices – because the price in this situation is not really determined by the marginal cost of providing the service (for example, by fuel cost) but rather represents the equilibrium price of an oligopolistic market to which only a few players are granted access.

Online sharing platforms have challenged those markets, bringing competition through unorthodox channels: for a while, Uber and Lyft drivers did not need a medallion to operate a service in all respects very similar to that of taxi drivers. Facing such developments, public authorities should not ban platforms from operating the service altogether; neither should they adopt a hands-off approach. Instead, they should take the occasion to reconsider their local transport policy, evaluate whether changes in market structures are feasible (for example, lowering barriers to entry by expanding the supply of taxi medallions), and adapt the local regulatory framework to guarantee that the sharing economy services meet the same safety standards of traditional taxi services and abide by the same rules, such as fiscal or other legal obligations.

As Calo and Rosenblat (2017) put it:

"Regulators must find ways to characterize and address problematic behaviour. Regulators can accomplish this by drawing lines between acceptable and unacceptable (or harmful) conduct, as the law must often do, or else by attempting to better align the incentives of sharing economy firms with those of other participants".

I will analyse the potential policy solutions to labour markets and, more generally, to equality concerns in the context of the dedicated chapters (Chapter 12 for employment and Chapter 13 for equality). That is because the sharing economy's concerns are sufficiently general to merit a broader discussion. For example, platform workers may require stronger social protection nets. But that need is shared by many workers affected by the digital revolution. So Chapter 12 is more indicated to discuss those policy dilemmas.

Let us then move to the next section and focus on the actual European context specifically for the sharing economy.

11.4 The European Union's perspective

In Europe, countries have displayed a large array of different approaches to the sharing economy across different sectors, from the lax to the more confrontational. The relevant regulatory framework depends on the interplay between national and local regulations, judicial interpretation, and the application of existing laws and new ad hoc laws explicitly adopted to regulate the sharing economy. Such a patchwork of regulatory frameworks is in sharp contrast with the goal of a European Digital Single Market (see Chapter 1): it represents a significant obstacle for companies wishing to invest and develop across the continent. Most importantly, fragmentation is relatively heavier for smaller players, hindering the scale-up of potential challengers to established platforms. For example, Airbnb and Uber may find it challenging to implement different policies in different European countries. Still, they have the resources to deal with it. Instead, smaller new platforms would struggle to achieve anywhere near the same level of success, being unable to leverage a truly European scale.

There are EU laws that provide a basis for a more homogeneous approach to the sharing economy within the Single Market.[13] To the extent that online sharing platforms can qualify as "mere" electronic intermediaries, they are subject to the e-Commerce Directive (Directive 2000/31/EC) (extensively discussed in Chapter 9). By default, this implies no restriction of access by platforms to any EU market. Unless a Member State claimed that access must be restricted for reasons related to either public policy, protection of public health, public security, or protection of consumers or investors, and obtained the green light from the European Commission to do so.

Sharing platforms would also not be considered liable for the content they host (students may recall the discussion around Art. 14 of the e-Commerce Directive referred to in Chapter 9).

However, online sharing platforms are often rather involved in the process of provision of services and can therefore hardly qualify merely as intermediaries. The case of Uber, for example, has been scrutinized by the European Court of Justice (see Box 11.2 for a description). The ECJ concluded that because Uber "*exercises decisive influence over the conditions under which the drivers provide their service*" (for instance, Uber sets the tariff charged by the drivers), Uber is "*more than an intermediation service*", and therefore does not fall within the scope of the e-Commerce Directive. Ascertaining whether online sharing platforms qualify as pure intermediaries is necessarily an arbitrary process. It involves a certain degree of subjectivity, given that the boundaries between **intermediation** and **active service provision** are often blurred.

---

[13] For a comprehensive overview, see Hatzopoulos and Roma (2017).

Box 11.2   The European Court of Justice and Uber (Case C-434/15)

In 2014, a taxi drivers' association brought an action against Uber before a court in Barcelona. That court referred the case to the European Court of Justice (ECJ), asking for a preliminary ruling about whether Uber should be considered an information society service or a transport service. The ECJ took its decision in December 2017 (Court of Justice of the European Union, 2017). It stated that:

> "An intermediation service such as that at issue in the main proceedings, the purpose of which is to connect, by means of a smartphone application and for remuneration, non-professional drivers using their own vehicle with persons who wish to make urban journeys, must be regarded as being inherently linked to a transport service and, accordingly, **must be classified as "a service in the field of transport" within the meaning of EU law.** Consequently, such a service must be excluded from the scope of the freedom to provide services in general as well as the directive on services in the internal market and the directive on electronic commerce. It follows that [. . .] it is for the Member States to regulate the conditions under which such services are to be provided in conformity with the general rules of the Treaty on the Functioning of the EU".

In other words: Uber cannot be considered "just" an intermediary, and the e-Commerce Directive does not apply to it. To reach that conclusion, the ECJ noted that *"the application provided by Uber is indispensable for both the drivers and the persons who wish to make an urban journey* [and] *Uber exercises decisive influence over the conditions under which the drivers provide their service"*.

Similarly, in February 2021, the UK Supreme Court indicated that Uber drivers should be considered employees.[14]

Courts are thus naturally called upon to establish which relevant law applies. If, according to the Court, the activity of the platform falls outside the scope of the e-Commerce Directive, then the relevant EU framework would typically be based on the EU Services Directive (Directive 2006/123/EC).

If that is the case, then access to national markets is more difficult (compared to what it would be if the eCommerce Directive would apply). Indeed, according to the Service Directive, Member States can establish *"justified, necessary and proportionate"* requirements for reasons of public interest to allow a platform to operate. In other words, the Service Directive allows more leeway to the Member States who

---

[14] Uber BV and others (Appellants) v Aslam and others (Respondents) [2021] UKSC 5 On appeal from: [2018] EWCA Civ 2748. See press summary here: https://www.supremecourt.uk/press-summary/uksc-2019-0029.html

can more easily justify possible barriers to access that they may establish to prevent entry by sharing economy platforms.

In addition, platforms are also necessarily subject to other EU laws, such as data protection laws (see Chapter 5), consumer protection laws (see Chapter 10), and competition law (see Chapter 8).

Even though online sharing platforms tend to portray themselves as intermediaries connecting consumers with freelancers, they may sometimes qualify as "employers". In 2015, a UK court found that Uber runs a transportation business and its drivers should therefore be entitled to get payments according to the national living wage (Mr Y Aslam, Mr J Farrar and Others vs Uber). The decision was upheld by the UK Supreme Court in 2021.[15]

In the European Union, If drivers are considered Uber's employees, they are primarily subject to national legislation (labour markets are a competence of Member States). With some exceptions: EU laws regulate working conditions or mandate specific anti-discriminatory rules, for example.[16] In December 2021, the European Commission released a Directive proposal aimed to protect digital platform workers. According to the proposed text, platform workers should be presumed to be employees if certain conditions are met (such as: the platform sets the workers' remuneration or supervises their performance).

11.4.1 The EU Communication: A European Agenda for the Collaborative Economy

In June 2016, the European Commission released a Communication concerning the "collaborative economy" (a synonym of sharing economy, in this context) (European Commission, 2016). The aim was to provide guidance on how existing EU laws should be applied in the context of the sharing economy, encouraging a more harmonious EU approach by Member States. The Communication is, however, non-binding: Member States are therefore free to ignore it. It suggests several criteria to ascertain the laws that should apply to the activity of online sharing platforms for the most relevant issues (market access, liability, consumer protection, employment, and taxation—see Table 11.2 below for a summary). Still, it ultimately concludes that the relevant approach will have to be decided on a case-by-case basis. Generally speaking, the text of the Communication remained too high-level to provide concrete guidance, and it did not achieve much: Member States were only encouraged to find the right solution, with minimal guarantee that they would do it and, above all, that they would do it in a consistent manner.

Noting that the *"EU legislation does not establish expressly at what point a peer becomes a professional services provider in the collaborative economy"*, the Communication suggests that platforms should not be subject to authorization procedures if

---

[15] Uber BV and others (Appellants) v Aslam and others (Respondents) [2021] UKSC 5 On appeal from: [2018] EWCA Civ 2748. See press summary here: https://www.supremecourt.uk/press-summary/uksc-2019-0029.html

[16] For an overview, see Hatzopoulos and Roma (2017).

Table 11.2 Summary – The European Communication on the "Collaborative Economy"

Issue	Approach
Market Access	• Requirements to be established on the basis of the features of the collaborative economy business model • A key parameter of assessment is the level of control exerted by the platform over the service providers. Key criteria are: 　○ Price 　○ Contractual terms 　○ Ownership of assets • Member States should take the occasion to modernize market access requirements for all operators
Liability	• Collaborative economy platforms benefit from liability exemption for content they host (art. 14 e-Commerce Directive) • They are not exempted from liability for other services or activities they perform
Consumer Protection	• EU consumer law does not apply to consumer-to-consumer transactions, but only to transactions involving a trader • To qualify a service provider as trader, Member States should consider: 　○ Frequency of service 　○ Profit-seeking motive 　○ Level of turnover
Employment	• EU Court of Justice definition of employee: "*the essential feature of an employment relationship is that for a certain period of time a person performs services for and under the direction of another person in return for which he receives remuneration*" • To ascertain whether an employment relationship exists, Member States should look at the following conditions: 　○ The existence of a subordination link 　○ The nature of the work 　○ The presence of remuneration • Member States should: 　○ Assess the adequacy of their national employment rules considering the new digital paradigm 　○ Provide guidance on the applicability of their national employment rules
Taxation	• Member States are encouraged to facilitate and improve tax collection • Collaborative economy platforms should proactively collaborate without prejudice to the intermediary liability exception of the e-Commerce Directive • Member States encouraged assessing their tax rules to create a level playing field for business providing same services.

they act only as intermediaries, and that restrictions to their operations should only be imposed when strictly necessary to protect the public interest.

The **level of control that a platform exerts over the service providers** should be the critical parameter of assessment to ascertain whether a platform is more than a mere intermediary between peers. Key criteria in that respect are the following: the **price** (is the platform setting the tariff paid by users, only recommending it, or providing no indication at all?); the **contractual terms** (who sets the obligations and rights accompanying the service: the platform or the service provider?); and the **ownership** *of key assets* (is the service provider using their own, or the platform's, assets?).

Platforms that are considered intermediaries would benefit from the exception of liability provided by the e-Commerce Directive (see Chapter 9 for an extensive explanation). However, they would still be liable for the services that they offer in the first place (payment services, for example).

Users of online sharing platforms could benefit from the protection of EU consumer protection laws, but only to the extent that the service providers qualify as "traders", namely as persons "acting for purposes relating to his trade, business, craft or profession" (Directive 2005/29/EC). For the purpose of ascertaining whether the service providers qualify as traders, three main criteria of assessment are suggested in the Communication: the **frequency of the services** (the more regular the provision of a service, the higher the likelihood that a provider qualifies as a trader); the **profit-seeking motive** (providers that swap assets or only receive compensation for the cost they bear to provide the service would not usually qualify as traders); and the level of **turnover** (the higher the income from sharing economy activity, the more likely the provider is to qualify as trader).

As regards the existence of an employment relationship between online sharing platforms and the service providers, the reference should be the concept of "worker" as defined by the ECJ: "*the essential feature of an employment relationship is that for a certain period of time a person performs services for and under the direction of another person in return for which he receives a remuneration*". The criteria recognized by the European Commission as essential to establishing whether such an employment relationship exists are as follows: the **existence of a subordination link** (if the service provider is not free to choose how and when to provide the service they are more likely to qualify as employee of the platform); the **nature of the work** (the existence of an employment relationship would tend to be excluded if the activity of the service provider is marginal, with short duration, limited working hours, discontinuous work, or low productivity, for example); and the **presence of a remuneration** (service providers who merely volunteer or received compensation only for the costs they incur would tend not to be qualified as employees). As mentioned above, in December 2021 the European Commission released a proposal for an overall EU general framework to protect **platform workers** and workers in bogus self-employed relationships (the proposal also includes safeguards against the use of artificial intelligence to manage platform workers). Pressure to take concrete initiatives (possibly of a regulatory nature) to protect workers mounted during the Covid-19 pandemic: evidence showed that platforms were not compensating workers for lost income during lock-downs or providing them with sick leave, despite increased risks of health hazard (see also Chapter 3).

Finally, with regard to taxation, the European Commission suggests that Member States "should apply functionally similar tax obligations to business providing comparable services" and implement measures to increase transparency and facilitate the collection of taxes on revenues generated by online sharing platforms (see Chapter 10 for a discussion on platforms' taxation).

11.5 Case Study: Amsterdam's sharing economy action plan

Residents of the city of Amsterdam, in the Netherlands, have historically been very open to sharing their assets with each other. With the increasing popularity of the sharing economy, the city government was thus keen to exploit the new opportunities emerging thanks to the use of online platforms, while addressing potential risks. In 2015, Amsterdam backed the deployment of a consistent vision and action plan to foster the development of the sharing economy within the city.

The city's plan concerns several different activities, including housing, product sharing, individual shared mobility, and office spaces. At the time of writing, more than 150 sharing economy platforms were active in Amsterdam. Examples of local sharing platforms are: "Lena", a platform through which customers can share or rent expensive clothes or fashion items; "MotoShare", used for the sharing of vehicles such as motorbikes or cars; and "Peerby", a platform used for renting or borrowing of general-purpose items. The plan is well integrated with other city initiatives that complement each other, such as those related to the "circular economy" (i.e. aimed to minimize waste, incentivize re-use and reduce ecological impact), and support the city's start-up ecosystem.

More information about Amsterdam's sharing economy action plan can be found here: https://www.ellenmacarthurfoundation.org/assets/downloads/Amsterdam_-Case-Study_Mar19.pdf

11.6 Review questions

- On the basis of its history and the current economic context, what are the prospects of the sharing economy, in your view? Are current expectations inflated, is the hype due to fade, or do you expect the size of the sharing economy to continue growing?
- Provide three real-life examples of sharing economy platforms (or make up your own). For each of them, identify all the actors involved (service providers, users, and intermediaries) and explain its features in relation to the three dimensions of analysis discussed in the book: excess capacity, asymmetry of information, and oligopolistic profits.
- Is there a role that the European Union can play to protect the rights of workers in the sharing economy? Justify and explain your answer.
- Should local authorities have a say on which sharing economy platforms are allowed on the territory of their competence? What are the pros and cons of delegating that choice to them?
- In your view, which should be the main factors to consider to establish the "neutrality" of the intermediary, vis-à-vis service providers and users?

PART 4

DIGITAL SOCIETY

12

Technology and Employment

Abstract

Concerns about the ability of labour markets to adapt to the introduction of new revolutionary technologies are common in history. Technology can improve workers' productivity, but it can also make them redundant: if machines and algorithms can perform the same job faster and at a lower cost, why would anybody employ human workers? As it turns out, the previous industrial revolutions did not reduce the need for humans in labour markets. Instead, they induced a transformation of the jobs that workers were required to perform, creating new opportunities and tasks that only humans could pursue. It may be reasonable to expect that this time, with the Fourth Industrial Revolution brought about by technological progress, is not going to be any different. New jobs will be created, and technological adoption will not produce structural unemployment. However, even if this is the case, the transition is nevertheless costly and necessarily painful for a significant part of the working population. Thus, public policies are needed to protect workers temporarily displaced or in atypical employment contracts with wide and flexible social safety nets. Public policy should also create the conditions for a general upskilling of the workforce and provide incentives for workers and employers to respectively enrol in training programmes and offer continuous learning opportunities to their own employees. Lifelong learning may be the best way to ensure a smooth transition to labour markets 4.0.

12.1 Background

Few questions in digital policy so vividly strike the public imagination as to how technology will affect the future of work. Will machines take over the world, outperforming humans with lower production costs and better quality outcomes, rendering us redundant? Are the most vulnerable in society—the poor, the unemployed, the elderly—going to yet again be the ones hit the hardest and bear the burden of a digitized economy, being the easiest to replace with machines or sophisticated algorithms? Is humanity about to enter an era where nobody will have to work, and people will struggle to find meaning and purpose in their lives? Naturally, the high degree of emotions featured in this debate is a source to be exploited by commentators. The discussion has gradually polarized between those who anticipate apocalyptic scenarios, whereby the workforce will entirely be substituted by a "superior" artificial intelligence (see Chapter 15 for a discussion around AI

Digital Economic Policy. Mario Mariniello, Oxford University Press.
© Mario Mariniello (2022). DOI: 10.1093/oso/9780198831471.003.0012

and "singularity"), and those who dismiss such fears as just an instinctual, albeit irrational, reaction, as seen frequently in the history of economic development. After all, automated looms and cars did not generate massive unemployment, despite their significantly disruptive effect on the textile and transport markets. Calculators did not replace mathematicians. ATM machines did not put bank tellers on the street; instead, their job was transformed, with more time dedicated to direct personal advice and less cash handling.

The **Fourth Industrial Revolution** (see Chapter 1) is having profound implications for labour markets, but the reality is more nuanced than it is often depicted. Neither theory nor the currently available empirical evidence can provide complete clarity about what to expect in the medium and long term. We can, however, analyse patterns, identify the main issues that are likely to arise, and use theoretical design to provide a basis for effective policy action today. In this chapter, I illustrate the different issues around work and technological development. The aim is to provide students with a solid anchor to serve as a basis for further research (and hopefully spare them from becoming captured by the emotional framework surrounding this discussion).

12.1.1 Is this time different?

We know from Chapter 1 that it has become customary to identify four main waves of technological innovations in recent human history:

- the **"first industrial revolution"**, with the emergence of the steam engine
- the **"second industrial revolution"**, which transformed manufacturing through electricity
- the **"third industrial revolution"**, driven by electronics and Information Communication Technologies (ICT), and, finally
- the **"fourth industrial revolution"**, the one we are witnessing today, propelled by artificial intelligence and machine learning.

Each of these waves generated strong disruptive effects in labour markets. At the time, they all ultimately drove leading thinkers to believe that the new technologies would reduce the demand for human workers in the long term. In less than a century, between 1820 and 1913, employment in agriculture in the United States went from representing 70% of the total employed workforce to 27.5%, and it is currently around 2% (United Nations, 2021b). John Maynard Keynes, in 1930, famously wrote: "*the increase of technical efficiency has been taking place faster than we can deal with the problem of labour absorption*".[1]

---

[1] Keynes (1930).

As it turns out, history proved those who believed that humans would have an ever-decreasing role in the production of goods and services wrong. After the shock of transition, when displacement effects may in principle accompany the introduction of technologies, demand for labour grows stronger than ever, with a general increase of the proportion of the population participating in the work force (in the past, this also happened thanks to the opening of labour markets to women).[2]

A particularly telling case study is quoted by Bessen (2015), who noted that machines do not necessarily replace workers but may relocate them to perform tasks that require different sets of skills. The number of automated teller machines (ATM) installed over the US territory increased by four times between 1995 and 2010; however, no drop in the number of bank tellers was observed (Figure 12.1). The number of tellers per branch dropped from 20 to 13 between 1988 and 2004; however, the decreased costs implied a significant increase in the number of bank branches (an increase of 43% in urban areas). In addition, competition between banks increased the relative value of those skills that could not be automated, and tellers moved from cash-handling tasks to tasks requiring human relationship skills. Thus, the emergence of ATM triggered a change in the role of bank tellers rather than causing a layoff of the workforce. Bessen (2016) generalizes the conclusion from the case study reporting empirical evidence that the number of jobs grew faster in computer-intensive occupations than the rest of the economy.

In the next section, I will further explore the economics that may explain such dynamics, namely: how intuitive **displacement effects** (e.g. a machine that can do the work of ten employees in half the time can be reasonably expected to put 19 workers on the street) can be offset by **productivity, growth, and innovation effects**.

Before getting to that level of granularity, however, a general question comes to mind: could it be that the current industrial revolution is somehow different from

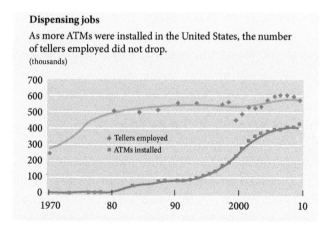

Figure 12.1 The impact of ATMs on bank tellers in the US
Source: Bessen, James. 2015. "Toil and Technology." Finance and Development 52(1).

---

[2] For a thorough review see Mokyr, et al. (2015).

the previous ones? If that were the case, the possibility of a general shrinking of the human labour force in the long term should naturally not be excluded.

The triggering force of the fourth industrial revolution is a technology that is rapidly becoming **a General Purpose Technology** (or GPT). That is: artificial intelligence and machine learning are increasingly pervasive, embedded in people's everyday life (consider the use of smartphones, for example), and are therefore reshaping much of the economy and society. The same happened with the previous technological revolutions, such as with electricity and steam power. Yet, the nature of the technology is fundamentally different this time. From Chapter 5 on the data economy, we know that data is *non-rivalrous*. While electricity or steam power deplete their value with use, the value of data does not decrease when processed through machine learning. Actually, its value may exponentially grow, with expanding datasets (the more data fed into the process, the more the process generates data) and marginal production costs approaching zero.[3] This suggests that the competitive pressure exerted by technology on human workers may be comparatively stronger this time, technology being much cheaper to use once set up.

Another notable difference is the **speed of transformation,** a leitmotiv of this book (see Chapter 1, for example). Figure 12.2 illustrates how much more quickly the current technological revolution is spreading in the economy compared to similarly revolutionary technologies in the past. This means that *this time* will be somehow more difficult for educational systems to adjust to the structural changes in the economy to equip workers with the necessary skills that future employers require. **Labour markets now have much less time to adapt to a highly dynamic environment**. With hindsight, we know today that early commentators could not anticipate the vast number of new jobs that appeared later on after adopting steam power and electricity. This applies to us today, too. In addition, there are good indications that numerous new professions will appear in the near future. They will also keep on changing at a frenetic pace, which is unprecedented in history. If anything, this reinforces the call for effective public policies geared to equipping future generations of workers with tools to deal with uncertainty, a structural characteristic of the future economy (see Section 12.3 below).

12.1.2 The hollowing-out of the middle-class

The current technological revolution also appears to exacerbate a phenomenon that was first observed in the second half of the twentieth century: the "**hollowing-out**" of the middle class (Autor, et al., 2006). Employers can get the most from automation when they implement it to perform tasks entailing repetitive work or the use of mental abilities such as the ability to read, remember, and acquire new knowledge. **Routine and cognitive tasks** tend to be found in jobs in the middle of the

---

[3] For a discussion, see Martens and Tolan (2018).

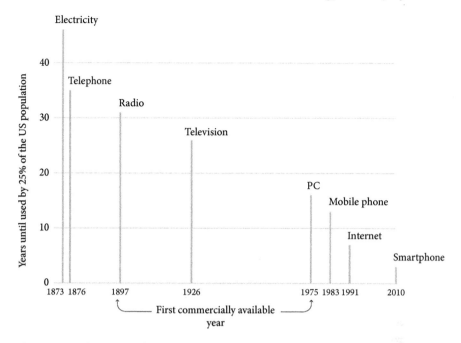

Figure 12.2 The speed of technological development
JRC 2019 https://ec.europa.eu/jrc/en/publication/eur-scientific-and-technical-research-reports/
changing-nature-work-and-skills-digital-age

wage ranking, for example: machinery mechanics in manufacturing, shop salespersons and routine office workers. At the two extremes of the wage scale are jobs where tasks tend to be less predictable, requiring *also* the use of non-cognitive skills such as creativity, resilience, teamwork, empathy, and flexibility. Examples of **non-routine, non-cognitive** jobs at the bottom of the wage scale are cleaning personnel, home care personnel, food-preparation workers, bartenders, and beauticians. At the other end of the scale, highly paid jobs such as managers, technical specialists, doctors, researchers, lawyers, and data analysts, also tend to require the ability to perform non-routine, non-cognitive tasks (on top of demanding high investment in education). The result is that the wave of automation brought about by technological advancement has polarized the distribution of jobs, destroying opportunities for the middle-class while increasing the demand for jobs at the two extremes of the wage spectrum (Figure 12.3).

The hollowing-out of the middle-class is a widespread phenomenon—it affects developed as well as developing countries with few exceptions. It creates the premises for social attrition, with workers exiting the mid-wage range exercising pressure on the poorer segment. The hollowing-out of the middle class also explains why wage inequality is on the rise: the supply of work for jobs at the bottom of the scale is increasing, exerting downward pressure on wages. At the same time, on the other side, at the upper end of the scale, it is the demand for work by employers that is increasing, creating upward pressure on wages for highly skilled jobs. Students should not overlook the link between the current ongoing technological disruption, job

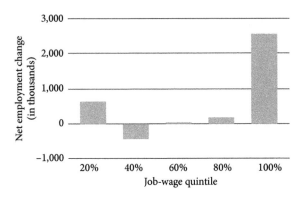

Figure 12.3 Net employment change (in thousands) by job-wage quintile in the EU between Q2 2011 and Q2 2015

Source: https://www.researchgate.net/figure/Net-employment-change-in-thousands-by-job-wage-quintile-EU-2011-Q2-2015-Q2_fig1_304246760

polarization, and wage inequality and the rise of populism. Moreover, an increasing gap between labour productivity and real wages (sometimes dubbed as "**the great decoupling between productivity and wages**" (Brynjolfsson & McAfee, 2015)) has been observed in the last decades, contributing to substantiate the origin of discontent: productivity increases have generated higher economic value, but that value was captured mainly by the owners of capital, not workers, creating a legitimate sentiment of frustration (Piketty, 2015). I will discuss these subjects extensively in Chapter 13.

Generally speaking, significant technological advances redistribute economic value from those whose competencies are made obsolete to those who can exploit the potential untapped by technology. Digitization is shifting value from those who have skills that can be substituted by machines (routine, cognitive) to those who have skills complemented or enhanced by machines (non-routine, non-cognitive). As Brynjolfsson and McAfee (2011) put it: *"There's never been a better time to be a worker with special skills or the right education, because these people can use technology to create and capture value. However, there's never been a worse time to be a worker with only "ordinary" skills and abilities to offer, because computers, robots, and other digital technologies are acquiring these skills and abilities at an extraordinary rate."* Other authors point out that technology has exacerbated inequality by disproportionally allocating higher wages to top earners within certain occupations that require computer-related skills. Since schools cannot keep up with providing the skills that employers seek, those who learn them through self-teaching and on-the-job experience have a significant comparative advantage with respect to the median employee, resulting in skewed wage distribution.[4]

It is worth noting that this redistributive effect also occurs at a geographical level: countries with a higher proportion of the workforce employed in manufacturing as

---

[4] See for example Bessen (2015) and Bessen (2016).

opposed to services, for example, are set to experience higher levels of disruption in their labour markets. Geographic diversity is a structural feature of Europe (Slovak Republic and Slovenia are certainly more exposed to automation risks than the Scandinavian countries, for example). Therefore, intervention at the EU level through the Digital Single Market strategy has the additional goal of ensuring that technological development does not exacerbate inequality within the European Union (see Section 12.4).

The direct effect that new technologies may have on the demand for human workers is a major concern for many, and it calls for the design of public policies to mitigate potential harm. However, it is important to keep in mind that technology may affect labour markets in several different ways. For example, it can increase the quality and the quantity of labour supply: technological advancement allows a broadening of the geographic scope to match workers and employers (teleworking, for example, makes it easier to reach workers in countries where labour is cheaper); augmented reality allows workers to carry out tasks they do not have the means to perform on their own; the boom in courses taught online can significantly raise the education potential for societies; employers can use social networks (for example, LinkedIn) to increase the speed and accuracy of their search. Digitalization also promises to significantly affect businesses' internal organization introducing radical changes in the employer-employee relationship (see also Chapter 15 for a discussion around artificial intelligence and monitoring at the workplace). For example, employers are confronted with the fact that technology is reshaping the manager-employee relationship from vertical to horizontal. Managers find it increasingly difficult to exclusively rely on employment contracts to retain valuable workforce. Companies tend to build their retention strategies on other aggregating factors, such as shared values and a common culture linked to the company's purposes, or developing a sense of community. A higher degree of flexibility is valuable to both the supplier and the taker of labour service (think about freelancing, for example). Still, it also increases workers' vulnerability and poses new challenges to employers as well. The emergence of the "platform" or "sharing" economy, whereby individual workers supply their work service to their employers outside a standard employment contractual framework, calls into question the effectiveness of traditional social safety nets. Independent workers are often unable to access the same benefits enjoyed by "employed" workers or can access them only at prohibitively high costs: unemployment benefits, health insurance, pension systems, to mention a few (see Chapter 11 for a detailed discussion).

12.2 Opportunities and challenges

In this section, we will have a closer look at the effects generated by automation on the demand for human labour. It is important to remember—as seen in Section 12.1—that automation is just one part of the picture, not the whole

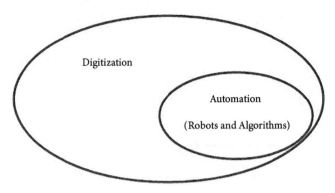

Figure 12.4 Automation is a subset of digitization

(Figure 12.4). In other words: in this section I discuss the effect that technology has on labour to the extent that technology can directly replace the work carried on by humans. We do not look at how technology is reshaping labour markets affecting the relationship between employers and employees, improving the quality of labour supply, and facilitating vacancy filling.

Broadly speaking, automation can have the following six major effects on the demand for labour (summarized in Figure 12.5):[5]

1) It can **displace** human workers through substitution: a machine or an algorithm may perform the job of one or more humans achieving higher quality outcomes in a smaller amount of time (Box 12.1 reports the estimates of the share of jobs at risk of automation that the economic literature has so far proposed)

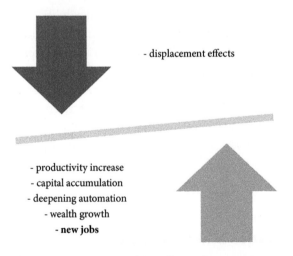

Figure 12.5 Summary of the effects of automation on labour demand

---

[5] This classification follows Acemoglu and Restrepo (2019) and United Nations (2017).

2) It can complement human workers by **increasing their productivity**: technology may help humans to improve their performance while carrying on tasks that cannot be automated. It, therefore, increases the demand for workers that can perform those tasks

3) It can **increase the incentives to invest in capital**. This "capital accumulation effect" can increase the demand for workers to the extent that capital and labour are in a complementary relationship: consider, for example, "cobots" or "collaborative robots" that help accelerate production. Universal Robots reports about an "Italian power tool manufacturer, Rupes, [that] made a bold commitment to eliminating defects and waste on its production line, whilst improving the working conditions of employees. The small company installed UR cobots to handle screw insertions, helping it achieve a 'zero defect' goal in the production process" (Von Hollen, 2019)

4) It can **deepen automation,** increasing the performance of machines that have already substituted humans in the past. This effect does not entail any displacement of human workers. If anything, this has already happened in the past. But it increases the demand for workers through increased productivity of existing machines or algorithms

5) At an aggregate level, automation has a positive effect on **wealth growth**. Wealth growth implies higher real incomes and greater production and demand for goods and services in the whole economy, fostering a positive push for labour demand. In the nineteenth century, the weaving industry underwent deep restructuring, with 98% of it becoming automated. Yet, because the demand for textile products was very elastic, it boomed in response to the dramatic reduction in prices. The resulting effect was a net increase in labour demand in textile markets

6) Finally, technology can dramatically **expand the set of available jobs** by generating a demand for new tasks to perform. Acemoğlu and Restrepo (2016) find that, between 1980 and 2010, the introduction of new tasks and job titles could explain about half of the employment growth in the US.

It turns out that displacement effects ((1) above) can be strong and hard to counterbalance with complementarity effects (from (2) to (5) above). An excellent empirical analysis is by Acemoğlu and Restrepo (2020) who use refined econometric techniques to identify and measure the causal relationship between the introduction of industrial robots and changes in employment in US local labour markets between 1990 and 2007. The researchers find that one more robot per thousand workers reduces the employment to population ratio by about 0.2 percentage points, and wages by 0.42 %. A logical (albeit somewhat counterintuitive) conclusion reached by the same authors in another paper is that, from the perspective of human workers, the introduction of brilliant technologies is to be preferred to the introduction of technologies that only marginally improve productivity (Acemoğlu & Restrepo, 2019). In the latter case, the productivity gain and the complementarity effects are certainly not sufficient to offset the displacement effects and are therefore more likely to reduce employers' demand for human workers.

Yet the majority of observers would agree that, in the medium and long term, it is the effect (number (6) in the above list), the **creation of new jobs and tasks** triggered by the revolutionary technologies' adoption wave, that usually tilts the balance, leading the economy to a new equilibrium where the need for human workforce is not reduced. We can hardly figure it out now. Certainly, new jobs are emerging in the area of data analytics and artificial intelligence: data analysts, trainers, ethicists, digital architects, AI programmers, 3D printer specialists. Perhaps, though, in just a couple of decades, we will witness the emergence of professions that may look absurd in the present day: synthetic food creators, drone or space pilots, psychological counsellors for robot-human relationship crises. We simply do not, and cannot, know, in the same way that early commentators during the first industrial revolution could unlikely imagine that the children of their children would become website designers a few years down the road. Or even, as bank tellers could not anticipate the new tasks that they would have been asked to perform after the introduction of ATM machines. Mokyr et al. (2015) brilliantly summarize this insight with the following words:

> "In the end, it is important to acknowledge the limits of our imaginations. Technophobic predictions about the future of the labor market sometimes suggest that computers and robots will have an absolute and comparative advantage over humans in all activities, which is nonsensical. The future will surely bring new products that are currently barely imagined, but will be viewed as necessities by the citizens of 2050 or 2080. These product innovations will combine with new occupations and services that are currently not even imagined. Discussions of how technology may affect labor demand are often focused on existing jobs, which can offer insights about which occupations may suffer the greatest dislocation, but offer much less insight about the emergence of as-yet-nonexistent occupations of the future. If someone as brilliant as David Ricardo could be so terribly wrong in how machinery would reduce the overall demand for labor, modern economists should be cautious in making pronouncements about the end of work".

Box 12.1 Who will lose their job?

We cannot know what the future will bring, but we may guess what it will take away from us. A number of researchers have attempted to infer which jobs will be made obsolete by technology by extrapolating information from current automation trends. In Section 12.1 of this chapter, we have seen that machines and algorithms are more likely to be used to perform routine and cognitive tasks. Therefore, logically, if an existing job implies performing many routine and cognitive tasks, that job must be more vulnerable to displacement by technology adoption. Researchers have classified jobs based on the proportion of automatable tasks that their accomplishment entails and ended up defining a ranking whereby jobs are classified according to the risk of disappearing. One of the first papers applying this technique is Frey and Osborne (2013), concluding that, in the following 10 to 20 years, almost half of all jobs in the US are at high risk of disappearing because of automation. The authors, however, look at aggregated "occupation" level: they assume that a job with a significant number of automatable tasks will disappear. Other researchers have shown that looking at a more disaggregated "task" level would suggest less alarmist scenarios. The vast majority of jobs just becoming partially automated, with only some of their currently associated tasks performed by machines rather than by humans. That explains why Arntz et al. (2016), for example, estimate that just 9% of jobs in OECD economies are at risk of being completely displaced by technology (Figure 12.6 summarizes the findings of the most recent published papers on this subject).

While the task-based logic may appear sound, students should be cautious about taking those estimates only as a general suggestion and not as a reliable indication of the exact proportion of jobs that will disappear in the future. That is because occupation-based and task-based models rely on subjective methodology:

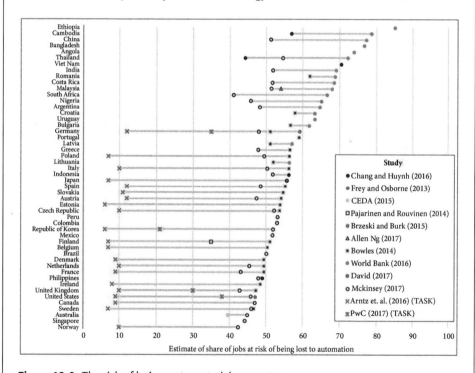

Figure 12.6 The risk of being automated, by country

Source: UNDESA, 'Frontier Issues: The impact of the technological revolution on labour markets and income distribution' (29 August 2017), p. 29.

continued

Box 12.1 *continued*

- in the identification of the tasks (who decides whether a machine can really perform a task better than a human worker can and whether the performance/costs trade-off suggests that a worker will always be replaced?);
- and in the identification of the right level of aggregation of tasks for any given job (who decides whether the proportion of tasks that will be automated is such that the job will disappear rather than transform, losing some of the currently performed tasks while acquiring new ones?).

12.3 Dilemmas for policymakers

While we still do not really know how technology will affect labour markets, the conclusion from the previous two sections is that there are good indications that the net effect on human labour demand will ultimately be positive, at least in the long term.

For two reasons, however, policymakers should take both scenarios (a *net increase* and a *net decrease* in the demand for human workers) equally seriously: first, the second scenario of a reduction in the need for human workers cannot be ruled out yet. Second, there is an issue with citizens' perception of the risk of massive unemployment induced by technology. Economists often downplay people's worries in face of the uncertainty. They point to the low likelihood that technological advancement would leave workers without a job—even if they lost the occupation they are currently employed in, they would get a new one, workers are often told. This strategy has, however, so far proven unsuccessful, at least judging from the wave of scepticism towards technology and work that is shattering the world (72% of European citizens believe that "robots steal people's jobs", according to a 2017 Eurobarometer survey (European Commission, 2021i)). And yet, one key task of public policy is to directly address citizens' fears and reassure them that public authorities "*have a plan*" should the worst-case scenario materialize.

For didactic purposes, let us artificially split the analysis of the policy solutions for the two scenarios into two separate sections, bearing in mind that solutions often overlap. The distinction between one scenario and the other is not so neat in real life.

12.3.1 Scenario 1: Technology will increase labour demand in the long term

If technology will increase the demand for human workers, this does not mean that everybody will be better off. Quite the contrary: transitions are costly, at least for

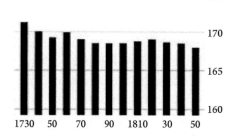

Mean height of English soldiers
Aged 20–23 years old. cm

Figure 12.7 The effect of nutrition quality on soldiers during the first Industrial Revolution
https://www.economist.com/free-exchange/2013/09/13/did-living-standards-improve-during-the-industrial-revolution

some. The early Industrial Revolutions were generally not accompanied by public policies aimed at addressing the cost of transition for the more vulnerable classes, and the unstable employment situation translated into a short-term decrease in the average quality of life. For example, it led to lower nutrition quality, as a decrease in the average height of Europeans in the years following the first Industrial Revolution in 1760 presumably suggests (see Figure 12.7).

It is, therefore, reasonable to expect that the Fourth Industrial Revolution will also negatively affect the quality of life for some. Even if more jobs are created than destroyed, not all who lose their jobs will get a new one. In addition, technology has distributional effects, shiftingeconomic value from those who have skills that can be substituted by machines (such as routine-based) to those who have skills that are complementary to machines, potentially exacerbating inequality. Finally, technology has an impact on the quality of jobs, even if job-holders retain them. For example, it can improve employers' ability to monitor and control employees, with potentially significant negative effects on their wellbeing (I will discuss the effect of technology on the workplace in Chapter 15 on artificial intelligence). Or it can give rise to new types of jobs that are hard to classify in traditional categories such as "employee" or "self-employed", and therefore give rise to issues that are more difficult to tackle through traditional social protection tools (this is the case for *sharing economy workers*—see Chapter 11 for an analysis).

Two key intervention areas can help navigate the transition while minimizing societal costs:

- public policies in support of reskilling and reforms of the educational sector; and
- public policies that protect and support workers who have temporarily been displaced facilitating their reintegration into labour markets.

12.3.1.1 The importance of education and life-long learning

Skills are the obvious starting point for public policies tackling issues with the future of work. We know from Chapter 2 that European labour markets are very much unprepared for the technological revolution. The latest Digital Scoreboard from the European Commission indicates that approximately 43% of the EU population in 2017 had an insufficient level of digital skills, with 10% of the EU labour force having no digital skills at all. 30% of the workforce does not have the minimum basic digital skills that are often required to perform a job; it is estimated, for example, that in 2016 half of the jobs in the construction sector required basic digital skills to be performed. Meanwhile, EU employers lament their inability to find workers with the set of skills they need to further digitize their business. The European Commission has estimated a growing deficit of ICT professional skills, forecasted to reach 595,000 for EU27 in 2020. Furthermore, 56.7 % of EU companies with more than 250 employees report a digital skill gap at the workplace (Joint Research Centre, 2019b).

Tellingly, researchers have shown that technological advancement pushes employers to look for workers possessing a medium to a high level of digital skills and, most importantly, social or non-cognitive skills. A definition for the former is found in the European Digital Competence Framework (Council of the European Union, 2018):

> *"**Digital competence** involves the confident, critical and responsible use of, and engagement with, digital technologies for learning, at work, and for participation in society. It includes information and data literacy, communication and collaboration, media literacy, digital content creation (including programming), safety (including digital well-being and competences related to cybersecurity), intellectual property related questions, problem solving and critical thinking".*

Social and non-cognitive skills may include: competence in cross-cultural settings, adaptive thinking, entrepreneurship, resilience, flexibility, curiosity, creativity, inclination to strive under pressure, and the ability to excel in team work.

Deming (2017) identified an increasing gap between the wage premium for social skills and maths-based skills, including Science Technology Engineering and Mathematics (STEM) disciplines: between 1980 and 2012, the share of jobs in the US labour force requiring high levels of social interaction grew by almost twelve percentage points.

A natural response to the skills shortage in the labour force is through policies aimed to improve the educational system and foster knowledge of new technologies amongst the post-schooling population. The benefits of early high-quality education with small children and of the provision of life-long learning opportunities should be emphasized. Successful learning programs require the involvement and concerted engagement of all key stakeholders: governments, employers, employees, parents, and students.

Educational systems require radical rethinking: currently, schooling programmes are most often geared towards disseminating knowledge to pupils.[6] That is

---

[6] A notable exception is Finland—discussed in section 12.3.2.

the logical consequence of the fact that modern educational systems are born out of the need to provide the future workforce with the knowledge necessary to perform tasks in *routine-oriented* labour markets. Future labour markets will instead need workers that can handle uncertainty, as we have just seen. So educational systems should shift from simply providing direct knowledge to students to providing the non-cognitive tools needed to acquire new knowledge autonomously. And to implement it in a volatile environment or to creatively identify solutions to problems that cannot yet be foreseen.

Eurostat defines **life-long learning** as the set of "*all learning activities undertaken throughout life with the aim of improving knowledge, skills and competences, within personal, civic, social or employment-related perspectives*" (Eurostat, 2019). The provision of learning opportunities for workers who possess skills substitutable by machines, rather than complementing them, is a cornerstone of any strategy aimed to smoothen the transition towards economy 4.0. Yet data shows that those workers with greater need, namely: those at higher risk of automation, belonging to vulnerable categories such as low-skilled, older, and unemployed, tend to participate *less* in training opportunities (see Figure 12.8).

This apparent inconsistency, those who need training/upskilling the *most* are those who get it the *least*, can be explained by the fact that mobility tends to be easier for the high-skilled, and that their training tends to be more specific and purpose-oriented. It turns out that the highly skilled have a higher incentive to enrol in training programmes. Likewise, there is an awareness issue, with the low-skilled being less aware of the availability of general upskilling programmes and the benefit for their career. This asymmetry in the distribution of learning opportunities taken is an **apparent market failure**, begging for public intervention. Policies are needed to ensure that especially low-skilled workers are willing and able to take up learning opportunities. Such as policies that:[7]

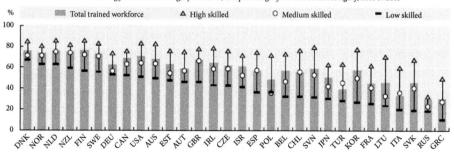

Fewer low-skilled workers receive training than medium- and high-skilled workers
Workers receiving firm-based training, by skill level, as a percentage of workers in each category, 2012 or 2015

Figure 12.8 Low-skilled workers tend to train less than medium and high-skilled
OECD digital challenges Going Digital: Shaping Policies, Improving Lives – 2019

---

[7] The below suggestions are based on the OECD work on the future of work and, in particular: OECD (2019f) and OECD (2019g).

- Incentivize companies to **reach out and communicate** to workers about internal and external upskilling opportunities. Likewise, bigger companies should invest significant resources in the **provision of upskilling opportunities or the financing of external learning,** and possibly include in their organizations a one-stop-shop office guiding workers on their career prospects. Companies should foster a new mindset, **a culture of continuous learning** amongst employees
- Facilitate cross-company recognition of acquired skills. Mutual recognition can be achieved through the establishment of educational standards and the establishment of certification schemes. Training rights and acquired qualifications should be made **easily portable** from one company to another so that workers do not lose them when they change job
- Support the introduction of **flexible opportunities** such as learning programmes, consisting of self-contained learning modules so that adults can arrange their learning path to best fit their individual background, preferences, and ambitions
- Provide **financial backing for employees and employers,** partially or fully compensating them from foregone earnings and social security contributions during training time

12.3.1.2 Social safety net 4.0

Reskilling schemes aim to empower workers to reduce the likelihood that technology will displace them. Social safety nets instead protect those workers who would nevertheless be displaced, helping them to find new employment and supporting them during the transition period. A major challenge here is represented by how technology is reshaping workers' employment status, blurring the distinction between being an employee versus being self-employed and therefore making coverage by public social insurance tools often uncertain (see Chapter 11 on the sharing economy for further discussion). A logical policy response should be based on two prongs: clarifying social protection inclusion criteria and facilitating self-employed workers to enter insurance schemes. More generally, the Fourth Industrial Revolution exerts increasing pressure on governments to move towards a *"flexicurity"*-kind of approach.[8] That is: models that entail a high level of support for the unemployed on a universal basis, while allowing employers more leeway when needing to dismiss their workforce. Such models have proven successful in Scandinavian countries, ensuring access by all citizens to essential welfare goods and services such as housing, health care, and education, while providing for the necessary flexibility needed in particular by highly dynamic and evolving markets.

At the same time, labour market policies should facilitate displaced workers' access to job search services. They should provide workers with *"tailored"* support that

---

[8] For an analysis of flexicurity, see: Boeri, et al. (2012).

would not only increase the chance that they would find a new job, it would also provide guidance to allow workers to better understand how they could get the most out of their profile, thanks to their expertise and the acquisition of new skills via reskilling programmes.

12.3.2 Scenario 2: Technology will decrease labour demand in the long term

In this scenario, machines and algorithms would replace human workers to an extent such that, in the long term, labour markets will need fewer humans in order to properly function. Alternatively, there could be a significant reduction in the *amount* of work performed by humans, for example, through a decrease in the average number of working hours, something that occurred after the previous industrial revolutions.[9]

A possible public policy response to structural unemployment consists of adopting **Universal Basic Income (UBI)** schemes whereby citizens would be entitled to receive a monthly income by the state unconditionally, no matter their wealth or employment condition. UBI has the advantage to guarantee that nobody is excluded from the state's support. However, whether UBI would be welfare-enhancing is a highly controversial matter. The first, relatively intuitive, problem is that UBI may lower citizens' incentive to work in the first place: why would people work if they can receive an income for the mere fact that they are citizens of a country with a "generous" government? Experimental evidence seems to back that intuition.[10] Finland, for example, has run a 2-year trial from January 2017 to December 2018 in which the government granted a monthly salary of €560 to a sample of 2,000 unemployed people aged 25 to 58 years old. It was observed that the grant did not trigger any positive effect on employment, and the experiment was terminated (with some general disappointment).

Second, UBI is, by definition, very expensive. It, therefore, requires a heavy fiscal adjustment, with increased taxes and, in parallel, a significant shrinking of public services. Thus, it does not come as a surprise that UBI finds great support in Silicon Valley circles. In effect, UBI is just another way through which governments can redistribute value to citizens, substituting services with a direct monetary transfer. As we have seen in Chapter 8, a restricted number of digital companies are acquiring an increasingly powerful role in service markets. At the same time, these companies are boosting their ability to extract value from individuals through the information they gather about them (see Chapter 5 on the Data Economy). Therefore, in this context, UBI can make people more vulnerable, rather than empowering them. The

---

[9] In the US, an average working week decreased from almost 60 hours in 1900 to 50 hours in 1930—see Golden (2009).

[10] Hoynes and Rothstein (2019) argue that ongoing pilot studies on UBI are not designed to address the most relevant questions generated by UBI; namely, those related to distributional effects.

most vulnerable segments of societies (e.g. citizens with a lower level of digital skills) would access fewer services while having little bargaining power vis-à-vis digital service providers when spending their UBI (for example, because they are less able to switch between competing services).

More generally, the OECD has shown that a budget-neutral UBI (that is: a UBI policy accompanied by a parallel increase in taxes and cut in services) would have direct distributional effects (OECD, 2017b). Middle-income households are more likely to gain with UBI, as they do not qualify for means-tested benefits (and therefore benefit from receiving UBI even if it is financed through cutting other types of income support or public services which depend on means-testing), and they are less affected by net tax increases compared to high-income households. On the other hand, lower-income segments are more likely to be hit by cuts in means-tested income supports. In the UK, OECD calculates that a financially sustainable UBI would amount to a monthly income of £230 per person, an amount far below the poverty line of £702 and 28% less than the currently guaranteed minimum-income benefits. In the OECD simulation, 15% of the UK population would be in poverty with a budget-neutral UBI, compared to 10% under the existing system (OECD, 2017b).

Another rather primitive potential policy measure proposed to prevent structural unemployment is introducing a **robot tax**: such an approach would inevitably slow down the pace of technological adoption, rebalancing the cost-benefit comparison between human workers and machines. Moreover, the tax income could be invested in retraining programmes so that workers would increase their chances to retain their job in the future. However, the logic of the robot tax is flawed: as we have seen throughout this book, the adoption of new technologies gives rise to many concerns, but the solution is not to raise barriers to it. Instead, policymakers should create a setting where digital can thrive while addressing the issues that may arise with it. On the contrary, slowing down adoption would be detrimental to the very workers that the tax would be supposed to protect. It would reduce European companies' incentives to digitize their production process, reduce their productivity, and expose them to international competition. It would be a meagre consolation for workers: to retain their job because their company does not digitize its production but lose their job because their employer goes bankrupt due to the unsustainable competitive pressure by Chinese or US counterparts.

A broader approach is necessary. There is no doubt that digitization can significantly positively affect the size of the metaphorical pie, generating tremendous value for the economy and society. Public policy efforts should therefore be directed to incentivize technological adoption, even if that entails structural unemployment. The critical problem to address is how the generated value is distributed. As we have seen in Chapter 8, competition policy can, in that respect, have an important role since it addresses digital markets' dysfunctionalities, favouring a fairer allocation of value to all stakeholders. In the specific case of companies and workers, presumably mechanisms should be designed to allow workers to earn their fair share of the benefits yielded by the automation of their company, for example, by incentivizing stock options in salary packages. As suggested in Lowitzsch (2016): "*A solution to the dilemma of machines substituting for humans and reducing labour demand would be for European citizens to acquire a significant share of co-ownership in the robots competing with them on the labour market, subsequently providing them with a second source of income independent of their labour. This is in line with the most recent support of the European Commission for Employee Ownership.*" I will further discuss these issues in the following Chapter 13 on digital inequality.

12.4 The European Union's perspective

The European Union has a small room for manoeuvre in labour markets: *employment* is a shared competence with the Member States, whereby the EU plays a coordinator role and supplements national policies where countries have not yet intervened. Therefore, the active role of the European Commission is mainly limited to the surveillance, monitoring, and assessment of what Member States do in terms of labour market regulation, labour taxation and incentives, and wage policy developments, particularly given the overall impact on the development of the Single Market. The European Commission can suggest to Member States to adopt specific policies affecting their domestic labour markets. Indeed, it systematically does so in the *European Semester*, for example, through which the European Commission and the Member States design common policies to achieve growth targets. In practice though, countries remain broadly free to ignore the European Commission's recommendations.

EU law can, however, establish **minimum standards** in terms of social affairs and employment within the Union's territory: EU provisions regulate health and safety at work, equal opportunities and discrimination bans, working conditions such as working hours, part-time, and fixed-term contracts. In addition, EU law ensures respect of the four fundamental freedoms enshrined in the Treaty of the European Union: freedom of movement for *persons, capital, goods, and services*. Therefore, it regulates the conditions upon which workers from different Member States can access other EU countries' labour markets.

That being said, EU policies are instrumental in addressing the concerns about the impact of technology on labour markets analysed in the previous sections. On the one hand, digitization is inherently an international phenomenon, begging for a coherent supranational approach. Think about the crucial importance of network effects and scale in teaching and research. More coordination between educational systems, consistency in training programmes, smooth cross-border mobility between universities and the business sector by graduates can limit unemployment risk while responding to the need to favour the technological development of European companies, and increase their productivity.

On the other hand, there is a relatively good awareness among European citizens about the role of the European Commission as the Single Market's gatekeeper. Thus, it would be hard to accept a European Union only concerned with fostering digitization, favouring the inflow of foreign competitive digital services, but not with the protection of those vulnerable segments of society that are most likely to be harmed by technological progress.

In 2017, the major EU institutions (the European Commission, the European Parliament, and the Council of the EU) proclaimed the **European Pillar of Social Rights** with the aim to "*serve as a guide towards efficient employment and social outcomes when responding to current and future challenges which are directly aimed at fulfilling people's essential needs, and towards ensuring better enactment and implementation of social rights*". The implementation of the Pillar's 20 principles[11] is a shared responsibility by all the signatories (see Chapter 13 on inequality). From the side of the European Union, the concrete initiatives with direct relevance to the challenge posed by the digitization of society aligned with the Pillar's goals are:

- A **Directive on Transparent and Predictable Working Conditions**. The main goal of the Directive is to set minimum standards of protection for workers in more precarious jobs. It, therefore, responds directly to the emergence of new forms of employment featured by the increased flexibility required of workers
- A **Directive on work-life balance for parents and carers**. The Directive introduces greater flexibility for working parents and carers, with minimum paternity leave, parental leave, and carers' leave rights
- The creation of the **European Labour Authority**, tasked with the goal of facilitating workers' cross-border mobility
- A **Council Recommendation on Access to Social Protection**, with the goal of supporting people in non-standard forms of employment or self-employed people who may not get sufficient cover by social security schemes (see Chapter 11 on the Sharing Economy for a discussion).

For the purposes of the issues examined in this chapter, the most important initiative taken by the European Commission is the **New Skills Agenda** adopted in June 2016 (European Commission, 2016l). As we observed in the previous sections, a key issue where public policy intervention could potentially bring significant improvements concerns the mismatch between what employers ask for and what employees and job-seekers can offer. At the root of that mismatch lies a European workforce lacking digital skills. Therefore, it is not surprising that the Digital Single Market Strategy identifies that as a core area of action in its chapter on "*building an inclusive e-society*". It says:

> "*The responsibility for curricula lies with the Member States which need urgently to address the lack of essential digital skills. The Commission will support their efforts and will play its*

---

[11] The first principle of the European Pillar of Social rights recites: "*Everyone has the right to quality and inclusive education, training and life-long learning in order to maintain and acquire skills that enable them to participate fully in society and manage successfully transitions in the labour market*".

role in enhancing the recognition of digital skills and qualifications and increasing the level of ICT professionalism in Europe. The Commission will address digital skills and expertise as a key component of its future initiatives on skills and training".

It is also worth noting that, despite their growing importance, non-cognitive skills are rarely taught as competences areas around Europe. For example, the Joint Research Centre (2019b) reports that social and emotional learning is not mandatory in curricula among 17 Member States analysed. Only half of the adult EU population can positively recognize a relevant role for school education in helping them developing *initiative* and *entrepreneurship* skills.

The New Skills Agenda is a Communication laying down a package of ten actions to improve the provision of training and the access to it throughout the European Union, to facilitate the display of workers' competencies, and to guide individuals in their career and life-long learning choices (see Box 12.2). All actions were subsequently followed by the adoption of concrete legislative or administrative measures that would implement them. Particularly relevant are: the **Skill Guarantee** (rebranded **Upskilling Pathways** in the European Council Recommendation adopted in December 2016 (The Council of the European Union, 2016). The review of the **European Qualifications Framework** in May 2017 (European Commission, 2016m). And the set-up of a "**Digital Skills and Jobs Coalition**" in December 2016 (European Commission, 2021j), relaunching the previous "Coalition for Digital Jobs" from 2013.

Box 12.2   The New Skills Agenda's 10 key actions (European Commission, 2016n)

---

1. A **Skills Guarantee** to help low-skilled adults to progress towards an upper secondary qualification.
2. A review of the **European Qualifications Framework** to ensure consistency in the appreciation of skills in the European labour market.
3. The "**Digital Skills and Jobs Coalition**" encompassing Member States and industry stakeholders to foster the creation of a wide digital talent pool and provide individuals with adequate digital skills.
4. The "**Blueprint for Sectoral Cooperation on Skills**" to address specific economic sectors' skill needs.
5. A "**Skill Profile Tool for Third Country Nationals**" to identify skills and qualifications of migrants.
6. A revision of the **Europass Framework** to guide individuals in their career and learning choices and provide them with an easier way to highlight their skills.
7. Enhancing opportunities for **Vocational Education and Training (VET)**.

continued

Box 12.2 *continued*

8. A review of the **Recommendation on Key Competences** to facilitate the acquisition of the core set of skills that will be mostly needed in future labour markets.

9. An initiative on **graduate tracking** to better monitor graduates progress' in labour markets.

10. A proposal to improve the **exchange of best practices** to effectively address "brain drain".

The **Skill Guarantee** aims to support low-skilled adults to acquire minimal levels of literacy, numeracy, and digital skills. It does so through a three-step procedure: adults would first identify their skill needs and define their learning needs. They would then receive a "tailored" training offer adapted to their identified needs. And, finally, there would be a framework to validate and allow the recognition of the newly acquired skills. The responsibility for the implementation of the guarantee schemes rests with the existing structures across the Member States, with the EU offering guidance and financial support through several funding channels (the Employment and Social Innovation programme (European Commission, 2021k), the Structural Reform Support Programme (European Commission, 2021l), the European Social Fund (European Commission, 2021m), and some other EU funds). For example, €27 billion of funding from the European Social Fund was planned to support *education, training, skills, and life-long learning* from 2014 to 2020.

The **European Qualification Framework** (EQF) is a reference system used to allow international comparison of qualifications. It is, therefore, an important tool to facilitate learners' and workers' mobility throughout the EU territory. The EQF defines eight reference levels for learning outcomes for "knowledge", "skills", and "responsibility and autonomy". Level 1 corresponds with basic general knowledge, basic skills to perform simple tasks, or work under direct supervision in a structured context. Level 8 corresponds with knowledge at the most advanced frontier, possessing highly advanced skills and techniques, or demonstrating substantial authority, innovation, and autonomy to develop new ideas or processes at the forefront of a certain field of work or study.

The European Commission has developed two specific frameworks for Digital Competences and Entrepreneurial Competences named *DigComp*[12] and *EntreComp*.[13]

The **Digital Skills and Jobs Coalition** is a platform bringing together EU countries and stakeholders such as industrial players, non-profit organizations, or educational institutions. The Coalition was set to pursue four goals by 2020: train one million young unemployed people for vacant digital jobs through internships or

---

[12] See https://ec.europa.eu/jrc/en/digcomp
[13] See https://ec.europa.eu/social/main.jsp?catId=1317&langId=en

apprenticeships programmes; support small and medium enterprises to attract and retain digital talents; favour the uptake of digital tools within students and teaching personnel in schools; and promote the use of funding to support the development of digital skills. The Coalition, for example, contributes to the design and implementation of "digital opportunity traineeship" schemes, targeting students from all over Europe with allowances for up to twelve months and facilitating companies willing to open vacancies for trainees with lower administrative burden, EU funding contributions, and easier access to a cross-border pool of potential candidates.

In November 2020, the European Commission officially launched the **Pact for Skills.**[14] Similarly to the digital skills and jobs coalition, the idea is to invite public and private entities to join forces to promote upskilling and reskilling of the European workforce. The stated goals of the pact are four: (1) promoting a culture of lifelong learning for all; (2) building strong skills partnerships; (3) monitoring skills supply/demand and anticipating skills needs; (4) working against discrimination and for gender equality and equal opportunities. The Commission has committed to supporting the signatories of the pact in their upskilling and reskilling actitivies as of 2021, for example, through financing or facilitating access to knowledge and information sharing.

Finally, in 2020 the European Commission launched its **Digital Education Action Plan**[15] for 2021–2027. It lays out several actions that should be taken in the years to come to update European countries' educational and training systems, making them fit for a digital economy. It is important to note that the plan was drafted after the outbreak of the Covid-19 pandemic crisis. Therefore, it attempts to incorporate the lesson from the pandemic. For example, it envisages support to facilitate access and use of distant learning technology (almost 60% of respondents to a European Commission's consultation stated that they had no experience with distant learning before the pandemic).

The plan focuses on two priority areas:
1. *Foster the quality of the digital education ecosystem*
2. *Enhancing digital skills and competences*

In area 1 ("**foster the quality of the digital education ecosystem**"), actions focus on improving access to connectivity infrastructure and technological equipment, such as in schools, or enhancing the quality of learning content offered, including through the upskilling of teachers. In area 2 ("**Enhancing digital skills and competences**"), actions focus on providing pupils with basic digital skills from an early age, incentivize the adoption of technological topics in teaching programs (including how to address challenges in the digital space, such as disinformation), or fostering the uptake of advanced courses in ICT, particularly by women (who, as we have seen, tend to be under-represented in the technological sector).

---

[14] See https://ec.europa.eu/social/main.jsp?catId=1517&langId=en
[15] https://ec.europa.eu/education/education-in-the-eu/digital-education-action-plan_en

The plan successfully identifies the key areas that require policy intervention. However, it struggles with the structural limitation of the EU role in educational matters that, as we have seen, tend to fall in the Member States' sphere of competence. Thus the envisaged actions in the Digital Educational Action Plan are primarily geared towards the provision of teaching guidelines, the strengthening of cross-border cooperation, information sharing (for example, through the establishment of a *European Digital Education Hub*), and mutual recognition of qualifications (for example, through the creation of a *European Digital Skills Certificate*).

On their part, countries around Europe are starting to pay attention to skills training and life-long learning as core tools to face the challenges posed by digitization. The OECD (2019h) reports that some countries, for example, are attempting to pull down barriers to training for workers in atypical contractual relationships. A rather common practice is to allow training costs to be filed as business expenses that can thus be deducted from tax bills. Other actions include the 2016 French "*Loi Travail*" obliging online platforms to finance platform workers' training and help them obtain recognition of previously acquired skills. In Austria, self-employed workers may access regional funds to finance their training needs, provided that they fulfil certain conditions that make them more likely to be in an atypical employment contractual relationship. For example, they may need to be insured under the Commercial Social Security Act and holding a "contract for work" without a trade license. Perhaps most importantly, several countries are experimenting with the **portability of training rights** (see Section 12.3 above). Since 2015 France has adopted the *Compte Personnel de Formation* or CPF (from 2018 also opened to self-employed). The CPF is a repository of all training activities undertaken by a worker from their first employment to their retirement; it is personal, and it allows a smooth transfer of the workers' training rights from one employer to another. At the time of writing, Portugal, Spain, and the Netherlands have plans to introduce a similar system of individualized learning accounts.

✳✳✳✳

12.5 Case Study: The "hybrid" future of work

In an effort to contain the spread of Covid-19, governments around the world have forced people to stay home for the bigger part of the years 2020 and 2021. Workers that could perform their job's tasks remotely did so. During the pandemic, two very clear indications came across from labour markets; first, before the pandemic many workers were teleworking less than they could. Indeed, the experience during lockdowns showed that productivity levels were not affected by telework; in other words: the pandemic helped to uncover untapped potential. Second, while many found permanent teleworking exhausting, a significant number of employers and employees flagged their intention to retain at least part of the flexibility after the emergency was over. A majority of workers signalled, for example, that, after the pandemic, they would enjoy working from home two or three days per week. A post-pandemic scenario in which a significant part of the workforce is regularly working in remote may bring considerable benefits. But it also poses the challenge of creating work environments where physical and virtual presence is efficiently blended. Depending on the nature of tasks performed and workers' own personal needs or preferences, employees and managers need to find new ways of working that combine the benefits of face-to-face contact with the flexibility of telework. Moreover, the increased geographical mobility of workers may give rise to significant macro-economic effects, such as downward pressure on house pricing in cities and an increase in the economic growth of peripheral and countryside areas. In 2021, the story of the tiny Spanish village of Gósol broke the news. Before the pandemic, Gósol risked disappearing as all its inhabitants had either died or left. During the pandemic, many came to the village to enjoy its quiet life. The pandemic repopulation effect also allowed Gósol to save its school from closing.

For a good coverage on the future of hybrid work see this article from the New Yorker: https://www.newyorker.com/magazine/2021/02/01/has-the-pandemic-transformed-the-office-forever

12.6 Review questions

- Explain the phenomenon known as "the hollow-out of the middle class" emphasizing the role of technology (i.e. how technology has contributed to eroding salaries in the middle of the wage distribution). Provide two examples of jobs for each of these three wage categories: low-wage, medium-wage, high-wage, and describe the effect that technological progress may have had on each of them.
- A new technology allows a manufacturing plant to produce the same quantity of wooden tables employing half of the human resources needed before. If that technology is adopted, what do you expect to be the net effect on employment at that manufacturing plant and why? Justify and explain your answer in detail.

- What are the potential benefits and drawbacks of adopting a Universal Basic Income scheme? Illustrate your answer with an example (make up your own).
- Imagine the following scenario. The European Commission has just proposed introducing a new support scheme to favour the adoption of certain digital technologies that promise to significantly increase productivity and reduce the need for the human workforce. The Council must adopt the proposal before entering into force. What would be, in your view, the primary source of disagreement between the Member States and why? Justify and explain your answer.
- Explain why basic (non-technological) education in school may, in the long term, affect the impact of technology on labour markets.

13

Digital Inequality

Abstract

Technological development is often presented as a powerful way to enhance the human condition, particularly for the most vulnerable segments of the population. Digital technologies can improve the efficiency of general interest services, most notably in the health care and educational sectors. They generate opportunities and reduce costs for consumers, workers, and small entrepreneurs. New technologies provide for incredibly effective communication channels, enhancing political participation and amplifying the voice of those who are the margin of society. On the contrary, history shows that the most recent technological development cemented and even exacerbated off-line inequalities, contributing to polarising societies and widening the gap between the haves and the have-nots. A key driver of this extremely worrying phenomenon is the digital divide, defined as individuals' different exposure to the opportunities offered by technology, both in terms of access and ability to use it and profit from it. Policymakers must deploy policy solutions that would promote wider access to technology within the population and a more symmetric distribution of the benefits that stem from it. Policy should drive technological development to correct off-line inequality rather than exacerbate it.

13.1 Background

In the previous chapter, we looked at the effect that technological progress has on labour markets. In this chapter, I take a broader look and study the interplay between technology and equality, being aware of the role that work has to determine income and wealth distribution within the economy.

I use the term *equality* in this context not to indicate a state of the world where everyone shares the same degree of happiness or wealth. Instead, for *equal society* I consider one where all of its members have an equal opportunity to satisfy their will, regardless of their background and endowment.[1] An asymmetric distribution of wealth should not be considered a problem in itself. Instead, it may be a *symptom* of an asymmetry in the distribution of opportunities within society. That is the real problem that needs addressing by policymakers.

Students should not be surprised to discover that digital policy plays a significant role with respect to equality in society. Digitization is a key vehicle of opportunity.

---

[1] For an excellent review of the discussion around the utilitarian paradigm and equality of opportunity paradigm, see: Peragine and Ferreira (2015).

Digital Economic Policy. Mario Mariniello, Oxford University Press.
© Mario Mariniello (2022). DOI: 10.1093/oso/9780198831471.003.0013

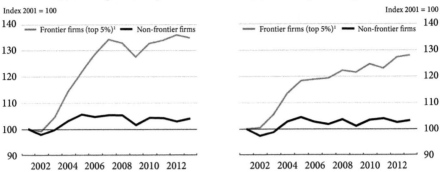

Figure 13.1   Firms' productivity polarization correlates with wage dispersion
OECD Economic Outlook, Volume 2017, Issue 1 – Chapter 2

It is, indeed, often presented as such: a digitized society, an "Eldorado" for citizens, who can get better, tailored services, and for companies, who can significantly increase their productivity (in Chapter 5, for example, we have seen how data can generate significant value for those who have the means to process and analyse them). Accordingly, digitization could contribute to correct asymmetries in the value distribution of society, enhancing the means available for those who lack them. But it could also increase inequality dramatically if only some, possibly the most wealthy, can reap its benefits.

Presumably, reducing inequality should be a policy goal in itself. It features amongst the United Nations' Sustainable Development Goal (Goal n. 10) (United Nations, 2021a), and it is thus broadly considered an important objective to pursue to achieve shared prosperity (the Sustainable Development Goals are endorsed by the European Union too). Addressing inequality does not, however, have only an ideological basis. Economies with significant differences between individuals in terms of well-being are also inherently more unstable and prone to conflict and violence, which can further aggravate the poorer and most vulnerable individuals' conditions, in a vicious cycle. Populism, nationalism, and protectionism find fertile ground in the generalized feelings of being unfairly treated, insecurity, and stress that inequality contributes to generating. We have seen in Chapter 12 how polarization of skill demand driven by technological progress has hollowed out the income distribution, affecting, in particular, the middle-class segment, with a significant detriment to society's stability. The rise of populism, the election of US President Trump in 2016, and Brexit are phenomena that can be linked to this sense of insecurity (Inglehart & Norris, 2016).

Inequality has also been linked with slower economic growth. Because inequality may be seen as the price to pay to incentivize innovation investment and risk-taking initiative, the theoretical economic literature has not been unanimously supportive of that finding. Yet, most empirical studies back the existence of a causal link between inequality of opportunities and the amount of value that a society can produce. This is mainly driven by the lost opportunities in terms of human capital, which is not acquired by low-income; inability to access financial markets; inability to move the societal ladder; and misallocation of skilled employees that are more vulnerable to external shocks in unequal societies (IMF, 2019).

Inequality is defined along with a number of different dimensions (European Commission, 2021o):

- **Economic inequality** is often measured with reference to wealth or income distribution. A classic indicator for it is the *Gini Coefficient* which takes values between zero, in the (theoretical) case of perfectly symmetric distribution of income or wealth, and one, in case of perfect inequality (i.e. a society where all wealth is concentrated in the hands of one single individual). All developed economies have seen the Gini coefficient increase significantly in the last half-century, showing that economies have become more unequal
- **Social inequality** is measured by looking at differences in access to education, employment opportunities, or social positions. It can relate to the quality of working conditions or health care that individuals can access to. Social inequality is strongly related to economic inequality. Still, it can be driven by discrimination of gender, sexual orientation, race, religion, social class, geographical origin, residence, income, age, or any other features signalling belonging to a minority
- **Political inequality** measures asymmetries in the ability to influence political decisions over the territory where individuals reside, affecting their level of civic participation as well as the chance to promote their interests and protect their rights
- **Environmental inequality** indicates differences in exposure to environmental risk or health hazard, such as pollution; it also records individuals' asymmetric access to natural resources such as fresh water or city green spaces.

Likewise, inequality can be measured across individuals within a specific territory (*vertical inequality*) or across different groups of individuals, for example, minorities or individuals with a well-defined geographical belonging, such as urban vs rural areas residents (*horizontal inequality*).

Looking at Europe Eurofound (2021), the European Commission (2021p), and Blanchet et al. (2019) find that income inequality has increased in the majority of European countries, with the top 1% income bracket growing twice as fast as the bottom 50%, capturing 17% of European income growth. The 2020 pandemic has exacerbated inequality both between countries, slowing down their convergence in income levels, and within countries. Eurofound (2021) indicates pay and income inequality, as well as the significant number of working poor amongst EU workers, as the most worrying social trend for Europe. Similar trends are observable on other dimensions of inequality. People in the low-income segments struggle to improve their social mobility or general quality of life (with better access to health and education, for example), compared to the higher-income households. The European Institute for Gender Equality 2020 annual report indicates that, at the current pace, it would take 60 years to achieve full equality of opportunities, regardless of gender. It points to segregation in education and work as one of the main drivers of gender symmetry: only 20% of ICT jobs are taken up by women, while only 15% of jobs in nursing, midwifery, and personal care in health services are taken up by men, for example (European Institute for Gender Equality, 2020).

The purpose of this chapter is to look at inequality from the lens of digital policy. Before looking at the role that technological development can play in addressing differences between individuals, or exacerbating them (see the next section), let us introduce some key terminology.

The relationship between inequality and digitization has been described along the lines of two concurrent hypotheses (van Deursen, et al., 2017):

(1) the **normalization hypothesis**, according to which digitization triggers a redistribution of resources from the more wealthy to the less wealthy
(2) the **stratification hypothesis**, suggesting that digitization reflects and helps cement inequalities that are present in the analogic/offline world.

Two mechanisms are conducive to the stratification hypothesis: a *power law* channel, according to which the returns from digital are not linear; they are instead increasing more than proportionally with the level of access to technology. For example, being able to connect to the Internet via basic broadband (see Chapter 4) can allow surfing the Internet and interact via email, yielding considerable benefit to the user. However, having access to high-speed connectivity may allow to work or study remotely. That increase in return may be much bigger than what could have been expected with a simple upgrade of that user's Internet speed connection. The second channel is the *amplification* mechanism, whereby inequalities are exacerbated by digitization. Amplification is thus a natural corollary of the power law. Sociologists studying digital inequality also refer to the **Matthew effect**, by means *"the richer get richer, and the poor get poorer"*.

The expression **Digital Divide** has been used to indicate the unequal distribution of opportunities between individuals, households, companies, and geographic areas to access information and communication technologies, and to the benefit gained from them (OECD, 2006); particularly relevant to this is individuals' ability to prosper in the online environment. The bigger the digital divide, the stronger is the amplification effect and the stratification outcome on inequality.

A Digital Divide can be observed at three levels:

- *Level 1*: relates to individual **access to technology**, such as infrastructure or computing facilities. A level 1 digital divide can materialize if people cannot access technology or if the quality of their access is poorer than the one of others. Connectivity speed and reliability is a classic example.

- *Level 2*: relates to **skills and usage**. Assuming individuals (or even firms, as the digital divide can be applied to corporate or public entities as well) would be placed in the same conditions of technical access, they may have a different ability to use that technology. A senior man may have the latest laptop with the highest computing power in the market but may find it challenging to use it to access his bank account online or fill in a form for a public service.

- *Level 3*: relates to individuals' **ability to extract different amounts of value** from the services that they are able to use. This may depend on users' overall ability but could also be driven by contingent conditions or structural characteristics conducive to discrimination, such as their race or gender. Continuing with the above example: a kid from a low-income household in a poor area may not be able to access the Internet because of lack of connectivity (level 1). A senior man may be ok at level 1, with good access to ICT, but may be unable to use it (level 2). A well-educated young black woman may have good access to technology and possess the skills to use it; however, she may be unable to get the same chances to land a job by surfing available vacancies than her white, male peers because she is discriminated.

Simply put: level 1 in digital divide is about *access*, level 2 is about *use*, and level 3 is about *outcomes*. Notably, the term *Digital Divide* was coined in 1995 by the US National Telecommunication and Information Administration agency (NTIA, 1995) in a report that primarily focused on differences between American urban and rural areas in access to telecom infrastructure—hence level 1. But with infrastructure access becoming increasingly widespread, scholars that research the domain of digital inequality have been progressively expanding their focus to study also level 2 and level 3.

However, this should not mislead students to believe that level 1 is, today, less relevant than it was in 1995. Asymmetry in infrastructure access is still very much present in developed economies, as we have seen in Chapter 2 and 4 as regards Europe, for example. And it is all the more a significant issue for emerging economies. In 2018 Europe recorded a level of **Internet penetration** (the number of households with access to the Internet over the total number of households) equal to 85%, compared to an average of 36% for African countries, and 49% for Asian countries (Robinson, et al., 2020a). In its 2019 affordability report, the **Alliance for Affordable Internet** (an international organization pursuing the goal of granting universal access to the Internet) stated: "*While Internet access is considered a basic good by many, almost half of the world's population remains unable to connect. The primary barrier to Internet access is cost. In low and middle-income countries, 1GB data costs 4.7% of average income—more than double the UN threshold for Internet affordability. Across Africa, this figure rises to 7.1%, making access unaffordable for millions*" (A4AI, 2020), see also Figure 13.2.

Moreover, the meaning of ICT access is evolving too. Lutz (2019) for example, considers how the evolution of Internet use changes the meaning and relevance

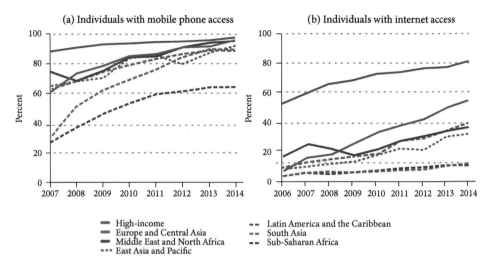

Figure 13.2 Unequal internet access: developed vs developing countries

World Bank. 2016. World Development Report 2016: Digital Dividends. Washington, DC: World Bank.
doi:10.1596/978-1-4648-0671-1

of the infrastructure that users can access. Consider the possibility of identifying a "mobile Internet underclass", that is: a class of users who can only access the Internet through their mobile devices. These users may be unable to access certain content or services; they may be unable to use certain key functionalities, such as drafting a document online or accessing smaller scale, local websites. Another example concerns next-generation smart speakers such as Amazon's Alexa or Apple's Siri. As they struggle to capture dialects and accent, their use by less-educated minorities is de facto limited.

13.2 Opportunities and challenges

The recent technological "revolution", from the emergence of the Internet to artificial intelligence—*Industry and Society 4.0* (see Chapter 12)—was accompanied by the promise of long-lasting and shared prosperity for everybody. As it turns out, digitization has created significant value, but not everyone has been able to tap into it. This asymmetry, in many ways, is not an obvious outcome: if we focus on inequality, it could go both ways. The *normalization* and the *stratification* hypotheses are, from the outset, equally potentially valid. The fact that digitization is currently having the effect of cementing inequality (thus validating the stratification hypothesis) is due to how markets have evolved and the role that has been played by political action (or lack thereof).

Thus let us first look at how digitization can help address inequality, possibly creating opportunities that are particularly beneficial to low-income individuals. After that, I will describe the challenges, or how the digital divide is increasing societal asymmetries.

13.2.1 Opportunities (the normalization hypothesis)

Every chapter of this book points to an area where digitization can bring significant benefit if market failures are addressed through sensible policy action. That applies to everybody, the poor and the rich alike. To validate the normalization hypothesis, it may be helpful though to focus on the aspects of digitization that are most likely to bring significant benefit to low-income individuals.

Following von Braun (2019) (Figure 13.3), the following effects thus merit to be singled out. A digitized economy entails:

- **An expansion of educational opportunities**. Digitization opens new doors allowing students to access educational tools from potentially anywhere in the world even if they cannot travel, at low prices or even for free. Digital services reduce dramatically the cost of attending educational courses (for example through *MOOC*, "massive online open courses"). The Internet makes it much more affordable to get informed, consult scientific production, and read newspapers. Artificial intelligence-enabled translation can allow overcoming language barriers. Intuitively all these opportunities carry stronger benefits for those who possess fewer means: families who cannot enrol their kids in school because of living in remote areas or not having the necessary finances; individuals lacking the educational background to access information in another language; kids with learning disabilities who, thanks to digital technologies, can be provided with tailored support by teachers
- **More affordable and good quality products and services**. The platform economy has disrupted traditional economic sectors. That generated a number of

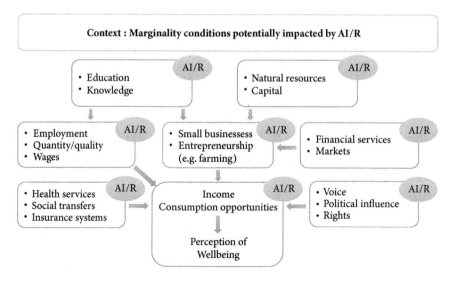

Figure 13.3 Channels for well-being in low-income households. Von Braun, J. (2019). AI and Robotics Implications for the Poor. Available at SSRN 3497591.

new issues, as we know from Chapter 8, for example. But it also entailed increased competition at the retail level, which translated in lower prices and increased competition. Taking urban transport as an example: sharing economy services have made on-demand transport more accessible, benefiting in particular those who could not afford a taxi ride. More generally, the dataization of the economy goes hand-in-hand with price discrimination (see the appendix). Price discrimination may be used to extract more value from buyers by companies. But it can benefit those users who have a lower ability to pay: if suppliers know that a certain group of buyer is low-income, they may use that information and their ability to change the price to charge lower prices to be able to sell their product while still making a profit. Note that, of course, this is only one aspect of discrimination which can be in favour of vulnerable individuals; vulnerabilities can indeed also lead to higher prices (think, for example, about the case of health insurances: the price increases with individual's health risk)

- **More business opportunities.** Digitization enlarges the spectrum of economic opportunities for those who lack the resources that would be considered essential in a traditional, "analogic", economy. We have seen in the e-commerce chapter how digitization can allow even micro family-run businesses to go global without the need for any physical asset. Cheaper, sophisticated technologies can allow increasing the profitability of small assets. Consider, for example, precision farming (see Chapter 15) and how it could help farmers and owners of small crops to significantly increase their production. The sharing economy allows individuals to leverage what they have, increase their flexibility, and match their household needs. This is particularly relevant for female participation in the workforce, which is traditionally restricted by housework and child-care, more so in low-income areas and emerging economies

- **Better access to health and well-being services.** Digital can pull down barriers to access to health services. Telemedicine can reach geographically remote areas. Information retrieved online, if well-screened (see Chapter 14), can complement medical advice. Good online information can foster competition and reduce the cost of medical treatment. Savings and improvements in hospital services generated by technology can translate into significant benefits for those most in need, such as those affected by chronic pathologies. AI and robotics can help people with disabilities accessing services online. On-the-job safety can be improved by shifting dangerous tasks (traditionally performed by low-wage workers) to machines. Technology can improve detecting and preventing malnutrition in impoverished areas. The potential gains for well-being are considerable

- **Better financing.** Digitization increases competition in the financial sector; it makes it easier and cheaper to open a bank account with online banking, for example, while a significant proportion of low-income households, particularly in emerging economies, cannot access banking services. Loans and insurances may become more affordable if data analytics is used to lower the risk of credit, for example, providing accurate information on credit-worthiness, which does not require the possession of physical collaterals. Digital currencies such as bitcoin can lower transaction costs. The benefit of reduced transaction costs is most compelling in the case of remittances by migrants: in 2017, the average global cost for migrants' remittance was more than 7% of the transferred amount. Digitization has the potential to reduce that cost to zero

- **Give political voice.** The Internet and social networks, in particular, are powerful means of freedom of expression. They are tools that everybody can use and be potentially heard by decision-makers. If used well, they can break segregation, cast light on unfair practices, and create movements to fight injustice and exclusion. They can generate unprecedented opportunities for political achievement (see Chapter 14 for an extensive analysis)
- **Better data for policy action.** Finally, data analytics can improve decision making—backing policy action with quantitative data. Data analytics can significantly affect low-income individuals, helping authorities identify those in need, craft targeted programmes that help lift individuals from poverty, for example, and evaluate ex-post their effectiveness. If inclusiveness and shared prosperity are core goals of policymakers, data analytics and technology make it easier to define a strategy to reach them and implement it.

13.2.2 Challenges (the stratification hypothesis)

Despite the potential described above, digital technologies have not helped shrink the gap between the haves and the have-nots (even though they may have generated absolute benefits for the poor). Quite the contrary: within-country inequality is increasing in all developed economies, despite the emergence of sophisticated technologies and the relative paradigm shift that is described throughout this book. What has come to be known as the Fourth Industrial Revolution did not seem to revert a tendency in the distribution of wealth which is rewarding the richer segments of society. That trend started in the 1970s without actually ever having stopped.

This observation is a consideration based on simple correlation: technological development is not the only factor affecting wealth distribution in the economy. Factors such as social policies, taxation, and financial markets all play a role. Yet, it would have been reasonable to expect to observe more generalized prosperity from the digital revolution, at least based on how policymakers often present technological development to citizens: as something *necessary* for the progress of human civilization.

Part of the problem is that lack of political will or ability to address the concerns we have analysed throughout this book led the digital economy to disproportionally reward economic power. Consider the following example: as we will see in Chapter 15, artificial intelligence can open a world of opportunities for employers and employees alike. Yet, the generated value may not be allocated symmetrically between the two parties. AI could allow a machine operator to have more flexibility, for example allowing her to use her smartphone to do certain operations she had to perform onsite before. At the same time, her employer could limit that flexibility by imposing physical presence even when not strictly necessary, while at the same time using technology to monitor more accurately employees' performance. Therefore, in this example, the value generated by AI has accrued mainly on the employer's side. And the explanation for that relies on the fact that labour and social protection laws have not evolved at the same pace of technology, leaving workers more vulnerable than before to exploitation.

The most apparent effect is, however, through the direct asymmetry in the distribution of digital means. That is: the increase in inequality can be primarily explained through the digital divide on all the three levels that I have described in Section 13.1. The Covid-19 pandemic is a perfect illustration of that – as we have seen, children with poor Internet access are those who experienced the most significant loss in terms of missed educational opportunities during lock-downs. Lower knowledge capital today leaves the prospect of even bigger income differences in the future.

As described in Van Deursen and Helsper (2015), studies have shown that in a societal context where Internet usage is asymmetric, those who access the Internet more intensively tend to experience higher wages. Engaged Internet users have an advantage in finding information about job opportunities. Individuals with a higher level of Internet skills access services and buy products at lower prices. More skilful Internet users are more likely to capitalize on social media to find new friends or romantic encounters; engaged digital users can more easily participate in discussions in local communities.

The digital divide should not only be seen from the perspective of individual citizens. There is a growing digital divide within the business sector between companies, which has important implications for welfare distribution within the economy and society. Nobel Prize for Economics Robert Solow once famously pointed out that "*you can see computers everywhere but in productivity statistics.*" (Solow, 1987). That came to be known as the "Solow Paradox": technological development promises to improve the economy's performance greatly. But economists are observing a long trend of generalized slowdown in the growth productivity (namely: the amount of outcome produced by companies given the capital and labour input they employ) in all developed economies (World Bank, 2018). The Solow Paradox can be best explained through the digital divide: technology improves companies' performance by far. It is just that only a tiny proportion of the economy is digitized and can reap the benefits of technological development. Figure 13.1 at the beginning of this chapter shows the significant difference in labour productivity (that is, the average amount of outcome produced by one hour of work) between the frontier firm and non-frontier firms. That difference is reflected in differences in wages. That is: inequality in workers' earnings manifest itself between companies, not within them (Brookings, 2019).

There are many reasons that can explain the lack of technological diffusion: we have seen them throughout the pages of this book. Companies may lack access to infrastructure; they may unable to employ the workers with the right skill; they may lack financing support. One key factor is market structure: where the market is concentrated, technological adoption is less symmetric, divergence in firms' productivity is more accentuated, and aggregate productivity grows at a slower pace (Brookings, 2019).

13.3 Dilemmas for policymakers

Throughout this section, let us be more specific about how the digital divide can manifest itself: the link between the different ways the digital divide materializes and the overall policy solutions described throughout the book should, ultimately, appear straightforward.

The following categorization is based on Robinson et al. (2015), (2020a), and (2020b):

- *Life cycle inequalities*

The digital divide can hamper the ability to extract value from digital technologies throughout the entire life cycle of an individual, albeit in different ways. Children and teenagers may lack access to the infrastructure needed to pursue their studies (the case of the pandemic and distance schooling is emblematic). But they may also be experiencing a divide in their type and level of exposure to digital technologies. It has been reported, for example, that kids from low-income families spend on average 2 hours more than their wealthy peers every day in front of a screen (Vox, 2019). Excessive exposure may affect school performance and may have other long-term adverse effects on well-being.

Young adults entering the workforce may be segregated according to their digital skills, with digital-savvy workers more likely to be employed in a white-collar job than a blue-collar job. A divide can also materialize between those workers who can master the boundaries between work and personal time, boundaries that are challenged by the increased use of digital communication technology. Middle-age individuals may experience a difference in their ability to use digital technologies to cater for multiple responsibilities such as work and family caretaking. Finally, elderly people run a significant risk of being cut off by an increasingly digitalized society, often lacking the means and the skills to access online services (see, for example, the discussion around digitized public services in Chapter 6).

- *Gender*

Women may experience the same level of access as men, but they are more likely to experience a second and third level divide. Women tend to have fewer opportunities online and use technology with a lower frequency and intensity. Women, on average, possess lower acquired digital knowledge than men. In 2015, only one out of four graduates in engineering and ICT were women. This skill difference naturally translates into a workforce that is not representative of the population, with 8 out of 10 ICT specialists that are men. Only 0.5% of girls wish to become ICT professionals at 15 years old, compared to 5% of boys (Publications Office of the EU, 2019). Quite tellingly, these differences are not due to differences in an alleged structural or genetic inclination that would make males more attracted to ICT. Instead, at the root of the difference, there often lies a cultural background: women are often expected to follow a stereotypical role, within their families, at school or within society at large. They are often encouraged to develop skills that belong more to the sphere of personal care and education (nursing, secretarial, or teaching).

- *Economic inequalities, entrepreneurship, and consumption*

Digital skills may give access to better jobs. However, the reverse is also true: employees with better jobs have more opportunities to develop their digital skills; because of direct on-the-job training offered by their employers; because they enjoy higher time-flexibility that can be used to develop further their digital skills; or because they tend to use their digital skills more at work, and hence they improve through experience. From an entrepreneurial point of view, digital skills may affect individuals' likelihood of business success. For example, their ability to translate their off-line networks into a business advantage increases with their ability to operate in the digital environment. On the buyer side, the digital divide can manifest itself in the degree of confidence that consumers show online, in their ability to access the best offers, both in terms of price and quality, and in their exposure to misleading information (see also next Chapter 14 on disinformation). Different skills online thus translate in an asymmetric distribution of the benefits that online purchases may bring; it can actually shift costs from one category of consumer to the other, through price discrimination, for example. For instance, consider the case of low-cost airlines. Airlines may advertise very low-price tickets (e.g. €9.99 for a short-haul flight) and reveal to the buyer at the time of paying that, when including other options such as luggage or seat booking, the actual price they need to pay is much higher. De facto, those companies exploit customers' behavioural biases to "trick" them into the purchase. Once a buyer has already made the mental process leading to the decision of buying the ticket, she is much less likely to change her choice, even if the price is increased. Customers that can anticipate online companies' strategies and can easily compare offers across different digital platforms not only get lower prices; they are also somehow subsidized by those customers who do not possess the same skills. Low-cost airlines would go bust if every customer were able to avoid the extra charges that are added to the final ticket price, either at the time of purchase or at the time of flying. Hence, they rely on customers who cannot avoid their "trick" to have a viable business. In that sense, digital skills drive a reallocation of value from the less-skilled to the more skilled.

- *Health care and disability*

We know from the previous section that access to health services can be facilitated by digitalization: its quality increases, as well as its reach and affordability. However, the most vulnerable groups, those who are the most in need of health services, also tend to be the less likely to exploit digital opportunities. A key driving factor is lower familiarity with the digital domain, determined by the cultural and educational background and, possibly, by physical or mental disability. Studies have shown that young, white women tend to have a higher likelihood to search for medical advice on the Internet. The lower the education level, the lower is the likelihood of relying on eHealth services.

- *Geography*

Where you are born and where you live is a strong predictor of your ability to profit from digital technologies. Again, the divide is evident between developed and emerging economies, as I pointed out above: Africa has a clear issue with Internet infrastructure, access and affordability, for example. The median mobile broadband download speed in Africa is 2.7 megabits per second (Mbits/s), roughly half the global median of 5.2 Mbits/s, and the monthly cost of a fixed broadband connection is 36.6% of gross national income, compared with 14.5% globally. But also within developed economies, there are strong differences. For example, between urban and rural areas—the latter being on average significantly less covered by high-quality connectivity infrastructure, with fewer digital public services available, and fewer educational and work opportunities in the digital area for their residents. Likewise, poor suburban areas do not offer their inhabitants the same opportunities as wealthier urban areas in terms of access and potential quality of online experience. That translates off-line inequalities to inequalities in the online world, and magnifying overall wealth differences within the population.

The description of the various shapes that the digital divide can take reported above has one straightforward implication: a comprehensive approach is necessary to tackle digital inequality. It would not help much if low-income households had access to high-speed Internet but not have the knowledge to prosper online. Likewise, enhancing buyers' protection online would not significantly affect the wealth distribution gap if the poor cannot access digital technologies and infrastructure.

Throughout this book, we have seen policies that, if well designed, would have the ultimate effect of reducing the gap between the haves and have-nots. **Telecom** policy and regulation (Chapter 4) aims to reduce the connectivity gap across the territory, notably creating the incentives for telecom service providers to build infrastructure in areas where profits are insufficient to tilt the trade-off in favour of investment. Likewise, telecom regulation ensures that services are affordable and meet specific quality standards, for everybody. In Chapter 12 we have looked at the importance of **digital re-skilling** and **educational policies**, together with policies to protect and empower workers in a context of "digital disruption". Even in the optimistic context of a positive net effect of technology on demand for jobs, a significant group of workers will not be better off. They will either not be able to reshape their expertise to fit new professions, they will go through a costly transition, or they will find themselves performing a job where their well-being is reduced. Policies to **foster competition,** especially within the platform economy (Chapter 8), are necessary to incentivize digital adoption by the broader economy. More competition can particularly benefit small and medium enterprises, and it can contribute to a more symmetrical distribution of the value created by technology, addressing the *Solow Paradox* described in the previous section. **Online platform workers** (Chapter 11) should get access to the same level of protection that has historically been guaranteed to employees while retaining the flexibility prompted by new economic models. Appropriate regulatory frameworks are necessary to ensure that the **data economy** (Chapter 5) and **artificial intelligence** (Chapter 15) are not conducive to gender or race-based discrimination. Public policies can be tailored to use data analytics to promote inclusion rather than increase the profitability of frontier digital companies' already very profitable business. **Digital taxation** (Chapter 6) can help to re-allocate value between large digital companies and the rest of society, ensuring that the nature of their business does not allow them to escape the methods traditionally used by states to address asymmetric wealth distribution within the economy. The **digitization of public services** should be primarily concerned with not leaving anyone out: increasing citizens' participation is one key goal of a digitized public sector (Chapter 6). Well-suited regulatory action can **protect online buyers** (Chapter 10) and prevent the **spread of illegal content** or **otherwise harmful (dis)information** online, which is most harmful to vulnerable categories, e.g. individuals with lower education level. **Cybersecurity** policies (Chapter 7) are concerned with creating an environment that is safe for everybody, not just those who can afford the best protecting hardware or software tools or expertise.

The overarching conclusion is a compelling one: there is no apparent reason to believe that policies aimed at fostering technological progress of a country like the ones analysed in this book should conflict with the goal of promoting inclusion and shared prosperity for all. Quite the contrary: well-designed digital policies are inclusive by nature, and their most straightforward outcome is to **fill the inequality gap**. Since the observed trend is of widening wealth and income gap between the rich and the poor, there is only one possible explanation: digital policy so far has failed to accomplish its job.

13.4 The European Union's perspective

For the reasons I just mentioned at the end of Section 13.3, it could be pointed out that the Digital Single Market strategy, *as such*, is a strategy aimed at addressing the digital exclusion and at prompting more social equality through the use of technology. Hence all the EU policies I have described throughout the book could equally fit this section too, as all of them have important implications for inequality, along the lines of what we have seen in the previous sections.

Thus, it may be helpful to use this section to look at those policies that are not explicitly directed to the digital domain but where digital plays an important role. Below I discuss the European Pillar of Social Rights and the European Commission's Digital4Development initiative.

13.4.1 The European Pillar of Social Rights

As anticipated in Chapter 12, the **2017 European Pillar of Social Rights** (European Commission, 2017i) is a joint declaration by the European Parliament, the Council, and the Commission. It identifies a set of principles and values at the core of the EU project and relates to ensuring better working and living conditions for everyone in Europe. It is structured in three chapters:

1. Chapter 1, on Equal opportunities and access to the labour market
2. Chapter 2, on Fair working conditions
3. Chapter 3, on Social protection and inclusion

The principles enshrined in the European Pillar of Social Rights are, by nature, broad and general. All of them can, however, be linked to specific areas of concern in the digital domain.

In particular, Chapter 1 indicates that:

- Everyone should have the right to education, training and life-long learning to nurture the necessary skills to fully participate in society and to transit from one job to another
- Women and men should have the same rights and access to equal career opportunities

- Discrimination based on gender, ethnic origin, religion, belief, disability, age, or sexual orientation to access employment, education, or social protection is banned
- Everyone should get access to opportunities for reskilling and retraining and should be able to transfer social protection and training entitlements during professional transitions.

As we know from the previous discussion and from Chapter 12, the development of digital skills, retraining, and life-long learning programs are central to any strategy aimed to facilitate the adaptation of labour markets to the new digital paradigm. Likewise, the transferability of social protection and training entitlements is crucial in an environment where the relationship between employers and employee is less stable, over time, and tend to acquire a multitude of different shapes which cannot be easily associated with traditional forms of employment (think about employment within the *sharing economy*, for example, see Chapter 11). Finally, we have seen how digital technology can facilitate discrimination by enhancing employers' ability to grasp information about their employees (see also Chapter 15 on artificial intelligence).

Furthermore, Chapter 2 states (amongst other things) that:

- Workers should have the right to fair and equal treatment regarding working conditions, access to social protection, and training
- Innovative forms of work that ensure quality working conditions should be encouraged. So should be entrepreneurship and self-employment. And occupational mobility should be facilitated
- Workers' personal data should be protected.

Again, the signatories of the Pillar seem to have in mind the emerging business' types, particularly in the digital *platform* economy. It is notable the reference to the protection of workers' personal data, which is considered indispensable for creating a healthy and safe work environment.

Finally, Chapter 3 includes the following provisions:

- Workers and self-employed (under comparable conditions) should have the right to adequate social protection regardless of the type and duration of their employment relationship
- Preventive and curative health care of good quality should be made accessible by everyone
- People with disabilities should access services that enable them to participate in the labour market and in society
- Everyone should be able to access essential services of good quality, including digital communications (inter alia). Furthermore, support for access to such services should be available for those in need.

Here, note the role that digital services may have to enable access to services, such as health care, that are considered essential rights for everyone and how digital technology can trigger more inclusivity for individuals with disabilities. The last statement on digital technologies is a clear reference to the need to bridge the digital divide and is tantamount to establishing a universal right to digital connectivity.

With the declaration, the EU institutions and Member States took responsibility to deploy concrete policy initiatives to implement the principles stated in the three chapters. Initiatives include updating national and EU law where necessary; improving enforcement; supporting social dialogue between all different stakeholders: citizens, workers, employers, private and public sector alike; enacting a monitoring program to record progress; deploying financial instruments such as the European Social Fund to support the implementation of the adopted policies.

In March 2021, the European Commission published an **Action Plan** proposing several concrete follow-up actions to implement the Pillar of Social Rights' principles by 2030 (European Commission, 2021). The action plan attempts to translate the principles—adapting them to the evolving social context, particularly given the digitization of the economy. For example, the European Commission's plan includes to:

- Put forward a legislative proposal to protect platform workers (see Chapters 11 and 12) and allow them to negotiate better working conditions collectively without infringing competition law
- Propose a regulation for artificial intelligence that would protect employees at the workplace (see Chapter 15)
- Propose initiatives in support of *individual learning accounts*
- Support workers' right to disconnect
- Publish a report on the application of the employment equality and racial equality directives
- Develop health data spaces and foster digitization of public health services (see Chapter 6)
- Improve portability of social security rights building on e-ID solutions (see Chapter 6).

The list of actions is long.[2] More generally, the action plan fixes three minimum headline targets to be reached by 2030: (a) 78% of people aged 20 to 64 in employment; (b) 60% of all adults participating in training every year; (c) a reduction of the number of people at risk of poverty or social exclusion by 15 million. Achieving the targets appears feasible, but the success of the social pillar actions in the digital context heavily depends on the effective implementation of the whole digital agenda, as we have noticed multiple times throughout the book.

---

[2] Students can keep track of the European Commission's progress with the action plan follow up by visiting https://ec.europa.eu/info/strategy/priorities-2019-2024/economy-works-people/jobs-growth-and-investment/european-pillar-social-rights/european-pillar-social-rights-action-plan_en

13.4.2 Digital4Development

The other notable EU initiative relevant from a digital inclusion perspective but that we have not covered elsewhere in this book is the European Commission's **Digital4Development** strategy.

In 2017 the European Commission published a Staff Working Document titled: "Digital4Development: mainstreaming digital technologies and services into EU Development Policy" (European Commission, 2021q) (the "D4D paper"). The Commission's paper defines a framework to support global sustainable development and inclusive growth through the use of digital technologies. Thus, while the Digital Single Market strategy focuses on creating a digital economy within the European Union, the D4D paper primarily aims to promote digitization outside the EU, particularly for emerging economies.

The framework identifies four priority areas on which the Commission planned to intervene:

1. Promote access to affordable and secure broadband connectivity and digital infrastructure, including the necessary regulatory reforms
2. Promote digital literacy and skills
3. Foster digital entrepreneurship and job creation
4. Promote the use of digital technology to enable sustainable development

According to the D4D paper, global connectivity is hampered: by underdeveloped terrestrial networks, in particular in the case of small islands or land-locked countries; by the absence of supporting public strategies, policies, and enabling regulatory frameworks; by low population density over the territory; by lack of market competition; by poor radio spectrum management (see Chapter 4) and high international connectivity prices; and by exposure to cybersecurity threats.

Accordingly, to **increase connectivity**, the D4D paper indicates the need to support the installation of submarine cables, cross-border fiber connection, and Internet Exchange Points (see Chapter 4), to foster international connectivity. The D4D paper encourages the endorsement of efficient and innovative spectrum management policies to foster mobile connectivity, particularly where infrastructure investment is less profitable (e.g. in rural areas). For example, it is suggested to use "TV White Spaces" (or frequencies not used locally by TV services) for local mobile telecommunication services. Finally, the D4D paper underlines the importance of capacity-building in the area of cybersecurity, adoption, use, and regulation of digital technology. Countries that are catching up in terms of technological development need to expand their technical and regulatory know-how to govern the process properly and, in particular, address the digital divide.

To **facilitate the development of digital literacy and skills,** the D4D paper pledges for reforms of educational and training systems in developing economies and the introduction of training for digital skills, such as coding and digital entrepreneurship, to pupils already from primary school age.

To **help develop entrepreneurial activities**, the D4D paper emphasizes the need to create the right "interconnected" environment, with connectivity infrastructure, computing facilities, talent, and financing capital in support of the emergence of hubs – digital ecosystems where start-ups and small-medium enterprises can access the resources they need to grow and leverage on synergies to cut their costs.

To **foster sustainable development**, the D4D paper identifies the following areas of actions: promoting gender equality and inclusivity addressing discrimination and improving girls' and women's access to digital skills and literacy; addressing climate change and environmental issues through more efficient technologies and use thereof; favouring the adoption of secure and digital identity systems that would help citizens (in particular in developing economies) to exercise their rights and fully access public services; investing in digital capacity building for governments; promoting the use of digital technologies for sustainable agricultural projects; incentivizing the use of digital technologies for the enhancement of educational systems, including through personalization and better targeting to address educational deficiencies in disadvantaged population groups; using technologies in the eHealth area to increase preventive and curative health services' efficiencies, monitor and address epidemics, and raise awareness about health hazards in the population.

The D4D paper does not have a dedicated budget line but relies on existing European Union funding instruments such as the European Development Fund (European Commission, 2021r). In the years since its launch, it has prompted the launching of several initiatives backed by the European Commission. Most notably, the creation of the "D4D Hub", launched in December 2020 and supported by five Member States (Germany, France, Belgium, Estonia, and Luxembourg) and initially directed at enhancing cooperation and sharing of best practices in the digital domain between the African Union and the European Union (D4D Hub, 2021).

****

13.5 Case Study: fair access to vaccines

There are many channels through which the Covid-19 pandemic has contributed to exacerbating inequality. Access to vaccine is one of those channels. Generally speaking, poorer, less-educated people, who lack access to or familiarity with digital infrastructure, tended to experience difficulties in accessing online vaccine booking systems and got vaccinated later than their richer, educated, digitally-savvy peers. It is not hard to spot an irony here, since the poorer or less-educated are also the ones who were hit harder by the pandemic. For example because they could not telework (white-collars' job tasks tend to be more "teleworkable" than blue-collars' tasks). Or because they tended to live in overcrowded housing conditions. EU countries have implemented different distribution strategies without necessarily ensuring that the least digitally savvy are not left behind. For example, a web portal used by five German provinces to book a vaccine jab slot forced visitors to go through 10 online steps and two-factor authentication: a cumbersome process, especially for the elderly. It has been suggested that vaccine online reservation systems should not rely on a first-come-first-served approach. Fairer solutions could entail a continuous collection of applications for slots; when slots become available, the system could use algorithms that blend randomness with priority criteria based on the characteristics of the applicant.

More information on fair access to vaccine can be found here:
https://www.bruegel.org/2021/03/fair-vaccine-access-is-a-goal-europe-cannot-afford-to-miss/

13.6 Review questions

- What are the implications of a more unequal society for digital progress? Does more inequality favour or impede technological development? Justify and explain your answer.
- List three reasons for which technology should reduce inequality (do not use the examples given in the book).
- Provide two examples for each of the three levels of the "digital divide" (make up your own; do not use the ones proposed in the book).
- What is the relation between market structure and the inequality generated by technological adoption? Which policies could be implemented to address the illness (failures in technological markets) rather than the symptoms (observed inequality in the distribution of the value generated by technology within society)?
- Which economic reasons should motivate the European Union to address the digital divide in Africa?

14
Disinformation in the Digital Age

Abstract

Disinformation is an ancient phenomenon that digitization boosted. It is impossible to say whether the average quality of information is higher or lower online than what it was before, when news could only circulate through print, radio, or TV. Today, however, the game has changed: it is far easier to generate and spread information to reach wide audiences in the Internet age. And the predominant online business model, highly dependent on web traffic and advertisement, undoubtedly generates high incentives to maximize audience, possibly by eliciting emotional engagement in users and arousing them to share false stories on social media. Markets seem unable to curb disinformation by themselves. Thus, public policy is needed to reduce the spread of false information online and defuse its potentially harmful effects. Measures include fact-checking and enabling access to high-quality media, forcing platforms to become more transparent and forthcoming, for example, allowing researchers to access their data. Furthermore, promising actions include empowering users with educational tools to overcome their "behavioural biases" and increase their wariness towards what they read or view online.

14.1 Background

The fabrication and promotion of false stories is an ancient phenomenon. It has featured in most societies throughout the history of humankind: the Romans practised "disinformation wars" (Financial Times, 2021), as did state governments during the major conflicts of the twentieth century. Disinformation is, however, considered one of the most salient phenomena of the digital age, possibly because its consequences are vastly exacerbated by the shift of societies to the digital paradigm.

The public debate has progressively migrated to online platforms, with an increasing proportion of citizens acquiring their information on the web through search engines, social networks, or messaging apps. Unfortunately, this shift has exposed societies to the risk that those channels are used to magnify the reach of fabricated or otherwise false information, with potentially dramatic repercussions.

Thanks to digital infrastructure, false stories, rumours, and conspiracy theories can spread like wildfire. A well-organized campaign on major social networks can steer public opinion to believe falsehoods and have a pivotal role in the outcome of elections and historical referenda (Independent, 2018). State actors can attempt to condition other countries' elections (The New York Times, 2021) or destabilize

Digital Economic Policy. Mario Mariniello, Oxford University Press.
© Mario Mariniello (2022). DOI: 10.1093/oso/9780198831471.003.0014

their political establishment (European Parliament, 2019). Fake remedies popular on the web can misguide people to attempt ineffective therapies while dealing with cancer (Shi, et al., 2019). Unfounded theories on alleged links between vaccination and autism can gain great traction online, leading to outbreaks around the globe (Burki, 2019). Genocides can be incited through the spread of false stories on social networks (Mozur, 2018).

Yet, despite clear-cut evidence of harm, disinformation is a phenomenon that is hard to pin down and public decision-makers often struggle to develop and implement tools that effectively address it.

Defining "disinformation" is a naturally elusive exercise, and this is probably the most significant challenge faced by policymakers attempting to address the phenomenon. It is very hard to draw sharp boundaries between what society can accept in terms of freedom of expression and what, instead, should be considered illegitimate because it's likely to cause significant harm. To what extent *departing from the "truth"* (assuming that it is possible to know what the "truth" is, an assumption that has been called into question by more than one philosopher)[1] is *acceptable*?

Defining disinformation is an inherently subjective question for which public policy is challenged to provide an objective answer.

For the purpose of this chapter, I will adopt the definition of disinformation suggested by the European Commission in its 2018 Communication "Tackling online disinformation: a European Approach" (European Commission, 2021s) (see Section 14.4 for an analysis):

> *"Disinformation is understood as **verifiably false or misleading information** that is created, presented and disseminated for **economic gain** or to **intentionally deceive** the public, and **may cause public harm**. (. . .) Disinformation does not include reporting errors, satire and parody, or clearly identified partisan news and commentary".*

Thus, the definition used by the European Commission hinges on **three necessary conditions to identify an act of disinformation**:

- *It must be false or misleading*—hence the departure from the truth must be inherent to its **nature**;
- At its origin, there must be the intention to achieve an *economic profit* or to otherwise *benefit from it*—hence it must have a **purpose** to serve;
- It may *cause harm* to the public—hence it may have a (possibly observable) **general effect**.

Note that when false information is spread unknowingly, with no purpose or explicit intent, that is normally called **misinformation**. Hence we could say that *disinformation* is *misinformation with intent*.

---

[1] See, for example, the work of Bruno Latour, who in fact doubts whether truth can be identified through scientific methodologies; for a profile, see Kofman, A. (2018).

The proposed definition of disinformation is clearly narrow by design. It aims to exclude from the scope of public intervention instances where, for example, news reporting is not accurate because of lousy reporting (note that "news reporting" is not the only source of potential disinformation, as we will see shortly). Or instances where the bias of the promoter of the false story is clear upfront, such that deception is unlikely unless the audience is consciously willing to be deceived (consider, for example, the joke of a comedian). Without such a narrow definition, it would be hard to find anything on the web that *would not* fall in the category of disinformation.

Still, even with a narrow definition, it is often difficult to categorize a story as disinformation, particularly regarding the qualification of harm. For example, it could often be argued that it is more harmful to society to have a commentator's right to freedom of expression limited rather than let her say what she would like to, even though it may not be factually correct.

Let us look at the three elements of the definition in greater detail.

14.1.1 Nature

Disinformation must, by construct, relate to an act that distorts the representation of reality. Therefore, it has often been associated with the term **"fake news"**, or news that is not factually correct. Consistently with an approach that has emerged in the literature on disinformation,[2] I will not use the term *fake news*. That choice is due to two reasons: first, because *fake news* is an inaccurate term. It does not encompass hybrid forms of disinformation, whereby real facts are blended with mixed facts. Second, it does not account for the large set of methodologies that can be used to distort the truth, for example, manipulating on purpose the reputation of a source. Additionally, in what has become its common use to indicate an act of partisanship, *fake news* has escaped its original meaning: to indicate an act of disinformation. The term has been appropriated by many in the public domain, from public commentators to politicians, to exponents of authoritarian regimes, in order to undermine the credibility of the media, particularly when subject to their criticism.

Academics have made various attempts to classify news in the context of an act of disinformation while **avoiding being trapped by the pitfalls of terminology**. A notable example is from the researchers of the Computational Propaganda Project,[3] who suggest relying on the term *junk news*. Junk news is defined as disinformation possessing at least three of the following five elements:

(1) professionalism, i.e. outlets do not employ the standards and best practices of professional journalism, refraining from providing information about real authors, editors, publishers and owners, lacking transparency and accountability

---

[2] See, for example, the final report of the High Level Expert Group on Fake News and Online Disinformation (European Commission, 2018), more on that below in Section 14.4, or Bradshaw (2019).
[3] See https://comprop.oii.ox.ac.uk/faq/

(2) style, i.e. the use of emotionally-driven language, including emotive expressions, hyperbole and ad hominem attacks

(3) credibility, i.e. outlets that rely on false information or conspiracy theories, often strategically, without resorting to fact-checking

(4) bias, i.e. outlets are highly biased, ideologically skewed, or hyper-partisan, and

(5) counterfeit, i.e. outlets mimic established news reporting, including fonts, stylistic content strategies, and branding.

For the purpose of the design of public policy, I need to make an important clarification. Public policy addressing disinformation should be designed specifically to tackle online behaviour that cannot be deemed "illegal" according to the current state of the law in the affected jurisdiction. This is because *illegal content* can be tackled in other ways (see Chapter 9) and arguably does not pose a challenge with a comparable level of complexity. When specific content is classified as "illegal", it means that the legislator has already called the trade-off between freedom of expression and harm risk. In other words, the legislator has established by law that the risk of harm for society trumps the risk of endangering freedom of expression.

Figure 9.1 in Chapter 9 provides a helpful illustration. Online content that belongs to area A is illegal and cannot be qualified as disinformation: copyright infringement is a straightforward example. Online content that belongs to area B can be qualified as disinformation because of its nature, purpose, and likelihood of harm; but it is also illegal (potentially deemed so in court). An illegal act of defamation would fall in this category. Content that pertains to area C is disinformation which is not illegal or not yet deemed so by a court. An example could be a fabricated piece of news suggesting that vaccines can cause autism in small children.

(A + B) and (C) are two very different problems: the former, (A+B), is dealt with in Chapter 9. This chapter, instead, focuses exclusively on non-illegal disinformation content, namely area C of Figure 9.1.

Note that the judicial system's role and its relationship with the online world (particularly with online platforms) are crucial in this context. As discussed in Section 14.4, disinformation laws may tackle content that is not yet illegal but has a high potential to be so. The problem is that, as we shall see, if courts have not yet expressed a judgement about the legality of the content, platforms may be required to exert a quasi-judicial role, taking a decision about which content should be removed and which should be kept online based on their inevitably subjective assessment.

14.1.2 Purpose

Identifying the purpose of disinformation requires understanding *cui bono* or who stands to gain from it. A diverse variety of different actors populates the universe of disinformation. As outlined by Marwick and Lewis (2017) and Tucker et al. (2018), a non-exhaustive list could include the following actors:

Independent and hired trolls. Trolls are actors who "*intentionally bait others to elicit an emotional response*" (Tucker, et al., 2018). They may do so for their own leisure, possibly using false stories to provoke criticism of mainstream outlets or institutions, or they may be paid to intervene in public fora on social networks. The mastermind may be, for example, a private actor, such as a company looking for ways to advertise its product, or a party, a politician, or a foreign state government attempting to spark emotional reactions or behaviours with the potential to destabilize the establishment. The trolling style of a site named 4chan, popular amongst disinformation actors, has been characterized by four distinct properties (see Marwick and Lewis (2017)): trolls use a deliberately offensive language; they show antipathy toward sensationalism in mainstream media; they attempt to trigger strong emotions in targets; and they tend to display an ambiguous attitude. In Internet culture, that is commonly known as *Poe's Law* (Wikipedia, 2021): trolls disguise their real intent, therefore making it impossible to understand whether what they say is a true manifestation of extremism or it is rather a parody of the extremism they mimic.

Hate groups and ideologues. Niche groups with a more or less open agenda to promote particular ideologies, cultural stances, or radical visions. They often implement aggressive strategies *against* well-defined targets: neo-nazi groups promoting white nationalism or white supremacy with anti-Semitic junk news, anti-feminist influencers, "incels" (involuntary celibates), paleomasculinists (who believe that men are naturally superior to women), and pick-up artists providing dating advice that qualify women as objects are just some examples (Marwick & Lewis, 2017).

Bots. Bots are software that employs AI-based technologies to create online content *de facto* pretending to be human. They can be used to increase the number of followers or the rate of approval of a certain influencer or politician. Bots can be programmed to run systematic attacks towards well-defined targets such as political dissidents. And they can manipulate search engines, inflating the ranking of specific websites or manipulating public opinion (Tucker, et al., 2018).

Conspiracy theorists. These actors leverage widespread anxieties to foster chaos in societies. They may insinuate that illegal immigrants are carrying illnesses or are treated better by the government than native workers. They can push forward stories suggesting that Jewish people control worldwide media. They can claim that planes release chemicals in the sky or that Big Pharma has secret agreements with the government to make useless and harmful vaccinations compulsory for kids. The emergence of conspiracy theories is not a new phenomenon; instead, it is yet another phenomenon amplified by the "megaphone" nature of the Internet. There is extensive research on conspiracy theories, particularly concerning the underpinning psychological and sociological dynamics that help explain why certain theories can gain significant popular traction.[4]

---

[4] See, for example: Goertzel (1994) or Sunstein and Vermeule (2009). For good reporting on recent conspiracy theories 'outbreaks' see: Harambam (2020).

Hyper-partisan news outlets. These are outlets with a specific agenda and a party political line. Their disinformation strategy is systematic: they aim to shape a world where every fabricated story or theory fits to corroborate the outlet's line. For example, a far-right outlet could plant false stories of immigrants harming the local economy. It could release a biased report on government spending where immigrants are indicated as the main beneficiaries of new subsidies. Or quote a local newspaper in Senegal to report that foreigners have been murdered for the sake of being white (without any fact-checking).

Junk news websites. Junk news websites are mostly driven by economic purposes. They promote false news to make a profit. As we will see in detail in the next section (and have already extensively discussed throughout this book, particularly in Chapter 8 on online platforms and Chapter 5 on the data economy), online businesses thrive on advertisements. Simply put: the more web traffic generated, the higher the appeal to advertisers, and the more profitable the platform. This dynamic creates the incentive to invent ad-hoc stories, which are likely to compel users to read, "click", and share the content. A most quoted example of such a strategy is the business that was put in place by some teenagers in a small town in North Macedonia, fabricating stories on Donald Trump and Hilary Clinton during their campaign for the US 2016 presidential election. While there is no clear evidence that their stories had a pivotal impact on the election results, it is factually correct to claim that the group of teenagers was very successful in putting thousands of dollars in their pockets.

Politicians. Dissimulation of facts is intrinsic to the nature of politics itself (Machiavelli, N., 1513). Yet, the online environment and, in particular, social networks have magnified the role of politicians in creating and promoting the spread of false claims. They may do so intentionally to inflate their number of followers. But they may also do it accidentally. That is because Internet has "cut out the middleman," and politicians eager to provide support to their claims have been increasingly sharing un-checked news, reacting with "their guts" rather than taking the time to double check the veracity of what they share and thus contributing to the spread of false claims. A prominent example is US President Trump's use of Twitter: "Trump's Twitter feed (contains) conspiracy-mongers, racists and spies" according to the New York Times (McIntire, et al., 2019).

Domestic and foreign governments. Domestic governments can use disinformation to reinforce their power. Foreign governments can use disinformation to destabilize the economy or the institutional setting of a rival country. Bradshaw and Howard (2019) report a significant increase in recent years in the use of social networks by state actors across the globe to suppress fundamental human rights, discredit political opponents, and drown out dissenting opinions. Autocratic regimes may use Facebook or Twitter, in particular, to affect other countries' public opinion, for example spreading destabilise messages designed to drive divisions within society. They show evidence of disinformation in 70 countries in 2019, compared to just 28 in 2017.

14.1.3 Effect

On March 27, amid the 2020 Covid-19 crisis, it was reported that "*nearly 300 people have been killed and more than 1,000 sickened by ingesting methanol across Iran [. . .] the poisonings come as fake remedies spread across social media [. . .] mixed with messages about the use of alcohol-based and sanitizers, some wrongly believed drinking high-proof alcohol would kill the virus in their bodies*" (Trew B., 2020).

Intuitively, the link between disinformation and harm is a no-brainer. A 2018 Eurobarometer survey of 26,576 EU citizens found that 83% of respondents consider "fake news" to represent a danger to democracy. The European Commission suggests that "(disinformation's) *public harm comprises threats to democratic political and policy-making processes as well as public goods such as the protection of EU citizens' health, the environment or security*" (European Commission, 2021s). The above-mentioned episode of disinformation in Iran is a case in point. However, the link between disinformation and harm is **less straightforward than it may appear**, certainly so from an economist's perspective.

It could be argued that the socially optimal level of disinformation is zero. However, pursuing such an objective would necessarily entail curbing freedom of expression without necessarily sparing harm (for example, because what is taken as an act of "disinformation" is ultimately harmless). At the same time, it cannot be presumed that false facts are necessarily "disliked" by citizens. If that were the case, addressing disinformation would mostly consist of tackling an asymmetric information problem. The problem would be "just" that the news "buyers" can be misled to listen to, view, or read stories with a lower quality than they expect (here, "quality" is intended as accuracy or closeness to reality; more on market failures in the next section).

However, that is not the only problem. False stories also exist because they, as such, appeal to individuals. Individuals may even *be aware* that a source is not particularly sound, but they may be looking for news or stories that are aligned with their view of the world or for pieces of evidence that allow them to support and spread their views amongst the contacts of their network. There is, in other words, **significant potential for a mismatch between the public interest and the individual interest**. Similar challenges are posed by the consumption of unhealthy and addictive products such as cigarettes or chips. Harm, in that case, is not only generated by the fact that consumers may be ignorant about the negative effects that cigarettes have on them. It also comes from the fact that individuals may *deliberately choose* to smoke to enjoy a short-term benefit despite the long-term risk of developing heart or lung diseases. Therefore, individuals may deliberately burden the collective through increased costs in health services (let alone through the increased disease risk for those who are forced to inhale their smoke passively).

In the case of disinformation, harm can likewise come directly from the effect on the target individual who *consumes* the false story, for example because she ends up drinking methanol to fight a viral infection. But it can also come indirectly, for example because a misinformed individual may be misled to cast a vote for a party that they would typically not support had they known the truth. Therefore, disinformation, distorting the democratic process, harms the whole collective.

More specifically, here are some examples of potentially harmful effects due to disinformation. Disinformation can:

- Push individuals to harm themselves through **misguidance** related to, among other things, health, safety, and security issues
- Lead individual to **vote** or make choices that are contrary to their interest, based on false or incorrect premises
- Dramatically **erode trust in news** reporting: when the disinformation noise is high, citizens do not believe anything anymore (it could be argued that the erosion of trust in mainstream media is often a primary goal of disinformation campaigns)
- **Polarize** public debate and foster the creation of "echo-chambers" (see Section 14.2 below)
- **Pollute political debate** and thwart the functioning of democracy
- Undermine support for actions pursuing objectives of **general public interest** such as the movement against climate change
- Stimulate hate and social **aggressiveness**
- Favour the aggregation and dissemination of **niche extremist content**
- **Exacerbate inequality** by having an amplified harmful effect on more vulnerable social categories (namely, individuals who, because of their demographics or educational background, tend to have fewer tools to spot disinformation online).

The analysis carried out in this section should suffice to illustrate why tackling *harmful purposely fabricated information* merits attention by policymakers. As mentioned at the beginning of the chapter, disinformation is an old and pervasive phenomenon. However, since this book is about digital policies, the focus of the following sections will specifically be on the dynamics of *(legal) disinformation online*. Our starting point should be to understand the implications of a digitalized society from a disinformation perspective.

14.2 Opportunities and challenges

The emergence of the digital paradigm has revolutionized information. It would be hard to assess objectively whether digitization has, on average, led to better or more poorly informed citizens. Indisputably, though, information in a digitized society is produced and consumed in a very different way than it was in a not-so-distant, "analogical", past. The 2019 Reuters Institute Digital News Report, the largest periodic survey of news consumption in the world, records that two-thirds of their

PROPORTION THAT SAID EACH WAS THEIR FIRST CONTACT
WITH NEWS IN THE MORNING BY AGE - SELECTED MARKETS

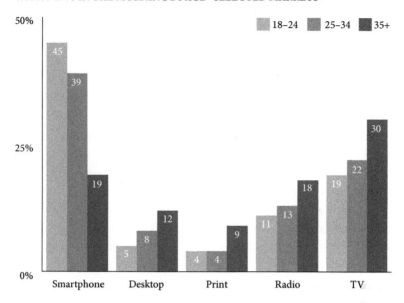

Figure 14.1 2019 Reuters Institute Digital News Report – Respondents'
first contact with news in the morning (% of respondents)
https://reutersinstitute.politics.ox.ac.uk/sites/default/files/2019-06/DNR_2019_FINAL_
1.pdf

cross-country sample use their smartphones to access news weekly. Using smartphones for such purpose has doubled in most countries between 2012 and 2019
(Newman, 2019). This tendency is powerful in the younger segment of the population. As Figure 14.1 shows, almost half of respondents younger than 25 years old said
that the first contact with the news in the morning was typically through a smartphone, instead of less than 20% for respondents older than 35 years old. News often
tends to be accessed through social media and messaging apps, too: Facebook or
Facebook's platforms, such as Instagram, Messenger, and WhatsApp, are used for
general purposes at least once per week by 84% of the sample, and for accessing
news by 57% of the sample.

Digitization has had a substantial impact on the news market, causing dramatic
changes both on the supply and demand sides. From a *supply* perspective:

- **Entry has become much easier**. Anybody can easily open up a "reporting outlet" on the web: bloggers, vloggers, and influencers can rely on online platforms
  and use more or less mainstream channels to reach wide audiences. Assets are
  no longer as relevant as they once were. Production costs are a very small fraction of what they have been in the past, particularly for those outlets that do not
  have a print circulation. It is also cheaper for news outlets to hire local reporters
  or photographers, as anybody can potentially become one by simply offering
  their reporting to the outlet

- **Scaling up is cheaper**. Thanks to the Internet, any outlet's potential reach is global, even for small, local publishers. Moreover, even outlets that target specific niche markets can now flourish, thanks to demand aggregation (as we have extensively discussed in Chapter 8 on online platforms). Demand aggregation dynamics explain why extremist content can be so successful online, for example
- As a natural corollary, the news-supply environment has become **hypercompetitive**. As a result, mainstream outlets now need to deal with potential competition from very small outlets or even single individuals who may break a Twitter story before they hear about it. This implies the need for sophisticated cross-platform strategies on social networks, search engines, email newsletters, and podcasts to keep customers engaged
- **Speed is exponentially higher** if compared to the time when news stories were primarily consumed in print format. With an analysis of the French market, Cagé et al. (2019) find that, on average, news is published in different online media outlets 169 minutes after being published on the website that first broke the news, but in less than 4 minutes in 25% of cases. They also note that most of the content published online is copied: only approximately one-third is original
- The **business model of news publishers has changed dramatically**. Advertisement has become a critical source of income for news or commentary providers, with subscriptions and pay-walls representing a small portion of the revenue stream for the vast majority of outlets. At the same time, outlets have lost much of their editorial control vis-à-vis their readership: customers tend to be their own "editors" by picking and consuming unbundled news from different sources. Facing a much more mobile customer base and being exposed to web traffic fluctuations (advertisements revenue increases with traffic), outlets have stronger incentives to publish "**clickbait**", attracting readers by arousing their emotions and curiosity with sensationalist titles or stories.

The "sensationalism phenomenon" has always riddled the news market. However, the incentives to boost attractiveness at the expense of quality and accuracy of the news are much higher within the new "digital" business model, because the outlet's reputation tends to be less relevant and customers do not incur monetary losses when clicking on links that turn out to be junk news. Often outlets aim to *go viral*, namely to produce stories that are then shared by an exponential number of individuals through social networks, therefore maximizing web traffic to their portal. This is an important dynamic explaining why disinformation can be so widespread in the digital environment.

Finally, it is helpful to recall from Chapter 9 on illegal content online, that online news outlets are in a symbiotic relationship with **online platforms**, such as web search engines, news aggregators, and social networks that often represent the main gateway to their outlets. In many ways, however, news providers tend to be in an asymmetric position, with much of the bargaining power laying in the hands of gatekeepers-platforms (Google, Facebook, and the like), on whose choices they significantly depend. A little tweak in their algorithms can have harsh repercussions on news providers' reach and income. In January 2018, for example, Facebook announced that it would change its algorithm to prioritize posts that, in the company's view, promote "meaningful conversations". These changes made news publishers less visible. The result on traffic was tangible: for example, publishers surveyed by parse.ly, a media analytics company, showed a drop of 28% in traffic from Facebook in 2018 compared to 2017 (Carr C., Arendt K., 2019).

Likewise, digitization had a strong impact on the *demand side* of the news market:

- Getting informed has never been **so cheap**. News seekers can often meet their needs without incurring any monetary costs (even though, as we know from Chapter 5, users may incur "hidden" costs such as those linked with the provision of personal data to publishers through "web cookies"). They may opt to subscribe to an outlet to access content that lies behind a paywall. However, even in that case, subscription costs tend to be much lower than they had been in the "pre-Internet" era when users had print subscriptions
- Readers can now access a much **wider offer**, both in terms of the type of content (the aggregation of the demand makes it possible to make it viable for specialized outlets to focus on the provision of niche content) and in terms of geography. For example, any reader with Internet access can read news from the US New Yorker,[5] Beijing News,[6] the Italian IlPost,[7] or the Nauruan Loop-Nauru.[8] Notably, web tools such as Google Translate allow readers to access news in any written language
- As pointed out above, **customers are now their own editors**: they can collect news from different sources without experiencing *lock-in effects*. As most news is now available for free, users can be entirely flexible, *multi-homing* and switching from one outlet to another. However, this does not necessarily translate to a fragmentation in the "demand" side of the news market: Mukerjee et al. (2018) find, for example, that consumption is rather catalysed by a reduced number of news outlets. In other words, readers tend to obtain information from a small group of reference outlets and possibly complement it with fringe news sources, but with lower intensity and less regularly
- Customers have a **higher passive exposure** to multiple sources of news, stories, or commentaries. For example, they are exposed to news when they scroll through their feeds on a social network because a friend shared a news link. Or they may get an unsolicited message with a news story on WhatsApp.

[5] https://www.newyorker.com/
[6] http://www.bjnews.com.cn/
[7] https://www.ilpost.it/
[8] http://www.loopnauru.com/

- Users **consume news differently**. Being your own editor also has drawbacks: users are confronted with an overabundance of information and have a limited attention span to dedicate to them. They may find it hard to decide on the "right" amount of time they should spend reading one source compared to others. They may be vulnerable to algorithmic manipulation and find themselves hooked to content, with platforms nurturing a kind of addiction to it (a simple example is YouTube's cyclical content feed—see Chapter 15 on artificial intelligence for an extensive discussion). Confronted with their own biases (see further below), they may consciously or subconsciously avoid news that challenges their world views, fostering what has become known as the **echo chamber** or **filter bubble** phenomenon. However, it is important to stress that the scientific literature has not reached a consensus regarding the existence of filter bubbles. This uncertainty is not surprising since digitization has implications in both directions: it allows content to be tailored more closely to a single individual's characteristics. It also allows a much richer and diversified news environment available to anybody connected to the Internet. In an environment where information from every angle of the Internet is overflowing users, echo chambers are a paradox challenging to grasp
- Finally, in the online world, news **users can also engage significantly more**. Users can take ownership of a story, supplementing it with a comment of their own before "tweeting" it or sharing it on other social networks. Users can leave comments at the bottom of the story, and they can often engage with other readers or viewers thanks to the ability to comment and engage with other readership. News propagation tends to correlate with the volume of comments and expression of sentiment by users (e.g. "likes") associated with it.[9] Brady et al. (2017) find that the presence of moral-emotional words in messages increases their diffusion by 20% for each additional word; the presence of moral-emotional language in political messages significantly boosts their spread, particularly within the same ideological "bubble". Tellingly, news **virility correlates with anger**, and the expression of *anger* seems to have been unlocked by the digital environment. Crockett (2017) argues that the online world, entailing physical distance, is fertile ground for the expression of moral outrage to flourish.

Revolutionary changes on both the supply and the demand sides of the market have had a strong impact on online content. It would probably be impossible to quantify all the effects in terms of the *average* quality and accuracy of news and stories. But it could be argued that, given the size and variety of supply and accessibility from a demand point of view, there is a high likelihood that the *maximum quality* potentially available to the interested reader is *higher today* than it was before the advent of the online news business model. In other words: digitization may or may

---

[9] See for example: Tan, et al. (2016).

not have lowered average news quality. But it almost certainly has increased the quality that any reader can theoretically access if holding the means to do so.[10]

However, the question is why the digital environment is riddled with disinformation and whether public intervention is needed to avoid harm.

14.2.1 Why does the market fail to counter disinformation?

Why does the market fail to counter disinformation? The simple answer is that the new business dynamics that we have just illustrated facilitate the generation and spread of disinformation. And market players do not have the incentive nor, often, the ability to curb that phenomenon.

Three primary sources of market failure can be identified in this context. All of these could likewise be found in the pre-online information world, but digitization has significantly magnified them:

- The presence of negative externalities
- Asymmetric information between news suppliers and news consumers
- Individuals' behavioural biases.

Negative externalities are generated each time that disinformation is created. For example, the supplier of a fabricated story can obtain a profit from its circulation. Notably, the decision to supply or spread the news is taken in isolation from the effect that the story can have on other players. To give an example, scientists have demonstrated that vaccines do not cause autism. However, spreading news about an alleged causal relationship between vaccines and autism can yield a reward to the source, for example extending the online influence of the publisher amongst an audience seeking ways to support their views. It may also cause an outbreak of measles, widespread death, or permanent disability in children, and higher costs for national health systems. But those costs are not borne by the source of the fabricated story. Therefore those costs do not dissuade the source from generating disinformation. Likewise, consuming junk news may reduce a voter's ability to cast a vote that reflects her preferences accurately; this could be seen as a cost for collective society because it undermines the democratic process. But such cost is not *internalized* by the consumer of the junk news, who may opt not to bother verifying the accuracy of its source.

Students may not be surprised to learn that *online platforms* play a central role in explaining the rise of the disinformation phenomenon.

At the core of disinformation's market failure is the misalignment of goals between online platforms and society. Platforms pursue their stakeholders' interest.

---

[10] Students should note here how, again, the expansion of possibilities brought about by digital can rewards those who have the tools to take them (e.g. higher educational background, Internet access, etc.) and penalize those who do not have them. See Chapter 13 on inequality.

Namely, they strive to maximize their profits. Profits in the online world are directly linked to the amount of web traffic that a platform aggregates. The higher the traffic to platforms, the bigger the advertisement revenue, the larger their dataset with information about users, the bigger the money flow (see Chapter 5 for an extensive analysis). At the same time, disinformation *boosts* web traffic: as we have seen above, fabricated stories tend to arouse emotional responses amongst users, stimulate engagement, and be shared quickly and extensively.

On the other hand, **platforms do not *internalize* the negative externality** that disinformation imposes on society: they do not bear the cost of the disinformation they host. Quite the contrary: curbing disinformation and preventing the circulation of false stories could not only imply forgoing profits in terms of loss of potential web traffic (an *opportunity cost*); it could also imply exposing themselves to criticism, for example for unwarranted "censorship", or even legal quandaries. For example, embarking in a quasi-editorial role could entail falling outside the remit of Article 14 of the E-commerce Directive. As we have seen in Chapter 9, platforms benefit from a safe harbour exempting them from liability for the content they host if they are unaware they are hosting it (see Chapter 9).

What could be the cost of allowing disinformation to riddle a platform? In principle, platforms could incur a *reputational* cost and become less appealing. However, as we know from Chapters 5 and 8, platform markets tend to exhibit a high concentration level, and alternatives are not really available to customers. In Western countries, turning away from Google's YouTube, Facebook, WhatsApp, Instagram, or Twitter because they host too much disinformation is hardly an option for anybody, given the absence of alternatives offering the same appeal. Hence, from a financial perspective, platforms have little to fear from not taking action against disinformation. That also explains why, in the public debate around the issue of disinformation, online platforms tend to place themselves on the freedom of expression side of the spectrum[11] (Figure 14.2).

Platforms may claim in the open that they do all they can to fight online disinformation, to preserve their public image. And yet, the evidence keeps coming to suggest that what is being done is not enough. For example, during the Covid-19 pandemic, Tech Transparency Project reported that YouTube ran adverts on videos promoting fake herbal remedies against the virus (Tech Transparency Project, 2020).

Freedom of Expression   Vs   *Safety and Security*

Figure 14.2 Freedom of Expression vs Safety and Security

---

[11] "*In the end you need to be careful once you have curtailed free speech—because once you have curtailed it you can't turn it back,*" he said, adding that Facebook's position is to "*err on the side of free expression where that fine line has to be crossed.*" Nick Clegg, Facebook's VP for Global Affairs, 20 January 2020. See: https://www.euractiv.com/section/digital/news/facebook-on-the-side-of-free-expression-as-eu-steps-up-disinformation-fight/

Google's YouTube executives have likewise been blamed for having let "toxic videos run rampant" despite internal warnings from its staff. Allegedly, proposals to change recommendations and curb conspiracies were sacrificed to maximize engagement and avoid falling outside the Communications Decency Act's safe harbour (a US law endorsing a similar principle of that of Art. 14 of the EU's E-commerce Directive, as we have seen in Chapter 9) (Bergen M., 2019). Notably, extremist content and "radicalization" does not flourish on YouTube only because YouTube's algorithm recommends viewers. On the contrary, YouTube (along with similar platforms) is a catalyst, a place where users with an extremist inclination may find other like-minded users, engage with them, and mutually reinforce their convictions. In that sense, content is just an excuse to attract, aggregate, nurture, and empower niches of users with very specific preferences (which, in the case of extremist content, conflict with the public interest).

Asymmetric information is present in news markets because news is, in the best-case scenario, an *experience good*. In other words, users can only assess the quality of a news item or story after having read, viewed, or otherwise experienced it. In a worse scenario, the quality of news is not grasped even after consumption. Indeed, users may not know the level of accuracy of content after reading it since they may lack the means, knowledge, or willingness to check whether the reporting is factually correct.

As we have seen in other chapters (see, for example, Chapter 7 on cybersecurity), asymmetric information is an important source of market failure. Because **outlets may find it hard to signal or guarantee the degree of accuracy of their sources**, they have no or little incentive to invest in increasing the quality of their content.[12] Asymmetric information is exacerbated in the digital environment because, as we have seen above, customer flows are much more volatile, users often do not incur monetary costs, are not locked into subscriptions, and are the "editors" of their own content, assembling content from different sources (*multi-homing*). Hence, they can be easily lured by "juicy" titles that hide little content behind them (the *clickbait* phenomenon). Branding and reputation still play a vital role in the online world, explaining why top news outlets still retain a strong incentive to invest in maximizing the quality of their reporting. But clickbait is also increasingly present in mainstream media, as shown in Rony et al. (2017, pp. 232–239), albeit being less common than elsewhere on the Internet.

Moreover, the fast pace at which news circulates online makes fact-checking very burdensome: pressed to release the news as fast as possible, publishers are often unable to provide full checking of their sources. This problem affects smaller outlets in particular since they lack the resources to speed up their fact-checking processes.

Finally, malicious actors may intentionally use bots to flood the market with low-quality, made-up stories with the purpose of aggravating the asymmetry of information. The purpose of a disinformation campaign may not be to mislead viewers

---

[12] See Akerlof's seminal paper: Akerlof, G. A. (1978).

or readers to believe a false story. Instead, the aim could be to **generate cacophony in the news market**, ultimately making it even more difficult for users to identify the sources they can rely on and generally erode trust in the media. "**Deepfakes**", for example, rely on artificial intelligence to induce viewers to believe that, say, a politician, is actually really saying what they hear in the fabricated video they are watching. But their ultimate aim may well be to make it more difficult to distinguish real videos. To the extent that deepfakes become endemic, there is a high likelihood that people would not believe in video reporting any longer, even real ones.[13]

Finally, news markets fail and disinformation prospers online because of humans' **behavioural biases**. Economic analysis usually assumes that agents are rational, and that they pursue their own interest based on the information that is available to them. Research has shown,[14] however, that a significant part of individual decision-making happens subconsciously. Often individuals do not optimize by picking the choice that is best for them. Instead, they are constrained by their *bounded rationality*.

The impact of limitations in our rational abilities is much stronger in an environment where users are overwhelmed by vast amounts of information. Where users are provided with great responsibility for selecting the content they are to consume (remember: they are their "own editors"). And where they are called to take an active role through constant engagement. Chris Wetherell, the inventor of the "retweet" button for Twitter, is reported to have once famously said about his invention: "*we might have just handed a 4-year-old a loaded weapon*" (Kantrowitz A., 2019).

Behavioural biases are such that readers may tend to look for information that confirms their own prejudice or to disregard information that challenges it (*confirmation bias*); they may attach a much higher value to short-term benefits despite overwhelming adverse effects in the long term, explaining for example why disinformation related to climate change is so widespread (*hyperbolic discount rate*); they may tend to align to the opinion of a group (*bandwagon effect*); or to overestimate their knowledge (*Dunning-Kruger effect*). A study on media literacy prepared for the European Commission in 2017 lists a number of biases that are particularly relevant to the disinformation phenomenon (see Figure 14.3) (European Commission, 2019f).

Bounded rationality explains why there would probably exist a market for fabricated stories even if there were no information asymmetry. Even if news-seekers could know upfront the quality of a source, they may still not opt for the most accurate, to the extent that accuracy is secondary to consistency with their own beliefs, for example.

---

[13] "*The more insidious impact of deepfakes, along with other synthetic media and fake news, is to create a zero-trust society, where people cannot, or no longer bother to, distinguish truth from falsehood. And when trust is eroded, it is easier to raise doubts about specific events*". See: Sample, I (2020).

[14] For a review, see the work of Daniel Kahneman, popularized in his book *Thinking, Fast and Slow* (Kahneman, D., 2011).

Heuristic or bias	Description	Domain
Fluency heuristic	A mental heuristic in which if one object is processed more fluently, faster, or more smoothly than another, the mind infers that this object has the higher value with respect to the question being considered	Decision-making
Confirmation bias	The tendency to look for or interpret information to confirm our existing beliefs	Decision-making
Consistency bias	Easy to integrate	Memory
Selective perception	The tendency of expectations to influence our perceptions	Decision-making
Status quo or default bias	The tendency to prefer that path of least resistance and therefore avoid change	Decision-making
Availability heuristic	The tendency to estimate the probability of an event based on its salience and easiness of retrieval in our memory rather than on its objective probability	Probability and beliefs
Overconfidence bias	The tendency to overestimate one's abilities of evaluation	Probability and beliefs
Ambiguity bias	In conditions of lack of information, the effect implies that people tend to select options for which the probability of a favourable outcome is known, over an option for which the probability of a favourable outcome is unknown	Decision-making
Bandwagon effect/social proof	The tendency to do (or believe) things because other people do or believe the same	Decision-making
Focalism	The bias to rely too heavily on one trait or piece of information when making decisions	Decision-making
Availability cascade	The self-reinforcing process in which a collective belief gains more and more plausibility through its increasing repetition in public situations	Probability and beliefs
Base rate fallacy	The tendency to ignore base rate information and focus on specific Information that is provided	Probability and beliefs
Belief bias	The evaluation of the logical strength of an argument is biased	Probability and beliefs
Continued influence bias	The tendency to believe previously learned misinformation even after it has been corrected	Probability and beliefs
Courtesy bias	To provide an opinion that is socially more correct than one's own opinion	Probability and beliefs
Curse of Knowledge	The bias of better-informed people to think about problems from the perspective of lesser-informed people	Probability and beliefs
Dunning-Kruger effect	The tendency for unskilled individuals to overestimate their own ability and the tendency for experts to underestimate their own capacities	Decision-making
Focusing bias	The bias to place too much importance on one (appealing) aspect of an event	Probability and beliefs
Framing bias	The bias of drawing different conclusions from the same information, based upon how the information is presented	Decision-making
Illusion of validity	Belief that our judgements are accurate, especially when the information is presented as consistent or intercorrelated	Probability and beliefs
Illusory correlation	Incorrectly perceiving relationships between two unrelated events	Probability and beliefs
Illusory truth effect	The tendency to believe that a statement is true because it is easier to process, or has been stated multiple times, regardless of its truthiness	Probability and beliefs

Figure 14.3 A selection of biases related to online media behaviour

European Commission, 'Study on Media Literacy' (28 October 2019), pp. 142–143. https://ec.europa.eu/digital-single-market/en/news/study-media-literacy-and-online-empowerment-issues-raised-algorithm-driven-media-services-smart

As pointed out in Flynn et al. (2017), the stream of psychological research on **directionally motivated reasoning** (another way to indicate confirmation bias), whereby individuals tend to seek or dismiss information that reinforces or contradicts their preferences, is particularly relevant to the disinformation phenomenon. They describe evidence that salience is a key factor strengthening directionally motivated reasoning (hence confirmation bias effects are more likely when strong emotions are aroused, such as in the context of a political discussion around immigration and security). They also report that, somewhat counterintuitively, directionally motivated reasoning is directly correlated to an individual's "sophistication", namely political knowledge and education. Highly sophisticated individuals tend to have stronger opinions, display stronger attachment to them, and have better tools to defend them and counter-argue opposing views. It appears that knowledge and education, in this case, could play against individuals' interest.

Directionally motivated reasoning may explain the existence of echo chambers. Particularly to the extent that individuals tend to be more inclined to believe information coming from sources closer to them (strong ties with the source of information are a significant predictor of the likelihood of influence of the target). However, recall that there is no agreement in the literature regarding echo chambers' existence. For example, Barberá (2015), using a large sample of Twitter data, found that users tend to be exposed to heterogeneous networks of ideologies, actually *reducing* the likelihood of echo chambers rather than increasing it, if compared with non-users. Moreover, it should be noted that disinformation is all the more harmful when targeting individuals *that are not* already aligned to the conveyed message. In that sense, the two phenomena of disinformation and echo chamber would offset one another to a certain extent.

Directionally motivated reasoning can also partially explain why the spread of disinformation online contributes to the ongoing tendency towards polarization in the political debate.[15] As pointed out by Tucker et al. (2018), there is a consensus in the scientific literature that elite behaviour is a major driver of political polarization. However, online "popular" communication has a role too: messages that endorse a group's stereotypes increase the likelihood of accepting inaccurate information about the out group, pushing individuals to lean on the extremes and, therefore, polarize. The stronger the emotional response in terms of anger aroused by those messages, the higher the risk of polarization. Anger can make individuals less likely to dismiss false information that is consistent with their views.

14.3 Dilemmas for policymakers

The challenge for policymakers is to eliminate or **defuse disinformation online while preserving freedom of expression**. Freedom of expression is a recognized right in the Universal Declaration of Human Rights. But it is also a highly subjective matter where boundaries often cannot be defined in absolute terms.[16] Students should, however, pay attention not to view information quality and freedom of expression as two faces of the same coin: for many reasons, the two are not necessarily mutually exclusive. Instead, even though curbing disinformation could entail undermining someone else's freedom, **the two largely complement each other**. To

---

[15] It is important to note here that digitization and social networks *are not* the only factors explaining polarization in the political debate. Economical, sociological, political, institutional, and historical factors interplay. See for example: Barber and McCarty (2015).

[16] United Nations (1948), Art. 19.

the extent that *"freedom of expression"* is a principle that should allow an individual to say something and *be heard,* it cannot be fully applied in a world riddled by disinformation: the overwhelming noise caused by the disinformation undermines communication. Likewise, accurate information is the outcome of free debate and trust in media. Leaning on accuracy by sacrificing freedom of expression is thus a dangerous path to walk: the cure can be worse than the illness, and a society that limits freedom risks cornering itself to being exposed to monochromatic information without having the antibodies to challenge it, as criticism is, by construct, prevented.

Policymakers are therefore not required to choose between freedom of expression and quality of online content. Instead, they need to deploy intelligent and sophisticated solutions that address disinformation from multiple angles to maximize the chance of success while minimizing negative spillovers on the exercise of human rights.

To frame the challenge of policymakers and provide some guidelines on potential policy avenues, let us go back to the definition of disinformation from the European Commission:

> Disinformation is understood as **verifiably false or misleading information** that is created, presented and disseminated for **economic gain** or to **intentionally deceive** the public, and **may cause public harm**.

In Section 14.1, we have identified three critical components in the definition: *nature, purpose,* and *effect.* Therefore, it would seem sensible to categorize policy action along the same lines.

14.3.1 Nature

The goal here is to **undermine the credibility of false or misleading information**. This can be done through **fact-checking**. Namely: third parties, such as independent NGOs or newspapers, verify the accuracy of news that has been published online or otherwise shared by a particular source. Fact-checkers not only identify and flag hoaxes; they usually also debunk them, shedding light on the origin of the misleading information and its possible purposes. The International Fact-Checking Network provides accreditation to fact-checking organizations, certifying that they abide by high-quality standards (Poynter, 2021). Public policies can be implemented to promote the emergence of fact-checking organizations, support their activities, and enhance their visibility online.

Fact-checking is a powerful and essential tool to address disinformation. It has, however, significant limitations. First of all, fact-checking takes time. As we have seen, though, junk news can travel very fast. Moreover, it travels at a faster rate than accurate stories, possibly thanks to the emotion it arouses (see Section 14.2, above). This means that fact-checking may be helpful to debunk a story, but it most often comes too late to slow down spreading by reducing the incentive of users to share the news.

Most importantly, there are strong indications in the literature suggesting that **fact-checking is often unsuccessful in changing the false belief that a fabricated story may have generated**. This is particularly true if the story's subject has highly emotional content (Flynn, et al., 2017) or when the fact-checking source is not perceived as ideologically close to the target user. In that sense, fact-checking prompted by a source within the group with whom the target may have strong ties (an ideologically similar user belonging to the same friends' network, for example) is more likely to defuse the effect of the false story on the target.

False beliefs, however, tend to be very persistent. In a study on a sample of French voters, Barrera et al. (2020) found that being exposed to strong rhetorical extreme-right content based on unsubstantiated facts significantly increases voting intention in favour of the extreme-right party's candidate, Marine Le Pen, *regardless* of whether they are accompanied by fact-checking. The researchers hypothesize the existence of a dynamic enacted by the *salience* of the topic mentioned. When a false statement regarding immigrants is made, that statement brings the issue to the attention of voters, making it more *salient* in their mind; therefore, it pushes them to support candidates with an anti-immigrant agenda, even if the statement is not based on actual facts *and this is known to the voter*. Fact-checking may also generate "*implied truth effects*": flagging news that has been fact-checked and proved unfounded on platforms, for example, can introduce a bias in users' assessment and induce them to overly trust news that has not been flagged but may still be unfounded (Pennycook, et al., 2020).

Nevertheless, fact-checking can be very helpful in contexts where targets do not have a strong ideological commitment towards the subject of the act of disinformation. Imagine, for example, a chain of disinformation regarding false remedies against Covid-19 growing on WhatsApp. Even if coming into play with a specific temporal lag compared to the release of the false story, fact-checking can help pour water on the wildfire and halt the sharing chain. Vosoughi et al. (2018) suggest that false stories spread quickly because of their novel content. Users that share them desire to acquire social status by showing to be "in the know" or to have access to "insider information". Suppose other users in the network can promptly post an article debunking the story. In that case, they can directly expose the original source to criticism, undermining their public reputation and "knowledgeable" social status, therefore providing an effective disincentive for the original source to share in the first place.

Another way to disempower disinformation is through **source ranking**, whereby sources get a mark or a certification by independent organizations indicating that their stories tend to be fact-checked and, thus, trustworthy. This form of indirect fact-checking has the advantage of being readily available when that news is released. Pennycook and Rand (2019) report evidence that ranking can even be based on crowdsourced judgements by social network users, suggesting that incorporating that assessment into social media ranking algorithms can help fight disinformation. It should be pointed out, however, that *source ranking* may be subject to a reverse implied truth effect: users may expect unranked sources to be less trustworthy than average. And this can constitute a barrier to entry for start-ups or novel news outlets which may have served to improve the quality of the news market.

14.3.2 Purpose

The goal here is to **make it less profitable to create, present or disseminate disinformation** by attacking revenue streams or generating potential costs (a straightforward example of the latter is regulatory enforcement through a fining policy).

Here online platforms play a primary role. In all respects, platforms are the key channels through which disinformation can reach large groups of individuals.

As we will see in Section 14.4, the European Commission has placed considerable pressure on online platforms to self-regulate, essentially pushing them to take responsibility for disinformation content they host. But as we have seen above, platforms do not have a strong incentive to do so: limiting disinformation on their own initiative would reduce their revenue and may even expose them to legal risks. Furthermore, it may even not be desirable to have platforms playing a de facto editorial role, potentially censoring content to avoid legal risk (we have seen in Chapter 9 the risk of *collateral censorship* and its effect on freedom of expression). During the Covid-19 pandemic, major social networks have taken a proactive approach to limit the spread of statements that could affect the health of millions. This included removing messages published by Head of States from their platforms. Regardless of whether platforms are correct in their assessment of content's potential to cause harm, one question remains. Should private entities (the platforms) that provide a quasi-universal service (they represent a major channel of communication to reach the population) be the ones calling the shots and prevent elected politicians or officials from sharing their messages publicly? The short-term benefit for public safety is as evident as the long-term risk for democracy.

However, platforms can certainly play a role to address disinformation. They can, for example, increase the visibility of fact-checked news using algorithms which favour fact-checked news. Or they can associate, visually, stories with high-risk subjects (such as health-related content) with information from official and verified sources. For example: a fake remedy story could be accompanied by links and excerpts from the World Health Organization's website. Platforms can also limit the spread of disinformation by curbing the use of unverified accounts and, in particular, the use of automated software—bots—on social networks. All major social networks with a meaningful presence in the European market have been taking action in this respect.[17] However, since platforms have been very reluctant to share data and information, it is very hard to assess the efficacy of those efforts.[18]

Platforms can significantly increase their transparency vis-à-vis the external world. A platform's transparency is a highly contentious issue since platforms tend to be wary not to disclose their "internal-cooking", with the risk of hampering their business by favouring potential competitors. But a certain degree of openness is necessary if one wishes to avoid policies forcing platforms to make their own call on content to be deemed harmful.

There are three crucial angles where increasing transparency can help in addressing online disinformation:

1. **Transparency vis-à-vis public authorities and fact-checking organizations.** Platforms can create and foster interfaces for monitoring disinformation and quick intervention by public authorities (namely, independent regulators). They can likewise provide raw anonymised data, transcripts of videos, and tools for data analytics to independent and certified NGOs to provide maximum support for their fact-checking activities

2. **Transparency regarding sources vis-à-vis users.** Platform users should have a clear understanding of the source of the story they view or read. That applies, particularly to political advertising. Platforms should make it visible *who pays* for an ad. This is all the more important when psychological profiling and ads micro-targeting (namely, advertisement tailored to a single individual's specific features or preferences) take place

3. **Transparency vis-à-vis the researcher community.** Disinformation online is a rapidly evolving phenomenon. Unfortunately, researchers are far away from fully understanding its dynamics.[19] But research is fundamental to inform public policy solutions. That is why there would be great benefits from platforms granting privileged access to their data to researchers, provided that the necessary safeguards for users' privacy are ensured.[20]

14.3.3 Effect

Finally, public policy should aim to defuse disinformation by empowering individuals, improving their ability to assess a source's accuracy, and expanding access to high-quality information.

---

[17] See, for example: Facebook (2020) and Twitter (2020).

[18] See, for example, the European Commission's assessment of the implementation of the Code of Practice on Disinformation (European Commission, 2021).

[19] For an example of the (many) research questions that are still open at the timing of writing of this book, see Tucker, et al. (2018).

[20] Initiatives in that sense have been taken place—see, for example: Facebook (2019).

In a 2020 report, the UK Telecom Regulator OFCOM (OFCOM, 2020) found that almost half of UK online adults had come across misleading information about the Covid-19 pandemic; yet 40% of people found it hard to know what is true or false about the virus. *Media literacy* indicates a set of skills that enhance users' ability to react critically, to be "constructively alerted", when they come across media. Investing in media literacy can thus prove to be a sensible strategy to defuse disinformation. However, it must occur at an early age to increase the chance that its effects persist over time. Finland and Italy, for example, have targeted programmes starting respectively at primary school (Henley J., 2020) and high school (Horowitz J., 2017).

At the same time, platforms could be required to take action to reduce the incentives of users to share false stories to gain a return in terms of social status or acceptance. One way to do so is through "**demetrication**", that is: hiding the number of "likes" or "re-share" of posts to curb virality (see Haidt and Rose-Stockwell (2019)). Likewise, platforms can **nudge** users away from posting inflammatory comments by activating pop-up messages requiring confirmation whenever the platform's algorithm detects a high degree of negative language. Simply pointing out to somebody that they may be about to post an offensive comment can dissuade them from going through with it. Researchers have shown that people surrounded by mirrors tend to be less likely to judge others based on stereotypes; if users are made self-aware, they may stop and think about what they are about to do (Angier N., 2008). Defusing emotional responses can be very effective in limiting the spread and speed of sharing of disinformation, as we have seen in Section 14.2.[21]

Finally, platforms can simply make it technically more challenging to share stories across wider audiences. For example, during the Covid-19 pandemic, WhatsApp prevented users from forwarding messages shared a certain number of times to multiple "chats" simultaneously to avoid the mass spread of messages. According to WhatsApp, such technical limits can significantly decrease the number of messages forwarded globally (WhatsApp, 2020).

14.4 The European Union's perspective

Countries worldwide have been increasingly deploying public policy and enforcement initiatives to address disinformation online (Poynter has an up-to-date list with categories of initiatives by country, see map in Figure 14.4).

Two notable examples in Europe, Germany and France, have recently placed themselves at the frontier of the experimentation with legislative action against disinformation, which did not spare the countries from harsh criticism. The German parliament passed a hate speech law named *Netzwerkdurchsetzungsgesetz* (NetzDG) in 2017 (the law came into force in January 2018). According to the law, platforms with more than two million users (such as YouTube, Facebook, or Twitter, at the

---

[21] Social networks have been experimenting with demetrication and nudging, though their implementation is not yet happening systematically and across the board. See, for example: Bryant, M (2019).

time of writing) have 24 hours to take down "obviously illegal" content. Failure to do so would risk a fine of up to €50 million. The law has been heavily criticised as the definition of "obviously illegal" content is entirely subjective. The risk is to end up with a strong incentive by platforms to err on the side of caution by censoring widely and potentially removing legal content to avoid the risk of being fined. Moreover, it should be noted that the two million cut-off threshold for the number of users may simply mean that content inciting hatred or violence would migrate from bigger to smaller platforms to circumvent the law.

Similarly, in 2020 the French government had proposed an "online hatred" bill. The proposed law was meant to oblige platforms to remove content that users had flagged as "hateful" within 24 hours. Failing to do so, platforms could have ended up with fines of up to 4% of their global turnover. However, the proposal was struck down by the French Constitutional Court. According to the Court the law would have generated an incentive for platforms to indiscriminately remove flagged content. The risk of compressing the right of freedom of expression was deemed evident, at least in this case.

Now let us turn to the policy experience at the European Union level.

14.4.1 The European Commission's plan to fight disinformation

The magnitude, scale, and cross-border dimension of disinformation and its ties with the proper functioning of democracies within the Single Market render it an

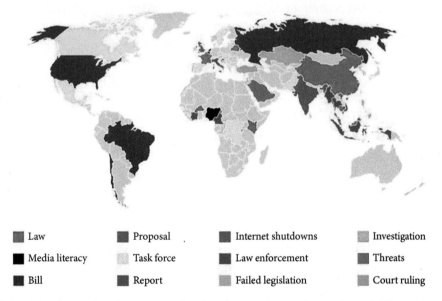

Figure 14.4 Map indicating actions taken by governments against online misinformation (by 2018)

Daniel Funke and Daniela Flamini, Poynter, 'A guide to anti-misinformation actions around the world'. https://www.poynter.org/ifcn/anti-misinformation-actions/

area suitable for action at the EU level. On disinformation, the European Commission has, since 2015, been taking a gradual approach. Its first initiatives concerned the narrower area of the external dimension, focussing on disinformation campaigns run by foreign powers to destabilize EU democracies. These early initiatives were often in the context of countering "hybrid threats" or threats deployed from different angles: military, domestic security, cybersecurity, and media influence. A Task Force named *East StratCom* was set up in March 2015 at the request of the European Council (European Council, 2015). East StratCom was the Council's way of responding to the growing attempts by Russia to interfere with EU Member States' democracies through large disinformation campaigns. The task force analyses disinformation trends and debunks false stories, attempting to foster awareness throughout Europe.[22]

The European Commission then sought to step up its efforts to improve understanding of the disinformation phenomenon as a whole, and not only related to the EU's external dimension. It did so in the usual European Commission's "way": through extended stakeholder dialogues, conferences, and consultations (European Commission, 2017g). The most notable outcome of that exploratory phase was the 2018 final report from the High-Level Group (HLG) of experts convened by the European Commission (European Commission, 2017h).

In the following phase, marked by its April 2018 Communication "Tackling online disinformation: a European approach", the Commission primarily aimed to involve stakeholders, in particular online platforms, to contribute to developing solutions and, most importantly, to take on a proactive role in fighting disinformation online (European Commission, 2018g). It increasingly "nudged" the industry to self-regulate, under the threat that it would swiftly shift to a more invasive regulatory approach, should self-regulation not yield the optimal social outcome.

As we have seen in the previous section, however, the chances of success of that approach were low from the outset. Online platforms may have an incentive to display publicly their efforts to address disinformation. But less certain is their interest in effectively curbing it, especially if this entails running legal risks while forgoing a significant source of revenue. The role and responsibility of online platforms is the object of the important ongoing discussion related to the **Digital Services Act**, which I have discussed in Chapter 9.

14.4.2 What has been done so far at EU level

By the time of writing, the most relevant contributions at EU level were:

- The High-Level Group Report of March 2018 (European Commission, 2018)

---

[22] See its website: https://euvsdisinfo.eu/

- The April 2018 Commission Communication on Tackling Online Disinformation
- The October 2018 Code of Practice on disinformation and its subsequent reporting/assessment
- The December 2018 Action Plan.

The **High-Level Group (HLG)** brought together representatives from large technological companies, the research community, institutions, civil society, journalists, and fact-checkers. It was set up to advise the Commission through an in-depth analysis of the current situation of the spread of disinformation online and to suggest policy solutions to tackle it. As it turns out, the report produced by the High-Level Group had a significant impact on the Commission's strategy.

The report was tellingly titled "**A Multi-Dimensional Approach to Disinformation**". The title suggests from the outset that disinformation is a multifaceted problem stemming from various causes and that regulation is certainly not the "silver bullet" that can unilaterally tackle it as a whole.

The critical policy suggestions of the report for a course of action against disinformation are:

- From the outset, **abandon the misleading fake-news terminology** (see Section 14.1 for a discussion)
- **Enhance transparency online,** mainly through the sharing of data between platforms and the fact-checking and research communities. Transparency should also be fostered by providing readers with information on sources (in particular in the case of political advertising). Source transparency indicators should also be deployed
- **Promote media and information literacy**, by supporting the teaching of key competences in EU schools, training teachers, and systematically evaluating progress
- **Empower users and journalists**, giving them smoother access to online data with specific interfaces, providing professionals with automatic content verification tools, and training journalists
- **Financially support** independent news media and the fact-checking community, including by funding "quality journalism" projects, to safeguard and promote diversity and sustainability of the European news media ecosystem
- Invest in improving our understanding of the phenomenon through, in particular, **strong support for research** geared to study disinformation across the EU (for example, facilitating the creation of an EU network of research centres).

Students may note a high degree of consistency between the HLG's suggestions and the policy solutions discussed in Section 14.3 of this chapter; a notable exception concerns financial support for the media environment. While help for quality media is, in principle welcome, direct support may hide a risk: to crowd out private invest-ment and end up financing the *"wrong winners"*—i.e. not the most efficient media that would have succeeded in a free and fair competitive market. Moreover, ensur-ing healthy and fair competition, even if disruptive, has the potential to stimulate the emergence of quality media in the market without the need for public inter-vention. This subject is covered extensively in Chapter 8 in the section dedicated to competition policy, and in Chapter 9 on illegal online content.

The subsequent European Commission Communication *"Tackling online dis-information: A European approach"* incorporates most of the HLG's advice, also elaborating ways to operationalize them.

The EC Communication is based on four overarching principles:

1. Improve **transparency** concerning the source of information, how it is created, supported and disseminated
2. Promote **diversity** of information online, in particular, supporting high-quality journalism
3. Foster **credibility** of information, increasing the visibility of assessments of quality, e.g. providing upfront indications to readers or viewers on the degree of trustworthiness of a publication
4. Design **inclusive** solutions requiring the involvement of all stakeholders, from platforms to advertisers, from institutions and public authorities, to journalists, fact-checkers, and single individuals.

The resulting concrete initiatives mapped onto those principles are as follows:

- the setting up of an EU-wide Code of Practice on Disinformation
- supporting the creation of an independent European network of fact-checkers
- the launch of a secure European online platform on disinformation
- encouraging voluntary online systems to allow the identification of suppliers of information
- coordinating and supporting the Member States to ensure secure and resilient election processes
- laying down several initiatives to promote media literacy, such as the launch of campaigns in schools involving fact-checker organizations
- exploring funding opportunities to promote media freedom and pluralism.

The Communication's principles are thus in line with the recommendations of the HLG Report. But the listed actions did not seem to have the potential to lead to concrete action: they are either very general and somehow superficial or consist-ing of unspecified support for initiatives where other stakeholders do the heavy lifting. The most significant of the listed initiatives is the **Code of Practice on Disinformation**: a self-regulatory tool that online platforms would agree to abide by on a *voluntary basis* (European Commission, 2020r). It sets out a wide range of commitments, grouped in five categories: (1) scrutiny of advertisement placements; (2) political advertising and issue-based advertising; (3) integrity of services; (4) empowering consumers; and (5) empowering the research community. A year after the launch of the Code, in October 2019, the Commission issued a preliminary assessment of the advances made. It recorded progress by platforms in identifying and setting up catalogues of political advertisers, labelling misinformation, providing data on the removal of content ordered by public authorities, expanding collaboration with the fact-checking community, investing in training of journalists, and supporting media literacy programmes.

But the outcomes achieved by platforms were far from satisfactory in terms of providing adequate transparency related to non-political advertisements and deploying an effective methodology, including accurate metrics, to evaluate the impact of self-regulatory measures. Platforms, above all, failed to supply granular data to researchers and fact-checking organizations, essentially hindering the latter in doing their job. At the time of writing, the Code of Practice was still subject to an ongoing assessment process. However, it is fair to say that, based on what can observed today, self-regulation does not seem to be enough to address the problem. Disinformation online is all the more evident today, and the public perception is that the phenomenon is only growing. The spread of disinformation during Covid-19 reinforced that perception. For that reason, in May 2021 the European Commission published a **Guidance to Strengthen the Code of Practice on Disinformation** (European Commission, 2021). With the guidance paper, the European Commission attempts to address some of the shortcomings of the Code of Practice identified during the pandemic crisis. The most relevant suggestions of the guidance paper (which remains non-binding) relate to content monetization and platform cooperation, and information sharing. For example, the guidance paper suggests that platforms could tighten their control of ads revenue linked to disinformation systematically posted by the same actors. The Commission also reinforces its call for more transparency by platforms towards the external world, including researchers and users, who should be helped to recognize and flag disinformation content.

At the time of writing, another action worth mentioning by the European Commission is from December 2018, when the Commission and the High Representative of the Union for Foreign Affairs and Security Policy presented a Joint Communication on an **Action Plan against Disinformation** (European Commission, 2018j). The Action Plan attempts to address the European Council's concerns about the impact of disinformation on Member States' democratic processes and the then-upcoming European Parliamentary elections, which took place in May 2019. The Action Plan builds on the Communication on Tackling Online Disinformation and focuses in particular on expanding the capabilities and strengthening cooperation and coordination between the Member States.

The plan rests on four pillars:

- **Improving the EU institutions' ability to detect, analyse, and expose disinformation.** This, in particular, entailed upscaling resources for strategic communication task forces and Union delegations within the Member States, for example with additional staff members
- **Strengthening coordinated and joint responses to disinformation.** This entailed the creation of a "rapid alert system" to provide alerts on disinformation campaigns in real-time across the EU and the designation by each Member State of a contact point for exchanges and coordination on disinformation issues
- **Mobilizing the private sector.** This contained a commitment to increasing pressure on the industry to abide by the Code of Practice
- **Raising awareness and improving societal resilience.** This notably entailed setting up targeted campaigns in Europe and beyond, and additional support for independent media and fact-checker networks at the Member State level.

The Action Plan did not provoke a breakthrough in EU policies against disinformation. Instead, it appears to be in total continuity with the approach of the April 2018 Communication. Russian groups target EU elections with continued and sustained disinformation activity, for example (Scott M., Cerulus L., 2019), even though the Action Plan's primary goal was to shield elections from the effects of disinformation.

Thus, it appears that the EU's response to growing concerns related to disinformation online has so far been too weak to yield any significant change. Finally, as we have seen in Chapter 9, in December 2020 the European Commission has proposed a Digital Services Act (DSA) with the aim to curb illegal content online. The DSA proposed text contains provisions to incentivize very large platforms to reduce the risk of abuse of their communication channels (and thus also to reduce the spread of disinformation, see Chapter 9). Whether these measures will be of help to tackle disinformation is yet to be seen. I tend to be sceptical, since they mostly rely on very large platforms' ability to self-impose limitations; as I have explained in this chapter: given platforms' diverging interests, this is unlikely to work.

****

14.5 Case Study: Lithuanian elves taking on Russian trolls

Lithuania is very much exposed to Russian propaganda (similarly to its Baltic neighbours, Latvia and Estonia). Disinformation online can be a way to manipulate local public opinion, for example to sugarcoat the USSR's history of oppression. Or disinformation can be spread to amplify the Russian sphere of influence and generate public support towards its foreign policies. Attempts of online manipulation are perpetuated by "*Russian trolls*", i.e. "users that intentionally bait others to elicit an emotional response." In response to those attempts, a large community of Lithuanian volunteers emerged. Borrowing from J.R.R. Tolkien's "Lord of the Rings" fictitious world (Tolkien, 2012), the volunteers call themselves "*elves*" (elves and trolls typically hate each other . . .). There are more than five thousand, among them professionals from the tech sector, students, business people, scientists, and journalists. The Lithuanian elves patrol the Internet looking for Russian-originated disinformation. Some of them work to debunk false information. Others proactively set up name-and-shame campaigns against pro-Russian propaganda trolls. Elves can also rely on a website called *Demaskuok.lt* that was created through a collaboration between media outlets, the military, and civil society. The website regularly scans thousands of articles per day against a dataset of false narratives that are commonly used by Russian trolls (such as that "Lithuania is a state occupied by NATO"). Once identified, the manipulative content is further reviewed and, where deemed necessary, debunked through concerted media efforts.

More information on the Lithuanian elves can be found here:
https://www.euronews.com/2017/09/28/lithuania-has-a-volunteer-army-fighting-a-war-on-the-internet

14.6 Review questions

- Explain the importance of terminology in the context of the policy debate around ways to limit the spread of disinformation online.
- Illustrate the phenomenon known as "filter bubble" or "echo chamber" with a real-life case (or make up your own example). Do filter bubbles amplify or limit the problem with online disinformation? Explain.
- Why may debunking disinformation not help mitigate most of the risk of harm for society? Explain your answer, emphasizing the role of the limits to human rational thinking.
- Discuss potential policy remedies to disinformation from the perspective of the expected timing with which their effect is supposed to become observable. Which policies are already effective in the short term? Which ones have effects that are only visible in the long term?
- A Member of the Parliament proposed a 30-minutes rule for take-down of harmful content when a platform detects it. Would that help to limit the spread of disinformation? Justify and explain your answer.

15

Artificial Intelligence

Abstract

Artificial intelligence (AI) holds the keys to unlocking a future of unconceivable prosperity for humankind: it may dramatically boost the performance of economies and provide unprecedented opportunities for citizens, companies, and the public sector. It may also advance our ability to address humanity's challenges, such as providing effective tools for disaster control, a weapon against climate change, or a cure for diseases like cancer. But AI also conceals the potential for a future at the other end of the spectrum. A future where citizens of dystopian societies undergo permanent monitoring for the way they behave or could behave. Where discriminatory treatment is a norm and fundamental rights are systematically ignored. A society where the gap between the haves and have-nots becomes unbridgeable. The role of public policy in the AI space is thus extremely important. Public policy can create the conditions for humanity to get the most out of AI while steering it away from the dystopian future, popularly depicted in science fiction books or films, by designing appropriate ethical and legal frameworks to protect society's core values. AI catalyses all of the promises and the fears entailed in the digital paradigm. It thus serves as the ideal conclusive chapter, where most of the issues and public policy solutions covered throughout this book come together.

15.1 Background

Artificial intelligence (or **AI**) can refer to any technology that aims to emulate biological intelligence, even just a feature of it, such as the ability to learn from the surrounding environment. AI could have a high impact on all economic sectors, profoundly affecting the structure and the functioning of future societies, comparably to the emergence of electricity and steam engines during the Industrial Revolution (Tani, S., 2016). AI is set to become endemic to our economies and societies: it holds the promise of boosting the quality of life of citizens, for example through better and quicker health diagnostics, of increasing companies' productivity, and improving our public services. Ultimately, AI may be the key to unlocking solutions to some of humanity's long-standing challenges such as cancer, climate change, world hunger, or disaster control. But AI's transformative power may come at a high price, exacerbating inequalities, increasing the opportunities for state or

Digital Economic Policy. Mario Mariniello, Oxford University Press.
© Mario Mariniello (2022). DOI: 10.1093/oso/9780198831471.003.0015

non-state actors to commit abuses, and ultimately endangering the survival of the human species, if left uncontrolled.[1]

It is no coincidence that the chapter on AI comes at the end of this book. It could be argued that AI is embedded in all of the promises and pitfalls that embracing the new digital paradigm entails. Thus, in many ways, this chapter also serves the purpose of reviewing the subjects we have covered throughout the text.

15.1.1 History of AI

The term "Artificial intelligence" was coined in the 1950s. Still, thinkers explored the potential of machines to emulate human intelligence much earlier than that, the ancient Greek philosopher Aristotle being a first vivid example.[2] Despite its long history, or perhaps because of it, the notion of AI remains somewhat nebulous still today: AI is a broad term that escapes any clear-cut definition. It could be said that AI refers to technologies (hardware or software) able to function autonomously in a specific environment, having the capacity to forecast what may happen next and react accordingly.[3] Or AI could come to indicate technologies that attempt to mimic human cognitive functions, such as interacting with others or learning from experience. According to the *Turing Test*,[4] a machine could be called "intelligent" if it can trick a human observer into believing that a human generates the answers she gets during the test. Often, the line between AI technologies and the *use* that is made of those technologies is blurred. As a result, often debates around AI tend to consider wider research fields and *areas of application* (such as robotics, autonomous driving, virtual assistants, natural language processing, computer vision), *approaches* (such as machine learning, rules-based game playing, expert systems) or specific *techniques and methods* (such as artificial neural networks, deep learning, clustering algorithms) as if they were conceptually similar.

In recent years, AI has become a buzzword in the business world as well as in the policy environment. The hype around AI technologies is well evidenced in investment figures. In 2017, the total funding from venture capital to AI tripled compared to 2016, reaching a total of €11 billion worldwide. Statista (2020b) estimates that, in 2023, the total worldwide spending in robotic/intelligent process automation (namely, software robot mimicking human action) and AI automation (i.e. software that mimics human intelligence) will surpass €30 billion, approximately six times more than total spending in 2016. Total revenue from the AI-driven hardware market is forecasted to increase from less than €18 billion in 2018 to approximately €210 billion in 2025: a ten-fold increase.

Historically, though, expectations around AI have not displayed a linear evolution. Instead, funding and interest in AI fluctuated from hype to lack of interest:

---

[1] For a goose-bump inducing read, see Bostrom (2017).
[2] For a comprehensive overview of the history of Artificial Intelligence, see Nilsson (2009).
[3] See Nilsson (2009).
[4] See Turing (2009).

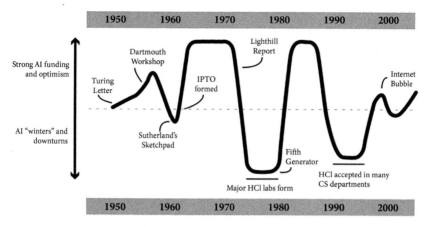

Figure 15.1 The history of artificial intelligence
https://pdfs.semanticscholar.org/e22b/e3642660d6a779e477124cae7cbfdfa5b0a5.pdf

the term "AI winter" refers to those periods (the late 1960s, the late 1970s and the 1990s, see Figure 15.1) when investors had abandoned hopes that AI would achieve any significant breakthrough, after an initial phase of euphoria and high hopes from the times of Turing in the 1950s. The current period could qualify as one of those moments where excitement peaks, with potential frustration lurking behind the corner, at the sudden realization that investors' expectations cannot be met within a sensible time horizon. However, three factors matured in the late 2000s which boosted AI's odds of becoming the game-changer it had promised to be (heralding the "*this time will be different*" motto):

- The emergence of **high network computational power**
- The development of highly **sophisticated algorithms**
- and, perhaps most importantly, the **availability of vast amounts of data** from many different sources (see Chapter 5).

These three factors taken together have allowed a technology that was already known in the 90s, called **Machine Learning**, to achieve results that, just a few years earlier, hardly anyone could hope to pursue. A most notable example is from 2016 when an AI-powered application named *AlphaGO* (from Google's DeepMind, one of the most successful AI-developing companies in the world (DeepMind, 2020)) won against Lee Sedol, the world champion of *Go*. *Go* is considered the most complex board game ever developed by humankind, with 10^{170} possible board con-figurations, more than the number of atoms in the universe (Akpan N., 2016). The achievement was not only remarkable in itself. It also sparked excitement across the globe. It was an eye-opener, particularly for Far East countries, where the culture of *Go* has its roots. An AI application developed by a Western company beat-ing a South Korean *Go* world champion while more than 280 million Chinese viewers were watching generated what experts in Asian affairs have dubbed a

"Sputnik moment" for China (Schiavenza M., 2018). Ever since, the Chinese government has committed itself to prevail in what countries often perceive as the "global race for AI supremacy" (more on this in Section 15.4).

15.1.2 AI technologies

Machine learning (ML)[5] enables computers to draw inferences from data and make decisions, predictions, or judgments without explicitly programming the path to the outcome. **Data mining** is the process through which potentially valuable information is extracted from raw data, and it is often used in ML processing.

ML is currently the AI technology with the most obvious disruptive potential: it finds its use in many applications, such as natural language processing, image recognition, and robotics (see further below). A sophisticated ML-based technology goes under the umbrella term of **Deep Learning**. A deep learning system is a neuronal network imitating the structure of the human brain. The nodes of the network are not programmed to perform a specific task. Instead, the system receives inputs from the external environment and re-adjusts the network's nodes to get closer to achieving the overarching goal set by the developers. It is "deep" because the neuronal networks are assembled in many layers. And it is "learning" because the more inputs it gets, the more refined the outcome it yields.

A popular type of ML processing is called **supervised learning**. With this approach, the developer sets a goal, supplies training data, and provides feedback to the machine (thus, the machine learns under the "supervision" of a developer). It is often used for categorization. For example, to teach a computer to recognize photographs of cats and dogs, photos are supplied (the more, the better), and the system is instructed of the goal. After each run, results are checked, and developers provide feedback: which photographs were classified correctly and which were not. After that, the system adjusts itself and tries again. This process continues until the desired level of confidence is achieved.

Reinforcement learning is used in complex environments where the system learns *by itself* to make the right decisions leading to desired outcomes. Under this approach, the system is not typically provided with examples of correct behaviour based on which it would improve (supervised learning). Faced with a complex environment, the system relies on trial and error, taking actions and learning from past interactions. The adjustment towards the desired outcome happens automatically as the system is "aware" of what success looks like (e.g. winning a Go game).

AlphaGO is an example of supervised learning. It was trained with a dataset of approximately thirty million Go moves labelled as good moves or bad moves to achieve the level necessary to beat Lee Sedol. AlphaGO Zero, a reinforcement learning version of AlphaGO, achieved the same level by playing against itself in fewer than

---

[5] See Mitchell, et al. (2013) for a general introduction to the technology.

four million matches, "just" a small fraction of the data needed by its older brother (DeepMind, 2017).

The most important conclusion we can draw from this brief description of AI-powered applications is that the outstanding results that have been achieved so far strongly rely on *data* and *computational power*. That marks a fundamental difference with the functioning of the human mind, even though neuronal networks in AI attempt to imitate the brain's structure. Humans are endowed with (most likely innate) "**cognitive models**" that allow them to create a narrative of reality based on their intuition and the interactions they observe.[6] A child learns to recognize a cat after seeing them a few times. They do not need to process a massive dataset of cats' images to learn what a cat looks like. "Go" masters became champions after having played a few thousand matches, not millions, as was the case with AlphaGO. In other words, if humans had the same computational power as machines, they would be far more efficient than deep learning algorithms.[7] While attempts are being made to emulate human intuition/model-based cognitive processing in machines (see, for example, the stream of research on "Boltzmann Machines" and probabilistic machine learning), there is currently no indication that algorithms will ever achieve this level of sophistication. According to some commentators, given the current state-of-the-art in AI research, "*super-intelligence*," or an intelligence that is superior to that of human beings, is as likely as time travel. Yet, a few experts, albeit a minority,[8] can envisage a future where machines will become cleverer than humans. This phenomenon, termed a "**singularity moment**," is seen as a potential turning point in human history: super-intelligent machines would arguably be able to programme ever more intelligent machines, triggering an exponential growth in AI's capabilities. In this scenario, machines could take over control from humans and become the "new dominant species" of the planet (Hern A., 2016), (Figure 15.2).

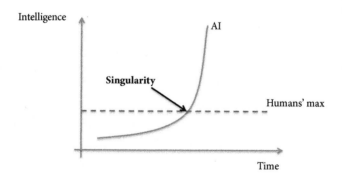

Figure 15.2 The AI Singularity Moment

---

[6] On cognitive models and artificial intelligence, see Amit (2018).

[7] See the interview to MIT's Joshua Tennenbaum extracted from a wonderful article by the online magazine Il Tascabile (only in Italian, unfortunately): Nosengo (2021).

[8] See, for example, a 2016 research paper where researchers surveyed a group of experts asking them: "The earliest that machines will be able to simulate learning and every other aspect of human intelligence": 41% replied 'Never'. 18% indicated less than 50 years. See Müller and Bostrom (2016).

While this Sci-Fi-like scenario may appear esoteric to the readership of this book, one should not underestimate its practical consequences for policymaking. For example, the European Parliament in 2017 prompted a debate around "robots' kill switches", i.e. buttons that any machine should have and that would allow humans to turn them off in case of emergency (European Paliament, 2017). It is easy to imagine that the singularity scenario could well have been in the back of the minds of the Members of the European Parliament during the debate.

Another way to frame this discussion is by introducing the concepts of "**narrow AI**" and "**general AI**".[9] "Narrow AI" refers to machines that are capable of carrying out a specific task, such as playing Go or spotting lung tumours in x-ray images. On the other hand, general AI is AI that would be capable of quickly adapting and responding to a changing environment, performing a variety of tasks that are not necessarily related, mimicking human consciousness. While the development of general AI is not in sight, narrow AI is a very concrete reality. When looking at specific tasks, narrow AI is already outperforming humans.

Gartner[10] categorizes narrow AI applications into three groups:

- **Automated Control/Internet of Things**: performing tasks such as robotics, self-driving cars, factory automation, traffic control, and game playing
- **Pattern Recognition**: performing tasks such as fraud detection, health care, demand prediction, automatic trading, credit scoring, and social media analysis
- **Customer Engagement**: performing tasks such as speech recognition, conversational interfaces, machine translation, and helpdesk automation.

Rather than Terminator-style robots wiping humanity from the face of the planet, AI is better represented by its applications that are becoming endemic to the everyday life of many. For example, in *prediction models*, a message in an email is analysed. The algorithm, trained to recognize patterns and regularities to grasp the meaning of the text, can then suggest possible meaningful answers. For example, in Figure 15.3, the AI employed by my email service provider suggested three possible replies to a message it correctly identified as related to a doctor appointment (sure, that was an easy one . . .).

Narrow AI should therefore be a primary concern for policymakers. The debate on public policy on AI should emphasize the role of AI as a **complement to humans** rather than its potential role as a **substitute** for them (even if substitution effects are still very important, as we have seen in Chapter 12 concerning workers' technological displacement).

The fear of robots replacing humans as the dominant species rests on the assumption that the world would be better off with humans left in charge. But, empowered by sophisticated machines, humans may have great potential to lead to catastrophic

---

[9] See Kaplan and Haenlein (2019) for a description of AI's "evolutionary stages", from narrow to superintelligence.

[10] https://www.gartner.com/en

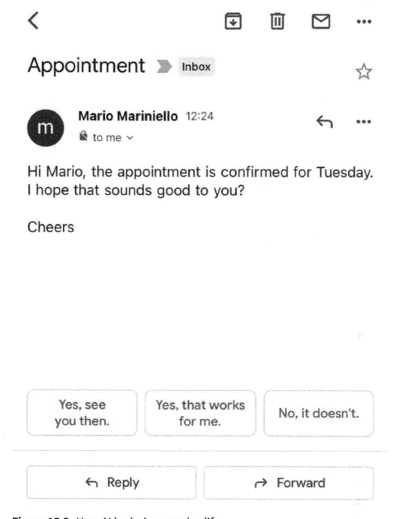

Figure 15.3 How AI looks in everyday life

scenarios, no less than machines left to their own devices. As Calo and Craw-ford (2016) put it: worries of a general artificial intelligence taking over the world may serve only to distract from other more pressing issues. The potential harmful consequences that AI in its narrow, task-specific shape can already have today.

Let us turn to the opportunities and challenges that AI offers as a complement to human beings.

15.2 Opportunities and challenges

15.2.1 Artificial intelligence's promises

Artificial intelligence is set to boost economies' performance around the world. Statista (2020b) forecasts that AI will be associated with more than a quarter of

China's GDP and 14.5% of North America's GDP in 2030. The greatest product enhancements and productivity gains are expected in public and personal services, consumer goods, accommodation, and food services.

AI has the potential to double annual economic growth rates and boost productivity by up to 40% by 2035 (Accenture, 2016). Industries adopting new automation techniques may increase their productivity by replacing routine tasks carried out by humans with efficient AI-powered machines (see Chapter 12). Automation generates significant cost-savings, for example, improving warehouse management or speeding up product distribution. Thanks to AI, companies can make accurate demand forecasts and plan their business accordingly. For example, the producer of packaged salads may rely on an AI-powered application to process data from restaurants, anticipate customers' trends, and plan the crop accordingly.[11] Major savings can also be obtained thanks to predictive maintenance (e.g., accurately estimating when to intervene before actual maintenance is needed) and optimizing manufacturing processes.[12] Offline, personalized promotions, optimized assortment, and tailor-made offers can contribute to increasing sales by 1–5%, while online profiling can lead to a 30% growth in sales.

The demand side has the potential for even more significant benefits. Citizens can benefit from personalized health diagnostics; road safety is maximized through driver assistance (and so are the health sector savings); students may be able to access tailor-made educational offers. The private and the public sector have the potential to become significantly more efficient and responsive to what people really need.[13]

But the most striking cases in favour of AI are made by the significant progress it yields in areas of primary concern for humanity. In January 2020, Google's DeepMind developed an AI system capable of surpassing human experts in predicting breast cancer (see McKinney et al. (2020); see also the case study at the end of this chapter). AI detection entailed a 5.7% absolute reduction in false positives and a 9.4% reduction in false negatives compared to human radiologists. An AI-powered application named BlueDot predicted the Covid-19 pandemic outbreak nine days before WHO released its warnings (Niiler E., 2020). The same algorithm had successfully predicted the outbreak of Zika in Florida. Similarly, AI helped researchers identify Covid-19 carriers, track their contacts, and sequence the virus protein structure (Dananjayan & Raj, 2020). Hao (2019) lists at least ten ways in which AI can contribute to addressing **climate change**. For example, AI can process satellite images to automatically identify where deforestation is taking place and help authorities stop illegal activity (assuming policymakers favour preventing deforestation). Or it can boost farmers' productivity through precision farming, limiting the use of nitrogen-based fertilizers, which can generate nitrous oxide, a greenhouse gas 300 times more detrimental than carbon dioxide.

---

[11] See EPSC (2018).

[12] The business consulting firm McKinsey has a number of useful examples and estimates. Check https://www.mckinsey.com/featured-insights/artificial-intelligence

[13] https://www.mckinsey.com/featured-insights/artificial-intelligence

15.2.2 Areas of concern

Artificial intelligence is deeply entangled with digital products and services. It can be found upstream in the value chain, providing inputs for production, such as key market forecasts. It can occur right in the middle of the value chain, transforming or processing services: imagine AI in precision farming, where tractors automatically adjust to ground conditions depending on the information captured by their sensors. But AI is also downstream, at the very end of the value chain, as the successful outcome of a cocktail of essential ingredients: connectivity (Chapter 4), data (Chapter 5), computing power (Chapter 1), and the implementation of sophisticated technological skills (Chapter 12).

Therefore, it is not surprising to realize that AI markets are exposed to all of the potential sources of market failures that we have covered throughout this book. AI markets suffer from issues generated by network externalities, asymmetry of information, moral hazard, lack of competition, geographical fragmentation, and the bounded rationality of users. However, the core of public concerns on AI is not strictly related to market frictions and market failures. Instead, the emphasis is on the wider societal implications that *complementary narrow*[14] *AI* can have. Implications that are undoubtedly exacerbated by market inefficiencies and the inability of markets to self-regulate. By augmenting the abilities of humans, AI dramatizes existing power asymmetries and biases, magnifying their negative effects on society. Because AI is a kind of "power multiplier", the gap between the haves and the have-nots is set to become larger with AI. In other words, AI has the potential to widen societal inequality (see Chapter 13).

Algorithms can affect the decisions taken by judges: ProPublica (see Angwin et al. (2016)) reported the existence of a bias against black people within the algorithm that US judges have used to predict the likelihood of future criminal action, for example. AI affects how people communicate through messaging apps: predictive text is changing the way people write to each other. AI can boost the popularity of a user on a social network; it can define a company's destiny by upgrading or downgrading its ranking on a web search engine; it can make a national election candidate visible or invisible to the public. Artificial intelligence is, in other words, becoming the analytical and communication infrastructure of our society. However, that infrastructure is not neutral: the way in which AI technology is developed and implemented can have a profound implication for society.

The *AI Now Institute* is a New York-based research institute examining the social implications of AI. Its annual reports are an invaluable resource to monitor the concerns raised by developing and adopting new technologies.[15] For example, in 2020, the institute demonstrated how employers are increasingly using AI to monitor employees constantly. The *AI Now* 2019 report states:

---

[14] The "substitution" effects are dealt with in Chapter 12 on the effect of automation on labour markets.
[15] All reports can be accessed on the AI Now Institute's website: https://ainowinstitute.org/

"Algorithmic systems [. . .] control everything from interviewing and onboarding, to worker productivity, to wage setting and scheduling. Whether inside Amazon's fulfilment warehouses, behind the wheel of an Uber, or interviewing for their first job out of college, workers are increasingly managed through AI, with few protections or assurances. AI systems used for worker control and management are inevitably optimized to produce benefits for employers, often at great cost to workers. New research also suggests that lower-wage workers, especially workers of colour, will face greater harm from labour automation in the years to come, whether from displacement or from the degradation of work, as workers are increasingly tasked with monitoring and tending to automated systems rather than completing the tasks themselves".

Citizens may also be the target of companies' discriminatory policies, which are driven by algorithms, either by design or by accident, because they're reflective of the implicit prejudices of the developers. Sweeney (2013) found that a black-identifying name was 25% more likely to get an advertisement related to an arrest record on Google search. For example a Google search for the name Trevon Jones may yield neutral suggestions such as "looking for Trevon Jones?" or leading suggestions such as "Trevon Jones, Arrested?". Sweeney showed that you are more likely to get the latter type of suggestion with a black name. Even the relationship between the public sector and citizens can be reshaped by AI, exacerbating inequalities. Algorithms based on users' data have been used to monitor urban areas requiring intervention, for example, to fill a pothole in the street. However, this resulted in skewed intervention, leaving some communities underserved, since the information used was mainly related to a particular group of citizens, namely users with a smartphone who engaged with the local administration by sending out pictures of areas requiring intervention (Crawford K., 2013).

One of the areas where concerns for AI applications are more prominent is **facial recognition**. Facial recognition is the process through which a person's identity is verified by capturing, analysing, and comparing that person's face with a potentially large dataset containing biometric data of a specific population. A further application of the AI technology that powers facial recognition applications is **affect recognition**: this involves detecting an individual's emotional state based on the analysis of an individual's micro-expressions or tone of voice (AI Now Institute, 2019). Facial recognition may be used for security purposes at airports, to substitute for passwords when unlocking a user's own device, identify criminals on the run, or search for missing children. Affect recognition can potentially be used to screen applicants at a job interview, verify whether an audience (e.g. a class of students) is paying attention to the speaker, or capture non-verbal expressions of pain in hospitalized patients (AI Now Institute, 2019).

An initial problem with facial recognition technologies is that they still tend to be fallible, despite having potentially dramatic consequences for individual human rights. Face recognition software may yield more accurate results than if a human being was entrusted with the task of recognizing a face. Yet researchers have reported systematic biases leading to violations of human rights and discrimination of minorities (Hartzog W., 2018). Rhue (2018) finds that popular emotion-recognition software systematically assigns a relatively more negative emotional ranking to black individuals, regardless of their facial expression.

Even if design and implementational issues were addressed and a yet-to-be-discovered superior technology yielded unbiased results, facial and affect recognition pose deep questions regarding their potential effect on society. As pointed out by Hartzog (2018), facial recognition technology is a "Trojan horse" that, despite several benefits and efficiencies (for example, in terms of enhanced security), could lead society towards a dystopian future: one where people would not feel free to be themselves in public, where governments would have a powerful tool to identify and repress criticism, where businesses would be able to grasp consumers' inner feelings and manipulate them with precision, or where employers could exert absolute control over their employees. The experience of China offers a glimpse of such a dystopian future. The Chinese government rolled out an obligatory "Social Credit System" for all its citizens by 2020. In the Social Credit System, an algorithm ranks users of digital services based on their behaviour offline and online and that of the friends in their network. Citizens with a higher score receive many privileges, such as easier access to credit or speedier public administrative processes when applying for travelling abroad. The price to pay for citizens is to live in a state of perennial government surveillance.[16]

A related area of concern is the implication of the use of automated aerial robots, commonly known as **drones**. With facial recognition technologies, drones can be used for aerial surveillance: the government's drones may fly over a crowd protesting in the streets and provide the government with an accurate identification of every protester. Drones can also be used to spy on individuals on their back garden as well as by the military, by terrorists, or in a significant number of criminal activities. "Swarm" drone attacks pose an increasingly severe threat to airport security, for example. "Killer robots", automated weapons used to pursue the killing of a human being, are being increasingly used by military forces worldwide such as the US, China, Israel, South Korea, Russia, and the UK, generating widespread concerns about their implication for human rights. Killer robots hold the power to decide who ought to live or die, but without the features that affect human behaviours in those ethically charged situations, such as the feeling of responsibility, compassion, and moral judgement (Campaign to Stop Killer Robots, 2021). Those concerns explain why calls for an outright ban of killer robots are increasingly popular, including amongst policymakers (European Parliament, 2018).

---

[16] To know more about the Social Credit System in China, see Liang, et al. (2018).

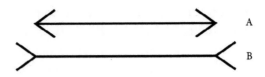

Figure 15.4 Muller-Lyer Illusion

15.2.3 AI bias and beyond

Biased datasets and biased technological development are crucial issues, often rooted at technology's inception.[17] A well-known issue with the **AI developer ecosystem** is that it does not reflect the demographic and cultural composition of the society where AI is embedded. The vast majority of developers behind the major globalized platforms are white males with a homogeneous cultural background (Harrison S., 2019). But those platforms are very popular across a wide global geographical area. Lack of representativeness is worrisome since a non-diverse environment inevitably replicates its own biases when de facto in charge of designing the infrastructure for a wider social setting.

Consider this simple illustration. Figure 15.4 is known as the "Muller-Lyer optical Illusion," from the name of the German psychologist who proposed it at the end of the nineteenth century. If I were to ask my students: *which segment is longer?* Virtually everybody in the room would reply "segment B". As it turns out, segments A and B are of exactly the same length. Most Western observers are tricked into believing that segment A is shorter because their brain has, since birth, been wired to assume that the size of segments with outward arrows is shorter than it really is and that the size of segments with inward arrows is longer than it really is.

In the 1960s, some South African anthropologists tested the Muller-Lyer illusion with members of a Zulu tribe, an ethnic group in southern Africa. The researchers were surprised to find that the Zulus did not fall for the illusion (Segall, et al., 1963). Show Figure 15.4 to a Zulu, and they would likely tell you that, indeed, segments A and B are of the same length. The reason is simple: European students are, from birth, surrounded by angles, and are thus used to inferences about the likely size of the squared objects they observe. The Zulu instead usually live in housing structures shaped like a round beehive with no square angles, so they have not been subconsciously programmed to extrapolate the length of the segment based on the arrows at either end.

The Muller-Lyer illusion illustrates how the nurturing environment we live in feeds into human judgement: we are hardly aware of the bias that conditions our world vision.[18] Moreover, even upon becoming aware of that bias, we are still

---

[17] On bias in AI, see for example: Osoba and Welser IV (2017). Leavy (2018) focuses specifically on gender bias.
[18] The 'nature vs. nurture' debate, or what is the impact of genes and that of the surrounding environment on human behaviour, is at the root of any science having humans as object of study: from philosophy to biology and from economics to anthropology and sociology. The related literature is therefore immense. I would thus limit

unlikely to self-correct or to be able to generate unbiased models that can become universal. Hence an inevitable step to addressing the bias of the AI programming ecosystem is to inject more diversity into it, allowing a diverse range of programmers to chip in, making it more representative of the society for which AI technologies are crafted.[19]

The concerns raised by narrow AI can, however, be even deeper. As with the case of facial recognition, let us assume that all narrow AI bias would one day vanish. No bias is a somewhat reasonable assumption to make: technology will become accurate to the maximum extent in the long term. Accuracy may not help, though, if the source of the problem does not lie in the composition of the data sample or the technology development process but, instead, reflects people's mentality or the structure of their society. Keep in mind that AI inevitably amplifies a society's unequal distribution of power. A good illustration is Google's "sentiment analysis," an AI-powered tool developed by Google to grasp the emotional charge of online discussions.[20] Google's sentiment analysis attributed a negative score/ranking to words such as "homosexual" or "Jew" (Thompson T., 2017). Unfortunately, this astonishing result was not due to biased technology and hence could not be easily "fixed." Instead, the technology accurately reflected that online chats are often riddled with derogative wording against minorities. In other words, the problem did not rest on the technology but the humans that the technology accurately analysed.

This observation leads to a fundamental question: should we aim for an "unbiased" AI and thus a neutral representation of society? Or should it instead be geared to correct society, for example, nudging fairer online conversations, even if this means introducing a little manipulation of the algorithm?

AI can bring the consequences of the existence of power asymmetries within a society to the extreme. Sophisticated algorithms may have strong economic (distributional) implications and fundamentally reshape human interaction. A critical underlying idea of algorithms is to be able to use a vast amount of data to anticipate better what could be the thoughts, needs, or preferences of human beings in their capacity as consumers, citizens, employees, or voters. This use of data allows the customization of supply of goods and services (see Chapter 5). Still, it also implies an **atomization of markets**: stretching this consideration to the maximum extent, each individual may become *a market in itself*, with its own individual features and a perfectly tailored supply.

Some individuals might be better off if algorithms allowed suppliers to grasp exactly who they are and what they want. The introduction of the Social Credit Score system in China, for example, finds support among those who would otherwise be

---

myself to suggest two favourite popular science readings of mine here, hoping to spark students' curiosity: Dawkins (2016) and Diamond (2013).

[19] Another problem with the current system is that programmers tend to come from developed economies; thus AI also exacerbate between countries (thanks to Marianna Wysocki for suggesting this point).

[20] Kiritchenko and Mohammad (2018) analyse gender and race bias in sentiment analysis.

unable to obtain a mortgage because they cannot offer enough collaterals to mitigate risks for the banks. Thanks to the Social Credit system, they can access credit by providing more accurate information about their online activity and the contacts in their network (this observation should sound familiar: check the discussion over the welfare effects of "price discrimination" in the appendix and Chapter 5). Other individuals may instead be worse-off: individuals with a higher probability of getting sick, for example, should expect their health insurance costs to rise with the use of AI technologies to refine insurers' ability to predict risk.[21]

By crafting the economy around each individuals' characteristics, AI directly challenges the principle of mutualization of risk between the members of society, questioning the fundamental principles on which it is based, such as respect of human rights and equality in opportunities. Without corrective measures, an AI-powered society is inherently polarized and possibly unstable.

Therefore, it is of utmost importance that the transposition of the values on which traditional societies are based on the new AI-powered society is not left in the hands of developers. Instead, this is the primary function of public policy, as we shall see in the following two sections.

15.3 Dilemmas for policymakers

It is fair to say that AI is a fantastic opportunity for the European economy. It can bring benefits to everybody: to citizens, businesses, and the public sector. Embracing the "AI revolution" is also an essential geostrategic move to make. Missing the "AI boat" while other economies are fully on-board (most prominently the US and China) could have catastrophic consequences for the competitiveness of the European economy. European companies would inevitably suffer the increased productivity of their competitors should they be left behind in the race for AI adoption.

At the same time, as we have seen in Section 15.2, AI can have profound destabilizing effects on society. That is why governments worldwide have increasingly been deploying "AI-strategies," as did the European Commission in 2018 (we will look at that closely in Section 15.4). An appropriately crafted AI strategy at the European level would thus be geared, on the one hand, towards fostering the development and uptake of AI in European countries and, on the other hand, towards addressing the social risks that come with it. Note that because AI markets tend to enjoy strong economies of scale and network economies, a supranational approach is often the most suitable to address these issues. That explains why the role of the European Union is so important in this context. Along with the significant impact of AI on the EU Single Market.

---

[21] For a general legal analysis of the implications of social credit systems, see Mac Síthigh and Siems (2019).

Before looking at the details of the set of actions that could fit an efficient AI strategy, let us pause a second to reflect on an important concept. Throughout the book, we have frequently been confronted with benefits and risks as two sides of the same coin when discussing technological innovation. Perhaps AI is a case where this contrast becomes more striking, given its inclination towards extremes: picture on one side of the coin "defeating cancer," and, on the other side, "dystopic government surveillance."

However, as we have seen often throughout this book, to a significant extent this is a false dichotomy, usually played up in discussions around the role of public policy by lobbies interested in defending their vested interests. Regulation defining the limits of applying new technologies may be seen as a potential disruption to innovation, for example. The reality is that addressing risks, if done correctly, can serve to stimulate the development and adoption of technology by reducing uncertainty and increasing trust. Likewise, working to facilitate investment in innovation can offer an opportunity to steer the evolution of technology towards a path that is compatible with society's values.

As an illustration, consider the Chinese Social Credit model, where safeguards for individuals' rights to privacy are minimal. And compare it with the European approach to personal data protection (see Chapter 5). Leaving aside the importance of protecting privacy *per se*, it could be argued that the Chinese economy has had a head start vis-à-vis European companies. The latter have access to significantly fewer data and must respect strict rules that constrain the use they can make of the data they obtain. For example, as we have seen in Chapter 5, the General Data Protection Regulation (GDPR) prevents the use of data for purposes that are different from the purpose for which the data subjects had originally given explicit consent to process. The advantage for non-privacy oriented jurisdictions may be real in the short term. However, an approach that neglects individual rights is hazardous in a fast-moving environment such as digital, where value-added of a service often comes from its ability to be tailored to individuals' preferences and needs. It is thus difficult to imagine a future of digital prosperity for countries that do not address issues related to the effect of technology on citizens' well-being early on in the development of new technologies. As we have seen, the GDPR is far from perfect. Yet its entry into force came in the immediate aftermath of the *Cambridge Analytica* scandal (Wired (2019)), and it came as a relief not only to citizens but also to the European business community, concerned that the drop in trust amongst users would slow down growth in the digital sector. Conversely, a Chinese Social Credit model may not only be subject to strong criticism from an ethical standpoint. It could also have long-term negative consequences on the Chinese digital economy, as it is difficult to predict how market demand for digital services will react should the tension between users and misuse of technology (by the public or private sector) blow up at a later stage.

For ease of exposition, let us group potential policy action for AI in two broad categories:[22]

    a. policies to stimulate AI innovation, development, and adoption, focusing on the *economic impact* of AI, and

    b. policies to address the risks of AI, focusing on its *social impact*.

15.3.1 Policies to stimulate AI innovation, development, and adoption

AI can be at the cutting edge of a country's technological development. To stimulate investment in AI, that country needs **digital infrastructure**. It requires widespread access to high power **computing** facilities, **connectivity**, and **data**. Access to computing facilities can be facilitated by supporting the creation of AI "innovation hubs" or one-stop-shop local organizations pulling together resources from different actors and responding to an aggregate demand of, in particular, smaller companies that cannot afford to invest in their own digital infrastructure. In Chapter 4, we have seen how the deployment of crucial wired and wireless infrastructures can be fostered through direct financial support, regulatory action, more intra-European coordination on wireless spectrum management, and demand pulling initiatives. Chapter 5 has looked at initiatives to favour the flow of data between actors and across the territories. **Data pools**, initiatives to share data vertically and horizontally across the value chain, and regulatory intervention to favour interoperability, data portability and access are valuable solutions to maximize the data available for AI applications in the economy. Legal clarity in key areas, such as the liability of actors involved in the data-powered application's value chain, can affect long-term investment and growth.

Likewise, we have seen in Chapter 6 the importance of opening up the public sector with P2B open data initiatives, which can create significant opportunities for AI developers. Ensuring a technologically **safe** and secure AI environment is equally important. AI is both offering new tools to cyber-attackers to perpetrate their criminal activity and creating new vulnerabilities. For example, attackers can trick algorithms by directly altering the dataset upon which they are relying. The measures that we covered in Chapter 7 for effective public policy action for cybersecurity are, therefore, instrumental for AI development too.

Support for AI research can take the form of facilitating coordination and information sharing between research institutions across Europe, leveraging the European scale, for example in terms of access to broader and more heterogeneous datasets. The European AI research context also requires deploying efficient

---

[22] Acemoğlu and Restrepo (2020) make the case for a joint approach: we should support the development and adoption of the "right" kind of AI, namely: the one which does not entail adverse social welfare effects.

frameworks that would strengthen its links with AI's commercial aspects without research being pre-empted by them. A traditionally significant limitation for technological research in Europe is its inability to have a commercial outcome, despite its ability to reach the highest quality standards. What is needed is more multi-directional communication between researchers, the business, and the public sector. That can be achieved through public action, for example supporting coordination tools at any geographical level, such as European, national, regional, and local *research–market* platforms. Finally, public support can prompt more research where there appears to be a stronger need based on the European economic context, of which European policymakers should have a better picture. For example, research streams aimed to address the challenge of relaxing AI dependence on data sample size (such as on "small data", transfer learning, augmented data learning, hybrid learning models (OECD, 2019c)) can be extremely valuable in a context where access to data is structurally limited (as is the case for small- and medium-sized enterprises (SMEs)).

Direct **financial support for AI adoption** by companies can be contemplated, particularly in the case of smaller, financially constrained companies, to internalize the positive externality (see the appendix) that AI may generate. AI and, generally speaking, *automation* can create a virtuous *data-multiplier* effect: the more automated are production processes, the more data are collected, the more data are potentially shared and available in the economy, the more powerful AI applications become, and the greater the potential productivity gains. Likewise, promoting the digitization of the public sector (see Chapter 6) would arguably generate more data to feed into the AI economy.

A survey of business managers by Gartner (2017a) found that a major obstacle to the adoption of AI within companies is a lack of access to the necessary **technical skills**. As shown in Figure 15.5, more than half of the interviewed managers claimed that "lack of necessary skills" is the biggest roadblock to AI adoption. Skills scarcity is a problem that is not unique to Europe: in 2017, the New York Times reported that fewer than ten thousand people in the world possess the skills that are required to perform advanced AI research (The New York Times, 2017). Therefore, public policy aimed to create, nurture, and attract AI talent is extremely important to ensure AI market's growth. All the policy options that we have analysed in Chapter 12, such as educational, life-long learning, and reskilling policies, can have a decisive impact on AI development in Europe.

Finally, policies that preserve or stimulate competition in the digital environment can trigger an expansion of the AI economy. The **enforcement of competition policy**, in particular, can prompt companies to innovate and invest more in new, AI-powered technologies. For one, it creates an incentive to do so by unleashing competitive pressure on market players: if they do not invest in AI, they may suffer competition and potentially be forced out of the market. But the enforcement of competition policy also ensures access to crucial inputs for the development

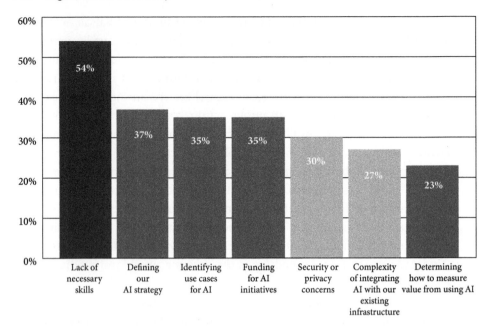

Figure 15.5 Answers to the question: 'What is the biggest roadblock to AI adoption?' (Share of respondents, %, 2017)

https://venturebeat.com/2017/11/04/the-biggest-roadblock-in-ai-adoption-is-a-lack-of-skilled-workers/

of AI-powered services and products, even if market counterparts hold significant market power (for a basic review of competition policy within the digital environment, see Chapter 8).

Competition policy enforcement places itself right at the intersection between AI economic policies and AI social policies. Consider the case of discrimination: competition between market players is possibly the strongest weapon against algorithmic-empowered discrimination since it limits the ability of suppliers to extract value from users to increase their profits. Consider, for example, the insurance market: AI can enable insurers to accurately predict potential customers' likelihood to get sick, as we have seen in the previous section. But if the insurance market is strongly competitive, insurers have a lower ability to leverage their AI-based superior knowledge to force high prices on customers. Thus, competition is, in a way, the best antidote to discriminatory AI (Motta, M., 2004). Similar effects can be obtained through ex-ante regulation aimed at increasing the level of competition in the market (see, for example, the case of the Digital Markets Act, discussed in Chapter 8).

15.3.2 Policies to address the risk of AI

Tackling the social risks posed by AI requires defining comprehensive ethical frameworks, extending the safeguards of the "analogical" world to the world of automation, and, where necessary, creating new rules to tackle novel issues as well as the legal tools to enforce them.

Progress in AI can have far-reaching consequences on the evolution of societies, affecting the quality of the relationship between human beings, as we have seen in the previous two sections. Thus, an overarching goal of policies dedicated to AI should be to steer the development of technology to protect and enhance the welfare of humanity. Using the wording of the High-Level Expert Group on Artificial Intelligence (European Commission, 2019g) set up by the European Commission (see further below, Section 15.4), AI needs to be "human-centric." To pursue that goal, a number of areas of action can be identified.

AI quality standards can be mandated. Standards may refer to privacy protection (see Chapter 5) or degree of **security** (see Chapter 7). Standards can tackle the issue of "black box" AI, whereby observers are not fully capable of grasping the functioning of AI and monitoring algorithmic processing, particularly in the case of neuronal "deep learning" networks. It may be possible to address the black box issue by fostering AI systems' transparency, explicability, and accountability. However, establishing criteria for transparency can be extremely tricky, given the structural features of machine learning. Doshi-Velez and Kim (2017) point out the absence of a consensus among experts on what "explicable AI" should look like. But they identify the cases in which explanation is needed (recall from Chapter 5 that, while mandated by the GDPR, explicability may be not considered necessary for the protection of human rights). According to the two researchers, explanation is not necessary where there are no significant consequences for unacceptable results or where the system can be trusted because the problem is sufficiently well-studied and validated in real applications. Conversely, explanation may be necessary if the problem tackled by the algorithm cannot be completely formalized. For example, preventing discrimination through accurate programming may not be feasible, as it may be the case that "fairness" (or absence of discrimination) is too abstract a concept to be encoded in the system. Hence, transparency is needed to correct a bias that the AI system cannot independently tackle from its inception.

Where possible, however, AI technologies could be compelled to be "**lawful by design**", and hence algorithms would be created by developers to minimize the likelihood that they would break the law. An illustrative example is algorithms prevented from fostering collusion by helping companies converge on the same (non-competitive) price levels. AI quality standards may also define the level of involvement of humans in the oversight of the algorithms. So that humans do not lose their autonomy vis-à-vis the technology and maintain a degree of responsibility throughout the implementation process, not only at the development or outcome stage. Approaches to human oversight include (European Commission, 2019g):

- **Human-in-the-Loop**, whereby humans can intervene at any time in every decision cycle of the algorithm
- **Human-on-the-Loop**, whereby humans can intervene during the design and monitor the whole process

- **Human-in-Command**, whereby humans can oversee the whole activity of the system and decide where and when to use, or not to use it.

A human-centric technology should never be endorsed with the responsibility of accomplishing a whole set of jobs without a parallel human fallback. Likewise, humans should not lose their ability to perform tasks that technology helps them carry out more efficiently. First, this would entail a loss of their ability to control and understand the process. Second, this would exacerbate the dependency of humans on technology, increasing the risk of harmful effects in case of technology's malfunctioning or breakdown. A dramatic example is offered by an airplane crash where 228 people lost their lives. On 1 June 2009, the Air France 447 crashed into the Atlantic Ocean because the plane hit a column of ice crystals in the sky, which induced the autopilot to be turned off. The ex-post assessment of the incident points to a human mistake, which would have been avoidable if the pilots had received enough training to replace the technology in case of its failure. **Human oversight** entails fostering complementarity with AI technologies, which are to be conceived to augment human abilities rather than fully substitute them. Surgeon robots would always need a surgeon. Medical software would need radiologists. Algorithms filtering platform content would need a reviser to complement and validate their selection. AI-powered courts decisions would need a judge taking responsibility for the process and its outcome. A self-driven car would need a human who could potentially take control of it. Human oversight principles must include periodic tests and retraining to ensure that humans would be able to perform a task in case of a malfunctioning in the technology.

Public authorities should monitor the development of AI technologies, anticipating the likely impact if introduced in specific social contexts and evaluating the impact ex-post to learn from implemented practices. Calo and Crawford (2016) propose the adoption of a methodology based on a systematic **social-system analysis**. In this model, researchers and experts with different backgrounds and expertise, representatives from collective associations, and actors from the public and private sectors should systematically evaluate the social and economic impact of the introduction of AI-powered technologies, for different communities, through different dimensions of analysis: economic, ethical, anthropological, sociological, and historical. Consider, for example, the introduction of the use of facial recognition software by local police in a specific geographical area. A social-system analysis would entail tackling the question of effect from a comprehensive set of angles for all affected community members.

Public policy can provide **support to independent research programmes** investigating AI societal implications. Support can take the form of financial aid or coordination between researchers or research institutions through the establishment of AI societal research networks. Note, however, that the research community may be affected by the same problem that we observed in Section 15.2 for the AI development ecosystem: it is hardly representative of the demographic composition of the society it aims to study. Therefore, public intervention should be steered to tackle the issue of representation, incentivizing the creation of a richer, more diverse development and research environment for AI to minimize the risk of biased outcomes.

A final comment relates to **international initiatives**. Consider, for example, the possibility of establishing an outright ban on autonomous weapons or a concerted action to draft universally valid principles for an "ethical" AI.[23] There is undoubtedly merit in pursuing a coordinated global action to define a consistent ethical framework for artificial intelligence to be observed worldwide. As we have seen, the reach of AI application is global, despite it being the expression of a tiny and homogenous cultural minority of developers. However, the risk is that such a globalized approach to AI ethics would be monopolized by dominant powers: the US, Europe, and China, in the first instance. Therefore, any global ethical code for AI should not only attempt to equally involve perspectives from different cultural, religious, and philosophical backgrounds,[24] it should also allow enough flexibility to be adapted "locally," where necessary, while still being entirely consistent with the overarching principle of a "human-centric" technology respectful of universal human rights.

15.4 The European Union perspective

Artificial intelligence is capturing the imagination of governments around the world. Commentators point to an "AI arms race," driven mainly by the polarization of trade relationships and an increasingly tense technological rivalry between China and the US. Hogart (2018) describes the emergence of a phenomenon he dubs "AI Nationalism," whereby countries will increasingly invest in AI to achieve a "technological supremacy." They would do so by nurturing their data economy or supporting infrastructure deployment and subsidizing and protecting their AI champions, blocking takeovers by foreign firms, and competing to attract the best AI talents. A closely related expression, "digital sovereignty", has come to indicate a country's efforts to limit its technological dependence on foreign countries, as we have seen in Chapter 1. Digital sovereignty applies particularly to AI, where hardware is as important as software. The semiconductor sector plays a critical strategic role in determining a country's likelihood of success in the AI race. Sophisticated AI software running on generic hardware tends to be inefficient. The future of AI development is dedicated hardware: on the *cloud,* the *edge,* and the *fog* (see Chapter 4). The major technological companies (such as Facebook, Baidu, Tencent, Amazon, Google, Microsoft), venture capitalists, investors, but also governments, such as China and the US, are well-aware of the importance of semiconductors. Thus, they invest massively in AI chips, making this a fundamental piece of their AI

---

[23] On the role of AI in warfare, see Cummings (2017).

[24] A worthy initiative in that respect is the one launched by the global engineering organization IEEE in 2016. See https://standards.ieee.org/industry-connections/ec/autonomous-systems.html

strategies.[25] The importance of chips explains the technological basis of the strategic geopolitical role played by Taiwan: both the US and Chinese "champions," Apple and Huawei, respectively, heavily rely on Taiwan's important semiconductor sector (Kirk H., 2020).

A significant number of countries around the world have developed or are developing *AI strategies*. According to the OECD (2019c), national AI strategies are generally focused on exploiting AI to foster the economy's productivity and competitiveness. National AI strategies may include the following priorities:

- increasing investment in AI skills
- the deployment of policies to attract talents
- supporting AI research
- identifying key sectors, such as transportation, healthcare, and public services, where the demand for AI-powered applications should be incentivized
- plans for massive infrastructure investment (connectivity, computing facilities, data facilities)
- supporting companies' uptake of AI
- and laying out legal and ethical frameworks to prevent social harm.

A strategy that is particularly compelling for the breadth of its ambition, as well as for its significance from a geopolitical perspective, is the one released by China's State Council in July 2017 titled "New Generation Artificial Intelligence Plan." The strategy formally recognizes the AI sector as a national priority. It identifies an ultimate goal for 2030: for China to become the world-leading AI power (Ding, 2018) (see Table 15.1 for an overview). The launch of the Chinese strategy has sparked fear worldwide, and it has undoubtedly incentivized European countries to accelerate their efforts to develop a robust technological sector. The goals of the plan set into motion by China's "Sputnik moment" (see Section 15.1) appears realistic to many commentators. China has a vibrant AI research outcome, with more AI papers published than anywhere else globally, a booming AI start-up ecosystem attracting significant external investment, and extensive infrastructure deployment supported by the government. Above all, China can count on a very favourable data environment, where companies and public institutions can access vast amounts of personal and non-personal data with fewer regulatory restrictions than in Europe. And it can also benefit from less cultural resistance: studies have demonstrated that Chinese citizens tend to attach less value to privacy than Europeans, for example.[26] The fact that the Chinese ambition for AI world leadership has excellent potential to bear fruit is all the more worrisome for the EU because the Chinese "AI model" (of which the Social Credit system is a striking example) collides with the EU's own

---

[25] My gratitude to Marco Ceccarelli for suggesting this point.

[26] For example, see McKinsey (2016) surveying car drivers and finding that 93% of Chinese respondents would be willing to share location data with car manufacturers to improve cars' performance, compared to 65% of German drivers and 72% of US drivers.

Table 15.1 Main Goals of the Chinese Artificial Intelligence Development Plan[27]

2020	2025	2030
Develop the next generation of AI technologies on big data, swarm intelligence, hybrid enhanced intelligence, and autonomous intelligence systems. Gather the world's leading talents together. Establish initial frameworks for laws, regulations, ethics, and policy.	Become the primary driver for China's industrial advances and economic transformation. Use AI in a wide range of fields – manufacturing, medicine, national defence. Become a leading player in research and development. Finalize laws, regulations, ethical norms, policies, and safety mechanisms.	Become the world's premier AI innovation centre. Develop major breakthroughs in research and development. Expand the use of AI through social governance and national defence. Create leading AI innovation and personnel training bases.

Source. "Next Generation Artificial Intelligence Development Plan", The State Council, The People's Republic of China

model, which is based on the protection of values lying at the core of the European project, such as privacy and non-discrimination. Moreover, being a first-mover in such a novel space, where rules are in the making, can yield considerable advantages, such as the opportunity to generate global standards that the whole world may end up following, as seen in the case of the GDPR (see Chapter 5). The Chinese AI strategy is, in other words, a potent source of pressure for the EU to get a move on in the AI space.

15.4.1 The European Union AI strategy

Squeezed between the AI race, pitted against its global competitors, and spurred by its own ambition to exploit AI as a wonder-tool to boost the productivity of its economy, the EU has taken an increasingly active role for AI in recent years. Most of the Digital Single Market initiatives, such as the free flow of data regulation, the telecom code, or the new skills agenda, are functional to developing key inputs for AI. These subjects are covered in previous chapters. Hence this chapter focuses on the ad hoc initiatives specifically designed for artificial intelligence. In particular:

- The European Commission Communication: "**Artificial Intelligence for Europe**" (April 2018) (European Commission, 2018k)
- The "**Ethics Guidelines for Trustworthy Artificial Intelligence**," prepared by the High-Level Group on Artificial Intelligence (April 2019) (European Commission, 2019g)
- The European Commission's "**White Paper on Artificial Intelligence**: a European approach to excellence and trust" (February 2020) (European Commission, 2020s).

The Communication "Artificial Intelligence for Europe" defines the **European Strategy for AI** and could be considered the European equivalent to the Chinese "New Generation Artificial Intelligence Plan." It is structured in three pillars:

1. Boosting EU technology and industrial capacity
2. Addressing AI's socioeconomic impact
3. Ensuring an appropriate human-centric ethical and legal framework.

The first pillar looks at AI as a tool to boost the competitiveness of the EU economy, enhancing the performance of the private and the public sector. The key measure proposed concerns stepping up investment, with the European Commission aiming to mobilize more than €20 billion from EU funds, Member States, and the private sector by the end of 2020. Note that, according to Statista (2017), in 2017, the total investment and financing in the Chinese AI sector was already above €24 billion. The contribution by the European Commission was set to be an investment increase by 80% between 2018 and 2020, tapping in the Horizon 2020 fund. The additional investment was designed to support research and innovation in AI technologies and funding AI research excellence centres, providing financial incentives for AI uptake across Europe, particularly by SMEs and public administrations. The longer-term perspective included measures to support the data economy, such as creating an industrial data platform to facilitate data sharing between companies—a measure incorporated in the EU's data strategy, as we have seen in Chapter 5. Such measures would finance the creation of *digital innovation hubs*, specialized on AI technologies and designed to provide small companies with access to cutting-edge expertise with an "AI-on-demand" platform. This latter measure, in particular, appeared far-fetched, as it assumed that the European Commission could leverage a superior knowledge in AI than that available to market players in the sector.

The second pillar is a very general overview of AI's disruptive potential from a social point of view (bear in mind that the European Union has limited competence regarding social policy compared to the Member States—see Chapter 12 for a discussion). It describes several initiatives prompted by the European Commission to support Member States to adjust labour markets and educational systems to address the disruption. In particular: the creation of dedicated retraining schemes; gathering analysis and expert inputs to anticipate changes in the labour market; and encouraging business-education partnerships.

The third pillar is possibly the most original and intriguing. It lays down the basis for the European Commission's efforts to design an ethical and legal framework to protect and empower individuals in the AI space. The plan of the European Commission entailed setting up a "European AI Alliance" to draft AI ethics guidelines. The alliance was intended to be an inclusive multi-stakeholder platform representative of European markets and society. The aim was to address some of the biases that we have identified in Section 15.2, although it is fair to say that open consultative platforms often tend to be dominated by the most powerful market players, thanks to the deeper resource pockets they can tap into. The Commission also envisaged issuing guidance on the interpretation of the product liability directive (see Chapter 5) and supporting research in the development of explainable AI. Finally, the Commission committed to improving its monitoring of AI development and uptake in Europe, encouraging collaboration between Member States, and taking the lead on international coordination for a global approach to the ethical challenges brought about by AI. As a first follow up, in December 2018, the EU Member States agreed on a Coordinated Plan on artificial intelligence titled "Made in Europe" (European Commission, 2018l).

In April 2019, the "**AI high-level expert group**," a group of experts nominated by the European Commission to steer the process, in cooperation with the European AI Alliance, released a revised version of their "Ethics Guidelines for Trustworthy Artificial Intelligence" (European Commission, 2019g). The final guidelines followed the publication of the first draft of the guidelines in December 2018, which received more than 500 comments in a public consultation). The European Commission endorsed the guidelines in its Communication "Building Trust in Human-Centric Artificial Intelligence" (European Commission, 2019h), making them the de facto ethical reference for AI in Europe. The guidelines are directed to stakeholders involved in the design, development, deployment, implementation, or use of AI and those affected by AI development, including businesses, the public sector, research institutions, and individuals. However, the guidelines are non-binding; they do not create any new legal obligations and, consequently, do not envisage any enforcement mechanism to ensure their application. Nevertheless, they can be considered a good starting point for defining an effective, ethical AI framework in Europe. They paved the way for the European Commission's proposed AI regulation (see further below) in April 2021.

The guidelines identify three key general features that a "trustworthy" AI must possess. AI must be:

(1) **lawful** – respecting all applicable laws and regulations
(2) **ethical** – respecting ethical principles and values
(3) **robust** – both from a technical perspective while taking into account its social environment.

These principles are translated into a set of critical concrete requirements that must be satisfied for AI applications to be considered trustworthy (Figure 15.6). The requirements are:

- *Human agency and oversight.* This requirement implies that AI applications should have user's well-being at the core of their system, ensuring the respect of fundamental rights and allowing appropriate control and oversight by humans
- *Technical robustness and safety.* AI applications should be reliable and secure. They should guarantee that their outcome is accurate and can be replicated

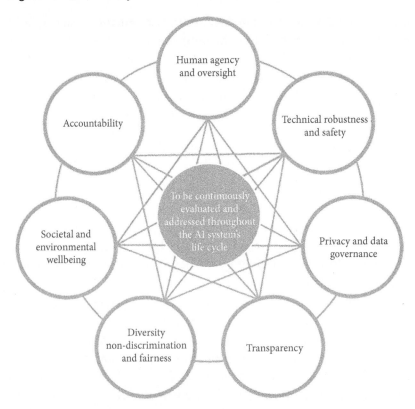

Figure 15.6 The interrelationship between the seven requirements
https://ec.europa.eu/newsroom/dae/document.cfm?doc_id=6041

- *Privacy and data governance.* Privacy and data protection should be ensured from inception to the end of any AI-powered process. Particular attention should be dedicated to ensuring the quality and integrity of the data used. In addition, access to data should be adequately regulated
- *Transparency.* AI applications must be traceable: it must be possible to observe how the process that led to a specific outcome unfolded. It should also be possible to explain the final outcome or decision to the maximum extent. And the features and limitations of the application should be clearly explained to stakeholders
- *Diversity, non-discrimination, and fairness.* To minimize bias, applications should be designed by diverse teams. They should envisage mechanisms that ensure large and representative participation, particularly by citizens
- *Societal and environmental well-being.* AI applications should consider not only their impact on the individual but also on the environment and society as a whole
- *Accountability.* AI applications should envisage a framework for allocating responsibility relative to their system, process, and outcome. Accountability can be ensured through mechanisms that allow AI applications to be audited, in

particular by external third parties. Adequate redress should be ensured to those negatively affected by AI applications.

Overall, the requirements appear sensible and consistent with the issues that we have identified in the previous sections. However, the guidelines have an intrinsic limitation: their *voluntary nature*. It is unclear why stakeholders would have the incentives to adhere to the guidelines. Particularly where they would entail a profit loss, for example because the scope of their data analytics would be further restricted beyond the existing constraints posed by GDPR. Besides that, the requirements tend to mix ethical imperatives with desirable features in AI, which could also be driven by market dynamics when there is no apparent general market failure that prevents them from arising. For example, AI developers would seem to have all the incentives to develop "technically robust" applications already: if they failed to do so, their business would fail to achieve its purpose. Conversely, possibly the most effective requirements are "transparency" and "accountability", as external evaluation creates pressure on AI developers and AI users to increase the quality of the AI systems they develop or rely on.

Aware of the limitations of the self-regulatory approach, in February 2020, the European Commission released its "**White Paper on Artificial Intelligence: a European approach to excellence and trust**" (European Commission, 2020s). In the White Paper, the Commission lays down several policy options for AI's trustworthy and secure development in Europe. The White Paper was designed to instigate a debate among stakeholders, who were encouraged to provide feedback.

The White Paper is structured around two building blocks: (a) actions to create an "ecosystem of excellence" around the AI value chain, and (b) actions to create an "ecosystem of trust." While the wording may be changing between different Commission's initiatives, students may realize that the structure of the thinking around AI remains the same: a set of actions to maximize AI's opportunities for the economy alongside a parallel set of actions to protect citizens from potential social disruption.

As regards the "ecosystem of excellence," foreseen actions include:

- the creation of excellence and testing centres combining European, national, and private investment; initiatives in support of reskilling, upskilling, and, in particular, attracting the best AI minds in the world to European universities
- a commitment to having at least one digital innovation hub per Member State with a high degree of specialization in AI; €100 million equity financing for innovative development in AI and a promise to scale up investment subject to the final agreement on the EU Multiannual Financial Framework (European Commission, 2020t)
- the set-up of a new PPP or "Public-Private Partnership" on AI, data, and robotics; incentives to promote the adoption of AI within the public sector

- and, finally, the promise to engage in international fora to increase cooperation among "like-minded" countries but also with other global players.

Regarding the "ecosystem of trust", the white paper proposes some possible changes in the EU legislative framework to address the risks posed by AI for the respect of fundamental rights and for individuals' safety and adjust the current liability framework. In particular, the European Commission suggests that the EU legislative framework should be updated to:

- ensure the effective application of EU law, for example in terms of enforcement of transparency rules
- extend the scope of current EU law to ensure that not only products but also services, are fully covered by EU safety legislation
- address risks generated by the overtime evolution of software (for example, with updates) that could not be foreseen at the time the AI application was marketed
- ensure certainty in the allocation of responsibility along the value chain
- adapt the concept of safety to account for the new risks generated by AI (such as cyber-threats and personal security risks).

Most notably, the White Paper puts forward a **risk-based approach**, which would determine the scope for the future EU regulatory framework. The idea is to identify AI applications that are to be considered "high risk" based on two cumulative criteria:

(1) AI is used in a critical sector where the magnitude of harm for society in case things go wrong is significant (for example, health sector, transport, public sector)
(2) and AI is used in such a way that risks are intrinsically higher (for example, during a surgery).

On this basis, AI used during a delicate surgery may be considered "high risk," while AI used to facilitate appointment scheduling in a hospital may not be. The Commission further suggests two illustrations of high risk AI applications: AI used to screen applicants for job opportunities and AI used for remote biometric identification (e.g. facial recognition applications).

With the White Paper, the European Commission took a new step towards a legal framework that would effectively bind market players. This was an important initiative, given, as we have seen previously, the lack of incentives for market players to comply with a non-binding ethical framework.

In April 2021, the European Commission finally proposed its **Artificial Intelligence Act** (European Commission, 2021). The Artificial Intelligence Act is an EU regulation: if adopted by the EU legislators, it would become enforceable everywhere in the EU27. The proposal follows the risk-based approach proposed in the White Paper.

It identifies specific AI uses that *can never* be accepted:

- governments' social credit systems (similar to the ones used in China and described above)
- the manipulation of a person's behaviour through subliminal techniques with a high likelihood to cause physical or psychological harm
- the exploitation of vulnerabilities of a specific group of persons due to their age or physical or mental disability
- real-time remote biometric identification systems in publicly accessible spaces. With the notable exceptions of: targeted search for potential victims of crime (such as missing children); the prevention of imminent threats to security such as in the case of terrorism; the identification of serious criminal offences.

The use of high-risk AI applications can instead be accepted if specific requirements are met. The high-risk category encompasses AI use in these areas:

- Biometric identification
- Management and operation of critical infrastructure
- Education and vocational training
- Recruitment, promotion, or termination of employment relationships
- Management of access to essential public and private resources
- Law-enforcement
- Immigration and border control
- Administration of justice and democratic processes.

The obligations to be satisfied by high-risk AI systems include:

- **The establishment of a risk management system**. This should consist of a continuous iterative process to be carried on throughout the whole life-cycle of the AI system. It should aim to identify and mitigate known and foreseeable risks.
- **The use of high-quality data where bias is minimized**. Training, validation, and testing data sets should be "*relevant, representative, free of errors and complete*".
- **Transparency guarantees**. Users must be able to interpret the system's outcome and use it appropriately. The proposal emphasizes the need to provide extensive information on the process, quality, and potential limitations of the AI system.
- **Human oversight**. Appropriate human–machines interface tools should be established to allow a natural person to oversee the use of the AI system, with the aim to minimize risks to health, safety, or fundamental rights.
- **Guarantees of high accuracy, robustness, and cybersecurity**.

The proposal indicates that enforcement should be carried over by Member States' national authorities (such as data protection authorities) under the coordination and supervision of an EU body called **European Artificial Intelligence Board** (the body's role echoes that of BEREC, the EU body responsible for telecom regulation, see Chapter 4). Fines for non-compliance can be as high as 6% of company global turnover. Also notable is the proposed establishment of an **EU database** that would register all high-risk AI applications used in Europe in an effort to increase transparency and public monitoring of AI developments and risks.

Undoubtedly, the AI Act proposal was a needed step by the European Commission for all the reasons that we have explored at length in this chapter. The Commission's proposed pragmatic approach to allow the concrete implementation of ethical principles is particularly commendable. Likewise, enforcement with adequate penalty measures, transparency, and coordination at the EU level all seem excellent and necessary features for an AI framework to be effective. However, the proposal has significant margins of improvements. For example, the obligations for high-risk applications are not always clearly identified. It is unclear, for example, what a "foreseeable" risk refers to in highly complex and fast-evolving environments. Imagine a worker subject to emotional monitoring through a high-risk AI technology. Can the long-term risk for the worker's mental well-being be considered foreseeable? It is, moreover, doubtful whether clear-cut boundaries can be established in the AI space, where issues with data or processing can easily spill over from one application to the other. Imagine an AI application used in a general research setting—possibly considered low risk—which ended up affecting the use of AI in a high-risk setting, such as in epidemic control (Nguyen, et al., 2020). Conversely, some requirements do not appear to be clearly mapped into well-defined market failures.[28] Accuracy or robustness requirements relate to AI quality features and may be redundant. If AI systems become more transparent (thanks to the other requirements imposed on high-risk AI systems), markets may efficiently select the most robust and accurate AI applications without the need for regulation.

Finally, the European Commission's proposal may be too optimistic as regards the role that regulation can play in mitigating harm. Some applications, such as biometric recognitions, may have dangerous implications in the context where they are used, even if technology would be perfectly unbiased, transparent, robust, and accurate (as we have seen in Section 15.2). More than carving out exceptions or imposing strict requirements on such technologies, the EU legislators should thus consider whether it would not simply be better to ban the use of those technologies from the outset.

****

---

[28] Readers may note that the 2019 Ethics Guidelines described above had the same issue.

15.5 Case Study: artificial intelligence against breast cancer

In 2020, 2.3 million women worldwide received a breast cancer diagnosis, and almost 700,000 deaths linked to breast cancer were recorded. At an early stage, breast cancer is localized and asymptomatic. However, if undetected, cancer can progress, invading surrounding breast tissue and ultimately spread to the rest of the body. Breast cancer treatment can be very effective, but its efficacy crucially depends on the timing of diagnosis. If breast cancer is detected before it has spread, it can be cured. Radiologists play a crucial role in cancer screening programs. They analyse a vast amount of images from mammography, breast ultrasound, or magnetic resonance imaging (MRI) every day, under pressure. An artificial intelligence-powered software developed by Siemens and called "syngo.Breast Care" helps radiologists at Radboud University Medical Center in the Netherlands to process images at a faster speed and higher level of accuracy. Siemens' algorithm scores images according to the likelihood of malignancy. It reduces the workload of radiologists by automatically attributing to each case a priority rank and improving diagnostics through interactive, colour-coded lesions scoring in the processed images. It has been shown that thanks to artificial intelligence, radiologists can be 15% to 20% faster in performing their evaluations. A software called "Mirai" and developed by a PhD student at MIT, Adam Yala, has been found to be more accurate than the usual statistical models used by practitioners to assess cancer likelihood: 42% of patients who developed cancer in five years were flagged as high risk by Mirai, as opposed to 23% with the most accurate of the standard statistical models.

More information on syngo.Breast Care can be found here:
https://www.siemens-healthineers.com/mammography/reading-reporting/syngo-breastcare

More information on Mirai can be found here:
https://news.mit.edu/2021/robust-artificial-intelligence-tools-predict-future-cancer-0128

15.6 Review questions

- What is the difference between "narrow artificial intelligence" and "broad artificial intelligence"? Illustrate your answer with real-life cases or examples of your own (do not use the examples proposed in the book).
- What would be the consequences for a country's economy if that country would call itself out of the "AI global race"? What role does AI play from a geopolitical point of view?
- Which EU policies that are not explicitly targeting artificial intelligence, as such, can have the strongest impact on AI development and uptake in Europe? Why?

- Does reducing bias in data help address discrimination by AI powered-application? Justify and explain your answer.
- Can adopting an "ethical approach" to AI (including a regulation aiming at curbing AI's social risk) affect a country's likelihood to innovate in that space? Justify and explain your answer.

Microeconomics: A Toolkit

Abstract

This appendix helps readers lacking a background in microeconomics navigate the technical concepts and terminology I have used in this book. By no means does it attempt to be exhaustive, covering all economic concepts that could be applied to analyse and describe digital markets' dynamics.[1] However, it can suffice to help non-economists grasp the intuition behind the given explanations throughout the book.

A.1 Supply, demand, and market equilibrium

In microeconomics, markets are often described in terms of the relationship between the supply of a particular good or service (let us call it: *the product*) and its demand. In their most basic theoretical shape, supply and demand in a market are defined by two curves representing how much of the product is up for sale or demanded for at different price levels (Figure A.1).

The market's aggregate supply curve is given by the sum of all the products that are up for sale by all sellers on the market; the market's aggregate demand curve is given by the sum of all potential buyers' purchasing intentions. Generally speaking, for the majority of products, when the price increases, the quantity supplied follows (that is why the supply curve in Figure A.1 is upward sloped) while the quantity demanded decreases (the demand curve in Figure A.1 is downward sloped).

When supply and demand match (point E*), the market is in equilibrium: a quantity of the product Q* is sold and a price P* is paid for each unit of the product by the buyers to the sellers.

Economists have a way to qualify the value which is produced by the market at the equilibrium.

The **dark grey triangle** in Figure A.1 represents the gain for sellers, the **profit**. The supply curve suggests that at any point of quantity smaller than Q*, there are sellers willing to sell for a lower price than P* (possibly because that price was still above their unit production costs). The difference between

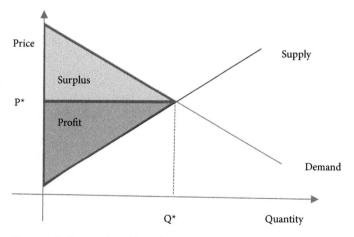

Figure A.1 Demand and Supply

---

[1] A classic textbook for microeconomics at graduate level is Mas-Colell, et al., (1995); the fundamental textbook reference for industrial organization is Tirole (1988).

P* and the price at which smaller quantities could have been sold times the total quantity sold corresponds to the area of the dark grey triangle. That is the value produced by the market and enjoyed by sellers.

The **grey triangle** instead represents the gain for buyers, their **surplus**. The demand curve suggests that at any point of quantity smaller than Q*, there are buyers willing to buy at a higher price than P*. The difference between that price (what buyers would have been willing to pay) and P* (what actually buyers pay, since that is the market equilibrium) times the total quantity purchased corresponds to the area of the grey triangle. That is the value generated by the market and enjoyed by the buyers.

The **elasticity** of the demand and supply curves gives a sense of how buyers and sellers respond to price increases by affecting the curves' steepness. If a curve is very steep, it means that it is not so elastic. Conversely, if it tends to be flat, it means that it is very elastic (with respect to price).

An elastic demand curve implies that, when price is slightly increased, many buyers will drop out and not buy the product. If the curve were inelastic, then price increases are absorbed by buyers with no great consequence on the quantity purchased. Sellers that face an elastic demand have, in other words, much less power in setting the price of the product they sell compared to the lucky ones who face an inelastic demand.

Naturally, the one described above is a very stylised abstraction that can nevertheless be used as a starting point for any microeconomic analysis.

For example, in the book, I often flag that digital services are challenging to measure in monetary terms. However, readers should not be puzzled by the use of price as one of the two key parameters to define equilibrium in Figure A.1. In a theoretical model, the price parameter could be used to represent anything that implies a cost for a "buyer" and a gain for the seller. Hence, for example, *price* could stand for the amount of personal information that a user of an online platform must share to get to use the service. Thus, even if joining a social network appears to be *for free*, at least in monetary terms, the theoretical dynamic underlying it can ultimately be linked back to the basic microeconomic model described in Figure A.1.

A.2 Market failures and their sources

In economics, the expression **market failure** is used to describe a situation in which markets are not generating as much value as they could from a broad societal perspective. That is: the equilibrium to which demand and supply converge is sub-optimal. In other words, there exist at least another market equilibrium where more value could be generated if the market's frictions (the sources of market failures) could be removed. Note that this does not have to be directly related to the *distribution* of that value between market players, buyers, or sellers. Instead, the sub-optimality of the equilibrium is defined just in terms of efficiency: when a market fails, available resources are not fully exploited, society could be more prosperous, the proverbial economic pie bigger (who gets to eat the pie is a different matter which does not directly relate to the efficiency of the market).

Market failures are a primary reason for public intervention. Public intervention is costly: it is financed through taxpayers' money, and it always entails the risk that public administrators do not get it right. Suppose, for example, that the government decides to subsidize a specific company to incentivize that company to innovate. But that company may not deserve to be rewarded, perhaps because its products turn out to be not as innovative as hoped for when public subsidies were allocated. For that reason, it is always preferable to abstain from intervening in markets that work efficiently (i.e. in markets that do not *fail*), perturbing the dynamics that lead to the generation of value (for example, affecting the production or the sale of products). From a public policy perspective, removing frictions in markets that fail is the *first best*. In markets that do not fail, public intervention would nevertheless have a role but mostly limited to redistributing the generated value (for example, through taxation policies).

Described this way, it would seem that the scope for public policy intervention is very narrow.

However, that is not the case because, in practice, **markets often fail**. In reality, no frictionless market exists and the idea that the best outcome for society can be achieved by leaving players entirely free to pursue their self-interest, letting Adam Smith's *market's invisible hand*[2] operate, is just a theoretical construct.

That theoretical construct is nevertheless handy because it helps give a logical structure to public intervention. When public administrators intervene, they should justify their intervention based on the market failure they intend to address. In other words, public policy is needed to correct the failure that prevents the market from converging to optimal outcomes by itself. Public intervention can take many forms: *legislation* (e.g. an EU Regulation aimed at reducing barriers to entry, to increase market competition); *taxation* or *subsidies*; *direct supply* of certain products that are considered important for society (e.g. schooling or health services); or *enforcement* (e.g. merger control by antitrust authorities).

There are many sources of market failures. Below I describe only those which I mentioned in the book.

A.2.1 Externalities

Externalities occur whenever a product's production or consumption affects a third party that is not directly involved in the production process or transaction. In the case of a **positive externality**, the third party *benefits* from it. For example, education is known to have strong positive externalities, as the direct beneficiaries (the students) contribute with their knowledge and skills to improve society. The members of society are the third-parties benefiting from education's positive externality. Another common expression in economics is **spillover**: through positive externalities, education has a *positive spillover* on society.

When a product has significant positive externalities, it is **non-rivalrous** (that is: it can be consumed without depleting its value), and it is **not excludable** (that is: it is unfeasible or too costly to exclude anybody from its consumption), then that product is said to be a **public good**. Police enforcement or environmental protection are classic public good examples.

Conversely, a **negative externality** is verified when the third party is *harmed*. Smoking a cigarette has negative externalities on passive smokers. Going to work by car has negative externalities on society due to pollution. Posting disinformation online linking vaccines to autism has a negative externality on immunosuppressed individuals, to the extent that it may dissuade parents from vaccinating their kids and thus contribute to the spread of diseases they are exposed to.

Externalities are a source of market failure because they are typically not taken into account by the primary actors who generate them when making their production or consumption decision.

Thus, without public policy intervention, a market would see an excessive amount of cigarettes smoked compared to what would be optimal from a social point of view. Smokers **do not internalize** the cost they impose on society when deciding how much to smoke: they would necessarily smoke less if they would. Likewise, online platforms do not internalize the cost that spreading disinformation has on society. Thus, at the equilibrium, too much disinformation is circulating on the web.

Perhaps counterintuitively, positive externalities also lead to market failure. Companies may, for example, invest in R&D (research and development) after careful consideration of the benefits they could get compared to the investment cost. However, they would not include among the companies' benefits the benefit that R&D may have for society and the economy. Therefore, without policy intervention, they would necessarily invest less than what would be desirable from a societal perspective. Likewise, students' engagement in learning activities would be only determined by their personal return, as the return of education from a society perspective is not taken into account when the single individual is deciding to enrol in a school or university course. In other words, markets affected by positive externalities tend to generate too little of the value they could produce.

A common way to deal with externalities is through taxation or subsidies. Taxing a good that produces negative externalities will reduce its production or consumption—aligning it to the optimal equilibrium from a societal perspective. Conversely, governments may subsidize the production

---

[2] Smith (1791).

or consumption of goods with positive externalities to increase them and approach the optimal equilibrium. Classic examples are R&D subsidies.[3]

A.2.2 Asymmetric information

Asymmetric information features a situation in which the parties involved in a transaction have a different degree of knowledge about the value of the concerned product. For example, a second-hand car seller may be aware that the car's engine has some structural deficiencies. The individual who is buying it may instead have no means to become aware of it. Thus the seller *knows more* than the buyer, and the market for used cars exhibits strong asymmetric information.[4] It should be not hard to see how this example can be extended to the digital environment. For example, users may use a free email service without knowing the quality of that service (here, quality could be represented by the degree of security against cyber-attacks or the guarantee that personal information is not used for commercial purposes). As we have seen in Chapter 8, online platforms often help address asymmetric information in traditional markets through the enaction of ranking mechanisms. For example, comments by former users may help travellers select a better accommodation—offering a validation test to the claims advertised by their potential host. Likewise, restaurants' reviews help reduce asymmetric information between restaurant owners and potential clients.

Asymmetric information is a source of market failure primarily because they trigger a perverse dynamic effect, resulting in a rush towards lower quality products ("lemons" in the words of Nobel-prize winner George Arthur Akerlof (Akerlof, G. A., 1978)). Imagine that the seller has no way to guarantee the quality of the product she sells, for example, because she cannot certify it or because there is no reputational mechanism that would increase her incentives to be sincere. Potential buyers anticipate that and thus tend to assume that the seller is selling a low-quality product. On the other hand, the seller would certainly not have any incentive to sell a high-quality product if she knows that buyers would not believe her and be ready to pay a premium for it. Hence sellers will all converge to sell low-quality products ("lemons" stand for cars discovered to be defective after purchase, in American slang).

The market fails because some buyers may have been ready to pay a premium for high-quality products. Without public intervention (such as certification schemes, standardization, consumer protection), that high-quality product market would not materialize. No high-quality products are found on the market also because high-quality sellers may exit the market. The market is, in other words, subject to **adverse selection**: only low-quality sellers sell products in a market riddled by asymmetric information.

A.2.3 Moral hazard

Moral hazard occurs any time a party in a transaction can cause a cost on the other involved parties without being detected. For example, an employee that is teleworking may have an incentive to declare that she was at her desk a longer time than she actually was, imposing a potential cost to her employer. Another classic example is insurances: after having been insured, the insured party has an incentive to engage in riskier behaviours, thus increasing expected costs for insurance companies (naturally, insurance companies anticipate that and impose premiums that compensate for that increased risk).

Moral hazard is a source of market failure because it has a cooling effect on the supply of a particular product or even prevents new markets from emerging from the outset. Consider the example of teleworking: a considerable amount of workers would telework without "cheating" on their employer; if anything, they may work more and be more productive at home (as data from the Covid-19 pandemic

---

[3] Note that R&D subsidies should not target a specific company to avoid running the risk mentioned above, i.e. that the wrong company is rewarded (an inefficient company which is not innovating as desired). Instead, R&D subsidies should be general and allocated to any company showing to be efficient and innovative.

[4] The second-hand car example is not coincidental, as it was used in Akerlof's seminal paper on asymmetric information: Akerlof, G. A. (1978, pp. 235–251).

period seem to support). Yet, employers may be reluctant to give teleworking opportunities to their employees because of potential moral hazard.

For example, public policy can intervene, increasing the cost of "misbehaving" for the agent that can engage in risky activities. For example, the General Data Protection Regulation forces companies to enact a system of protection for the personal data they host against potential data breaches. In case of a data breach, the company must swiftly report it. The company can face significant fines in case of non-compliance (see Chapter 5). Thus, the GDPR increases the cost of moral hazard: companies cannot be "sloppy" with the data they host after data subjects have given their consent to use it and leave it defenceless to a potential cyber-attack. Doing so could entail paying a hefty fine.

A.2.4 Market power

Another critical source of market failure is **market power**. Market power corresponds to a supplier's ability to define its market behaviour with a degree of independence from external constraints: the more independent the supplier, the higher its market power.

The constraint *par excellence* to market power is **market competition**. Generally speaking, the higher the number of competitors faced by the supplier, the lower is its market power. Market shares are usually a first good indication of power (albeit not conclusive). However, the importance of the competition constraint also depends on the "strength" of the competitors in the market, not only on their number. For example, suppose competitors are very small and do not have the production capacity to take over a significant share of the market from the dominant supplier. In that case, they may not meaningfully constrain its market power, even if numerous.

Competition may be limited in a market for many reasons. For example, barriers to entry, such as the investment needed to set up a production plan, may be very high, so that not many companies can afford to enter the market. Those barriers can also be artificial or created by public authorities with the specific purpose to control the number of players in the market. For example, a taxi driver may need to pay a high license fee to be able to drive in a specific city. Market players can also engage in activities that have the ultimate goal to reduce competition. For example, a dominant supplier could buy its competitors, eventually increasing market concentration (recall that, precisely for that reason, mergers of relevant size are subject to merger control by antitrust authorities).

Competition is, however, not the only constraint that can limit market power. Theoretically, also a **monopolist** (i.e. a company facing no competitors in the market) can have limited freedom to set the price or the quality of its products. This could happen, for example, in the case of a highly contestable market, where barriers to entry are very low. In that case, a monopolist could be concerned that increasing its prices too much would quickly trigger entry by potential competitors, and thus it may refrain from doing so in the first place.

Another source of constraint to market power is **demand elasticity**. A highly elastic demand implies that any price increase by the monopolist would entail a significant drop in sales, as many buyers would simply not purchase the product. Demand elasticity is one core element of Google's line of defence against antitrust investigations it has been subject to. Google has a quasi-monopoly of the market for *organic* and general-purpose web search in Europe. However, Google has claimed that "*competition is just one-click away*":[5] its users can easily switch to other search engines if they feel Google's quality is too low. Implicitly, Google is claiming that even if it would be considered a monopolist, it could not exert any market power because of the high demand elasticity of its users.

Sometimes products may have structural features that make them more suitable to be produced or supplied by a restricted number of sellers. An extreme case of this scenario is that of a **natural monopoly**, i.e. a market in which it is most efficient to have just one supplier. Utilities such as telecoms, water or gas distribution, or rail transport are typical examples.

Natural monopolies arise when extremely high fixed costs are necessary to start the supply of the product. For example, digging the ground to build a network of water pipes qualifies as such. But the advantage of having two overlapping networks of water pipes can hardly outweigh the duplication costs

---

[5] See for example: NBC BAY AREA (2011).

entailed by digging the ground twice. Hence, also from a societal perspective, it is often more efficient to have just one network supplying all potential users.

When fixed costs are high, the average cost of providing a service or good supply decreases in the number of units since those fixed costs are distributed over the total quantity sold. That corresponds to the definition of **economies of scale**. Note: every natural monopoly benefits from high economies of scale. However, many industries enjoy significant economies of scale without necessarily being natural monopolies. For example, production in a simple manufacturing plant is generally more efficient if it's close to full capacity. **Network economies** also typically feature natural monopolies: they refer to the benefit of having just one network to connect different buyers because for each of them, the value of the network is increasing in its size. Telecom markets tend to display strong network economies as users attach a high value to find the person they want to phone to on the same network of their telecom service provider. Note that regulators mandate telecom operators' network interoperability exactly to address that issue.

Even though having few or just one supplier in natural monopolies markets is more efficient than having many, natural monopolies are still not delivering the optimal outcome from a societal perspective. Thus, they tend to fail, which is why market regulation is required.

Understanding why market power is a source of market failure requires a dedicated discussion, which I undertake in the next Section A.3.

A.3 Market power and competition

Figure A.2 illustrates a core reason why market power is a source of market failure. To have a more straightforward illustration, it depicts the extreme case of a monopolist with full market power (the reasoning could be easily extended to *oligopolies* where players still enjoy a certain degree of market power without being the only players in the market). Left unconstrained, free to set the price that maximizes its profits, a monopolist would compare its **marginal costs** (i.e. the cost of producing one additional unit of product; represented by the upward line, which corresponds to the supply curve in a competitive market such as the one depicted in Figure A.1) and its **marginal revenue** (i.e. the revenue that each additional unit produced can bring if sold; downward sloping as the lower the price per unit, the lower is the revenue). To maximize its profits, the monopolist sets the quantity produced according to the point where the marginal cost and the marginal revenue curves match, namely at Q'. Producing more would entail an actual loss (the marginal cost is higher than the marginal revenue, so each unit sold costs more than it yields). Producing less than Q' would entail a loss of opportunity (since the marginal revenue is higher than the marginal cost, producing an additional unit is profitable, so it would be silly not to sell it). The price level corresponding to Q' is given by the demand, and it is equivalent to P'.

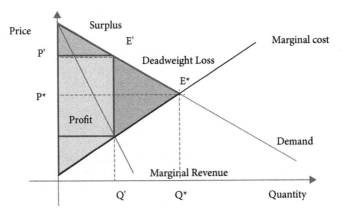

Figure A.2 Value loss due to market power

Similarly to what was described in Figure A.1, the buyers' surplus is given by the area of the grey triangle in Figure A.2 (it includes all buyers that could have been willing to pay a higher price than P'). The area of the light grey trapezoid gives the monopolist's profit: it is the total revenue (price P' times quantity sold Q') minus total cost.

The dark grey triangle conveys the key insight of Figure A.2. That is called **deadweight loss,** and it represents the amount of value that the market *could have produced* if it was competitive. With perfect competition (i.e. zero market power), at the equilibrium, the quantity produced and purchased would have been Q* (as in Figure A.1). At that level the total sum of profits and surplus corresponds to the blue and grey triangle of Figure A.1, namely the sum of the grey, light grey and dark grey area of Figure A.2.

Thus, in plain words, market power implies that fewer products are produced and consumed in the economy than they otherwise would have been if resources were allocated efficiently.

It is important to stress the absence of any political judgment here: the market does not fail because it is the monopolist who is better off (and thus could be considered *unfair*). Instead, it fails because, at an aggregate level, *the value produced is inferior to the value that could have been produced* in a competitive market. That is why market power generates a market failure.

The one described above is a classic textbook explanation of why it is desirable to have competition rather than monopolies. However, that explanation just focuses on **static effects,** i.e. effects that materialize in one specific point in time. Decreasing market power and increasing competition can, however, have also very important **dynamic effects**.

When subject to competition, companies tend to exert a higher effort to become more efficient, for example investing in production process innovation. They do so because they are aware that if they would not, they could be forced to exit the market. Thus competition pushes companies to become more efficient.

Similarly, competition dynamically selects the best companies and thus has a sectorial productivity effect. In the long term, companies that are not productive enough are forced to exit the market. If so, those that manage to "survive" and stay active in the market tend to have higher productivity levels. Thus, on average, competitive industrial sectors tend to be more productive than non-competitive ones.

Finally, competition may either reduce or increase incentives to innovate through its effect on potential profits. In an extreme (theoretical) scenario of perfect competition, the market profits approach to zero and products are sold at marginal costs. Thus, companies may be dissuaded to invest in those markets, as fixed costs may not even be offset by the little or zero profits they make. In this extreme scenario, competition dynamically reduces investment to innovate. However, it should be pointed out that in reality, markets rarely exhibit similar features, and the competition dynamic effects tend to actually incentivize innovation rather than dampen it (see, for example, the discussion on competition in telecom markets, Chapter 4, Section 4.2.1).

Moreover, even when competition squeezes profits towards the zero bound, it may still incentivize innovation. In fact, in such instances, companies may be pushed to invest in product innovation, to "escape" harsh competition in the market where they are and look for profits in other markets, or even create entirely new ones, where they can enjoy significant profits. For example, a European carmaker that was enjoying considerable profits in the diesel car market faces a sudden increase in competition due to the entry of two formidable competitors from China. Suddenly, the European carmaker cannot make any profit anymore through the sale of its diesel cars. Thus, it decides to invest heavily in developing a next-generation electric car model to seek profits in that market where competition is not as intense as in the diesel car market.

A.4 Artificial restriction of competition and competition policy

Antitrust authorities watch over markets. Their role is to prevent market players from implementing behaviours that may artificially restrict competition and thus reduce the value that those markets can produce for society, i.e. lead markets to fail. Their function in the context of digital markets is discussed extensively in Chapter 8, Section 8.3.2.[6]

---

[6] A classic textbook reference for the economics of competition policy is Motta, M. (2004).

For the purpose of this appendix, however, let us focus on just a few of the artificial restrictions that can be put in place by market players (namely those that are most relevant for the issues addressed throughout the book):

A.4.1 Mergers and agreements between market players

Market players can act unilaterally or coordinate to reduce market competition in many ways. The most obvious one is through mergers and acquisitions: a company may purchase a competitor and relieve some competitive pressure in the market (mergers may, however, be motivated by other purposes, such as increasing production efficiency).

They can also enter into explicit agreements, for example, to set a common industry standard. Or an "upstream" supplier or wholesaler may enter into an agreement with its "downstream" retail sellers, for example, to ensure that the retailer does not sell other suppliers' brands (these are called "exclusivity" clauses).

Generally speaking, **vertical restrictions** (that is: mergers or agreements between market players that are in a complementary relationship, such as between a wholesaler and a retailer) tend to generate fewer competition concerns than **horizontal agreements** (that is: mergers or agreements between market players that are in direct competition as they sell products that are substitute to each other, such as two smartphone manufacturers' brands). The former are indeed more likely to generate **efficiencies** that can reduce costs and thus potentially increase value for consumers and sellers alike.

A primary driver for that effect is related to an important economic concept called **double marginalization**. Double marginalization occurs whenever two complementary products are sold by two different suppliers, each enjoying a certain degree of market power. An example discussed in the book is that of international mobile roaming markets (see Section 4.2.2). When visiting Florence in Italy, a Belgian resident must purchase access to an Italian telecom network provider *and* a Belgian telecom network provider. The two providers are in a complementary relationship (our Belgian tourist needs both to place a call). Double marginalization occurs because each player in its own market exerts its market power to set its product price without considering that an increase in that price negatively affects the demand for the other complementary product. In other words, each of the two suppliers does not *internalize* the cost they impose on the other (see the parallel with externality discussion in Section A.2). In the case of roaming, the two telecom operators set the network access price without considering the overall dampening effect that this has on the Belgian tourist's willingness to place a call from Italy. In such circumstances (that actually are very frequent, in vertically related or complementary markets), a restriction of competition can make that effect disappear. The Belgian tourist would be better off having to deal with just one network rather than two. In other words, the vertical restriction (it could be a merger between the two network operators, for example) helps *internalize* the effect that the pricing behaviour of each player places on each other.

The existence of double marginalization is something policymakers must take into account when they speak about "breaking up" Big Tech as a way to address online platforms' market issues. Breaking up online platforms may increase competition at a certain level, but it can also entail inefficiencies. For example, generating double marginalization effects between complementary products that the same company is currently selling, such as a whole purpose web search engine and a vertical/specialized web search engine, (see Chapter 8.1.1). So the balance in favour of breaking up is not straightforward.

Note, however, that vertical restrictions may also be very harmful if they are crafted in a way to prevent competition to unfold. For example, through an exclusivity clause with retailers, a supplier may be able to keep a rival outside the market (for an accessible description of different scenarios in which vertical restrictions are harmful to competition, see the European Commission's brochure: "The competition rules for supply and distribution agreements"[7]).

A vertical restriction I have mentioned in the book is called **Most Favoured Nation** clause or MFN. Such a restriction most typically binds a company to offer products on the best terms offered in the market. For example, an online platform such as Booking.com could prevent hotels from advertising

---

[7] https://op.europa.eu/en/publication-detail/-/publication/c06dce20-7a0f-4611-b767-db9a5aa77f2c

rooms on their own websites at a lower price than the one asked for on Booking.com's platform. The MFN is a vertical restriction because hotels have a complementary relationship with Booking.com (they rely on the platform to reach a wider audience of potential travellers). MFNs may be harmful to competition. For example, because they help players collude (see below): companies have lower incentives to lower their prices if they know that their competitors are committed to matching that price (and no seller enjoys a *race to the bottom* or price war). MFN clauses, however, may be *pro-competitive* (that is: they may increase efficiency and have beneficial effects for society). For example, it is possible that without MFN, an online platform would not exist in the first place. Imagine the extreme situation in which every business on a platform uses the platform solely for advertising while incentivizing buyers to buy their products through other channels. The platform would surely go bust in a short amount of time. Similar reasons justify the existence of other restrictions such as **Resale Price Maintenance** (or RPM) clauses; that is, most typically: clauses that allow a producer to set the retail price of its products. Imagine a showroom furniture reseller: keeping a physical showroom active is costly. If clients could visit the showroom and then buy the same furniture online from another reseller at a lower price, no showroom shop would be viable. That is why a furniture maker may be willing to impose some kind of RPM clause to coordinate its resellers to a price that does not penalize showroom resellers, preserving the viability of their business.[8]

Conversely, the analysis of **horizontal restrictions** tend to be easier, although not always straight-forward. It is much more likely that direct limitations to competition between sellers that sell products that are potential substitutes to each other induce a market failure and thus harm social welfare. For example, imagine a market where there are just three main brands of smartphones, with other brands holding a small market share. Suppose two of the three main brands merge (a 3-to-2 merger). In that case, there is a high likelihood that prices for smartphones will increase and that their quality will decrease since *horizontal* competition has been significantly reduced.

Horizontal collusion is probably the most compelling amongst horizontal restrictions. Any antitrust law bans explicit agreements between direct competitors: they are considered *hardcore* competition policy infringements because there is little doubt that these agreements are harmful, and illegality is presumed.

Competition authorities pursue explicit collusive agreements through investigations, surprise in-spections, or *leniency programs*. Leniency programs are systems of impunity guarantees to incentivize the submission of information by cartels' whistleblowers.

Players, however, may not need to enter an explicit agreement in order to collude. **Tacit collusion** refers to a situation in which market players are able to coordinate to a cooperative equilibrium where they simply stop competing, for example, keeping their prices higher than expected in a competitive market and increasing their profits at the expense of their customers. Antitrust laws cannot pursue tacit collusion for obvious reasons. If there is no explicit agreement to break, collusion entirely relies on each company's unilateral choices. In that case, antitrust authorities cannot dictate how companies should behave in the market to compete with other players. That makes tacit collusion a particularly challenging problem to deal with.

The best way to deal with tacit collusion is to remove those market features that make it more likely. One of those conditions is **transparency**, which is why tacit collusion is mentioned in the book. When competitors can easily monitor each other's behaviour they also have a chance to quickly react should one of them be detected to deviate from the collusive equilibrium. For example, four laptop producers may have tacitly understood that €1,000 for a certain tier of laptop is the best price that maximizes their profits. If one of them could sell its laptops at €900 and remain unnoticed, it would be able to make a lot of profit – stealing a likely significant share of the market from its collusive partners that kept faith in the tacit agreement of €1,000 per laptop. However, suppose the market is very transparent. In that case, each manufacturer tends to resist the temptation to deviate and charge €900 for its laptops because as soon as it would do it, all the other players would likely detect it. Detection would spark a price war and a very counterproductive (from the sellers' point of view) *race to the bottom* in prices.

---

[8] The combination of MFN and RPM clauses may create the conditions for significant harm to competi-tion. See for example, the EU e-Book case: https://ec.europa.eu/competition/elojade/isef/case_details.cfm?proc_code=1_39847

For this reason, there is an increasing concern about the impact that online algorithmic monitoring may have on collusion. Artificial intelligence can dramatically increase market players' ability to detect deviations from collusive equilibria by their competitors and thus acts as a *tacit collusion* enabler (see Chapter 8).

A.4.2 Abuse of dominance

A company holding a significant degree of market power can qualify as **dominant**. "Abuses" by dominant companies are prohibited by antitrust laws.[9] Abuses primarily consist of strategies put in places by a company to prevent market competition from increasing. For example, a dominant company may bundle its products forcing buyers to buy them in a package, with the consequence of keeping a potential competitor out of the market of one of the two bundled products.

One abusive practice that I have mentioned several times in the book is called **price discrimination** (once again, pay attention: the word *price* is used for simplicity; discrimination can occur at different dimensions with different parameters, not necessarily selling price).

Price discrimination is defined as a seller's practice to charge a different price to two or more customers buying the same product, when differences in production or supply costs (such as, for example, delivery costs if customers are located in different geographical areas) do not explain the divergence in prices. Price discrimination is highly relevant in the digital context because *data,* as we know from Chapter 5, are at the core of the digital economy. And accurate information can enable discrimination. Companies know a great deal about their customers, thanks to data analytics. This knowledge can allow them to customize their services as well as discriminate *against* them, charging different prices or supplying different service quality.

The treatment of price discrimination from an economic perspective is tricky, as price discrimination does not have obvious welfare effects. To see this, consider the simple numeric example described in Table A.1.

Table A.1 describes a situation where two customers have a different "willingness to pay" for the same product (customer A is willing to pay 10 units, while customer B is willing to pay 5 units), even though the product is produced at the same cost (3 units). For example, imagine customer A being a young professional with a good salary and customer B being a penny-less student, both interested in buying a ticket for a movie night, but with an apparent different ability to afford it.

When price discrimination is allowed, the cinema owner charges 10 units to customer A and 5 units to customer B, to maximize its profits. The cinema owner makes $(10-3) + (5-3) = 9$ unit of profit. Both the young professional and the student get served and can enjoy the movie (just: the student had to show her student card to get the cinema discount).

When price discrimination is banned, the cinema can only charge one price. It is easy to see that the only price that makes sense for it is 10 units. In fact, charging 5 would generate profits equal to $(5-3) + (5-3) = 4$, while charging 10 would generate profits equal to $10-3 = 7$. Note that only the young professional is served in this scenario because the penny-less student cannot afford to pay 10 units for the movie.[10]

Table A.1 Customer payoff matrix

	Willingness to Pay	Cost of Supply
Customer A	10	3
Customer B	5	3

---

[9] For example, for the EU see Art. 102 of the Treaty on the Functioning of the European Union (TFEU).
[10] Any other price would not make sense: a price higher than 10 would imply no sale, as not even customer A would buy the ticket. A price lower than 10 but higher than 5 would decrease profits as it would not increase sales.

This example illustrates a universal property of price discrimination: more elastic customers (i.e. those who have a lower willingness to pay) tend to benefit from price discrimination as sellers tend to charge them a lower price.

More generally, price discrimination may create incentives to supply higher elasticity customers. It may favour competition for marginal customers, i.e. those ready to switch from one brand to another. It can also create the conditions for more investment by companies that anticipate that they will be able to enjoy more flexibility in their price setting to adapt to future market changes. But price discrimination can be used by companies to extract more value from customers, charging a price very close to the maximum they are ready to pay. And it can be used by dominant companies to preserve their market power, for example, excluding rivals through several sophisticated techniques (such as **predatory pricing,** i.e. loss-making prices that make competitors' businesses non-viable).

The essential takeaway here is that price discrimination rarely can be considered harmful or beneficial from the outset: it is always necessary to look at the market and how price discrimination has been used to conclude whether harm has been caused. However, one crucial general consideration can be made: the likelihood that price discrimination causes harm (leading to market abuse) is higher the higher is the discriminating seller's market power. The intuition behind that result rests on the fact that customers with low bargaining power tend to be less elastic vis-à-vis the supplier. If the supplier is a monopolist, customers do not have much of a choice: to buy from it or not buy at all. In this situation, the ability of the company to extract value from its customers is much higher. And so is the risk of harm.[11]

The natural corollary of this consideration is that it makes more sense to attempt to increase competition in online and data markets instead of using a blanket ban of discrimination. This is because increasing competition minimizes the risk that price discrimination is used to pursue abuses by dominant companies. But, at the same time, it does not prevent *good* discrimination from arising (such as the one that allows penny-less students to enjoy a movie night).

A.5 Empirical analysis

Let me finally make some concluding remarks regarding the use of statistical analysis for policymaking. **Econometrics** is a branch of economics focusing on applying statistical techniques to economic data for empirical inference. Similarly to any other social scientist, economists cannot validate their theories replicating social phenomena in a lab. They can only observe social dynamics and attempt to infer from them conclusions of general relevance.

Econometric techniques are used for that purpose. Their most compelling use aims to disentangle **causal effects** between different variables in well-defined patterns that are observed in data. For example, an econometrician may be interested in understanding whether adopting a regulation that banned specific behaviours by large online platforms had ultimately the *causal effect* of damping innovation or increasing online platforms' service quality.

Sophisticated techniques may involve complex modelling or the use of "structural breaks" in the data (i.e. *exogenous*, or independent, events that have no relationship with anything object of the study, such as the sudden breakout of a pandemic . . .) to identify clear causal relationships between variables. Even a general explanation of those techniques would fall outside the scope of this book. However, I believe it may be helpful to briefly describe a pitfall policymakers may fall into.

It is rather common for policymakers to be exposed to economic analysis produced by stakeholders to support their arguments, for example, in favour or against a certain regulation. Those analyses can prove helpful, at least to give a general idea of how markets work. However, they do not necessarily convey reliable normative suggestions if the data presented only records correlation relationships rather than causal ones.

---

[11] Here harm is considered from a consumer perspective, which is the perspective normally taken by antitrust authorities. When a *total* welfare perspective is taken (that is: attaching the same value to producers' profits and consumers' surplus), price discrimination may be considered to be welfare enhancing also if implemented by a monopolist. That is because it allows the monopolist to extract all surplus from customers and reduce the deadweight loss, as identified in Figure A.2.

A positive (negative) correlation relationship indicates that two variables tend to change in the same (opposite) way. When one increases, the other follows (decreases). Simple statistical regressions tend to capture correlations, not causality.

A classic example concerns *education* and *income*. It is relatively common to observe a high positive correlation between education and income: a higher level of education is associated with higher income levels. This correlation may be partially driven by a causal relationship. However, other factors can explain that relationship. For example, income and education may be affected by a common *confounding* variable with strong explanatory power for both, e.g. individuals' parents' income. Individuals from rich families have a higher chance of accessing good universities; they also have a higher chance of getting a good job, thanks to their parents' network or business' activity. In this case, the correlation between education and income is considered (at least partially) **spurious**.

Other statistical results may be affected by **reverse causality**: the analyst observes that variables A and B are highly correlated and conclude that A causes B; in reality, B is causing A. Consider the example I used in the book (Chapter 6): public administrations that adopt digital technologies tend to be more efficient. That is: adoption of technology (A) and efficiency (B) are highly correlated variables. However, it would be wrong to conclude that technology *causes* an increase in the administration's efficiency. The causal relationship is at least partially reversed. Efficient administrations are indeed more likely to adopt innovative technologies (hence A causes B and B causes A).

Another common challenge to statistical inference is **sample selection**: two variables may be highly correlated, but the driving factor of the correlation is the composition of the sample used for the analysis (that composition is not necessarily evident). For example, imagine observing that individuals who switch from employed work to self-employed work display a high level of work satisfaction (an argument that could be used by sharing economy platforms, for example, see Chapter 11). You could conclude that switching to being self-employed *causes* individuals to be, on average, happier with the work they do. However, that conclusion would not take into account the selection bias of the sample observed. Those individuals who decided to switch to be self-employed are not necessarily representative of the whole population of workers. They are actually people who value being independent more than others. That explains the effect on their job satisfaction, but that result cannot be generalized for the whole population of workers.

The ones illustrated above are just a few examples, and the list of potential ways in which descriptive analysis may mislead to the wrong conclusion is long. However, the important takeaway should be straightforward: policymakers (and their "digital advisers") should never take statistical analysis at face value. Before taking any conclusion on the actual or potential effect of a certain policy intervention, it is always necessary to verify that the analysis is backed by good econometrics (and validated by good econometricians).

****

Bibliography

A4AI, 2020. *Affordability Report*, s.l.: A4AI.

Ablon, L., Heaton, P., Lavery, D. & Romanosky, S., 2016. *Consumer Attitudes Toward Data Breach Notifications and Loss of Personal Information*, s.l.: RAND.

Accenture, 2016. *Why Artificial Intelligence is the Future of Growth.* [Online] Available at: http://s3.amazonaws.com/medias.ccei.quebec/ouvrage/Accenture-Why-AI-is-the-Future-of-Growth.PDF [Accessed 10/5/21].

Acemoğlu, D. & Restrepo, P., 2016. *The race between machines and humans: Implications for growth, factor shares and jobs.* [Online] Available at: https://voxeu.org/article/job-race-machines-versus-humans

Acemoğlu, D. & Restrepo, P., 2019. Artificial Intelligence, Automation and Work. In: *The Economics of Artificial Intelligence: An Agenda.* s.l.: University of Chicago Press, pp. 197–236.

Acemoğlu, D. & Restrepo, P., 2020. Robots and Jobs: Evidence from US Labor Markets. *Journal of Political Economy*, 128(6), pp. 2188–2244.

Acemoğlu, D. & Restrepo, P., 2020. The wrong kind of AI? Artificial intelligence and the future of labour demand. *Cambridge Journal of Regions, Economy and Society*, Volume 13(1), 25–35.

Acquisti, A., 2004. Privacy in electronic commerce and the economics of immediate gratification. In: B. J., a cura di *EC '04 Proceedings of the 5th ACM Conference on Electronic Commerce.* New York: Association for Computing Machinery, pp. 21–29.

Acquisti, A., Friedman, A. & Telang, R., 2006. *Is There a Cost to Privacy Breaches? An Event Study.* s.l., ICIS 2006 Proceedings, p. 94.

Aghion, P. et al., 2005. Competition and Innovation: an Inverted-U Relationship. *The Quarterly Journal of Economics*, 120(2), pp. 701–728.

Agrawal, D. & Fox, W., 2017. Taxes in an e-commerce generation. *International Tax and Public Finance*, Volume 24(5), pp. 903–926.

Ahmad, N. & Schreyer, P., 2016. Measuring GDP in a Digitalised Economy. *OECD Statistics Working Papers, OECD Publishing, Paris*, Volume No. 2016/07.

AI Now Institute, 2019. *AI Now 2019 Report*, New York: New York University.

Akerlof, G. A., 1978. *The market for "lemons": Quality uncertainty and the market mechanism. In Uncertainty in economics.* s.l.: Academic Press.

Akerlof, R., Holden, R. & Rayo, L., 2018. Network Externalities and Market Dominance. *unpublished manuscript.*

Akpan N., 2016. *Google artificial intelligence beats champion at world's most complicated board game.* [Online] Available at: https://www.pbs.org/newshour/science/google-artificial-intelligence-beats-champion-at-worlds-most-complicated-board-game [Accessed 10/5/21].

Akter, S. et al., 2016. How to improve firm performance using big data analytics capability and business strategy alignment?. *International Journal of Production Economics*, Volume 182, 113–131.

Al Hossain, F. et al., 2020. FluSense: a contactless syndromic surveillance platform for influenza-like illness in hospital waiting areas. *Proceedings of the ACM on Interactive, Mobile, Wearable and Ubiquitous Technologies*, 4(1), pp. 1–28.

Alexander J., 2019. *Youtubers and record labels are fighting and record labels keep winning.* [Online] Available at: https://www.theverge.com/2019/5/24/18635904/copyright-youtube-creators-dmca-takedown-fair-use-music-cover [Accessed 24/4/21].

Alharthi, A., Krotov, V. & Bowman, M., 2017. Addressing barriers to big data. *Business Horizons*, Volume 60(3), pp. 285–292.

Amit, K., 2018. *Artificial intelligence and soft computing: behavioral and cognitive modeling of the human brain.* s.l.: CRC press.

Ammu, N. & Irfanuddin, M., 2013. Big data challenges. *International Journal of Advanced Trends in Computer Science and Engineering*, Volume 2(1), pp. 613–615.

Anderson M., 2014. *88% Of Consumers Trust Online Reviews As Much As Personal Recommendations*. [Online] Available at: https://searchengineland.com/88-consumers-trust-online-reviews-much-personal-recommendations-195803 [Accessed 24/2/21].

Anderson, J. & Mariniello, M., 2021. *Regulating big tech: the Digital Markets Act*. [Online] Available at: https://www.bruegel.org/2021/02/regulating-big-tech-the-digital-markets-act/ [Accessed 24/4/21].

Anderson, R. & Moore, T., 2006. The economics of information security. *science*, Volume 314(5799), pp. 610–613.

Anderson, R., 2001. Why information security is hard-an economic perspective. *Seventeenth Annual Computer Security Applications Conference*, Volume (pp. 358–365). IEEE.

Angier N., 2008. *Mirrors Don't Lie. Mislead? Oh, Yes*. [Online] Available at: https://www.nytimes.com/2008/07/22/science/22angi.html [Accessed 10/5/21].

Angwin, J., Larson, J., Mattu, S. & Kirchner, L., 2016. *Machine Bias*. [Online] Available at: https://www.propublica.org/article/machine-bias-risk-assessments-in-criminal-sentencing [Accessed 10/5/21].

Armstrong, M. & Wright, J., 2007. Two-sided markets, competitive bottlenecks and exclusive contracts. *Economic Theory*, Volume 32(2), pp. 353–380.

Arntz, M., Gregory, T. & Zierahn, U., 2016. *The Risk of Automation for Jobs in OECD Countries: A Comparative Analysis*, Paris: OECD Publishing.

Autor, D. H., F Katz, L. & Kearney, M. S., 2006. The Polarization of the U.S. Labor Market. *American Economic Review*, 96(2), pp. 189–194.

Ayre, L. & Craner, J., 2017. Open data: What it is and why you should care. Public Library Quarterly, 36(2), pp. 173–184. *Public Library Quarterly*, Volume 36(2), pp. 173–184.

Balkin, J. M., 2013. Old-school/new-school speech regulation. *Harvard Law Review*, Volume 127, p. 2296.

Barber, M. & McCarty, N., 2015. Causes and consequences of polarization. In: *Political negotiation: A handbook*. 37 a cura di Washington: Brookings Institution Press, pp. 39–43.

Barberá, P., 2015. Birds of the same feather tweet together: Bayesian ideal point estimation using Twitter data. *Political analysis*, Volume 23(1), pp. 76–91.

Barrera, O., Guriev, S. & Henry, E. Z. E., 2020. Facts, alternative facts, and fact checking in times of post-truth politics. *Journal of Public Economics*, Volume 182, pp. 104–123.

Barter, P., 2013. *"Cars are parked 95% of the time". Let's check!*. [Online] Available at: https://www.reinventingparking.org/2013/02/cars-are-parked-95-of-time-lets-check.html. [Accessed 4/5/21].

Bauer, M., 2018. *Digital Companies and Their Fair Share of Taxes: Myths and Misconceptions*. [Online] Available at: https://ecipe.org/publications/digital-companies-and-their-fair-share-of-taxes/ [Accessed 3/5/21].

BBC, 2018. *Tim Cook: personal data being 'weaponised'*. [Online] Available at: https://www.bbc.com/news/av/technology-45969382 [Accessed 21/4/21].

Beck, R., Müller-Bloch, C. & King, J., 2018. Governance in the blockchain economy: A framework and research agenda. *Journal of the Association for Information Systems*, Volume 19(10), p. 1.

Belk, R., 2014. You are what you can access: Sharing and collaborative consumption online. *Journal of Business Research*, 67(8), pp. 1595–1600.

Bell L., 2018. *Europe is the world's biggest target for DDoS attacks, F5 Networks claims*. [Online] Available at: https://www.itpro.co.uk/security/30500/europe-is-the-worlds-biggest-target-for-ddos-attacks-f5-networks-claims [Accessed 21/4/21].

Belleflamme, P. & Peitz, M., 2018. Platforms and network effects. In: *Handbook of Game Theory and Industrial Organization*, (eds) Luis C. Corchón and Marco A. Marini, s.l.: Edward Elgar Publishing, Volume II, pp. 286–317.

Benner, K., 2017. *Inside the Hotel Industry's Plan to Combat Airbnb*. [Online] Available at: https://www.nytimes.com/2017/04/16/technology/inside-the-hotel-industrys-plan-to-combat-airbnb.html [Accessed 5/5/21].

BEREC, 2021. *Body of European Regulators for Electronic Comminications*. [Online] Available at: https://berec.europa.eu/ [Accessed 30/4/21].

Berg, J., 2016. *Income Security in the Collaborative Economy: Findings and Policy lessons from a survey of crowdworkers*, Geneva: International Labour Office.

Bergen, M., 2019. *YouTube Executives Ignored Warnings, Letting Toxic Videos Run Rampant.* [Online] Available at: https://www.bloomberg.com/news/features/2019-04-02/youtube-executives-ignored-warnings-letting-toxic-videos-run-rampant [Accessed 10/5/21].

Bergeron, R., 2020. *A non-profit is gathering laptops and other devices so hospital patients can say goodbye to their loved ones.* [Online] Available at: https://edition.cnn.com/2020/04/15/health/iyw-coronavirus-donating-devices-to-hospitals-trnd/index.html [Accessed 20/4/21].

Berkman, H., Jona, J., Lee, G. & Soderstrom, N., 2018. Cybersecurity awareness and market valuations. *Journal of Accounting and Public Policy*, Volume 37(6), pp. 508–526.

Bertolini A., 2016. *Liability and Risk Management in Robotics*, s.l., Presentation to the European Parliament.

Bessen, J., 2015. Toil and Technology. *Finance and Development*, 52(1), 16–19.

Bessen, J., 2016. How computer automation affects occupations: technology, jobs, and skills Working Paper No. 15–49. *Boston University School of Law and Economics*.

Blanchet, T., Chancel, L. & Gethin, A., 2019. *Forty years of inequality in Europe: Evidence from distributional national accounts.* [Online] Available at: https://voxeu.org/article/forty-years-inequality-europe

Boeri, J., Conde-Ruiz, I. & Galasso, V., 2012. The Political Economy of Flexicurity. *Journal of the European Economic Association*, 10(4), pp. 684–715.

Boogost I., 2018. *Welcome to the Age of Privacy Nihilism.* [Online] Available at: https://www.theatlantic.com/technology/archive/2018/08/the-age-of-privacy-nihilism-is-here/568198/ [Accessed 21/4/21].

Bostrom, N., 2017. *Superintelligence.* s.l.: Dunod.

Botsman, R. & Rogers, R., 2010. *What's Mine Is Yours: The Rise of Collaboratie Consumption.* New York: Harper Collins.

Botsman, R., 2010. *The case for collaborative consumption.* Sydnex: TEDxSydney.

Boudreau, K. & Hagiu, A., 2009. Platform Rules: Multi-sided Platforms as Regulators. In: A. Gawer, a cura di *Platforms, Markets and Innovation*. Cheltenham, UK: Edward Elgar Publishing Limited, pp. 163–191.

Bourreau, M. & de Streel, A., 2019. Digital Conglomerates and EU Competition Policy. *SSNR*, 3. Volume Available at SSRN 3350512.

Bourreau, M., De Streel, A. & Graef, I., 2017. Big Data and Competition Policy: Market power, personalised pricing and advertising. *Personalised Pricing and Advertising*.

Bradshaw, S. & Howard, P., 2019. *The Global Disinformation Order. 2019 Global Inventory of Organised Social Media Manipulation*, Oxford: Oxford Internet Institute.

Bradshaw, S., 2019. Disinformation optimised: gaming search engine algorithms to amplify junk news. *Internet Policy Review*, Volume 8(4), pp. 1–24.

Brady, W. J. et al., 2017. *Emotion shapes the diffusion of moralized content in social networks.* s.l., Proceedings of the National Academy of Sciences, 114(28), pp. 7313–7318.

Brookings, 2019. *Productive equity: The twin challenges of reviving productivity and reducing inequality.* [Online] Available at: https://www.brookings.edu/research/productive-equity-the-twin-challenges-of-reviving-productivity-and-reducing-inequality/ [Accessed 7/5/21].

Bryant M., 2019. *Instagram's anti-bullying AI asks users: 'Are you sure you want to post this?'.* [Online] Available at: https://www.theguardian.com/technology/2019/jul/09/instagram-bullying-new-feature-do-you-want-to-post-this [Accessed 10/5/21].

Brynjolfsson, E. & McAfee, A., 2011. *Race against the machine: How the digital revolution is accelerating innovation, driving productivity, and irreversibly transforming employment and the economy.* s.l.: Brynjolfsson & McAfee.

Brynjolfsson, E. & McAfee, A., 2015. The Great Decoupling. *Harvard Business Review*, Issue June 2015, pp. 66–74.

Brynjolfsson, E. & Oh, J., 2012. *The attention economy: measuring the value of free digital services on the Internet*, s.l.: s.n.

Brynjolfsson, E., Hitt, L. M. & Kim, H. H., 2011. Strength in numbers: How does data-driven decision making affect firm performance? *SSRN*.

Buiten, M. C., de Streel, A. & Peitz, M., 2020. Rethinking liability rules for online hosting platforms. *International Journal of Law and Information Technology*, Volume 28, pp. 139–166.

Bundeskartellamt, 2015. *Bundeskartellamt takes decision in ancillary copyright dispute*. [Online] Available at: https://www.bundeskartellamt.de/SharedDocs/Meldung/EN/Pressemitteilungen/2015/09_09_2015_VG_Media_Google.html [Accessed 24/4/21].

Bundeskartellamt, 2018. *Guidance on Transaction Value Thresholds for mandatory Pre-merger Notification*. [Online] Available at: https://www.bundeskartellamt.de/SharedDocs/Publikation/EN/Leitfaden/Leitfaden_Transaktionsschwelle.pdf?__blob=publicationFile&v=2 [Accessed 24/4/21].

Burki, T., 2019. Vaccine misinformation and social media. *The Lancet*, October.

Bursztein, E. et al., 2019. Rethinking the detection of child sexual abuse imagery on the Internet. *The World Wide Web Conference*, pp. 2601–2607.

Cagé, J., Hervé, N. & Viaud, M. L., 2019. The production of information in an online world: Is copy right? *SSNR*.

Calo, R. & Crawford, K., 2016. *There is a blind spot in AI research*. [Online] Available at: https://www.nature.com/news/there-is-a-blind-spot-in-ai-research-1.20805 [Accessed 10/5/21].

Calo, R. & Rosenblat, A., 2017. The taking economy: Uber, information, and power. *Colum. L. Rev.*, Volume 117, p. 1623.

Calzada J., Gil R., 2019. *News aggregators and the reform of the copyright legislation in Europe*. [Online] Available at: https://voxeu.org/article/news-aggregators-and-european-copyright-legislation [Accessed 24/4/21].

Camera, A., 2015. *Interrogazione a Risposta Scritta 4/09150*. [Online] Available at: http://aic.camera.it/aic/scheda.html?numero=4%2F09150&ramo=CAMERA&leg=17 [Accessed 5/5/21].

Campaign to Stop Killer Robots, 2021. *Who wants to ban fully autonomous weapons?*. [Online] Available at: https://www.stopkillerrobots.org/ [Accessed 10/5/21].

Carr C., Arendt K., 2019. *Facebook's biggest losers: Content hurt by the last product strategy update*. [Online] Available at: https://blog.parse.ly/post/8383/facebooks-biggest-losers-content-hurt-by-the-last-product-strategy-update/ [Accessed 10/5/21].

Cave, M., 2006. Encouraging infrastructure competition via the ladder of investment. *Telecommunications Policy*, Volume 30, pp. 223–237.

Cave, S. & ÓhÉigeartaigh, S., 2018. An AI race for strategic advantage: rhetoric and risks. *Proceedings of the 2018 AAAI/ACM Conference on AI, Ethics, and Society*, pp. 36–40.

Cavusoglu, H., Mishra, B. & S., R., 2004. The Effect of Internet Security Breach Announcements on Market Value: Capital Market Reactions for Breached Firms and Internet Security Developers. *International Journal of Electronic Commerce*, Volume 9, pp. 69–104.

Celikel Esser, F. et al., 2016. *The European Collaborative Economy: A research agenda for policy support*, Luxembourg: Publications Office of the European Union.

Chen, M. & Sheldon, M., 2015. Dynamic Pricing in a Labor Market: Surge Pricing and Flexible Work on the Uber Platform. *Ec*, Volume 455(10.1145), pp. 2940716–2940798.

Chen, T. & Kockelman, K., 2015. Carsharing's Life-Cycle Impacts on Energy Use and Greenhouse Gas Emissions. *Transportation Research Pard D Transport and Environment*, 47(August), pp. 276–284.

Chia, P., Chuang, J. & Chen, Y., 2016. *Whack-a-mole: Asymmetric Conflict and Guerrilla Warfare in Web Security*. s.l., Proceedings of the 15th Annual Workshop on the Economics of Information Security.

Chiou, L. & Tucker, C., 2017. Content Aggregation by Platforms: The Case of the News Media. *Journal of Economics and Management Strategy*, Volume 26(4): 782–805.

Choe, E. et al., 2014. Understanding quantified-selfers' practices in collecting and exploring personal data. *Proceedings of the SIGCHI conference on human factors in computing systems*, Volume pp. 1143–1152.

Cisco, 2021. *What Are the Most Common Cyber Attacks?*. [Online] Available at: https://www.cisco.com/c/en/us/products/security/common-cyberattacks.html [Accessed 21/4/21].

Coad, A. & Duch-Brown, N., 2017. Barriers to European cross-border E-commerce. *JRC Digital Economy Working Paper.*, Volume No. 2017–03.

Codagnone, C. & Martens, B., 2016. Scoping the Sharing Economy: Origins, Definitions, Impact and Regulatory Issues. *Institute for Prospective Technological Studies Digital Economy Working Paper*, 26 May. Volume 2016/01. JRC100369.

Cohen, B., Hall, B. & Wood, C., 2017. Data Localization Laws and Their Impact on Privacy, Data Security and the Global Economy. *Antitrust*, Volume 32, p. 107.

Cohen, P., Hahn, R. H. J., Levitt, S. & Metcalfe, R., 2016. Using big data to estimate consumer surplus: The case of uber. *National Bureau of Economic Research*, Issue (No. w22627).

Consolidated versions of the Treaty on European Union and the Treaty on the Functioning of the European Union - Part three: Union Policies and Internal Actions - Title VII: Common rules on competition, taxation and approximation of laws - Chapter 1: Rules on competition (.), OJ 2008 L 115.

Contreras, J., 2015. A brief history of FRAND: analyzing current debates in standard setting and antitrust through a historical lens. *Antitrust Law Journal*, Volume 80(1), pp. 39–120.

Coppel, J., 2000. E-Commerce: Impacts and Policy Challenges. *OECD Economics Department Working Papers*.

Cornell Law School, 2021. *47 U.S. Code § 230 - Protection for private blocking and screening of offensive material*. [Online] Available at: https://www.law.cornell.edu/uscode/text/47/230 [Accessed 24/4/21].

Correa, J. A. a. O. C., 2014. Competition & Innovation: Evidence from U.S. Patent and Productivity Data. *The Journal of Industrial Economics*, 62(2), pp. 258–285.

Correa, J. A., 2012. Innovation and Competition: An Unstable Relationship. *Journal of Applied Econometrics*, 27(1), p. 160–166.

Council Directive (EU) 2017/2455 of 5 December 2017 amending Directive 2006/112/EC and Directive 2009/132/EC as regards certain value added tax obligations for supplies of services and distance sales of goods, OJ 2017 L 348.

Council Directive (EU) 2019/1995 of 21 November 2019 amending Directive 2006/112/EC as regards provisions relating to distance sales of goods and certain domestic supplies of goods, OJ 2019 L 310.

Council of the European Union, 2018. *Council Recommendation of 22 May 2018 on key competences for lifelong leaerning (2018/C 189/01)*. [Online] Available at: https://eur-lex.europa.eu/legal-content/EN/TXT/PDF/?uri=CELEX:32018H0604(01)&from=EN [Accessed 10/5/21].

Council Regulation (EC) No 139/2004 of 20 January 2004 on the control of concentrations between undertakings (the EC Merger Regulation) (Text with EEA relevance), OJ 2004 L 24.

Court of Justice of the European Union, 2017. *Press Release No 136/17: Judgement in Case C-434/15 Asociacion Prfesional Elite Taxi v Uber Systems Spain SL*, Case C-434/15 [2017].

Craigen, D., Diakun-Thibault, N. & Purse, R., 2014. Defining cybersecurity. *Technology Innovation Management Review*, Volume 4(10), pp. 13–21.

Crawford K., 2013. *The Hidden Biases in Big Data*. [Online] Available at: https://hbr.org/2013/04/the-hidden-biases-in-big-data [Accessed 10/5/21].

Crémer, J., de Montjoye, Y. & Schweitzer, H., 2019. *Competition Policy for the Digital Era*, s.l.: European Commission.

Crockett, M. J., 2017. Moral outrage in the digital age. *Nature human behaviour*, 1(11), pp. 769–771.

Croll A., 2011. *Who owns your data*. [Online] Available at: http://mashable.com/2011/01/12/data-ownership/#X8U9fB5H8kq4 [Accessed 21/4/21].

Cummings, M., 2017. *Artificial intelligence and the future of warfare*. London: Chatham House for the Royal Institute of International Affairs.

Curry, E., 2016. The big data value chain: definitions, concepts, and theoretical approaches. In: *New horizons for a data-driven economy*. s.l.: Springer, Cham., pp. 29–37.

Czernich, N., Falck, O., Kretschmer, T. & Woessmann, L., 2011. Broadband infrastructure and economic growth. *The Economic Journal*, Volume 121(552), pp. 505–532.

D4D Hub, 2021. *D4D Hub*. [Online] Available at: https://toolkit-digitalisierung.de/en/partners/multilateral/d4d-hub/ [Accessed 7/5/21].

Dananjayan, S. & Raj, G. M., 2020. Artificial Intelligence during a pandemic: The COVID-19 example. *The International Journal of Health Planning and Management*.

Dartford, K., 2019. *Rural Greece enjoys the benefits as internet isolation comes to an end.* [Online] Available at: https://www.euronews.com/2019/11/18/rural-greece-enjoys-the-benefits-as-internet-isolation-comes-to-an-end [Accessed 20/4/21].

Darvas, Z., 2020. *COVID-19 has widened the income gap in Europe.* [Online] Available at: https://www.bruegel.org/2020/12/covid-19-has-widened-the-income-gap-in-europe/ [Accessed 20/4/21].

Datta, A. & Agarwal, S., 2004. Telecommunications and economic growth: a panel data approach. *Applied Economics*, Volume 36(15), pp. 1649–1654.

Daugherty, T., Eastin, M. S. & Bright, L., 2008. Exploring consumer motivations for creating user-generated content. *Journal of interactive advertising*, 8(2), pp. 16–25.

Dawkins, R., 2016. *The Selfish Gene.* s.l.: Oxford University Press.

Day, G. & Stemler, A., 2019. Infracompetitive Privacy. *Iowa L. Rev.*, Volume 105, p. 61.

De Groen, W. & Maselli, I., 2016. *The Impact of the Collaborative Economy on the Labour Market*, s.l.: CEPS working paper.

De Hert, P. et al., 2018. The right to data portability in the GDPR: Towards user-centric interoperability of digital services. *Computer Law & Security Review*, Volume 34.

De la Mano, M. & Padilla, J., 2018. Big Tech Banking. *Journal of Competition Law & Economics*, 20 12. Volume 14(4), pp. 494–526.

de Reuver, M., Sørensen, C. & Basole, R., 2018. The digital platform: a research agenda. *Journal of Information Technology*, Volume 33(2), pp. 124–135.

De Streel, A. et al., 2020. *Online Platforms' Moderation of Illegal Content Online: Law, Practices and Options for Reform.*, s.l.: STUDY requested by the IMCO committee - European Parliament.

DeepMind, 2017. *AlphaGo Zero: Starting from scratch.* [Online] Available at: https://deepmind.com/blog/article/alphago-zero-starting-scratch [Accessed 10/5/21].

DeepMind, 2020. *AI could be one of humanity's most useful inventions.* [Online] Available at: https://deepmind.com/about#our_story [Accessed 10/5/21].

Degeling, M. et al., 2018. We value your privacy. now take some cookies: Measuring the GDPR's impact on web privacy. *arXiv p*, Volume reprint arXiv:1808.05096.

Deming, D., 2017. The growing importance of social skills in the labor market. *The Quarterly Journal of Economics*, Volume 132(4), pp. 1593–1640.

Diamond, J., 2013. *Guns, germs and steel: a short history of everybody for the last 13,000 years.* s.l.: Random House.

Dickinson, G., 2018. *How the world is going to war with Airbnb.* [Online] Available at: https://www.telegraph.co.uk/travel/news/where-is-airbnb-banned-illegal/ [Accessed 10/5/21].

Ding, J., 2018. *Deciphering China's AI dream*, s.l.: Future of Humanity Institute Technical Report.

Directive (EU) 2019/771 of the European Parliament and of the Council of 20 May 2019 on certain aspects concerning contracts for the sale of goods, amending Regulation (EU) 2017/2394 and Directive 2009/22/EC, and repealing Directive 1999/44/EC, OJ 2017 L 136/28.

Directive (EU) 2016/1148 of the European Parliament and of the Council of 6 July 2016 concerning measures for a high common level of security of network and information systems across the Union, OJ 2016 L 194/1.

Directive (EU) 2017/541 of the European Parliament and of the Council of 15 March 2017 on combating terrorism and replacing Council Framework Decision 2002/475/JHA and amending Council Decision 2005/671/JHA, OJ 2017 L 88/6.

Directive (EU) 2018/1808 of the European Parliament and of the Council of 14 November 2018 amending Directive 2010/13/EU on the coordination of certain provisions laid down by law, regulation or administrative action in Member States concerning the provision of audiovisual media services (Audiovisual Media Services Directive), OJ 2018 L 303.

Directive (EU) 2018/1972 of the European Parliament and of the Council of 11 December 2018 establishing the European Electronic Communications Code, OJ 2018 L 321/36.

Directive (EU) 2019/1024 of the European Parliament and of the Council of 20 June 2019 on open data and the re-use of public sector information, OJ 2019 L 172.

Directive (EU) 2019/2161 of the European Parliament and of the Council of 27 November 2019 amending Council Directive 93/13/EEC and Directives 98/6/EC, 2005/29/EC and 2011/83/EU of the European Parliament and of the Council as regards the better enforcement and modernisation of Union consumer protection rules (Text with EEA relevance), OJ 2019 L 328.

Directive (EU) 2019/770 of the European Parliament and of the Council of 20 May 2019 on certain aspects concerning contracts for the supply of digital content and digital services (Text with EEA relevance), OJ 2019 L 136/1.

Directive (EU) 2019/790 of the European Parliament and of the Council of 17 April 2019 on copyright and related rights in the Digital Single Market and amending Directives 96/9/EC and 2001/29/EC (Text with EEA relevance.), OJ 2019 L 130.

Directive 2000/31/EC of the European Parliament and of the Council of 8 June 2000 on certain legal aspects of information society services, in particular electronic commerce, in the Internal Market ('Directive on electronic commerce'), OJ 2000 L 178.

Directive 2003/98/EC of the European Parliament and of the Council of 17 November 2003 on the re-use of public sector information, OJ 2003 L 345.

Directive 2005/29/EC of the European Parliament and of the Council of 11 May 2005 concerning unfair business-to-consumer commercial practices in the internal market and amending Council Directive 84/450/EEC, Directives 97/7/EC, 98/27/EC and 2002/65/EC, OJ 2005 L 149.Directive 2006/123/EC of the European Parliament and of the Council of 12 December 2006 on services in the internal market, OJ 2006 L 376.

Directive 2010/13/EU of the European Parliament and of the Council of 10 March 2010 on the coordination of certain provisions laid down by law, regulation or administrative action in Member States concerning the provision of audiovisual media services, OJ 2010 L 95.

Directive 2011/92/EU of the European Parliament and of the Council of 13 December 2011 on combating the sexual abuse and sexual exploitation of children and child pornography, and replacing Council Framework Decision 2004/68/JHA, OJ 2011 L 335/1.

Directive 2013/37/UE of the European Parliament and of the Council of 26 June 2013 amending Directive 2003/98/EC on the re-use of public sector information,, OJ 2013 L 175.

Dischinger, M. & Riedel, N., 2011. Corporate taxes and the location of intangible assets within multinational firms. *Journal of Public Economics*, 7–8(95), pp. 691–707.

Doshi-Velez, F. & Kim, B., 2017. Towards a rigorous science of interpretable machine learning. *arXiv preprint arXiv:1702.08608, 27*.

Duch-Brown, N. & Cardona, M., 2016. Delivery costs and cross-border e-commerce in the EU digital single market. *Institute for Prospective Technological Studies Digital Economy Working Paper*, Volume No. 2016/03.

Duch-Brown, N. & Martens, B., 2016. The economic impact of removing geo-blocking restrictions in the EU Digital Single Market. *Joint Research Centre*, Volume Digital Economy Working Paper 2016/02.

Duch-Brown, N., Grzybowski, L. R. A. & Verboven, F., 2020. Online Market Integration and European Policy. *VOXeu*.

Echikson, W., 2020. *Europe's Digital Verification Opportunity*, s.l.: CEPS Research Paper.

Edelman, B. & Luca, M., 2014. Digital discrimination: The case of Airbnb.com. *Harvard Business School NOM Unit Working Paper*, Volume, (14–054).

Edelman, B., Luca, M. & Svirsky, D., 2017. Racial discrimination in the sharing economy: Evidence from a field experiment. *American Economic Journal: Applied Economics*, Volume 9(2), pp. 1–22.

Einav, L. & Levin, J., 2014. Economics in the age of big data. *Science*, Volume 346(6210).

Eisenmann, T., Parker, G. & Van Alstyne, M., 2011. Platform Envelopment. *Strategic Management Journal*.

Elia, G., Margherita, A. & Passiante, G., 2020. Digital entrepreneurship ecosystem: How digital technologies and collective intelligence are reshaping the entrepreneurial process. *Technological Forecasting and Social Change*, Volume 150, pp. 119791.

ENISA, 2019. *ENISA Threat Landscape Report 2018*. [Online] Available at: https://www.enisa.europa.eu/publications/enisa-threat-landscape-report-2018 [Accessed 21/4/21].

ENISA, 2021. *Vulnerabilities and Exploits*. [Online] Available at: https://www.enisa.europa.eu/topics/csirts-in-europe/glossary/vulnerabilities-and-exploits [Accessed 21/4/21].

EPSC, 2018. *The Age of Artificial Intelligence*, Bruxelles: European Political Strategy Centre, European Commission.

Esmeijer, J., Bakker, T. & de Munck, S., 2013. *Thriving and surviving in a data-driven society*, s.l.: TNO.

EU Disinfo Lab, 2020. *Platforms' responses to COVID-19 mis- and disinformation.* [Online] Available at: https://www.disinfo.eu/resources/covid-19/platforms-responses-to-covid-19-mis-and-disinformation [Accessed 10/4/21].

Eurofound, 2019. *Virtual and augmented reality: Implications of game-changing technologies in the services sector in Europe.* [Online] Available at: https://euagenda.eu/upload/publications/untitled-262817-ea.pdf [Accessed 10/4/21].

Eurofound, 2020. *COVID-19 unleashed the potential for telework – How are workers coping?.* [Online] Available at: https://www.eurofound.europa.eu/fr/publications/blog/covid-19-unleashed-the-potential-for-telework-how-are-workers-coping [Accessed 30/4/21].

Eurofound, 2021. *Eurofound.* [Online] Available at: https://www.eurofound.europa.eu/ [Accessed 7/5/21].

European Commission, 2010a. *Communication from the Commission to the European Parliament, the Council, the European Economic and Social Committee and the Committee of the Regions - A Digital Agenda for Europe.* [Online] Available at: https://eur-lex.europa.eu/LexUriServ/LexUriServ.do?uri=COM:2010:0245:FIN:EN:PDF [Accessed 20/4/21].

European Commission, 2011. *Guidelines on the applicability of Article 101 of the Treaty on the Functioning of the European Union to horizontal co-operation agreements.* [Online] Available at: https://eur-lex.europa.eu/legal-content/EN/TXT/HTML/?uri=CELEX:52011XC0114(04)&from=EN [Accessed 21/4/211].

European Commission, 2013. *Communication on Cybersecurity Strategy of the European Union: An Open, Safe and Secure Cyberspace.* [Online] Available at: https://eur-lex.europa.eu/legal-content/EN/TXT/?uri=celex%3A52013JC0001

European Commission, 2014a. *Broadband Investment Guide.* [Online] Available at: https://ec.europa.eu/digital-single-market/en/news/broadband-investment-guide [Accessed 20/4/21].

European Commission, 2014b. *Towards a thriving data-driven economy.* [Online] Available at: http://ec.europa.eu/newsroom/dae/document.cfm?action=display&doc_id=6210 [Accessed 21/4/21].

European Commission, 2015. *Communication: The European Agenda on Security.* [Online] Available at: https://eur-lex.europa.eu/legal-content/GA/TXT/?uri=CELEX:52015DC0185

European Commission, 2015a. *Communication from the Commission to the European Parliament, the Council, the European Economic and Social Committee and the Committee of the Regions - A Digital Single Market Strategy for Europe COM/2015/0192.* [Online] Available at: https://eur-lex.europa.eu/legal-content/EN/TXT/?uri=celex%3A52015DC0192 [Accessed 20/4/21].

European Commission, 2015b. *New rules on roaming charges and open Internet.* [Online] Available at: https://digital-strategy.ec.europa.eu/en/news/new-rules-roaming-charges-and-open-internet [Accessed 20/4/21].

European Commission, 2015c. *Public consultation on the regulatory environment for platforms, online intermediaries, data and cloud computing and the collaborative economy.* [Online] Available at: https://ec.europa.eu/digital-single-market/en/news/public-consultation-regulatory-environment-platforms-online-intermediaries-data-and-cloud [Accessed 24/4/21].

European Commission, 2016a. *Communication from the Commission to the European Parliament, the Council, the European Economic and Social Committee and the Committee of the Regions - Digitising European Industry Reaping the full benefits of a Digital Single Market.* [Online] Available at: https://eur-lex.europa.eu/legal-content/EN/TXT/?uri=CELEX%3A52016DC0180 [Accessed 20/4/21].

European Commission, 2016b. *Communication from the Commission to the European Parliament, the Council, the European Economic and Social Committee and The Committee of the Regions European Cloud Initiative -Building a competitive data and knowledge economy in Europe.* [Online] Available at: https://eur-lex.europa.eu/legal-content/GA/TXT/?uri=CELEX%3A52016DC0288 [Accessed 20/4/21].

European Commission, 2016c. *Commercial sector: EU-US Privacy Shield.* [Online] Available at: https://ec.europa.eu/info/law/law-topic/data-protection/international-dimension-data-protection/eu-us-data-transfers_en [Accessed 21/4/21].

European Commission, 2016d. *Simplifying e-procurement and e-invoicing adoption.* [Online] Available at: https://ec.europa.eu/isa2/actions/simplifying-public-tenders_en [Accessed 20/4/21].

European Commission, 2016e. *Communication from the Commission: Connectivity for a Competitive Digital Single Market - Towards a European Gigabit Society.* [Online] Available at: https://ec.europa.eu/newsroom/dae/document.cfm?doc_id=17182 [Accessed 20/4/21].

European Commission, 2016f. *Communication from the Commission to the European Parliament, the Council, the European Economic and Social Committee and the Committee of the Regions EU eGovernment Action Plan 2016–2020 Accelerating the digital transformation of government.* [Online] Available at: https://eur-lex.europa.eu/legal-content/EN/TXT/?uri=CELEX:52016DC0179 [Accessed 20/4/21].

European Commission, 2016h. *A comprehensive approach to stimulating cross-border e-Commerce for Europe's citizens and businesses.* [Online] Available at: https://eur-lex.europa.eu/legal-content/EN/TXT/?uri=CELEX%3A52016SC0163 [Accessed 24/4/21].

European Commission, 2016i. *Communication on Online Platforms and the Digital Single Market Opportunities and Challenges for Europe.* [Online] Available at: https://ec.europa.eu/digital-single-market/en/news/communication-online-platforms-and-digital-single-market-opportunities-and-challenges-europe [Accessed 24/4/21].

European Commission, 2016j. *Commission Decision (EU) 2017/1283 of 30 August 2016 on State aid SA.38373 (2014/C) (ex 2014/NN) (ex 2014/CP) implemented by Ireland to Apple (notified under document C(2017) 5605).* [Online] Available at: https://eur-lex.europa.eu/eli/dec/2017/1283/oj [Accessed 4/5/21].

European Commission, 2016k. *Communication from the Commission to the European Parliament, the Council, the European Economic and Social Committee and the Committee of the Regions: A European agenda for the Collaborative Economy COM/2016/0356 final.* [Online] Available at: https://eur-lex.europa.eu/legal-content/EN/TXT/?uri=COM%3A2016%3A356%3AFIN [Accessed 4/5/21].

European Commission, 2016l. *Communication from the Commission to the European Parliament and the Council, the European Economic and Social Committee and the Committee of the Regions: A New Skills Agenda for Working together to strengthen human capital, employability (.).* [Online] Available at: https://eur-lex.europa.eu/legal-content/EN/TXT/?uri=CELEX:52016DC0381 [Accessed 7/5/21].

European Commission, 2016m. *Proposal for a COUNCIL RECOMMENDATION on the European Qualifications Framework for lifelong learning and repealing the Recommendation of the European Parliament and of the Council of 23 April 2008 on the establishment of the European Qualifications (.).* [Online] Available at: https://eur-lex.europa.eu/legal-content/EN/TXT/?uri=CELEX:52016DC0383 [Accessed 7/5/21].

European Commission, 2016n. *Ten actions to help equip people in Europe with better skills.* [Online] Available at: https://ec.europa.eu/esf/home.jsp [Accessed 7/5/21].

European Commission, 2016o. *The competition rules for supply and distribution.* [Online] Available at: https://ec.europa.eu/digital-single-market/en/news/full-synopsis-report-public-consultation-needs-internet-speed-and-quality-beyond-2020 [Accessed 7/5/21].

European Commission, 2017a. *Antitrust/Cartel Cases.* [Online] Available at: https://ec.europa.eu/competition/elojade/isef/case_details.cfm?proc_code=1_39740 [Accessed 21/4/21].

European Commission, 2017b. *Building a European Data Economy.* [Online] Available at: https://ec.europa.eu/newsroom/dae/document.cfm?doc_id=41205 [Accessed 21/4/21].

European Commission, 2017c. *Communication from the Commission to the European Parliament, the Council, the European Economic and Social Committee and the Committee of the Regions European Interoperability Framework – Implementation Strategy.* [Online] Available at: https://eur-lex.europa.eu/resource.html?uri=cellar:2c2f2554-0faf-11e7-8a35-01aa75ed71a1.0017.02/DOC_1&format=PDF [Accessed 21/4/21].

European Commission, 2017d. *Europeans' attitudes towards cyber security.* [Online] Available at: https://op.europa.eu/en/publication-detail/-/publication/388ac375-c438-11e7-9b01-01aa75ed71a1/language-en/format-PDF/source-50238852 [Accessed 21/4/21].

European Commission, 2017e. *Mergers: Commission fines Facebook €110 million for providing misleading information about WhatsApp takeover.* [Online] Available at: https://ec.europa.eu/commission/presscorner/detail/en/IP_17_1369 [Accessed 21/4/21].

European Commission, 2017f. *Tackling Illegal Content Online. Towards an enhanced responsibility of online platforms.* [Online] Available at: https://ec.europa.eu/newsroom/dae/document.cfm?doc_id=47383 [Accessed 21/4/21].

European Commission, 2017g. *Recordings of the multi-stakeholder conference on fake news.* [Online] Available at: https://digital-strategy.ec.europa.eu/en/library/recordings-multi-stakeholder-conference-fake-news [Accessed 10/5/21].

European Commission, 2017h. *Call for applications for the selection of members of the High Level group on Fake News.* [Online] Available at: https://digital-strategy.ec.europa.eu/en/news/call-applications-selection-members-high-level-group-fake-news [Accessed 10/5/21].

European Commission, 2017i. *European Pillar of Social Rights – booklet.* [Online] Available at: https://ec.europa.eu/info/publications/european-pillar-social-rights-booklet_en [Accessed 7/5/21].

European Commission, 2018. *Final report of the High Level Expert Group on Fake News and Online Disinformation.* [Online] Available at: https://digital-strategy.ec.europa.eu/en/library/final-report-high-level-expert-group-fake-news-and-online-disinformation [Accessed 10/5/21].

European Commission, 2018b. *Towards a common European data space.* [Online] Available at: https://eur-lex.europa.eu/legal-content/EN/TXT/PDF/?uri=CELEX:52018DC0232&from=EN [Accessed 21/4/21].

European Commission, 2018d. *The 2018 Ageing Report: Economic and Budgetary Projections for the EU Member States (2016–2070).* [Online] Available at: https://ec.europa.eu/info/publications/economy-finance/2018-ageing-report-economic-and-budgetary-projections-eu-member-states-2016-2070_en [Accessed 21/4/21].

European Commission, 2018e. *Blockchain for Government and the Public Services.* [Online] Available at: https://www.eublockchainforum.eu/sites/default/files/reports/eu_observatory_blockchain_in_government_services_v1_2018-12-07.pdf?width=1024&height=800&iframe=true [Accessed 21/4/21].

European Commission, 2018f. *Communication from the Commission to the European Parliament, the Council, the European Economic and Social Committee and the Committee of the Regions on enabling the digital transformation of health and care in the Digital Single Market.* [Online] Available at: https://ec.europa.eu/newsroom/dae/document.cfm?doc_id=51628 [Accessed 21/4/21].

European Commission, 2018g. *Tackling online disinformation: a European Approach.* [Online] Available at: https://eur-lex.europa.eu/legal-content/EN/TXT/?uri=CELEX:52018DC0236 [Accessed 10/5/21].

European Commission, 2018h. *Proposal for a Regulation of the European Parliament and of the Council on preventing the dissemination of terrorist content online.* [Online] Available at: https://eur-lex.europa.eu/legal-content/EN/TXT/?uri=SWD:2018:408:FIN [Accessed 24/4/21].

European Commission, 2018i. *A Europe that protects: Commission reinforces EU response to illegal content online.* [Online] Available at: https://ec.europa.eu/commission/presscorner/api/files/document/print/en/ip_18_1169/IP_18_1169_EN.pdf [Accessed 24/4/21].

European Commission, 2018j. *Action Plan against Disinformation.* [Online] Available at: https://digital-strategy.ec.europa.eu/en/library/action-plan-against-disinformation [Accessed 21/4/21].

European Commission, 2018k. *Artificial Intelligence for Europe.* [Online] Available at: https://ec.europa.eu/newsroom/dae/document.cfm?doc_id=51625 [Accessed 10/5/21].

European Commission, 2018l. *Coordinated Plan on Artificial Intelligence.* [Online] Available at: https://ec.europa.eu/newsroom/dae/document.cfm?doc_id=56018 [Accessed 10/5/21].

European Commission, 2018n. *Communication from the Commission to the European Parliament and the Council: Time to establish a modern, fair and efficient taxation standard for the digital economy COM/2018/0146 final.* [Online] Available at: https://eur-lex.europa.eu/legal-content/EN/TXT/?uri=CELEX%3A52018DC0146 [Accessed 4/5/21].

European Commission, 2018o. *Impact Assessment Accompanying the document Proposal for a Council Directive laying down rules relating to the corporate taxation of a significant digital presence (.).* [Online] Available at: https://ec.europa.eu/taxation_customs/sites/taxation/files/fair_taxation_digital_economy_ia_21032018.pdf [Accessed 3/5/21].

European Commission, 2018p. *Questions and Answers on a Fair and Efficient Tax System in the EU for the Digital Single Market*. [Online] Available at: https://ec.europa.eu/commission/presscorner/detail/sv/MEMO_18_2141 [Accessed 3/5/21].

European Commission, 2019. *Guidance on the Regulation on a framework for the free flow of non-personal data in the European Union COM/2019/250*. [Online] Available at: https://eur-lex.europa.eu/legal-content/EN/TXT/?uri=COM:2019:250:FIN

European Commission, 2019a. *European Commission adopts adequacy decision on Japan, creating the world's largest area of safe data flows*. [Online] Available at: https://ec.europa.eu/commission/presscorner/detail/en/IP_19_421 [Accessed 21/4/21].

European Commission, 2019b. *ICT-ENABLED PUBLIC SECTOR INNOVATION EU-funded projects on co-creation for the public sector*. [Online] Available at: https://ec.europa.eu/info/sites/info/files/research_and_innovation/contact/documents/egov_brochure_interactive_1.pdf [Accessed 21/4/21].

European Commission, 2019c. *Report from the Commission to the European Parliament and the Council assessing the consistency of the approaches taken by Member States in the identification of operators of essential services in accordance with Article 23(1) of Directive 2016/1148/EU* (COM (2019) 546 final). [Online] Available at: https://eur-lex.europa.eu/legal-content/EN/TXT/PDF/?uri=CELEX:52019DC0546&from=EN [Accessed 24/4/21].

European Commission, 2019d. *Mergers: Commission approves acquisition of Red Hat by IBM*. [Online] Available at: https://ec.europa.eu/commission/presscorner/detail/en/IP_19_3433 [Accessed 24/4/21].

European Commission, 2019e. *Antitrust: Commission imposes interim measures on Broadcom in TV and modem chipset markets*. [Online] Available at: https://ec.europa.eu/commission/presscorner/detail/en/IP_19_6109 [Accessed 24/4/21].

European Commission, 2019f. *Study on media literacy and online empowerment issues raised by algorithm-driven media services (SMART 2017/0081)*. [Online] Available at: https://digital-strategy.ec.europa.eu/en/library/study-media-literacy-and-online-empowerment-issues-raised-algorithm-driven-media-services-smart [Accessed 10/5/21].

European Commission, 2019g. *Ethics guidelines for trustworthy AI*. [Online] Available at: https://ec.europa.eu/newsroom/dae/document.cfm?doc_id=60419 [Accessed 10/5/21].

European Commission, 2019h. *Communication: Building Trust in Human Centric Artificial Intelligence*. [Online] Available at: https://digital-strategy.ec.europa.eu/en/library/communication-building-trust-human-centric-artificial-intelligence [Accessed 10/5/21].

European Commission, 2019i. *The New Deal for Consumers: What benefits will I get as a consumer?*. [Online] Available at: https://ec.europa.eu/info/sites/info/files/factsheet_new_deal_consumer_benefits_2019.pdf [Accessed 4/5/21].

European Commission, 2019j. *EU Science Hub: EntreComp: The entrepreneurship competence framework*. [Online] Available at: https://ec.europa.eu/jrc/entrecomp [Accessed 10/5/211].

European Commission, 2020. *Communication on The EU's Cybersecurity Strategy for the Digital Decade*. [Online] Available at: https://ec.europa.eu/newsroom/dae/document.cfm?doc_id=72164

European Commission, 2020. *Communication: A New Industrial Strategy*. [Online] Available at: https://eur-lex.europa.eu/legal-content/EN/TXT/?qid=1593086905382&uri=CELEX%3A52020DC0102

European Commission, 2020. *Proposal for a Directive on the resilience of critical entities*. [Online] Available at: https://eur-lex.europa.eu/legal-content/EN/TXT/?uri=COM:2020:829:FIN

European Commission, 2020. *Proposal for directive on measures for high common level of cybersecurity across the Union*. [Online] Available at: https://ec.europa.eu/newsroom/dae/document.cfm?doc_id=72166

European Commission, 2020a. *State of the Union Address by President von der Leyen at the European Parliament Plenary*. [Online] Available at: https://ec.europa.eu/commission/presscorner/detail/en/SPEECH_20_1655 [Accessed 20/4/21].

European Commission, 2020b. *Equipping Europe for world-class High Performance Computing in the next decade*. [Online] Available at: https://eur-lex.europa.eu/LexUriServ/LexUriServ.do?uri=SWD:2020:0179:FIN:EN:PDF [Accessed 20/4/21].

European Commission, 2020c. *I-DESI 2020: How digital is Europe compared to other major world economies?*. [Online] Available at: https://digital-strategy.ec.europa.eu/en/library/i-desi-2020-how-digital-europe-compared-other-major-world-economies [Accessed 20/4/21].

European Commission, 2020d. *Digital Economy and Society Index (DESI) 2020 Questions and Answers.* [Online] Available at: https://ec.europa.eu/commission/presscorner/detail/en/qanda_20_1022 [Accessed 20/4/21].

European Commission, 2020e. *The Digital Single Market.* [Online] Available at: https://ec.europa.eu/competition/sectors/telecommunications/overview_en.html [Accessed 30/4/21].

European Commission, 2020f. *Secure 5G networks: Commission endorses EU toolbox and sets out next steps.* [Online] Available at: https://ec.europa.eu/commission/presscorner/detail/en/IP_20_123 [Accessed 20/4/21].

European Commission, 2020g. *Cybersecurity of 5G networks.* [Online] Available at: https://ec.europa.eu/newsroom/dae/document.cfm?doc_id=64468 [Accessed 20/4/21].

European Commission, 2020h. *Report on the safety and liability implications of Artificial Intelligence, the Internet of Things and robotics.* [Online] Available at: https://ec.europa.eu/info/sites/info/files/report-safety-liability-artificial-intelligence-feb2020_en_1.pdf [Accessed 21/4/21].

European Commission, 2020i. *A European strategy for data.* [Online] Available at: https://ec.europa.eu/info/sites/info/files/communication-european-strategy-data-19feb2020_en.pdf [Accessed 21/4/21].

European Commission, 2020j. *Proposal for a Regulation of the European Parliament and of the Council on European data governance (Data Governance Act).* [Online] Available at: https://eur-lex.europa.eu/legal-content/EN/TXT/?uri=CELEX%3A52020PC0767 [Accessed 21/4/21].

European Commission, 2020k. *Report on the Impact of Demographic Change, European Commission.* [Online] Available at: https://ec.europa.eu/info/files/report-impact-demographic-change-commission-communication_en [Accessed 21/4/21].

European Commission, 2020l. *Communication from the Commission to the European Parliament, the Council, the European Economic and Social Committee and the Committee of the Regions Horizon 2020 - The Framework Programme for Research and Innovation.* [Online] Available at: https://eur-lex.europa.eu/legal-content/EN/ALL/?uri=CELEX%3A52011DC0808 [Accessed 21/4/21].

European Commission, 2020m. *Towards a European strategy on business-to-government data sharing for the public interest.* [Online] Available at: https://ec.europa.eu/newsroom/dae/document.cfm?doc_id=64954 [Accessed 21/4/21].

European Commission, 2020o. *Proposal for a Regulation of the European Parliament and of the Council on contestable and fair markets in the digital sector (Digital Markets Act) (COM (2020) 842 final), 2020/0374 (COD).* [Online] Available at: https://ec.europa.eu/info/sites/info/files/proposal-regulation-single-market-digital-services-digital-services-act_en.pdf [Accessed 24/4/21]

European Commission, 2020p. *Proposal for a Regulation of the European Parliament and of the Council on a Single Market For Digital Services (Digital Services Act) and amending Directive 2000/31/EC (COM (2020) 825 final).* [Online] Available at: https://ec.europa.eu/digital-single-market/en/news/proposal-regulation-european-parliament-and-council-single-market-digital-services-digital [Accessed 21/4/21]

European Commission, 2020r. *EU Code of Practice on Disinformation.* [Online] Available at: https://ec.europa.eu/newsroom/dae/document.cfm?doc_id=54454 [Accessed 10/5/21].

European Commission, 2020s. *White Paper on Artificial Intelligence - A European approach to excellence and trust.* [Online] Available at: https://ec.europa.eu/info/sites/default/files/commission-white-paper-artificial-intelligence-feb2020_en.pdf [Accessed 10/5/21].

European Commission, 2020t. *Multiannual financial framework 2021–2027.* [Online] Available at: https://ec.europa.eu/info/strategy/eu-budget/long-term-eu-budget/2021-2027/documents_en [Accessed 10/5/21].

European Commission, 2020u. *Explanatory Notes on VAT e-commerce rules.* [Online] Available at: https://ec.europa.eu/taxation_customs/sites/taxation/files/vatecommerceexplanatory_notes_30092020.pdf [Accessed 4/5/21].

European Commission, 2021. *2030 Digital Compass: the European way for the Digital Decade.* [Online] Available at: https://eur-lex.europa.eu/resource.html?uri=cellar:12e835e2-81af-11eb-9ac9-01aa75ed71a1.0001.02/DOC_1&format=PDF

European Commission, 2021. *Communication: The European Pillar of Social Rights Action Plan.* [Online] Available at: https://ec.europa.eu/social/BlobServlet?docId=23696&langId=en

European Commission, 2021. *Guidance on Strengthening the Code of Practice on Disinformation.* [Online] Available at: https://ec.europa.eu/newsroom/dae/redirection/document/76495

European Commission, 2021. *Proposal for a Regulation amending Regulation (EU) No 910/2014 as regards establishing a framework for a European Digital Identity* (COM (2021) 281 final), 2021/0136 (COD). [Online] Available at: https://eur-lex.europa.eu/resource.html?uri=cellar:5d88943a-c458-11eb-a925-01aa75ed71a1.0001.02/DOC_1&format=PDF

European Commission, 2021. *Proposal for a Regulation on Aritifical Intelligence (ARTIFICIAL INTELLIGENCE ACT).* [Online] Available at: https://eur-lex.europa.eu/legal-content/EN/TXT/?qid=1623335154975&uri=CELEX%3A52021PC0206

European Commission, 2021. *SWD (2020)180 Assessment of the Code of Practice on Disinformation.* [Online] Available at: https://ec.europa.eu/newsroom/dae/document.cfm?doc_id=69212

European Commission, 2021. *Updating the 2020 Communication: A New Industrial Strategy.* [Online] Available at: https://ec.europa.eu/info/sites/default/files/communication-industrial-strategy-update-2020_en.pdf

European Commission, 2021a. *The European Digital Strategy.* [Online] Available at: https://ec.europa.eu/digital-single-market/en/content/european-digital-strategy [Accessed 20/4/21].

European Commission, 2021b. *Data Visualisation Tool - Data & Indicators.* [Online] Available at: https://digital-agenda-data.eu/ [Accessed 20/4/21].

European Commission, 2021c. *Broadband Glossary.* [Online] Available at: https://digital-strategy.ec.europa.eu/en/policies/broadband-glossary#B [Accessed 20/4/21].

European Commission, 2021d. *Broadband strategy & policy.* [Online] Available at: https://ec.europa.eu/digital-single-market/en/broadband-strategy-policy [Accessed 30/4/21].

European Commission, 2021e. *European data strategy.* [Online] Available at: https://ec.europa.eu/info/strategy/priorities-2019-2024/europe-fit-digital-age/european-data-strategy_en [Accessed 20/4/21].

European Commission, 2021f. *The impact of demographic change in Europe.* [Online] Available at: https://ec.europa.eu/info/strategy/priorities-2019-2024/new-push-european-democracy/impact-demographic-change-europe_en [Accessed 20/4/21].

European Commission, 2021g. *Non-legislative measures to facilitate reuse.* [Online] Available at: https://digital-strategy.ec.europa.eu/en/policies/non-legislative-measures-facilitate-reuse [Accessed 20/4/21].

European Commission, 2021h. *Taxation and Customs Union: Business: VAT: Existing EU legal framework.* [Online] Available at: https://ec.europa.eu/taxation_customs/business/vat/existing-eu-legal-framework_en [Accessed 4/5/21].

European Commission, 2021i. *Attitudes towards the impact of digitisation and automation on daily life.* [Online] Available at: https://digital-strategy.ec.europa.eu/en/news/attitudes-towards-impact-digitisation-and-automation-daily-life [Accessed 5/5/21].

European Commission, 2021j. *Shaping Europe's digital future: Digital skills and job coalition.* [Online] Available at: https://ec.europa.eu/digital-single-market/en/digital-skills-jobs-coalition [Accessed 7/5/21].

European Commission, 2021k. *Employment, Social Affairs & Inclusion: EU Programme for Employment and Social Innovation (EaSI).* [Online] Available at: https://ec.europa.eu/social/main.jsp?catId=1081&langId=en [Accessed 7/5/21].

European Commission, 2021l. *Technical Support Instrument (TSI): About the TSI.* [Online] Available at: https://ec.europa.eu/info/funding-tenders/funding-opportunities/funding-programmes/overview-funding-programmes/structural-reform-support-programme-srsp_en [Accessed 7/5/21].

European Commission, 2021m. *European Social Fund.* [Online] Available at: https://ec.europa.eu/esf/home.jsp [Accessed 7/5/21].

European Commission, 2021n. *EU Science Hub: DigComp.* [Online] Available at: https://ec.europa.eu/jrc/digcomp [Accessed 7/5/21].

European Commission, 2021o. *International Partnerships: Reducing inequality.* [Online] Available at: https://ec.europa.eu/international-partnerships/sdg/reducing-inequality_en [Accessed 7/5/21].

European Commission, 2021p. *Eurostat*. [Online] Available at: https://ec.europa.eu/eurostat/web/european-pillar-of-social-rights/overview [Accessed 7/5/21].

European Commission, 2021q. *Digital4Development: mainstreaming digital technologies and services into EU Development Policy*. [Online] Available at: https://digital-strategy.ec.europa.eu/en/library/digital4development-mainstreaming-digital-technologies-and-services-eu-development-policy [Accessed 9/5/21].

European Commission, 2021r. *European Development Fund*. [Online] Available at: https://ec.europa.eu/info/strategy/eu-budget/eu-budget-news-events-and-publications/documents/european-development-fund_en [Accessed 7/5/21].

European Commission, 2021s. *Communication - Tackling online disinformation: a European Approach*. [Online] Available at: https://digital-strategy.ec.europa.eu/en/library/communication-tackling-online-disinformation-european-approach [Accessed 10/5/21].

European Council, 2015. *European Council meeting*. [Online] Available at: https://www.consilium.europa.eu/media/21888/european-council-conclusions-19-20-march-2015-en.pdf [Accessed 10/5/21].

European Institute for Gender Equality, 2020. *Gender Equality Index 2020: Digitalisation and the future of work*. [Online] Available at: https://eige.europa.eu/publications/gender-equality-index-2020-digitalisation-and-future-work [Accessed 7/5/21].

European Paliament, 2017. *Robots: Legal Affairs Committee calls for EU-wide rules*. [Online] Available at: https://www.europarl.europa.eu/news/en/press-room/20170110IPR57613/robots-legal-affairs-committee-calls-for-eu-wide-rules [Accessed 10/5/21].

European Parliament, 2018. *European Parliament speaks out against "killer robots"*. [Online] Available at: https://www.europarl.europa.eu/news/en/press-room/20180906IPR12123/european-parliament-speaks-out-against-killer-robots [Accessed 10/5/21].

European Parliament, 2019. *Disinformation and propaganda - impact on the functioning of the rule of law in the EU and its Member States*, s.l.: Policy Department for Citizens' Rights and Constitutional Affairs.

European Political Strategy Centre, 2017. *Enter the Data Economy*. [Online].

Eurostat, 2019. *Glossary: Lifelong learning*. [Online] Available at: https://ec.europa.eu/eurostat/statistics-explained/index.php?title=Glossary:Lifelong_learning [Accessed 5/5/21].

Eurostat, 2021. *European Statistics*. [Online] Available at: https://ec.europa.eu/eurostat/data/database [Accessed 20/4/21].

Evans, D. & Schmalensee, R., 2013. The antitrust analysis of multi-sided platform businesses. *National Bureau of Economic Research*, Volume No. w18783.

Evans, P. & Gawer, A., 2016. *The rise of the platform enterprise: A global survey*, s.l.: The Center for Global Enterprise.

Facebook, 2019. *First Grants Announced for Independent Research on Social Media's Impact on Democracy Using Facebook Data*. [Online] Available at: https://about.fb.com/news/2019/04/election-research-grants/ [Accessed 10/5/21].

Facebook, 2020. *Fake Accounts*. [Online] Available at: https://transparency.facebook.com/community-standards-enforcement#fake-accounts [Accessed 10/5/21].

Faroukhi, A., El Alaoui, I., Gahi, Y. & Amine, A., 2020. Big data monetization throughout Big Data Value Chain: a comprehensive review. *Journal of Big Data*, Volume 7(1), pp. 1–22.

Fenner, G. H. & Renn, R. W., 2010. Technology-assisted supplemental work and work-to-family conflict: The role of instrumentality beliefs, organizational expectations and time management. *Human Relations*, 63(1), pp. 63–82.

Fernandez, S. & Rainey, H., 2017. Managing successful organizational change in the public sector. *Debating public administration*, Volume (pp. 7–26). Routledge.

Filippas, A., Horton, J. & Golden, J., 2018. Reputation inflation. *Proceedings of the 2018 ACM Conference on Economics and Computation (pp. 483–484)*.

Financial Times, 2021. *Financial Times*. [Online] Available at: https://www.ft.com/content/aaf2bb08-dca2-11e6-86ac-f253db7791c6 [Accessed 7/5/21].

Finck, M. & Pallas, M., 2020. They who must not be identified—distinguishing personal from non-personal data under the GDPR. *International Data Privacy Law*, 10(1), pp. 11–36.

Fingas J., 2017. *Facebook knew about Snap's struggles months before the public.* [Online] Available at: https://www.engadget.com/2017-08-13-facebook-knew-about-snap-struggles-through-app-tracking.html [Accessed 24/4/21].

Finnis, J., 2011. *Natural law and natural rights.* s.l.: Oxford University Press.

Flynn, D. J., Nyhan, B. & Reifler, J., 2017. The nature and origins of misperceptions: Understanding false and unsupported beliefs about politics. *Political Psychology*, Volume 38, pp. 127–150.

Frenken, K. & Schor, J., 2019. Putting the sharing economy into perspective. In: *A research agenda for sustainable consumption governance.* s.l.: Edward Elgar Publishing, pp. 3–10.

Freudenberg, N. & Ruglis, J., 2007. Reframing school dropout as a public health issue. *Preventing chronic disease*, 4(4), pp. 1–11.

Frey, C. & Osborne, M., 2013. The future of employment: How susceptible are jobs to computerisation?. *Technological forecasting and social change*, Volume 114, pp. 254–280.

Frost and Sullivan, 2016. *Future of Carsharing Market to 2025: Technology Advancements, Market Consolidation and Government Initiatives to Influence Market Growth Over the Next Decade.* [Online] Available at: https://store.frost.com/future-of-carsharing-market-to-2025.html [Accessed 4/5/21].

Gartner, 2017a. *The biggest roadblock to AI adoption is a lack of skilled workers.* [Online] Available at: https://venturebeat.com/2017/11/04/the-biggest-roadblock-in-ai-adoption-is-a-lack-of-skilled-workers/ [Accessed 10/5/21].

Gartner, 2017b. *Top 10 Strategic Technology Trends for 2017: A Gartner Trend Insight Report*, s.l.: s.n.

Gartner, 2020. *Gartner Forecasts Global Government IT Spending to Decline 0.6% in 2020.* [Online] Available at: https://www.gartner.com/en/newsroom/press-releases/2020-08-05-gartner-forecasts-global-government-it-spending-to-de [Accessed 21/4/21].

Gawer, A. & Srnicek, N., 2021. *Online platforms: Economic and societal effects*, s.l.: EPRS - Panel for the Future of Science and Technology.

Gawer, A., 2014. Bridging differing perspectives on technological platforms: Toward an integrative framework. *Research policy*, Volume 43(7), pp. 1239–1249.

GC and Others v Commission nationale de l'informatique et des libertés (CNIL), Case C-136/17 [2019], ECLI:EU:C:2019:773.

Ge, Y., Knittel, C., MacKenzie, D. & Zoepf, S., 2016. Racial and gender discrimination in transportation network companies. *National Bureau of Economic Research.*, Volume No. w22776.

GilPress, 2016. [Online] Available at: https://whatsthebigdata.com/2016/05/30/a-few-Internet-of-things-iot-facts-infographic/ [Accessed 27/5/21].

Goertzel, T., 1994. Belief in conspiracy theories. *Political psychology*, 15(4), pp. 731–742.

Golden, L., 2009. A Brief History of Long Work Time and the Contemporary Sources of Overwork. *Journal of Business Ethics*, 84(2), pp. 217–227.

Google Spain SL and Google Inc. v Agencia Española de Protección de Datos (AEPD) and Mario Costeja González, Case C-131/12, [2014] ECLI:EU:C:2014:317.

Gordon, L. & Loeb, M., 2006. *Managing cybersecurity resources: a cost-benefit analysis.* (Vol. 1) a cura di New York: McGraw-Hill.

Görög, G., 2018. The Definitions of Sharing Economy: A Systematic Literature Review. Management. *Management* (18544223), 13(2).

Graef, I., 2015. Market definition and market power in data: The case of online platforms. *World Competition*, Volume 38(4).

Guetta-Jeanrenau, L. & Mariniello, M., 2021. *Fair vaccine access is a goal Europe cannot afford to miss.* [Online] Available at: https://www.bruegel.org/2021/03/fair-vaccine-access-is-a-goal-europe-cannot-afford-to-miss/ [Accessed 20/4/21].

Gupta, A. et al., 2013. The who, what, why, and how of high performance computing in the cloud. In 2013 IEEE 5th international conference on clo. *IEEE 5th international conference on cloud computing technology and science*, (Vol. 1, pp. 306–314). IEEE.

Gyarmathy, K., 2019. *Edge Computing vs. Cloud Computing: What You Need to Know.* [Online] Available at: https://www.vxchnge.com/blog/edge-computing-vs-cloud-computing [Accessed 30/4/21].

Hagiu A., & Wright J., 2015. Multi-sided platforms. *International Journal of Industrial Organization*, Volume 43, pp. 162–174.

Haidt J., Rose-Stockwell T., 2019. *The Dark Psychology of Social Networks*. [Online] Available at: https://www.theatlantic.com/magazine/archive/2019/12/social-media-democracy/600763/ [Accessed 10/5/21].

Hao K., 2019. *Here are 10 ways AI could help fight climate change*. [Online] Available at: https://www.technologyreview.com/2019/06/20/134864/ai-climate-change-machine-learning/ [Accessed 10/5/21].

Harambam, J., 2020. *Why we should not treat all conspiracy theories the same*. [Online] Available at: https://theconversation.com/why-we-should-not-treat-all-conspiracy-theories-the-same-140022 [Accessed 10/5/21].

Harrison S., 2019. *Five Years of Tech Diversity Reports - and Little Progress*. [Online] Available at: https://www.wired.com/story/five-years-tech-diversity-reports-little-progress/ [Accessed 10/5/21].

Hartzog W., 2018. *Facial Recognition Is the Perfect Tool for Oppression*. [Online] Available at: https://medium.com/s/story/facial-recognition-is-the-perfect-tool-for-oppression-bc2a08f0fe66 [Accessed 10/5/21].

Harvard, 2014. *Predicting Ebola's spread using cell phone data*. [Online] Available at: https://www.hsph.harvard.edu/news/hsph-in-the-news/predicting-ebolas-spread-using-cell-phone-data/ [Accessed 21/4/21].

Hatzopoulos, V. & Roma, S., 2017. Caring for sharing? The collaborative economy under EU law. *Common Market Law Review*, Issue 54(1), 81–127.

Hein, A. et al., 2019. Digital platform ecosystems. *Electronic Markets*, pp. 1–12.

Helsper, E., 2011. The emergence of a digital underclass: Digital policies in the UK and evidence for inclusion. *LSE media print*.

Henley J., 2020. *How Finland starts its fight against fake news in primary schools*. [Online] Available at: https://www.theguardian.com/world/2020/jan/28/fact-from-fiction-finlands-new-lessons-in-combating-fake-news [Accessed 10/5/21].

Hern A., 2016. *Stephen Hawking: AI will be 'either best or worst thing' for humanity*. [Online] Available at: https://www.theguardian.com/science/2016/oct/19/stephen-hawking-ai-best-or-worst-thing-for-humanity-cambridge [Accessed 10/5/21].

Hintze, M. & El Emam, K., 2018. Comparing the benefits of pseudonymisation and anonymisation under the GDPR. *Journal of Data Protection & Privacy*, Volume 2(2), pp. 145–158.

HM Treasury, 2018. *The economic value of data: discussion paper*. [Online] Available at: https://www.gov.uk/government/publications/the-economic-value-of-data-discussion-paper [Accessed 21/4/21].

Hogart, I., 2018. *AI Nationalism*. [Online] Available at: https://www.ianhogarth.com/blog/2018/6/13/ai-nationalism [Accessed 10/5/21].

Horowitz J., 2017. *In Italian Schools, Reading, Writing and Recognizing Fake News*. [Online] Available at: https://www.nytimes.com/2017/10/18/world/europe/italy-fake-news.html [Accessed 10/5/21].

Horton, J. J. & Tambe, P., 2015. Labor economists get their microscope: big data and labor market analysis. *Big data*, 3(3), pp. 130–137.

Hoynes, H. & Rothstein, J., 2019. Universal basic income in the United States and advanced countries. *Annual Review of Economics*, Volume 11, 929–958.

Huang, J. S., Yang, M. J. & Chyi, H. I., 2013. Friend or foe? Examining the relationship between news portals and newspaper sites in Taiwan. *Chinese Journal of Communication*, Volume 6(1), 103–119.

Hyman, L., 2018. *It's Not Technology That's Dirsupting Our Jobs*. [Online] Available at: https://www.nytimes.com/2018/08/18/opinion/technology/technology-gig-economy.html [Accessed 10/5/21].

ILO, 2021. *ILO Monitor: COVID-19 and the world of work. Seventh edition*. [Online] Available at: https://www.ilo.org/wcmsp5/groups/public/@dgreports/@dcomm/documents/briefingnote/wcms_767028.pdf [Accessed 20/4/21].

IMF, 2018. *Measuring the Digital Economy*. [Online] Available at: https://www.imf.org/en/Publications/Policy-Papers/Issues/2018/04/03/022818-measuring-the-digital-economy [Accessed 20/4/21].

IMF, 2019. *Inequality of Opportunity, Inequality of Income and Economic Growth*. [Online] Available at: https://www.imf.org/en/Publications/WP/Issues/2019/02/15/Inequality-of-Opportunity-Inequality-of-Income-and-Economic-Growth-46566 [Accessed 10/5/21].

IMF, 2020. *The Great Lockdown: Worst Economic Downturn Since the Great Depression*. [Online] Available at: https://ec.europa.eu/commission/presscorner/detail/en/qanda_20_1022 [Accessed 20/4/21].

Independent, 2018. *Independent*. [Online] Available at: https://www.independent.co.uk/news/uk/politics/final-say-brexit-referendum-lies-boris-johnson-leave-campaign-remain-a8466751.html [Accessed 7/5/21].

Inglehart, R. F. & Norris, P., 2016. Brexit, and the Rise of Populism: Economic Have-Nots and Cultural Backlash. *HKS Working Papers No. RWP16-026*, Volume No. RWP16–026.

iPropertyManagement, s.d. *Airbnb Statistics*. [Online] Available at: https://ipropertymanagement.com/research/airbnb-statistics [Accessed 4/5/21].

Ireland and Others v European Commission, Cases T 778/16 and T 892/16 [2020], ECLI: EU:T:2020:338

IT Governance, 2021. *Types of cyber threat in 2021*. [Online] Available at: https://www.itgovernance.co.uk/cyber-threats [Accessed 24/4/21].

Itsme, 2021. *Itsme app*. [Online] Available at: https://www.itsme.be/ [Accessed 21/4/21].

Jang-Jaccard, J. & Nepal, S., 2014. A survey of emerging threats in cybersecurity. *Journal of Computer and System Sciences*, Volume 80(5), pp. 973–993.

Janowski, T., 2015. Digital government evolution: From transformation to contextualization. *GOVERNMENT INFORMATION QUARTERLY*, Volume 32, iss. 3 (2015), pp 221–236.

Janssen, M., Charalabidis, Y. & Zuiderwijk, A., 2012. Benefits, adoption barriers and myths of open data and open government. *Information systems management*, Volume 29(4), pp. 258–268.

Jenik C., 2020. *A Minute on the Internet in 2020*. [Online] Available at: https://www.statista.com/chart/17518/data-created-in-an-internet-minute/ [Accessed 20/4/21].

Jesse, F. & Maurits, M., 2019. *The new dot com bubble is here: it's called online advertising*. [Online] Available at: https://thecorrespondent.com/100/the-new-dot-com-bubble-is-here-its-called-online-advertising/13228924500-22d5fd24 [Accessed 21/4/21].

Jo, A.M., 2017. The effect of competition intensity on software security—an empirical analysis of security patch release on the web browser market. *Proceedings of the 16th Annual Workshop on the Economics of Information Security*.

Johnson, G. & Shriver, S., 2020. Privacy & market concentration: Intended & unintended consequences of the GDPR. *SSNR*.

Joint Research Centre, 2019a. *Exploring Digital Government transformation in the EU - Analysis of the state of the art and review of literature*. [Online] Available at: doi:10.2760/17207 [Accessed 21/4/21].

Joint Research Centre, 2019b. *The changing nature of work and skills in the digital age*, Luxembourg: Publications office of the European Union.

Joint Research Centre, 2020. *Assessing the impacts of digital government transformation in the EU*, Luxembourg: Publications Office of the European Union.

Joskow, P. L., 2007. Regulation of natural monopoly. In: *Handbook of law and economics*. s.l.: Elsevier, pp. 1227–1348.

Kahneman D., 2011. *Thinking, Fast and Slow*. New York: Farrar, Straus and Giroux.

Kalantari, M., 2017. Consumers' adoption of wearable technologies: Literature review, synthesis, and future research agenda. *International Journal of Technology Marketing*, Volume 12(3), pp. 274–307.

Kaldestad Ø., 2016. *The Consumer Council and friends read app terms for 32 hours*. [Online] Available at: https://www.forbrukerradet.no/side/the-consumer-council-and-friends-read-app-terms-for-32-hours/ [Accessed 21/4/21].

Kannan, P. 2., 2017. Digital marketing: A framework, review and research agenda. *International Journal of Research in Marketing*, Volume 34(1), pp. 22–45.

Kantrowitz A., 2019. *The Man Who Built The Retweet: "We Handed A Loaded Weapon To 4-Year-Olds"*. [Online] Available at: https://www.buzzfeednews.com/article/alexkantrowitz/how-the-retweet-ruined-the-internet [Accessed 10/5/21].

Kaplan, A. & Haenlein, M., 2019. Siri, Siri, in my hand: Who's the fairest in the land? On the interpretations, illustrations, and implications of artificial intelligence. *Business Horizons*, Volume 62(1), 15–25.

Katz, M., 2018. *Why Are New York Taxi Drivers Killing Themselves?*. [Online] Available at: https://www.wired.com/story/why-are-new-york-taxi-drivers-committing-suicide/ [Accessed 10/5/21].

Keith, M., Maynes, C. & Lowry, P. B. J., 2014. Privacy fatigue: The effect of privacy control complexity on consumer electronic information disclosure. *International Conference on Information Systems*, Volume (ICIS 2014), Auckland, New Zealand, pp. 1–18.

Kenney, M. & Zysman, J., 2016. The rise of the platform economy. *Issues in science and technology*, Volume 32(3), p. 61.

Keynes, J., 1930. Economic possibilities for our grandchildren. In: *Essays in persuasion*. London: Palgrave Macmillan, pp. 321–332.

Khan, A., 2016. Electronic commerce: A study on benefits and challenges in an emerging economy. *Global Journal of Management and Business Research*.

Kilhoffer, Z. et al., 2019. *Study to gather evidence on the working conditions of platform workers VT/2018/032 Final Report 13 December 2019.*, s.l.: Study Commissioned by the European Commission - VT/2018/032 Final Report 13 December 2019.

Kiritchenko, S. & Mohammad, S. M., 2018. Examining gender and race bias in two hundred sentiment analysis systems. *arXiv preprint*, Volume arXiv:1805.04508.

Kirk H., 2020. *The Geo-Technological Triangle Between the US, China, and Taiwan.* [Online] Available at: https://thediplomat.com/2020/02/the-geo-technological-triangle-between-the-us-china-and-taiwan/ [Accessed 10/5/21].

Kofman A., 2018. *Bruno Latour, the Post-Truth Philosopher, Mounts a Defense of Science.* [Online] Available at: https://www.nytimes.com/2018/10/25/magazine/bruno-latour-post-truth-philosopher-science.html [Accessed 10/5/21].

Kosseff, J., 2019. *The twenty-six words that created the internet.* s.l.: Cornell University Press.

Krämer, J., Senellart, P. & de Streel, A., 2020. *Making data portability more effective for the digital economy*, s.l.: CERRE Report.

Kritikos, M., 2020. *Workplace Monitoring In The Era Of Artificial Intelligence.* [Online] Available at: https://epthinktank.eu/2020/12/22/workplace-monitoring-in-the-era-of-artificial-intelligence/ [Accessed 20/4/21].

Kshetri, N., 2014. Big data's impact on privacy, security and consumer welfare. *Telecommunications Policy*, 38(11), pp. 1134–1145.

Kunreuther, H. & Heal, G., 2003. Interdependent security. *Journal of risk and uncertainty*, 26(2–3), pp. 231–249.

Kwilinski, A. et al., 2019. E-Commerce: Concept and Legal Regulation. *Modern Economic Conditions. Journal of Legal, Ethical and Regulatory Issues*, Volume 22, pp. 1–6.

Laguarta, J., Hueto, F. & Subirana, B., 2021. *COVID-19 Artificial Intelligence Diagnosis using only Cough Recordings.* [Online] Available at: https://www.embs.org/ojemb/articles/covid-19-artificial-intelligence-diagnosis-using-only-cough-recordings/ [Accessed 20/4/21].

Lambrecht, A. et al., 2014. How do firms make money selling digital goods online?. *Marketing Letters*, Volume 25(3), pp. 331–341.

Lancet, 2020. *COVID-19 transmission—up in the air.* [Online] Available at: https://www.thelancet.com/journals/lanres/article/PIIS2213-2600(20)30514-2/fulltext [Accessed 20/4/21].

Lazer, D., Kennedy, R., King, G. & Vespignani, A., 2014. Google Flu Trends still appears sick: An evaluation of the 2013–2014 flu season. Volume Available at SSRN 2408560.

Leavy, S., 2018. Gender bias in artificial intelligence: The need for diversity and gender theory in machine learning. Proceedings of the 1st international workshop on gender equality in software engineering, Volume pp. 14–16.

Lee, I., 2017. Big data: Dimensions, evolution, impacts, and challenges. *Business Horizons*, Volume 60(3), pp. 293–303.

Lefouili, Y. & Madio, L., 2021. The economics of platform liability. No. 8919 (CESifo Working Paper).

Lezzi, M., Lazoi, M. & Corallo, A., 2018. Cybersecurity for Industry 4.0 in the current literature: A reference framework. *Computers in Industry*, Volume 103, pp. 97–110.

Liang, F., Das, V., Kostyuk, N. & Hussain, M. M., 2018. Constructing a data-driven society: China's social credit system as a state surveillance infrastructure. *Policy & Internet*, Volume 10(4), 415–453.

Liu-Thompkins, Y., 2019. A decade of online advertising research: What we learned and what we need to know. *Journal of advertising*, Volume 48(1), pp. 1–13.

Lloyd's London, 2018. *Sharing risks, sharing rewards: A study on how customers, service providers and platforms perceive risk in the sharing economy model.* [Online] Available at: https://www.lloyds.com/news-and-insights/risk-reports/library/sharing-risks-sharing-rewards [Accessed 4/5/21].

Lomas, N., 2018. *WTF is GDPR?.* [Online] Available at : https://techcrunch.com/2018/01/20/wtf-is-gdpr/

López González, J. & Ferencz, J., 2018. Digital Trade and Market Openness. *OECD Trade Policy Papers*, Volume No. 217. https://www.researchgate.net/profile/Javier-Lopez-Gonzalez-4/publication/328601819_Digital_Trade_and_Market_Openness/links/5bd810f892851c6b2799096f/Digital-Trade-and-Market-Openness.pdf

Lowitzsch, J., 2016. *Automation, digital revolution and capital concentration: The elephant in the room - A race for the machine?.* European Parliament Hearing, s.n.

Lutz, C., 2019. Digital inequalities in the age of artificial intelligence and big data. *Human Behavior and Emerging Technologies*, Volume 1(2), pp. 141–148.

Lyons K., 2020. *Coca-Cola, Microsoft, Starbucks, Target, Unilever, Verizon: all the companies pulling ads from Facebook.* [Online] Available at: https://www.theverge.com/21307454/unilever-verizon-coca-cola-starbucks-microsoft-ads-facebook [Accessed 24/4/21].

Mac Síthigh, D. & Siems, M., 2019. The Chinese social credit system: A model for other countries?. *The Modern Law Review*, Volume 82(6), 1034–1071.

Machiavelli, N., 1513. *The prince.* s.l.: s.n.

Maffei L., 2016. *Pokémon Go will soon get ads in the form of sponsored locations.* [Online] Available at: https://techcrunch.com/2016/07/13/pokemon-go-will-soon-get-ads-in-the-form-of-sponsored-locations/ [Accessed 20/4/21].

Majcher, K. & Mariniello, M., 2020. Harnesing Risk in the Era of Big Tech. European Political Strategy Centre, European Commission, Unpublished manuscript.

Manyika, J. et al., 2016. *Independent work: Choice, necessity, and the gig economy. McKinsey Global Institute, 2016, pp. 1–16.,* s.l.: McKinsey Global Institute, 2016.

Marcus, J. S. & Petropoulos, G., 2017. *Extending the scope of the geo-blocking prohibition: an economic assessment.* [Online] Available at: https://www.bruegel.org/2017/02/extending-the-scope-of-the-geo-blocking-prohibition-an-economic-assessment/ [Accessed 4/5/21].

Mariniello M., 2014. *Cold water on Europe's digital dream.* [Online] Available at: https://www.bruegel.org/2014/07/cold-water-on-europes-digital-dream/ [Accessed 30/4/21].

Mariniello M., 2020. *A timid start for European Union data governance.* [Online] Available at: https://www.bruegel.org/2020/11/a-timid-start-for-european-union-data-governance/ [Accessed 21/4/21].

Mariniello, M. & Salemi, F., 2015. Addressing fragmentation in EU mobile telecom markets. *Bruegel Policy Contribution*, Issue 3.

Marr, B., 2016. *Big data in practice: how 45 successful companies used big data analytics to deliver extraordinary results.* s.l.: John Wiley & Sons.

Martens, B. & Tolan, S., 2018. Will This Time Be Different? A Review of the Literature on the Impact of Artificial Intelligence on Employment, Incomes and Growth. *JRC Digital Economy Working Paper*, 19 December.Volume 2018–08. https://www.econstor.eu/bitstream/10419/202236/1/jrc-dewp201808.pdf

Martens, B., 2016. An economic policy perspective on online platforms. Bertin Martens (2016) An Economic Policy Perspective on Online Platforms. *Institute for Prospective Technological Studies Digital Economy Working Paper*, Volume 5. https://www.econstor.eu/bitstream/10419/202222/1/jrc-dewp201605.pdf

Martin, E. & Shaheen, S., 2011. Greenhouse gas emission impacts of carsharing in North America. *IEEE Transactions on intelligent transportation systems*, Volume 12(4), pp. 1074–1086.

Marwick, A. & Lewis, R., 2017. *Media manipulation and disinformation online.* New York: Data & Society Research Institute.

Mas-Colell, A., Whinston, M. D. & Green, J. R., 1995. *Microeconomic theory.* New York: Oxford University Press.

Matheu-García, S.H.-R. J., Skarmeta, A., & Baldini, G., 2019. Risk-based automated assessment and testing for the cybersecurity certification and labelling of IoT devices. *Computer Standards & Interfaces*, Volume 62, pp. 64–83.

Maxwell, W. J. & Bourreau, M., 2015. Technology neutrality in internet, telecoms and data protection regulation. *Computer and Telecommunications Law Review*, 21(1), pp. 1–4.

Mazzella, F., Sundararajan, A., d'Espous, V. & Möhlmann, M., 2016. How digital trust powers the sharing economy. *IESE Business Review*, 26(5), pp. 24–31.

Mazziotti, G., 2015. Is geo-blocking a real cause for concern in Europe?. *EUI Department of Law Research Paper*, Volume 2015/43. https://cadmus.eui.eu/bitstream/handle/1814/38084/LAW_2015_43.pdf?sequence=1&isAllowed=y

McCarthy, N. 2020. The Composition Of Coronavirus Misinformation. Statista. Statista Inc. Accessed: April 12, 2021. https://www.statista.com/chart/22527/composition-of-covid-19-misinformation/. Made available under the Creative Commons License CC BY-ND 3.0

McIntire, M., Yourish, K. & Buchanan, L., 2019. *In Trump's Twitter Feed: Conspiracy-Mongers, Racists and Spies*. [Online] Available at: https://www.nytimes.com/interactive/2019/11/02/us/politics/trump-twitter-disinformation.html [Accessed 10/5/21].

McKinney, S. M. et al., 2020. International evaluation of an AI system for breast cancer screening. *Nature*, 577(7788), pp. 89–94.

McKinsey, 2016. *Would you like to learn more about our Automotive & Assembly Practice?*. [Online] Available at: https://www.mckinsey.com/industries/automotive-and-assembly/our-insights/will-car-users-share-their-personal-data#

Melchor O. H., 2008. *Managing change in OECD governments*, s.l.: OECD.

Melnick J., 2018. *Top 10 Most Common Types of Cyber Attacks*. [Online] Available at: https://blog.netwrix.com/2018/05/15/top-10-most-common-types-of-cyber-attacks/#Phishing%20and%20spear%20phishing%20attacks [Accessed 21/4/21].

Mishra, S., Clark, J. & Perrault, C. R., 2020. *Measurement in AI Policy: Opportunities and Challenges*. [Online] Available at: https://arxiv.org/abs/2009.09071 [Accessed 20/4/21].

Mitchell, R., Michalski, J. & Carbonell, T., 2013. *An artificial intelligence approach*. Berlin: Springer.

Mokyr, J., Vickers, C. & Ziebarth, N., 2015. The History of Technological Anxiety and the Future of Economic Growth: Is This Time Different?. *Journal of Economic Perspectives*, 29(3), pp. 31–50.

Moore, G. E., 1965. *Cramming more components onto integrated circuits*. s.l.: s.n.

Moore, G. E., 1975. *Progress in digital integrated electronics. In Electron devices meeting (Vol. 21)*. s.l.: s.n.

Moore, T., 2010. The economics of cybersecurity: Principles and policy options. *International Journal of Critical Infrastructure Protection*, 3(3–4), pp. 103–117.

Motta, M., 2004. *Competition policy: theory and practice*. s.l.: Cambridge University Press.

Mozur, P., 2018. *The New York Times*. [Online] Available at: https://www.nytimes.com/2018/10/15/technology/myanmar-facebook-genocide.html [Accessed 7/5/21].

Mr Y Aslam, Mr J Farrar and Others *vs* Uber, Case numbers 2202551/2015 & Others [2016]

Mukerjee, S., Majó-Vázquez, S. & González-Bailón, S., 2018. Networks of audience overlap in the consumption of digital news. *Journal of Communication*, 68(1), pp. 26–50.

Mulcahy, D., 2016. *The gig economy: the complete guide to getting better work, taking more time off, and financing the life you want. Amacom*. s.l.: Amacom.

Müller, V. & Bostrom, N., 2016. Future progress in artificial intelligence: A survey of expert opinion. In: *Fundamental issues of artificial intelligence* . Cham: Springer, pp. 555–572.

NBC BAY AREA, 2011. *Schmidt on Antitrust: Competition is One Click Away*. [Online] Available at: https://www.nbcbayarea.com/news/national-international/schmidt-on-antitrust-competition-is-one-click-away/1901637/ [Accessed 20/4/21].

Neighbour, J., 2002. Transfer pricing: Keeping it at arm's length. *OECD Observer*, Issue 1.

Newman, N., 2019. *Executive Summary and Key Findings of the 2019 Report*, s.l.: Reuters Institute and University of Oxford.

Nguyen, T. et al., 2020., 2020. Artificial intelligence in the battle against coronavirus (COVID-19): a survey and future research direction. *arXiv preprint arXiv:2008.07343*.

Niiler E., 2020. *An AI Epidemiologist Sent the First Warnings of the Wuhan Virus*. [Online] Available at: https://www.wired.com/story/ai-epidemiologist-wuhan-public-health-warnings/ [Accessed 10/5/21].

Nijland, H. & van Meerkerk, J., 2017. Mobility and Environmental Impacts of Carsharing in the Netherlands. *Environmental Innovation and Societal Transitions*, 23(June), pp. 84–91.

Nilsson, N., 2009. *The quest for artificial intelligence*. s.l.: Cambridge University Press.

Nosengo, N., 2021. *Ripensare l'Intelligenza Artificiale*. [Online] Available at: https://www.iltascabile.com/scienze/ripensare-intelligenza-artificiale/

NTIA, 1995. *FALLING THROUGH THE NET: A Survey of the "Have Nots" in Rural and Urban America*, Washington D.C.: NTIA.

OECD, 2003. *The e-Government Imperative, OECD e-Government Studies, OECD Publishing, Paris,*. [Online] Available at: https://doi.org/10.1787/9789264101197-en [Accessed 21/4/21].

OECD, 2006. *Glossary of Statistical Terms*. [Online] Available at: https://stats.oecd.org/glossary/detail.asp?ID=4719 [Accessed 7/5/21].

OECD, 2015. *Big Data for Growth and Well-Being*, Paris: OECD Publishing.

OECD, 2015. *Data-Driven Innovation: Big Data for Growth and Well-Being*, Paris: OECD Publishing.

OECD, 2015b. *Addressing the Tax Challenges of the Digital Economy, Action 1–2015 Final Report*. [Online] Available at: http://dx.doi.org/10.1787/9789264255258-en [Accessed 10/5/21].

OECD, 2015c. *Digital Security Risk Management for Economic and Social Prosperity*. [Online] Available at: https://www.oecd.org/sti/ieconomy/digital-security-risk-management.pdf [Accessed 24/4/21].

OECD, 2016. *Consumer Protection in E-commerce*. [Online] Available at: http://dx.doi.org/10.1787/9789264255258-en [Accessed 3/5/21].

OECD, 2017a. *Trust and Public Policy: How Better Governance Can Help Rebuild Public Trust*. [Online] Available at: https://doi.org/10.1787/9789264268920-en [Accessed 21/4/21].

OECD, 2017b. *Basic income as a policy option: Can it add up?*. [Online] Available at: https://www.oecd.org/social/Basic-Income-Policy-Option-2017.pdf [Accessed 10/5/21].

OECD, 2019. Unpacking E-commerce: Business Models, Trends and Policies, Paris: OECD Publishing, Paris.

OECD, 2019a. *The Path to Becoming a Data-Driven Public Sector, OECD Digital Government Studies*. [Online] Available at: https://doi.org/10.1787/059814a7-en [Accessed 21/4/21].

OECD, 2019b. *Unpacking E-commerce: Business Models, Trends and Policies*, Paris: OECD publishing.

OECD, 2019c. *Artificial Intelligence in Society*. [Online] Available at: https://www.oecd.org/going-digital/artificial-intelligence-in-society-eedfee77-en.htm [Accessed 10/5/21].

OECD, 2019d. *Action 1 Tax Challenges Arising from Digitalisation*. [Online] Available at: https://www.oecd.org/tax/beps/beps-actions/action1/ [Accessed 10/5/21].

OECD, 2019e. *Public consultation document: Secretariat Proposal for a "unified Approach" under Pillar One*. [Online] Available at: https://www.oecd.org/tax/beps/public-consultation-document-secretariat-proposal-unified-approach-pillar-one.pdf [Accessed 10/5/21].

OECD, 2019f. *Getting Skills Right: Engaging low-skilled adults in learning*. [Online] Available at: https://www.oecd.org/employment/emp/engaging-low-skilled-adults-2019.pdf [Accessed 10/5/21].

OECD, 2019g. *Going Digital: Shaping Policies, Improving Lives*. [Online] Available at: https://www.oecd.org/publications/going-digital-shaping-policies-improving-lives-9789264312012-en.htm [Accessed 10/5/21].

OECD, 2019h. *Policy Responses to New Forms of Work*, Paris: OECD Publishing.

OECD, 2020a. *OECD Digital Economy Outlook 2020*. [Online] Available at: https://www.oecd-ilibrary.org/science-and-technology/oecd-digital-economy-outlook-2020_bb167041-en [Accessed 20/4/21].

OECD, 2020b. *A Roadmap toward a common framework for measuring the Digital Economy, Report for the G20 Digital Economy Task Force*, s.l.: s.n.

OECD, 2020c. *E-commerce in the time of COVID-19*. [Online] Available at: https://www.oecd.org/coronavirus/policy-responses/e-commerce-in-the-time-of-covid-19-3a2b78e8/ [Accessed 30/4/21].

OECD, 2020d. *OECD Policy Responses to Coronavirus (COVID-19) - Education and COVID-19: Focusing on the long-term impact of school closures, June 2020.* [Online] Available at: https://www.oecd.org/coronavirus/policy-responses/education-and-covid-19-focusing-on-the-long-term-impact-of-school-closures-2cea926e/#biblio-d1e280 [Accessed 20/4/21].

OECD, 2021. *Going Digital Toolkit.* [Online] Available at: https://goingdigital.oecd.org/ [Accessed 20/4/21].

OFCOM, 2020. *Half of UK adults exposed to false claims about coronavirus.* [Online] Available at: https://www.ofcom.org.uk/about-ofcom/latest/features-and-news/half-of-uk-adults-exposed-to-false-claims-about-coronavirus [Accessed 10/5/21].

Oliveira, T., Alhinho, M., Rita, P. & Dhillon, G., 2017. Modelling and testing consumer trust dimensions in e-commerce. *Computers in Human Behavior*, Volume 71, pp. 153–164.

OPSI, 2018. *New OPSI guide to blockchain in the public sector.* [Online] Available at: https://oecd-opsi.org/new-opsi-guide-to-blockchain-in-the-public-sector/ [Accessed 21/4/21].

Osoba, O. A. & Welser IV, W., 2017. *An intelligence in our image: The risks of bias and errors in artificial intelligence.* s.l.: Rand Corporation.

Oulton, N., 2012. Long Term Implications of the ICT Revolution: Applying the Lessons of Growth Theory and Growth Accounting. *Economic Modelling*, 29(5), p. 1722–1736.

Our World in Data, 2021. *Coronavirus Pandemic (COVID-19).* [Online] Available at: https://ourworldindata.org/coronavirus [Accessed 30/4/21].

Oussous, A., Benjelloun, F., Lahcen, A. & Belfkih, S., 2018. Big Data technologies: A survey. *Journal of King Saud University-Computer and Information Sciences*, Volume 30(4), pp. 431–448.

Papacharissi, Z. & Gibson, P., 2011. Fifteen minutes of privacy: Privacy, sociality, and publicity on social network sites. *Privacy online*, Volume Springer, Berlin, Heidelberg, pp. 75–89.

Papandropoulos, P., 2007. How should price discrimination be dealt with by competition authorities?. *Droit&économie Concurrences*, Volume N° 3-2007, pp. 34–38.

Parcu, P., 2020. New digital threats to media pluralism in the information age. *Competition and regulation in network industries*, Volume 21(2), pp. 91–109.

Parker, G., Van Alstyne, M. & Choudary, S., 2016. *Platform revolution: How networked markets are transforming the economy and how to make them work for you.* New York: WW Norton & Company.

Peitz, M., 2018. s.l.: CERRE.

Peña-López, I., 2017. *OECD digital economy outlook 2017*, s.l.: OECD.

Pennycook, G. & Rand, D., 2019. Fighting misinformation on social media using crowdsourced judgments of news source quality. *Proceedings of the National Academy of Sciences*, Volume 116(7), pp. 2521–2526.

Pennycook, G., Bear, A., Collins, E. T. & Rand, D. G., 2020. The implied truth effect: Attaching warnings to a subset of fake news headlines increases perceived accuracy of headlines without warnings. *Management Science.*

Penttinen, J. T., 2015. *Telecommunications Handbook: Engineering guidelines for fixed, mobile and satellite systems.* s.l.: John Wiley & Sons.

Peragine, V. & Ferreira, F., 2015. Equality of opportunity: Theory and evidence. *World Bank Policy Research Paper*, Volume 7217. http://www.siepweb.it/siep/wp/wp-content/uploads/repec/1427104309Ferreira_Peragine_WP_SIEP_693.pdf

Perrault, R. et al., 2019. *The AI Index 2019 Annual Report, AI Index Steering Committee*, Stanford, CA,: Human-Centered AI Institute, Stanford University.

Pesole, A. et al., 2018. *Platform Workers in Europe Evidence from the COLLEEM Survey*, Luxembourg: Publications Office of the European Union.

Petrova A., 2019. *The impact of the GDPR outside the EU.* [Online] Available at: https://www.lexology.com/library/detail.aspx?g=872b3db5-45d3-4ba3-bda4-3166a075d02f [Accessed 21/4/21].

Pierrakakis, K., Gkritzali, C., Kandias, M. & Gritzalis, D., 2015. 3D printing: a paradigm shift in political economy. *Proc. of the 65th International Studies Association's Annual Convention.*

Piketty, T., 2015. About capital in the twenty-first century. *American Economic Review*, 105(5), pp. 48–53.

Poynter, 2021. *The International Fact-Checking Network.* [Online] Available at: https://www.poynter.org/ifcn/ [Accessed 10/5/21].

Pradhan, R., Arvin, M., Norman, N. & Bele, S., 2014. Economic growth and the development of telecommunications infrastructure in the G-20 countries: A panel-VAR approach. *Telecommunications Policy*, Volume 38(7), pp. 634–649.

Pradhan, R., Mallik, G. & Bagchi, T., 2018. Information communication technology (ICT) infrastructure and economic growth: A causality evinced by cross-country panel data. *IIMB Management Review*, Volume 30(1), pp. 91–103.

Propeller, 2021. *Meet Propeller. The doctor-recommended way to manage your asthma or COPD.* [Online] Available at: https://www.propellerhealth.com/ [Accessed 21/4/21].

Publications Office of the EU, 2019. *10 trends shaping the future of work.* [Online] Available at: https://op.europa.eu/en/publication-detail/-/publication/e77a1580-0cf5-11ea-8c1f-01aa75ed71a1/language-en/format-PDF/source-121729338 [Accessed 7/5/21].

PwC, 2016. *The Wearable Life 2.0 Connected living in a wearable world.* [Online] Available at: https://www.pwc.com/us/en/industry/entertainment-media/assets/pwc-cis-wearables.pdf [Accessed 20/4/21].

Regulation (EU) 2016/679 of the European Parliament and of the Council of 27 April 2016 on the protection of natural persons with regard to the processing of personal data and on the free movement of such data, and repealing Directive 95/46/EC (General Data Protection Regulation), OJ 2016 L 119/1.

Regulation (EU) 2018/1807 of the European Parliament and of the Council of 14 November 2018 on a framework for the free flow of non-personal data in the European Union, OJ 2018 L 303.

Regulation (EU) 2018/1971 of the European Parliament and of the Council of 11 December 2018 establishing the Body of European Regulators for Electronic Communications (BEREC) and the Agency for Support for BEREC (BEREC Office), OJ 2018 L 321.

Regulation (EU) 2018/302 of the European Parliament and of the Council of 28 February 2018 on addressing unjustified geo-blocking and other forms of discrimination based on customers' nationality, place of residence or place of establishment within (.) (Text with EEA relevance), OJ 2018 L 601.

Regulation (EU) 2018/644 of the European Parliament and of the Council of 18 April 2018 on cross-border parcel delivery services (Text with EEA relevance), OJ 2018 L 112.

Regulation (EU) 2019/881 of the European Parliament and of the Council of 17 April 2019 on ENISA (the European Union Agency for Cybersecurity) and on information and communications technology cybersecurity certification and repealing Regulation (EU) (Text with EEA relevance), OJ 2019 L 151.

Regulation (EU) 330/2010 of 20 April 2010 on the application of Article 101(3) of the Treaty on the Functioning of the European Union to categories of vertical agreements and concerted practices (Text with EEA relevance), OJ 2010 L 102.

Regulation (EU) No 910/2014 of the European Parliament and of the Council of 23 July 2014 on electronic identification and trust services for electronic transactions in the internal market and repealing Directive 1999/93/EC, OJ 2014 L 257.

Reilly, M., 2017. *Google Now Tracks Your Credit Card Purchases and Connects Them to Its Online Profile of You.* [Online] Available at: https://www.technologyreview.com/2017/05/25/242717/google-now-tracks-your-credit-card-purchases-and-connects-them-to-its-online-profile-of-you/ [Accessed 21/4/21].

Retail Touch Points, 2016. *Data-Driven Personalization Drives Advanced Pricing Strategies.* [Online] Available at: https://retailtouchpoints.com/resources/data-driven-personalization-drives-advanced-pricing-strategies [Accessed 21/4/21].

Rhue, L., 2018. Racial influence on automated perceptions of emotions. *SSRN 3281765.*

Richter, F. (2018). Music Piracy Still Prevalent in the Age of Streaming. Statista. Statista Inc. Accessed: April 16, 2021. https://www.statista.com/chart/15764/prevalence-of-music-piracy/. Made available under the Creative Commons License CC BY-ND 3.0

Richter, F. (2020). Video Chat Apps Rise to Prominence Amid Pandemic. Statista.

Ricketson, S. & Ginsburg, J., 2006. *International copyright and neighboring rights: the Berne convention and beyond.* s.l.: Oxford University Press

Roberts, A., 2015. Too much transparency? How critics of openness misunderstand administrative development. *Fourth Global Conference on Transparency Research, Università della Svizzera Italiana.*

Roberts, D., Hughes, M. & Kertbo, K., 2014. Exploring consumers' motivations to engage in innovation through co-creation activities. *European Journal of Marketing.*

Robinson, L. et al., 2015. Digital inequalities and why they matter. *Information, communication & society,* Volume 18(5), pp. 569–582.

Robinson, L. et al., 2020a. *Digital inequalities 2.0: Legacy inequalities in theinformation age,* Chicago: University of Illinois.

Robinson, L. et al., 2020b. *Digital inequalities 3.0: Emergent inequalities in the information age,* Chicago: University of Illinois.

Rocher, L., Hendrickx, J. & de Montjoye, Y., 2019. Estimating the success of re-identifications in incomplete datasets using generative models. *Nature Communications,* 10(1).

Rochet, J.-C. & Tirole, J., 2003. Platform Competition in Two-Sided Markets. *Journal of the European Economic Association,* Volume 1(4): 990–1029.

Rochet, J.-C. & Tirole, J., 2006. Two-Sided Markets: A Progress Report. *The Rand Journal of Economics,* Volume 37(3): 645–667.

Roller, L. & Waverman, L., 2001. Telecommunications infrastructure and economic development: A simultaneous approach. *American economic review,* Volume 91(4), pp. 909–923.

Rony, M. M. U., Hassan, N. & Yousuf, M., 2017. *Diving deep into clickbaits: Who uses them to what extents in which topics with what effects?.* s.l., Proceedings of the 2017 IEEE/ACM International Conference on Advances in Social Networks Analysis and Mining.

Rosenblat, A. & Stark, L., 2016. Algorithmic labor and information asymmetries: A case study of Uber's drivers. *International journal of communication,* Volume 10, p. 27.

Rouvroy, A. & Poullet, Y., 2009. The right to informational self-determination and the value of self-development: Reassessing the importance of privacy for democracy. In: *Reinventing data protection?* . Dordrecht: Springer, 45–76.

Saggi, M. & Jain, S., 2018. A survey towards an integration of big data analytics to big insights for value-creation. *Information Processing & Management,* Volume 54(5), pp. 758–790.

Sample, I., 2020. *What are deepfakes – and how can you spot them?.* [Online] Available at: https://www.theguardian.com/technology/2020/jan/13/what-are-deepfakes-and-how-can-you-spot-them [Accessed 10/5/21].

Sartor, G., 2017. *Providers Liability: From the eCommerce Directive to the future,* s.l.: EUI.

Satariano A., 2020. *Europe's Privacy Law Hasn't Shown Its Teeth, Frustrating Advocates.* [Online] Available at: https://www.nytimes.com/2020/04/27/technology/GDPR-privacy-law-europe.html [Accessed 21/4/21].

Savoldelli, A., Codagnone, C. & Misuraca, G., 2014. Understanding the e-government paradox: Learning from literature and practice on barriers to adoption. *Government Information Quarterly,* Volume 31, pp. 63–71.

Schiavenza M., 2018. *China's 'Sputnik Moment' and the Sino-American Battle for AI Supremacy.* [Online] Available at: https://asiasociety.org/blog/asia/chinas-sputnik-moment-and-sino-american-battle-ai-supremacy [Accessed 10/5/21].

Schwab, K., 2017. *The fourth industrial revolution. Currency.* s.l.: s.n.

Scott M., Cerulus L., 2019. *Russian groups targeted EU election with fake news, says European Commission.* [Online] Available at: https://www.politico.eu/article/european-commission-disinformation-report-russia-fake-news/ [Accessed 10/5/21].

Scott M., Clark N., 2015. *European Publishers Play Lobbying Role Against Google.*

Scott M.; Cerulus L., 2018. *Europe's new data protection rules export privacy standards worldwide.* [Online] Available at: https://www.politico.eu/article/europe-data-protection-privacy-standards-gdpr-general-protection-data-regulation/ [Accessed 21/4/21].

Scott, M., Palmer, D., Heikkila, M. & Braun, E., 2020. *Threat of EU-US trade war grows amid digital tax stand-off.* [Online] Available at: https://www.politico.eu/article/europe-us-digital-tax-trade-war/ [Accessed 4/5/21].

Sebastian, I. et al., 2020. How big old companies navigate digital transformation. *Strategic Information Management.*

Segall, M. H., Campbell, D. T. & Herskovits, M. J., 1963. Cultural differences in the perception of geometric illusions. *Science*, 139(3556), pp. 769–771.

Selby, J., 2017. Data localization laws: trade barriers or legitimate responses to cybersecurity risks, or both?. *International Journal of Law and Information Technology*, Volume 25(3), pp. 213–232.

Sen, R., 2018. Challenges to cybersecurity: Current state of affairs. *Communications of the Association for Information Systems*, 43(1), p. 2.

Shapiro, C. & Varian, H., 1998. *Information Rules A Strategic Guide to the Network Economy*. s.l.: Harvard Business Press.

Shapiro, C., 2011. Competition and Innovation: Did Arrow Hit the Bull's Eye?. In: J. L. a. S. Stern, a cura di *The Rate and Direction of Inventive Activity Revisited*. s.l.: University of Chicago Press, p. 361–404.

Shapiro, C., 2018. Antitrust in the age of populism. *International Journal of Industrial Organisation*.

Shi, S., Brant, A., Sabolch, A. & Pollom, E., 2019. False News of a Cannabis Cancer Cure. *Cureus*, Volume 11(1). https://assets.cureus.com/uploads/original_article/pdf/16818/1612428425-1612428420-20210204-18590-1jtoyvd.pdf

Singer, P. & Friedman, A., 2014. *Cybersecurity: What everyone needs to know*. USA: OUP.

Skjelvik, J., Maren Erlandsen, A. & Haavardsholm, O., 2017. Environmental Impacts and Potential of the Sharing Economy. *TemaNord*, 2017(5).

Smith, A., 1791. *An Inquiry into the Nature and Causes of the Wealth of Nations*. s.l.: (Vol. 1). Librito Mondi.

Soesanto, S., 2018. *A hammer in search of a nail: EU sanctions and the cyber domain*. [Online] Available at: https://jia.sipa.columbia.edu/online-articles/hammer-search-nail-eu-sanctions-and-cyber-domain [Accessed 24/4/21].

Solow, R., 1987. We'd Better Watch Out. *The New York Times*, 12 July, p. 36.

Sostero, M., Milesi, S., Hurley, J., Fernandez Macias, E., Bisello, M., 2020. *Teleworkability and the COVID-19 crisis: a new digital divide?*, Seville: European Commission, JRC.

Sridhar, K. S. & Sridhar, V., 2007. Telecommunications Infrastructure and Economic Growth: Evidence from Developing Countries. *Applied Econometrics and International Development*, Volume Vol. 7, No. 2, pp. 37–61.

Stanford HAI, 2020. *Who's leading the global AI race?*. [Online] Available at: https://aiindex.stanford.edu/vibrancy/ [Accessed 20/4/21].

Statista Inc.. Accessed: April 12, 2021. https://www.statista.com/chart/21268/global-downloads-of-video-chat-apps-amid-covid-19-pandemic/. Made available under the Creative Commons License CC BY-ND 3.0

Statista, 2017. *Artificial intelligence (AI) investment and financing in China from 2013 to 1Q'18*. [Online] Available at: https://www.statista.com/statistics/941152/ai-investment-and-funding-in-china/ [Accessed 10/5/21].

Statista, 2020a. *Internet of Things (IoT)*. [Online] Available at: https://www.statista.com/study/27915/internet-of-things-iot-statista-dossier/ [Accessed 20/4/21].

Statista, 2020b. *Artificial Intelligence (AI)*. [Online] Available at: https://www.statista.com/study/38609/artificial-intelligence-ai-statista-dossier/ [Accessed 10/5/21].

Statista, 2020c. *Value of the global sharing economy 2014–2025*. [Online] Available at: https://www.statista.com/statistics/830986/value-of-the-global-sharing-economy/ [Accessed 4/5/21].

Statista, 2021. *Digital Media Report*. [Online] Available at: https://www.statista.com/study/44526/digital-media-report/ [Accessed 20/4/21].

Stelitano, L. et al., 2020. *The Digital Divide and COVID-19: Teachers 'Perceptions of Inequities in Students' Internet Access and Participation in Remote Learning*, s.l.: RAND.

Stiglitz, J. E., Sen, A. & Fitoussi, J. P., 2010. *Mismeasuring our lives: Why GDP doesn't add up*. s.l.: The New Press.

Stolton S., 2018. *A 'fifth freedom' of the EU: MEPs back an end to data localisation*. [Online] Available at: https://www.euractiv.com/section/data-protection/news/a-fifth-freedom-of-the-eu-meps-back-end-of-data-localisation/ [Accessed 20/4/21].

Sunstein, C. R. & Vermeule, A., 2009. Conspiracy theories: Causes and cures. *Journal of Political Philosophy*, 17(2), pp. 202–227.

Sweeney, L., 2013. Discrimination in online ad delivery. *Queue*, 11(3), pp. 10–29.

Taddeo, M. & Floridi, L., 2015. The debate on the moral responsibilities of online service providers. *Science and Engineering Ethics*.

Tan, C., Friggeri, A. & Adamic, L., 2016. *Lost in propagation? Unfolding news cycles from the source*. s.l., Tenth International AAAI Conference on Web and Social Media.

Tani, S., 2016. *AI to be the 'new electricity,' says Baidu chief scientist*. [Online] Available a t: https://asia.nikkei.com/Business/AI-to-be-the-new-electricity-says-Baidu-chief-scientist [Accessed 10/5/21].

Tapscott, D., 1996. *The digital economy: Promise and peril in the age of networked intelligence (Vol. 1)*. New York: McGraw-Hill.

Tech Transparency Project, 2020. *Google is Paying Creators of Misleading Coronavirus Videos*. [Online] Available at: https://www.techtransparencyproject.org/articles/google-paying-creators-of-misleading-coronavirus-videos [Accessed 10/5/21].

Teffer, P., 2017. *EU bans 'geo-blocking' - but not (yet) for audiovisual*. [Online] Available at: https://euobserver.com/digital/139964 [Accessed 4/5/21].

Teubner, T., Hawlitschek, F. & Dann, D., 2017. Price Determinants on Airbnb: How reputation pays off in the sharing economy. *Journal of Self-Governance and Management Economics*, 5(4), pp. 53–80.

The Council of the European Union, 2008a. *Council Framework Decision 2008/913/JHA of 28 November 2008 on combating certain forms and expressions of racism and xenophobia by means of criminal law*. [Online] Available at: https://eur-lex.europa.eu/legal-content/EN/TXT/?uri=celex:32008F0913 [Accessed 24/4/21].

The Council of the European Union, 2008b. *Framework Decision on combating certain forms and expressions of racism and xenophobia by means of criminal law*. [Online] Available at: https://eur-lex.europa.eu/legal-content/EN/TXT/?uri=LEGISSUM%3Al33178 [Accessed 24/4/21].

The Council of the European Union, 2016. *Council Recommendation of 19 December 2016 on Upskilling Pathways: New Opportunities for Adults*. [Online] Available at: http://eur-lex.europa.eu/legal-content/EN/TXT/?uri=OJ:JOC_2016_484_R_0001 [Accessed 7/5/21].

The Economist, 2017a. *Internet firms' legal immunity is under threat*. [Online] Available at: https://www.economist.com/business/2017/02/11/internet-firms-legal-immunity-is-under-threat [Accessed 24/4/21].

The Economist, 2017b. *The world's most valuable resource is no longer oil, but data*. [Online] Available at: https://www.economist.com/leaders/2017/05/06/the-worlds-most-valuable-resource-is-no-longer-oil-but-data [Accessed 24/4/21].

The Economist, 2018. *American tech giants are making life tough for startups*. [Online] Available at: https://www.economist.com/business/2018/06/02/american-tech-giants-are-making-life-tough-for-startups [Accessed 24/4/21].

The European Observatory on Infringements of Intellectual Property Rights, 2020. *Status Reports on IP Infringement*. [Online] Available at: https://euipo.europa.eu/ohimportal/en/web/observatory/status-reports-on-ip-infringement [Accessed 24/4/21].

The New York Times, 2017. *Tech Giants Are Paying Huge Salaries for Scarce A.I. Talent*. [Online] Available at: https://www.nytimes.com/2017/10/22/technology/artificial-intelligence-experts-salaries.html [Accessed 10/5/21].

The New York Times, 2020a. https://www.nytimes.com/2020/05/06/technology/employee-monitoring-work-from-home-virus.html. [Online] Available at: https://www.nytimes.com/2020/05/06/technology/employee-monitoring-work-from-home-virus.html [Accessed 24/4/21].

The New York Times, 2020b. *The Hot New Covid Tech Is Wearable and Constantly Tracks You*. [Online] Available at: https://www.nytimes.com/2020/11/15/technology/virus-wearable-tracker-privacy.html [Accessed 24/4/21].

The New York Times, 2021. *Russian Hacking and Influence in the U.S. Election*. [Online] Available at: https://www.nytimes.com/news-event/russian-election-hacking [Accessed 7/5/21].

The New Yorker, 2021. *Inside the Making of Facebook's Supreme Court*. [Online] Available at: https://www.newyorker.com/tech/annals-of-technology/inside-the-making-of-facebooks-supreme-court [Accessed 24/4/21].

The Ranking Digital Rights, 2018. *Corporate Accountability Index*. [Online] Available at: https://rankingdigitalrights.org/index2018/ [Accessed 20/4/21].

Thompson T., 2017. *Google's Sentiment Analyzer Thinks Being Gay Is Bad.* [Online] Available at: https://www.vice.com/en/article/j5jmj8/google-artificial-intelligence-bias [Accessed 10/5/21].

Thouvenin, F., Weber, R. & Fr, A., 2017. *Data ownership: taking stock and mapping the issues. In Frontiers in data science.* s.l.: (pp. 111–145). CRC Press.

Tirole, J., 1988. *The theory of industrial organization.* s.l.: MIT press.

Tiwana, A., Konsynski, B. & Bush, A., 2010. Research commentary—Platform evolution: Coevolution of platform architecture, governance, and environmental dynamics. *Information systems research,* Volume 21(4), pp. 675–687.

Toffler, A., 1970. *Future shock.* s.l.: Bantam.

Tolkien, J., 2012. *The Lord of the Rings: One Volume.* s.l.: Houghton Mifflin Harcourt.

Trew B., 2020. *Coronavirus: Hundreds dead in Iran from drinking methanol amid fake reports it cures disease.* [Online] Available at: https://www.independent.co.uk/news/world/middle-east/iran-coronavirus-methanol-drink-cure-deaths-fake-a9429956.html [Accessed 10/5/21].

Tucker, J. A. et al., 2018. Social Media, Political Polarization, and Political Disinformation: A Review of the Scientific Literature. SSNR.

Tullock, G., 2004. *The selected works of Gordon Tullock,* s.l.: Liberty Fund.

Turing, A., 2009. Computing machinery and intelligence. In: *In Parsing the turing test Springer, Dordrecht.* Dordrecht: Springer, pp. 23–65.

Twitter, 2020. *Platform Manipulation.* [Online] Available at: https://transparency.twitter.com/en/reports/platform-manipulation.html#2020-jan-jun [Accessed 10/5/21].

Twizeyimana, J. D. & Andersson, A., 2019. The public value of E-Government–A literature review. *Government Information Quarterly,* 36(2), pp. 167–178.

UNCTAD, 2021. *UNCTAD Stat.* [Online] Available at: https://unctadstat.unctad.org/wds/ReportFolders/reportFolders.aspx?sCS_ChosenLang=en [Accessed 24/4/21].

UNESCO, 2021. *ROAM-X Indicators.* [Online] Available at: https://en.unesco.org/internet-universality-indicators/roamx-indicators [Accessed 24/4/21].

UNICEF, 2020. *Two thirds of the world's school-age children have no internet access at home, new UNICEF-ITU report says.* [Online] Available at: https://www.unicef.org/press-releases/two-thirds-worlds-school-age-children-have-no-internet-access-home-new-unicef-itu [Accessed 30/4/21].

United Nations, 1948. *Universal Declaration of Human Rights.* [Online] Available at: https://www.un.org/en/about-us/universal-declaration-of-human-rights [Accessed 10/5/21].

United Nations, 2017. *Frontier Issues: The impact of the technological revolution on labour markets and income distribution.* [Online] Available at: https://www.un.org/development/desa/dpad/publication/frontier-issues-artificial-intelligence-and-other-technologies-will-define-the-future-of-jobs-and-incomes/ [Accessed 5/5/21].

United Nations, 2021a. *Sustainable Development Goals.* [Online] Available at: https://www.un.org/sustainabledevelopment/ [Accessed 7/5/21].

United Nations, 2021b. *Frontier Issues Artificial Intelligence and Other Technologies Will Define the Future of Jobs and Incomes.* [Online] Available at: https://www.un.org/development/desa/dpad/publication/frontier-issues-artificial-intelligence-and-other-technologies-will-define-the-future-of-jobs-and-incomes/ [Accessed 5/5/21].

Urbinati, A., Bogers, M., Chiesa, V. & Frattini, F., 2019. Creating and capturing value from Big Data: A multiple-case study analysis of provider companies. *Technovation,* Volume 84, pp. 21–36.

USA Facts, 2020. *4.4 million households with children don't have consistent access to computers for online learning during the pandemic.* [Online] Available at: https://usafacts.org/articles/internet-access-students-at-home/ [Accessed 30/4/21].

Van Deursen, A. & Helsper, E., 2015. A nuanced understanding of Internet use and non-use among the elderly. *European Journal of Communication,* Volume 30(2), pp. 171–187.

Van Deursen, A., Helsper, E., Eynon, R. & van Dijk, J., 2017. The Compoundness and Sequentiality of Digital Inequality. *International Journal of Communication,* Volume 11, pp. 452–473.

Van Dijck, J., 2009. Users like you? Theorizing agency in user-generated content. *Media, culture & society,* Volume 31(1), pp. 41–58.

Varghese, B. & Buyya, R., 2018. Next generation cloud computing: New trends and research directions. *Future Generation Computer Systems,* Volume 79, pp. 849–861.

Verizon, 2017. *2017 Verizon Data Breach Investigations Report (DBIR) from the Perspective of Exterior Security Perimeter.* [Online] Available at: https://www.verizondigitalmedia.com/blog/2017-verizon-data-breach-investigations-report/ [Accessed 24/4/21].

Verizon, 2020. *2020 Data Breach Investigations Report.* [Online] Available at: https://enterprise.verizon.com/resources/reports/dbir/# [Accessed 24/4/21].

von Braun, J., 2019. AI and Robotics Implications for the Poor. *SSNR.*

Von Hollen, J., 2019. *How cobots are levelling the manufacturing playing field.* [Online] Available at: https://www.universal-robots.com/blog/how-cobots-are-levelling-the-manufacturing-playing-field/ [Accessed 5/5/21].

Vosoughi, S., Roy, D. & Aral, S., 2018. The spread of true and false news online. *Science,* 359(6380), pp. 1146–1151.

Vox, 2019. *Poor kids spend nearly 2 hours more on screens each day than rich kids.* [Online] Available at: https://www.vox.com/recode/2019/10/29/20937870/kids-screentime-rich-poor-common-sense-media [Accessed 7/5/21].

Vu, K., Hanafizadeh, P. & Bohlin, E., 2020. ICT as a driver of economic growth: A survey of the literature and directions for future research. *Telecommunications Policy,* 44(2), pp. 1–20.

Wachsmuth, D. & Weisler, A., 2018. Airbnb and the Rent Gap: Gentrification Through the Sharing Economy. *Environment and Planning A: Economy and Space,* 50(6), pp. 1147–1470.

Wachter, S., Mittelstadt, B. & Floridi, L., 2017. Why a Right to Explanation of Automated Decision-Making Does Not Exist in the General Data Protection Regulation. *International Data Privacy Law,* Volume 7(2), pp. 76–99.

Warzel, C. & Mac, R., 2018. *These Confidential Charts Show Why Facebook Bought WhatsApp.* [Online] Available at: https://www.buzzfeednews.com/article/charliewarzel/why-facebook-bought-whatsapp [Accessed 24/4/21].

Watanabe, C., Naveed, K., Tou, Y. & Neittaanmäki, P., 2018. Measuring GDP in the digital economy: Increasing dependence on uncaptured GDP. *Technological Forecasting and Social Change,* 137, pp. 226–240.

Weiss, R. & Mehrotra, A., 2001. Online dynamic pricing: Efficiency, equity and the future of e-commerce. *Va. JL & Tech.,* Volume 6, p.1.

Welby, B., 2019. The impact of digital government on citizen well-being. *OECD.*

WhatsApp, 2020. *Search the Web.* [Online] Available at: https://blog.whatsapp.com/?lang=en [Accessed 10/5/21].

Whish, R. & Bailey, D., 2015. *Competition law.* s.l.: Oxford University Press, USA.

Wiener A., 2020. *Trump, Twitter, Facebook, and the Future of Online Speech.* [Online] Available at: https://www.newyorker.com/news/letter-from-silicon-valley/trump-twitter-facebook-and-the-future-of-online-speech [Accessed 24/4/21].

Wikipedia, 2021. *Poe's law.* [Online] Available at: https://en.wikipedia.org/wiki/Poe%27s_law [Accessed 10/5/21].

Wired, [2019]. *The Cambridge Analytica Story, Explained.* [Online] Available at: https://www.wired.com/amp-stories/cambridge-analytica-explainer/ [Accessed 10/5/21].

World Bank, 2016. *World Development Report 2016: Digital Dividends.* [Online] Available at: https://elibrary.worldbank.org/doi/abs/10.1596/978-1-4648-0671-1 [Accessed 20/4/21].

World Bank, 2018. *Global Economic Prospects, June 2018: The Turning of the Tide?.* s.l.: World Bank.

World Bank, 2019. *Digital Business Indicators.* [Online] Available at: https://www.worldbank.org/en/research/brief/digital-business-indicators [Accessed 20/4/21].

Wu, T., 2003. Network neutrality, broadband discrimination. *Journal of Telecommunications and High Technology Law,* Volume 2, p. 141.

Yapar, B., Bayrakdar, S. & Yapar, M., 2015. The role of taxation problems on the development of e-commerce. *Procedia-Social and Behavioral Sciences,* Volume 195, pp. 642–648.

Zervas, G., Proserpio, D. & Byers, J., 2017. The rise of the sharing economy: Estimating the impact of Airbnb on the hotel industry. *Journal of marketing research,* Volume 54(5), pp. 687–705.

Zervas, G., Proserpio, D. & Byers, J., 2021. A first look at online reputation on Airbnb, where every stay is above average. *Marketing Letters,* Volume 32(1), pp. 1–16.

Zoepf, S., Chen, S., Adu, P. & Pozo, G., 2018. The economics of ride-hailing: driver revenue, expenses, and taxes. *CEEPR WP*, Volume 5, pp. 1–38.

Zorn, Z., 2019. *100+ Sharing Economy Apps and Websites You Don't Want to Miss.* [Online] Available at: https://www.moneynomad.com/100-sharing-economy-apps-websites/ [Accessed 4/5/21].

Zuiderwijk, A. & Janssen, M., 2014. Open data policies, their implementation and impact: A framework for comparison. *Government Information Quarterly*, Volume 31(1), pp. 17–29.

Glossary

3D printing – technology used to manufacture three-dimensional objects through the help of robot-arm printheads

3G, 4G, 5G – wireless communication technologies, respectively of the third, fourth, and fifth generation. Worldwide, 3G was first launched in 2002, 4G in 2009, and 5G in 2019. 3G, 4G, and 5G are the technology standards that allow mobile phones to connect to the Internet

Abuse of dominance – generally refers to the conduct of a player that holds a dominant position (see *dominance*) in the market and that leverages that power to hamper competition (for example, preventing competitors from accessing key production inputs at market prices). Art. 102 of the Treaty on the functioning of the European Union prohibits abuse of dominance

Access node – in telecoms, refers to the last distribution point in a network aggregating all the connections to final users in a nearby area

Acquirhire – refers to acquiring a company with the primary purpose of recruiting the target's company employees (for example: talented, highly skilled artificial intelligence developers)

Active equipment – refers to devices that need to be powered by a source of energy. Examples in telecoms are routers used to provide wireless services

Actual competition – level of competition currently observed in the market. It is often opposed to *potential competition*, i.e. competition that is not yet observed

Adequacy decision – refers to a decision taken by the European Commission determining that a country outside the European Union has an adequate level of data protection, consistently with the General Data Protection Regulation

Adverse selection – economic phenomenon observed when players involved in a possible transaction have different information on the value of the good traded. Such *asymmetry of information* may trigger a selection in the players that are willing to trade, namely: only players selling low-quality goods remain in the market

Affect recognition – (also known as *emotion recognition*) in this book, the term is used to refer to artificial intelligence applications attempting to identify human feelings, personality, mental and emotional engagement through actual monitoring (for example, through the scanning of facial expressions) or through data processing (for example, through the scanning of email text)

Ancillary right – in copyright law, ancillary rights arise from the exploitation of copyrighted content in a different shape than the one originally copyrighted. For example, a poster with a picture extracted by a movie may qualify as an ancillary right

Anonymization – process used to remove information from a dataset so that the original source of the data cannot be anymore identified

Anti-competitive agreement – agreement between market players resulting in a decrease of competition. A typical example are price cartels, where market players agree not to deviate from an agreed price level

Application Programming Interface – (usually abbreviated with *API*) software allowing different applications to communicate with each other smoothly

Artificial intelligence – a technology attempting to emulate biological intelligence learning from the surrounding environment and reacting to unforeseen circumstances with a certain degree of autonomy

Asymmetric information – in economics, refers to a situation in which two players have access to a different degree of information on a condition that is relevant to a potential transaction between them (for example, the quality of the good traded or the likelihood that a player behaves in a certain way)

Augmented reality – technology blending computer-generated images with real-world objects, enhancing users' experience. For example, a smartphone's camera can be pointed to a building to return the image of that building with a map of the electric cables running through its walls

B2B – refers to companies interacting with companies

B2C – refers to companies interacting with consumers

B2G – refers to companies interacting with public administrations (G stands for "government")

Backbone network – (also known as *core network*) in telecoms, a backbone network aggregates high capacity circuits (usually a ring of fibre optic cables) at the local/regional level. All telecom connections of a major city would connect to a backbone network, which would then connect to the rest of the world (the Internet)

Backhaul – in telecoms, refers to the segment connecting the *backbone network* (->) and local terminals, *access nodes* (->) to which Internet users connect

Bandwagon effect – psychological phenomenon whereby an individual's probability of implementing a particular behaviour is affected by the number of other individuals implementing it

Bandwidth – maximum amount of data that can be transferred in a given amount of time

Behavioural bias – belief or cognitive process leading to irrational choices, namely: choices that are not optimal in pursuing the goals or preferences of the individual who makes them. See also: *bounded rationality*

Belt and Road Initiative – refers to a strategic plan adopted by the Chinese Government in 2013 and entailing the creation of a global infrastructure connecting China to a significant number of countries around the world (in particular: Asian and African countries)

Big data – general term used to indicate technologies and techniques used for the collection, processing, and analysis of large datasets that traditional data-processing applications cannot handle

Biometric data – information on an individual physical, physiological, or behavioural features, often used for identification or authentication purposes. See also *face recognition*

Bitcoin – digital currency relying on *blockchain* technologies to finalize *peer-to-peer* transfers between users

Bitstream access – in telecoms, refers to a virtual, non-physical access to a physical network

Blockchain – dataset aggregating transactions in blocks "chained" with each other. Modifying a block or transaction would require altering the entire chain. For that reason, blockchain technologies are considered very secure. Blockchain is the underlying technology of *bitcoin*. See also *digital ledger technology*

Blue-collar – employment classification. Generally refers to jobs requiring to perform manual tasks. See also: *white-collar*

Boltzmann Machine – neural network connecting symmetric autonomous nodes. When activated, nodes can respond to information to which they have not been exposed before based on a probability distribution learned from an input dataset

Bot – software performing automated tasks over the Internet

Botnet – network of computers hijacked by cyber-attackers to pursue a malicious action in the cyber-space

Bounded rationality – generally refers to humans' inability to make entirely rational choices. Namely: to make the choice that maximizes the probability to achieve one's goals, conditional on available information. See also *behavioural bias*

Broad artificial intelligence – (also known as *strong artificial intelligence*) refers to artificial intelligence capable of performing a wide range of unspecified tasks, similarly to human intelligence

Broadband – high-speed telecom system. In the European Union, *basic* broadband guarantees up to 30 Megabytes per second (Mbps) of download speed; *fast* broadband has minimum of 30 Mbps download speed; *ultrafast* broadband has minimum of 100 Mbps download speed

Burden of proof – expression used in a legal context to indicate the allocation of responsibility between parties to provide evidence supporting a determinate legal claim. For example, in EU merger control, the European Commission has the *burden of proof* to show that the merger is anti-competitive (see: *anti-competitive agreement*)

Caching – storing of files in a storage location for a limited amount of time

Causal effect – in econometrics, a causal effect is defined as the difference in outcomes when exposed and when not exposed to a particular treatment. It is usually opposed to *correlation*, whereby the relationship between outcome and treatment is not strictly due to the treatment itself

Chip – set of electronic circuits integrated on a silicon base. Chips are essential to any electronic device and are therefore indispensable for the fabrication of appliances such as smartphones, personal computers, and Internet of Things appliances

Clickbait – term usually used to indicate content placed online to lure users into clicking on a link and redirecting them to a specific web page

Cloud – technology used to provide computing services over the Internet. Those services may include data storage, use of software, data processing, and analytics, for example

Cognitive task – usually used in a work context. A cognitive task is a task requiring the use of a mental process. That may entail reading, remembering, or acquiring new knowledge, for example

Collateral censorship – in the context of intermediaries' liability, refers to the removal of content that is not illegal from online platforms' servers to reduce platforms' exposure to potential liability risks

Complementary – two products are in a *complementary* relationship if the ability to access one of them increases the value of the other one. For example, bread and butter are in a *complementary* relationship

Communication from the European Commission – non-binding act published by the European Commission, typically to present a strategy or action plan. The Digital Single Market Strategy, for example, is a Communication from the European Commission

Confirmation bias – (also known as *directionally motivated reasoning*) refers to individuals' tendency to filter information according to its adherence to their preconceived beliefs. For example, a judge that has already made up her mind that a defendant is guilty tends to attribute a lower value to new evidence in support of the defendant's innocence

Connected cars – a general category that refers to vehicles capable of automatically interchanging information with the outside world through the Internet

Conspiracy theory – unfounded theory attempting to explain events of general interest rejecting mainstream views. Conspiracy theories tend to hinge on the role that small, powerful political groups may have played in the event

Consumer welfare – (also known as *consumer surplus*) indicates the value that the consumption of a particular good or service generates from consumers' perspective, minus the cost that those consumers need to bear to access it. Simple economic models often represent consumer welfare with the difference between how much a consumer is willing to pay for a good and how much she actually pays for it. Consumer welfare, however, also depends on goods' qualitative features

Contestable market – a market is contestable if companies can quickly enter it and challenge incumbent suppliers. In a perfectly contestable market, a monopolist sets competitive prices, as any price above the competitive level would automatically induce entry by competitors (note: this is a theoretical illustration of an unrealistic extreme scenario, as entering a market always entails some fixed costs)

Co-regulation – regulatory approach whereby public authorities define an overarching goal, such as improving the functioning of a specific market, and the market players active in that market choose and implement the measures needed to pursue that goal. For example, the European Commission may set the goal of reducing *disinformation* in online platform markets, and online platforms may be required to pursue that goal with adequate measures, such as removal of harmful content from their servers

Correlation – in econometrics, two variables are correlated if they tend to display values that are in direct relationship with each other. For example, when the variable "education level" increases, the variable "salary" increases too (that is: education and salary are positively correlated), while the variable "unemployment likelihood" tends to decrease (that is: education and unemployment are negatively correlated). Correlation coefficients vary between 1 (perfect positive correlation) and −1 (perfect negative correlation)

Council of the European Union – institution representing EU Member States' governments. The *Council* is where national ministers from each EU country meet to adopt laws and coordinate policies

Counterfactual scenario – state of the world that materializes absent the action that is the object of analysis. For example, a competition authority assessing the effect of a merger on the market needs to evaluate the counterfactual scenario if the merger is not allowed. In the counterfactual scenario, the company that is being acquired could go bust and exit the market, for example. Thus, in that case, a merger that prima facie may have appeared to lower *actual competition* may not have anti-competitive effects, as it is not altering the number of players

compared to the *counterfactual scenario* (where only one company is active anyway)

Counter-notice – in response to a take-down action (see *notice and take-down*) whereby a host server has removed certain online content, affected parties may submit a *counter-notice* to appeal against the take-down and ask to reinstate the content

Country of origin principle – the *country of origin principle* is at the cornerstone of the *EU Single Market*. It predicates that the applicable law to a service performed in an EU *Member State* is the country's law from which that service originates. The country of origin principle has thus the potential to simplify companies' scale up in Europe. For example, a company wishing to supply all 27 EU Member States would only need to deal with its country of origin legislation and not with 27 different country laws

Covid-19 – stands for "Coronavirus Disease 19". Covid-19 is caused by *SARS-CoV-2*, a virus provoking severe acute respiratory syndromes. The World Health Organization declared the Covid-19 pandemic in March 2020. The pandemic is still ongoing at the time of writing this book

Cryptojacking – refers to a type of malicious activity in the cyberspace: the unauthorized use of others' computers to mine cryptocurrency, such as *bitcoin*

Cyber-attack – a general term indicating a malicious action in the cyberspace, usually perpetrated by hackers

Cyber-espionage – refers to a type of malicious activity in the cyberspace, namely: the acquisition of non-public information without the consent of the source

Cybersecurity – a general term indicating the protection of networks and information systems against malicious attacks, human mistakes, natural disasters, and technical failure

Dark Web – content that is retrievable online but is not indexed by mainstream online search engines. In addition, the content in the dark web is encrypted so that its users and their location are not traceable (thus, the *dark web* tends to be associated with illegal activity online). The dark web is a subset of the *deep web*

Data breach – a data breach occurs whenever personal information is lost, stolen, or involuntarily disclosed by the entity that stores or control that information

Data broker – a company whose business consists of collecting personal or non-personal data from a variety of public and private sources, aggregating it and selling it or licensing its use to users

Data centre – a physical infrastructure aggregating high computational power such to allow the storage, processing, and analysis of very large data sets

Data controller – in the General Data Protection Regulation's terminology, a *data controller* is an entity (a person, a company, a public authority) which, alone or jointly with others, determines the purposes and means of the processing of personal data

Data lake – centralized repository of raw data, typically used by organizations to optimize data storage and avoid cost duplications. For example, different organizational departments may not need to collect the same information, if the first department that collects it makes it available in the *data lake*. A *data hub* serves a similar purpose within an organization, but differently from data lakes, *data hubs* contain refined, ready-to-use information in a high-quality format

Data mining – process aimed to extract useful information from large datasets

Data pool – a group of two or more entities sharing data through a common data repository

Data portability right – refers to the right to individuals to export information they sourced from the entity that host it and use it for their own purposes

Data subject – according to the General Data Protection Regulation, a *data subject* is a natural person who can be identified, directly or indirectly, through the information available in a particular dataset

Dead weight loss – in microeconomics, the term refers to the amount of value that a market could generate if it would be possible to remove frictions that give rise to a *market failure*, such as *market power*

Deep learning – neuronal network imitating the structure of the human brain. The attribute "deep" refers to the fact that neuronal networks are organized in layers (hence at different depth levels); "learning" refers to the fact that the neuronal networks are progressively readjusted when processing new external input to improve the accuracy of the application's outcome

Deep Web – content that is retrievable online but is not indexed by online search engines. The *deep web* may contain illegal or legal content (illegal content is usually located in the *dark web*)

Deepfake – artificially altered video where a person's face or body is manipulated to let viewers believe that they belong to someone else. *Deepfakes* require artificial intelligence-powered technologies

Demetrication – used in social media, refers to the removal of certain kinds of users' public feedback to users' posts. For example, the number of likes expressed for a post on Facebook or a user's number of followers on Twitter

DESI – stands for Digital Economy and Society Index. It is a composite index created by the European Commission to summarize indicators on Europe's digital performance periodically

Digital divide – a general term used to indicate the gap between individuals who can access technology and prosper from it and those who cannot

Digital innovation hub – "one-stop-shop" for companies willing to use digital technologies to improve their business strategy, production process, products, or services. Digital innovation hubs aggregate technologies, expertise and services to help companies, for example with access to technology, technical knowledge, training, skill development, or financing advice

Digital Single Market – extension of the *Single Market* concept to the digital space. Namely:

a territorial area encompassing all EU *Member States* where digital goods and services are free to flow, facing no border or regulatory restriction to movement

Digital sovereignty – broad concept that refers to a country's ability to be autonomous in the digital space regardless of its relationship with other countries. It applies, for example, to access to raw materials, such as rare earths, considered indispensable for computing technologies. See also *strategic autonomy*

Digital Subscriber Line – (often abbreviated with *DSL*) telecom technology used to allow data transfer over traditional telephone lines

Disinformation – verifiably false or misleading information that is created, presented, and disseminated for economic gain or to deceive the public intentionally, and that may cause public harm

Distributed Denial of Service – a malicious activity in the cyberspace consisting of overwhelming a target network or computing facility with an unbearable amount of Internet traffic, so to hamper its functioning

Distributed ledger technology – (commonly referred to as *DLT*) a database replicated across different locations and users, eliminating the need for a central validation authority or intermediary. *Blockchain* is a type of digital ledger technology

Dominance – terminology used in competition policy to indicate market players that can operate with a significant degree of autonomy vis-à-vis other actual or potential market players and final consumers

Double marginalization – economic phenomenon verified when two different market players, each holding some market power, are supplying complementary inputs required for the production of a good or service. Double marginalization tends to inflate costs, and it is thus often quoted as an important reason to back vertical mergers (namely: mergers between companies supplying complementary products). A vertical merger eliminates double marginalization (though it may generate concerns of other natures)

Downstream – term used to indicate markets at the end of the value chain, close to final customer. For example, a car retailer is *downstream* compared to the car manufacturer, which is *upstream*

Drone – aerial vehicle that can be piloted remotely without the need of a human pilot on board

Dunning-Kruger effect – *behavioural bias* according to which low-skilled individuals have a tendency to overestimate their capabilities

Dynamic effect – in microeconomics, refers to an effect that we cannot immediately observe; instead, the effect can be observed after a certain (often unspecified) interval of time has elapsed

Dynamic pricing – business practice consisting in allowing the price of supplied goods or services to vary more or less frequently over time, for example, in response to surges or decreases in demand

Echo chamber – (also known as *filter bubble*) term often used in social media communication. It refers to users' (conscious or subconscious) selective exposure to information that matches or reinforce their preexisting beliefs

E-Commerce – following the definition proposed by *OECD,* e-Commerce refers to the sale or purchase of goods or services, conducted over computer networks by methods specifically designed to receive or place orders

Economies of scale – economic phenomenon whereby average costs of production or supply decrease in the number of units produced or supplied

Edge computing – refers to the practice of storing and processing information at the edge of a network (that is: close to the origin of that information or to where that information is used or consumed)

E-government – general term to indicate the digitalization of the public sector

eHealth – refers to the use of digital technologies to reduce costs, increase accessibility and improve the quality of health services

eID – national electronic identification scheme used by *Member States* in the European Union

Elasticity – in microeconomics, term used to indicate a variable's sensitivity to a change in a different but related variable. For example, the demand for a good is considered "elastic to price" if a change in price generates a significant change in the demand for that good

Endogenous variable – in econometrics, an *endogenous variable* is affected by the other variables used in the model. For example, in a model attempting to study the relationship between outbreaks of Covid-19 and job losses, the variable "job losses" is endogenous to the model (because a Covid-19 outbreak may force companies to shut down and layoff part of the workforce). Conversely, the variable "Covid-19 outbreak" is *exogeneous*

EU co-legislative process – ordinary procedure used by EU legislators to adopt new EU law. According to it, the *European Commission* submits a draft proposal which then must be adopted by the *European Parliament* and the *Council of the European Union*

EU Directive – legislative act setting out a goal that all *EU Member States* must pursue. Directives, however, leave it up to each Member State to craft its laws to reach that goal

EU Regulation – legislative act directly applied across the *European Union* without the need of a legislative intervention by *Member States* (Member States may still be required to adopt measures that favour the implementation and enforcement of a regulation)

European Commission – (often abbreviated with *EC*) executive branch of the *European Union*

European Council – collegiate body defining the overall political directions and priorities of the *European Union*. It comprises the leaders of all 27 EU *Member States*

European Parliament – *European Union* body co-exercising the EU legislative power, together with the *Council of the European Union*. It is the EU's only institution directly elected by EU citizens

European Semester – 6-month cycle of economic, fiscal, labour, and social policy coordination within the European Union

European Union – (often abbreviated with *EU*) political and economic union between 27 European countries covering most of the European continent

Ex-ante – in the regulatory context, term used to indicate an approach hinging on the definition of rules before a specific event has occurred. It is usually juxtaposed to *ex-post*

Excludability – in microeconomics, refers to a property of goods. A good is *(non) excludable* if it is (not) possible to prevent access to it ("possible" in economics is a relative term: it implies that it is not too costly to prevent access)

Exogenous variable – (often used interchangeably with *structural break*) in econometrics, an *exogenous variable* is not affected by the other variables used in the model. For example, in a model attempting to study the relationship between outbreaks of Covid-19 and job losses, the variable "Covid-19 outbreaks" is exogenous to the model (because presumably, job losses do not cause Covid-19 outbreaks). Conversely, the variable "job losses" is *endogenous*

Experience good – product with quality features that cannot be observed before consumption. For example, a Bolgheri red wine must be tasted before being able to judge whether it was worth its price. *Experience goods* are often juxtaposed to *search goods*

Ex-post – in the regulatory context, term used to indicate an approach hinging on the role of enforcement authorities after a particular event has occurred. It is typically juxtaposed to *ex-ante*

Externality – positive or negative consequence affecting a third party that is not involved in the process that originated the effect. For example, the consumption of a cigarette produces a (negative) *externality* on a third party, the passive smoker, that is not actively involved in smoking

Facial recognition – usually refers to an artificial intelligence-powered application implemented to automatically recognize a human face matching it with a preexisting dataset of personal identifiers

Fact-checking – validation process used to verify that the factual information in support of a specific claim or news are correct

Fair, Reasonable, and Non-Discriminatory – (often abbreviated in *FRAND*) expression often used in licensing contexts when licensing prices cannot be defined before parties enter an agreement. *FRAND* commitments postulate that the licensing party must ask a reasonable price when it becomes possible to formulate a concrete offer

Fake news – false information staged as news. Public commentators and politicians have appropriated the expression *fake news* to undermine the media's credibility. Therefore, *disinformation* experts have progressively abandoned it

Fibre – cable made of glass or plastic that allows connectivity over light over long distances with very high data speed and quality. Frequently abbreviated with the acronym *FTTx*, where x can be H to indicate *fibre to the household*; B to indicate *fibre to business*, and so on

Filter-bubble – see *echo chamber*

Flexicurity – term used to indicate welfare systems that tend to promote flexibility for business and social and economic security of workers at the same time. *Flexicurity* welfare systems are typical of Scandinavian countries

Fog computing – decentralized computing infrastructure where data storage and processing can occur anywhere between the place where the information originates and the cloud

Foreclosure – in competition law, typical *abuse of dominance* whereby a *dominant* company leverages its *market power* to prevent a competitor from entering the market.

Foresight analysis – methodology used to scan the future analysing macro-trends and developing possible long-term scenarios. The analysis does not necessarily frame scenarios in terms of their likelihood. Instead, *foresight analysis* considers all possible scenarios and

uses them as reference for testing and discussing ideas concerning the future

Fourth Industrial Revolution – used to indicate the ongoing transformation of economy and society induced by the progressive automation of industries, adoption of artificial intelligence, and consumption of interconnected digital technologies

G2B – Acronym used to indicate a relationship between public administration (G stands for "government") and business

G2G – Acronym used to indicate a relationship between public administrations (G stands for "government")

G7 – Informal group of 7 rich countries. The group includes Canada, France, Germany, Italy, Japan, the UK, and the US.

GAFAM – Acronym colloquially used to indicate a group of US companies dominating online platform markets in the US and Europe: Google, Amazon, Facebook, Apple, and Microsoft

General Purpose Technology – indicates a technology introducing radically new production and consumption processes with profound transformational effects on the entire economy. Examples are electricity or information technology

Geo-blocking – practice used by companies to discriminate online users based on their geographical location, most of the time applying different access conditions or price terms

Geoengineering – refers to the development and deployment of large scale technologies to counteract climate change. For example, large scale mirrors to reflect sunlight and reduce global warming

Gigabyte – commonly used unit of computer storage capacity, equivalent to 1,000 megabytes. Roughly equivalent to the storage needed to host a 1h 40min–2h movie of average quality

Gini coefficient – statistical index measuring the dispersion of income in a well-identified population. It varies between 0 (perfect symmetric distribution of value where every individual in the population has the same share) and 1 (perfect inequality)

Gold-plating – terminology used to indicate a Member State's practice to implement an EU Directive using legislative or non-legislative acts (such as guidelines) that are not strictly necessary to implement the directive. Instead, the acts are artificially crafted to favour domestic interests, such as national market players

Good Samaritan clause – in the context of regulatory approaches to tackle harmful content online, *good Samaritan clauses* are used to incentivize online platforms to pro-actively identify content to be removed without losing protection from the e-Commerce Directive *safeharbour*. In fact, according to the e-Commerce Directive, online platforms cannot be held responsible for harmful content they host without being aware of it

Gross Domestic Product – (usually abbreviated with *GDP*) indicator providing a measure of the size of a specific area's economy. It is equal to the sum of the gross values added of all institutional units resident in that area and engaged in production, plus taxes and minus subsidies on products

Hacker – individual with a high degree of informatics knowledge using an informatic system to pursue a specific goal

Hate group – organization of formal or informal nature dedicated to the spread of content with the ultimate goal of inciting hatred towards single individuals or a particular group of people

Hate speech – content often to be found online expressing hate or inciting violence towards a single individual or group of people

High-performance computing – (often abbreviated with *HPC*; also referred to as *supercomputers*) computing systems capable of processing extremely high amounts of information and solving highly complex problems

Horizontal agreement – in competition policy, refers to an agreement between market players operating at the same level of the production or supply chain (and that are thus most likely *actual* or *potential* competitors)

Horizontal search outcome – (also known as *universal search outcome*) outcome by a web search engine that is general and not specific to a particular sector or area of interest (that is the case of *vertical search outcome*)

Human-in-command – refers to the role of humans vis-à-vis artificial intelligence applications. With *human-in-command*, a human can oversee the overall activity of the artificial intelligence system and decide when and how to use the system

Human-in-the-loop – refers to the role of humans vis-à-vis artificial intelligence applications. With *human-in-the-loop*, a human can intervene in every decision cycle of the system

Human-on-the-loop – refers to the role of humans vis-à-vis artificial intelligence applications. With *human-on-the-loop*, a human can intervene during the design cycle of the system and monitor the system's operation

Hyperbolic discount rate – in economics, used to indicate a tendency to significantly overestimate short-term gains compared to long-term losses strongly, to an extent such to result in counter-productive (irrational) choices for the individual who makes them

Infodemic – term used to indicate the rapid and far-reaching spread of information and *disinformation* related to a specific subject. The spread occurs primarily via *online platforms* (in particular, *social networks*)

Information and communication technologies – (usually abbreviated with *ICT*) general term encompassing any communication technology, the Internet, network and telecom infrastructure, computing facilities, hardware, and software used in any digital application

Intellectual property right – (usually abbreviated with *IPR*) right recognized to individuals, private, or public entities for creations of individuals' minds. The owner of an *IPR* can exclude others from accessing her creation for a well-defined period

Interim measure – in the context of EU competition law, refers to a condition imposed by the European Commission on a company before having concluded that the company's behaviour is *anti-competitive*. Interim measures are used to avoid potentially anti-competitive behaviours to cause irreversible harm

Internet of things – general term used to indicate a system of devices capable of exchanging information with each other

Internet penetration – statistical indicator used to represent the level of connectivity of a community over a well-defined geographical area. The index is typically computed as the number of Internet users over the total population

Internet protocol – (usually abbreviated with *IP*) methodology used to transfer data from one computer to another. An *IP address* is a unique identifier that identifies a specific device or network

Internet service provider – (usually abbreviated with *ISP*) entity, usually a telecom operator, supplying the necessary services to connect and exchange data through the Internet

Interoperability – refers to the ability to easily exchange information between different computing systems, devices, applications or platforms

Killer robot – fully autonomous technologies developed to cause harm without the need of control by a human being

Killer acquisition – merger or acquisition of a typically promising, innovative small company by a large, incumbent company. In a *killer acquisition*, the objective of the incumbent is to prevent the emergence of a potential future competitor

Latency – in telecoms, refers to the delay which is to be expected from the moment in which the command to start the data transfer is given to the moment in which the actual traffic begins

Level playing field – expression typically used in trade contexts. It underlines the need of establishing rules that apply symmetrically to all market players, without favouring a specific category of players. For example, telecom companies have been concerned about the absence of a *level playing field* in the EU Single Market because *online platforms* are allegedly subject to lighter regulatory constraints than telecom operators

Life-long learning – broad expression that refers to all education and training an individual can receive during a lifetime, including initial education, training and adult learning

Local loop unbundling – (often abbreviated with *LLU*) in telecom regulation, refers to a regulatory provision that allows telecom operators to compete for providing the service in the "last mile" of the telecom connection (that is: between the final user and the *access node*)

Machine learning – type of artificial intelligence that autonomously learns from the new information it processes and thus constantly improves the accuracy of the outcome it returns

Machine to Machine – (often abbreviated with *M2M*) refers to wired or wireless communication between devices. See also *Internet of things*

Malware – general term used in cyber-security to indicate any software developed to pursue one or more malicious actions in the cyberspace

Marginal cost – typically the cost of producing one extra unit of a determinate product

Market failure – in economics, terminology used to describe a situation in which markets are not generating as much value as they could, from a broad societal perspective

Market power – in economics, *market power* relates to a seller's ability to define its market behaviour with a degree of independence from external constraints: the more independent the supplier, the higher its *market power*

Massive online open courses – (usually abbreviated with *MOOC*) educational courses available online and open to anyone wishing to follow them for free

Matthew effect – in sociology, refers to an amplification effect whereby a particular phenomenon results in increasing the gap between the rich and the poor

Member State – (often abbreviated with *MS*) one of the 27 countries belonging to the *European Union*

Merger – business transaction resulting in two companies becoming one. It usually takes place in the form of acquisition, whereby an acquiring company purchases a target company

Misinformation – information that is false or inaccurate. Note the difference with *disinformation*: *misinformation* is not necessarily conceived to cause harm

Mobile network operator – (usually abbreviated with *MNO*) company supplying wireless voice and data communication services for its subscribed mobile users

Mobile virtual network operator – (often abbreviated with *MVNO*) mobile operator that provides wireless connectivity services to its users but does not own the network. *MVNOs* normally rent their network access from *mobile network operators*

Monopoly – market player supplying the totality of the market where it operates

Moore's law – observation according to which the number of transistors on a microchip tends to double every two years. *Moore's law* emphasizes the quick pace at which computing systems increase their computing power and decrease their size

Moral hazard – in economics, refers to a scenario where a party in a transaction has an incentive to increase her exposure to risk, shifting part or all expected costs to the other party involved in the transaction

Most favoured nation clause – (often abbreviated with *MFN clause*) in competition policy, a *MFN* clause binds a supplier of a good or service to sell its product at the best conditions offered in the market (often *MFN* clauses refer to pricing terms)

Multiannual financial framework – (often abbreviated with *MFF*) refers to the *EU's* long-term budget, usually covering a seven-year period. It defines the maximum amount of resources for each major category of EU spending for the period it covers

Multi-homing – in this book, the term is used in the context of online platform markets. It refers to users' ability to use two or more online platforms at the same time for the same purpose

Multi-sided – used in the context of online platform markets, it refers to platforms' role as intermediary between two or more different groups of customers (the "sides" of the market)

Narrow artificial intelligence – (also known as *weak artificial intelligence*) refers to artificial intelligence developed to perform a single specific task

Natural monopoly – in economics, it defines a scenario where it is most efficient to have one single seller to supply a good or service in the market, rather than two or more

Neighbouring right – see *ancillary right*

Net neutrality – in telecom regulation, regulatory principle preventing *Internet service providers* from discriminating data traffic depending on users, type of content, application used, geographical location, etc. For example: an Internet service provider should not slow down the speed of data transfer just because a user is streaming a movie from a well-defined source rather than another

Network economies – economic principle by means of which the value of consuming a product increases with the number of players who are consuming it. For example: from the perspective of the single user, the value of a telecom service is increasing in the number of users she can reach within the same network

Network sharing agreement – agreement between telecom operators to share the use of the networks they own in order to gain *economies of scale* and *network economies*

Next generation access network – (usually abbreviated with *NGA* or *NGN*) telecom network at least partially made of optical cables. *NGAs* can deliver a higher connectivity speed and quality compared to legacy copper networks (normally *NGAs* guarantee at least 30 Megabyte per second of download speed)

Nexus – in the context of taxation policy, refers to the link between the entity that must pay the tax and the taxing authority in a defined geographical area. The nexus legitimizes the taxing authority to enforce the payment of taxes

Non-cognitive task – usually used in a work context. A *non-cognitive task* requiring the use of soft-skills, or skills that relate to a worker's personality and emotions. Examples include: creativity, resilience, teamwork, empathy, and flexibility

Non-personal data – any information that cannot be considered *personal data*. Non-personal data can originate from machines or any other non-human source. Or they can originate in humans but be subsequently anonymized to prevent re-identification of the original source

Normalization hypothesis – in the context of the study of the impact of technology on society, refers to technology's ability to reduce inequality

Notice and take-down – in the context of online market regulation, refers to a procedure put in place by online platforms and consisting in removing access from content they host on their servers after having received notice that the content is illegal

Nudging – in behavioural economics, refers to the effect that the architecture of a certain (physical or virtual) environment has on steering individuals behaviors towards determinate choices

Oligopoly – in economics, refers to a market dominated by a restricted number of players that hold significant *market power*

Online platform – undertaking operating in a *multi-sided* market that uses the Internet to let two or more well-defined groups of users interact, generating value for the involved groups

Open data – refers to information that is held by public administration and is made available for free to the general public, normally with no constraint on its use

Open-source software – software with a source code that is publicly accessible to anyone willing to inspect it, change it, further develop it or share it

Operating system – (often abbreviated with *OS*) software allowing a computer's hardware to run. It is the key interface between users and the computer's hardware: any software or application used must run over a computer's *operating system*

Organic search result – (also known as *natural search result*) refers to the outcome returned by web search engine and which is not affected by paid advertising

Organisation for Economic Cooperation and Development – (often abbreviated with OECD) intergovernmental organization of 37 member countries pursuing the goal of stimulating economic development worldwide

Over-the-top player – (often abbreviated with *OTT*) streaming service using the Internet to supply content over the top of other platforms. In this book, *OTT* is used often in the telecom context to indicate messaging service platforms such as WhatsApp or Telegram

Passive infrastructure – in telecoms, refers to essential network equipment that does not require power to be activated, such as:masts, ducts, and copper or optic cables

Peer-to-peer communication – refers to the direct data transfer between peer computers in the same network. All peer computers share the same responsibility to handle the data transmission between each other, without the need of a central server to mediate or host the data that is transferred

Permanent establishment – concept used for the allocation of taxing rights in relation of profits made by companies which are active in more than one country. The *OECD* definition is the most commonly used. Accordingly, a *permanent establishment* means a fixed place of business through which the business of an enterprise is wholly or partly carried on

Personal data – information that relates or can be related to an individual person

Personal Information Management Systems – (often abbreviated with *PIMS*) systems allowing users to store, use and control their personal data locally. They are considered a potential privacy-friendly alternative to online platforms users' personal data hovering. *PIMS* revert a common logic: it is not the user who provides the data to the application (e.g. a social network); it is the application that runs locally on a user's PIMS, using the data where they are and "leaving them" there

Phishing – term indicating a malicious action in the cyberspace. It consists of reaching out to a potential victim with a fabricated message (an email, a phone text message) in order to lure her to share sensitive information, such as banking details or passwords

Platform economy – a general term indicating any economic activity which relies on *online platform's* business models

Poe's Law – internet slang used to indicate that, in online contexts, a parody of an extreme content or views is always misinterpreted by at least some online users. Those users ultimately believe that the author of the parody means what she wrote literally. For example, an internet user could tweet that "any person over 40-years-old should be killed" to allow the reopening of the economy during the Covid-19 pandemic. Typically at least some users would take that tweet seriously.

Potential competition – competition that is not yet observed in the market but that it is likely to emerge in the future in the scenario of reference. It is often opposed to *actual competition* i.e. competition that is currently observed in the market

Predatory pricing – in competition policy, abusive practice by a *dominant* company consisting in setting prices at a low, unprofitable level, incurring losses in the short-term, with the purpose of driving competitors out of the market. Short-term losses are then recovered in the long-term, when the company which implemented the abusive conduct is able to enjoy larger market shares

Price discrimination – in economics, refers to the practice of charging different prices for products that have the same production and distribution costs

Primary liability – in the context of online intermediaries' liability, refers to the intermediary's direct responsibility for the content it deliberately uses (and not for the content that

it hosts because a third party uploaded it). For example: an online platform is primarily liable for the copyrighted content it uses to supply its service

Prosumer – expression used to underline the role of consumers of a product in contributing to its production. In the data economy, consumers are typically *prosumers*, as the data they produce while consuming the product contribute to its production. For example, usually, smartphone apps require users' data to function optimally

Pseudonymization – process through which certain information is transformed so that it cannot be re-associated with its original source (unless a "key code" or additional information is used to "crack" the pseudonym)

Public good – good or service that is *non-excludable* and *non-rivalrous*. Simple examples are environmental resources, such as water quality or biodiversity

Public-private partnership – (often abbreviated with *PPP*) contractual agreement between a public administration and a private entity for the supply of a service, infrastructure or asset, in which the public and private parties share risk and management responsibilities

QR code – graphic barcode used to convey complex information in a machine-readable format. It is used to issue Digital Covid-19 Certificates, for example

Quantum technologies – technologies that rely on quantum mechanics principles. In particular, *quantum computing* is considered capable of overcoming some of *HPC's* limitations. For example, *HPC* need to process every possible combination to solve a complex combinatory problem and this can be cumbersome. Quantum computing can overcome that by creating multidimensional spaces where the complexity of such problems is reduced

Radio spectrum – well-defined interval of frequencies of electromagnetic energy used to transmit information through space wirelessly. Typical use of *radio spectrum* are TV, radio, or mobile communication

Real-time bidding – (often abbreviated with *RTB*) auction process through which advertisement slots on web pages are sold and bought while a web page is loading

Regulatory fragmentation – term used to stress the existence of multiple regulatory frameworks in a particular geographical area of reference. The term is often used in *EU* jargon to indicate that the *Single Market* is not yet complete because of *Member States*' different regulatory approaches

Reinforced learning – refers to the learning process of specific artificial intelligence applications that are allowed to "experiment" solutions in a complex and novel environment (such as a board game setting) and are rewarded or punished depending on the outcome they achieve

Resale price maintenance – (often abbreviated with *RPM*) contractual clause in an agreement between a producer and retailer. An *RPM* clause allows the producer to determine the retail price

Reskilling – the process of providing a worker with new skills to perform new tasks or take up a new job

Reverse causality – in econometrics, refers to a potential source of misinterpretation of a model's outcome. Econometric models aim to identify a causal relationship between two variables. Namely: researchers aim to understand whether *A* may cause *B*. When the model is affected by *reverse causality*, researchers may observe a strong relationship between A and B, but it is *B* causing *A* and not the reverse. For example, a researcher might be interested in knowing if higher levels of digitization *cause a* higher level of efficiency in public administrations. If she finds strong *correlations*, these may be due also to *reverse causality* because efficient public administrations tend to digitize more

Right to be forgotten – right enshrined in the EU General Data Protection Regulation. It postulates that a *data subject* has the right to have her personal data erased by the *data controller* where certain conditions apply

Rivalry – in microeconomics, the terms refers to a property of goods. A good is (non) *rivalrous*

if its consumption (does not) depletes its value. A glass of wine is *rivalrous* (if I drink it, nobody else can). The sea is *non-rivalrous* (if I swim, I do not affect others' chance to swim too)

Roaming – in telecoms, refers to a wireless connection mediated by a different network than the default, home one. *International roaming* refers to the use of mobile connectivity in a country different from the one in which the user has her mobile service subscription

Robot tax – expression used colloquially to indicate a taxation regime aimed to discourage employers from replacing human workers with autonomous machines

Routine task – usually used in a work context. A *routine* task requires a regular and consistent repetition of the same process. For example, operating a metal-press machine may involve repeating always the same action. A *non-routine* task requires changing approach based on the situation faced. For example, hairdressing requires a different cut for each new customer

Safe harbour – legal expression used to indicate a set of conditions that guarantee impunity if satisfied. For example, according to the *EU* e-Commerce Directive, online platforms are not liable for the illegal content they may host if they are not aware of it. This lack of knowledge gives rise to the e-Commerce's Directive *safe harbour*

Sample selection – in econometrics, expression used to indicate a potential source of misinterpretation of a model's outcome. *Sample selection* occurs when the data used for inference is not representative of the whole population. For example, a researcher may wish to study the effect of becoming self-employed on a worker's well-being. Running the econometric model on a dataset of workers who turned from being employee to being self-employed would not, however, provide indications for the whole population of workers because workers who decide to become self-employed have different features from those who did not. In other words: self-employed workers *self-select* themselves to be in the sample that the researcher is studying

SARS-CoV-2 – Severe acute respiratory syndrome coronavirus 2. SARS-CoV-2 is the virus causing *Covid-19*

Science, Technology, Engineering, and Mathematics – (often abbreviated with *STEM*) general term used to indicate a group of scientific disciplines that are deeply interlinked, thus often studied together

Search good – product with quality features that can be observed before consumption. For example, a signed photo by photographer Susan Meiselas is a *search good* since you already consume the photo before buying it by viewing it. *Search goods* are often juxtaposed to *experience goods*

Secondary liability – in the context of online intermediaries' liability, refers to the intermediary's indirect responsibility for the content uploaded by a third party on its servers. For example, a video streaming service infringing copyright because of a video uploaded by one of its users

Security Operations Centre – (often abbreviated with SOC) internal department of a private or public entity monitoring and analysing that entity's exposure to cyber-threats. SOC is also responsible to react and deploy a response after a cyber-incident took place

Self-regulation – refers to a regulatory approach based on market players entering voluntary agreements aimed to improve the functioning of the market. Public authorities may offer some guidance to market players, but there is no enforcement mechanism to ensure that the agreements are respected

Semiconductor – Material used to ensure conductivity between conductors and insulators. Silicon, for example, is a semiconductor. Semiconductors are essential for the fabrication of microchips or *chips*. See also *Silicon Valley*

Sentiment analysis – technology based on natural language processing and used to identify subjective assessments through the scanning and processing of a text

Sharing economy – (also known as *collaborative economy*, *peer-to-peer economy*, and *gig economy*) refers to a typology of business based on

an online platform that allows private individuals to respond to a demand in the market for the supply of certain services or for the use of assets those individuals own

Silicon Valley – geographic area largely identifiable with the southern part of the San Francisco Bay area in Northern California, US. The name is suggestive of the high level of technological development and innovation of the companies established there. It alludes to silicon, a typical *semiconductor* material used for fabricating *chip*s

Single Market – the *Single Market* is a core goal of the *European Union*. It refers to the creation of a territorial area encompassing all EU *Member States* where people, goods, services, and capital can move freely with no restriction, internal border, or regulatory obstacle

Singularity – in the artificial intelligence context, refers to a specific moment in the evolution of technology. That is the moment in which humans would create a more intelligent machine than the most intelligent among humans. The singularity theory rests on the assumption that, at that moment, such a *super-intelligent* machine would be able to program an even more intelligent machine, kicking off an exponential growth in machines' intelligence. Ultimately this path would lead to machines superseding humans as the Planet's dominant species

Small and Medium Enterprise – (often abbreviated with *SME*) in the EU, refers to companies with fewer than 250 employees and yearly turnover smaller than €50 million (*medium* enterprises) or companies with fewer than 50 employees and yearly turnover smaller than €10 million (*small* enterprises)

Snippet – small excerpt, often representative of the content from which it is excerpted. In the book, the term is used with reference to the EU Copyright Directive, whereby online platforms should pay publishers *neighbouring rights* for the use of *snippets* from their news outlets

Social credit system – (also known as *social scoring*) system that assigns a score and ranks citizens based on their online and offline behaviour. It may also take into account other factors, such as citizens' interpersonal relationships. A citizen ranking may affect her probability of finding a job or getting a bank loan, for example. China implemented a social credit system as of 2014

Social network – in the digital context, the expression indicates a network enabled by an online platform and used by users to communicate and interact with each other. For example, communication may occur through writing posts or commentaries, posting of images, videos or links, re-posting of content uploaded by other users, oral interaction, expression of feelings through symbols or emoticons

Solow Paradox – expression used to emphasize the absence of a significant correlation between investment in technology and aggregate levels of productivity in an economy. Nobel-winner economist Robert Solow first made that observation in 1987, noting that "computers are everywhere except for productivity statistics"

Spam – unsolicited message spread over the Internet often with a commercial purpose

Spill-over – in economics, refers to a second-order effect related to parties not directly involved in a transaction or event. For example, a library has a direct educational effect on its users. The library also fosters its users' civic sensitivity; it thus has a positive *spill-over* effect on the neighbourhood area. The concept of *spill-over* is closely related to the concept of *externality*

Spurious correlation – in econometrics, refers to the existence of a *correlation* between two variables that is not driven by a *causal* relationship

Standard-setting body – (also known as *standard-setting organization*) organization pursuing the primary goal of coordinating industry players to develop and adopt a technological standard

Startup company – small company starting to develop its business

Static effect – in microeconomics, refers to the effect that we can actually observe immediately after having taken a particular action

Strategic autonomy – refers to a country's ability to independently define its priorities in areas such as economic and foreign policy or security and to implement decisions accordingly, regardless of other countries' political or economic interest

Stratification hypothesis – in the context of the study of the impact of technology on society, refers to technology's tendency to exacerbate inequality. The *digital divide* is the primary driver of technology's stratification effect

Substitution – two products are in a *substitution* relationship if the ability to access one of them decreases the value of the other one. For example, rail transport and cars are in a *substitute* relationship

Sunk investment – investment that cannot be recovered. For example, plugging in a telecom cable below the ground entails bearing some costs that cannot be recovered in the future, such as the cost of digging the ground

Superintelligence – refers to hypothetical autonomous machines possessing an intelligence level which is higher than that of the most intelligent human being. This concept is closely related to that of *singularity*

Supervised learning – type of *machine learning* based on training artificial intelligence with labelled data. Contrary to *reinforced learning* the system is not allowed to play with itself. Instead, it receives information that the developer has already categorized

Tacit collusion – tacit agreement between competitors in a market. For example, companies in a market may all converge to charge a higher price than the one that would emerge in a competitive environment without the need to communicate explicitly. Competition authorities cannot go after tacit collusion because of its informal nature

Techlash – backlash against major players in the digital space (particularly: the *GAFAM* players). The backlash started in the second half of the second decade of the twenty-first century, primarily because of users' concerns about the use of their personal data, online disinformation, and loss of democratic control

Technology neutrality – in telecom regulation, refers to the principle according to which regulators should be agnostic as regards the specific technological solution that citizens, business, or other public administrations choose for the supply of a connectivity service

Telework – refers to workers performing their job's tasks from multiple physical locations thanks to the use of remote technology

Theory of harm – in competition policy, refers to the economic reasoning adopted by a competition authority to explain why a specific company's conduct is anticompetitive and thus results in a reduction of *consumer welfare*

Total welfare – (also known as *total surplus*) indicates the value that the sale and consumption of a particular good or service generates, minus the cost of production and distribution

Trade and Technology Council – (also referred to as TTC) council launched by the EU and US in September 2021 with the aim to promote cooperation between the two economies, particularly on global technological issues, through periodic high-level meetings between Senior EU and US officials

Transfer price – price used to indicate the value of transactions within a particular organization, primarily for book-keeping purposes. Transfer pricing can be used for tax avoidance purposes, such as transferring a multinational company's taxable value to a department of that company located in a jurisdiction where taxation is lighter

Troll – term used in the online environment to indicate a user that intentionally baits others to elicit an emotional response

Trusted flagger – refers to an entity of private or public nature that has demonstrated to have the necessary expertise and competence to flag the presence of illegal content online

Tweet – short message containing text, images, or videos and posted on Twitter. According to Twitter's current policy, a tweet can contain a maximum of 280 characters

Unicorn – *startup company* with a market value of $1 billion or more

Uniform Resource Locator – (often abbreviated with *URL*) web address

Universal basic income – (often abbreviated with *UBI*) a public subsidy system consisting in granting to any adult citizen a certain amount of money on a regular basis and unconditionally

Upstream – term used to indicate markets at the beginning of the value chain, far from the final customer. For example, a car manufacturer is *upstream* compared to car retailers that are *downstream*

User-generated content – (often abbreviated with *UGC*) content that an Internet user has contributed to create and that is retrievable online. It may consist of a video, an image, or a post on a social network, for example

Value gap – expression used in the context of the public debate around copyright obligations for online platforms. Copyrighted work shared on online platforms generates profits. The *value gap* is the difference between the share of that value that goes to platforms and the share that goes to copyright holders

Vectoring – technology used to enhance telecom connectivity speed and quality of legacy copper cables

Venture capital – type of equity investment usually used to finance small or *startup companies* which are expected to have significant long-term growth potential (thus venture capital investment tend to be very risky)

Vertical restriction – in competition policy, refers to an agreement between two market players that operate at different levels of the value chain. They thus sell products that are not in direct competition but may instead complement each other

Vertical search outcome – (also known as *specialized search outcome*) outcome by a web search engine that is specific to a particular sector or area of interest

Virality – refers to the replication of audiovisual content online, usually thanks to users reposting it or forwarding it to their online social network

Virtual reality – technology used to create a fictitious three-dimensional environment and to allow individuals to perform actions and interact in that environment

Wearable technology – electronic device worn by individuals to monitor their health status or activity

Web cookie – small file containing an Internet user's information such as her username, password, or a record of websites previously visited. Websites may collect *cookies* to identify a user's profile and to tailor ads to match that user's preferences, for example

Web crawling – refers to automated software scanning the Internet to collect certain information

White-collar – employment classification. Generally refers to jobs performed in an office, such as desk or administrative work. See also: *blue-collar*

White spaces – *radio spectrum* frequencies that are assigned but are not used at the local level

Wired connectivity – refers to connectivity enabled by a network of physical cables

Wireless connectivity – refers to connectivity enabled by transmission over the air (it includes mobile communication, satellite, but also Bluetooth, for example)

Zettabyte – unit of computer storage capacity, equivalent to one trillion *gigabytes*

Index